Participation and Covenant

Participation and Covenant
Contours of a Theodramatic Theology

DICK MOES

WIPF & STOCK · Eugene, Oregon

PARTICIPATION AND COVENANT
Contours of a Theodramatic Theology

Copyright © 2024 Dick Moes. All rights reserved. Except for brief quotations in critical publications or reviews, no part of this book may be reproduced in any manner without prior written permission from the publisher. Write: Permissions, Wipf and Stock Publishers, 199 W. 8th Ave., Suite 3, Eugene, OR 97401.

Wipf & Stock
An Imprint of Wipf and Stock Publishers
199 W. 8th Ave., Suite 3
Eugene, OR 97401

www.wipfandstock.com

PAPERBACK ISBN: 979-8-3852-0458-8
HARDCOVER ISBN: 979-8-3852-0459-5
EBOOK ISBN: 979-8-3852-0460-1

Unless otherwise indicated, Scripture quotations are from the ESV® Bible (The Holy Bible, English Standard Version®), © 2001 by Crossway, a publishing ministry of Good News Publishers. Used by permission. All rights reserved. The ESV text may not be quoted in any publication made available to the public by a Creative Commons license. The ESV may not be translated in whole or in part into any other language.

Scripture quotations marked (NIV) are taken from the Holy Bible, New International Version®, NIV®. Copyright © 1973, 1978, 1984, 2011 by Biblica, Inc.™ Used by permission of Zondervan. All rights reserved worldwide. www.zondervan.comThe "NIV" and "New International Version" are trademarks registered in the United States Patent and Trademark Office by Biblica, Inc.™

For Elsina,
Fellow partaker of the divine nature.

Table of Contents

Acknowledgements ix

Introduction 1

1. Design Features of a Theodramatic Framework 15

2. Michael Horton's Covenantal Framework 61

3. An Evaluation of Horton's Covenant Theology 119

4. Participating in the Life of God and Divine-human Covenants: The Drama of God's Mission for His Glory 189

5. Outlining a Theodramatic Framework 257

6. Communicating the Gospel and Shaping our Christian Identity and Practice 307

Conclusion 339

Bibliography 341

Subject Index 385

Author Index 403

Scripture Index 415

Acknowledgements

I WOULD LIKE TO extend my sincere thanks to the North-West University in Potchefstroom for offering me a scholarship to pursue a PhD in theology at their university. I had no intention of embarking on a PhD study after having completed my Doctor of Ministry. However, the offer of this scholarship stimulated me to do so.

I am deeply grateful for my supervisors. I met Dr. Sarel van der Walt when I attended the Fourth General Synod of the Reformed Churches in South Africa as a fraternal delegate of the United Reformed Churches in North America. When I discussed the possibility of doing a PhD in dogmatics, he agreed to be my second supervisor. Thank you for your guidance and counsel, which enabled me to bring this project to completion.

Because of Dr. Hans Burger's deep knowledge of union with Christ and covenant theology, I asked him to be my first supervisor. Thank you for the pedagogically and theologically sound feedback you gave on each chapter. Your probing questions continued to stimulate me to strive for beauty and excellence.

Several people sent me pdf documents of manuscripts, some published and some (as yet) unpublished, that I needed to consult for this study. Thank you Dr. Dmytro Bintsarovskyi, Dr. Hans Burger, Drs. Nynke Dijkstra-Algra, Dr. Jos Douma, Dr. Arnold Huijgen, Dr. Mark Jones, Dr. Larry Perkins, Dr. Audy Santoso, Dr. Koert van Bekkum, Drs. Harry Wendt, and Dr. Paul Williamson.

I would like to extend my sincere gratitude to Mrs. Jane de Glint-Sneep and Mr. Doug Field for the editorial work you did on earlier versions of this thesis, and to Mr. John Barach for the excellent job in editing the final version with a keen eye for bibliographic detail.

I gratefully acknowledge the assistance of the librarians of the Norma Marion Alloway Library at Trinity Western University (TWU). Your help was especially appreciated during the research and writing of the second half of my thesis throughout the COVID pandemic when you arranged contactless holds pickup.

Mr. Apko Nap deserves special thanks for the encouragement he gave during this project.

I am deeply grateful to my family for their encouragement. My wife Elsina continually encouraged me and, because she worked at TWU, often picked up books at the library for me. Mary-Anne and Reuben helped me with some of the formatting of the final version of my thesis. My brother-in-law, Jan Houweling, arranged the purchase of numerous books in The Netherlands.

Above all, I give my deepest thanks to my triune God, whose hand I continually and sometimes mysteriously felt upon me as I worked on my thesis. Thank you for keeping me safe during the COVID pandemic. Thank you also for allowing me to participate in your divine nature in Christ through the fellowship of the Holy Spirit.

Introduction

THIS BOOK IS A work of what used to be called "theological encyclopedia." While we think of an encyclopedia today as a set of volumes covering topics alphabetically, theological encyclopedia is the old name of a particular branch of theology.

Theological encyclopedia isn't the study of theology itself, so much as it is the study of how to study theology. It deals with methodology, with how various topics in theology relate to each other and form a unified whole, with the order in which the various topics ought to be considered. For instance, should we talk first about the existence of God and his attributes and only later add that he is triune, or should we introduce the doctrine of the Trinity from the beginning and discuss his attributes in the light of it?

An introduction to a systematic theology textbook might deal with these things briefly, and we skim those pages on our way to the "real theology" later on. Few seminaries, if any, offer a course in theological encyclopedia. Few books on the subject are written and, I suspect, fewer still are read.

But while theological encyclopedia might sound like an arcane topic that only an ivory tower theologian could waste much time on, it is essential. The methodology we apply to theological study has everything to do with the results of our study. The framework within which we consider theological topics—the way we think they relate to each other so that they aren't just a bunch of unrelated ideas but are instead a unified whole—affects the conclusions we come to with regard to each of these topics.

More than that, our theological framework affects our lives and those of others around us. It affects how we communicate—and how clearly we communicate—the gospel. And it affects our own understanding of and growth in our Christian identity.

In this book, I outline a theodramatic framework that has participation in the life of God with Christ through the Spirit as its integrative center. In doing so, I enter into conversation with covenant or federal[1] theology, particularly as presented by Michael Horton, in which the integrative center is the concept of the covenant.

The goal of this conversation is to determine which theological framework, with its integrative center, is better able to give direction to the Christian life, to help us clearly communicate the gospel and to properly shape our Christian identity and practice so that we become fitting participants in the life of God.

WHY I WROTE THIS BOOK

I have been interested in the topic of participation or dwelling in the life of God for some time. My interest was sparked by a personal crisis in my life and by subsequent reading about union with Christ and life in the Spirit.

In September 2003, I embarked on a Doctor of Ministry program in Spiritual Formation and Leadership, which culminated in a dissertation entitled *Cultivating a God-Generated Life: Being Embedded with Christ in the Father through the Advance Installment of the Holy Spirit*. The term "God-generated life" was inspired by Calvin's understanding of union with Christ as a substantial ontological union, in which the incarnate humanity of Christ is the channel through which the fullness of salvation in Christ is communicated.[2] The purpose of that study was to examine the nature and significance of this ontological or real union in connection with developing a God-generated life in which, because we are born of God, we become people and places where heaven and earth meet.

When North-West University in Potchefstroom offered me a scholarship toward a PhD in theology, I decided to pursue a design study— that is, a study focused on the question "What should the structure of a systematic theology look like?"[3]—in which I would outline a theodramatic framework or the contours of a theodramatic systematic theology.

---

1. The word "federal" comes from the Latin *foedus*, which means "covenant."

2. Calvin, *Institutes*, 3.24; 4.17.19; Billings, *Calvin, Participation, and the Gift*, 62–65; Evans, *Imputation and Impartation*, 23–29.

3. A design study is therefore different from a biblical-theological study ("How does the Bible speak about a theological theme?"), a contextual study ("How are a theological theme and related themes viewed in our context?"), a conceptual study ("What would a certain theological concept look like?"), and a historical-theological study

INTRODUCTION

At this time, there is no systematic theology that has participation in the life of God as its integrative center. There is, however, a growing interest in this topic. Billings speaks of substantially participating in the life of God through faith in Christ,[4] and Burger about being in God through being in Christ.[5] Canlis focuses on pneumatologically participating in the life of God through faith in Christ.[6] Evans emphasizes participating in the life of God through being united to the incarnate humanity of Christ through the Holy Spirit by faith.[7] Fairbairn considers the heart of the Christian faith to entail sharing in the Son's relationship with his Father.[8] Letham speaks about our partaking of the divine nature through our union with the person of Christ,[9] and Vanhoozer about participating in the divine nature as participating in the Son's communion with the Father and the Spirit.[10] This study, then, should be seen in the context of this growing interest and as a contribution to the further development of the theme of participation in the life of God.[11]

At this time, there is also no theodramatic systematic theology. There is, however, a growing interest in understanding the Christian faith as essentially dramatic. Balthasar has written a five-volume study in which he approaches Scripture through the lens of theater and drama.[12] Building on this study, Vanhoozer has developed his own theodramatic framework for communicating the gospel.[13] N. T. Wright suggests that we can divide the theodrama of Scripture into five acts: (1) Creation,

---

("How has a theological theme been thought about in history?").

4. Billings, *Calvin, Participation, and the Gift*, 53–65.
5. Burger, *Being in Christ*, 537; *Life in Christ*, 216–19.
6. Canlis, *Calvin's Ladder*, 14.
7. Evans, "Three Current Reformed Models," 27–30.
8. Fairbairn, *Life in the Trinity*, 13–37.
9. Letham, *Systematic Theology*, 788; *Union with Christ*, 127.
10. Vanhoozer, *Remythologizing Theology*, 293; *Faith Speaking Understanding*.
11. For a recent exploration into Paul's theology of union with Christ and participation, see Thate, Vanhoozer, and Campbell, eds., *"In Christ" in Paul*. Macaskill, *Union with Christ*, provides a comprehensive examination of union with Christ and participation in God in the New Testament, as well as in the early church fathers, contemporary Orthodoxy, and the Lutheran and Reformed traditions. Bowsher, *Life in the Son*, explores participation and union with Christ in John's Gospel and Letters. Beale, *Union with the Resurrected Christ*, provides a virtual encyclopedia of union with the resurrected Christ in the New Testament.
12. Balthasar, *Theo-Drama*.
13. Vanhoozer, *Drama of Doctrine*; "Drama-of-Redemption Model"; *Faith Speaking Understanding*; and "At Play."

(2) Fall, (3) Israel, (4) Jesus, and (5) Church.[14] Wells divides the acts up differently: (1) Creation, (2) Israel, (3) Jesus, (4) Church, and (5) Eschaton.[15] Bartholomew and Goheen, on the other hand, divide Scripture's theodrama into six acts: (1) Creation, (2) Fall, (3) Redemption Initiated, (4) Redemption Accomplished, (5) Church, and (6) Redemption Completed.[16] Christopher Wright expands the theodrama into seven acts: (1) Creation, (2) Rebellion, (3) Promise, (4) Christ, (5) Mission, (6) Judgment, (7) New Creation.[17] Harris proposes a theatrical hermeneutic for reading Scripture.[18] Vander Lugt promotes an interpretative improvisation or performance of the Christian faith on the stage of this world.[19] And Farlow believes that it is best to dramatize theology because God's revelatory action is inherently dramatic.[20] This study should be seen in the context of this growing interest in theodrama and as contributing to the further development of an essentially dramatic understanding of the Christian faith.

GOD'S FUNDAMENTAL RELATIONSHIP WITH HUMANITY

Covenant theology has the concept of the covenant as its integrative center.[21] At the heart of covenant theology are three overarching covenants: the pretemporal covenant of redemption, the covenant of creation (often seen as a covenant of works), and the covenant of grace. The covenants with Noah, Abraham, Israel, and David, as well as the new covenant, are classified under these three covenants.[22]

Michael Horton's dogmatic studies clearly seek to contrast a covenant ontology with a participatory ontology.[23] Rather than affirming

---

14. Wright, "How Can the Bible Be Authoritative?" 7–32; *New Testament and the People of God*, 140–43.
15. Wells, *Improvisation*, 52–57.
16. Bartholomew and Goheen, *Drama of Scripture*.
17. Wright, *The Great Story*, 12–37.
18. Harris, *Theater and Incarnation*.
19. Vander Lugt, *Living Theodrama*.
20. Farlow, *Dramatizing of Theology*.
21. Horton, *God of Promise*, 13–14; Macleod, "Covenant Theology," 214.
22. Horton, *God of Promise*, 77–107; Macleod, "Covenant Theology," 215–17.
23. Horton, *Lord and Servant*, 10–16; "Participation and Covenant," 107–32; *Covenant and Salvation*, 153–215; *Christian Faith*, 602–19.

God's ontological or real unity with the world and our ontological participation in or dwelling in the life of the Trinity, Horton sees God's unity with the world as a strictly covenantal or ethical unity.[24] But are these two ontologies mutually exclusive, as Horton thinks, or are they intimately intertwined?

In this book, I argue that because God's fundamental relationship with humanity does not entail a covenantal ontology, but a participatory ontology—an ontology of participating in God's loving presence in Christ through the Holy Spirit through a listening and thankful filial spirit, characterized by the openness and responsiveness of faith—a theodramatic framework that incorporates a reframed understanding of divine-human covenants and has participation in the life of God in Christ through the Spirit as its integrative center is better able to give direction for properly shaping our Christian identity and practice and making us effective communicators of this gospel in our secular culture than Horton's framework of covenant theology. In fact, as we will see, a participatory ontology—an ontology of mutual indwelling—and a covenantal ontology are not mutually exclusive but intimately intertwined.[25]

CRITICAL REFLECTION ON THE PRACTICES OF THE CHURCH

"Theology," says Hans Burger, "is critical reflection on the practice of the church aimed at helping to communicate the gospel of Jesus Christ as clearly as possible and to enable the members of the church to live in Christ and in the Spirit in communion with God and with each other to the glory of God."[26]

This definition implies that theological reflection is embedded in theory-laden practice—that is, a practice laden with our assumptions

---

24. Horton, *Lord and Servant*, 84.

25. We can participate in or dwell in God's loving presence in Christ through the Holy Spirit cosmologically as well as soteriologically. Vanhoozer articulates these two levels of participation as follows: "We therefore have to distinguish two kinds of 'being in' or participation in Christ: a general cosmological participation in the Son through whom all things were made (Col. 1:16) and a more particular christological [or soteriological] abiding in the Son in whom there is reconciliation (2 Cor. 5:17)" (*Remythologizing Theology*, 281–82). Since this study is about the practice of communicating the gospel and living the Christian life, however, the emphasis here is on our soteriological participation in Christ.

26. Burger, *Being in Christ*, 7.

and perspectives[27]—beginning with theory-laden practical concerns and questions, going to theory, and then back to theory-laden practice again.

The reflection in this study goes through six hermeneutical movements. It begins in the rest of this introduction by describing and interpreting the theory-laden empirical reality of our secular culture and the church within this culture that gives rise to concerns and questions about how to communicate the gospel and how our identity and practice as Christians should be shaped.

It then explores how certain design features of a theodramatic framework shape our Christian identity and practice so that we become fitting participants in the life of God and effective communicators of the gospel in our secular culture (chapter 1).

It goes on to analyze and evaluate Michael Horton's covenant theology, examining the implications of its structural design for our communication of the gospel and our Christian identity and practice (chapters 2 and 3), before sketching the contours first of a theodramatic biblical narrative (chapter 4) and then of a theodramatic systematic theology (chapter 5) that have participation in the life of God as their integrative center and incorporate a reframed understanding of divine-human covenants.

Finally, this theological reflection returns to the theory-laden practice that raised concerns and questions at the outset to show how this theodramatic framework of biblical narrative and systematic theology does shape our Christian identity and practice and enable us to communicate the gospel effectively in our secular culture (chapter 6).[28]

Since all knowing is historically and linguistically situated,[29] this study will be done from the perspective of the Reformed tradition. The canonical Scriptures will be read as the Word of God that is the ultimate normative voice for theology.

OUR SECULAR CULTURE

In his influential work *A Secular Age*, Charles Taylor presents the word "secular" as having three senses. The first refers to the retreat of religion from public places, such as politics and the marketplace, while religion

---

27. For an example of how theological reflection is embedded in the hermeneutical questions of life, see Thiselton, *Hermeneutics of Doctrine*.

28. This methodology was inspired by Burger, *Being in Christ*, 8, 24–25, and Browning, *Fundamental Practical Theology*, 5–9, 35–54.

29. Gadamer, *Truth and Method*, 278–90, 301–22; 414–23, 455–506.

remains present in sacred places. The second refers to the decline of religious belief and practice as an outcome of modernity.[30] These first two uses of the term "secular" Taylor considers merely the subtraction of religious belief, but the third use of "secular" includes the change in the conditions of belief or the plausibility structures of society. It involves "a move from a society where belief in God is unchallenged and, indeed, unproblematic, to one in which it is understood to be one option among others, and frequently not the easiest to embrace." "Secularity" in this sense answers the question "Why was it virtually impossible not to believe in God in, say, 1500 in our Western society, while in 2000 many of us find this not only easy, but even inescapable?"[31]

Taylor discusses culture in terms of its "social imaginary" and its "plausibility structures." A social imaginary is "the way ordinary people imagine their social surroundings ... often not expressed in theoretical terms, [but] carried in images, stories, legends, etc."[32] Though they wouldn't use this term, it is the way ordinary people intuitively imagine meaning and significance. Plausibility structures are all the things—beliefs, practices, institutions, rituals, shared assumptions, and so on—that make certain ideas or beliefs make sense or seem more believable. A society considers something to be believable based primarily on how well it fits with its social imaginary.

While our secular culture is not monolithic, it can be described in terms of its social imaginary and plausibility structures, as Taylor has shown.

First, our secular culture is a *disenchanted* culture in which people live as enclosed, individual, rational, buffered selves. By "buffered," Taylor means that they are closed off to anything transcendent, "not open and porous and vulnerable to a world of spirits and powers."[33] They live within an immanent frame of life in which they seek the meaning,

---

30. Taylor, *Secular Age*, 2–4, 14–15, 20

31. Taylor, *Secular Age*, 3, 25; cf. 26–29. Helpful introductions to and engagements with the work of Charles Taylor include Burger and Spijker, *Open for God*; Colorado and Klassen, *Aspiring to Fullness*; Hansen, *Our Secular Age*; Root, *Faith Formation*; Smith, *How (Not) To Be Secular*; and Warner et al., *Varieties of Secularism*.

32. Taylor, *Secular Age*, 171–72; see also Taylor, *Modern Social Imaginaries*, 23–30.

33. Taylor, *Secular Age*, 27. Taylor adds that a "buffered" self is "essentially the self which is aware of the possibility of disengagement. And disengagement is frequently carried out in relation to one's whole surroundings, natural and social" (*Secular Age*, 42; cf. 38–42). For the genealogy of the rational, individual "buffered" self, see Taylor, *Sources of the Self*.

significance, and fullness of their lives in a natural and material world that has lost contact with the transcendent beyond themselves.[34]

As such, people no longer consider the ontological structure of creation to be enchanted[35] and suffused with the presence of God and angels, having a "natural" (i.e., inherently compatible) porous[36] relationship with God by living in his loving presence and participating in his life, but instead consider creation—and the ontological structure of humanity—to be intrinsically self-sufficient. Accordingly, they consider exclusive humanism a viable option. "A secular age," says Taylor, "is one in which the eclipse of all goals beyond human flourishing becomes conceivable; or better, it falls within the range of an imaginable life for masses of people. This is the crucial link between secularity and a self-sufficing humanism."[37]

But with the loss of transcendence comes a sense of malaise—indeed, as Taylor shows, three malaises: "(1) the sense of the fragility of meaning, the search for an over-arching significance; (2) the felt flatness of our attempts to solemnize the crucial moments of passage in our lives; and (3) the utter flatness, emptiness of the ordinary."[38] Taylor sums up this sense of malaise with the words of Peggy Lee's song "Is that all there is?"[39]

Second, our secular culture is an *expressive* culture, in which people pursue authenticity by following their desires and defining for themselves what it means to be human.[40] People no longer want to realize their humanity and identity in conforming to external norms, institutions, and values, but instead by living it out or expressing it in their own way. To

---

34. An immanent frame is the self-sufficient natural order of a closed world structure as contrasted to a supernatural frame. Taylor, *Secular Age*, 542; cf. 539–93.

35. On the enchanted world, see Taylor, *Secular Age*, 29–43; *Dilemmas and Connections*, 287–302.

36. Clarifying his distinction between a "buffered" and a "porous" self, Taylor writes, "My point was that that disenchantment did not consist in a change in *beliefs*, but rather a shift in which the immediate experience was reconfigured, so that a new issue could arise around belief or non-belief in spirits" (Response, 300).

37. Taylor, *Secular Age*, 19–20.

38. Taylor, *Secular Age*, 309. In an earlier work, Taylor included the threat of the loss of public freedom as one of the malaises (*Ethics of Authenticity*, 8–10).

39. Taylor, *Secular Age*, 311, 507, 509.

40. On the expressivist turn, see Taylor, *Sources of the Self*, 368–90.

be truly human or authentic is ultimately a matter of discovering and choosing one's own self-definition and doing one's own thing.[41]

Taylor writes, "The 60s provide perhaps the hinge moment, at least symbolically. ... As well as moral/spiritual and instrumental individualisms, we now have a widespread 'expressive' individualism." He adds, "This is, of course, not totally new. Expressivism was the invention of the Romantic period in the late eighteenth century. Intellectual and artistic elites have been searching for the authentic way of living or expressing themselves through the nineteenth century. What is new is that this kind of self-orientation seems to have become a mass phenomenon."[42]

The expressive culture, with its emphasis on being and doing whatever you want, however, results in loneliness, a loss of communion, and the fragmentation of people's lives. Moreover, it leads to the perpetration of injustice and the proliferation of victims of this injustice. Doing your own thing, it turns out, often hurts others.

Third, our secular culture is an *experiential* culture that seeks its sources of morality and truth within itself more through personal experience than theory. Accordingly, people's own lived experience often guides how they interpret reality and shape their lives.[43] Story or narrative is viewed as central in the experience of the personal and the expression and explanation of these personal experiences because we have a narrative identity.[44] Root writes, "When someone tells her story, she reveals her person. Stories are the tentacles of personhood that reach out to share and be shared in. We enter each other's lives . . . through the words of our stories, and entering into these stories binds us to one another.[45]

While story or narrative is indeed central—we are narrative people, whose lives are stories—often these narratives are nothing more than a smorgasbord of small narratives that lead to a fragmented understanding of oneself. A person's understanding of her own story is limited—we know only the story so far, never the whole story, let alone the story of everyone at all times—and so secular culture tends to reduce morality

---

41. Taylor, *Secular Age*, 473–504; cf. 440–72, 505–35; see also Taylor, *Ethics of Authenticity*.

42. Taylor, *Secular Age*, 473; Root, *Faith Formation*, 9.

43. Taylor, *Secular Age*, 4–5, 10–14, 16–18.

44. Root, *Faith Formation*, 143; *Relational Pastor*, 169–202; Taylor, *Sources of the Self*, 25–52.

45. Root, *Faith Formation*, 143; see also Taylor, *Language Animal*, 291–319.

and truth to "what's true for me"—except, inconsistently, when confronting anyone who wants to hold the speaker to a code of morals or a truth the speaker finds offensive. One's own story cannot be generalized into a moral code and one's own truth cannot be applied to—or effectively criticized by—anyone else.

Fourth, our secular culture is a *distracted* culture because it is a technological culture. "Flashing lights, vibrations, bells ringing, little red dots, email alerts, notifications, pop-up windows, commercials, news tickers, browser tabs—everything is designed to capture our attention."[46] Constant distraction does not encourage deeper reflection on beliefs and tends, then, to foster a superficial experience of one's beliefs. Attempting to combat the frenzy of their distracted lives, people turn to meditation techniques, such as mindfulness.[47]

Fifth, our secular culture is a *pluralistic* culture where every ultimate belief, including belief in God, is one option among others and thus contestable and contested because of the change in the social imaginary and plausibility structures of society. Ever since the 1960s, Taylor says, we have been "living in a spiritual super-nova, a kind of galloping pluralism on the spiritual plane."[48] Elsewhere, he speaks of the "steadily widening gamut of new positions—some believing, some unbelieving, some hard to classify—which have become available options for us."[49]

This pluralism of beliefs leads to a mutual fragilization or destabilization of beliefs.[50] Rishmawy describes this fragilized pluralism this way: "Belief has become less of an on/off switch, and more of a series of dials you can set in various degrees (post-secular, humanist, Romantic, libertarian, eco-feminist, and on and on)."[51]

Enclosed in an immanent framework as they are, people have nevertheless not forgotten the transcendent. They experience the cross-pressures of "openings to transcendence" and "the closure of immanence" in their search for meaning, significance, and fullness.[52] The multiple

---

46. Noble, *Disruptive Witness*, 19.
47. Noble, *Disruptive Witness*, 15–30.
48. Taylor, *Secular Age*, 300.
49. Taylor, *Secular Age*, 423.
50. Taylor, *Secular Age*, 303–4.
51. Rishmawy, "Millennial Belief," 51.
52. Taylor, *Secular Age*, 594–617. Writing to Christians, Smith says, "While stark

options caused by these cross-pressures have led many people to consider themselves to be "spiritual, but not religious," a phrase that, as Bass puts it, "is the contemporary way of trying to explain some sort of connection to God"—or at least something transcendent or supernatural— "separate from, in tension with, or in opposition to religious institutions."[53] The church and the Bible no longer seem plausible, but Tarot cards might.

"Some people," Taylor says, "will undoubtedly feel that the immanent frame calls out for one reading . . . the obvious, the 'natural' one," that is, to "see immanence as admitting of no beyond."[54] But the secularist spin[55] that tips the immanent frame towards "closed world structures" is not the only way to live in a secular age. There is also another take[56] possible that tips the immanent frame towards openness to transcendence as "answering to our deepest craving, need, fulfillment of the good."[57]

THE CHURCH IN A SECULAR CULTURE

What about the church? While the church in our secular culture is also not monolithic, it can be described as having the following characteristics.

First, many in the church have a faith that can be described as "Moralistic Therapeutic Deism,"[58] that is, they perceive the God of the Christian faith as "one who exists, created the world, and defines our general moral order, but not one who is particularly personally involved

---

fundamentalisms—either religious or secular [e.g., new atheists]—get all the press, what should interest us are these fugitive expressions of doubt *and* longing, faith *and* questioning. These lived expressions of 'cross-pressures' are at the heart of the secular" (*How (Not) To Be Secular*), 14.

53. Bass, *Christianity after Religion*, 87.

54. Taylor, *Secular Age*, 550.

55. Smith describes this spin as a "construal of life within the *immanent* frame that does not recognize itself as a construal and thus has no room to grant plausibility to the alternative" (*How (Not) To Be Secular*, 143). Examples of this closed secularist spin would include Dawkins, *God Delusion*, and Hitchens, *God Is Not Great*. However, see McGrath and McGrath, *Dawkins Delusion*, and McGrath, *Why God Won't Go Away*.

56. A "take" is a "construal of life within the *immanent frame* that is open to appreciating the viability of other takes" (Taylor, *Secular Age*, 143).

57. Taylor, *Secular Age*, 548; see also Taylor, *Varieties of Religion Today*.

58. For this term, see Smith and Denton, *Soul Searching*. While the focus of their sociological study is the religious lives of American teens, the results of their study have implications for the religious lives of American adults because most American teens follow the religious practices of their parents. Smith and Denton, *Soul Searching*, 56, 96, 102, 115–16, 120, 261; see also Dean, *Almost Christian*, 4, 39, 47, 52, 54, 81, 109, 111, 194, 201.

in one's affairs—especially affairs in which one would prefer not to have God involved"[59]—but who wants them to be good in order to feel good. Doctrine isn't so much downplayed as it is simply ignored. The Christian life, instead of involving living in union with Christ and performing the life of God and living for the other, becomes "a kind of individualized, consumer spirituality."[60]

Second, Christians within certain church traditions often live with a partial Jesus who determines their past and future, but not their present. Instead of realizing that faith joins them to Christ so that they are objectively relocated in the risen and ascended Christ so that it is no longer they who live, but Christ Jesus who lives in them (Gal 2:20), many consider Jesus to be someone who died for their sins in the past and who secured their future.

But "the Christian faith is not just about the past or the future," Burger insists. "Jesus Christ is not the great absentee in the present; the present is not empty. We are new creations in Christ, as Paul says . . . (2 Corinthians 5:17)."[61]

Third, because many in the church have difficulty perceiving their world in biblical terms, they experience a disconnect between the world they live in and the world depicted in Scripture. Consequently, many are more formed by the social imaginary of the secular culture they live in than the imaginary of Scripture and they do not use the biblical imaginary as their main plausibility structure to understand their life in this world.[62]

Kevin Vanhoozer writes, "In his essay 'The Demise of Biblical Civilization,' historian Grant Wacker claims that during the twentieth

---

59. Smith and Denton, *Soul Searching*, 164. The de facto creed of Moralistic Therapeutic Deism has the following tenets: "1. A God exists who created and orders the world and watches over human life on earth. 2. God wants people to be good, nice, and fair to each other, as taught in the Bible and by most world religions. 3. The central goal of life is to be happy and to feel good about oneself. 4. God does not need to be particularly involved in one's life except when God is needed to resolve a problem. 5. Good people go to heaven when they die" (*Soul Searching*, 162–63; see also Moes, *Cultivating a God-Generated Life*, 8; Dean, *Almost Christian*, 14).

60. Root, *Faith Formation*, xvi. Root considers Moralistic Therapeutic Deism to be "a tumor that is wrapped around many organs and bones of twentieth- and twenty-first century American life" (*Faith Formation*, 93–94). For Taylor on the therapeutic turn, see *Secular Age*, 618–23.

61. Burger, *Life in Christ*, vii; cf. 1–5. See also Terlouw, *Real Faith*, 125–34; Hiestand, "Not 'Just Forgiven,'" 47–66.

62. Vanhoozer, *Pictures at a Theological Exhibition*, 17–20; *Doers and Hearers*, 109–13.

century, the average American did not renounce the Bible but simply stopped using it as the primary plausibility structure with which to make sense of the world. People began to understand the meaning of events in terms of this-worldly historical processes rather than in terms of divine providence." He adds, "The demise of biblical civilization was a failure of the imagination to read our world in terms of God's word. The demise of biblical civilization is related to the replacement of *sola Scriptura* in the social imaginary of the West by other stories."[63]

FRAMEWORK FOR THE FUTURE

Given the state of the world and of the church in the world, is there hope? Taylor believes so. "There is a large element of hope. It is a hope that I see implicit in Judaeo-Christian theism (however terrible the record of its adherents in history), and its central promise of a divine affirmation of the human, more total than humans can ever attain unaided."[64]

As Taylor has highlighted, human beings inescapably live within a framework or a moral space.[65] The question is what that framework will be, and that is a question that has everything do with the framework of our theology. Far from being an unimportant topic to be skimmed over or skipped entirely when it appears in a systematic theology, theological encyclopedia—the question of the framework of our systematic theology—turns out to be crucially important for our lives and for our world.

---

63. Vanhoozer, *Doers and Hearers*, 109.

64. Taylor, *Sources of the Self*, 521. Elsewhere he writes, "I foresee another future, based on another supposition. This is the opposite of the mainstream view. In our religious lives we are responding to a transcendent reality. We all have some sense of this, which emerges in our identifying and recognizing some mode of what I have called fullness, and seeking to attain it." He adds, "Modes of fullness recognized by exclusive humanisms, and others that remain within the immanent frame, are therefore responding to transcendent reality, but misrecognizing it. They are shutting out crucial features of it. So the structural characteristic of the religious (re)conversions that I described above, that one feels oneself to be breaking out of a narrower frame into a broader field, which makes sense of things in a different way, corresponds to reality" (*Secular Age*, 768).

65. Taylor, *Sources of the Self*, 3–52. Commenting on what he had written in *A Secular Age*, Taylor writes, "My book lays out, unashamedly, a master narrative. The adverb bespeaks the view I hold, that we can't avoid such narratives. The attempt to escape them only means that we operate by an unacknowledged, hence unexamined and uncriticized narrative. That's because we (modern Westerners) can't help understanding ourselves in these terms" (Response, 300).

Covenant theology, as presented and modified by Michael Horton, offers one framework. But because God's fundamental relationship with humanity does not entail a covenantal ontology, but a participatory ontology—an ontology of participating in God's loving presence in Christ through the Holy Spirit through a listening and thankful filial spirit, characterized by the openness and responsiveness of faith—a theodramatic framework that incorporates a reframed understanding of divine-human covenants and has participation in the life of God in Christ through the Spirit as its integrative center is better able to give direction for properly shaping our Christian identity and practice and making us effective communicators of this gospel in our secular culture than Horton's framework of covenant theology. In fact, as we will see, a participatory ontology—an ontology of mutual indwelling—and a covenantal ontology are not mutually exclusive but intimately intertwined.

My hope is that outlining a theodramatic framework or the contours of a theodramatic systematic theology that incorporates a reframed understanding of divine-human covenants and that has participation in the life of God in Christ through the Spirit as its integrative center will benefit not only the church but the world, as well. Our secular culture, with its social imaginary and its plausibility structures, needs the church to communicate the gospel clearly, and to do so we need to grow and be shaped as fitting participants in the life of God.

As Vanhoozer says, "The task of evangelism, and theology, is to take every imagination captive to Scripture, nurture it and help it indwell the drama of the Christ. We must taste, discern and act in the world as it is—made new in Christ. For this we need a theodramatic framework and a biblically invigorated imagination."[66]

---

66. Vanhoozer, *Pictures at a Theological Exhibition*, 177.

1

Design Features of a Theodramatic Framework

WHAT DO WE MEAN when we speak about a theological framework, let alone a theodramatic framework? A theological framework is more than just the Table of Contents of a systematic theology textbook: first this doctrine, then that doctrine.

The framework is more foundational than the Table of Contents or even what is said about various doctrines. It has to do with the presuppositions and beliefs with which and on the basis of which we theologize. It has to do with what integrates our theological work, so that we aren't discussing a bunch of unrelated doctrines but a unified whole. It has to do with what theology is and what theology does.

This chapter outlines how certain design features of a theodramatic framework—or what we might call the contours of a theodramatic systematic theology—give direction to our communication of the gospel in our secular culture and shape our Christian identity and practice so that we become fitting participants in the life of God.

Because Scripture contains the gospel we communicate and shapes us for life in God and indeed is the basis of all of our theologizing, I will start by considering the nature of *Scripture*. But because the gospel must be understood and interpreted, we must also consider the nature of *hermeneutics*. Because doctrine reconceptualizes the speech acts of Scripture into "thought-acts" or "mental habits," through which we interpret and experience God's speech acts in Scripture and in Jesus Christ in terms of theodramatic imagination and action, a consideration of the nature of *doctrine* follows. And because the structure of systematic theology is the intentional pedagogical form we give to our communication of the gospel and shapes our Christian identity and practice, I will conclude with an examination of the nature of *structure*.

THE NATURE OF SCRIPTURE

The narrative approach to reading Scripture

Scripture contains many different books with separate narratives, but all of these different books and all of these narratives are blended into a rich intertextual whole that allows us to discern the theological worldview that runs through Scripture.[1]

Not everyone agrees that there is a theological worldview that gives a narrative unity to Scripture. The historical-critical method of biblical interpretation, for instance, tries to locate the meaning of the text in historical referents behind the text of Scripture instead of seeking it in the narrative world of the text of Scripture itself.[2] Postmodern readers are not only suspicious of grand unifying narratives but also reject them as totalizing attempts to control one's behavior. They thus believe only in their own local, contextual narratives.[3] And Jews, who embrace only the Old Testament as their Scriptures, would see no narrative unity between these Scriptures and the New Testament Scriptures.

But Luke tells us that Jesus, on the road to Emmaus, opened the Scriptures and, "beginning with Moses and all the Prophets, he interpreted to them in all the Scriptures the things concerning himself" (Luke 24:27). He did something similar on the evening of that same day when he appeared to his disciples and opened their minds to understand what Scripture—the Law of Moses, the Prophets, and the Psalms—said about him: "Thus it is written, that the Christ should suffer and on the third day rise from the dead, and that repentance for the forgiveness of sins should be proclaimed in his name to all nations, beginning from Jerusalem" (Luke 24:46–47). Both of these statements imply that, according to Jesus, God acts in the history of this world and that these acts have been recorded in Scripture in such a way that there is a rich theological narrative unity to the whole of Scripture.[4]

---

1. Klink and Lockett, *Understanding Biblical Theology*, 23–24, 98.
2. Frei, *Eclipse of Biblical Narrative*, 103–4.
3. Grenz, *Primer on Postmodernism*, 44–49.
4. Reading the Bible in the light of its narrative unity is not new (Childs, *Biblical*

When reading Scripture as a narrative unity, it is important to discern the plotline and see how the individual parts of the story fit into the narrative whole. In doing so, we discover the theological worldview in this narrative.[5]

There are various ways to discern that plotline. Richard Hays, for instance, attempts to do so by reading the Bible backwards.[6] That is, he reads the Old Testament retrospectively, in the light of its fulfillment in the ministry of Jesus Christ. The Old Testament, he says, is the manger that contains Jesus Christ, prefiguring or foreshadowing the deep meaning of his person and ministry. The New Testament teaches us how to read the Old Testament, and the Old Testament teaches us how to read the New Testament. Reading this way requires an imagination converted by the death and resurrection of Jesus Christ, so that we hear echoes of the Old Testament Scripture in the New and an intertextual fusion occurs between them.[7]

N. T. Wright does not consider this approach to be sufficiently historical.[8] History and faith mutually inform each other. Wright looks for all the available evidence that sheds light on the historical Jesus, including the synoptic Gospels. Using the scientific method of hypothesis and verification, he endeavors to discern how everything fits together into a

---

Theology, 30–51; Fesko, "Antiquity of Biblical Theology," 443–77; Klink and Lockett, *Understanding Biblical Theology*, 94–95; cf. Irenaeus, *Against Heresies*, I.8.1; I.9.2, 3; I.10.1–3; 326, 332; Augustine, *On Christian Doctrine*, 2.9.14). What is new is the emphasis on narrative as a literary and philosophical category (Klink and Lockett, *Understanding Biblical Theology*, 95). For the influence of the so-called linguistic turn to narrative interpretation of texts, see Heidegger, *Being and Time*, 144–49; Ricoeur, *Time and Narrative*, I-3, 52–87; Wittgenstein, *Philosophical Investigations*, section 6 and 18; Magee, *Great Philosophers*, 331; Smith, "Who's Afraid of Postmodernism?," 221–25. For the deep dissatisfaction felt with the historical-critical method of biblical interpretation influencing the turn to narrative, see Frei, *Eclipse of Biblical Narrative*, 103–4; Klink and Lockett, *Understanding Biblical Theology*, 96. For the influence of our identity increasingly being experienced in terms of narrative, see Bartholomew and Goheen, *Drama of Scripture*, 12; Ricoeur, "Narrative Identity," 188–99; *Oneself as Another*, 113–68; Stroup, *Promise of Narrative Theology*, 99–198; van Dusseldorp, *Preken tussen de verhalen*, 172–76.

5. Klink and Lockett, *Understanding Biblical Theology*, 96–97.

6. Hays, *Reading Backwards*, 1–16.

7. Hays, *Echoes of Scripture*, 23–33; "Reading Scripture," 216–38. Christopher Seitz, however, objects to Hays's method because he thinks it limits the use of the Old Testament to mere background to the New Testament, while he considers the Old Testament to have a Christian message of its own apart from the use of the Old Testament in the New (*Character of Christian Scripture*, 11, 20, 139–40, 156, 203).

8. Borg and Wright, *Meaning of Jesus*, 19–26.

coherent and simple worldview. He looks for a big picture, much as one assembles the bits and pieces of a jigsaw puzzle into the unified whole it is meant to depict.[9]

Faith, for Wright, is the knowledge one has of Christ through having a personal relationship with him. In this personal knowledge of Christ, we also come to know about the historical Jesus. According to Wright, "the Jesus I know in prayer, in the sacraments, in the faces of those in need, is the Jesus I meet in the historical evidence—including the New Testament, of course, but the New Testament read not so much as the church has told me to read it but as I read it with my historical consciousness fully operative."[10] Through this scientific method of hypothesis and verification, in which faith and history mutually inform each other about Christ, our knowledge of him is increasingly supported and expanded.[11]

According to Wright, the story of Israel is decisive for understanding Jesus. God appointed Abraham and Sarah to be a new Adam and Eve, through whom he would restore his creation by dealing with the disorder and evil caused by Adam's sin.[12] In order to guide and shape Israel—Abraham's descendants—in living the truly human life that God intended them to live and to witness to this kind of life to the nations around them, God gave his people the law or Torah as a way of life.[13] Israel, however, failed in living out its vocation by failing to be guided and shaped by the Torah. Consequently, God sent his people into exile, just as he expelled Adam and Eve from the Garden of Eden. After their geographical return from exile, Israel did not rule the world but was under the oppression of pagan nations. Moreover, Israel's God did not

---

9. Wright (*New Testament and the People of God*, 109–12; 122–26; *Jesus and the Victory of God*, 137–44; *Paul and the Faithfulness of God*, 24–36) defines worldviews as lenses through which we look at the world and generated by story, symbols, praxis, and a set of questions. The questions are: Who are we?, Where are we?, What's wrong?, What's the solution?, and What time is it?

10. Borg and Wright, *Meaning of Jesus*, 26.

11. Hays ("Knowing Jesus," 61) sums up the difference between Wright and himself as follows: "On the one hand, Tom insists that without historical investigation of the factuality of the Gospels, the story is vacuous, not least at the level of concrete action in the world. I insist, on the other hand, that without the canonical form of the story, we could never get the historical investigation right in the first place." For serious objections to Wright's historiographical method, see Evans, "Methodological Naturalism," 180–205.

12. Wright, *New Testament and the People of God*, 260–62. See also Beale, *Union with the Resurrected Christ*, 112.

13. Wright, *New Testament and the People of God*, 228–29.

DESIGN FEATURES OF A THEODRAMATIC FRAMEWORK

return to Zion and become king as promised (Isa 52:8). As a result, most first-century Jews would have believed that Israel was still in a state of exile.[14] But they also believed that God would one day keep that promise. He would establish his kingdom, restore his creation, and either welcome the Gentiles into his people or destroy them. Thus, he would vindicate Israel as his true people.[15]

Within this first-century historical context, Jesus should be understood as "a prophet mighty in deed and word" (Luke 24:19), proclaiming and embodying that through him God was defeating evil, bringing the exile to an end, and putting things right by inaugurating his kingdom or rule over creation in Israel and the world.[16] Moreover, he saw himself as Israel's Messiah, called to act as its representative by fulfilling its calling and enduring suffering and death on the cross in order to defeat evil and bring Israel's exile to an end.[17] With Jesus' resurrection from the dead, God demonstrated his faithfulness to his creation and his covenant by vindicating Jesus as Israel's Messiah who has ended the exile by defeating sin and death and who now is the Lord of the world whom all nations are summoned to obey.[18]

Thus, the narrative approach to Scripture—unlike the historical-critical, postmodern, and Jewish approaches—reminds us that Scripture blends God's acts in history recorded in the different books of Scripture into a rich, intertextual whole that articulates a comprehensive theological worldview.

The redemptive-historical approach to reading Scripture

The redemptive-historical approach to Scripture goes beyond the narrative approach. As we saw earlier, when Jesus explained Scripture to the two men on the road to Emmaus and later to his disciples, he implied

14. Wright, *New Testament and the People of God*, 268–70; *Jesus and the Victory of God*, xvii–xviii, 126–27, 203–6.

15. Wright, *New Testament and the People of God*, 267–68, 332–34.

16. Wright, *Jesus and the Victory of God*, 172, 191–96.

17. Wright, *Jesus and the Victory of God*, 540–611.

18. Wright, *Jesus and the Victory of God*, 612–53; *Resurrection*, 581, 726–31. Wright elaborates on this story (*Paul and the Faithfulness of God*, 474–537), but the storyline is essentially the same. He now refers to the outer story being about God and creation and to the various subplots that need to be understood within this outer story. For a helpful summary of Wright's theology, see Kuhrt, *Tom Wright for Everyone*, 31–64. For a theological evaluation of Wright's theology, see Holland, *Tom Wright*.

that Scripture has a narrative unity. He taught them that the three parts of the Old Testament—the Law, the Prophets, and the Psalms—had to be read in the light of his suffering, death, and resurrection.[19] The difference between the narrative approach and the redemptive-historical approach, however, is that the former considers the narrative unity of Scripture to be a quality of the narrative structure of Scripture itself. The latter considers the unity of Scripture to lie in the progressive unfolding of God's acts in the history of redemption in Christ.

When Jesus tells the two disciples on the road to Emmaus that his suffering and death were necessary to fulfill the three parts of the Old Testament Scriptures, he was indicating to them that his death and resurrection were the fulfillment of God's history with Israel. He was implying, then, that we must read Scripture backwards in the light of its fulfillment in his death and resurrection and that the Old Testament Scriptures are rightly understood only if they are read as pointing forward to his death and resurrection.

Thus, when Moses says to Israel, "The Lord your God will raise up for you a prophet like me from among you, from your brothers—it is to him you shall listen" (Deut 18:15), we should read this as pointing forward to Jesus Christ. When Isaiah says, "Behold, the virgin shall conceive and bear a son, and shall call his name Immanuel" (Isa 7:14) and "For to us a child is born, to us a son is given; and the government shall be upon his shoulder, and his name shall be called Wonderful Counselor, Mighty God, Everlasting Father, Prince of Peace" (Isa 9:6), we should read this as pointing forward to Jesus Christ. And when the psalmist says, "I will tell of the decree: The Lord said to me, 'You are my Son; today I have begotten you. Ask of me, and I will make the nations your heritage, and the ends of the earth your possession. You shall break them with a rod of iron and dash them in pieces like a potter's vessel'" (Ps 2:7–9), we should see this statement as pointing forward to Jesus Christ.

Reading the Old Testament Scripture backwards, in the light of its fulfillment in Jesus' death and resurrection, and forward, as pointing to his death and resurrection, illustrates that there is a progressive unfolding of God's acts in the history of redemption in Christ. Reading Scripture this way shows us why this redemption was necessary.

Ever since the fall into sin, there have been three mortal dangers in this world: sin, death, and the devil. Sin makes us guilty and deserves to

---

19. Cf. the Nicene Creed: "and the third day he arose again, according to the Scriptures."

be punished. Sin defiles and pollutes us. Sin is an addictive power that can destroy us. Sin erects partitions that isolate us from God and each other.[20] Because of sin, death came into this world. Death manifests itself in the fact that creation, including ourselves, is subjected to futility and is in bondage to corruption, so that all creation groans to be delivered (Rom 8:20–23). In addition, there is the danger of the devil who has a powerful grip on this world and holds it and its people in captivity.

Because God loves his world and its people, he promises that he will remove these three mortal dangers by dealing with each through the Lord Jesus Christ. In doing so, he restores and transforms humanity as the ruler and priest of his good creation in him. Paul refers to this restoration and transformation of humanity and creation as God uniting all things in heaven and earth in Christ Jesus (Eph 1:10). The author to the Hebrews refers to this restoration and transformation as fulfilling God's intention of bringing many sons to glory together with the Lord Jesus Christ (Heb 2:5–10).

This redemption was achieved through the suffering, death, and resurrection of Jesus, in accord with the Scriptures. Isaiah 53, for instance, prefigured his suffering and death, Psalm 118 his rejection, death, and vindication, and Psalm 16 his resurrection from the dead.[21] Jesus Christ has redeemed his fallen creation and has united all things in him in a new creation by his death and resurrection.

The theodramatic approach to reading Scripture

The theodramatic approach to reading Scripture enriches the narrative reading by viewing Scripture's narrative structure as being of a theodramatic nature.[22] The difference between a narrative and a theodramatic approach to Scripture has been described as follows:

> Though both narratives and dramas share a common story shape, they represent stories differently. Narratives use narrators and typically recount their stories in the third person (he, she, they) and thus can be kept at arm's length. Dramas, by way of contrast, show rather than tell and are typically enacted in the first person and second person, the language of personal

---

20. Gumbel, *Questions of Life*, 44–47.
21. Hays, "Reading Scripture," 230.
22. Burger, "Theologische hermeneutiek," 43.

interaction (e.g., "You shall be holy, for I am holy" [1 Pet. 1:16; cf. Lev. 19:2]). And this is perhaps the most important difference, the element that makes drama more suitable than narrative to serve as handmaid to theology: though stories can entrance us and invite us into their worlds, dramas insert us into the action and demand that we say or do something.[23]

The theodramatic approach also enriches the redemptive-historical approach by considering the progressive unfolding of God's acts in the history of redemption in Christ to be dramatic.

Hans Urs von Balthasar is one of the first to have given a sustained treatment of the concept of theodrama.[24] According to him, divine revelation is best understood through the lens of theater and drama because revelation does not just present us with words but, in and through words, also presents us with action.[25] The triune God, Father, Son, and Holy Spirit, together produce the theodrama. The Father, from whom the whole theodrama proceeds, is the author of the theodrama, in which he himself is also included and for which he takes responsibility.[26] The Son is the chief actor, who creatively actualizes the Father's theodramatic script, making it present and causing it to be embodied on the stage of this world.[27] The Holy Spirit is the director who guides the performance of the theodrama, enabling the drama to come alive in obedience to the script and reach its goal and purpose.[28] In addition to the production of the theodrama, there is its realization in presentation, the audience, and its horizon of meaning. When the Father, Son, and Holy Spirit present the theodrama on the stage of this world, they do so with a view to drawing us into it.[29]

As a result, we are not just spectators, but become participants, actors. As we do so, our life in this world is illuminated and a new

---

23. Vanhoozer, *Faith Speaking Understanding*, 252; cf. Vanhoozer, "Drama-of-Redemption Model," 156–61; Vander Lugt, *Living Theodrama*, 8. Treier ("Holy Scripture," 557) adds that "drama is distinct from narrative generally, with its action moving forward by means of speech."

24. For a helpful introduction to Balthasar's theological dramatic theory, see Nichols, *No Bloodless Myth*; *Key to Balthasar*, 49–88; Wigley, *Balthasar's Trilogy*, 73–121.

25. Balthasar, *Theo-Drama*, 1:15.

26. Balthasar, *Theo-Drama*, 1:19, 270, 279–80, 319; 2:62, 78, 271–84; 3:530, 535; cf. 3:525–35.

27. Balthasar, *Theo-Drama*, 1:281, 285; 2:87; *Glory of the Lord*, 1:303.

28. Balthasar, *Theo-Drama*, 1:298–99; 3:533–34.

29. Balthasar, *Theo-Drama*, 1:309–10.

horizon is opened up for us with regard to the meaning and nature of our existence.[30]

Drawing on Balthasar's understanding of Scripture through the lens of theater and drama, Kevin Vanhoozer has developed a theodramatic framework for communicating the gospel.[31] The theodrama has its beginning in the triune God, Father, Son, and Holy Spirit, who live in an eternal fellowship and communication of love with one another and who create a world and humanity so that they can participate in this fellowship and communication of love in Christ through the Spirit.[32] The world is the stage on which God's glory is manifested. History is the theater of the gospel, in which God dialogically engages humanity with his speech acts. He prompts them to participate faithfully and fittingly in the theodrama that is being played out in the history of the world and the history of their lives. God executes his eternal decree, moving history forward toward the future consummation of history in the kingdom of God.[33]

Scripture is the inspired transcript that witnesses to the unfolding drama of redemption. It communicates the profound meaning of this theodrama. Moreover, Scripture prescribes and describes the church's participation in the theodrama. It gives both positive and negative lessons for the church today. To interpret this theodrama, we need to increasingly make the world depicted in the transcript our own by inhabiting or living in it.[34] Only in this way will we be able to perform the theodrama today faithfully and fittingly, by putting on Christ through the direction and prompting of the Holy Spirit.[35]

---

30. Balthasar, *Theo-Drama*, 1:308, 314–15.

31. Vanhoozer does differ from Balthasar at points. A major difference between Vanhoozer and Balthasar is that the latter imports the economic drama of redemption into the inner life of the Trinity in the form of an eternal kenosis. Balthasar writes, "The immanent Trinity must be understood to be that eternal, absolute self-surrender where God is seen to be, in himself, absolute love." He adds, "the Father strips himself, without remainder, of his Godhead and hands it over to the Son" (*Theo-Drama*, 4:323; cf. Vanhoozer, "At Play," 12). According to Vanhoozer, God's love is not characterized by self-emptying, but by fullness ("At Play," 14). Moreover, he writes, "In employing a theatrical model I am not subscribing to a particular theory of drama but rather deploying a number of themes and concepts that will prove fruitful in our search for Christian understanding" ("Drama-of-Redemption Model," 155).

32. Vanhoozer, *Remythologizing Theology*, 57, 156, 268–71, 280–83.

33. Vanhoozer, *Faith Speaking Understanding*, 66, 244; *Doers and Hearers*, 128–32.

34. Vanhoozer, *Faith Speaking Understanding*, 24, 246.

35. Vanhoozer, *Faith Speaking Understanding*, 236, 250.

Several unifying themes of the drama of Scripture have been suggested.[36]

First, Greg Beale defends the unity of *the drama of new creation*. According to Beale, as Adam and Eve lived in God's presence in his cosmic temple in the Garden of Eden, so God's new humanity will live in his presence in his city-temple or new creation. The life, death, and resurrection of Jesus Christ launched the fulfillment of this eschatological new creation—a fulfillment that is already now, but not yet as full as it will be—and it is available to those who embrace Jesus Christ through faith.[37]

Second, N. T. Wright presents the *drama of the kingdom*. According to Wright, the Old Testament is a story in search of an ending, the ending in which God would return to Zion and become king. This happened in and through Jesus' life, death, and resurrection.[38]

Third, Christopher J. H. Wright argues for the unifying theme of the *drama of God's mission for his glory*. Because God has a mission for his glory, he created and redeemed the world and humanity to glorify and enjoy him forever.[39] The Bible, then, is a product of God's mission that witnesses to the drama of that mission for his glory.[40]

Fourth, William Dumbrell presents the unifying theme of the *drama of covenant*. According to Dumbrell, when God speaks about "establishing my covenant" with Noah in Genesis 6:18, that phrase has to do with continuing or maintaining a covenant relationship and thus refers to God's pre-existing covenant relationship with creation, which then progressively unfolds in the other covenants in Scripture with a view to bringing creation and humanity into the eternal Sabbath rest.[41] The next

---

36. For the importance of knowing the unifying theme that gives coherence to the various acts of the theodrama of Scripture and theatrical performance, see Stanislavski, *An Actor Prepares*, 116–19, 273, 276; cf. Vander Lugt, *Living Theodrama*, 101–2; Vanhoozer, *Drama of Doctrine*, 371–74, 379; *Faith Speaking Understanding*, 118.

37. Beale, *Temple and the Church's Mission*, 25; *New Testament Biblical Theology*, 15–16; Beale and Kim, *God Dwells Among Us*, 17–28, 135–40; cf. Leder, "Presence, Part 1"; "Divine Presence, Part 2"; "Divine Presence, Part 3"; Alexander, *From Eden to the New Jerusalem*; Alexander, *City of God*.

38. Wright, *How God Became King*, 240–45; cf. Goldsworthy, *According to Plan*; Dempster, *Dominion and Dynasty*.

39. Wright, *Mission of God*, 62–65, 188, 404; *The Great Story*, 119-24.

40. Wright, "Mission as a Matrix," 103–4, 120–22, 137; *Mission of God*, 22, 51; *The Great Story*, 5-9; cf. Hamilton, *God's Glory*; VanDrunen, *God's Glory Alone*.

41. Dumbrell, *Covenant and Creation*, 26, 34–35, 42–43; *End of the Beginning*, 40, 176–79; cf. Hahn, *Kinship by Covenant*; Gentry and Wellum, *Kingdom through Covenant*.

two chapters will address how classical covenant theology, sometimes called "federal theology," handles this unifying theme of covenant.

Fifth, Kevin Vanhoozer uses the unifying theme of a covenantal courtroom drama to integrate the themes of new creation, kingdom of God, and covenant.[42] While it is not his unifying theme, Balthasar too mentions God's lawsuit as a theme in dramatic theology found in the prophetic literature and the Pauline epistles and discusses how this theme was used by Marcus Barth to structure a five-act play.[43]

These themes need not be in conflict with each other and there is considerable overlap. In this study, we will consider the unifying theme that gives coherence to the various acts of the theodrama of Scripture and history—including our lives—to be God's mission for his glory, a glory accomplished by having creation and humanity live in his loving presence and participate in his life in Christ through the Holy Spirit (Ps 104:30; Acts 17:28; Col 1:17; Heb 1:3).

This theme expresses the fundamental relationship God has—and intends to have—with his creation and humanity. God's goal in the theodrama is to bring creation and humanity into the Sabbath rest of the fullness of God's loving presence in Christ through the Spirit in the coming kingdom of God, that is to say, the new heaven and new earth where God will be all in all (Isa 11:9; Hab 2:14; 1 Cor 15:28). The beginning of the fullness of this Sabbath rest in the kingdom is experienced today through faith as we entrust ourselves to Jesus Christ and allow him to form himself in us through his Holy Spirit (Gal 2:20; 4:19).[44] Covenant, then, is God's commitment to secure and guarantee this purpose.[45]

Using this theme thus integrates the themes of the presence of God (Beale, Leder, Alexander), Sabbath rest (Dumbrell), new creation (Beale, Alexander), courtroom drama (Vanhoozer, Balthasar, Barth), the kingdom of God (N. T. Wright), covenant (Dumbrell, Leder, Williamson), mission (Christopher Wright), and the glory of God (Christopher Wright).

---

42. Vanhoozer, *Faith Speaking Understanding*, 102–10; see also *Drama of Doctrine*, 50–56.

43. Balthasar, *Theo-Drama*, 2:152–59; cf. Barth, *Justification*.

44. See the further discussion of the unifying theme of God's mission for his glory in chapters 4 and 5.

45. Leder, "Divine Presence, Part 2," 207–20; Williamson, *Sealed with an Oath*, 11–12, 43.

The theological approach to reading Scripture

The church has always practiced a theological interpretation of Scripture in one form or another.[46] Reading Scripture was experienced as a spiritual discipline through which one entered into the depth of the text of Scripture by intensively engaging and reflecting on the words of Scripture in order to be caught up in them and transformed by them.[47]

Moreover, since Jesus Christ is considered the key to all of Scripture, the Old Testament has been read as prefiguring Christ through the Christocentric reading strategies of allegory and typology.[48] Through the practice of *lectio divina* (divine or prayerful, contemplative reading of Scripture) and the use of the interpretive method of the fourfold sense of Scripture—literal, allegorical, tropological, and anagogical—Scripture was read with a view to certain kinds of application to Christian practice.[49] What is more, Scripture was read through the theological lens of the apostolic teaching.[50]

But over the course of time, this sort of reading has been discontinued by many. Some trace the beginning of the change to the abandonment of the premodern sacramental mindset, which viewed creation as participating in eternal realities. According to them, as a result of Thomas Aquinas's acceptance of "pure nature" (i.e., nature conceived apart from its final end) and Duns Scotus's affirmation of univocity of being (i.e., we talk about God in the same way we talk about human beings, thus making creation independent of God), God's relationship with the world began to be viewed as merely external, his governing of the world was seen as based on his will separated from his being, and people came to believe that "universals do not have a real existence in the mind of God, but are simply names that we assign to particular objects."[51] The Enlightenment, with its insistence on objectivity and neutrality, finalized this abandonment of the sacramental mindset.[52]

---

46. Bartholomew and Thomas, *Manifesto for Theological Interpretation*, 1; Treier, *Introducing Theological Interpretation*, 39–77.

47. Treier, *Introducing Theological Interpretation*, 41–45.

48. Treier, *Introducing Theological Interpretation*, 45–51.

49. Treier, *Introducing Theological Interpretation*, 51–55.

50. Treier, *Introducing Theological Interpretation*, 57–58.

51. Boersma, *Heavenly Participation*, 80; cf. 19–25, 65, 68–83; Levering, *Participatory Biblical Exegesis*, 18–25; Balthasar, *Glory of the Lord*, 4:395–96; 5: 9–29.

52. Treier, *Introducing Theological Interpretation*, 27, 47; Goheen and Wright, "Mission and Theological Interpretation," 171.

Nevertheless, what was discontinued has re-emerged, stimulated, according to some, by Barth's theological engagement with Scripture in his commentary on Romans and his subsequent exegetical work in other commentaries and his *Church Dogmatics*.[53] Like Barth, many had become disenchanted with the secular mode of reading Scripture as practiced by the historical-critical method, which imagined that it could interpret Scripture in a neutral manner, without any theological assumptions, and imposed limits on the interpretation of Scripture by "subjecting it to the demands of methodical naturalism."[54]

This dissatisfaction with historical-critical interpretation led to a movement known as the theological interpretation of Scripture, which wanted to read Scripture once more within "the conceptual world of the text itself" as "an instrument of God's communicative presence in this world."[55]

The conceptual world of the text itself is read within the parameters of the *regula fidei* or rule of faith. This rule of faith does not predetermine the meaning of Scripture, nor is it a superstructure placed upon Scripture or simply a summary of Scripture. Rather, it is the underlying unity of Scripture that serves as a "horizon of interpretive preunderstanding," guiding the church in its interpretation of Scripture.[56] As such, the rule of faith clarifies the scope and limit of the message of Scripture. Moreover, it points to what God does in Jesus Christ through the Holy Spirit as its narrative center.[57]

This movement does not completely reject the historical-critical method because it does provide helpful insights into the historical world behind and in the linguistic world of the text. But it considers it to be insufficient in itself for the task of truly understanding Scripture.[58] Accordingly, the church must always "recontextualize historical-critical studies," as Billings says, because "history is a theater of divine action."[59]

---

53. Bartholomew and Thomas, *Manifesto for Theological Interpretation*, 1; Paddison, "History and Reemergence," 29; Treier, *Introducing Theological Interpretation*, 7–20.

54. Rae, "Theological Interpretation," 109; Billings, *Word of God*, 49, 147.

55. Rae, "Theological Interpretation," 94; Billings, *Word of God*, 180.

56. Green, *Practicing Theological Interpretation*, 77–80; Swain, *Trinity, Revelation, and Reading*, 111; cf. Gadamer, *Truth and Method*, 289–96, 302, 311–18, 384, 464–65.

57. Billings, *Word of God*, 22–23; Vanhoozer, *Drama of Doctrine*, 19.

58. Paddison, "History and Reemergence," 29; Billings, *Word of God*, 225; Plummer, *40 Questions*, 315; Balthasar, *Glory of the Lord*, 1:538.

59. Billings, *Word of God*, 225.

The theological interpretation of Scripture can be characterized as follows.

First, it considers Scripture to be a divine communication or address of God to the church. More precisely, Scripture is the Spirit's instrument through which the church is called to listen and respond to the voice of God in obedience of faith, for this God desires communion with those he has created. He wants people to participate in his life in Christ through the Spirit.[60]

Second, theological interpretation considers God to be communicatively present in Scripture, desiring to draw us into an ever-deeper communion with himself in Christ through the Spirit. As God is providentially present in the world, so he is providentially present in Scripture, working out his purpose in our lives.[61]

Third, theological interpretation is a practice of the church. Since the church of today is not the first to read Scripture, it draws on earlier, premodern theological interpretation of Scripture and reads Scripture in communion with those who have read it before. Accordingly, the current practice of reading Scripture is sustained and nourished by the wisdom of previous generations found in the tradition of the church.[62]

Fourth, theological interpretation has as its goal the formation of the moral character of the reader, so that he grows in his love for God and his neighbor. The more we know the Christ about whom Scripture speaks, the more we will learn to love God and our neighbor as Christ did for the sake of the world.[63] In addition, the more we know the Christ about whom Scripture speaks, the better we will know our place with regard to Scripture: not as those who proudly master it, but as those who humbly submit and attend to it.[64]

---

60. Paddison, "History and Reemergence," 29, 33–39; Thomas, "Telos," 198, 204; Holt and Spears, "Ecclesia as Primary Context," 82–93; Demptser, "Canon," 143–48; Bartholomew, *Introducing Biblical Hermeneutics*, 19–24; Billings, *Word of God*, 80, 103, 199–206; Swain, *Trinity, Revelation, and Reading*, 7, 16, 61, 96; Fowl, *Theological Interpretation*, 9; Vanhoozer, *Doers and Hearers*, 74; cf. Huijgen, *Lezen en laten lezen*, 24–34.

61. Paddison, "History and Reemergence," 30–31, 39–42; Billings, *Word of God*, 206–13.

62. Treier, *Introducing Theological Interpretation*, 31, 42–45; Holt and Spears, "Ecclesia as Primary Context," 72–81; Green, *Practicing Theological Interpretation*, 73–74, 126; Fowl, *Theological Interpretation*, 52; Swain, *Trinity, Revelation, and Reading*, 99–118.

63. Treier, *Introducing Theological Interpretation*, 32, 45–46; Thomas, "Telos," 204–7; Billings, *Word of God*, 224–25; Green, *Practicing Theological Interpretation*, 126; Vanhoozer, *Doers and Hearers*, 72–75, 80–85; cf. Huijgen, *Lezen en laten lezen*, 34–40.

64. Green, *Practicing Theological Interpretation*, 126.

Conclusion

All of these approaches contribute to our understanding of Scripture and therefore also to our understanding of how we ourselves are shaped to be fitting participants in the life of God and effective communicators of the gospel.

The narrative approach reminds us that while Scripture contains many different books with separate narratives, all of them are blended into a unified whole that presents a comprehensive theological worldview. The gospel we proclaim and by which we ourselves are shaped in our Christian identity cannot be reduced to "the message of Paul" or of any other portion of Scripture, let alone to the forgiveness of sins. The whole Bible tells the story by which we are shaped, the story that we communicate to the world, a story moving from creation through Israel to the new creation, brought about through Jesus, that is already breaking into our broken present by the Spirit who is the power by whom we are shaped and live.

The redemptive-historical approach reminds us that Jesus' death, resurrection, and outpouring of the Spirit were the fulfillment of God's history with Israel, and beyond that with Adam, a history unified by the progressive unfolding of God's redemptive purposes, so that we can read Scripture as Jesus and the apostles did, understanding the Old Testament in light of its fulfillment in Jesus and seeing it as pointing forward to him and to his victory over sin, death, and the devil.

The theodramatic approach reminds us that we are not outside the story but are ourselves actors in the story. Scripture is a drama that inserts us into its action and demands that we say or do something in response, so that through Scripture and through our response to it God carries out his mission for his glory, bringing creation and humanity to live in his loving presence and to share his life in Christ by the Spirit. The theodramatic approach thus shapes our identity as actors in the drama who are inviting others to take up their proper role in Christ.

The theological approach reminds us that Scripture is the Spirit's instrument, in which God himself is communicatively present and by which we are called to listen and respond in the obedience of faith. As we read Scripture, we grow in our communion with God in Christ so that our moral character, too, is formed and we grow in our love for God and our neighbor.

THE NATURE OF HERMENEUTICS

Hermeneutics as the art of understanding and interpretation

To say that hermeneutics is the art of understanding and interpretation implies that hermeneutics is not just about developing a set of rules and methods for interpreting texts (epistemology) but also focuses on who the understanding person is and under what conditions he is able to understand.[65] Two significant ontological factors that play a role in our interpretation and therefore also shape our identity and affect our communication of the gospel in the world are time and history and the body and finitude.

Time and History. We are not disengaged beings who experience a value-neutral world on which we impose meaning. Rather, we are engaged selves who participate in and are shaped by the stream of history in which we are embedded from our birth. Consequently, interpretation is not something we do occasionally but rather something that belongs to our human condition. To be is to interpret and understand![66] Our perception of the world, then, is not primarily theoretical, neutrally examining objects from a distance, but rather is practical, understanding how the web of relations in which we are embedded is meaningful to us.[67] And because we participate in the stream of history and are shaped by it, tradition as such is not a hindrance to understanding but rather the precondition of it.[68]

Body and Finitude. God created us as embodied, finite human beings, and therefore we do not have a God's-eye view of reality. Our understanding is always a subjective and limited interpretation of reality. Our finitude and embodiment are reflected in the way we receive the world. The world is given to us already interpreted through an intricate

---

65. "Hermeneutics" also refers to "the philosophical discipline of analyzing the conditions for understanding" (Zimmermann, *Hermeneutics*, 6; cf. Burger, "Foundation or Perspective?," 36; de Bruijne, "Kunst van het verstaan," 22). This section engages with hermeneutics as a philosophical discipline. For the application of this insight to the hermeneutics of doctrine, see Thiselton, *Hermeneutics of Doctrine*.

66. Gadamer, *Truth and Method*, 288–89, 311–18, 506; Heidegger, *Being and Time*, 144–49; Zimmermann, *Hermeneutics*, 30–32.

67. Heidegger, *Being and Time*, 138–49; Gadamer, *Truth and Method*, 318–87; Zimmermann, *Hermeneutics*, 8, 39.

68. Gadamer, *Truth and Method*, 289–96; Zimmermann, *Hermeneutics*, 50. While tradition as such is not a hindrance for understanding but a precondition of it, it can become a hindrance at times because, like all human activity, tradition is ambivalent.

web of words and concepts that have developed over time. We do not use language as a toolbox of labels that we attach to things in the world in a disengaged, instrumental manner. Instead, we use language as the medium through which we relate to and interpret our experience of life and our being in the world.[69] Our being in the world, then, is like a conversation in which we creatively appropriate pre-existing conceptual vocabulary and dialogically seek to come to an understanding of our experience of life.[70]

But because God created us this way, he can communicate with us by his Word and Spirit. God is not hampered by our creatureliness. He made us embodied and finite beings who participate in and are shaped by the stream of time and history and who use the medium of language to relate to and interpret our experience of life and our being in the world and who—even when interpreting God's speech to us—use a greater context to influence how we understand a particular part.

When we interpret a text, then, there is always a creative movement between our understanding of our life experience and the world of the text that we are attempting to interpret, with the parts creatively clarifying the greater context and the greater context creatively clarifying the parts. This is known as the hermeneutical circle or spiral.[71]

Because we are not only formed by the ontological factors of time and history and of body and finitude but are also *mal*formed by them, they do not always play a positive role. God does not approve of everything that happens and not all understanding is therefore correct. In order to be shaped to participate in the life of God and in order to communicate the gospel clearly to our secular culture, we may not simply interpret Scripture in terms of our life experience but must allow Scripture to change us and our understanding, including our understanding of our life experience.

This shift of focus to the subject—the one doing the understanding—and the conditions under which we understand does not entail relativism. "After all, to claim that all knowledge is relative to a personal standpoint is not all the same as claiming that only individual

---

69. Gadamer, *Truth and Method*, 401–506, 568–75; Heidegger, *Being and Time*, 155–61; Zimmermann, *Hermeneutics*, 13–15, 42–43.

70. Gadamer, *Truth and Method*, 401–7, 412, 462, 480, 569–70; Zimmermann, *Hermeneutics*, 41–43, 45–47.

71. Osborne, *Hermeneutical Spiral*, 32, 417–19; Thiselton, *Hermeneutics of Doctrine*, 14; Zimmermann, *Hermeneutics*, 26, 37, 51, 67, 129.

perspectives exist and are all of equal value. It is only to claim that we are not gods who look down on our world, but finite creatures deeply affected by the course of history."[72]

Moreover, understanding through personal engagement is more like playing a game or performing a piece of music. When we play a game or execute a musical score, we cannot simply make up our own rules or play whatever we want. We have to play the game according to the preexisting rules of the game. We perform the piece of music according to the musical score. And so too when we interpret a text, we cannot simply make up the meaning of the text. We must interpret it according to its linguistic structure.[73]

Hermeneutics is thus the art of understanding and interpretation.[74] It is not the skill of obtaining epistemological certainty scientifically. It is the art of realizing how, given the ontological factors of time and history, body and finitude, God uses Scripture—or other means of communication outside Scripture—in the process of understanding. This art of understanding and interpretation is thus a gift of the Holy Spirit,[75] who gives us the mind of Christ (1 Cor 2:16).

Hermeneutics and the mind of Christ

With the fall into sin, humanity closed themselves off to living in God and each other's loving presence and instead became turned in on themselves and self-enclosed, which leads to a hermeneutical groaning that has consequences for our understanding (see Rom 8:22–23; cf. 1:18–23). Understanding, too, needs to be seen in the light of salvation.

God the Father, in principle, redeems us from our hermeneutical groaning by sending us Jesus Christ and the Spirit. As the "radiance" and the "exact imprint of [God's] nature" (Heb 1:3), "the true light, which

---

72. Zimmermann, *Hermeneutics*, 18.

73. Gadamer, *Truth and Method*, 111; Ricoeur, *Hermeneutics*, 159; Zimmermann, *Hermeneutics*, 42. Ricoeur, however, criticized Gadamer because he "paid too little attention to how linguistic structures both limit and facilitate the interpretation" (Zimmermann, *Hermeneutics*, 62). The personal situation of the reader does the same. For instance, the significance of a text may be different for a person in a state of joy and excitement than for someone experiencing grief and sadness.

74. De Bruijne, "Kunst van het verstaan," 19, 23; Gadamer, *Truth and Method*, 163, 185, 191, 194, 279, 302; Thiselton, *Hermeneutics of Doctrine*, 1–5; Zimmermann, *Hermeneutics*, 1–2.

75. Kwakkel, "Kun je wel zeggen."

gives light to everyone" (John 1:9), and "the light of the world" (John 8:12; 9:5), the Son is ultimately the one who breaks open our enclosed selves and enlightens our darkened minds, enabling us to hear and understand his Father and to desire to listen to his Father and do his will.[76] He can do this because, when he took on human flesh and lived among us, he lived on earth with the same filial openness and responsiveness as he had in heaven.[77] He did this as our representative and our substitute, with the sacrifice of his life and of his death.

The Father demonstrated that he had in principle redeemed us from our hermeneutical groaning by raising his Son from the dead as the first fruits of his new creation (1 Cor 15:20, 23). When Christ ascended into heaven, he did so as the resurrected and glorified Christ, in whom the moral order of creation had been restored and transformed.[78]

Because we were united with Christ in his death, resurrection, and ascension, our subject is objectively relocated in the risen and ascended Christ. We participate in his position in the moral order of the renewed creation.[79] Our old self has died and our new self has come to life in him (Rom 6:3–11; Gal 2:20; Eph 4:20–24; Col 3:5–11). And this has implications also for the healing and renewal of our understanding, for in the risen Christ are hidden all the treasures of wisdom and knowledge (Col 2:3).[80]

God the Father also in principle redeems us from our hermeneutical groaning by sending us the Spirit. The Spirit groans for the fulfillment of God's new creation purpose in the resurrected Christ and helps us in our weakness (Rom 8:26).[81] He can do so because he is the Spirit who searches the deep things of God and who gives life (John 6:63; 1 Cor 1:10). This life includes the life of our hermeneutical renewal. The Spirit

---

76. Vanhoozer, *Faith Speaking Understanding*, 64–65.

77. Swain and Allen, "Obedience of the Eternal Son," 123–24, 129; Boyer, "Articulating Order," 258–59, Torrance, *Incarnation*, 176–77; Vanhoozer, "At Play," 15–16, 20; Balthasar, *Theo-Drama*, 2:256, 259, 269; cf. 2:243–71; Webster, "God's Perfect Life," 144–45, 147, 149, 151.

78. O'Donovan, *Resurrection and Moral Order*, ix, xv–xviii, 13–15, 17, 19–20, 31–32, 53–67.

79. O'Donovan, *Resurrection and Moral Order*, 22, 25, 76–97, 247–48; *Finding and Seeking*, 14, 40–41; Burger, "Transformatie door de vernieuwing," 100–101; Vanhoozer, "Imprisoned or Free?," 29.

80. Burger, "Theologische hermeneutiek," 40–41; Vanhoozer, "Imprisoned or Free?," 24–29.

81. O'Donovan, *Finding and Seeking*, 1.

renews us in this way by doing in us what Christ has done for us, "so that it is no longer [we] who live, but Christ who lives in [us]" (Gal 2:20).

Consequently, our union with Christ in his death and resurrection in history slowly begins to take form in our lives as our old self increasingly dies and our new self increasingly comes to life. The Holy Spirit opens our enclosed selves and joins us to the risen Christ, mysteriously communicating his mindset of filial openness and responsiveness to us so that we begin to hear, listen to, understand, and do the will of his heavenly Father just as he did and does.

In short, in opening up our enclosed selves and joining us to the risen Christ, the Spirit enables us to share subjectively in his position in the moral order of the renewed creation.[82] In this way, the Spirit causes us to receive the perspective of the mind of Christ, so that we no longer interpret and understand according to the flesh, but rather according to the Spirit (Rom 12:2; 2 Cor 4:16; Eph 4:23; Col 3:10).[83]

While we are primarily passive as the Father carries out this work of hermeneutical redemption, he does use the means of faith to join us to Christ (John 6:57; Rom 1:17; Gal 2:21).[84] In filial openness and dependence, faith considers the Father's address to us in Christ in his Word to be trustworthy so that we entrust ourselves to Christ, and this faith is ultimately the filial dependence and responsiveness of the faith of Christ.[85] The more we put on Christ by faith, the more Christ communicates to us his own filial openness and responsiveness so that, by the Spirit, we more and more have the mind of Christ.[86]

Putting on Christ through faith in this way is a discipline or activity that needs to be nurtured.[87] The nurturing disciplines include celebration (Exod 5:1; Ps 145:7; Phil 4:4), confession (Num 5:7; Ps 32:5; Jas 5:16), fasting (Ps 69:10; Zech 8:19; Matt 6:16–18), fellowship (Ps 133:1–3; Acts

---

82. Burger, "Receiving the Mind," 55–62; O'Donovan, *Resurrection and Moral Order*, 22–26, 76, 101–20, 247–48.

83. Burger, "Theologische hermeneutiek," 41–42; Dalferth, *Theology and Philosophy*, 85–88, 158–61, 212–13, 219–23; O'Donovan, *Resurrection and Moral Order*, 22–27, 85, 87, 101–5, 109, 111–13, 140–41; *Self, World, and Time*, 93–97.

84. Burger, "Theologische hermeneutiek," 46; Dalferth, *Theology and Philosophy*, 219–23; O'Donovan, *Finding and Seeking*, 40–41; cf. 24–69.

85. Cf. Allen, *Justification and the Gospel*, 83–89.

86. Evans would include this model of union with Christ under "pneumatological-incarnational realism" (Evans, "Three Current Reformed Models," 27–30).

87. Burger, "Soteriological Perspective," 201–3; "Receiving the Mind," 70–71; "Foundation or Perspective?," 50–51.

2:42; Rom 12:4-17; Eph 4:15-16; Col 3:8-17), meditation (Pss 1:2; 63:6; Phil 4:8), prayer (2 Kgs 19:15-19; Matt 5:44; Acts 2:42; Eph 6:18), silence (Ps 62:1, 5), solitude (Matt 14:23), submission (Col 3:18-24; Heb 13:17; Jas 4:7), worship (Ps 99:5; Acts 13:1-3; Heb 12:28), and the use of the sacraments (Rom 6:1-11; Gal 3:27; Luke 24:30-31, 36; Acts 2:46).[88] However, even though putting on the mind of Christ is a discipline we must engage in, our understanding in this life will always be "provisional and open to correction."[89]

Our hermeneutical starting point, then, must be participation in Christ. That is to say, our starting point in hermeneutics is not epistemology but soteriology. All other hermeneutical reflection should be built upon this soteriological basis.[90]

---

88. Books helpful in cultivating spiritual disciplines or practices include Andrews, ed., *Kingdom Life*; Calhoun, *Spiritual Disciplines Handbook*; Chandler, *Christian Spiritual Formation*; Douma, *Beholding the Glory*; Foster, *Celebration of Discipline*; *Streams of Living Water*; Nouwen, *Only Necessary Thing*; *Selfless Way of Christ*; Smith, *Desiring the Kingdom*; *Imagining the Kingdom*; Troost, *Mindful met Jezus*; Warren, *Liturgy of the Ordinary*; Willard, *Spirit of the Disciplines*; *Renovation of the Heart*. For a biblical theology of personal transformation, see Millar, *Changed into His Likeness*. For biblical, practical approaches to spiritual formation, see Boa, *Life in the Presence of God*. For spiritual formation in theological perspective, see Greenman and Kalantzis, *Life in the Spirit*.

89. Vanhoozer, *Is There a Meaning*, 300; cf. 367-452; Burger, "Soteriological Perspective," 199-200.

90. Burger, "Soteriological Perspective," 199-204. Much more could be said about soteriology, rather than epistemology, as our hermeneutical starting point. For classical or strong foundationalism as an epistemological starting point for justifying knowledge claims, see Burger, "Foundation or Perspective?," 59-60; Grenz and Franke, *Beyond Foundationalism*, 30-31; Frame, *Doctrine of the Knowledge of God*, 386; Murphy, "Epistemology," 191; Plantinga, *Warranted Christian Belief*, 82-85; *Knowledge and Christian Belief*, 13-15; Wolterstorff, Introduction to Plantinga and Wolterstorff, *Faith and Rationality*, 1-5; *Reason within the Bounds*, 28-30; Wood, *Epistemology*, 78, 84-85. For the weaknesses of classical or strong foundationalism, see Burger, "Foundation or Perspective?," 60; Frame, *Doctrine of the Knowledge of God*, 105, 386-91; Plantinga, "Reason and Belief in God," 59-63; *Warranted Christian Belief*, 93-99; *Knowledge and Christian Belief*, 15; Wolterstorff, *Reason within the Bounds*, 58-62. For the eclipse of the agency of God in classical or strong foundationalism, see Bowald, *Rendering the Word*, 1, 16-17, 19, 179; Burger, "Foundation or Perspective?," 59-63. For the church's reaction and adaption to classical foundational epistemology's demand for undisputed, self-evident, value-neutral, basic or foundational beliefs in order to be able to justify beliefs and have epistemological certainty with regard to knowledge in general, see Bowald, *Rendering the Word*, 23, 74-181; Burger, "Foundation or Perspective?," 63; Huijgen, *Lezen en laten lezen*, 27, 122, 157-59; Sarot, "Christian Fundamentalism," 261-62. For the use of the word "foundation" as a soteriological and ecclesiological metaphor for our salvation in Christ and for the church being the body of Christ, see Burger, "Soteriological Perspective," 197, 204; "Foundation or Perspective?," 61-62, 65. For the relationship between

PARTICIPATION AND COVENANT

Hermeneutics and the use of language

As we have seen above, the world is given to us already interpreted through an intricate web of words and concepts that has developed over time. The use of language is thus important for the process of understanding. Words are tools or instruments that determine how we think about and give meaning to our life in the world from within the context of the actual situations of our everyday life. Thus, we will understand a particular sentence only within the rules of the "language game" or the context within which a word is used.[91]

Language can be compared to a toolbox with which we do things. According to the philosopher J. L. Austin, we can distinguish between three different linguistic or speech acts. First, we perform a *locutionary* act with a sentence—that is, we are uttering a sentence that has a certain reference or meaning, such as "The dog wants to go out." Second, we are also performing an *illocutionary* act with that sentence—that is, we are saying something with a certain force; we want to affect the hearer in some way, to elicit some sort of response. When we say "The dog wants to go out," we may intend the hearer to get up and let the dog out. Or maybe we just want to let the hearer know what that strange whining sound is. Third, if our illocutionary act is successful, we are performing a *perlocutionary* act, actually eliciting a response, bringing about or achieving something with the sentence we uttered. Perhaps the person we are speaking to gets up and opens the door for the dog. Or perhaps she settles back in her chair and stops wondering about the noise she's been hearing.[92]

---

seeing understanding in the light of soteriology and clearly communicating the gospel in our secular, pluralist society, see Burger, "Soteriological Perspective," 201–3; "Foundation or Perspective?," 60–64. For reading Scripture with the mind of Christ as not implying an anti-realist, postmodern perspectivism that claims that there is no truth, but only relative truths, see Burger, "Foundation or Perspective?," 64; Grenz, *Primer on Postmodernism*, 93, 110. For reading Scripture with the mind of Christ as not implying playing off Scripture against the perspective of the mind of Christ, see Burger, "Foundation or Perspective?," 64. For reading Scripture with the mind of Christ and a critical-realist epistemology, see Burger, *Being in Christ*, 7, 23; cf. Wright, *New Testament and the People of God*, 35; Vanhoozer, *Is There a Meaning*, 300–302, 322–23.

91. Vanhoozer, *Is There a Meaning*, 208.

92. Austin, *How to Do Things with Words*, 94–132. Building on Austin, John Searle proposes the classification of illocutionary acts into five basic categories: representatives or assertives, directives, commissives, expressives, and declarations ("Taxonomy of Illocutionary Acts," 354–58). By this classification, Searle is contending that "speaking a language is engaging in a rule-governed form of behaviour" that we need to

It is probably more accurate to say that instead of performing three different speech acts in a sentence, we are performing one speech act—we utter a locution with an intention—and the response of the hearer is not a perlocutionary act of the speaker but rather the effect of the sentence.[93] But the distinction between the content of a sentence (locution) and the intent of the sentence (illocution) helps us see that speech cannot be disconnected from the intent of the speaker.[94]

What applies to speech acts in the use of ordinary language applies also to texts. According to Paul Ricoeur, a text is "a discourse told by somebody, said by someone to someone else about something."[95] What applies to human texts in general also applies to Scripture in particular. Scripture, too, is "a discourse told by somebody, said by someone to someone else about something." The focal point of this text is not primarily language as an abstract system or codes of interrelated meaning, but the concrete message that emerges when the system or code of language is used in the form of a speech act in sentences. When Scripture says something (*locution*), it is said with an intention (*illocution*) that is meant to elicit a particular response (*perlocution*).

Scripture is addressed not only to one person, as a personal conversation or a personal letter would be, but also to all who read and engage it according to the rules of the genre of its written discourse.

Moreover, Scripture's frame of reference has been extended beyond the frame of its immediate situation to include the situation of any reader of the text. On the one hand, Scripture is addressed to its original audience. For instance, Haggai 1 is addressed specifically to Jews who have returned to the land after the exile and have given up on the rebuilding of the temple. But on the other hand, Scripture also addresses the church through all ages. The Lord is not rebuking us, through Haggai, for not

---

learn and internalize (*Speech Acts*, 12, 16, 22, 39–42; Vanhoozer, *Is There a Meaning*, 209–10). Moreover, he is asserting that there are not "an infinite or indefinite number of language games or uses of language," as Wittgenstein claimed (Searle, "Taxonomy," 369; Vanhoozer, *Is There a Meaning*, 209). Instead, "there are a rather limited number of basic things we do with language: we tell people how things are, we try to get them to do things, we commit ourselves to doing things, we express our feelings and attitudes, and we bring about changes through our utterances. Often we do more than one of these at once in the same utterance" (Searle, "Taxonomy," 369; *Expression and Meaning*, 29; Vanhoozer, *Is There a Meaning*, 209).

93. Burger, "Theologische hermeneutiek," 53.
94. Vanhoozer, *Is There a Meaning*, 209.
95. Ricoeur, *Interpretation Theory*, 30.

rebuilding the temple in Jerusalem—we are not the original audience—but he is still speaking to us and calling forth a response from us.

In its speech, then, Scripture projects "a new way of being in the world," which needs to be appropriated by those who dialogically engage it. It mediates a fusion between the horizon of the author (the world behind the text) and the reader (the world in front of the text), through which the reader comes to a new understanding of himself.[96]

Most importantly, when we read Scripture, we do not just have an encounter with the language of a text. We encounter God himself, the author of this language. God uses the text as a medium through which he speaks to and addresses the readers of Scripture, intending to say something to them. When Scripture speaks, God speaks.[97] God can do this because he is communicatively present in Scripture, desiring to draw us into an ever-deeper communion with himself in Christ through the Holy Spirit. When God speaks to us through the medium of the text of Scripture, he is appropriating and accepting the words of humans as his own words.[98]

Kevin Vanhoozer anchors God's divine discourse in the immanent and economic Trinity. Our view of Scripture, according to Vanhoozer, is predicated upon our view of God and his providence in the history of the world.[99] God's being is a dynamic, communicative activity between

---

96. Ricoeur, *Interpretation Theory*, 37.

97. *Contra* Ricoeur who separates the author(s) of Scripture from the text of Scripture so that Scripture has a semantic autonomy of its own. I agree with Vanhoozer: "On the one hand, Ricoeur detaches meaning from authors. The written text is autonomous of its author; it sets out on a career of its own. On the other hand, he affirms the text as discourse. These two moves may, in the end, prove contradictory. . . . Ricoeur's analysis of discourse tacitly appeals to the author throughout: as originator of the event, as artisan of the work, as proposer of its world. His definition of discourse, therefore, ought to be expanded in order to make these implicit appeals more explicit. Discourse, I submit, is 'something said *by someone* to someone about something.' After all, things do not get said on their own" (*Is There a Meaning*, 214, 216). In a similar vein, Vanhoozer writes that Gadamer cannot separate the intention of the text from the intention of the author (*Is There a Meaning*, 107, 142, 201–80; *Drama of Doctrine*, 157).

98. Wolterstorff, *Divine Discourse*, 51–54; Burger, *Being in Christ*, 15–16. God's speech, according to Wolterstorff, cannot be reduced to revelation because when God reveals, he dispels ignorance, while when he speaks, he takes a normative stance towards us and demands things of us (*Divine Discourse*, 23, 35). It is beyond the scope of this section to determine why God appropriated the texts he did and not others, as well as how the process of appropriation took place. For helpful insights in this regard, see Burger, "God spreekt," 142–44.

99. Vanhoozer, *First Theology*, 131.

the Father, Son, and Spirit[100] and God's communicative activity in the economic Trinity reveals his communicative activity in the immanent Trinity.[101] Scripture, then, is God's communicative action in and through which God speaks as a communicative agent, addressing and engaging those who hear and read it through "a rainbow of divine communicative acts."[102]

In this way, Vanhoozer locates Scripture in the economy of redemption and gives it a mission in this economy analogous to the missions of the Son and the Spirit. As the Son was sent on a mission, so Scripture is sent on a mission. As God's communicative action was embodied in Jesus, so his communicative action is verbalized in Scripture. As God sent Jesus to draw people into the new covenant community to participate in his divine life in Christ, so God sent Scripture to do the same. As God's communicative action in Jesus was accompanied by the Spirit and requires the Spirit, so his communicative action in and through Scripture is also accompanied by the Spirit and requires the Spirit so that it can extend Christ's communicative action.[103]

This makes Scripture God's covenant document, which contains the unified speech act of a single speaker through the speech acts of different human authors that "both recount the history of God's covenant dealings with humanity and regulate God's ongoing covenantal relationship with

---

100. "To communicate (Lat. *communicare*) is to 'share' or 'make common'" (Vanhoozer, *Remythologizing Theology*, 203, 207, 211).

101. When Vanhoozer writes that the economic Trinity reveals the immanent Trinity, he means that "the economic Trinity corresponds to but does not exhaust or encompass the reality of the immanent Trinity" (*Remythologizing Theology*, 203).

102. Vanhoozer, "Ascending the Mountain," 35; cf. 9-13, 202, 291-92; cf. Huijgen, *Lezen en laten lezen*, 24-31. Taking his cue from Barth, who identified God the Father as the revealer, God the Son as the revelation, and God the Holy Spirit as the revealedness, Vanhoozer identifies God the Father as the locution or the agent who initiates communication, God the Son as the illocution or the content of the communication, and God the Holy Spirit as the perlocution or consequence of the communication (*First Theology*, 154-56, 291-92). Bowald indicates that there may be theological problems with this correspondence between the three persons of the Trinity and the three forms of speech acts but does not state what the problem may be (*Rendering the Word*, 200). Burger states that because the Father always addresses us in Christ through the Spirit, identifying the three persons of the Trinity with the three different forms of speech acts has its limitations ("Foundation or Perspective?," 40).

103. Vanhoozer, *Drama of Doctrine*, 60, 70-71, 228.

his people."[104] As such, Scripture is not only a binding and authoritative witness to God's revelation but is itself also revelation.[105]

As God's covenant document through which God communicates and reveals himself, with a mission analogous to the missions of the Son and the Spirit, Scripture has stability of meaning. Meaning is "the result of communicative action, of what an author has done intending to certain words at a particular time in a specific manner." This leads to a literal or literary sense of meaning, where the "literal [or literary] sense of an utterance of text is the sum total of those illocutionary acts performed by the author intentionally and with self-awareness." Understanding a text, then, "consists in recognizing illocutionary acts and their results," and "interpretation is the process of inferring authorial intentions and of ascribing illocutionary acts."[106]

Yet there is more to the meaning of a text than the literal or literary meaning. Because the Word of God is embodied in Jesus Christ in the New Testament, and because of the continuity of God's acts in his Word, later revelations can be prefigured in earlier texts. Thus, typological or figural meanings of Scripture are possible.

Further, because of the close relationship between Christ—the incarnate Word of God, into whose image God wants to transform us—and the Scriptures as the Word of God, God can use Scripture to transform us into Christlikeness. This leads to a transfigural reading of Scripture, because the more we see the glory of Christ in Scripture, the more we can be transformed in his image.[107] In this approach, the literal or literary sense of particular texts does not change but is extended to Scripture as an organic whole.[108]

---

104. Vanhoozer, *Drama of Doctrine*, 137, cf. 68

105. Vanhoozer, *Drama of Doctrine*, 38, 147, 267, 276. Like Wolterstorff, Vanhoozer does not reduce Scripture to revelation (*Drama of Doctrine*, 45, 48).

106. Vanhoozer, *First Theology*, 202–3.

107. Vanhoozer, "Ascending the Mountain," 795–97.

108. Storer helpfully compares Vanhoozer and Henri de Lubac and notes that whereas Vanhoozer emphasizes God's communicative action through the literal, canonical sense of Scripture, de Lubac emphasizes God's communicative action through the spiritual sense of Scripture that illuminates the great allegory of Christ. For Vanhoozer, this implies that the meaning of a text is determinate, bound to the locutions and illocutions of a text; for de Lubac, the meaning of a text is infinite because Scripture mediates the infinite mystery of God revealed in Christ. Behind these two approaches to determining the meaning of a text lie two different ontologies: a communicative/covenantal ontology for Vanhoozer and a sacramental ontology for de Lubac (Storer, *Reading Scripture to Hear God*, 1–102). For a critique of a "spiritual reading" of Scripture

However, this redemptive-historical context of Scripture includes not only the text of Scripture but the reader of Scripture as well, for it shows how he "figures" in the story and is related to Christ in the history of redemption.[109] Accordingly, Vanhoozer says, when we behold "the glory of the Lord in the face (i.e., literal sense) of the biblical text . . . the Spirit uses [this] to effect our own transfiguration 'from one degree of glory to another'" (2 Cor 3:18). In doing so, "the Spirit uses Scripture to form interpreters into active actors in the theodrama [of Scripture]."[110] Thus, the "economy of communication terminates not in the text, but in us."[111] As active actors, we complete the text when we perform it.[112]

---

that departs from the literal text, see Provan, *Reformation*, 199–225. For his criticism of a Christian-platonic sacramental ontology, see Provan, *Reformation*, 416–23.

109. Burger aptly shows how the fourfold sense of Scripture can be reconfigured to give a fourfold perspective on how the reader is included in the theodrama of Scripture. He is included historically in the literal reading of Scripture. He is included allegorically because he participates in the story of Jesus Christ. He is included morally or tropologically because he lives his life today in the tension of the already and not yet. He is included anagogically because he longs for the fulfillment of God's new creation in the coming kingdom of heaven ("Foundation or Perspective?," 60–61). In the light of the fact that allegorical interpretation has a history of finding fanciful different (*allos*) interpretations of a text that arbitrarily change its literary sense, I would prefer to speak of being typologically included in the theodrama of Scripture because we participate in the story of Jesus, since typology does not change the literary sense of the text but only its referent (Vanhoozer, "Ascending the Mountain," 786–87).

110. Vanhoozer, "Ascending the Mountain," 797; Burger, "Foundation or Perspective?," 59–60. To use the language of speech act theory, this is the perlocutionary effect of God's speech acts in Scripture. Because the perlocutionary effect refers to the effects or significance of the meaning of a speech act, it does not change the determinate meaning of the speech act. It simply shows that there is an abundance of significance or application in the meaning of Scripture for all the different readers of Scripture. Vanhoozer refers to this perlocutionary effect of the meaning of the speech act as the significance of the text distinguishing it from the meaning of the text (*Is There a Meaning*, 259–63). However, he also refers to it as the extended meaning of the text (*Is There a Meaning*, 262; cf. "Ascending the Mountain," 797).

111. Vanhoozer, "Drama-of-Redemption Model," 74.

112. Hart links the word "performance" to "*parfournir* (to accomplish entirely, achieve, complete)" (Hart and Guthrie, *Faithful Performances*, 5; Farlow, *Dramatizing of Theology*, 9).

THE NATURE OF DOCTRINE

Doctrine as grammar

In *The Nature of Doctrine*, George Lindbeck challenged two models of the nature of doctrine that, after years of teaching doctrine and of ecumenical work, he found to be conceptually and practically problematic in meeting the challenges that changing situations continue to present to the church.[113] The first is the *cognitive-propositional* model, "in which church doctrines function as informative propositions or truth claims about objective realities."[114] The second is the *experiential-expressive* model, which "interprets doctrines as noninformative and nondiscursive symbols of inner feelings, attitudes, or existential orientations."[115] Instead, Lindbeck proposed a third model for understanding the nature of doctrine, the *cultural-linguistic* model.

Earlier, I noted that some of those influenced by the linguistic turn in philosophy and impacted by Wittgenstein rejected the idea that words get their meaning by standing for external objects or being associated with ideas in the mind. Instead, they emphasized that words are tools or instruments that determine how we think about and give meaning to our life in the world from within the context of the actual situations of our everyday life. Moreover, I noted that because language is part of the world we inhabit, we have no point of view outside of language from which we can evaluate the relationship between language and the world.

Lindbeck's cultural-linguistic model needs to be understood within this linguistic framework, for this model emphasizes that "religions resemble languages together with their correlative forms of life and are thus similar to cultures (insofar as these are understood semiotically as reality and value systems—that is, as idioms for the constructing of reality and the living of life)." If religion resembles languages and cultures, then the "function of church doctrines that becomes most prominent in this perspective is their use, not as expressive symbols or as truth claims, but as communally authoritative rules of discourse, attitude, and action."[116]

---

113. Lindbeck, *Nature of Doctrine*, 7.
114. Lindbeck, *Nature of Doctrine*, 16.
115. Lindbeck, *Nature of Doctrine*, 16.
116. Lindbeck, *Nature of Doctrine*, 18–19; cf. Vanhoozer, *Drama of Doctrine*, 10.

Understanding doctrine as rules of discourse does not deny that doctrines express propositional convictions.[117] But these are "second-order rather than first-order propositions and affirm nothing about extra-linguistic or extra-human reality." Thus, as second-order propositions they make "intrasystematic rather than ontological truth claims." Consequently, this approach "does not locate the abiding and doctrinally significant aspects of religion in propositionally formulated truths, . . . but in the story it tells and in the grammar that informs the way the story is told and used. . . . On this view, doctrines acquire their force from their relation to the grammar of a religion." These doctrines "illustrate correct usage rather than define it."[118] Learning doctrine, therefore, is like learning a language through participating in its use by speaking that language.[119]

Seeing doctrines as second-order propositions that make intrasystematic truth claims helps us understand what is at stake when a religion's first-order statements change because of the challenges posted by our changing situations. According to Lindbeck, when this happens it does not change the ontological truth claims as such, but it requires only an application of the grammar or rules of discourse of doctrine to these ontological truth claims so that they are expressed in a different way—speaking, for instance, of Jesus as "the Messiah," the "incarnate Logos," the "Man for others," or "the humanity of God."[120] "Yet, amid these shifts in Christological affirmations and in the corresponding experiences of Jesus Christ, the story of passion and resurrection and the basic rules for its use remain the same."[121] Moreover, "Christians allow their cultural conditions and highly diverse affections to be molded by the set of biblical stories that stretches from creation to eschaton and culminates in Jesus' passion and resurrection."[122]

This emphasis on the biblical story shaping social and ecclesial practice involves a priority of practice over theory, a "performance interpretation" or "embodiment" of the biblical story where our secular culture does not absorb the biblical story but the biblical story absorbs our

---

117. There is a debate as to whether this is Lindbeck's own view, but it is beyond the scope of this study to adjudicate this debate.
118. Lindbeck, *Nature of Doctrine*, 80–81.
119. Lindbeck, *Nature of Doctrine*, 81.
120. Lindbeck, *Nature of Doctrine*, 82.
121. Lindbeck, *Nature of Doctrine*, 83.
122. Lindbeck, *Nature of Doctrine*, 84.

secular culture.[123] However, because of the variety of perspectives within the biblical story, "the meaning ascribed to texts is underdetermined to the extent that their use in shaping life and thought is unspecified."[124] Thus, to be able "to appeal to Scripture as a whole for the contemporary guidance of the church," the church needs a norm outside of Scripture "to decide *which* part of Scripture to apply in any given situation and how."[125]

For Lindbeck, this norm lies in the church's use of the narrative.[126] It is the church's use of the biblical narrative that makes doctrine normative.[127] This is how doctrine regulates the Christian faith or functions as the grammar of the language of the Christian community that illustrates its correct usage in meeting the church's continually varying challenges. This cultural-linguistic model of doctrine does not suffer from the conceptual and practical problems in meeting those challenges that the cognitive-propositional and emotional-expressive models of doctrine have.

Lindbeck's approach, however, has problems of its own. Vanhoozer considers Lindbeck's model to be reductionistic, with a reductionistic view of doctrine in general, of the cognitive-propositional model in particular, and of the cognitive dimension of doctrine. He believes Lindbeck's model fails to distinguish between the meaning of the biblical story and the significance of the story for the church community. Moreover, because the church community often lacks a consensus on how to apply the rules to new problems and challenges, the church in reality is often unable to provide the stability for church doctrine that Lindbeck thinks his model gives it.[128]

---

123. Lindbeck, "Atonement," 222–25; *Nature of Doctrine*, 118.

124. Lindbeck, "Postcritical Canonical Interpretation," 36.

125. Lindbeck, "Postcritical Canonical Interpretation," 36; cf. Vanhoozer, *Drama of Doctrine*, 172.

126. Lindbeck, *Nature of Doctrine*, 80.

127. Vanhoozer, *Drama of Doctrine*, 172. While for Lindbeck the church's use of the biblical narrative is what makes doctrine normative, after reading Wolterstorff's *Divine Discourse* (1995), he was also open to authorial-discourse functioning as a norm for doctrine (Lindbeck, "Postcritical Canonical Interpretation," 40–49). However, he made no effort to show how these two norms can function side by side (Vanhoozer, *Drama of Doctrine*, 167, 173, 183–84).

128. Vanhoozer, *Drama of Doctrine*, 84–88, 96–97, 121, 141; cf. McGrath, *Genesis of Doctrine*, 15–20.

Doctrine and drama

Even though Lindbeck's cultural-linguistic approach to doctrine is open to significant criticism, the benefit of his approach is its emphasis on ecclesial practice and the performance of doctrine.[129] To do justice to this emphasis, Vanhoozer develops his alternative model, which he aptly calls a canonical-linguistic approach. This model is meant to integrate the best of the cognitive-propositional model with its emphasis on information, the emotional-expressive model with its emphasis on expression, and the cultural-linguistic model with its emphasis on rules for Christian practice.[130] Doctrine, on Vanhoozer's view, is dramatic or theatrical direction for fitting participation in or performance of the drama of redemption.[131]

While the theater is not mentioned very often in Scripture (e.g., Acts 19:29, 31), there are at least five reasons for comparing doctrine to drama—though it must be emphasized that the comparison is not necessary but expedient for the purpose of ministry.[132]

First, because "the essence of drama is persons presenting themselves to one another, largely through language, but also through deeds," Scripture is dramatic both in its form and its content.[133] It is dramatic literature that resembles a play and can be compared to a script or transcript, and so comparing doctrine to drama is "not imposing an external model (i.e., the theater) onto Scripture."[134]

As we have seen above, Scripture is ultimately a drama of God's mission for his glory in which he brings creation and humanity to live in his loving presence and participate in his life in Christ through the Spirit.

---

129. Vanhoozer, *Drama of Doctrine*, xiii.

130. Vanhoozer, *Drama of Doctrine*, 106.

131. Vanhoozer, *Drama of Doctrine*, 30–33. Vanhoozer writes, "A drama is a *doing* (from *drao* = 'I do')" (*Remythologizing Theology*, 195). Considering doctrine to be dramatic or viewing it as theatrical direction for fitting participation in or performance of the drama of redemption does not imply advocating drama in the worship service, however (Vanhoozer, *Faith Speaking Understanding*, 242).

132. Vanhoozer, *Faith Speaking Understanding*, 21.

133. Vanhoozer, *Faith Speaking Understanding*, 27; "The Voice and the Actor," 91. Wright writes, "... the Israelites did certainly have the idea that the mighty acts of God in and through them were *visible* to the nations, who are often portrayed as spectators and witnesses of the story as it proceeds, whether in salvation or judgment. The idea of the world as an open stage on which Yahweh God was at work in Israel and the nations in the great drama of history would not have been foreign to the Israelite imagination" (*The Great Story*, 15; see also *Mission of God*, 467–74).

134. Vanhoozer, *Drama of Doctrine*, 244–46.

As God sent Jesus to accomplish this goal, so he also sent Scripture to do the same.

Accordingly, Scripture is "part of the drama itself."[135] Scripture is God's communicative action in Christ through which he wants to draw us into an ever-deeper communion with Christ through the Holy Spirit. Since "theology's method should be appropriate to its theo-dramatic subject matter," it naturally follows that doctrine that is the result of reflection upon this theodramatic subject matter and gives direction for continuing the theodrama should also be dramatic.[136]

Second, it is natural to compare doctrine with drama because both doctrine and God's relationship with humanity are dialogical.[137] As a God of communicative action, God dialogues with humanity, communicating with them by way of his speech acts, through which he asserts things to them, directs them, promises things to them, expresses his feelings to them, and declares things to them—all toward his goal of having people participate in his mission for his glory by living in his loving presence and sharing his divine life in Christ by the Spirit. Humanity, in turn, is to live in a dialogical relationship with God, responding to him with a spirit of filial receptiveness by obediently participating in God's mission.

Third, comparing doctrine with drama appeals to our imagination.[138] While imagination as such is "the power of forming mental images of what is not really present," a biblically informed imagination "is the ability to form mental images of what is *really* present . . . even though it cannot be perceived empirically with the senses."[139] It is "the power of synoptic vision: the ability to synthesize heterogeneous elements into a unified whole. . . . It is the ability to discover connections."[140]

---

135. Balthasar, *Theo-Drama*, 2:112; cf. 2:102–15; Vanhoozer, *Drama of Doctrine*, 70–71.

136. Vanhoozer, *Drama of Doctrine*, 38; "The Voice and the Actor," 91; *Faith Speaking Understanding*, 28–29; *Pictures at a Theological Exhibition*, 228–29.

137. Vanhoozer, "The Voice and the Actor," 91; *Faith Speaking Understanding*, 68–72.

138. Vanhoozer, "The Voice and the Actor," 91, 94; *Faith Speaking Understanding*, 25.

139. Vanhoozer, *Drama of Doctrine*, 416; see also Farlow, *Dramatizing of Theology*, 125–66.

140. Vanhoozer, *Drama of Doctrine*, 416, 281; *Pictures at a Theological Exhibition*, 23–27, 133, 165, 177, 232; *Doers and Hearers*, 56, 108.

As such, the imagination is "a cognitive[141] faculty for creating meaning."[142] As an integrative faculty, it "engages the will and emotions as well as the mind.[143] As an organ of meaning, the biblically informed

---

141. Vanhoozer explains: "By 'cognitive' I simply mean what pertains to mental rather than bodily action." He adds, "To imagine something is to think of it as possibly being so" (*Pictures at a Theological Exhibition*, 26). Smith, however, believes the imagination is fundamentally noncognitive: "Because we are affective before we are cognitive (and even while we are cognitive), visions of the good get inscribed in us by means that are commensurate with our primarily affective, imaginative nature." He adds, "Rather than being pushed by beliefs, we are pulled by a *telos* that we desire. It's not so much that we're intellectually convinced and then muster the willpower to pursue what we ought; rather, at a precognitive level, we are attracted to a vision of the good life that has been painted for us in stories and myths, images and icons. It is not primarily our minds that are captivated but rather our imaginations that are captured" (*Desiring the Kingdom*, 53–54).

Vanhoozer believes that understanding the imagination as fundamentally noncognitive is too sharp a dichotomy. He writes, "I am less willing to distinguish thinking from imagining so sharply or to prioritize the latter [i.e., desire] over the former [i.e., thinking]. Although I agree that 'what we love is a specific vision of the good life, an implicit picture of what we think human flourishing looks like,' I think this picture, like the imagination itself, is fundamentally cognitive, not non-cognitive, as Smith maintains" (*Pictures at a Theological Exhibition*, 25).

Having asserted that "faith is the enduring ability to imagine God, the world and ourselves in the light of the biblical story of salvation," he sums up his key claims as follows: "(1) Only the imagination—the ability to grasp meaningful patterns or conceive unified wholes out of apparently unrelated elements—enables us to 'see' God and the kingdom of God at work in the world. (2) It is faith that enables this imagination—and faith comes by *hearing*, and hearing from the word of Christ (Rom 10:17)" (*Pictures at a Theological Exhibition*, 17).

Vanhoozer's understanding of the imagination as primarily a cognitive faculty is corroborated by Egan. He writes, "So, the imagination is the capacity to think of things as possibly being so; it is an intentional act of mind; . . . it is not distinct from rationality but rather a capacity that greatly enriches rational thinking" (*Imagination*, 43). Regarding the imagination as a faculty concerned with possibility, Bailey writes, "The imagination perceives possible ways of being in the world, is captivated by other possibilities, and seeks to negotiate a space for life amid possibility." He adds, "The imaginative faculty moves us forward by facilitating three things: (1) an orienting vision *for* the world, (2) an aesthetic experience *of* the world, and (3) a poetic [i.e., dramatic] participation *in* the world" (*Reimagining Apologetics*, 89–90, 102; see also Gould, *Cultural Apologetics*, 106–10; Ordway, *Apologetics and the Christian Imagination*, 15–20). For the imagination granting a more textured access to reality than reductive materialism, see Tyson, *Seven Brief Lessons*, 36–41.

142. C.S. Lewis compares reason and imagination as follows: "For me, reason is the natural organ of truth, imagination is the organ of meaning. Imagination, producing new metaphors or revivifying old, is not the cause of truth, but its condition." In other words, metaphors and analogies are necessary to enable us to understand the meaning of our words (Lewis, "Bluspels and Flalansferes," 265; cf. Vanhoozer, "In Bright Shadow," 94).

143. Vanhoozer, "In Bright Shadow," 99; *Pictures at a Theological Exhibition*, 24, 166;

imagination functions by metaphorically explaining the unfamiliar in terms of the familiar, such as saying "God is my rock" or "the Lord is my shepherd."

It also functions eschatologically, to allow us to recognize something that will be perfect only in the future as already being partially present, as in Paul's statement, "Therefore, if anyone is in Christ, he is a new creation. The old has passed away; behold, the new has come" (2 Cor 5:17). Vanhoozer refers to what C. S. Lewis says about growing to be like Christ by pretending to be like Christ and says, "What Lewis calls 'good pretending' is not the fictive *what if* but the eschatological *what is*. Though the naked eye can't see it, the eyes of the heart see God's transferring saints from the old age to the new, from the kingdom of darkness to the kingdom of light (Col 1:13)."[144]

In this way, the biblically informed imagination is the ability to see things as they really are in Christ.[145] Consequently, the theodramatic imagination is the ability to see the drama of God's mission of intratrinitarian glorification being enacted on earth as it is in heaven and our participation in or performance of this drama of mutual glorification as one unified drama through our union with Christ by faith.

Fourth, the comparison of doctrine to drama reminds us that the Christian life is filled with "tension and urgency."[146] Every day, we are confronted with situations, problems, and challenges new and old that require putting on Jesus Christ. They require embodying the Christian faith so that we can take our part in God's mission for his glory. Often, we have to improvise creatively to meet these challenges wisely and deal with problems in a way that is faithful to the authorial intent of God's divine discourse in Scripture.[147]

Doers and Hearers, 107; *Drama of Doctrine*, 12. Vanhoozer adds, "Paul perhaps has the imagination in mind when, in Ephesians 1:18, he speaks of 'having the eyes of your hearts enlightened.' The Spirit alone can open the eyes of our heart, but we then have to make the effort to keep them open by maintaining a vital relationship with the object of our heart's desire: the Lord Jesus Christ'" ("In Bright Shadow," 99). For a holistic understanding of the imagination as the eyes of the heart, see Searle, *Eyes of Your Heart*.

144. Vanhoozer, "In Bright Shadow," 100; *Pictures at a Theological Exhibition*, 27. On Lewis's understanding of the imagination and his sacramental view of reality, see Williams, *C. S. Lewis*, 79–189.

145. Vanhoozer, "In Bright Shadow," 99–101.

146. Vanhoozer, "The Voice and the Actor," 91; *Faith Speaking Understanding*, 21; Balthasar, *Theo-Drama*, 1:260–61. Drama, says Balthasar, illuminates human existence (*Theo-Drama*, 1:259–68).

147. In addition to Scripture, the church has the "classic productions" or "masterpiece

DESIGN FEATURES OF A THEODRAMATIC FRAMEWORK

In addition, there is the tension of living in between the times, in the already and not yet. The life, death, and resurrection of Jesus Christ launched the fulfillment of God's eschatological goal and already now we live in God's loving presence and share in his life—but not yet as we will when Christ returns and God will be all in all. It is the tension between the already and the not yet that propels the drama of God's mission. This dramatic tension includes the urgency of our own daily repentance and the call to others to repent and believe because the kingdom of heaven is near. Without faith and repentance, there will be no entrance into this coming kingdom. Comparing doctrine to drama, then, reminds us that in this dramatic tension "the Spirit uses Scripture to form interpreters into active actors in the theodrama."[148]

Fifth, comparing doctrine to drama reminds us that reading and interpreting Scripture redemptive-historically includes not only the text of Scripture but also the reader of Scripture, because it shows how he figures in the story and is related to Christ in the history of redemption. As such, doctrine as drama bridges the gap between theory and practice.[149]

This conforms to what I wrote earlier about the perlocutionary nature of speech acts. While an illocutionary speech act has to do with the rhetorical force of an utterance or what it intends to accomplish, a perlocutionary speech act refers to the way the illocutionary speech act elicits a response, the effect it has in the life of a person of community. Accordingly, Scripture is not only a text but also a script that regulates God's continued communicative action through us as we seek to perform it.[150]

It is precisely the fact that the script of Scripture regulates the church's performance of the theodrama of Scripture that distinguishes this ecclesial performance from Lindbeck's, where the goals and interests

---

theater" of the ecumenical councils and the "classic productions" or "regional theater" of the confessional theology of a particular denomination and of other denominations (Vanhoozer, *Drama of Doctrine*, 449–53; "Drama-of-Redemption Model," 74–175; *Faith Speaking Understanding*, 147–49). On the relevance of doctrine and creeds, see Sayers, *Creed or Chaos* and *Letters to a Diminished Church*, 1–79.

148. Vanhoozer, "Ascending the Mountain," 797.

149. Vanhoozer, *Faith Speaking Understanding*, 4, 20, 33–37; *Pictures at a Theological Exhibition*, 226–28.

150. Vanhoozer, *Drama of Doctrine*, 234–36; Balthasar, *Theo-Drama*, 1:20. Faced with objections that biblical interpretation is not about performing texts, Vanhoozer clarifies: "strictly speaking, *we do not perform the text/script but the world/theodrama that the text/script presupposes, entails, and implies*" (Vanhoozer, "Drama-of-Redemption Model," 166).

of the interpreting community rule and regulate the church's performance.[151] Thus, there is no need to place authorial discourse interpretation over against performance interpretation. We bring them together and place them side-by-side.[152]

Doctrine as dramatic direction

Scripture contains God's speech acts. Doctrine reconceptualizes these speech acts into "thought-acts" or "mental habits." Through these, we interpret and experience God's speech acts in Scripture and in Jesus Christ in terms of theodramatic imagination and action.[153] The purpose of these thought-acts or doctrinal habits is to draw us into the theodrama of redemption so that we participate in this drama as it continues in the life of the church until Jesus Christ returns.[154]

Doctrine therefore has a pastoral function. It was always meant to be more about training in wisdom and life with God than in abstract truth.[155] Seeing doctrine as dramatic direction or as pastoral instruction in wisdom reminds us of the catechetical instruction in the early church, where catechumens were not only taught the substance of the Christian faith but were also taught how this faith directed them to participate in the reality to which the substance referred. Then, when they were baptized, they were visibly and dramatically initiated into this reality—the drama of redemption—which served as a frame of reference for the rest of their lives.[156]

---

151. Vanhoozer, *Drama of Doctrine*, 165–76.

152. Vanhoozer, *Drama of Doctrine*, 184. Wolterstorff does place authorial discourse interpretation over against performance interpretation (*Divine Discourse*, 171–82). For the performance of Scripture, see also Lash, *Theology on the Way*; Young, *Art of Performance*. Wells places improvisation over against performance (Wells, *Improvisation*, 61–65). However, when we understand improvisation as the improvisation of a transcript, performance of a transcript and improvisation of a transcript go hand in hand (Vanhoozer, *Drama of Doctrine*, 335).

153. Vanhoozer, *Drama of Doctrine*, 90, 377–78; *Faith Speaking Understanding*, 25–27, 31–32; *Doers and Hearers*, 109–13, 132–36; Vander Lugt, *Living Theodrama*, 13–14.

154. Vanhoozer, *Faith Speaking Understanding*, 87–89.

155. Charry, *By the Renewing*; Huijgen, *Lezen en laten lezen*, 70; Vanhoozer, *Drama of Doctrine*, 13–14; *Doers and Hearers*, 217.

156. Vanhoozer, *Drama of Doctrine*, 103. For the importance of character formation for theatrical formation, see Stanislavski, *An Actor Prepares* and *Building a Character*; cf. Vander Lugt, *Living Theodrama*, 33–36, 45; Vanhoozer, *Drama of Doctrine*, 369–74; "At Play," 118.

Doctrine as dramatic direction is meant to lead to *fitting* participation in or performance of the drama. *First*, it must comport with the whole drama of redemption as it has been communicated to us in Scripture, the script of the theodrama, which has its dramatic center in Jesus Christ.[157] God communicates this whole theodrama as a differentiated wholeness through a variety of literary forms or genres.[158] These genres do not function just as literary classifications, but as "literary games" or rule-governed communicative social practices that engage reality in a way that is meant to achieve certain communicative goals and responses. As such, the canonical script of Scripture is like an "atlas" that contains a "collection of maps" having "the same basic orientation" but reflecting different perspectives that provide "an interpretive framework" or a way of participating in the drama of redemption.[159]

Lindbeck's cultural-linguistic model of doctrine has us participating in the language game or rule-governed life of the church community in order to understand the meaning of the biblical narrative. The canonical-linguistic model of doctrine that Vanhoozer proposes, which views doctrine as dramatic direction, has us participate in the literary games (genres) or rule-governed communicative social practices of the canon in order to understand the meaning of the biblical narrative and respond appropriately to it.[160] If we want to participate in God's drama of redemption in a way that fits with the whole drama as it has been communicated to us in Scripture, we must become apprentices to these diverse canonical practices or canonical maps and learn how they inform doctrine, which directs us to participate fittingly in the theodrama of Scripture.

Second, dramatic direction for fitting participation in the drama of redemption must not only demonstrate faithfulness to the canonical text; it must also demonstrate faithfulness to the contemporary context. Because the canonical script is the living and active word of God (Heb 4:12), it can do that by enabling us to make wise judgments that fittingly transpose the meaning of the text into a different cultural key. Moreover, because the canonical practices of Scripture and the drama of redemption

---

157. Vanhoozer, *Drama of Doctrine*, 258–59; "Drama-of-Redemption Model," 179–81; *Faith Speaking Understanding*, 145–47.

158. Vanhoozer, *Drama of Doctrine*, 272–76.

159. Vanhoozer, *Drama of Doctrine*, 295–97; *Pictures at a Theological Exhibition*, 88–90, 100–101.

160. Vanhoozer, *Drama of Doctrine*, 213–15, 282–91.

communicated in Scripture are transcultural, they are relevant for everyone in every culture.¹⁶¹

Fittingly transposing the canonical text into a different cross-cultural key will involve improvising and creatively and imaginatively extending the meaning of the text in ways that develop the theodramatic action in new situations and that reincorporate the new situation into the theodrama. Jesus creatively and imaginatively extended the meaning of the Old Testament and developed the theodramatic action further, incorporating himself and his ministry into it. The apostle Paul creatively and imaginatively did the same with regard to the inclusion of the Gentiles into the people of God.¹⁶² This does not lead to a "fusion" of horizons, as Gadamer would have us believe, because transposing the meaning of the text into new context does not entail the "merging or mixing" of cultures, but rather the enrichment of each culture, since each culture retains its particularity.¹⁶³

Fittingly transposing the meaning of the canonical text into a different cultural key also entails being prophetic, since often there are dissimilarities between the canonical text and the contemporary situation. Many people in our contemporary culture participate in a different drama. Fitting transposition protests against these competing dramas that work against the theodrama of Scripture. It speaks out against them and does not accommodate or capitulate to them. Moreover, fitting transposition prophetically protests against these competing dramas by faithfully and compellingly bearing witness to the eschatological resurrection life that has broken into the world in Christ and his Spirit. In doing so, the church participates in Christ's prophetic ministry by being his eyes, ears, mouth, hands, and feet in this world—being people and places where heaven and earth meet.¹⁶⁴

---

161. Vanhoozer, *Drama of Doctrine*, 313–14, 317–18; *Faith Speaking Understanding*, 199–204.

162. Vanhoozer, *Drama of Doctrine*, 335–40, 388–89; "Drama-of-Redemption Model," 172–74; *Faith Speaking Understanding*, 193–94; *Doers and Hearers*, 154–55; Wells, *Improvisation*, 65–66, 150–51; Vander Lugt, *Living Theodrama*, 72–73; cf. 69–78.

163. Vanhoozer, *Drama of Doctrine*, 352. For the importance of theodramatic availability, openness, and receptivity for creatively and imaginatively extending the meaning of the text, see Balthasar, *Glory of the Lord*, 5:106, 112–13; *Theo-Drama*, 2:288; Vander Lugt, *Living Theodrama*, 29–60. Vander Lugt rightly states that this openness and receptivity needs to be an openness and receptivity "to the triune God, Scripture, the church, tradition, unbelievers, and local contexts that produces readiness for theodramatic performance" (*Living Theodrama*, 44; cf. 47)

164. Vanhoozer, *Drama of Doctrine*, 356–59.

For instance, Vanhoozer concludes that transsexuality does not extend the meaning of the text to develop the theodrama faithfully and fittingly in a new situation. It is

> bad improvisation in which, forgetting what happened in Act One (creation), one strikes out in one's own technologically clever (but self-determined) direction, ontologically ad-libbing, laughing all the way to the organ bank. To perform sex reassignment surgery is to encourage the worst kind of playacting: hypocrisy. The irony, as with all sin, is that in trying to find oneself, one loses oneself. Those who seek to rewrite their roles make God a bit player in a drama that exchanges the gospel for the pottage of self-determination.[165]

He adds, "To be sure, all of us have sinned and have manifested a tendency to script-write our own lives. Transsexuals are not 'worse' sinners than anyone else, though the symptoms of their self-alienation may be more conspicuous.[166]

Doctrine and the formation of Christian identity and practice

Narrative reconfigures our identity in terms of a biographical story that has meaning and purpose because it is placed within the overarching narrative of Scripture. Doctrine reconceptualizes the speech acts of Scripture into thought-acts or mental habits by which we interpret and experience God's speech acts in Scripture and in Jesus Christ in terms of theodramatic imagination and action, and by these thought-acts or mental habits doctrine also reconfigures our narrative identity. Our Christian identity and practice, therefore, are essentially theodramatic.[167] Consequently, "who we are is ultimately defined in terms of Jesus' person and work." We are united to Christ or in Christ, and we have the task to increasingly become like Christ.[168]

Doctrine, then, is a mental habit that directs us in imaginatively and creatively understanding our identity in Christ. For instance, the doctrine of the Trinity directs us to remember that God's being is a dynamic missional activity of love, life, and glorification between the Father, Son, and

---

165. Vanhoozer, "Drama-of-Redemption Model," 196–97.
166. Vanhoozer, "Drama-of-Redemption Model," 214.
167. Balthasar, *Theo-Drama*, 1:645–48; cf. 1:481–643; 2:335–46; 3:149–259.
168. Vanhoozer, *Drama of Doctrine*, 392; "Putting on Christ," 147–71.

Spirit and that God's missional activity in the economic Trinity reveals his missional activity in the immanent Trinity, so that what is being done on earth is what happens in heaven.[169] The doctrine of creation directs us to remember that God created this world and humanity so that it and we could share in his fellowship of love with his Son through the Holy Spirit and join him in his mission for his glory by living in his loving presence and participating in his life.[170] The doctrines of the fall and redemption direct us to remember God's intention for us to do what Adam and Eve did not do, to spread the blessing of living in God's loving presence and sharing in his life throughout the world by dealing with the chaos and disorder caused by sin.[171]

Indeed, the doctrine of redemption after the fall—together with our eschatological expectation—reveals to us that the theodrama is not a tragedy, "because Jesus' life is not taken from him but freely laid down (John 10:17–18). Moreover, Jesus' death loses its sting when the Father vindicates him by raising him from the dead, the first step in putting all injustice to rights (1 Cor. 15:55)." Instead, it is a divine comedy, because

> comedy often turns social conventions on their heads; indeed, such comic inversion is often the focus of the play. The divine comedy of Christ's exchanging the form of God for the form of a slave (Phil. 2:5–8) represents the greatest inversion of all. The difference between comedy and tragedy is, in the final analysis, a matter of endings: tragedy begins well but ends badly; comedy begins with a complication but ends well—in this case, with every knee in heaven and on earth bending at, and every tongue confessing, the name of Jesus Christ as Lord (Phil. 2:10–11).[172]

---

169. Vanhoozer, *Faith Speaking Understanding*, 73–75, 80–82, 89–90, 110; "At Play," 3, 14–17, 20–21, 26–27; Balthasar, *Theo-Drama*, 3:505–35; 5:61–109, 111–88; *Glory of the Lord*, 2:74–75.

170. Balthasar, *Theo-Drama*, 5:425–29; *Glory of the Lord*, 1:618; cf. 1:605–18; 6:87–143.

171. Cf. Balthasar, *Theo-Drama*, 3:192–93; cf. 3:178–211.

172. Vanhoozer, *Faith Speaking Understanding*, 94–95. Adams claims that Christianity is "*tragi-comic:* grim realism that wins through to a happy ending" (Adams, "Eucharistic Drama," 217). Siding with Shakespeare, Balthasar writes about the genre of the drama, "In accordance with the Christian principle of forgiving mercy, the dramatist causes the Good to predominate without feeling it necessary to reduce the totality of world events to some all-embracing formula. Just as, in his central plays, he takes up a position beyond tragedy and comedy, because the world he portrays is a mixture of both elements, so he also rises above justice and mercy by allowing both of them to persist, partly in each other and partly in opposition to each other. But all the time he is utterly certain that the highest good is to be found in forgiveness" (*Theo-Drama*,

DESIGN FEATURES OF A THEODRAMATIC FRAMEWORK

But doctrine is not only a mental habit that directs us in understanding our identity in Christ; it is also a mental habit that directs us to become more and more what we are in Christ, under the direction and by the power of the Holy Spirit. Our Christian identity leads to Christian practice that bears witness to all that is in Christ.[173]

For instance, the doctrine of the Trinity directs us to perform what is in Christ by putting on Christ and clothing ourselves with him, so that we act out the splendor of God's perfect life of love in Christ through the Holy Spirit and do heaven on earth, just as the Father, the Son, and the Spirit—the author, the leading actor, and the director of the drama—do.

In fact, putting on Christ is the fundamental issue in our acting out our part in God's drama of redemption. Doing so is not acting mechanically or hypocritically. Rather, it is living out our true identity in Christ by the Spirit. As Vanhoozer puts it,

> Christ is more than a costume, more than something that Christians hide behind. Nor is Christ an external (moral) example that disciples must emulate. On the contrary, . . . disciples act out only what is first inside them. To "put on" Christ is to acknowledge that the life of Christ has been conceived within us. In acting out Christ we are, through the Spirit, letting Christ live in and through our lives.[174]

Clothed in Christ, we participate in his threefold office of prophet, priest, and king, becoming cruciform and victorious agents of reconciliation and renewal in this world.

The doctrine of the church directs us to become an interactive theater of the gospel, bearing witness to the reality of God in this world and embodying hope for the world.[175]

4:478; cf. 4:413–78).

173. Vanhoozer, *Faith Speaking Understanding*, passim; *Pictures at a Theological Exhibition*, 46, 180–99; Balthasar, *Glory of the Lord*, 1:28–29; 4:399–431.

174. Vanhoozer, *Faith Speaking Understanding*, 136–37; cf. 115–38; *Doers and Hearers*, 217–21. The biblical concept of "imitating Christ" needs to be understood in this light (Vanhoozer, *Faith Speaking Understanding*, 123–25; Habets, *Anointed Son*, 273). For the dynamic interplay between formation as availability, openness, receptivity and performance as fitting participation in the theodrama of Scripture, see Vander Lugt, *Living Theodrama*, 29–60.

175. Vanhoozer, *Faith Speaking Understanding*, 139–206; *Doers and Hearers*, 137–43; Balthasar, *Theo-Drama*, 1:119; cf. 4:361–423; 5:118–41; *Glory of the Lord*, 4:32–484, 507–26, 543.

Doctrine is thus a form of spiritual formation that helps us become spiritually fit, training our thinking and imagination so that we see this world and our task in it in eschatological terms—that is, in terms of what God has done in Christ and is doing in Christ.[176] Accordingly, doctrine is a spiritual discipline that helps us cultivate the mind of Christ through faith so that Christ generates in us his own filial dependence and responsiveness. He grants us his mind or moral attitude by the Spirit so that with great theodramatic vision we know who we are and what we have to do. We know what story we are a part of, just as Christ knew who he was and what he had to do because he knew the story of which he was a part.[177]

THE NATURE OF STRUCTURE

If we want to design a theoretical framework that helps us clearly communicate the gospel and that properly shapes our Christian identity and practice, we need not only a good understanding of the nature of Scripture, of hermeneutics, and of doctrine but also a good understanding of the nature of structure—and specifically the pedagogical nature of structure.

As we saw earlier, doctrine has a pastoral function. It reconceptualizes God's speech acts in Scripture into thought-acts or mental habits that direct our participation in or performance of the ongoing theodrama in the world today. Doctrine was always meant to be more about training in wisdom and life with God than in abstract truth.

The same can be said about the structure of a systematic theology. It too is pastoral—or should be. A work of theological encyclopedia, as we noted at the beginning of the book, may be dry as dust, a topic guaranteed not to be a bestseller, the stuff in the first few pages of the textbook that you skip to get into the theology itself. But like doctrine, theological encyclopedia—the consideration of the structure of theology—has everything to do with training in wisdom and life because it has to do with how to organize the various doctrines in a certain order, a coherent whole, in a way that is pedagogically helpful for the spiritual formation of the members of the church.

---

176. Vanhoozer, *Drama of Doctrine*, 371–77.

177. Vanhoozer, "Drama-of-Redemption Model," 171; *Faith Speaking Understanding*, 188–90; MacIntyre, *After Virtue*, 216.

DESIGN FEATURES OF A THEODRAMATIC FRAMEWORK

Until the nineteenth century, theological writing was oriented and organized for the sake of pedagogy, the upbuilding of Christians, though not all could be characterized as systematic theology. This sort of organization of smaller parts into a coherent whole for the sake of pedagogy can even be seen already in the finalization of the canon. Heide writes, "The process of inclusion or exclusion involved a great deal more than simply deciding the authorship or date of a particular text. It also included fitting the text into the whole of the canon so that the works might function as a unit in their witness to the gospel." He adds, "While this is something quite different from putting together a whole/complete system of doctrines in the modern (i.e., Hegelian) sense, it nevertheless demonstrates a concern for orderliness and consistency in the testimony."[178]

This pedagogical concern for orderliness and consistency between Scripture as a whole and its various parts can also be seen in the use of the *regula fidei* or rule of faith, which served as a "horizon of interpretive preunderstanding," guiding the church in its interpretation of Scripture.[179] As such, it clarified the scope and limit of the message of Scripture, pointing to what God does in Jesus Christ through the Holy Spirit as its narrative center. Accordingly, when confronted with Gnostics who supported their teachings by parts of Scripture taken out of their context, Irenaeus appealed to this rule of faith as a guide for correctly understanding the meaning of Scripture.[180] "While it is true that the rule-of-faith was not a written document or a formal formulation of doctrine, it does appear to contain the seeds of doctrinal formulation and certainly serves in a manner similar to the later doctrinal formulations (e.g., the creeds) used to demarcate heresy."[181]

Theological handbooks continued through the centuries to manifest this pedagogical concern for orderliness and coherence for the sake of the spiritual formation of the members of the church. Origen systematically responded to the challenges of the heretical teachers of his time and when members of the church read Scripture in the light of the questions their context posed, he responded to their questions with answers that the rule of faith did not supply.[182] Melanchthon pedagogically structured

---

178. Heide, *Timeless Truth*, 14.

179. Green, *Practicing Theological Interpretation*, 77–80; Swain, *Trinity, Revelation, and Reading*, 111; cf. Gadamer, *Truth and Method*, 289–96, 302, 311–18, 384, 464–65.

180. Irenaeus, *Against Heresies*, I.8.1; I.9.2, 3; I.10.1–3.

181. Heide, *Timeless Truth*, 23.

182. Heide, *Timeless Truth*, 27; Reeling Brouwer, *Grondvormen*, 40–42; cf. Origen,

his orderly and systematic account of the Christian faith around the themes of sin, law, grace, and the gospel.[183]

Calvin organized doctrine as he did because it is meant to spiritually form members of the church in wisdom.[184] While his first edition of the *Institutes* followed the Lutheran lead and considered the themes of sin, law, grace, and the gospel as central to the Christian experience and the integrative center of an orderly account of the Christian faith, later editions began with the knowledge of God and made that the integrative center.[185] In the final edition in 1559, Calvin pedagogically uses the Apostles' Creed to further unpack this knowledge of God, focusing on the knowledge of God the creator (book 1), on the knowledge of God the redeemer in Christ (book 2), on the way we receive grace in Christ (book 3), and on the external means by which God invites us into the society of Christ (book 4).[186] Each of the titles of the last three books contains the name "Christ," while the first does not—and that too is for pedagogical reasons. Calvin wanted his readers to realize that their knowledge of God the creator would do them no good unless faith in Christ was added to this knowledge, so that their knowledge of God would become knowledge of the eternal Father of the Lord Jesus Christ who had become their God and Father in Christ.[187] Moreover, Calvin—again for pedagogical purposes—makes the themes of sin, law, and gospel part of the knowledge of God the redeemer in Christ, rather than the integrative center of the Christian faith as a whole.[188]

The structure of a systematic theology, then, organizes the various doctrines of Scripture into a coherent whole pedagogically, for the sake of the spiritual formation of the members of the church. Burger summarizes this pedagogical function of structure aptly when he writes:

> Themes are selected, these themes are put together in a certain order, relations are made between these themes.... This is what we always do when we explain the gospel to someone else ... in a way that communicates the message effectively. We do the same in education, but also in systematic theology ... putting

---

De Principiis, 239.

183. See Melanchthon, *Commonplaces*, 7, 13; Reeling Brouwer, *Grondvormen*, 196.
184. Calvin, *Institutes*, 1.4.
185. Reeling Brouwer, *Grondvormen*, 212–14, 216, 220.
186. McNeill, Introduction to Calvin, *Institutes*, xi–xvii.
187. Calvin, *Institutes*, 2.6.1; Reeling Brouwer, *Grondvormen*, 227, 232.
188. Calvin, *Institutes*, 2.7–8; Reeling Brouwer, *Grondvormen*, 229.

theological themes together in a certain structured way. . . . We always have a certain point of view from which we select and order theological themes, choosing words and images that fit our purposes. This is done in response to certain questions, which are being asked in our context.[189]

CONCLUSION

The nature of Scripture, of hermeneutics, of doctrine, and of structure all shape our Christian identity and practice as well as our communication of the gospel.

All the different books of Scripture form one book, a unified whole with a comprehensive theological worldview, telling a story that moves from creation to the new creation. Because the gospel that shapes us and that we communicate to the world is the announcement of that new creation that is present in Christ because of his victory over sin, death, and the devil and that is already breaking forth in this world by the Spirit, our theological framework should stress the eschatological reality of our participation in this new creation today through faith and by the Holy Spirit.

Jesus' death, resurrection, and outpouring of the Spirit were the fulfillment of God's history with Israel, and beyond that with Adam, and so our theological framework should be redemptive-historical in scope. More than that, Scripture is a drama and we are not mere spectators but actors who are caught up in the story, and our theological framework ought to cultivate participation in or performance of this redemptive drama, joining God in carrying out his mission for his glory so that we and others live in God's loving presence. And because Scripture is the Spirit's instrument by which he fosters communion with God as we share in his life in Christ, the integrative center of our theology ought to be participation in or dwelling in the life of God.

The nature of hermeneutics determines the sort of theological framework we need, too. We are creatures limited by time and history, body and finitude, and so our theology needs to highlight that our understanding will always be a subjective and limited interpretation of reality. At the same time, God breaks open our self-enclosed fallen mindset and relocates us in the risen and ascended Christ, renewing our understanding and interpretation, and so our theology must also emphasize the fundamental importance of receiving the mind of Christ for our

189. Burger, "Gospel Presentation," 269.

understanding and interpretation, rather than epistemological certainty, with the goal of becoming good readers of Scripture.

As we do so, we ought also to become good actors in the drama. Doctrine is dramatic direction for our roles in God's theodrama, and our theological framework ought to promote the church's performance of the gospel. To that end, it should appeal to our theodramatic imagination and encourage us to improvise and perform the theodramatic transcript of Scripture creatively, fittingly, and faithfully in new situations. It must be normed by the canonical practices of Scripture but also incorporate our cultural situation into the biblical narrative, giving us direction as to how we can communicate the gospel effectively and live out our Christian identity in the new situations we encounter.

Since our goal, both in the shaping of our Christian identity and practice and in our communication of the gospel, is to bear witness to all that is in Christ, our theological framework ought to emphasize—and require—that we put on Christ and clothe ourselves with him in order to act out the perfection of God's eternal life and do heaven on earth. Because doctrine has more to do with training for wisdom and life with God than it does with abstract truth, the structure of our theology must be pedagogical, aimed at helping Christians grow to become fitting participants in the life of God and effective communicators of the gospel in our secular culture.

It is my contention that a theodramatic framework with these characteristics can help us do so, and I will flesh out this claim further in chapter 6. But first I turn to an analysis of Michael Horton's theological framework, a form of classical covenant theology, to see how it gives direction to our communication of the gospel and to the shaping of our Christian life.

2

Michael Horton's Covenantal Framework

INTRODUCTION

Who is Michael Horton?

MICHAEL HORTON WAS BORN on May 11, 1964. He was raised in an Arminian, dispensationalist setting and began to embrace Reformed theology when he was in high school, in part due to the profound influence of the book of Romans.[1] He received his B.A. at Biola University, his M.A.R. at Westminster Seminary in Escondido, California, where he studied under Meredith Kline, and his Ph.D. from the University of Coventry and Wycliffe Hall in Oxford, where he did doctoral research under the supervision of Alister McGrath on the Puritan Thomas Goodwin. He completed a post-doctoral research fellowship at Yale University Divinity School between 1996 and 1998. In 2016, he was awarded an honorary Doctor of Divinity from Grove City College in Grove City, Pennsylvania.

Horton is founder and editor-in-chief of Sola Media, home of the White Horse Inn, an internationally syndicated radio broadcast, *Modern Reformation* magazine, Core Christianity, and Theo Global. Since 1998, he has been the J. Gresham Machen Professor of Systematic Theology

---

1. Horton writes, "The year I was twelve, things began to change in my life—not all at once, but gradually. I had been involved in family devotions and Bible reading, but suddenly, the Bible sprang to life for me." He continues, "The Book of Romans began to shatter my earlier notions about reality. Every time I read from Romans I found myself searching for a deeper understanding of God's purpose and grace" (*Mission Accomplished*, 13–14).

and Apologetics at Westminster Seminary in California.[2] He is also an ordained minister in the United Reformed Churches in North America.

Why Michael Horton?

To show the value of the theodramatic approach I am proposing, it helps to compare and contrast it to another theological framework. I chose to interact with Michael Horton's for several reasons.

First, Horton is a covenant theologian, working in the historic line of covenant theology that has developed since the Reformation, even though he does criticize this theology or seek to reformulate it at certain points. This theological approach has the concept of the covenant as its integrative center.[3] By contrast, the framework I am proposing here has participation in the life of God as its integrative center, entailing a reframed understanding of divine-human covenants.

Second, Horton's dogmatic studies and systematic theology clearly seek to contrast a covenant ontology with a participatory ontology.[4] Rather than affirming God's ontological unity with the world and our ontological participation in the life of the Trinity, he sees God's unity with the world as a covenantal or ethical unity, since there can be no "natural" (i.e., inherently compatible) communion between God and humanity because of their ontic distance.[5] But are those two ontologies mutually exclusive or, as I will propose, intimately intertwined?

Third, Horton puts post-Reformation covenant scholastics of the sixteenth and seventeenth centuries in dialogue with current biblical studies, systematic theology, and philosophical theology. He considers these post-Reformation scholastics to be good conversation partners in his interaction with modern theology, because "for the most part [Protestant scholasticism] represents the period of refinement and systematization that ordinarily follows periods of discovery" and consolidated the ideas of the Reformation "as an ecclesiastical form of life and thought" with its confessions, liturgies, and church orders.[6] Horton's goal "is not

---

2. https://solamedia.org/team-member/michael-horton/; https://wscal.edu/academics/faculty/michael-s-horton.

3. Horton, *God of Promise*, 13–14; Macleod, "Covenant Theology," 214.

4. *Lord and Servant*, 10–16; "Participation and Covenant," 107–32; *Covenant and Salvation*, 153–215; *Christian Faith*, 602–19.

5. Horton, *Lord and Servant*, 84; *God of Promise*, 10, 29.

6. Horton, *Covenant and Eschatology*, 3; *Christian Faith*, 31.

to repristinate the achievements of these classic systems of the sixteenth and seventeenth centuries, but to harvest some of [their] basic insights" in order to engage a dislocated, modern theology that has become increasingly fragmented and unsure of its location in academic (or even ecclesiastical) discourse as a result of the doubt and criticism in the wake of deconstruction.[7] Moreover, he believes that a postmodern environment that has left modern foundationalism behind is open to confessional covenant theology.[8] With Horton, I share a desire to equip Christians to share the gospel faithfully and fittingly in our secular culture. But are the post-Reformation scholastics the best conversation partners to fit us for this task?

THE COVENANT FRAMEWORK OF HORTON'S THEOLOGY

The law-gospel distinction in Horton's covenant theology

Horton makes a sharp distinction between law and gospel: "When we speak of the distinction between law and gospel," Horton explains, "... we are referring to different illocutionary stances that run throughout all of the Scriptures—everything in both Testaments that is in the form of either an *obligatory command* or a *saving promise* in Christ.... The law functions differently," he continues, "depending on the covenant in which it is operative. In a covenant of works (a law-covenant), law prescribes what is to be performed, personally and perfectly, on penalty of death.... In a covenant of grace, law has no power to condemn, since its stipulations have been fulfilled (personally and perfectly) and its penalties for violation have been borne in our place by our covenant head, Jesus Christ." Even though the law is also a guide for our life of thankfulness, "it must first cut off all hope of life by our personal obedience."[9] Thus, while "law and gospel are not inherently antithetical, ... with respect to the question as to how sinners may be justified before God, law and gospel are not only different but totally antithetical principles."[10] To Horton,

7. Horton, *Covenant and Eschatology*, 3.
8. Horton, *Covenant and Eschatology*, 4.
9. Horton, *Christian Faith*, 137–38.
10. Horton, *Christian Faith*, 395–96; see also 429, 755; *Law of Perfect Freedom*, 21, 269–70; *Beyond Culture Wars*, 109–14; *In the Face of God*, 131, 135; *Thomas Goodwin*, 203–4; *We Believe*, 77–78, 225, 236, 268–72, 279, 296, 345, 425; *Covenant and*

this sharp contrast is necessary as a demonstration of God's holiness and justice and to protect the integrity of the doctrine of justification.[11]

The three covenants in Horton's covenant theology

Horton operates with the post-Reformation scholasticism's distinction between three covenants: the covenant of works, the covenant of grace, and the covenant of redemption.[12]

The covenant of works

The covenant of works, in post-Reformation scholasticism and in Horton's covenant theology, is a covenant between God and Adam before the fall into sin.

Horton prefers to call it a covenant of creation, because this description "is the least controversial and most broadly useful"[13] and because God sovereignly ordered his relationship with creation and humanity covenantally by his dynamic and interactive speech, on the one hand, and the response of creation and humanity in utter dependence upon him, on the other hand.[14] Thus, for Horton, the covenant of works does not begin with the so-called probationary command in Genesis 2:16–17 but with creation itself. Moreover, because human existence is intrinsically covenantal, being human "is ultimately a narrative-ethical rather than a metaphysical-ontological question."[15]

This covenant of works, not added to creation but inherent and essential to it, can be seen in the fact that Adam was created in the image of

---

Eschatology, 136, 195; *Better Way*, 66, 70–71, 74, 151, 155; "Classical Calvinist View," 40–41; *Lord and Servant*, 102, 196; *God of Promise*, 53; *Covenant and Salvation*, 80–101, 148–52; *Gospel-Driven Life*, 131; *Gospel Commission*, 165, 225; *Core Christianity*, 128–29; "Reflections on Gospel Theology," 86–89; *Justification*, 1:282–98.

11. Horton, *Lord and Servant*, 133; *God of Promise*, 84; *Covenant and Salvation*, 64, 120.

12. For this section, I made use of Kim, *Michael Horton's Covenant Theology*, 116–220.

13. Horton, *God of Promise*, 83.

14. Horton, *Christian Faith*, 332–34; see also 138, 385, 415–23, 446, 541, 575; *Lord and Servant*, 66–76; *God of Promise*, 10.

15. Horton, *Lord and Servant*, 94.

God.[16] For Horton, this means that Adam was created to be obedient and was given dominion over creation "to lead the whole creation into God's everlasting shalom, signified and sealed by the Tree of Life."[17] In this covenant, the "principle of inheritance" is law performance ("works").[18] Hence, because law and gospel involve different principles of inheritance and stand in antithetical relationship to each other with regard to justification, Horton sees the covenant of works as in an antithetical relationship to the covenant of grace.[19]

The "everlasting shalom" or eschatological rest in store if Adam had been successful would have been a higher quality of life than Adam's life in the garden. "Creation was the stage—the 'beautiful theater'—for God's drama, not an end in itself. Life in the garden was not intended to simply go on in perpetuity but was merely the point of departure for the great march of creation behind God's vice-regent into the everlasting life of God's own Sabbath-rest."[20]

In leading the whole of creation into God's own Sabbath rest, Adam was meant to act as the covenantal or federal head of humanity, earning—by his works—not only his right to enter into this rest, but also the right for all of his posterity.[21] In other words, his obedience would be imputed to them. Conversely, his disobedience and its effects would likewise be imputed to them.[22] As the image of God, Adam did not need any grace to be able to obey God and fulfill his covenant commission as

16. Horton, *Christian Faith*, 332, 380–81; *God of Promise*, 10.

17. Horton, *Christian Faith*, 380–81; see also 384, 386–91, 397; *Lord and Servant*, 79–80, 94; *Christless Christianity*, 290–91; Kline, *Kingdom Prologue*, 19, 33–41, 107–17.

18. See, e.g., Horton, *God of Promise*, 31, 88, 176; *Covenant and Salvation*, 20, 24, 97; "Covenant and Justification," 23–24; *Justification*, 2:140, 436.

19. See Horton, *God of Promise*, 35–50; "Post-Reformation Reformed Anthropology," 49–51; *Covenant and Salvation*, 11–36; "Which Covenant Theology?," 211–21; *Christian Faith*, 137–38, 418, 420, 439–40, 463, 609, 617, 716, 789; *Justification*, 1:298–310. For the dogmatic use of the law and gospel distinction as two ways of being saved, see Renihan, *From Shadow to Substance*, 17–67. He distinguishes this dogmatic use of this distinction from the historical use as "referring to two historical time periods, the Old and the New Testaments" (*From Shadow to Substance*, 19).

20. Horton, *Christian Faith*, 386; see also *Lord and Servant*, 79–80; *God of Promise*, 106; *Christian Faith*, 403–4, 419–20, 441, 906; *Pilgrim Theology*, 122–23, 138, 145–46, 446, 452–58. Because the goal of redemption is not simply restoration, but consummation, Horton asserts that eschatology precedes soteriology (Horton, *Lord and Servant*, 79–80, 220).

21. Horton, *Christian Faith*, 415, 421, 688; *Lord and Servant*, 129.

22. Horton, *Christian Faith*, 424; *Lord and Servant*, xii, 53; *Putting Amazing Back into Grace*, 151.

the covenantal head of the human race because he had been created in a state of integrity.[23]

Thus, law precedes grace in the meritorious covenant of creation or of works.[24] This covenant of works is still in effect today, and humanity can be aware that it is under this covenant because the law is written on their consciences.[25]

"'Law,'" says Horton, "refers to any command, from Genesis to Revelation [while] Gospel refers to any place in either testament where the promise of salvation by grace alone through faith alone is found."[26] To fail to see and adhere to this law-gospel hermeneutic, on Horton's view, is to confuse law and gospel.[27] Putting it another way, it is to confuse what God has done and what we do.

Consequently, on Horton's view, because it has the same principle of inheritance—law performance—Horton considers the Mosaic covenant or covenant with Israel at Mount Sinai to be, in some sense, a covenant of works. Drawing on the studies of G. E. Mendenhall and Meredith Kline, who interpret biblical covenants against the background of a certain phase of ancient Near Eastern international politics,[28] Horton asserts that in Scripture (e.g., Gal 4:21–31), "two different types of covenants form distinct riverbeds cutting synchronically through the same biblical history: a purely promissory oath on God's part and a conditional suzerainty-vassal relationship on the other."[29]

---

23. Horton, *Christian Faith*, 411, 424; *Lord and Servant*, 83–84, 94, 100; *God of Promise*, 54; "Post-Reformation Reformed Anthropology," 49; "Obedience Is Better Than Sacrifice," 316.

24. Horton is also arguing against Barth's "grace precedes law" and Roman Catholicism's "grace perfects nature" (*Christian Faith*, 336; Kim 125).

25. Horton, *Christian Faith*, 138, 140–42, 387, 979; *God of Promise*, 92–93, 118, 191; *Covenant and Salvation*, 35, 88, 92; *Christless Christianity*, 125, 209; "In Praise of the Profanity," 261; *Gospel-Driven Life*, 253; *Gospel Commission*, 237; *Core Christianity*, 84–85, 90; *Justification*, 1:62, 295; 2:63, 75, 136–37.

26. Horton, *Law of Perfect Freedom*, 21; *Christian Faith*, 137, 665.

27. Horton, *Christless Christianity*, 107–19, 122, 124, 157, 247, 250; *Gospel-Driven Life*, 35, 210; *Christian Faith*, 439; *Putting Amazing Back into Grace*, 159, 214, 226, 260; *Gospel Commission*, 227; *Core Christianity*, 129; *Justification*, 2:94, 97.

28. See Van Bekkum, "Biblical Covenants," 43–78.

29. Horton, *Lord and Servant*, 150; see also vii–x; "Classical Calvinist View," 32–33; *God of Promise*, 36; cf. 35–50; *Covenant and Salvation*, 11–36, 80–101; *Christian Faith*, 44–45, 151–52. Horton uses Hittite suzerainty treaties in particular as a template to help interpret biblical covenants. Thus, he writes, "It is not surprising then that God adapted the international treaty as the template for his relationship to creatures" (*God of Promise*, 29; see also 23–34; *Covenant and Salvation*, 13; *Christian Faith*, 44, 151, 424,

The Sinai covenant, then, is a conditional suzerainty law covenant as Israel's national oath of allegiance clearly illustrates. "The land was *given* to Israel," Horton writes, "but for the purpose of fulfilling its covenant vocation. Remaining in the land is therefore conditional on Israel's personal performance [as a nation] of the stipulations that the people swore at Sinai."[30] The conditional language of this law performance covenant is also clearly illustrated by the constant reminder that if Israel would do what God commanded, it would live, but if it failed to do this, it would die (e.g., Lev 18:5; Deut 4:1).

In this sense, the Mosaic covenant is essentially a republication of the covenant of creation/works God made with Adam in the Garden.[31] Horton sees this continuity between the covenant of creation and the Sinai covenant confirmed in Hosea 6:7, which he understands to mean that Israel transgressed as Adam had done. He further sees continuity between the two covenants in the fact that both Adam and Israel had similar functions in the history of redemption. "Since Israel was a theocracy typological of the eschatological Paradise of God, its national existence was a repetition of the covenant of creation," Horton writes. He adds: "Israel was called to see itself as a new theocratic garden of God's presence and as a new creation in the sense of representing humanity before God—all of this typological of the true Israel, the faithful Adam, who is also the true heavenly temple and everlasting Sabbath of God."[32]

Because Israel failed as a nation in fulfilling its covenant vocation, its history primarily has a revelatory function—that is, it reveals our human sinfulness.[33] But because individual Israelite believers were justified by faith, Israel's history also has a typological function, prefiguring salvation in Jesus Christ.

782–83). However, he also makes the following concession, "It is probably unwise to make the law-covenant/promise-covenant too heavily dependent on formal similarities with ancient Near Eastern treaties. Regardless of parallels, only the exegesis of particular covenants in Scripture can determine its basis and terms" (*God of Promise*, 45).

30. Horton, *Covenant and Salvation*, 15; *God of Promise*, 20; *Christian Faith*, 154, 420, 440–41, 492, 539, 778; *For Calvinism*, 100.

31. Horton, *Covenant and Eschatology*, 133; *Lord and Servant*, xii, 120, 151, 159; *God of Promise*, 31–33, 97; *Covenant and Salvation*, 13–15, 17, 97; *Christian Faith*, 420, 541, 712, 778; *Justification*, 2:57–95.

32. Horton, *Christian Faith*, 419–20. Horton does, however, recognize some discontinuities between the covenant of creation and the Sinai covenant (*God of Promise*, 32–33).

33. Horton, *Christian Faith*, 440–43.

Horton thus distinguishes between Old Testament believers being individually justified by faith and Israel as a nation remaining in the land by works. He writes, "While it is true that Old Testament saints were justified by faith according to the Abrahamic promise, the theocracy itself was to be maintained and vindicated by strict adherence to the Torah."[34] On his view, then, the Sinai covenant was essentially two-layered, one layer belonging to the covenant of grace and pertaining to personal salvation through faith and the other layer belonging to the covenant of creation/works and pertaining to staying in the land as a nation and involving a form of corporate covenant nomism.[35]

The covenant of grace

While the covenant of works is a conditional covenant comparable to ancient Near Eastern suzerainty-vassal treaties, where a suzerain places conditions upon a vassal, the covenant of grace is an unconditional promissory covenant comparable to ancient Near Eastern royal grant or gift covenants, where the vassals are beneficiaries of an inheritance because of a victory of the suzerain.[36]

There is one overarching covenant of grace, in which Christ, as the last Adam, fulfills the principle of personal law performance of the covenant of creation/works, which Adam failed to do, and thereby earns the inheritance—for himself and for us—of the eternal Sabbath rest, having satisfied God's justice with his perfect obedience and sacrifice as our perfect Mediator. As a result, the principle of personal law performance is now replaced by the principle of faith.[37]

This covenant of grace, therefore, depends upon the covenant of works and the principle of merit. As Meredith Kline writes,

> The parallel which Scripture tells us exists between the two Adams would require the conclusion that if the first Adam could not earn anything, neither could the second Adam. But, if the obedience of Jesus has no meritorious value, the foundation of the gospel is gone. If Jesus' passive obedience has no merit, there

---

34. Horton, *God of Promise*, 74–75; see also *God of Promise*, 50; Kline, *Kingdom Prologue*, 109.

35. Horton, *Covenant and Salvation*, 50.

36. Horton, *Christian Faith*, 537, 779.

37. Horton, *Lord and Servant*, 220, 226–27, 239; *God of Promise*, 105; *Covenant and Salvation*, 20, 24, 97; *Justification*, 2:140, 436.

has been no satisfaction made for our sins. If Jesus' active obedience has no merit, there is no righteous accomplishment to be imputed to us.[38]

Horton expresses the same idea when he writes, "It is in the Reformed doctrine of the covenant of works that God's glory, the original rectitude of humanity in creation, and the imputation of Christ's active as well as passive obedience can be maintained."[39]

This overarching covenant of grace is announced to Adam and Eve after their fall into sin as the so-called *protevangelium* or promise of redemption in Genesis 3:15.[40] This promise is then formally ratified by God in history with Abraham by a unilateral oath as an unconditional royal grant covenant for him and his descendants.[41]

This covenant with Abraham is then renewed with David, once more in the form of a unilateral, unconditional promise from God's side.[42] Although the Davidic covenant was made while the Sinai covenant was still in force, the two are distinct. Horton writes, "The Sinai covenant was something each family participated in, while the covenant with David

---

38. Kline, "Covenant Theology under Attack"; see also *Kingdom Prologue*, 138.

39. Horton, *God of Promise*, 87.

40. Horton, *Christian Faith*, 45, 152–53; *God of Promise*, 68, 74, 102, 105.

41. Horton, *Christian Faith*, 778–81; "Classical Calvinist View," 32; *God of Promise*, 40–42, 78. While from the human side, God's covenant with Abraham belongs to the royal grant type covenants, from God's side, it is a suzerain type covenant. Horton writes, "It is as if from the divine side, the covenant made with Abraham is a suzerainty treaty in which God swears unilaterally to personally perform all of the conditions and suffer all of the curses for its violation, but from the human side, the same covenant is a royal grant, an inheritance bestowed freely and in utter graciousness on the basis of the Great King's performance" (*God of Promise*, 41–42). While there are so-called conditions in this covenant of grace with Abraham, the fulfillment of these stipulations is not necessary to enjoy the salvific blessings of this covenant. For instance, concerning the stipulation of circumcision, Horton writes, "This rite is not treated as a condition of inheritance but as a sign and seal of the inheritance for the heir who is already entitled to it" (*God of Promise*, 42). Concerning the stipulation that Abraham offers up his son Isaac, Horton writes, "This [obedience of Abraham] is not the basis of Abraham's salvation, but the means through which that blessing [i.e., the fulfillment of God's promises to Abraham] comes to Abraham's heirs" (*God of Promise*, 45). Moreover, Horton considers Abraham's obedience to be "typological of Christ, who would merit by his obedience the reward of everlasting life" (*God of Promise*, 45). Thus, Abraham's obedience does not pertain to his own personal salvation (Kim, *Michael Horton's Covenant Theology*, 175–76).

42. Horton, *Christian Faith*, 447; *God of Promise*, 44–50, 56–57, 73–76.

(like that with Abraham and Noah) was something they heard about—a pact that had been made in their interest but without their partnership."[43]

These promises made to Adam and Eve, Abraham, and David are then fulfilled in the promissory, unconditional royal grant new covenant made with all believers, God's last will or testament, promised by the prophets and inaugurated by Christ's death.[44] When those in this covenant of grace believe in Christ, the active and passive obedience of Christ is imputed to them.[45]

But while the new covenant is a royal grant covenant, Horton says, it does contain conditions that need to be met for the final salvation of believers. These conditions, however, are not the basis for entering into the eternal Sabbath rest, but rather are the fruit of having received a new heart by the Holy Spirit. Thus, for Horton, the new covenant is both unconditional and conditional. It is unconditional in its essence, but conditional in its administration.[46] These conditions of the new covenant are the moral law summarized in the Ten Commandments written on our consciences.[47]

Because Christ has fulfilled the demands of the covenant of works, with the inauguration of the new covenant with all believers the old or Sinai covenant with Israel has become obsolete.[48] Because of Israel's typological function, then, God's covenant with Israel as a national entity was a passing phenomenon, an interlude or parenthesis in God's redemptive history that provided "the scaffolding for the building of the true and everlasting temple."[49] However, Horton does not consider the church to be a replacement of Israel but sees it rather as the "fulfill[ment of] the promise God made to Abraham that in him and his seed all the nations

---

43. Horton, *God of Promise*, 48.

44. Horton, *Christian Faith*, 45, 153, 538, 541; *God of Promise*, 51–76.

45. Horton, *God of Promise*, 71, 76; *Covenant and Salvation*, 102–25; *Christian Faith*, 587–647; *For Calvinism*, 98–105; *Justification*, 2:321–66, 397–493.

46. Horton, *God of Promise*, 182; cf. 173–94; *Christian Faith*, 575–86, 615–19, 653–80; *Putting Amazing Back into Grace*, 150–54, 156–60; *Gospel Commission*, 152; cf. 150–53; *Covenant and Salvation*, 148–52, 263–66.

47. Horton, *God of Promise*, 178.

48. Horton, *God of Promise*, 59; "Obedience Is Better Than Sacrifice," 327; *Christian Faith*, 152, 447, 796, 862, 948.

49. Horton, *God of Promise*, 47; 69; see also *Christian Faith*, 152–53, 337, 384, 420, 448, 493, 528, 537, 539, 959, 986; *Justification*, 2:81.

would be blessed."[50] He also believes that Romans 11 seems to argue for an extensive ingrafting of Jews into the church.[51]

The covenant of redemption

Horton defines the covenant of redemption as "an eternal pact between the persons of the Trinity. The Father elects a people in the Son as their mediator to be brought to saving faith through the Spirit."[52] He asserts that if we hold to the doctrine of the Trinity and the doctrine of unconditional election, "it is unclear what objection could be raised in principle to describing this divine decree in terms of the concept of an eternal covenant between the persons of the Godhead."[53]

In Horton's view, such a covenant of redemption is implied when, in the New Testament, "the Son is represented (particularly in the fourth Gospel) as having been given a people by the Father (John 6:39; 10:29; 17:2, 4–10; Eph. 1:4–12; Heb. 2:13; citing Isa. 8:18) who are called and kept by the Holy Spirit for the consummation of the new creation (Rom. 8:29–30; Eph. 1:11–13; Titus 3:5; 1 Peter 1:5)." Furthermore, it is implied by the fact that "the Son's self-giving and the Spirit's regenerative work were the execution of the Father's eternal plan." He sees this confirmed when "Christ himself is spoken of as 'the Lamb slain from the foundation of the world' (Rev. 13:8 KJV)."[54]

The covenant of grace is made in history with believers and their children: "Not everyone in the covenant of grace is elect: the Israel below is a larger class than the Israel above. . . . It is possible to be in the covenant externally but not to be actually united to Christ through faith"[55] But it is the pre-temporal intra-trinitarian covenant of redemption that upholds the sovereign grace of God in bringing his elect to salvation in the history of redemption. As such, it is the basis for the temporal

---

50. Horton, *Christian Faith*, 730.
51. Horton, *Christian Faith*, 945–50.
52. Horton, *God of Promise*, 78; cf. Horton, *Lord and Servant*, xi, 66; "Participation and Covenant," 46–48; *God of Promise*, 14, 16, 19, 35, 45, 77–82, 87–88, 134; *Covenant and Salvation*, 136–39; *Christian Faith*, 45, 141, 236, 250, 303, 309, 321, 446, 486–87, 510–11, 518, 558, 575, 566, 587, 615–16, 644, 717–18, 854, 870.
53. Horton, *God of Promise*, 79.
54. Horton, *God of Promise*, 79–80.
55. Horton, *God of Promise*, 182, 185.

covenant of grace and for Christ's fulfillment of the covenant of works for the salvation of the elect.[56]

The covenant ontology of Horton's covenant theology

The philosophical context of Horton's covenant ontology

Ontology is the study of reality. It deals with questions such as "What is reality?" and "What is the nature of the relationship between God and the world?"

Horton describes the nature of reality and of the God-world relationship *covenantally*. Drawing on Paul Tillich's typology of ontology and adding something of his own, Horton distinguishes between three ontological grand narratives: "overcoming estrangement" (hyper-immanence), "the stranger we never meet" (hyper-transcendence), and "meeting a stranger" (covenantal).

The first ontological narrative—represented in Platonism, Gnosticism, mysticism, and process theologies—tends to erase "the infinite qualitative distinction between God and creatures." While its starting point lies in a strong dualism between God and the world, "the goal is to reestablish the unity of all reality." Rather than God entering into the world he has made, "all of reality *emanates* from this divine principle of unity like the rays of the sun." Consequently, redemption is essentially a form of inner self-actualization or "overcoming estrangement" by ontological participation in the life of the divine through the spark of divinity within you.[57]

The second ontological narrative, represented by atheism and deism, makes God either a projection of our psychological needs or someone who is not actively involved in history or nature. Accordingly, God—either existent or non-existent—is "the stranger we never meet."

Both of these ontological grand narratives share a univocal understanding of being—that is, "there is only one kind of reality or existence." In the pantheistic version of the "overcoming estrangement" model, the spiritual world is real, while the physical world is "a weak projection of an eternal (real) world." In the atheistic version of "the stranger we never

---

56. Horton, *God of Promise*, 105, 109, 182, 185.

57. Horton, *Christian Faith*, 36; cf. 36–39; *Lord and Servant*, 4–6; "Participation and Covenant," 110–12; *Covenant and Salvation*, 153–70.

meet," the physical world is real, while the spiritual world is a weak projection originating from the needy physical world.

Neither ontological grand narrative allows for a personal God "who transcends creaturely reality yet enters freely into relationship with it." Nor does either ontological grand narrative allow for "the personal intervention of God in nature and history." As such, both ontologies protect and affirm human autonomy. In doing so, they avoid God as the stranger.[58]

In contrast to these two deficient ontological grand narratives, Horton places his third option, "meeting a stranger." God is a stranger in a positive and negative sense. In a positive sense, God is a stranger because he is holy. As such, he "is *qualitatively* distinct from creation—not just more than, but different from, his creatures." As a result of this ontological difference, creation is God's good gift to humanity that is dependent upon him, while God is and remains sovereign over his creation.[59]

In a negative sense, God is a stranger because he is *ethically* distinct from his creation. This ethical difference is the result of humanity's fall into sin. Consequently, God is "morally *opposed* to us," and we are estranged from him. Redemption, therefore, is not achieved through inner self-actualization and human ascent, but through the descent of the Word of God in Christ Jesus.[60]

The ontological implications of Horton's "meeting a stranger" ontology are that the God-world relationship is not framed as an ontological union or participation in the being of God—an ontology of mutual indwelling—but as a covenantal union, a legal/ethical union with God by virtue of the covenant. On Horton's view, this covenantal union is not something added to the creation but rather something intrinsic to our being created in the image of God.[61]

Horton refers to this legal/ethical union as a covenantal ontology,[62] distinguishing it from a participatory ontology.[63] Nevertheless, Horton

---

58. Horton, *Christian Faith*, 40; cf. 39–41; *Lord and Servant*, 6–9; "Participation and Covenant," 112–15.

59. Horton, *Christian Faith*, 42.

60. Horton, *Christian Faith*, 42.

61. See Kline, *Kingdom Prologue*, 14–21.

62. McCormack describes covenantal ontology as "an ontology of correspondence," i.e., the correspondence of our will to the will or intention of God ("What's at Stake," 115; cf. Horton, *Christian Faith*, 90, 161, 389, 510, 674, 771).

63. Horton, *Christian Faith*, 42; cf. 41–42, 384; *Lord and Servant*, 10–16, 84; "Participation and Covenant," 115–23; *Covenant and Salvation*, 3, 7, 153–56, 181–215; cf.

does speak of a covenantal form of participation when he writes, "Just as the covenant of creation included every person 'in Adam,' and the covenant of grace includes all of the elect 'in Christ,' so also all things hold together (participate) in Christ, yet in different ways." He adds, "The proper antithesis is therefore not between participation and covenant, but between different accounts of both."[64]

The heart of Horton's covenant ontology

The heart of Horton's covenantal ontology is the doctrine of justification.[65] He believes that his revised doctrine of justification can better secure the *extra nos* character of our justification and combat the charge that the Protestant understanding of justification entails a legal fiction—a believer being declared righteous when, in fact, he has not become righteous—than the classical understanding of this doctrine, without sacrificing Reformed insights or being influenced by medieval participatory metaphysics, such as the classic understanding that regeneration precedes faith through the infusion of a new habit or the principle of new life.[66]

The idea of the infusion of habits, in Horton's view, involves the infusion of a divine substance, leading to the fusion of the divine and the creature,[67] and opens the door for a non-forensic source of justification that obscures the *extra nos* basis of justification, and therefore should be abandoned.[68] Put another way, this causal ontology—justification grounded in the infusion of habits—should be replaced with a communicative ontology.[69]

For Horton, God's judicial verdict of justification, announced in the effectual call, is the generative source of the whole *ordo salutis* or order of salvation.[70] He illustrates this as follows: "I am suggesting that we view

---

216–310; "Why Are We Celebrating?," 29, 34.

64. Horton, *Covenant and Salvation*, 164–65; cf. 129–52, 168, 200.

65. Horton, *Covenant and Salvation*, 1–2, 139, 143, 147, 198–99.

66. Horton, *Christian Faith*, 573, 595, 599, 606, 608–12, 669, 708; *Pilgrim Theology*, 286; *Covenant and Salvation*, 146–47, 176, 191–98, 216–42, 256–63.

67. Horton, *Covenant and Salvation*, 111; *Christian Faith*, 393, 764.

68. Horton, *Covenant and Salvation*, 197.

69. Horton, *Covenant and Salvation*, 217.

70. Horton, *Christian Faith*, 588, 597, 610–12, 710, 708; *Covenant and Salvation*, 129, 138–39, 143, 147–48, 198, 201, 203, 216–17, 247, 264; *Justification*, 1:209, 219.

all the items in the Pauline *ordo* as constituting one train, running on the same track, with justification as the engine that pulls adoption, new birth, sanctification, and glorification in tow." He adds, "This means that we never leave the forensic domain even when we are addressing other topics in the *ordo* besides justification proper. Although there is more to the new birth, sanctification, and glorification than the forensic, all of it is forensically charged."[71]

In Horton's view, there is a "schizophrenic tendency" in Protestant soteriology. It uses a forensic ontology to answer the problem of our guilt, but a participatory ontology (e.g., infused habits) to answer the problem of our corruption. Thus, he writes, "If the tendency in Roman Catholicism and Orthodox theologies is to confuse justification and sanctification, the tendency in Protestant theologies is sometimes to treat these two events more like two trains running on parallel tracks."

"In the latter case," he continues, "justification is seen as the answer to one soteriological problem (viz., guilt), and inner renewal (regeneration and sanctification) is seen as the answer to a different one (viz., corruption)." He concludes, "I think this problem is motivated by a schizophrenic tendency to allow a thoroughgoing forensicism with respect to justification while presupposing a different ontology as the basis for other elements in the *ordo*."[72]

He articulates the same concern when he writes, "The danger of the second move [i.e., distinguishing regeneration from effectual calling through the Word], however, was that justification and regeneration/sanctification were given different ontological fields of discourse that allowed them to drift apart like tectonic plates."[73]

Horton defines the *ordo salutis* as follows: "The Latin phrase *ordo salutis* means 'the order of salvation' and refers to how the Spirit applies the benefits of Christ to individuals" (*Christian Faith*, 312, 535, 536, 591, 998). He understands effectual calling as the "Spirit's sovereign work of raising those who are spiritually dead to life in Christ through the announcement of the gospel" (*Christian Faith*, 572). About the semantic content of the effectual call, Horton writes, "The Word that is spoken in effectual calling is not only a discourse about justification but *is* God's announcement of the justification of the sinner, received by faith" (*Covenant and Salvation*, 203).

71. Horton, *Christian Faith*, 708; cf. 575, 597, 610–12, 677, 706, 710; *Covenant and Salvation*, 139, 143, 147–48, 198, 216, 292–93; "Calvin's Theology of Union," 91, 93; "Covenant and Justification," 184; *Justification*, 1:273; 2:361, 470–71, 493. In some places, however, Horton has union with Christ preceding justification (*Christian Faith*, 587, 622; *Justification*, 2:470–71).

72. Horton, *Covenant and Salvation*, 301–2; cf. 216.

73. Horton, *Covenant and Salvation*, 236.

Drawing on the work of Kevin Vanhoozer and speech act theory, Horton asserts that the judicial verdict of justification, announced in the effectual call, occurs when the Father speaks in the Son through the Spirit or, putting it in speech act terms, when God's illocutionary act of justification is combined with the perlocutionary work of the Holy Spirit, issuing forth into repentance and faith. In other words, God's declaration "creates the reality it declares" and is constitutive of what it declares.[74] "Justification," Horton writes, "is not simply one doctrine among others; it is the Word that creates a living union between Christ, the believer, and the communion of saints."[75]

The charge of legal fiction no longer applies, then, because God's declaration of righteousness is a judicial verdict that generates transformative change, even though the transformative change itself is not part of God's declaration of righteousness or the basis of it.[76] "In effectual calling," Horton writes, "the Spirit grants the faith to receive Christ for justification and for sanctification, but analogous to God's performative utterance in creation, it is the forensic verdict ('Let there be!') that evokes the inner renewal that yields the fruit of the Spirit ('Let the earth bring forth . . .')."[77] "Justification is the fiat declaration, 'Let there be righteousness!'"[78]

Moreover, on Horton's view, regeneration and effectual calling are synonymous.[79] The concept of the infusion of habits is eliminated because it is no longer necessary.

But because God's judicial verdict of justification is the generative source of the whole *ordo salutis*, Horton distinguishes between what he considers the "gospel" and the "effects" of the gospel. He writes, "The Gospel produces new life, new experiences, and a new obedience, but too often we confuse the fruit or effects with the Gospel itself. Nothing that

---

74. Horton, *Covenant and Salvation*, 135, 138, 198, 201–3, 220–30, 240; *Christian Faith*, 610–11, 645, 649, 892; *Justification*, 2:361. The expression quoted is from McCormack, "What's at Stake," 107.

75. Horton, *Covenant and Salvation*, 138.

76. Horton, *Covenant and Salvation*, 139, 189–204, 243–46, 250; *Christian Faith*, 620, 646; cf. 620–47; *Justification*, 2:361.

77. Horton, "Calvin's Theology of Union," 91; cf. *Covenant and Salvation*, 203; *Christian Faith*, 159, 575, 621, 662–63; "Let the Earth Bring Forth . . . ," 127–149.

78. Horton, *Christian Faith*, 621. For God's declaration of justification being a speech act analogous to the act of creation *ex nihilo*, see Horton, *Covenant and Salvation*, 203; *Christian Faith*, 326, 611, 621, 645, 753.

79. Horton, *Covenant and Salvation*, 197; cf. 195–204, 232–42; *Christian Faith*, 610; cf. 608–12, 669–70, 572–75.

happens within us is, properly speaking, 'Gospel,' but it is the Gospel's effect."[80]

Horton wants his covenantal ontology to be a rival paradigm to a participatory ontology. "Covenant is not something added to a metaphysics and ontology derived from some other source," he writes, "but generates a worldview of its own. Covenant is not simply a theme, but an ontological paradigm in its own right."[81] As a rival paradigm, it protects the church against the risk of pantheistic and panentheistic mysticism associated with the participatory model.[82]

The essence-energies distinction undergirding Horton's covenant theology

Eastern Orthodox theology is well known for its distinction between the essence of God and the energies of God.[83] This distinction is considered to be the most important feature that distinguishes Eastern theology from Western.[84] While some early church fathers used this distinction, Bintsarovskyi explains, it "received its classical formulation in the works of Gregory Palamas (1296–1359). Seeking to give a theological account of the experience of monks who claimed to contemplate the uncreated divine light, Gregory postulated a distinction between God's essence, which always remains inaccessible and imparticipable, and God's uncreated energies, in which the saints do participate."[85] Distinguished from the essence of God, these uncreated energies are considered to be the "things around God," through which he manifests himself in this world and which can be apprehended by us.[86]

---

80. Horton, "Law and the Gospel"; "Reflections on Gospel Theology," 76–79. In addition to "properly speaking," however, he does also use the distinction of the broader and narrower sense of the gospel ("Reflections on Gospel Theology," 77–79).

81. Horton, *Covenant and Salvation*, 3; cf. 153–55, 160–65, 180; *Christian Faith*, 777; Michelson, "Covenantal History and Participatory Metaphysics," 408; cf. 391, 395.

82. Horton, *Christian Faith*, 36–39, 57, 102, 233, 237, 612, 615, 690–92; *Pilgrim Theology*, 30, 330; *Lord and Servant*, 11, 27; "Participation and Covenant," 129, 131–32; *Covenant and Salvation*, 214.

83. In this section, I make thankful use of Bintsarovskyi, *Hidden and Revealed*, 5–30.

84. Bradshaw, *Aristotle East and West*, xi.

85. Bintsarovskyi, *Hidden and Revealed*, 7.

86. For a genealogy of the usage of the term ἐνέργειαν in Greek philosophy and how the Christian tradition received and interpreted it, see Bradshaw, *Aristotle East and West*; "Concept of Divine Energies," 27–49.

Horton regrets that Western theology has usually used only two categories to describe reality. Either something belongs to the category of God's essence or it belongs to the category of creation. Eastern theology, however, has the third category of God's energies, which Horton, following Palamas, compares to the rays of the sun.

He writes, "The sun's rays are not the sun itself, but they are also not the ground that is warmed by the sun. Rather, they are the shining forth or effulgence of the sun." He adds, "Similarly, God's energies (*energeia*) are neither God's essence (*ousia*) nor a created effect but are God's knowledge, power, and grace directed toward creatures."[87]

Horton considers this distinction to be comparable to what Reformed theology teaches about the fact that we know God not in his essence but in his works. Thus, he writes, "God's works are neither God's essence nor merely the created effect of his action, but God's effective agency, . . . [or] God's workings. God's act of creating the world by his Word is neither an emanation of God's being nor itself part of creation. Rather, it is God's activity."[88]

Horton draws further comparisons to Reformation theology. "Eastern Orthodoxy," Horton writes, "has appealed to Exodus 33 for its distinction between the revelation of God in his essence (inaccessible glory) and in his energies (gracious acts), just as the Reformers did for their contrast between a theology of glory and a theology of the cross, and as their heirs did for the further distinction between archetypal and ectypal theology."[89] He implies that this is what Calvin meant when he wrote, "Thereupon his powers are mentioned, by which he is shown to us *not as he is in himself, but as he is toward us*: so that this recognition of him consists *more in living experience than in vain and high-flown speculation*."[90]

These resemblances between Eastern Orthodox and Reformed theology lead Horton to conclude that the essence-energies distinction

---

87. Horton, *Christian Faith*, 130; cf. 52, 228, 237, 613, 690, 817; *Covenant and Salvation*, 212, 268, 270; *People and Place*, 137. In addition to speaking about God's essence, Horton speaks about God's "hidden essence" (*Christian Faith*, 45, 52, 111, 123, 131, 234, 363, 373), God's "being" (*Christian Faith*, 43, 54, 130, 225, 234, 237, 241, 252, 256, 327, 340, 604, 690, 978, 991), and God's "nature" (*Christian Faith*, 241, 331, 323, 505). He uses these expressions interchangeably.

88. Horton, *Christian Faith*, 130; see also 574, 690; *Lord and Servant*, 117; *Covenant and Salvation*, 212, 231, 274–75.

89. Horton, *Christian Faith*, 131.

90. Horton, *Christian Faith*, 50, emphasis added by Horton; cf. the discussion on 50–52.

is where the two theological traditions intersect, despite their other significant differences.[91] In his view, even though Reformed theology does not explicitly mention this distinction, it presupposes it. Accordingly, he considers this distinction to be indispensable to Reformed theology, since it forms "the necessary metaphysical underpinning of many ideas and doctrines."[92]

THE DESIGN FEATURES OF HORTON'S THEOLOGICAL FRAMEWORK

In the previous chapter, I outlined four design features of a theodramatic framework, examining how the nature of Scripture, the nature of hermeneutics, the nature of doctrine, and the nature of structure shape our communication of the gospel and our Christian identity and practice.

Michael Horton's covenantal theological framework also involves an understanding of each of these design features, an understanding that overlaps with the theodramatic framework I have presented at some points and in some ways but that also differs with it in other significant ways.

The nature of Scripture in Horton's theology

The narrative nature of Scripture

The narrative approach to Scripture reminds us that while Scripture contains many different books with separate narratives, all of these books are blended into a rich intertextual whole, a single story that articulates a unified theological worldview that runs through the whole of Scripture. In the theodramatic framework I outlined earlier, this theological worldview should stress the eschatological reality—already through faith and by the Holy Spirit—of our participation in the resurrection life of the new creation.

Horton also has a narrative approach to reading Scripture, for he considers that Christianity is "the greatest story ever told," the story that

---

91. Horton, *Christian Faith*, 613; *Covenant and Salvation*, 212, 214. Horton outlines areas of agreement and disagreement with the Orthodox tradition in "Eastern Orthodoxy," 115–43. Ultimately, he considers the traditions to be incompatible.

92. Bintsarovskyi, *Hidden and Revealed*, 26; cf. Horton, *Christian Faith*, 612.

"interprets all other stories" because it has its origin not in philosophy but in revelation.[93]

The narrative plot of Horton's theology

The narrative plot that guides Horton's reading of Scripture is the worldview story of creation, fall, redemption, and consummation.[94] God freely created the world as a cosmic temple by his personal, living speech, which reflects his glory. He created human beings as his image, communicative beings who can respond to his living speech and who would live in a covenant of works with him as his prophets, priests, and kings, reflecting his glory as they bear witness to him and his works. He gave them the task of being fruitful and multiplying and having dominion over the earth in order to lead creation into the eschatological reward of God's Sabbath.[95]

Humanity, however, fell into sin by following Satan's advice instead of listening to God. Because Adam was the head of the human race and represented all of humanity and creation in the covenant of works, the whole human race sinned in him and suffered the consequences of his sin. Yet God promised a victory over Satan so that history could continue to move toward the eternal Sabbath rest through the outworking of the covenant of grace God would make in his covenants with Abraham, Israel, David—and eventually the promised new covenant.[96]

When Israel failed in its calling to reflect God's glory in the world, God sent his own Son to bear faithful witness to him and his works as the great prophet, priest, and king and to inaugurate the new covenant. As the head and mediator of the covenant of grace, Christ inaugurated the new covenant by fulfilling the conditions of the covenant of works for elect sinners by his active obedience and suffering the sanction of the covenant of works for them by his passive obedience, bearing the curse

---

93. Horton, *Christian Faith*, 14, 17. Horton speaks of the Christian story being a meganarrative, not a metanarrative, not only because its origin is in revelation and not philosophy, but also because "metanarratives give rise to ideologies, which claim the world's allegiance even, if necessary, through violence. The heart of the Christian narrative, however, is the gospel—the good news concerning God's saving love and mercy in Jesus Christ" (*Christian Faith*, 17).

94. Horton, *God of Promise*, 13; *Gospel-Driven Life*, 171; "Obedience Is Better Than Sacrifice," 35; *Christian Faith*, 17, 59; *Gospel Commission*, 169.

95. Horton, *Lord and Servant*, 66–119; *Christian Faith*, 331–34, 379–81, 396–406.

96. Horton, *Lord and Servant*, 121–55; *Christian Faith*, 408–16, 423–34, 437–42, 447, 541–42.

of the law and thereby satisfying God's justice on their behalf. Moreover, by so doing, he defeated Satan and his demonic powers, fulfilling the promise made in the covenant of grace.[97]

When Christ arose from the dead, ascended into heaven, and poured out his Spirit, he began his eschatological reign of grace as prophet, priest, and king in the new covenant, applying the benefits of salvation—justification, adoption, sanctification—to his new covenant church by his Word and Spirit by effectually calling people and uniting them, through faith, to himself.[98]

When Christ returns, he will reign in glory, judging the living and the dead and ushering in the eternal Sabbath rest in the kingdom of God, where humanity and creation will be elevated by being glorified or transfigured[99] into the likeness of the resurrected and glorified Christ.[100]

THE CENTER AND *TELOS* OF HORTON'S NARRATIVE PLOT

Becoming a partaker of the resurrection life of God's new creation in Christ, which breaks forth from the age to come into the presence, is the goal of creation and thus also the center and *telos* of the biblical narrative.

For Horton, Adam being created in the image of God meant that Adam was created to be obedient and was given dominion over creation "to lead the whole creation into God's everlasting shalom, signified and sealed by the Tree of Life."[101] This everlasting shalom or eschatological rest will be a higher quality of life than the life God created in the Garden. "Life in the garden was not intended to simply go on in perpetuity," Horton says, "but was merely the point of departure for the great march of creation behind God's vice-regent into the everlasting life of God's own Sabbath-rest."[102]

As the second Adam, Christ "undoes the curse of the first Adam and fulfills the *covenant of creation* for his elect, thereby winning the right to

---

97. Horton, *Lord and Servant*, 159–270; *Christian Faith*, 446–67, 483–520.

98. Horton, *Christian Faith*, 551–687.

99. Following others, Horton refers to this transfiguration as deification or *theosis* (*Covenant and Salvation*, 267–69, 272, 284, 302, 306, 308; *Rediscovering the Holy Spirit*, 285–86; *Justification*, 1:49, 52, 208, 250, 364; 2:488–93).

100. Horton, *Lord and Servant*, 242–70; *Covenant and Salvation*, 267–307; *Christian Faith*, 984–90; *Rediscovering the Holy Spirit*, 284–88.

101. Horton, *Christian Faith*, 380–81.

102. Horton, *Christian Faith*, 386.

be not only the risen head but the resurrection-life-giving Lord."[103] It is especially his resurrection that validates that the eschatological life of the future has broken into the historical present.[104]

Christ's ascension into heaven grounds the significance of eschatology by reminding us that we are now already seated with Christ in the heavenly places, though we do not yet see him face to face. It grounds the significance of pneumatology by reminding us that the Spirit now mediates Christ's presence through the preaching of the Word and the administration of the sacraments. And it grounds the significance of ecclesiology by reminding us that the church is a pilgrim community on its way to the new heaven and new earth.[105] Because the goal of redemption is not simply restoration but consummation, Horton asserts that eschatology precedes soteriology.[106]

The eschatological resurrection life of the future that is breaking into the historical present is also tied to Horton's understanding of the kingdom of God. He sees the roots of this concept in the Old Testament, where God is depicted as the king of all the earth and the people of Israel are portrayed as a kingdom of priests and a holy nation.[107] The concept of the kingdom of God, according to Horton, "issues chiefly in remission of sins, the new creation, and the new relationship to God (fatherhood-sons), and these are all thoroughly eschatological, not abstract and static concepts."[108]

When Jesus announced the arrival of the kingdom, he was announcing the arrival of the new covenant.[109] Unlike the kingdom of God in the Old Testament, which was a reign of law, the kingdom of God in the New Testament is a reign of grace in which Christ applies the benefits of his redemptive work to believers through the Spirit, creating a new covenant community or church. He applies these benefits in his threefold office as prophet, priest, and king. As prophet, he confronts his people with the law and the gospel. As priest, he intercedes for his people. And as king, he rules all things through his Word and Spirit. In this new covenant

---

103. Horton, *Christian Faith*, 446.
104. Horton, *Covenant and Eschatology*, 116.
105. Horton, *Christian Faith*, 534–35.
106. Horton, *Lord and Servant*, 79–80, 220.
107. Horton, *Christian Faith*, 539.
108. Horton, *Christian Faith*, 538.
109. Horton, *Christian Faith*, 539, 542.

community or church, the kingdom of God is already truly present, but not yet fully present in its consummated form.[110]

Horton distinguishes between the way Christ rules in the church and the way he rules in the world. He bases this distinction on the difference between the cultural mandate and the Great Commission, as well as the antithetical relationship between law and gospel with regard to justification.

The cultural mandate to be fruitful, multiply, and exercise dominion over the earth through the cultural activity of pursuing one's vocation is the law that was given to all humanity in the covenant of creation. It is grounded in God's general revelation, ruled by natural law, and enabled by God's common grace.

On the other hand, the Great Commission or cultic mandate to be fruitful, multiply, and exercise dominion over the earth was given in the covenant of grace to the church after humanity's fall into sin, along with God's gospel promise of a Savior. It is enabled by special grace. The church fulfills this commission by announcing the fulfillment of this promise through God gathering a church for himself from all the nations of the world by the Word and sacraments and, in this way, spreading the kingdom or rule of God.[111]

The redemptive-historical nature of Scripture

The redemptive-historical approach to Scripture reminds us that, because Jesus saw his death, resurrection, and outpouring of the Spirit as the fulfillment of God's history with Israel, the unity of Scripture lies in the progressive unfolding of the history of redemption in Christ. In our communication of the gospel, we must read Scripture backwards, as Jesus did, understanding it in the light of his death and resurrection—and also read the Old Testament Scriptures forward, seeing them pointing toward his victory over sin, death, and the devil through his death and resurrection.

---

110. Horton, *Christian Faith*, 235, 237, 541; 529-47; cf. 551-903; *Pilgrim Theology*, 221-28; *Lord and Servant*, 264-70; *People and Place*, 1-13; *Thomas Goodwin*, 129-44; *Better Way*, 61-79; *Core Christianity*, 68-71.

111. Horton, *God of Promise*, 111-26; *Christian Faith*, 712-15, 719, 728; *Gospel-Driven Life*, 161-65; *Gospel Commission*, 62-64.

Horton's Redemptive-Historical Method of Biblical Interpretation

Horton speaks of his methodology as "redemptive-historical/eschatological." By "redemptive-historical," he has in view "the organic unfolding of the divine plan in its execution through word (announcement), act (accomplishment), and word (interpretation)." Revelation is "the servant of redemption" as it "exegetes divine action and human response in actual historical contexts." By "eschatological," he means that the character of redemptive history does not progress in "a straight line of horizontal development... [but] unfolds through apocalyptic 'irruptions' in the fabric of ordinary history, particularly (though not exclusively) connected with the people of Israel." Thus, "God's work progresses on the vertical as well as the horizontal plane."[112]

Reading and interpreting Scripture in a redemptive-historical/eschatological manner is a constant reminder that theology should always be a theology of the cross, rather than a theology of glory, because the eschatological new creational goal of the kingdom of God is not yet fully realized[113] and revelation comes primarily through proclamation and hearing, not manifestation and vision.[114] Horton relates seeing to "seizing, grasping, dissecting, comprehending, mastering, and possessing its object," while hearing is related to placing ourselves "at the disposal of the covenant Lord, submitting to his Word."[115]

According to Horton, the redemptive-historical/eschatological approach to biblical interpretation, with its emphasis on God's acts in history, is superior to "a Platonizing version of Christian theology."[116] This "Platonizing version" is generally "ontological and cosmological in nature," with an ontological dualism between the eternal realm of the unchanging forms and the temporal realm of the changing appearances. This ontological dualism, in turn, leads to an epistemological dualism "in which the knowing subject seeks to transcend the realm of appearances (i.e., time and space) and contemplate the eternal ideas by means of recollection."[117]

---

112. Horton, *Covenant and Eschatology*, 5–6.
113. Horton, *Covenant and Eschatology*, 5.
114. Horton, *Too Good to Be True, passim*; "Better Homes and Gardens," 134.
115. Horton, *Christian Faith*, 81, 85; cf. 81–94; *In the Face of God*, 171–94.
116. Horton, *Covenant and Eschatology*, 7.
117. Horton, *Covenant and Eschatology*, 31.

Over against this ontological dualism Horton places his eschatological dualism: "Against Plato's irrepressible 'two worlds,' accentuated again in Kant, appears Paul's 'two ages.' Ontological dualism is replaced with eschatological dualism. Instead of the 'true world' of eternal perfection versus the 'apparent world' of temporal change we find 'this present age' and 'the age to come.'"[118]

The theodramatic nature of Scripture

The theodramatic approach to reading Scripture reminds us that Scripture is a drama that inserts us into its action and demands that we say or do something. Scripture intends to cultivate participation in and performance of its redemptive drama. Horton, too, views Scripture as a theodrama.

THE COVENANT CONTEXT OF THE DRAMA

Horton frames his understanding of the God-world relationship not as an ontological union involving participation in God—an ontology of mutual indwelling—but as a covenantal union, involving a legal/ethical relationship to God by virtue of the covenant. It should not surprise us, then, that he considers covenant to be the context or "architectonic structure, a matrix of beams and pillars," of God's counterdrama of redemption.[119] He summarizes this counterdrama as follows:

> It speaks of the triune God who existed eternally before creation and of ourselves as characters in his unfolding plot. Created in God's image yet fallen into sin, we have our identity shaped by the movement of this dramatic story from promise to fulfillment in Jesus Christ. This drama also has its powerful props, such as preaching, baptism, and the Supper—the means by which we are no longer spectators but are actually included in the cast. Having exchanged our rags for the riches of Christ's righteousness, we now find our identity "in Christ." Instead of God being a supporting actor in our life story, we become part of the cast that the Spirit is recruiting for God's drama.[120]

---

118. Horton, *Covenant and Eschatology*, 32; cf. 211–12.

119. Horton, *God of Promise*, 13; *Covenant and Eschatology*, 12; *Lord and Servant*, vii; "Participation and Covenant," 128; *Covenant and Salvation*, 2–3.

120. Horton, *Christian Faith*, 19; cf. *Covenant and Eschatology*, 92; *Better Way*,

He adds,

> The Christian faith is, first and foremost, an unfolding *drama*. Geerhardus Vos observed, "The Bible is not a dogmatic handbook but a historical book full of dramatic interest." This story that runs from Genesis to Revelation, centering on Christ, not only richly informs our mind; it captivates the heart and the imagination, animating and motivating our action in the world. When history seems to come to a standstill in sin, guilt, and death, the prophets direct God's people to God's fulfillment of his promise in a new covenant.[121]

Scripture, then, is the authoritative script of the drama that incorporates us into God's counterdrama and rescripts our lives.[122]

THE CULTIVATION OF OUR PARTICIPATION IN THE DRAMA

The primary means by which our participation in God's covenantal counterdrama of redemption is cultivated is the Sunday worship service. Here, the covenantal drama is liturgically enacted in a dialectical and dialogical manner, in which "theology and praxis, the individual and communal solidarity, history and eschatology, transcendence and immanence, come together dramatically."

In this liturgy, God performatively speaks through his greeting of grace and peace, the reading of the law, the pronouncement of absolution, the sermon, and the benediction, while the people respond with singing, confession, and prayer. This covenant renewal service, in which God's covenantal drama is enacted, "offers the only service in which God promises to make the new creation a reality among his people."[123]

In this covenant renewal service, God also gives his people the sacrament of baptism and the sacrament of the Lord's Supper as performative signs and seals of his goodwill toward them and as testimonies of the promises of his grace, in addition to the proclamation of the Word, through which he strengthens them in their faith. Baptism is a sign and seal of believers and their children being "incorporated into the divine

---

10–17, 128; *Lord and Servant*, xiii; *Covenant and Salvation*, 6; *People and Place*, ix; *Christian Faith*, 14–19; *Pilgrim Theology*, 14–18.

121. Horton, *Christian Faith*, 19.

122. Horton, *Covenant and Eschatology*, 171, 178; *Better Way*, 33–45; "Better Homes and Gardens," 114; *Christian Faith*, 24, 26, 32, 161–62, 373, 643, 660.

123. Horton, *Covenant and Eschatology*, 265, 269; *Better Way*, 33–92.

drama, rescripted from 'strangers and aliens' into 'the people of God,' grafted onto Jesus Christ as their life-giving vine." The Lord's Supper, likewise, is a sign and seal of their communion with Christ and their incorporation into God's drama of redemption. However, these visible signs and seals have only a proclamatory function and are never "the backdoor to a theology of vision and manifestation."[124] When members of the covenant community use these sacraments in faith by putting on Jesus Christ, they participate in the reality that is signed and sealed and take up their new role in God's drama of redemption.[125]

In addition to preaching and the sacraments, God gives his people church order and discipline to keep them faithful to the script of the drama. Church discipline is meant "to correct bad performances through good coaching." When a church member continues to refuse to participate in this script, he is writing himself out of the drama. Upon repentance, he is rewritten into it. Church discipline "enables the drama to continue without disintegrating into scattered performances." Moreover, it enables outsiders to see that the church "is in fact the transformative-performative production that *God* has performed in history."[126]

The theological nature of Scripture

The theological approach to reading Scripture reminds us that Scripture is the Spirit's instrument in which God himself is communicatively present. Through Scripture, the church is called to listen and respond to the voice of God in the obedience of faith because this God desires communion with those he has created and wants them to participate in his life in Christ through the Spirit. The theological approach draws on earlier, premodern interpretations of Scripture, reading Scripture in communion with those who have read it before. Its goal is the formation of the moral character of the reader so that he grows in love for God and his neighbor.

Horton also has a theological approach to Scripture. But instead of having ontological participation in the life of God as its integrative center, as the theodramatic framework does, Horton's approach is centered

---

124. Horton, *Covenant and Eschatology*, 270.

125. Horton, *Covenant and Eschatology*, 271; *Better Way*, 93–124. Horton emphasizes that the church's weekly public ministry needs to be supplemented and supported by ordinary family and private devotions of prayer, singing, instruction, and Bible reading (*Ordinary*, 181; *Gospel-Driven Life*, 156; Peterson, "Ordinary Spiritual Growth," 6–7).

126. Horton, *Covenant and Eschatology*, 272.

on the covenant, since he considers that to be the fundamental relationship between God and humanity.

Horton's understanding of the canon of Scripture

Horton considers Scripture to be the church's authoritative canon that comes from the Father, has the Son as its content, and has the Holy Spirit as its perfecting agency.[127] It is the Father's means of grace by which he speaks in order to have his people respond in faith.[128]

Drawing on the work of Meredith Kline, Horton asserts that Scripture is a covenant document whose form and content (e.g., historical prologues, stipulations, and sanctions) are modelled after ancient Near Eastern suzerainty treaties.[129] Accordingly, this canon is closed to revision by the vassals, God's people, while it is open to revision or fulfillment by the suzerain, God.[130]

Through this covenant canon, the Father not only creates a people for himself by his locution or speech but also regulates and rules their faith and practice. As such, the canon belongs to the church. This covenant canon is inspired in both its form and content and therefore is inerrant in its original autographs.[131]

Scripture has the Son as its content because it is centered on Christ's person and work as the mediator of the covenant of grace. This one covenant of grace is administered in the Old and the New Testament. Horton considers Israel to be a typological theocracy, offering typological sacrifices pointing to the person and work of Christ.[132] Israel's corporate history is a parenthesis in the history of redemption and, as such, primarily functions to reveal our human sinfulness.[133]

---

127. Horton, *Christian Faith*, 156–57.
128. Horton, *Christian Faith*, 120, 154, 147.
129. Horton, *God of Promise*, 132; *Christian Faith*, 210.
130. Horton, *God of Promise*, 134. Horton approvingly cites Kline who writes, "Another corollary of covenantal canonicity is that the Old Testament is not the canon of the Christian church. From a strictly legal standpoint, the Old Testament viewed in its identity as the historical treaty by which God ordered the life of pre-messianic Israel belongs to the church's historical archives rather than to its constitution" (cited in Horton, *God of Promise*, 134). This does not, however, make the Old Testament any less authoritative than the New Testament.
131. Horton, *Christian Faith*, 152, 160–61, 173, 180.
132. Horton, *Christian Faith*, 153, 156–57.
133. Horton, *Christian Faith*, 440–43; cf. 152–53, 337, 384, 420, 448, 493, 528, 537,

Scripture has the Spirit as its perfecting agency because it is "the primary means of grace, through which the Spirit applies redemption to sinners in the present." Horton asserts that "as the Spirit hovered over the waters in creation to prepare a place for the covenant partner, and 'overshadow[ed]' Mary so that she would conceive the incarnate Son, the same Spirit breathed out these texts—and illumines hearers now to receive them as the Word of God."[134]

The nature of hermeneutics in Horton's theology

Hermeneutics as the art of understanding and interpretation

Understanding and interpreting the gospel—the work of hermeneutics—is not the skill of obtaining epistemological certainty scientifically. It is rather the art of realizing how our subjectivity and context play a role in our linguistic analysis and interpretation of Scripture. Through hermeneutics, we understand how God uses Scripture and is actively present in Scripture to call us to listen and respond to his voice in the obedience of faith.

For a theodramatic framework, this means that the ontological factors of time and history, body and finitude mean that we do not have a God's eye view of reality and our understanding will always be subjective and limited—and yet God is not hampered by these factors but is able to communicate truly and effectively to us so that we also can communicate the gospel to others.

While Horton defines hermeneutics as "the study and practice of interpretation," he does acknowledge that subjective factors are involved.[135] "Like any science," he writes, "theology is not free to determine its own content and shape but is constrained by reality. No less than genetics or astronomy, theology involves subjectivity (i.e., the act of interpreting from one's own background and presuppositions) while aiming at objective reality."[136]

Moreover, Horton agrees with Gadamer that we are not disengaged selves who experience a value-neutral world in which we impose meaning, but we are engaged selves who are shaped by the stream of history

---

539, 959, 986; *God of Promise*, 47, 69; *Justification*, 2:8.

134. Horton, *Christian Faith*, 156, 157.

135. Horton, *Christian Faith*, 995.

136. Horton, *Christian Faith*, 30.

in which we are embedded from birth. Consequently, a text never speaks for itself. Instead, we bring our prejudice or preunderstanding as we seek to understand it. As a result, interpreting a text involves a hermeneutical circle or spiral, in which the parts clarify the whole and the whole clarifies the parts.[137] Nevertheless, given his definition of hermeneutics, his emphasis is primarily on the study and practice of interpretation.

The Analogical Mode of Theological Discourse

"A covenantal ontology requires a covenantal epistemology," Horton says,[138] and the heart of that that epistemology, according to Horton, is the analogical mode of theological discourse. This analogical mode of discourse gives us ectypal theology, not archetypal. The latter entails absolute knowledge and is identical with God's being or essence, while the former is finite knowledge, knowledge that belongs to creatures.[139] Analogical thinking identifies certain aspects of the unknown in terms of the known.[140]

Following John Calvin, Horton believes that God accommodates his revelation to our human weakness.[141] We do not know God as he is in himself, but only as he has revealed himself. Accordingly, the analogical mode of theological discourse "is appropriate but approximate, allowing us to make assertions concerning God's being and action without allowing access to the inner life (i.e., 'hiddenness') of God." We do not need access to the "inner essence" of God, because our concern is with "God's revealed character, intentions, and actions made explicit in Christ." Moreover, we cannot have access to this "inner essence" of God because his "essence can never be known in this life, or in the next."[142]

---

137. Horton, *Covenant and Eschatology*, 149–51.

138. Horton, *Christian Faith*, 54; *Lord and Servant*, 16–20.

139. Horton, *Lord and Servant*, 16–18; "Better Homes and Gardens," 136; *Christian Faith*, 54, 77–79, 128–29, 210.

140. Horton, *Covenant and Eschatology*, 8.

141. Horton, *Covenant and Eschatology*, 8; cf. 184–91.

142. Horton, *Covenant and Salvation*, 282; *Covenant and Eschatology*, 190; cf. *Christian Faith*, 131, 603, 694; *Rediscovering the Holy Spirit*, 25; Bintsarovskyi, *Hidden and Revealed*, 28.

Hermeneutics and the mind of Christ

As we saw in the previous chapter, with the fall into sin, our *nous* or mindset became turned in on itself and self-enclosed, so that our understanding and interpretation became futile and darkened. But God breaks open our enclosed selves, relocates us in the risen and ascended Christ, and subjectively renews our understanding by giving us the *nous* or mind of Christ, enabling us to understand and interpret the gospel from that new perspective. In the theodramatic framework, then, our focus in communicating the gospel and the basis of our Christian identity and practice is not epistemological certainty but rather acquiring the mind of Christ by being united with him through faith and the Holy Spirit.

Horton's covenant ontology leads him to adopt a hermeneutic that fits with the analogical mode of theological discourse.[143] We do not know God as he is in himself, in his "inner essence," but only as he reveals himself in his condescension. Our interpretation and understanding, then, are not characterized by epistemological certainty. On the contrary, "the demand for absolute epistemic certainty not only is idolatrous in its illicit demand for archetypal knowledge that belongs to God alone; it also reflects an overrealized eschatology—that is, a premature announcement that the consummation has arrived."[144] Faith is not "an immediate certainty, like the knowledge of logical, geometrical, or mathematical axioms or of sense experience.... Faith is clinging to Christ."[145]

While the phrase "the mind of Christ" is virtually absent in Horton's writing and he does not speak about us being ontologically relocated in the risen and ascended Christ, he does speak about the Holy Spirit indwelling believers[146] and about the Spirit's enlightening ministry.[147] So while the concept of the mind of Christ may not be Horton's hermeneutical starting point, it does function once he has started on his hermeneutical journey.

---

143. Horton, *Covenant and Eschatology*, 181–219.
144. Horton, *Christian Faith*, 91.
145. Horton, *Christian Faith*, 585.
146. Horton, *Rediscovering the Holy Spirit*, passim. The Kindle edition of this book lists no fewer than 81 references.
147. Horton, *Rediscovering the Holy Spirit*, 151, 260, 276.

Hermeneutics and the use of language

Understanding and interpreting the gospel involves recognizing the rules of the "language game" and the intent of God's speech acts as he communicates through the various genres of Scripture so that we become good readers of Scripture.

Horton agrees. He asserts that God literally acts in history by his Word and Spirit,[148] and this action includes speech.[149] Revelation is thus a divine communicative action, coming from the outside, by which God reveals himself. This divine activity is not a manifestation of God's essence nor is it simply the effect of his action. It is the manifestation of his energies or "energetic Word" and Spirit in this world, through which he "words" us.[150]

Because God has bound himself to his covenant people through his covenant speech, they are entitled to believe that he speaks to them and that they can interpret what he has said. Drawing on the hermeneutically sensitive insights of Nicholas Wolterstorff, Horton says that God's covenant community is justified in believing that God speaks to them through the medium of the text of Scripture because God has appropriated and accepted the words of humans as his own words. Drawing on John Calvin's understanding of the testimony of the Holy Spirit, Horton writes that God's covenant community is persuaded that God speaks through the medium of Scripture because the Spirit convinces them that he has done so and is doing so.[151]

Horton also views Wolterstorff's authorial discourse interpretation as the best method to understand the meaning of a text. We approach Scripture as a unified whole, allowing God to interpret his divine discourse according to the analogy of faith, through the linguistic structure of the text.[152] The literal sense of the text, then, has priority over other senses. The figural interpretation of promise and fulfillment is an

---

148. Horton, *Christian Faith*, 130, 159, 237, 612, 690; *Covenant and Salvation*, 211–15, 231, 268–70, 274–75, *People and Place*, 133; Bintsarovskyi, *Hidden and Revealed*, 27.

149. Horton, *Christian Faith*, 117–22.

150. Horton, *Christian Faith*, 129–32, 136, 154, 159, 164, 166, 166, 181, 574, 751, 753, 758; *Covenant and Salvation*, 302; *People and Place*, 101; Bintsarovskyi, *Hidden and Revealed*, 27.

151. Horton, *Covenant and Eschatology*, 144.

152. Horton, *Covenant and Eschatology*, 156–64.

extension of the literal meaning of the text, giving a fuller sense to that literal meaning.[153]

Because Scripture is God's speech, it is self-authenticating, giving itself divine authority and constituting itself as canon or normative rule "for the proper invocation of God's name for salvation and true worship."[154] It is the covenant, according to Horton, that "constitutes the biblical canon as canon."[155] Scripture does "not simply contain a covenant or covenants, but as a whole can be said to constitute the covenant document itself."[156]

This canon or covenant document is essentially perspicuous or clear, as well as sufficient.[157] It is verbally, completely, and organically inspired by God with the Father as its locutionary source, the Son as its illocutionary content, and the Holy Spirit as its perlocutionary effecting agency.[158] In the original manuscripts, the Scriptures are also inerrant "in all their real affirmations."[159]

It is through this accommodated, analogical divine discourse that God encounters his covenant community. He lays his claim upon them, unilaterally constituting them as his covenant people. He summons them to respond to his divine address in faith and incorporates them into his redemptive-historical/eschatological drama through this response of faith.

Accordingly, God's covenant community receives the meaning of its life from God instead of trying to create this meaning on its own. The text of Scripture first interprets the covenant community, rather than the covenant community first interpreting the text of Scripture.[160] We do not try to make Scripture relevant to our experience, but rather understand our experience in the light of Scripture. Thus, "the priority of the horizon of the text (at least in determining the textual sense) circumvents 'the fusion of horizons.'"[161]

---

153. Horton, *Covenant and Eschatology*, 177–80; *Core Christianity*, 77–79.

154. Horton, *Christian Faith*, 151.

155. Horton, *Covenant and Eschatology*, 177; cf. *Christian Faith*, 196–98; cf. 186, 195, 198.

156. Horton, *Covenant and Eschatology*, 207; see also 180; *Christian Faith*, 152–53.

157. Horton, *Covenant and Eschatology*, 177; *Christian Faith*, 196–98; cf. 186, 195, 198.

158. Horton, *Christian Faith*, 156–66.

159. Horton, *Covenant and Eschatology*, 177; cf. 173–81.

160. Horton, *Covenant and Eschatology*, 183, 191–206, 218.

161. Horton, *Covenant and Eschatology*, 165.

While the meaning of the text of Scripture can be grasped without the illumination of the Spirit, true understanding of the text depends on the Spirit. This illumination is not given as a secondary source alongside Scripture and in addition to it, but is given from within Scripture as it "unites us to Christ, the *res* of scripture so that we inevitably hear the voice of mere mortals *as* the voice of the Shepherd himself." Accordingly, Scripture and the Spirit are united in bringing Christ to the covenant community.[162]

While the Spirit through Scripture is the ultimate norm for true understanding, the Spirit also works with the interpretive community or tradition in coming to this true understanding. However, the *sensus communis* of the interpretive community arises out of the *sensus literalis* of Scripture and not the reverse.[163]

Horton considers preaching, as the primary means of communicating the gospel, to be truly practical when it encourages the listeners to become good readers of Scripture by having their lives rescripted by this covenantal discourse of God's speech acts.[164]

The nature of doctrine in Horton's theology

Doctrine as grammar

In the previous chapter, I considered doctrine as the grammar of the faith, the rules that govern the church's discourse for the sake of the church's practice and performance of the biblical narrative and its communication of the gospel to others.

Horton also views doctrine as grammar. Doctrine, for Horton, summarizes the accomplishments of God in the unfolding drama of redemption and gives meaning to them by defining and refining our understanding of these accomplishments. When we are learning a new language, through which we will interpret reality and our lives, we have to learn its vocabulary and grammar—the rules that govern how words work together meaningfully. A new job, an unfamiliar sport, a form of technology may all use words in distinctive ways, following distinctive rules that we must learn in order to participate fully. And so too with the

---

162. Horton, *Covenant and Eschatology*, 210.
163. Horton, *Covenant and Eschatology*, 216; cf. 215–19.
164. Horton, *Better Way*, 51–60, 69–80; *Christless Christianity*, 129–33, 142–48.

Christian faith. Doctrine is the grammar—the vocabulary and its rules—of the language game of the Christian faith.[165]

Horton finds that cognitive-propositionalist theories of doctrine tend "to reduce faith to *doctrine*, understood as propositional statements." Experiential-expressivist theories of doctrine tend "to reduce faith to *doxology*, which erupts from within the self's own religious experience." The problem with Lindbeck's cultural-linguistic model, Horton says, is that "it gives pride of place to ecclesial practice (*discipleship*)." And narrative models of doctrine tend to reduce faith to the unfolding dramatic narrative of redemption.[166]

Over against these reductionist theories of doctrine, Horton places a covenantal model of doctrine, in which God is qualitatively distinct from creatures, his revelation comes to us from outside ourselves, and Scripture is God's authoritative norm.[167]

With this model, Horton seeks to integrate the emphases of the other models. First, because God reveals what he is like in real history, "doctrine grows out of the biblical *drama*." Second, because God teaches us how he acts through the use of verbs, "the drama yields [the nouns of] specific *doctrine*." Thus, doctrine tells us "what the drama means for us." Third, "when God writes us into the script by interpreting what it means for us, we are not just astonished; we are overwhelmed with gratitude," which leads to doxology or praise and worship, through which we internalize the drama. Fourth, "living in this drama, informed by the doctrine, and shaped by the experience of true worship, we are able to live out our part in the story wherever God has placed us" as doxology leads to discipleship.[168]

Doctrine as drama

Viewing doctrine as drama reminds us that doctrine is the result of reflection on the theodramatic nature of Scripture that then appeals to our imagination so that we creatively improvise and perform the script of Scripture in new situations. In particular, as we saw earlier, while imagination as such is "the power of forming mental images of what is not

---

165. Horton, *Christian Faith*, 20–22.
166. Horton, *Christian Faith*, 209.
167. Horton, *Christian Faith*, 210.
168. Horton, *Core Christianity*, 17–18; see also *Christian Faith*, 210–19.

really present," theodramatic imagination "is the ability to form mental images of what is *really* present . . . even though it cannot be perceived empirically with the senses."[169] Theodramatic imagination allows us to connect to the greater context in which we live and to the transcendent reality in which we participate.

While Horton does not use the term "theodramatic imagination," the concept is certainly present in his theology. He understands that the narrative structure of Scripture is theodramatic—that is, that Scripture is a drama that inserts us into its action and demands that we say or do something. We are rescripted as performers of this drama. Furthermore, he understands the sacraments of baptism and the Lord's Supper as signs and seals of our incorporation into God's drama of redemption.[170]

Horton does not make a verbal appeal to the theodramatic imagination or speak about creatively improvising in new situations, but he does speak about theology as wisdom (*sapientia*) because it is "oriented toward a proper *relationship*—with God and with each other." Theology is thus "chiefly wisdom *concerning Christ*," based on revealed doctrines and practices that shape our interpretation of reality for "invoking the Father, in the Son, and by the Spirit, for salvation and life."[171]

Doctrine as dramatic direction

Doctrine is meant to give direction to our imagination and our action so that we participate in the theodrama of Scripture in a way that fits with the script we have in Scripture, as we extend the meaning of the canonical text to develop the theodramatic action in new situations.

Horton, as we have seen, considers doctrine to be a summary of the accomplishments of God in the unfolding drama of redemption, a summary that defines and refines our understanding of these accomplishments. But he presents doctrine more as an interpretive lens through which we understand reality and our lives in the world than as dramatic direction, though he does, of course, believe that our Christian identity and practice should always be normed by Scripture.

---

169. Vanhoozer, *Drama of Doctrine*, 416. For the relation between theodramatic imagination and the mind of Christ, see Vanhoozer, "Putting on Christ," 147–71.

170. Horton, *Better Way*, 93–124.

171. Horton, *Christian Faith*, 104–5, 110.

Nevertheless, Horton does speak about God's ongoing counterdrama of redemption and our role in it. Because this counterdrama shapes a specific covenant praxis or culture, we should not accommodate it to the culture of the metanarratives of this passing age in an attempt to make it "conceptually accessible and relevant to contemporary culture"—for example, by focusing more "on our own personal experience, rather than what God has done for us in history," attempting "to translate the gospel into contemporary language," seeing "the inward transforming work of the Spirit as the key element of Christianity" instead of the external announcement of "the objective facts of the gospel in history," and confusing law and gospel by speaking to people "about *living* the gospel, *doing* the gospel, even *being* the gospel" without first having them experience "the trauma of God's holiness" through the law that condemns us and then God's liberating grace of justification through faith in Christ.[172]

Instead, we should confront and challenge the presuppositions of this culture by performing the script of God's counterdrama on the stage of the history of this world. When we do so, "the drama of redemption unfolds as a play-within-a-play." While the drama of world history may seem to be the most significant drama, the play-within-a-play "ends up becoming the all-encompassing divine drama that seeps the entire natural creation and its history into its action and plot." Theology is thus a theology for pilgrims on the way.[173]

Knowledge of God's counterdrama thus leads to discipleship that relocates our identity from the narratives of this passing age into God's counterdrama, so that we become players who bear witness "to the Word made flesh for our salvation."[174] God's covenantal counterdrama of redemption, which is liturgically enacted in the Sunday worship service, is performed by the members of the church during the week in their various concrete contexts, making the church a theater of God's grace

---

172. Horton, *Christless Christianity*, 18, 152, 240; cf. 124–48; *Ordinary*, 120; "Enduring Power," 35–38; *Gospel Commission*, 27; "Why Are We Celebrating?," 27–32. For a helpful summary, see Frame, *Escondido Theology*, 28–47.

173. Horton, *Covenant and Eschatology*, 14, 45; see also *Christian Faith*, 13, 91; cf. 201–5; "T.V. Gospel," 21–31; "Toward a Second Reformation," 123–50; *Made in America, passim*; "Union with Christ," 327–53; *Beyond Culture Wars, passim*; *Where in the World, passim*; *In the Face of God, passim*; *Better Way*, 43–45, 211–41; *Too Good to Be True, passim*; *Christless Christianity, passim*; *Gospel-Driven Life*, 191–218; *Place for Weakness, passim*; *Calvin on the Christian Life, passim*.

174. Horton, *Christian Faith*, 20–21; cf. *Gospel Commission*, 133–60; *Core Christianity*, 17–21.

and the "counterdrama of genuine human existence and community" that offers hope to this world.[175]

Doctrine and the formation of Christian identity and practice

Doctrine, as we saw earlier, is a form of spiritual formation that prompts us to put on Christ and clothe ourselves in him so that we perform our identity in Christ, acting out the perfection of God's eternal life and performing heaven on earth. For a theodramatic framework, our Christian identity and practice should be cultivated so that they bear witness to what is in Christ.

Horton agrees. He speaks about bearing witness to the inbreaking of the kingdom of Christ in this world. "Descending into our history," he writes, Christ "has forever transformed it, opening up a fissure in that history of death by his resurrection. By his Spirit, Christ keeps that fissure opened for the proclamation of the gospel, so that our lives even now become united to the new history of everlasting joy that he has already entered as our pioneer."

He adds, "It is neither the ascent of the soul nor the gradual ascent of humanity toward a better world but the in-breaking of the kingdom of Christ to which the church bears witness. Christ has redefined history for us and for the whole earth."[176]

Elsewhere, he writes, "The calling of the church is not to witness to its own piety or to transform the world into Christ's holy kingdom. In the words of Dietrich Bonhoeffer, 'The intention of the preacher is not to improve the world, but to summon it to belief in Jesus Christ and to bear witness to the reconciliation which has been accomplished through Him and His dominion.'"[177]

For Horton, then, bearing witness to Christ is fundamentally bearing witness to what he did in history so that we might be justified—restored to a right legal and ethical standing before God—rather than bearing witness to all that is in Christ, including his work in us, transforming us so that we live out the new life we have in him, the life that is participation in the life of God by the Spirit.

---

175. Horton, *Covenant and Eschatology*, 274; cf. 273, 275.
176. Horton, *Gospel Commission*, 297–98.
177. Horton, *Christian Faith*, 868.

The nature of structure in Horton's theology

Structure, as we saw in the previous chapter, has a pedagogical purpose. A theodramatic theology ought to be designed in such a way that it trains us more in wisdom and life with God than in abstract truth.

Horton considers theology be "chiefly wisdom *concerning Christ.*"[178] It is "the wisdom that we need for invoking the Father, in the Son, and by the Spirit, for salvation and life."[179]

To teach this wisdom, Horton structures his systematic theology in terms of the redemptive-historical/eschatological development of the covenant, which is the integrative center of his theology:[180]

- The covenant maker as the God who lives
- The covenant partner as the God who creates
- The covenant mediator as the God who rescues
- The covenant blessings as the God who reigns in grace
- The covenant's consummation as the God who reigns in glory[181]

The covenant maker as the God who lives

While there is only one God—a unity of essence—he exists in a plurality of persons who live in each other covenantally and thus know themselves in and through the other. This covenantal relationship is also manifested in the covenant of redemption in which "the Father, the Son, and the

---

178. Horton, *Christian Faith*, 104–5.

179. Horton, *Christian Faith*, 110.

180. Horton combines these two aspects of his theology in the title of the first volume of his dogmatic studies: *Covenant and Eschatology*. In the second volume, he says that God's covenantal relationship with humanity serves as a "hermeneutical guide" for systematic theology (*Lord and Servant*, vii).

181. Cf. Horton, *Covenant and Eschatology*, 17; *Christian Faith*, 21, 307, 445, 549, 905. Horton uses the five verbs in the surface structure of this systematic theology because, together with Walter Brueggemann, he believes that "strong verbs give rise to stable nouns." He adds, "This is another way of saying that the drama gives rise to particular doctrines" (*Christian Faith*, 225; cf. Brueggemann, *Theology of the Old Testament*, 145–266). Horton compares systematic theology to "the box top of a jigsaw puzzle" that shows how the various pieces fit together or "a street map, pointing out the logical connection between various doctrines spread throughout Scripture" (*Christian Faith*, 27, 29).

Spirit... turn toward us, with a purpose to create, redeem, and gather a church for everlasting fellowship."

Accordingly, "all of God's purposes are understood in terms of" this covenant of redemption. All things proceed from the Father in the Son and through the Spirit, who himself proceeds from the Father and the Son. As a result, the works of the Trinity in the world (economic Trinity) analogically reveal the inner life of the Trinity (immanent Trinity).[182]

The covenant partner as the God who creates

The covenant partner is the God who sovereignly predestines. He is sovereign over everything that happens in the Son through the Spirit. His predestination includes election and reprobation, and his election is unconditional.[183]

As the God who sovereignly predestines, God also freely creates *ex nihilo* and covenantally—that is, legally and ethically—ordering creation for his glory through his loving and creative speech or energies in a continual dialectic of gift, gratitude, and obedience. As the Father eternally speaks forth the Son in the Spirit, so he speaks the world into existence through the Son in the Spirit, making creation an analogy and theater of the intratrinitarian communion.[184]

The God who creates is also the God of providence, who not only works upon creation and history but also within it, covenantally sustaining and governing it with his energies. God's providence is part of his common grace, through which he restrains sin, restrains his wrath, and is good to all, giving gifts and abilities to humanity in Christ and by the Spirit, thus enabling life to flourish on this earth.[185]

Creation is a cosmic temple, reflecting the glory of God because he dwells in it by his Spirit. Created in the image of God, humans are miniature temples where God dwells by his Spirit, too. "The image of God (*imago dei*) is not something *in* us... but something *between* us and

---

182. Horton, *Christian Faith*, 309; *Pilgrim Theology*, 89–105; *Thomas Goodwin*, 52–55; *Core Christianity*, 39–52.

183. Horton, *Christian Faith*, 309–23; *Mission Accomplished*, 44–66, 82–87; *For Calvinism*, 53–79.

184. Horton, *Christian Faith*, 332; cf. 324–49; *Pilgrim Theology*, 107–10; *Lord and Servant*, 69–76, 85; cf. 66–87.

185. Horton, *Christian Faith*, 350–72; *Pilgrim Theology*, 110–16; *Rediscovering the Holy Spirit*, 54, 58; cf. 47–80.

God that constitutes a covenantal relationship. . . . We have been created . . . with a special commission, for a special relationship [or covenant] with God."[186]

This covenant of creation was a covenant of works because it promised Adam and his posterity the right to the inheritance of eternal life if he would not transgress the probationary command by eating of the fruit of the tree of the knowledge of good and evil.[187]

Created to be an obedient prophetic witness to God and his works as keepers of God's covenant, Adam and Eve became false witnesses and broke God's covenant of creation. Indeed, says Horton, "Adam's first sin was not in eating the forbidden fruit but in allowing the false witness to become a resident of the garden in the first place."[188] Their disobedience resulted in the breakdown of the covenantal fabric of life.

Because Adam was the head of the human race and represented all of humanity and creation, his false witness and false representation had bearing not only on his relation to God but also on his relation to the whole human race and all of creation. In Adam, every human being also participated in his sin and thus is guilty with him for his sin and is corrupted with him by his sin.

Instead of immediately confirming the human race in everlasting death, God graciously delayed the consummation of history by promising victory over Satan so that history could continue to move to the eternal Sabbath rest. God calls Abraham and renews his promise of victory over Satan and universal blessing in him. God's call to and relationship with Abraham is continued in his relationship with Israel, which recapitulates God's relationship with Adam and Eve. As God promised victory over Satan when Adam fell, so he promises the making of a new covenant with Israel so that history could continue to move to the eternal Sabbath rest.[189]

God also unconditionally promises to uphold creation with his common grace in his covenant with Noah, his descendants, and all living

186. Horton, *Christian Faith*, 381.

187. Horton, *Christian Faith*, 381, 384, 386; cf. 373-407, 421, 425, 440-42, 688; *Pilgrim Theology*, 116-29, 131-41; *People and Place*, 260-65; *God of Promise*, 83-94; *Lord and Servant*, 91-121, 128-33, 151-152, 159-60; *Mission Accomplished*, 21-31; *Core Christianity*, 82-85.

188. Horton, *Christian Faith*, 410.

189. Horton, *Christian Faith*, 408-43; *Pilgrim Theology*, 131-57; *Lord and Servant*, 120-55; *Mission Accomplished*, 32-43; *God of Promise*, 9; *For Calvinism*, 35-52; *Core Christianity*, 85-97.

creatures. However, this is not a redemptive covenant, but a covenant of law that enables believers and unbelievers together to fulfill the cultural mandate and engage in cultural activity.[190]

Since the fall into sin, this cultural activity belongs to the common or secular realm and pertains to the temporal, not the eternal, while the cultic mandate belongs to the sacred realm and pertains to the eternal. These two realms exist parallel to or alongside each other. As a result, Christians are dual citizens, fulfilling their cultural vocation in the common kingdom in a common way, like unbelievers, with the natural law as their source of revelation, and fulfilling their cultic vocation in the sacred kingdom in a special way with Scripture as their source of revelation.[191]

The covenant mediator as the God who rescues

The covenant mediator, who is the God who rescues, is the person of Christ, in whom "all of God's covenantal purposes converge." As the eternal ontological Son who would take on our humanity, he "is the eternal Mediator of the *covenant of redemption*." As the second Adam and true Israel, he "undoes the curse of the first Adam and fulfills the *covenant of creation* for his elect, thereby winning the right to be not only the risen head but the resurrection-life-giving Lord." As the incarnate, crucified, and risen Christ, he "is the mediatorial head" of the covenant of grace. As the son of David, he is the messianic Savior who fulfills the Abrahamic and Davidic covenants and who will unite all God's people in an eternal kingdom of righteousness and peace. As the servant of the Lord, he fulfills "Israel's corporate office of covenant servant" and secures the redemption promised in the covenant of grace through his suffering and obedience.[192]

Jesus Christ, through whom God rescues, has a threefold office. As a prophet of God's covenant lawsuit, he speaks and actuates God's covenant blessings and curses into history by confronting Israel with the law and gospel.[193]

190. Horton, *God of Promise*, 114-28; *Christian Faith*, 364-68, 712-15, 925-27; "Time Between," 45-65; *Gospel-Driven Life*, 245-66; *Gospel Commission*, 210-46, 282.

191. Horton, *Where in the World*, 91; Horton, *God of Promise*, 114-15; "In Praise of the Profanity," 252-66; cf. Kline, *Kingdom Prologue*, 66-67, 153-60.

192. Horton, *Christian Faith*, 446, 455; cf. 447-52, 455-57; *Pilgrim Theology*, 164-66, 168-70.

193. Horton, *Christian Faith*, 483-86; *Pilgrim Theology*, 183-86; *Lord and Servant*, 209-19.

As priest, he represents the elect—in covenant solidarity with them and as a living sacrifice of active obedience to God's covenant will—in the eternal covenant of redemption, being born under the covenant of creation and its recapitulation at Sinai in order to redeem those under the dominion of sin and the curse of the law.[194]

Now, as an everlasting priest, Jesus is a mediator of the better covenant of God's unchangeable oath to Abraham, rather than the Levitical priesthood of the Mosaic covenant, which depended "on the obedience and mediator of sinful human beings."[195] As their substitute, Christ made satisfaction for the sins of God's elect, bearing their judicial sentence in their place and propitiating the wrath of God by the shedding of his blood of the covenant to reconcile them to God and usher in the new creation. This satisfaction of God's justice is the legal basis on which "Christ's victory over death, hell, and Satan is possible."[196]

Christ Jesus also has the office of king. As the eternal Son of God, he already exercises his kingship in creation by being the source of creation. He continues to exercise his kingship in redemption. Christ publicly displayed his royal office of king with his defeat of Satan and his demonic powers by his death, fulfilling the promise made in the covenant of grace. He continued to exercise this royal office in his triumphant resurrection from the dead as the source, head, and mediator of a new creation within this old creation as the anticipation of the renewal of the whole earth.[197]

Jesus Christ continues to exercise his threefold office of prophet, priest, and king after his ascension into heaven. From heaven, he carries out his office as prophet by confronting his people with the law and the gospel, his office of priest by interceding for his people, and his office of king by ruling all things by his Word and Spirit.[198]

---

194. Horton, *Pilgrim Theology*, 192–96; *Lord and Servant*, 219–32.

195. Horton, *Christian Faith*, 487; *Pilgrim Theology*, 186–87; *Lord and Servant*, 232–34.

196. Horton, "Traditional View," 121; see also *For Calvinism*, 81, 84–85, 90; *Christian Faith*, 492–500; *Pilgrim Theology*, 196–208; *Lord and Servant*, 234–39.

197. Horton, *Christian Faith*, 525–26; cf. 500–501, 521–29; *Pilgrim Theology*, 187–89, 206–7, 213–21; *Lord and Servant*, 242–64; *Mission Accomplished*, 96–100; *Thomas Goodwin*, 105–27.

198. Horton, *Christian Faith*, 529–47; *Pilgrim Theology*, 221–28; *Lord and Servant*, 264–70; *People and Place*, 1–13; *Thomas Goodwin*, 129–44; *Better Way*, 61–79; *Core Christianity*, 68–71.

The covenant blessings as the God who reigns in grace

The God who reigns in grace effectually calls people to be saints through the Holy Spirit and regenerates those whom the Father chose in eternity, bringing them into union with Christ through faith in him by the preaching of the gospel. Union with Christ "is a way of speaking about the way in which believers share in Christ in eternity (by election), in past history (by redemption), in the present (by effectual calling, justification, and sanctification), and in the future (by glorification)."

However, "our subjective inclusion in Christ occurs when the Spirit calls us effectually to Christ and gives us the faith to cling to him for all of his riches." This mystical, legal, organic union with Christ is the "matrix" or "proper habitat" of the *ordo salutis* or order of salvation. By using these terms—"matrix" and "proper habitat"—Horton means that "union with Christ is not a 'moment' in the *ordo salutis* like election, effectual calling, justification, sanctification, and glorification but is a more general way of speaking about all of our spiritual blessings being found in Christ rather than in ourselves."[199] We cannot, however, be united to Christ's essence. We can be united only to his energies. In this way, we participate in the fellowship of the Trinity and become partakers of the divine nature.[200]

God unites believers to Jesus Christ by justifying them through faith, imputing the active and passive obedience of Christ to them. Because God's declaration of justification by faith creates the reality it declares, this declarative verdict of God is the basis or generative source of all the transformative aspects of our union with Christ. As those who are justified by faith in Christ, we are also adopted as holy and righteous sons of God in Christ, who are legally entitled to his eschatological inheritance. As God's adopted sons, we are daily called to put on Christ by faith so that we are increasingly conformed to his image.[201]

Because union with Christ in the covenant of grace is the application in time of the eternal covenant of redemption secured by Christ's finished

---

199. Horton asserts that this is also Calvin's understanding of union with Christ ("Calvin's Theology of Union," 90).

200. Horton, *Christian Faith*, 587; cf. 587–619, 673–74, 700; *Pilgrim Theology*, 271–78; *Justification*, 2:366, 447; cf. 2:447–93; *Covenant and Salvation*, 121–52, 181–215, 285, 302; cf. 272–307; "Union with Christ," 107–15.

201. Horton, *Christian Faith*, 620–47; *Pilgrim Theology*, 279–301; *For Calvinism*, 86–88, 93–95, 98–105, 159–62, 293; "Calvin's Theology of Union," 88–94; cf. 72–88; *Justification*, 2:447–93; *Covenant and Salvation*, 102–25; *In the Face of God*, 89–94.

work, the God who reigns in grace by justifying believers through faith also sanctifies them and enables them to persevere in the faith.

As we work out our salvation according to the standard of God's moral law, we always need to hear the law's condemnation of all of our efforts to find salvation in keeping this moral law. At the same time, we always need to hear the gospel's assurance of our justification and sanctification in Christ. God will enable those he has chosen in Christ, redeemed in Christ, and effectually called into union with Christ to persevere to the fullness of the eschatological life of glorification in Christ.[202]

The doctrine of glorification, along with the other transformative aspects of our union with Christ, also finds its ground in the doctrine of justification. Whereas Adam failed to earn the reward of eternal life, Jesus Christ, "as the Last Adam and True Israel, . . . joyfully embraced his calling, fulfilled his trial, bore our debts, and entered the glory of the everlasting Sabbath day in triumphal procession as our representative head." What is already true for our covenant head is also true for those who are in Christ through faith. However, while they are already glorified in Christ their covenant head, this reality will be experienced in its fullness on the day of the resurrection of the body, which is at the same time the Day of Judgment.[203]

The God who reigns in grace works out his salvation in the church. Scripture describes the character and task of the church with several different metaphors that are all rooted in the church's covenantal relationship with God in Christ through his Spirit. The church is the servant of the covenant Lord, the chosen missionary people of God, the Israel of God, and the body of Christ.[204]

God brings about the new creation of his church through his redemptive speech. While God is sacramentally present with his covenant people in the preaching of the Word, he is not sacramentally present with

---

202. Horton, *Christian Faith*, 648–87; cf. 615–19; *Pilgrim Theology*, 303–24; *Covenant and Salvation*, 80–101, 243–66; *Mission Accomplished*, 121–29, 130–40; *In the Face of God*, 161–63; *For Calvinism*, 115–50; *Core Christianity*, 157–68.

203. Horton, *Christian Faith*, 688; cf. 688–710; *Pilgrim Theology*, 325–41; *Rediscovering the Holy Spirit*, 45, 284–88; *Covenant and Salvation*, 267–307.

204. Horton, *Christian Faith*, 711–50; *Mission Accomplished*, 108–20; *Beyond Culture Wars*, 169–85; *Where in the World*, 45–51, 189–204; *Thomas Goodwin*, 175–98; *Gospel Commission*, 35–80, 210–46; "The Church," 363–84; *Rediscovering the Holy Spirit*, 289–321.

them in the same way, because the word of the covenant law silences and convicts while the word of the covenant gospel justifies and renews.[205]

In addition to the proclamation of the Word, God gives his people the sacraments of baptism and the Lord's Supper as signs and seals of his goodwill toward them, by which he strengthens them in their faith. Because the substance of our covenantal union with the mediator of the covenant of grace is the same in both the old and new covenants, children belong to the covenant of grace in the Old Testament as well as the New Testament. However, those who have not yet been united to Christ through faith are related to the covenant only externally and are thus circumcised and baptized "*unto* repentance and faith." Baptism remains effectual for those who reject God's goodwill toward them in Christ, but this effect will not be mercy and life but rather judgment and death.[206]

As a sign and seal of God's goodwill toward us in Christ, the Lord's Supper communicates Christ and all his benefits to us by faith, through "the energies of [his] life-giving flesh," enabling us to be mysteriously nourished with Christ's body and blood through the Holy Spirit, while at the same time giving us a foretaste of the eschatological marriage feast of the Lamb.[207]

Because God is working out his salvation in the church by the proclamation of the Word and the administration of the sacraments, the church is "not an aggregate of individuals who have determined to form such a society," but rather is the covenant assembly that "is summoned, gathered, and called out by God's electing, redeeming, justifying, and renewing grace." Accordingly, the church finds its catholicity and unity in fellowship with this triune God, and this catholicity and unity is evident wherever the Word is faithfully proclaimed and the sacraments are administered according to Christ's command. The covenant model "favors a connectional polity or form of government" that is neither hierarchical

---

205. Horton, *Covenant and Eschatology*, 269; *Christian Faith*, 753, 763, 755; cf. 751–87; *Pilgrim Theology*, 343–66; *People and Place*, 37–98; *In the Face of God*, 134–39; *Thomas Goodwin*, 199–215; *Better Way*, 10–17, 61–90, 229; "Church," 313–22.

206. Horton, *Covenant and Eschatology*, 270; cf. 265–76; *Christian Faith*, 763, 789, 794; cf. 788–98; *Pilgrim Theology*, 367–78; *People and Place*, 99–152; *Better Way*, 93–109.

207. Horton, *Christian Faith*, 816; cf. 798–827; *Pilgrim Theology*, 374–86; *Covenant and Salvation*, 11–36; *People and Place*, 99–152; *In the Face of God*, 139–42; *Better Way*, 111–22. Horton asserts that the view that the Spirit communicates the energies of Christ's life-giving flesh is also Calvin's position (*People and Place*, 133; *Christian Faith*, 816–18).

nor democratic, but presbyterial—that is, ruled by the broader assembly of elders who represent the Lord. The covenant model of the church locates the holiness of the church not in the institution of the church or the members of the church, but in Christ, the head of the covenant of grace.[208]

From this covenantal perspective, the church finds its apostolicity in conformity to the apostles' teaching and practice. The extraordinary ministry of the apostles and prophets is now continued through the ordinary ministry of pastors and teachers who equip the members of the congregation for works of service as prophets, priests, and kings. Extraordinary gifts, such as the gift of healing and speaking in tongues as signposts and confirmations of the arrival of God's eschatological kingdom, have ceased because the foundation of the church has been laid. Through the faithful execution of the marks of the church—the faithful preaching of the gospel, the faithful administration of the sacraments, and the faithful administration of church discipline—the church fulfills its mission in the world by opening and shutting the kingdom by the keys of the kingdom. Thus, the marks of the church are the mission of the church.[209]

The covenant's consummation as the God who reigns in glory

The God who reigns in glory consummates his covenant with his people as he brings them into the dwelling place of their eternal Sabbath rest immediately when they die and then into the fullness of this Sabbath rest when they are raised from the dead with glorified bodies like Jesus Christ.[210]

God will reign in full glory when Christ returns on the clouds of heaven and judges the living and the dead. This may very well be preceded by a widespread reingrafting of Jews into the church.[211] Moreover,

---

208. Horton, *Christian Faith*, 828, 854; cf. 828–71; *Pilgrim Theology*, 393–410; *People and Place*, 190–220; *Better Way*, 141–87; "Gathered, Protected, and Preserved," 129–34; "Church," 322–33.

209. Horton, *Christian Faith*, 872–903; *Pilgrim Theology*, 387–419; *People and Place*, 221–56; *Gospel Commission*, 165–78, 189–99; "Gathered, Protected, and Preserved," 134–46; "Church," 333–38.

210. Horton, *Christian Faith*, 906–18; *Pilgrim Theology*, 421–25; *Core Christianity*, 148–50.

211. Horton, *Christian Faith*, 949; cf. 919–56; *Pilgrim Theology*, 421–46; *Thomas Goodwin*, 142–48, 217–40; *God of Promise*, 131–32; *Core Christianity*, 150–56.

at that time he will cleanse the earth and usher in a new heaven and a new earth where everything will be holy to the Lord. He will reign in glory, enthroned in the midst of his deified people in the eternal Sabbath rest.[212]

CONSEQUENCES OF THE DESIGN OF HORTON'S THEOLOGY

This survey of Horton's theology reveals a number of ways in which it agrees with the theodramatic framework outlined in the previous chapter. Both emphasize a redemptive-historical reading of Scripture, for instance. Both see Scripture as the script of a theodrama in which we are not just spectators but actors, called to take up our roles in the drama while remaining faithful to Scripture. Both see theology as grammar, as drama, as wisdom. Both understand the structure of a systematic theology to be pedagogical, aimed not so much at the communication of abstract truth as at the growth and maturation of God's people.

I do not want to diminish or downplay the parallels between my vision for theology and Horton's theological framework, nor is my evaluation of his theology and what I see as its consequences entirely negative. The frequent appearance of the word "rightfully" in what follows is intended to highlight its positive consequences.

Nevertheless, the design of Horton's theology—not only its content, but also its form, the way it is structured—has some significant negative consequences for both our communication of the gospel and for the shaping of our Christian identity and practice.

Consequences for the communication of the gospel

Legal/ethical and ontological participation in the life of God

Horton describes his covenant ontology as "meeting a stranger," in contrast to the hyper-immanent Platonic/mystical model of "overcoming estrangement" and the hyper-transcendent atheistic or deistic model of "the stranger we never meet."

---

212. Horton, *Christian Faith*, 957–90; *Pilgrim Theology*, 446–58; *People and Place*, 259–307; *Thomas Goodwin*, 149–54, 217–40; "Kingdom of God," 389–91; *Core Christianity*, 150–56.

God is a stranger, Horton says, both because he is qualitatively distinct from us—the creator rather than the creature—and because he is ethically distinct from us due to our sin. Christ brings about a fundamentally legal/ethical union with God, overcoming the distinction caused by sin.

While Horton does say that "the proper antithesis is ... not between participation and covenant, but between different accounts of both,"[213] the contrast he makes between his view and the Platonic ontology can lead to a presentation of the gospel in which covenant and participation are opposed, as if a legal/ethical fellowship with God and an ontological participation in the life of God are mutually exclusive.

Knowledge of God's nature or being

Horton undergirds his covenant ontology with the metaphysical distinction between the essence and energies of God, which leads him to adopt—rightfully—the analogical mode of theological discourse. But because in Horton's view this means that we know God only in his works and our knowledge of him is only and always analogical, we can never have any knowledge of God in his essence—that is, his being or nature.

Horton's theology, then, can lead to a communication of the gospel in which we know only God's works and God as he is in himself always remains unknown.

The nature of our image of God

Horton draws a sharp contrast between law and grace. Law is a reflection of God's holiness and justice and it precedes grace in the covenant of creation, which is therefore a covenant of meritorious works.

In the covenant of grace, according to Horton, Christ, as the last Adam and our mediator, had to fulfill the covenant of creation by his meritorious works (active obedience), thereby earning the inheritance of the eternal Sabbath rest, and had to satisfy God's justice by bearing the sentence that God's elect deserved for breaking that covenant of creation and for their own sins by his suffering and sacrifice as their substitute (passive obedience), thereby propitiating the wrath of God to reconcile them to God and usher in the new covenant.

---

213. Horton, *Covenant and Salvation*, 164–65; cf. 129–52, 168, 200.

The design of Horton's theology, then, can lead to a communication of the gospel in which God is presented primarily as a God of law and justice and only secondarily, in connection with Christ's work, as a God of mercy and grace.[214]

The foundational nature of our relationship with God and creation

Horton's theology is centered on his doctrine of the covenant, which he views as a legal/ethical union with God. The first covenant in time, in Horton's view, was a covenant of works in which Adam would either earn God's blessing through obedience or merit his curse through disobedience in a *quid pro quo* manner. This covenant of works is still in effect today, and people are wired to know its reality through the voice of conscience, their longing for eternal life, and their daily experience of the benefits of God's common grace.

Furthermore, because the foundational nature of our relationship with God and creation is determined by this covenant of works, it also determines the nature of the work of Christ. The covenant of grace itself depends on the fulfillment of the covenant of works. Christ perfectly did what Adam failed to. By his obedience, he merited eternal life for himself and for us.[215]

As with our image of God, so with our image of humanity and our relationship to God. The design of Horton's theology, with the covenant of works as foundational to everything else, can lead to a communication of the gospel in which humanity's fundamental relationship to God and creation is one of law and justice, in which God's blessing must be earned through obedience or his curse will be merited through disobedience.[216]

Our knowledge of sin and salvation

To demonstrate God's holiness and justice and to protect the integrity of the doctrine of justification, Horton's covenant theology makes a sharp distinction between law and gospel. While these two principles are not inherently antithetical, they are antithetical with regard to how we are justified and inherit eternal life. This sharp antithetical relationship leads

---

214. See Burger, "Gospel Presentation," 274–77.
215. See Burger, "Theology without a Covenant of Works," 332–34.
216. See Burger, "Theology without a Covenant of Works," 341.

Horton to assert that the law alone tells us that we are sinners, while the gospel alone tells us that we are pardoned and saved.

In a discussion with Tim Keller, Horton illustrates what he means. "The power of the gospel comes in two movements," Keller says. "It first says, 'I am more sinful and flawed than I ever dared believe,' but then quickly follows with, 'I am more accepted and loved than I ever dared hope.'" Horton responds:

> But shouldn't we say that it is the law that handles that first movement, not the gospel? Keller rightly emphasizes that idolatry is the common denominator of these sins. Yet the first work that needs to be done here is a penetrating and soul-searching "first use" of the law—to expose our sin and show our need for Christ. The law reveals our idolatry, and the gospel proclaims freedom from its condemnation and power. The gospel needs the law to do its job.[217]

On this view, then, for the gospel to be communicated, we must first confront people with the law so that they can learn that they are sinners. Only then do we present the gospel to them so that can come to know that they are pardoned and saved.

The problem of our guilt

Horton rightfully stresses the eschatological reality of our participation in the resurrection life of God's new creation already in the present through faith and the Holy Spirit. He also rightfully connects the eschatological resurrection life of the future that is breaking into the historical present to the concept of the kingdom of God, in which Christ applies the benefits of his redemptive work to believers by his Word and Spirit, creating a new covenant community or church, where Christ's reign in grace is already truly present, though not yet fully present in its consummated form.

Horton also rightfully stresses that Christ made satisfaction for the personal sins of God's elect by his blood of the covenant, bearing their judicial sentence in their place and propitiating the wrath of God to reconcile them to God and usher in the new covenant.

But, as we have seen, the heart of Horton's covenantal ontology is the doctrine of justification, which deals with the problem of our guilt.

---

217. Horton, "Reflections on Gospel Theology," 89.

Indeed, Horton considers God's justification of sinners to be, essentially, the gospel. Justification is the generative source of the whole *ordo salutis* or order of salvation.

As a result, a consequence of the design of Horton's theology can be that, in spite of what he says about our share in the resurrection life of God's new covenant and the church and kingdom, the weight he places on justification can lead to a communication of the gospel that focuses on the individual and narrows the gospel—and the use of the term "gospel"—to the forgiveness of sins and the declaration that an individual is righteous.[218]

The twofold soteriological structure of earning and applying benefits of salvation

Horton's view of the covenant of grace depends upon his view of the covenant of creation. For there to be a covenant of grace in which God's elect experience justification, sanctification, and glorification, Jesus Christ had to fulfill the requirements of the covenant of creation, which is, in Horton's view, a covenant of works. Jesus thus had to earn or merit blessing by his obedience in order to share all God's blessings with God's elect. Having earned blessing and resurrection life in glory, Christ now applies the benefits of his redemptive work to believers through the Spirit, creating a new covenant community or church.

This twofold soteriological structure is evident also in the redemptive-historical structure of Horton's systematic theology, which Horton has adopted for pedagogical reasons, to train believers in wisdom for the knowledge of God. First, he deals with the covenant mediator as the God who rescues. Only then does he deal with the covenant blessings coming from the God who reigns in grace, applying the blessings the covenant mediator earned and bestowing them in a certain logical order (*ordo salutis*).

This structure—first Christ earns benefits and then he bestows them to God's elect who respond in faith—can lead to a communication of the gospel in which Christians are thrown back on themselves, wondering whether the benefits of salvation are for them or not.[219]

---

218. The influence of the sacrament of penance on the individualizing impact of the emphasis on the problem of our guilt will be analyzed in the next chapter.

219. Cf. Burger, *Life in Christ*, 10–11, 17–18.

The nature of the kingdom of God

Horton links the eschatological resurrection life of the future that is breaking into the historical present to the concept of the kingdom of God. When Jesus announced the arrival of the kingdom, he was announcing the arrival of the new covenant, in which he reigns in grace as he applies the benefits of his redemptive work to believers through the Spirit, creating a new covenant community or church.

Horton's theology, then, can result in a communication of the gospel in which the kingdom of God primarily entails Christ's rule in the church, including his bestowal of forgiveness and other benefits on believers.

The Mosaic covenant and God's relationship with Israel

Horton follows the typical distinction covenant theology makes between the covenant of works and the covenant of grace. Because law and gospel stand in antithetical relationship to each other with regard to justification, Horton considers the Mosaic covenant—the covenant with Israel at Mount Sinai—as in some sense a covenant of works.

God gave Israel the land of Canaan to fulfill its covenant vocation but remaining in the land was conditional on Israel's obedience to the stipulations of the Sinai covenant. In this sense, the Mosaic covenant is essentially a republication of the covenant of works God made with Adam in the Garden. Because Israel failed in its covenant vocation, its history primarily functions to reveal our human sinfulness. Moreover, God's covenant with Israel as a national entity was a passing phenomenon or parenthesis in God's redemptive history.

Burger writes, "Within the threefold scheme of federal theology, Israel is easily forgotten. The law was already given to Adam before the fall, and the covenant of grace already began in Genesis 3. This evokes the question as to why Israel cannot be overlooked." However, Burger adds, "The other possibility is that the covenant of Israel is understood as a republication of the covenant of works. In that case, it becomes difficult to understand the existence of Israel as the consequence of the covenant of the promise and of grace made with Abraham. Israel only functions as the dark background of the new covenant."[220]

---

220. Burger, "Theology without a Covenant of Works," 339; cf. "'Theirs Are the Covenants,'" 6–9; "Story of God's Covenants," 272, 299.

Thus, a consequence of the design of Horton's theology can be that it leads to a communication of the gospel in which God's concrete dealing with Israel as a nation has no place. It appears to be difficult to understand Israel's existence as a consequence of the covenant God made with Abraham. One could just as easily skip from creation and fall to Christ and redemption and leave Israel out of the story altogether.

The nature of the new covenant

Horton's theology operates with a pretemporal intratrinitarian covenant of redemption in which the Father elects a people in the Son to be brought to faith by the Spirit. In his view, too, the covenant of grace is unconditional in its essence, though it is conditional in its administration. Those in the church who have not yet been united to Christ through faith are only externally related to the covenant of grace. Only the elect who have come to faith are internally related to the covenant of grace.

Thus, the design of Horton's theology can lead to a communication of the gospel in which the nature of the new covenant is governed by God's decretal election, leading to uncertainty about whether one is elect, whether one's faith is genuine, and whether one is therefore internally in the covenant of grace or only externally related to it.

Consequences for the shape of our Christian identity and practice

The nature of our self-image

As I noted above, Horton does rightfully stress the eschatological reality of our participation in the resurrection life of God's new creation already in the present through faith and by the Spirit. But he lays more stress on our guilt and the removal of our guilt, leading to a communication of the gospel that focuses on the individual's justification and functionally narrows the gospel to the forgiveness of sins.

This consequence with regard to the communication of the gospel also affects the nature of our self-image, fostering a focus on one's guilt and the wrath of God that it deserves. Horton's theology can thus shape our Christian identity so that we view ourselves, first and foremost, in legal and ethical terms.

The nature of union with Christ

This legal and ethical focus affects not just our self-image but also our understanding of our relationship to Christ. Horton stresses that God's fundamental relationship with humanity is an ontology of correspondence, the correspondence of our will to the will or intention of God. Our relationship with God is covenantal, which, in Horton's approach, means that it is legal/ethical.

On Horton's view, God legally unites believers to Christ through justification by faith and vitally unites them to Christ through sanctification by the Spirit. But because the divine energies of God are distinguished from his essence as the rays of the sun are distinguished from the essence of the sun, we cannot be united to God's essence but only to his energies. Accordingly, Christ does not dwell in us essentially, but only by the energies of his Spirit.

The consequence can be that even believers—the elect who have come to faith and who are therefore not only in external relation to the covenant of grace but who are internally related to it—still have only an outward or external union with Christ.

The generative source of our Christian identity

The heart of Horton's covenant ontology is the doctrine of justification. While union with Christ is, as Horton puts it, the matrix or proper habitat of the *ordo salutis*, justification is the forensic basis of this union and the generative source of the whole order of salvation. The consequence can be that our Christian identity is shaped by looking to our justification as the source of our transformation, rather than to our union with Christ.

The practice of spiritual formation through spiritual disciplines

Horton rightfully considers Scripture to be drama that inserts us into its action and demands that we say or do something in response. Moreover, he rightfully considers the primary means by which our participation in God's covenantal counterdrama of redemption is cultivated to be the Sunday worship service. There this covenantal drama is liturgically enacted as God performatively speaks through his greeting of grace and peace, the reading of the law, the pronouncing of absolution, the sermon, the administration of the sacraments, and the benediction, while the people respond with singing, confession, and prayer. Horton also rightfully insists that the church's weekly public ministry needs to be supplemented and supported by ordinary private and family devotions of prayer, singing, instruction, and Bible reading.

According to Horton, however, when we supplement the Sunday service and the ordinary private and family devotions with spiritual formation through spiritual disciplines of contemplative spirituality, such as being silent before God, we may tend to focus our attention on what is happening within us rather than what happened for us outside ourselves in and through Christ.

Consequently, he writes, "Instead of drawing us outside of ourselves, this trajectory [of spiritual disciplines] takes us deeper into ourselves, clinging to what is happening within us rather than what happened for us, outside of us, two thousand years ago." He adds, "The most important, most real, most lasting work is not accomplished in the depths of our heart but in the depth of history, under Pontius Pilate. It is precisely because of that accomplishment that we have every reason to meditate on the riches of our inheritance each day. And because of Christ's work outside of us, in history, we are not only justified but are being transformed from the inside out."[221] As he writes elsewhere, "Nothing that happens within us is, properly speaking, 'Gospel,' but it is the Gospel's effect."[222]

Horton's theology can thus lead to a discouragement of the practice of spiritual formation through spiritual disciplines of contemplative spirituality. Instead of viewing these disciplines as a means of training ourselves for and cultivating our participation in God's drama of redemption, they may be viewed as distractions from the gospel.

The practice of Christian cultural engagement

Horton draws a sharp distinction between the way Christ rules in the church and the way he rules in the world. Cultural activity, in Horton's view, belongs to the common or secular realm and pertains to the temporal, while the cultic mandate belongs to the sacred realm and pertains to the eternal. Because the church's calling to be a missionary people is given in the covenant of grace and is enabled by saving grace and guided

---

221. Horton, *Gospel-Driven Life*, 158; see also *Christless Christianity*, 151–52.
222. Horton, "Law and the Gospel"; cf. "Reflections on Gospel Theology," 76–79.

by special revelation, this calling must be distinguished from Christians' cultural calling in society, which is given in the covenant of creation and is enabled by common grace and guided by general revelation.

Failing to distinguish between the cultural and cultic calling, in Horton's view, is not only a confusion of these two realms, but also a confusion of kingdoms, of Christ and culture, of general and special revelation, and of law and gospel.[223]

The church fulfills its mission in the world by opening and shutting the kingdom of heaven by the use of the keys of the kingdom through the faithful execution of the marks of the church—the faithful preaching of the gospel, the faithful administration of the sacraments, and the faithful exercise of church discipline. Consequently, in Horton's view, the mission of the church consists of the marks of the church.

This view has consequences for the shaping of our Christian identity and practice. Christians fulfill their cultic vocation in the sacred kingdom in a special way with Scripture as their source of revelation. But they fulfill their cultural vocation in the common kingdom in a common way, alongside and even like unbelievers, with the natural law as their source of revelation.

Moreover, because our vocations outside the church have bearing on the temporal only, not the eternal, they are considered "creation" work and not "kingdom" work. In fact, Horton does not believe there should be "Christian institutions" (other than the church), nor are there "Christian" vocations.[224]

"Christianity," Horton says, "is not a culture . . . [but] a system of truth claims."[225] Elsewhere, he writes, "We do not need more 'Christian' influence in Washington. . . . Rather, we need more Christianity in the churches and a more secular (though not secularist) influence in all areas of culture by Christians freed to pursue their secular vocations."[226]

On this view, then, Christians should not try to apply the gospel to social issues. "The Gospel is not the answer to everything," Horton says,

---

223. See Horton, *Beyond Culture Wars*, 107–27; *God of Promise*, 17, 121–28; *Christless Christianity*, 114, 124, 157, 206; *Gospel-Driven Life*, 253–54, 263; cf. 245–66; *Gospel Commission*, 84, 86, 100, 118, 212, 226–28, 238, 245, 271, 286.

224. Horton, "Transforming Culture"; "How the Kingdom Comes"; *Calvin on the Christian Life*, 228; however, cf. "Christ and Culture Once More."

225. Horton, "Beyond Culture Wars," 26; cf. *Beyond Culture Wars*, 32–35.

226. Horton, "In Praise of the Profanity," 264.

and saying it is trivializes the gospel. Rather, societal issues "are temporal problems demanding temporal solutions."[227]

Horton's view also shapes the Christian practice of evangelism and discipleship. The church should not try to make disciples by being a people who are active in the world by embodying the gospel. Doing so easily distracts from the church as the place where Christ is the active party, forgiving and renewing sinners.

In fact, Horton sees being a missional church through missional engagement with society by embodying the gospel as a form of "mission creep," which he defines as "the expansion of a project or mission beyond its original goals, often after initial success."[228]

Thus, the design of Horton's theology can lead to a compartmentalization of the Christian life by driving a wedge between activities in the "common" and the "sacred" realm.

Horton's theology has some overlap with the theodramatic framework I presented in the previous chapter—not least that we both see theology in terms of drama. There are, of course, many areas in which Horton and I agree. By no means do I think he is wrong across the board!

At the same time, however, as we have seen, the design of his theology—both its form and its content—have some negative consequences not only for our communication of the gospel but also for the shaping of our Christian identity and practice. In the following chapter, then, I will investigate to what extent these consequences may be the result of systemic problems in Horton's covenant theology.

---

227. Horton, *Beyond Culture Wars*, 202.
228. Horton, *Gospel Commission*, 8; cf. 247–93.

3

An Evaluation of Horton's Covenant Theology

MICHAEL HORTON'S DOGMATIC STUDIES clearly seek to contrast a covenant ontology with a participatory ontology.[1] Rather than affirming God's ontological unity with the world and our ontological participation in or dwelling in the life of the Trinity, Horton sees God's unity with the world as a strictly covenantal or ethical unity.[2]

Horton's covenant ontology is a form of classical Reformed covenant theology, even though he criticizes this tradition at certain points. This tradition has the concept of the covenant as its integrative center.[3] At the heart of classic covenant theology are three overarching covenants: the pretemporal covenant of redemption, the covenant of creation (often seen as a covenant of works), and the covenant of grace. The covenants with Noah, Abraham, Israel, and David, as well as the new covenant, are classified under these three covenants.[4]

We have considered some of the consequences the design of Horton's theological structure, centered on his view of the covenant, has for

1. Horton, *Lord and Servant*, 10–16; "Participation and Covenant," 107–32; *Covenant and Salvation*, 153–215; *Christian Faith*, 602–19.

2. Horton, *Lord and Servant*, 84.

3. Horton, *God of Promise*, 13–14; Macleod, "Covenant Theology," 214.

4. Horton, *God of Promise*, 77–107; Macleod, "Covenant Theology," 215–17. There are, of course, covenant theologians who do not hold to all three of these covenants, who do not view the pre-fall covenant as a completely distinct covenant from the later covenant of grace, who do not believe the pre-fall covenant involved meritorious works, and so on. But our concern here is with Horton's theology, and Horton is operating, with some modifications, within a historical tradition that he, at least, would view as classical covenant theology.

our communication of the gospel and for the shape of our Christian identity and practice in the previous chapter. Now, we turn our attention to problems with classical Reformed covenant theology.

PROBLEMS WITH COVENANT THEOLOGY

The meaning of the word bĕrît

Covenant or federal theology has been defined as a "system of theology in which the relationship between God and humanity is described in covenantal terms."[5] The Westminster Confession of Faith 7.1 says that a "voluntary condescension on God's part" bridged the "distance between God and the creature" and made this covenantal relationship possible.

The covenant theology of the sixteenth and seventeenth centuries viewed "covenant" as a form of relationship, whether between two human parties or between God and humanity. Many more recent theologians, too, see "covenant" (Hebrew: *bĕrît*) as either referring to a relationship or to the establishment of a relationship.

Herman Bavinck, for instance, writes, "In Scripture 'covenant' is the fixed form in which the relation of God to his people is depicted and presented."[6] Louis Berkhof agrees and anchors this understanding of covenant and relationship in the life of the Trinity: "The archetype of all covenant life is found in the trinitarian being of God, and what is seen among men is but a faint copy (ectype) of this."[7]

---

5. McGowan, *Adam, Christ, and Covenant*, 9; cf. Macleod, "Covenant Theology," 215; Van Asselt, "Covenant Theology as Relational Theology," 65–84; Weir, *Origins of the Federal Theology*, 3–5. For limited introductions into covenantal theology, see Allen, *Reformed Theology*, 34–53; Macleod, "Covenant Theology," 214–18; McGowan, *Adam, Christ, and Covenant*, 9–21; Rhodes, *Covenants Made Simple*; Wright, "Covenant Theology," 33–43. For more comprehensive studies, see Belcher, *Fulfillment of the Promises*; Golding, *Covenant Theology*; Lillback, *Binding of God*; Strehle, *Calvinism, Federalism, and Scholasticism*; Vos, "Doctrine of the Covenant," 234–67; Waters, Reid, and Muether, *Covenant Theology*; Weir, *Origin of the Federal Theology*; and Woolsey, *Unity and Continuity*. Allen helpfully notes that "the doctrine of the covenant was viewed not only as an organizing principle for uniting Old and New Covenant, but also as an anthropological principle to relate creation, sin, and redemption" (Allen, *Reformed Theology*, 39). For an annotated bibliography of Reformed reflection on the covenant, see Muether, "Annotated Bibliography," 599–622.

6. Bavinck, *Reformed Dogmatics*, 2:568.

7. Berkhof, *Systematic Theology*, 263–64; see also Bavinck, *Reformed Dogmatics*, 3:214; Letham, *Systematic Theology*, 437; Loonstra, *Verkiezing, verzoening, verbond*, 194–95.

Horton likewise defines covenant as "a union based on an oath" or "a relationship under sanctions."[8] In fact, for Horton, "covenant" is "not simply a metaphor for a relationship but *is* the relationship between God and creation."[9] Horton, too, thinks that the archetype of all covenantal life is found in the life of the Trinity: "God's very existence is covenantal: Father, Son, and Holy Spirit live in unceasing devotion to each other, reaching outward beyond the Godhead to create a community of creatures serving as a giant analogy of the Godhead's relationship."[10]

The concept of covenant as a relationship between God and humanity functions as the integrative center of covenant theology. This can be seen in the three central covenants that typically make up the structure of this system of theology: the covenant of redemption (*pactum salutis*), the covenant of works, and the covenant of grace.[11] Accordingly, all God's actions must be understood within a covenantal framework.

This is also how the concept of covenant functions in Horton's systematic theology. For Horton, the architectonic structure of covenant ties together "ecclesiology (the context of the covenant), theology proper (the covenant maker), anthropology (the covenant partner), Christology (the covenant mediator), soteriology (the covenant blessings), eschatology (the covenant's consummation)."[12]

---

8. Horton, *Christian Faith*, 44; cf. *God of Promise*, 10; *Core Christianity*, 83; see also Bartholomew, "Covenant and Creation," 13–14, 18, 21–29; Bartholomew and Goheen, *Drama of Scripture*, 24–25, 50–51, 55–56, 72; Brown and Keele, *Sacred Bond*, location 237; De Graaf, *Promise and Deliverance*, 1:23, 36; *True Faith*, 33–36; de Jong, *Van oud naar nieuw*, 89–92; DeYoung, "Why Covenant Theology," 589; Frame, *Systematic Theology*, 17–20; Goheen, *Light to the Nations*, 34–36, 43; Hyde, *Welcome to a Reformed Church*, 52; Jones, *Living for God*, 35–36; cf. 33–44, 72; Paas, *Vrede op aarde*, 319, 361-62; Packer, *Concise Theology*, 87; Robertson, *Christ of the Covenants*, 3–15; Schilder, *Wat is de hel?*, 187–88; Looze kalk, 66; Schreiner, *New Testament Theology*, 13–14; Smith, *Eternal Covenant*, 49–53; Stam, *Covenant of Love*, 29–30; VanDrunen, *Divine Covenants and Moral Order*, 84; Van Genderen and Velema, *Reformed Dogmatics*, 394; Vanhoozer, *Drama of Doctrine*, 135–37; Vanhoozer, *Remythologizing Theology*, 68, 442–44; Vanhoozer, "At Play," 18; Vanhoozer, *Faith Speaking Understanding*, 101; Van Til, "Covenant Theology," 240; Ward, *God and Adam*, 17; Williams, *Far as the Curse Is Found*, 44–46, 143, 236.

9. Horton, *Christian Faith*, 426. So also, Paas, *Vrede op aarde*, 362

10. Horton, *God of Promise*, 10; see also Smith, *Eternal Covenant*, 49–53; Van Til, "Covenant Theology," 240.

11. The word "typically" is used intentionally. Allen writes, "In due course, the 'federal theology' typically (though not unanimously) acknowledged the presence of three covenants within Holy Scripture" (*Reformed Theology*, 40).

12. Horton, *Covenant and Eschatology*, 17; see also *God of Promise*, 13–14.

However, the view that the Hebrew word for "covenant" (*bĕrît*)[13] is simply synonymous with "relationship" has been rightly challenged. While *bĕrît* can refer to the establishment of a relationship, it refers primarily to a commitment to an existing relationship, shaping it in one way or another.[14]

The etymology of *bĕrît* is unclear, but even if it was clear, the etymology of a word "may have absolutely no bearing on the semantic function of the word as used by subsequent speakers and authors (in this case, those who authored and compiled the Old Testament)."[15]

When we examine how the word is used, though, we find that, as McKenzie concludes, "Broadly, the word [*bĕrît*] refers to an arrangement of some kind between two or more parties. But the exact nature of the arrangement is not always clear."[16] In some cases, Hugenberger notes, "the making of a covenant seems to presuppose an existing relationship."[17]

Kutsch argues that *bĕrît* does "not indicate a 'relationship,' but is the 'determination,' 'obligation,' accepted by the subject of the *bĕrît*. . . . The subject of the *bĕrît* places another, the one with whom a *bĕrît* is 'cut,' under obligation."[18]

---

13. By and large, *bĕrît* is translated with *diathēkē* in the Septuagint. The New Testament follows this practice. Williamson writes, "Strictly speaking, this refers to a promissory obligation, and is commonly used in ancient Greek literature of a last will or testament, rather than some kind of formal agreement or treaty—for which *synthēkē* might seem the more appropriate term." He explains that because *synthēkē* implies a mutual initiative whereas *diathēkē* a unilateral initiative, the biblical authors may have preferred the latter word to the former for their translation of *bĕrît*" (*Sealed with an Oath*, 37).

14. E.g., Burger, "'Theirs Are the Covenants,'" 10; "Story of God's Covenants," 273–74; "Tussen atomisering en samenklontering," 22–24; "Theology without a Covenant of Works," 340–41; Goldingay, *Israel's Gospel*, 181; Kwakkel, "Verplichting of relatie," 119–20, 128; Stek, "'Covenant' Overload," 39–40; Williamson, *Sealed with an Oath*, 43.

15. Williamson, *Sealed with an Oath*, 37; cf. Barr, "Some Semantic Notes," 23–38; McConville, "Berit," 747; Nicholson, *God and His People*, 99.

16. McKenzie, *Covenant*, 3; see also Kalluveettil, *Declaration and Covenant*, 90–91; McCarthy, *Treaty and Covenant*, 11; Williamson, *Sealed with an Oath*, 35.

17. Hugenberger, *Marriage as a Covenant*, 169. While Hugenberger criticizes identifying *bĕrît* with relationship, however, he does consider relationship to be the primary sense of the term, while regarding "a shared commitment to a stipulated course of action" a less frequent sense of the word (*Marriage as a Covenant*, 171–73).

18. He adds, "It is theologically significant that the OT does not know of a reciprocal *bĕrît* that pairs God and people—a *bĕrît* in which both God and people accept mutually enforceable responsibilities" (Kutsch, "Berit," 258–59, 264). Others have criticized Kutsch for overstating his case (Barr, "Some Semantic Notes," 24–25, 37; Hugenberger, *Marriage as a Covenant*, 170; Kwakkel, "Verplichting of relatie," 119–20, 125–26, 129;

Burger writes, "A *berit* confers to a relationship a formal, regulated status; it regulates, shapes, or directs that relationship." He adds, "A *berit* involves obligations for one or both parties in the relationship. Exegesis should determine which obligations exist and to whom they pertain."[19] Consequently, the context in which the word is used should be decisive for its meaning.[20]

A first systemic problem with Horton's covenant theology, then, is that the word *bĕrît* ("covenant") is not synonymous with "relationship," as his theology presupposes.

Relationality and creation

Covenant theology asserts that since there can be no "natural" (i.e., inherently compatible) communion between God and humanity because of their metaphysical distance—the distinction between the Creator and the creature—God voluntarily condescends and establishes a covenant relationship with them.[21]

As a result, God's fundamental relationship with humanity needs to be secured with a covenant.[22] Bavinck, for instance, writes, "Among rational and moral creatures all higher life takes the form of a covenant."[23]

Horton agrees that because of the metaphysical distance between Creator and creature, there can be no "natural" communion between God and humanity. But instead of seeing the covenant relationship as added to created reality, he understands it to be part of created reality itself. God constituted Adam and Eve as covenant beings by voluntarily

---

McCarthy, *Treaty and Covenant*, 16–22; Nicholson, *God and His People*, 104–9). Barr says Kutsch's research in this area "seems dominated by a strong sense of the opposition between grace and law, promise and law" ("Some Semantic Notes," 37).

19. Burger, "Story of God's Covenants," 274.

20. Burger, "'Theirs Are the Covenants,'" 10; see also "Story of God's Covenants," 273; McConville, "Berit," 747; Van Bekkum, "Biblical Covenants."

21. See Westminster Confession of Faith 7.1: "The distance between God and the creature is so great, that although reasonable creatures do owe obedience unto Him as their Creator, yet they could never have any fruition of Him as their blessedness and reward, but by some voluntary condescension on God's part, which He hath been pleased to express by way of covenant."

22. Bavinck, *Reformed Dogmatics*, 2:568–72; Berkhof, *Systematic Theology*, 215; Horton, *God of Promise*, 10, 29; Oliphint, *God with Us*, 111; Fesko, *Theology of the Westminster Standards*, 138; cf. Stek, "'Covenant' Overload," 12–16.

23. Bavinck, *Reformed Dogmatics*, 2:568; cf. Burger, "Theology without a Covenant of Works," 330.

creating them in his image, with the commission to lead all of creation into the eschatological reward of God's Sabbath rest.[24] As we saw above, for Horton, covenant "*is* the relationship between God and creation."[25]

The idea that God's fundamental relationship with humanity needs to be secured with a covenant—whether added at creation or inherent in creation—can best be understood against the background of late medieval nominalist covenant theology and the political and social thought that resulted in social contract theory.

Nominalism makes use of the distinction between *potentia absoluta*, what God can theoretically do because of his absolute power, and *potentia ordinata*, what God in actual fact does and will do because he has determined to act—and revealed that he will act—in a certain manner. Accordingly, history is a dialectic between God's absolute power and his ordained power.

The key to understanding this dialectic of causation is a covenant or contract God has made with creation and a covenant or contract he has made with the church. In the former, God binds or restricts his absolute power and obliges himself covenantally "to uphold his created universe and the laws that govern it, in spite of their contingent nature or the sinfulness of man. This is in the area of natural causation." In the latter covenant, "God commits himself to a process of salvation which, in spite of its contingent nature or the basic unacceptability of man, he will uphold. This is in the area of theological causation."[26]

In nominalist theology, then, a person merits the grace of eternal life, not based on his innate natural powers or the innate value of a good work, but on God's covenant promises. A person "who does what is in him can trust God's [covenant] promises."[27] Nominalism thus entails voluntarism, a theory where the will takes precedence over the intellect. When God rewards something, he does so not because he knows that the moral act has some inherent worth but because he freely wills to do so.[28]

The nominalist dialectic between God's absolute power and his ordained power in the order of salvation was meant to protect both God's

---

24. Horton, *Christian Faith*, 381, 384, 421, 425, 440–42, 688; *God of Promise*, 10, 83–84.

25. Horton, *Christian Faith*, 426.

26. Courtenay, "Covenant and Causality," 117.

27. Courtenay, "Covenant and Causality," 118; cf. 118. For the medieval concept of merit, see McGrath, *Iustitia Dei*, 138–50.

28. McGrath, *Christian Theology*, 53.

sovereignty and his trustworthiness.[29] But because only a person who did his best or did what was in him (*facere quod in se est*) could trust God's covenant promises with regard to the grace of eternal life, this nominalist covenant theology was essentially semi-Pelagian.[30] Nevertheless, the continuity between this late medieval covenant theology and Reformed covenant theology is clear.[31]

Irons, for instance, argues that this voluntarist nominalist concept of covenantal or congruous merit plays a role in covenant theology's covenant of works, where God voluntarily condescends and superimposes a covenant upon the created order, promising humanity a reward for obedience that is less than God's strict standard of justice would. The merit required in the covenant of works, says Iron, is *ex pacto* merit—covenantal merit—as opposed to condign merit, merit according to strict justice.[32]

Political and societal structures also shaped people's understanding of covenant theology. Burger writes, "The doctrine of the covenant developed in a voluntarist climate, in which many important relationships were understood as covenantal. Relationality was considered an extra, added by a voluntary act of free subjects."[33]

For instance, in the medieval feudal economy, a landowner protected his interests and those of his renters by entering into feudal covenants that were legally binding. Just as a soldier's oath of allegiance in those days was referred to as a *sacramentum*, so was a feudal covenant. Thus, it should not surprise us that a feudal covenant "would develop distinctive theological implications."[34]

---

29. Woolsey, *Unity and Continuity*, 197.

30. Burger, "Theology without a Covenant of Works," 327; Courtenay, "Covenant and Causality," 102–10; Woolsey, *Unity and Continuity*, 198.

31. Burger, "Theology without a Covenant of Works," 326–29; Irons, "Redefining Merit," 256–65; Lillback, *Binding of God*, 46–55; Strehle, *Calvinism, Federalism, and Scholasticism*, 6–82, Woolsey, *Unity and Continuity*, 194–200. Burger notes, "Some Reformed theologians have problems with affirming a continuity between nominalist and Reformed covenantal thinking. Nevertheless, the fact that the magisterial reformers opposed the pelagian tendencies of late medieval nominalism does not imply a discontinuation with a tradition of divine self-binding, thinking in terms of promise and covenant" ("Theology without a Covenant of Works," 328; cf. Woolsey, *Unity and Continuity*, 199). Horton does not appear to see this continuity (Horton, *Covenant and Salvation*, 60; cf. Burger, "Theology without a Covenant of Works," 328).

32. Irons, "Redefining Merit," 262–63.

33. Burger, "Theology without a Covenant of Works," 338.

34. Lillback, *Binding of God*, 31; see also Reeling Brouwer, "Adam als koopman,"

What was true for economic life was also true of political life. Political life, too, was seen in the context of a covenant where king and people were bound to one another in a social contract. Huijgen writes, "The very invention of 'covenant' cannot be isolated from Swiss theologians' familiarity with the Swiss federation or *Eidgenossenschaft*, in which covenant or *Bund* was a central idea, and which provided a heuristic framework for God's covenant with humans."[35]

So, too, God's relationship with humanity was viewed as a contractual relationship that had to be secured with a mutually binding covenant.[36] When the Westminster Confession 7.1 says that "the distance between God and the creature is so great, that although reasonable creatures do owe obedience unto Him as their Creator, yet they could never have any fruition of Him as their blessedness and reward, but by some voluntary condescension on God's part, which He hath been pleased to express by way of covenant," this assertion needs to be seen against the background of this nominalist covenant theology and the voluntarist medieval societal and political structures. Relationality was not considered to be natural; it had to be added by a voluntary act of God.

Thus, a second systemic problem with Horton's covenant theology is precisely this view that there can be no "natural" (i.e., inherently compatible) relationship between God and humanity and so God must condescend to secure a relationship with humanity by means of a covenant. In the Bible, however, we find that God's loving presence precedes the covenants he makes,[37] which, as this study will show, are redemptive instruments that secure and guarantee God's missional intent for humanity and creation, often during times of uncertainty.

The intratrinitarian covenant of redemption

Covenant theology typically finds the unity of salvation in the pretemporal intratrinitarian covenant of redemption between the Father and

---

161–73; "Karl Barth's Encounter," 199–203.

35. Huijgen, "Covenant Theology as Trinitarian Theology," 301–2.

36. Lillback, *Binding of God*, 29–37; Burger, "Theology without a Covenant of Works," 328; Woolsey, *Unity and Continuity*, 185–94.

37. Leder, "Presence, Part 1"; "Divine Presence, Part 2"; "Divine Presence, Part 3"; Burger, "Theology without a Covenant of Works," 341.

the Son and the Holy Spirit, in which it "is arranged that humans will be saved, how they will be saved and who will be saved."[38]

The Father, Son, and Holy Spirit make an agreement to purchase the redemption and glory of sinners who have been elected to receive salvation and glory. In this agreement, the Son voluntarily agrees to become the representative head and guarantor of these elect sinners, taking upon himself the responsibility not only to meet their legal obligations but also to purchase their salvation by his death on a cross; the Father promises the Son that he will receive all that he needs for this task; and the Holy Spirit voluntarily agrees to apply the purchased benefits of salvation to the elect so that they inherit the eternal life the Son has earned for them.[39] Horton, too, operates with a covenant of redemption.[40]

---

38. Huijgen, "Covenant Theology as Trinitarian Theology," 333.

39. See Allen, *Reformed Theology*, 40–41; Bavinck, *Reformed Dogmatics*, 3:212–15; Beach, "Doctrine of the *Pactum Salutis*," 101–42; Beeke and Jones, *Puritan Theology*, 237–58; Beeke and Smalley, *Revelation and God*, 982; Berkhof, *Systematic Theology*, 265–71; De Graaf, *True Faith*, 67, 74; Edwards, *Observations*; Fesko, *The Covenant of Redemption*; *Trinity and the Covenant of Redemption*; Frame, *Systematic Theology*, 59–60; Grudem, *Systematic Theology*, 518–19; Hodge, *Systematic Theology*, 358–62; Kamphuis, *Aantekeningen bij J.A. Heyns dogmatiek*, 62–63; Kline, *Glory in Our Midst*, 222, 235–36; *Kingdom Prologue*, 145; Loonstra, *Verkiezing, verzoening, verbond*, 332–51; Macleod, *Faith to Live By*, 126–28; Muller, *Triunity of God*, 265–67; O'Donnell, "Not Subtle Enough"; Richard, "Covenant of Redemption," 43–62; Schilder, *Wat is de hemel?*, 262–68; *Heaven*, 96–99; *Heidelbergse Catechismus*, 383–84, 397; Swain, "Covenant of Redemption," 107–25; Turretin, *Institutes*, 2:177–78; VanDrunen and Clark, "Covenant before the Covenants," 167–96; Van Genderen and Velema, *Reformed Dogmatics*, 200–208; Vanhoozer, *Remythologizing Theology*, 258–59, 269; *Faith Speaking Understanding*, 77–80; "At Play," 17–19; Vos, "Doctrine of the Covenant," 245–52; Witsius, *Economy of the Covenants*, 2:60–107.

For Reformed scholastic resources on the covenant of redemption, see Heppe, *Reformed Dogmatics*, 376–78, 382–84. For locating the origin of the concept of the *pactum salutis*, see Muller, "Toward the *Pactum Salutis*." For the place of the doctrine of the *pactum salutus* in covenant theology, see Woo, *Promise of the Trinity*, 14–23. For whether the *pactum salutis* involves not only the Father and the Son, but also the Spirit, see Allen, *Extent of the Atonement*, 40; Williamson, "*Pactum Salutis*," 260–62.

40. Horton, *God of Promise*, 78–82, 87; *Covenant and Salvation*, 136–39; *Christian Faith*, 303, 309, 446, 487, 510–11, 518, 587, 616, 717–18, 854.

In addition to other problems,[41] however, this supposed covenant of redemption is highly speculative and its alleged biblical support is weak.[42]

The main exegetical support offered for the covenant of redemption

There is no passage in Scripture that speaks explicitly about a covenant between the members of the Trinity for the redemption of the elect. Fesko asserts that, like the doctrine of the Trinity itself, "the doctrine is not based upon one or two isolated texts but rather an entire web of texts spread across the canon of Scripture . . . creating a tapestry of the work of the trinity in the redemption of fallen humanity. . . . On exegetical grounds, not speculative, various theologians detected covenantal language in the various parts of Scripture that reported and revealed the intra-trinitarian deliberations regarding salvation."[43] Muller puts it this way: "The notion of an eternal covenant of redemption between the Father and the Son is established primarily by way of conclusions drawn from a collation of various texts that present the nature of the work of redemption."[44]

In the Old Testament, exegetical support for this doctrine is inferred mainly from the Psalms, which speak about God's covenantal relationship with the anointed king, and from the Prophets, which speak about God's covenantal relationship with the suffering Servant and the messianic Branch.

Yahweh's relationship with the anointed king in the Psalms involves not only God's historical relationship with Israel's king but also his covenantal relationship with Jesus Christ, the one David represents and foreshadows. Because Jesus is also the pre-existent Son of God, this

---

41. For an overview of criticism of the theologoumenon of the covenant of redemption, see Loonstra, *Verkiezing, verzoening, verbond*, 140–84; Woo, *Promise of the Trinity*, 24–28, cf. 31–38, 85–89, 139–42, 187–90, 235–39. When the covenant of redemption and the covenant of grace are collapsed into one covenant (Kersten, *Reformed Dogmatics*, 233), the result is a soteriological determinism that does not do justice "to what the Bible says about God's interaction in time with all those with whom he concludes the covenant of grace" (Van Genderen and Velema, *Reformed Dogmatics*, 207; Van Asselt, "Covenant Theology as Relational Theology," 81–82).

42. In what follows, I have drawn on Williamson, "*Pactum Salutis*"; Woo, *Promise of the Trinity*.

43. Fesko, *Covenant of Redemption*, 81.

44. Muller, "Toward the *Pactum Salutis*," 19; see also 22, 28; VanDrunen and Clark, "Covenant before the Covenants," 194

covenantal relationship between God and the king implies a covenantal intratrinitarian relationship between Father and Son before the creation of the world.

Thus, when Psalm 2:7 says, "I will tell of the decree: The Lord said to me, 'You are my Son; today I have begotten you,'" this not only refers to the historical covenantal relationship between God and David and God and Jesus Christ, but it also alludes to a pretemporal intratrinitarian covenant between the Father and the Son.[45]

When Psalm 40 says, "In sacrifice and offering you have not delighted, but you have given me an open ear. Burnt offering and sin offering you have not required. Then I said, 'Behold, I have come; in the scroll of the book it is written of me: I delight to do your will, O my God; your law is within my heart,'" this not only refers historically to David and Jesus, whom David represents and foreshadows, but it also alludes to the Son's pretemporal willingness to obey the Father's will for him for the sake of the salvation of the elect.[46]

When Psalm 89:3–4 says, "You have said, 'I have made a covenant with my chosen one; I have sworn to David my servant: "I will establish your offspring forever, and build your throne for all generations"'" (see also vv. 28–29, 34–37, 49), it not only refers to God's historical covenant with David and his historical new covenant with Christ, but it also alludes to the pretemporal covenant between the Father and the Son "which these historical covenants 'disclose.'"[47]

This is true also of Psalm 110:4: "The Lord has sworn and will not change his mind, 'You are a priest forever after the order of Melchizedek.'"[48] In fact, Fesko believes this verse refers only to a pretemporal oath made by the Father to the Son, since the New Testament itself does not directly mention this oath.[49]

---

45. Fesko, *Trinity and the Covenant of Redemption*, 93–94; Kline, *Glory in Our Midst*, 235–36.

46. Fesko, *Trinity and the Covenant of Redemption*, 14–15; Cocceius, *Doctrine of the Covenant*, 87; Turretin, *Institutes*, 2:177–78; VanDrunen and Clark, "Covenant before the Covenants," 181–82, 192–94.

47. Williamson, "Pactum Salutis," 266; Fesko, *Trinity and the Covenant of Redemption*, 14.

48. Fesko, *Trinity and the Covenant of Redemption*, 104–6; Cocceius, *Doctrine of the Covenant*, 87; Kline, *Glory in Our Midst*, 226–27; Turretin, *Institutes*, 2:177; VanDrunen and Clark, "Covenant before the Covenants," 186–87, 192–94.

49. Fesko, *Trinity and the Covenant of Redemption*, 103. However, see Williamson, "Pactum Salutis," 266–67.

So, too, when we turn to the Prophets, God's covenantal relationship with the suffering Servant not only involves God's historical covenantal relationship with Christ but also includes the pretemporal intratrinitarian covenant relationship between the Father and the Son. Thus, when Isaiah 53:10 says, "Yet it was the will of the Lord to crush him; he has put him to grief; when his soul makes an offering for guilt, he shall see his offspring; he shall prolong his days; the will of the Lord shall prosper in his hand," this "will of the Lord" alludes to an intratrinitarian plan between the Father and the Son that the Son voluntarily accepted and that underlies his actions and accomplishments in history.[50]

God's covenantal relationship with the messianic Branch also implies a pretemporal covenant relationship between the Father and the Son. Thus, when Zechariah 6:13 says, "It is he who shall build the temple of the Lord and shall bear royal honor, and shall sit and rule his throne. And there shall be a priest on his throne, and the counsel of peace shall be between them both," the phrase "counsel of peace" is an allusion to the pretemporal *pactum salutis* that undergirds the historical peace that the coming Messiah would bring.[51]

In the New Testament, exegetical support for the intratrinitarian covenant of redemption is inferred mainly from Luke 22:29; John 6:39; 10:29; 17:2, 6, 24; Ephesians 1:3–14; 1 Timothy 1:9–10; and Hebrews 7:20–22.

In Luke 22:29, Jesus says to the disciples, "I assign to you, as my Father assigned to me, a kingdom." Williamson writes, "Theodore Beza (1519–1605) introduced Luke 22:29 into the discussion, when he rejected Jerome's translation of διατίθημι as 'appoint' (Latin: *dispone*) in favour of: 'I therefore *covenant* to you, just as my Father *covenanted* to me, a kingdom.'"[52] This covenantal appointment is considered to have occurred pretemporally in the intratrinitarian *pactum salutis*.[53]

---

50. Fesko, *Trinity and the Covenant of Redemption*, 269; Cocceius, *Doctrine of the Covenant*, 86; Kline, *Glory in Our Midst*, 226–27; Turretin, *Institutes*, 2:178; VanDrunen and Clark, "Covenant before the Covenants," 182–83, 192–94.

51. Fesko, *Trinity and the Covenant of Redemption*, 77; Cocceius, *Doctrine of the Covenant*, 85–86; VanDrunen and Clark, "Covenant before the Covenants," 187–89, 192–94; Witsius, *Economy of the Covenants*, 2:61; cf. 2:61–62). For an overview of the exegesis of Zechariah 6:13 as support for the *pactum salutis* from Jerome to modern exegesis, see Woo, *Promise of the Trinity*, 62–76.

52. Williamson, "Pactum Salutis," 270.

53. Fesko, *Trinity and the Covenant of Redemption*, 120; Cocceius, *Doctrine of the Covenant*, 88; VanDrunen and Clark, "Covenant before the Covenants," 190, 192–94;

John 6:39; 10:29; and 17:2, 6, 24 all speak about those given by the Father to Jesus. Horton believes that a covenant of redemption is implied when "the Son is represented (particularly in the fourth Gospel) as having been given a people by the Father (John 6:39; 10:29; 17:2, 4–10; Eph. 1:4–12; Heb. 2:13, citing Isa. 8:18) who are called and kept by the Holy Spirit for the consummation of the new creation (Rom. 8:29–30; Eph. 1:11–13; Titus 3:5; 1 Peter 1:5)."[54]

Ephesians 1:3–14, which states that the Father "chose us in [Christ] before the foundation of the world" and "has blessed us in Christ with every spiritual blessing," is considered an allusion to a pretemporal intratrinitarian covenant of redemption because it is located in the pretemporal realm ("before the foundation of the world") and is read through the lens of Psalms 2 and 110 and Zechariah 6.[55]

A similar inference is drawn with regard to 1 Timothy 1:9–10. Paul says that God "saved us and called us to a holy calling, not because of our works but because of his own purpose and grace, *which he gave us in Christ Jesus before the ages began,* and which now has been manifested through the appearing of our Savior Christ Jesus, who abolished death and brought life and immortality to light through the gospel." The statement that God had a purpose and gave us grace "in Christ Jesus before the ages began" is considered an allusion to the pretemporal covenant of redemption.[56]

Hebrews 7:20–22 says that, while "those who formerly became priests were made such without an oath," Jesus is "the guarantor of a better covenant" because of the oath God swore in Psalm 110:4. This ordination of Jesus as priest with a divine oath is considered to have occurred in eternity.[57]

Turretin, *Institutes*, 2:177; Witsius, *Economy of the Covenants*, 2:60).

54. Horton, *God of Promise*, 79–80.

55. Fesko, *Trinity and the Covenant of Redemption*, 116–17; cf. 108–10.

56. Fesko, *Trinity and the Covenant of Redemption*, 120.

57. Fesko, *Trinity and the Covenant of Redemption*, 104; Coccieus, *Doctrine of the Covenant*, 87–88; VanDrunen and Clark, "Covenant before the Covenants," 187, 193; Witsius, *Economy of the Covenants*, 2:4–60).

Evaluation of the main exegetical support offered for the covenant of redemption

The Old Testament defense of the intratrinitarian covenant of redemption is based on a typological exegesis that not only points forward to the historical Jesus but also points backward to him as the pretemporal Son. Ordinarily, however, typological exegesis involves analogical correspondences that point forward.[58] This does not mean, however, that an Old Testament passage can never refer to God's eternal decisions unless those decisions are mentioned explicitly. For instance, when the Old Testament says something about the relationship between God and someone prefiguring Christ, what is said of Christ is true of the Son in his eternal relationship to the Father within the Trinity because God does not change. But eternal decisions do not necessarily imply a *covenant*.

Second, not only is this bi-directional typological hermeneutic unusual; it is also unwarranted. The Old Testament texts that traditionally have been used to support the covenant of redemption do not point backward but forward. "A key issue addressed by the Psalter," writes Williamson, "is the apparent failure of God's promises concerning the Davidic dynasty (cf. Ps. 89). But these two psalms (2 and 110), along with others (e.g., Pss. 72; 132) affirm that God's promises will not fail. Rather, such hopes would yet be realized—in a future, ideal Davidic ruler." He adds: "And the NT leaves us in no doubt as to when and in whom such fulfilment took place."[59]

Thus, the Lord's decree in Psalm 2, the covenantal oath in Psalm 89, and the twin oracles in Psalm 110 allude only to God's promises to David concerning his offspring, promises that were ultimately fulfilled in his greater son. Likewise, Psalm 40:7–9 refers only to David's submissive attitude, which was perfectly fulfilled in the submissive attitude of his greater son, Jesus. Isaiah 53, too, has in mind God's covenant with David and only how God's new covenant with Israel fulfills the realities foreshadowed in this chapter. In the same way, Zechariah 6 has in view God's covenant with David and only the future harmonious relationship between the messianic Branch and the Lord whose temple he will build and on whose throne he will rule for the sake of the peace of his people.[60]

---

58. Beale, *Handbook*, 14; Williamson, "*Pactum Salutis*," 272

59. Williamson, "*Pactum Salutis*," 274.

60. Williamson, "*Pactum Salutis*," 274–78

AN EVALUATION OF HORTON'S COVENANT THEOLOGY

As for the alleged exegetical support from the New Testament, when Luke 22:29 speaks about God conferring or covenanting the kingdom to the Son, this might simply refer to God's covenant promise to grant the kingdom to the offspring of Abraham and David. Or it could refer to God's pretemporal decree to do so. But a decree is not necessarily a covenant.

When, for instance, John 6:39; 10:29; and 17:2, 6, 24 speak about the Father giving the elect to the Son, these passages are referring to the pretemporal plan of salvation, but not to a pretemporal *covenant*. When Ephesians 1:3–14 speaks about the pretemporal nature of our election in Christ and our predestination according to God's eternal plan, Paul is alluding only to a pretemporal divine decree. He says nothing about a covenant. When 2 Timothy 1:9–10 speaks about God's saving plan "before the ages began," it likewise refers only to a pretemporal decree.

When Hebrews 7:20–22 says that Jesus was made a priest with an oath, it is not referring to an oath made in eternity but rather one made in time, after the giving of the Mosaic law, and in all likelihood the one God swore to David and fulfilled in his greater son (Heb 7:28; cf. Ps 110).[61] To make Hebrews 7:28 fit with his pretemporal interpretation of the making of the oath, Fesko explains this verse as referring not to the making of the oath itself, but rather to the "word" or "revelation" of the oath, which came after the giving of the law.[62] But Williamson rightly observes that, "while it is true that the text does indeed refer to 'the word of the oath' (ὁ λόγος δὲ τῆς ὁρκωμοσίας), there is nothing to demand a peculiar understanding of the Greek syntax here, that would make the 'revelation,' rather than the 'oath' itself, the subject of the following clause. Surely it is the divine oath, rather than merely the revelation thereof, that 'appointed the Son'?"[63]

When the New Testament speaks, as it often does, about "the Father sending the Son and/or the Son's voluntary obedience to the will of the Father,"[64] this obedience can easily be explained on the basis of the Son's

---

61. Williamson, "*Pactum Salutis*," 278–80.
62. Fesko, *Trinity and the Covenant of Redemption*, 104.
63. Williamson, "*Pactum Salutis*," 280.
64. John 3:17, 34; 4:34; 5:23–24, 36–38; 6:29, 38–39, 44, 57; 7:16, 18, 28–29, 33; 8:16, 18, 26, 29, 42; 9:4; 10:18, 36; 11:42; 12:44–45, 49; 13:20; 14:24; 15:21; 16:5; 17:3–4, 8, 18, 21, 23, 25; 20:21. See also Matt 10:40; 15:24; Luke 4:43; 9:48; 10:16; Rom 8:3; Gal 1:4; 4:4; 1 John 4:9–10, 14.

filial responsiveness to the Father's will and not on the basis of a formal intratrinitarian covenant.[65]

Baugh asserts that in Galatians 3:19–20, "Paul moves briefly but most profoundly behind the historical development of the covenant of grace into the eternal realm." In verse 19, Paul reflects on the Son's preincarnate existence, while in verse 20 he speaks of "the intratrinitarian life of God as the foundation of the covenant with Abraham," rooting the inheritance of God's promises in the *pactum salutis*.[66]

But verse 20 does not allude to an intratrinitarian covenant. It simply underscores Paul's argument that, because it is not a human opinion but God's opinion that Gentile Christians become children of Abraham by receiving the Spirit through faith in Jesus Christ and not through works of the law, this should not be tampered with, just as you do not tamper with a human will or covenant—and all the more so because God's promise came unilaterally, directly, and orally from God and not through a human mediator.[67]

Vanhoozer seems to suggest that the expression "eternal covenant" in Hebrews 13:20 refers to the eternal covenant of redemption.[68] However, the expression "eternal covenant" is, in fact, a reference to the lasting character of the new covenant (cf. Heb 9:11–15).[69]

In the end, although several of the passages adduced as support for a pretemporal intratrinitarian covenant of redemption do show something of a unified act of the Father and the Son, they are not strong enough to bear the weight of a *pactum salutis* between the Father and the Son and the Holy Spirit in which covenant theology finds the unity of salvation.[70]

---

65. Lewis and Demarest, *Integrative Theology*, 3:333; *contra* Köstenberger and Swain, *Father, Son, and Spirit*, 169; Swain, "Covenant of Redemption," 119–20; VanDrunen and Clark, "Covenant before the Covenants," 180, 193.

66. Baugh, "Galatians 3:20," 69.

67. Van Bruggen, *Galaten*, 110; cf. 105–10; *contra*: Clark, "Do This and Live," 191; Woo, *Promise of the Trinity*, 79–82.

68. Vanhoozer, *Faith Speaking Understanding*, 78.

69. Van Bruggen, "Volhouden op de weg," 316.

70. Swain charges those who draw this conclusion with falling into the pitfall of underinterpretation ("Covenant of Redemption," 118). On the contrary, those who advocate a *pactum salutis* on the basis of these passages fall into the pitfall of overinterpretation (Williamson, "Pactum Salutis," 281). Loonstra agrees that there is no exegetical warrant for the *pactum salutis* (*Verkiezing, verzoening, verbond*, 187–90), but he still argues for the use of the concept of a *pactum salutis* as an explanation of the voluntary humiliation and submission of the Son to the Father (*Verkiezing, verzoening, verbond*, 341–51). Robertson argues that presenting God's decree in covenantal terms has "a

None of these passages speaks of a *covenant* or necessarily implies the existence of one. There is no need to frame whatever is included in the *pactum salutis* in covenantal terms. The most that can be said is that Scripture speaks about God's eternal plan or decree for our salvation. However, "this divine plan or decree must not necessarily be understood as covenantal, implying a more formalized agreement or contractual relationship between the persons of the Trinity."[71]

Thus, a third systemic problem with Horton's covenant theology is that it grounds the unity of salvation in a pretemporal intratrinitarian covenant that does not have the biblical support he alleges it has.

The covenant of works

In addition to operating with a pretemporal covenant of redemption between the persons of the Trinity, classical covenant theology also operates with a covenant of works.[72] This covenant is sometimes called a covenant

---

sense of artificiality" about it and "extend[s] the bounds of scriptural evidence beyond propriety" (*Christ of the Covenants*, 54). While new covenant theology rejects the covenant of redemption (Vlach, *New Covenant Theology*, 205–6; Lehrer, *New Covenant Theology*, 37–38), progressive covenantalism does not (Gentry and Wellum, *Kingdom through Covenant*, 77–79).

71. Williamson, "Pactum Salutis," 280; Lehrer, *New Covenant Theology*, 37; Letham, *Systematic Theology*, 433–39; Murray, "The Adamic Administration," 130–31; "Systematic Theology," 234–38.

72. Allen, *Reformed Theology*, 41–42; Bavinck, *Reformed Dogmatics*, 2:564–79; Beeke and Jones, *Puritan Theology*, 217–36; Beale, *New Testament Biblical Theology*, 42–43, 174, 917–18; Belcher, "Covenant of Works," 63–78; *Fulfillment of the Promises*, 23–35; Berkhof, *Systematic Theology*, 211–18; Bolt, "Why the Covenant of Works," 171–89; Estelle, "Covenant of Works," 89–135; Fesko, *Adam and the Covenant of Works*; Gentry and Wellum, *Kingdom through Covenant*, 79–84, 211–58, 667–70; Grudem, *Systematic Theology*, 516–18; Hodge, *Systematic Theology*, 117–22; Kline, *Kingdom Prologue*, 107–17; Letham, *Systematic Theology*, 349–65; Macleod, *Faith to Live By*, 121–22; Muller, *Triunity of God*, 175–89; Packer, *Concise Theology*, 87; Schilder, *Wat is de hel?*, 193–95; *Wat is de hemel?*, 246–52; *Heaven*, 90–92; Schreiner, *New Testament Theology*, 19–30; Turretin, *Institutes*, 1:569–89; Vos, "Doctrine of the Covenant," 237–45; Vos, *Anthropology*, 18, 32–36, 40–46, 54, 107, 114, 120, 130–34, 137; Spykman, *Reformational Theology*, 260–63; VanDrunen, *Divine Covenants and Moral Order*, 40; cf. 39–94; Waters, "Covenant of Works," 79–97; Williams, *Far as the Curse Is Found*, 70–75; Witsius, *Economy of the Covenants*, 1:16–29.

For Reformed scholastic resources on the covenant of works, see Heppe, *Reformed Dogmatics*, 281–300. On the origin of the theologoumenon of a covenant of works, see Muller, *Triunity of God*, 175–89; Weir, *Origins of the Federal Theology*, 1–36; Woolsey, *Unity and Continuity*, 80–158. On Irenaeus and Augustine's views regarding a pre-fall covenant, see Woolsey, *Unity and Continuity*, 164–66, 170–82; Lillback, *Binding of God*, 38–45.

of nature, a covenant of creation, or a covenant of innocence.[73] On this view, God promised Adam and his posterity the right to eternal life if he did not eat of the fruit of the tree of the knowledge of good and evil.

The Westminster Standards gave confessional status to this covenant, but while the Confession refers to it as "a covenant of works" (7.2), the Larger Catechism calls it a "covenant of life" (Q&A 20). Both passages, however, agree that in this covenant "life was promised to Adam; and in him to his posterity, upon condition of perfect and personal"—the Larger Catechism adds "and perpetual"—"obedience" (WCF 7.2).

Adherence to a covenant of works is considered by some to be "the identifying feature of the federal theology,"[74] and it is a feature of Horton's theology.[75]

The law-gospel distinction underlying the covenant of works

To understand the covenant of works, it is helpful to view it against the background of Luther's breakthrough in his understanding of the doctrine of justification by faith alone.

Throughout the late Middle Ages, justification was understood as a cooperative effort between God and humanity. This is exemplified, for instance, in the sacrament of penance, which, after baptism and the Eucharist, was probably the most important sacrament in the life and discipline of the church.[76] Penance was considered to be the paradigmatic way in which God and humanity interacted in terms of God's justice and his grace. God was viewed as a righteous judge who demanded perfect obedience from humanity.[77] At the final judgment, the books would be opened to see whether obedience outweighed disobedience. This doctrine of a righteous God demanding strict obedience was accentuated and reinforced by the Doom painting of the final judgment on the walls

---

Fesko mistakenly claims that Schilder does not hold to a covenant of works (Fesko, *Covenant of Redemption*, 182–84; cf. De Jong, *Church Is the Means*, 174). Schilder did, however, not consider the covenant of works to be a *quid pro quo* contract (*Wat is de hel?*, 194).

73. Muller, *Triunity of God*, 175.

74. Weir, *Origins of the Federal Theology*, 22, 29; cf. Burger, "Theology without a Covenant of Works," 326.

75. Horton, *Lord and Servant*, 93–119; *God of Promise*, 83–104; *Christian Faith*, 138, 385, 415–18, 420, 437, 446, 487, 506, 506, 541, 575, 609.

76. Pelikan, *Growth of Medieval Theology*, 210.

77. Pelikan, *Emergence of the Catholic Tradition*, 330.

of medieval cathedrals, depicting Christ judging souls and sending them either to heaven or to hell.[78]

The sacrament of penance enabled a person to make things right before the final judgment through confession of sin and making satisfaction in a manner that had been determined by the priest to be fitting for sins the person committed after his baptism.[79] But even though the satisfaction of Christ was decisive, had a person really ever contributed sufficiently to this satisfaction by his penance? Moreover, if it was ultimately the genuineness of his repentance that was decisive in this regard, how did one know whether his repentance was genuine enough? It is understandable that this teaching about penance would lead to massive uncertainty about one's salvation.[80]

In the context of this medieval spirituality, Luther received his liberating breakthrough, the realization that salvation was by grace alone, through faith alone, and in Christ alone. As a result of this breakthrough, Luther made a sharp contrast between law and gospel. "The Law," Luther wrote, "is the hammer of death, the thunder of hell, and the lightning of God's wrath to bring down the proud and shameless hypocrites . . . [and] to tear in pieces that monster called self-righteousness."[81] Consequently, "the Law and the Gospel are contrary ideas . . . [and] have contrary functions and purposes. . . . The Law has nothing to give. It demands, and its demands are impossible." On the other hand, "the Gospel . . . brings on the gift of the Holy Ghost, because it is the nature of the Gospel to convey good gifts. . . . The Gospel brings donations. It pleads for open hands to take what is being offered."[82] What is offered in the gospel is the righteousness of Christ.[83] Accordingly, "the first sermon, and doctrine, is the law of God. The second is the gospel. These two sermons are not the same."[84] The law tells us that we are sinners. The gospel tells us that we are pardoned and saved.

78. Burger, "Gospel Presentation," 273.

79. Pelikan, *Growth of Medieval Theology*, 210. For the move from public to private penance and the influence of Irish missionaries in this regard, see *Catechism of the Catholic Church*, ¶1447; Vorgrimler, *Sacramental Theology*, 208-9. However, Kate Dooley challenges the theory that private penance was an original institution of the Irish church ("From Penance to Confession," 390-411).

80. Burger, "Gospel Presentation," 273-74; *Life in Christ*, 12, 17.

81. Luther, *Commentary on Galatians*, 91; see also 88, 113.

82. Luther, *Commentary on Galatians*, 63.

83. Luther, *Commentary on Galatians*, 11, 53, 57-58, 104, 134.

84. Luther, *Basic Theological Writings*, 125; cf. Kim, *Michael Horton's Covenant*

The law-gospel distinction developed differently in Lutheran and Reformed theology. While both traditions employed this distinction, it developed in the Lutheran tradition into a hermeneutic in which the distinction is used "as a filter for all of sacred Scripture, arguing that all of Scripture is either Law or Gospel, and typically this amounts to identifying all conditional passages—i.e., biblical passages which contain obligations, or in which eternal life is conditional in some sense on the believer's obedience or perseverance—as 'law, not gospel.'" Within the Reformed tradition, on the other hand, this distinction typically developed in a more redemptive-historical manner.[85] Horton, however, believes that the Lutheran and Reformed understanding of the law-gospel distinction is essentially the same.[86]

In spite of the differences in the ways Lutherans and the Reformed developed and applied it, however, this distinction between law and gospel as two different ways of being saved typically underlies covenant theology's distinction between the covenant of works and the covenant of grace. Horton writes, "The architects of federal theology clearly recognized that their covenant of works-grace scheme arose from their prior commitment to the distinction between the law and the gospel."[87] Whereas the way of salvation in the covenant of works is by law and works, the way of salvation in the covenant of grace is by the gospel and faith.

The order—first law, then gospel; first works, then grace—as well as the claim that in order for us to enjoy the benefits of the covenant of grace, Christ first had to earn our salvation and all of God's blessings by meritorious obedience under a covenant of works, shapes our image of God, leading us to view him, first and foremost, as a God of law and justice, who demands strict obedience, and only then as a God of mercy and grace.

Theology, 2.

85. Garcia, Response to Horton's "Law and Gospel," 172; 171; McGraw, "Threats of the Gospel," 79–86.

86. Horton, *Christian Faith*, 137; "Calvin and the Law-Gospel Hermeneutic," 27–42. For more on this distinction, see Renihan, *From Shadow to Substance*, 17–67; Burger, "'Theirs Are the Covenants,'" 2; McGowan, "In Defense of 'Headship Theology,'" 183–89; *Adam, Christ, and Covenant*, 19–21, 69–70, 179–82; Sandlin, "Gospel of Law," 193–247.

87. Horton, *God of Promise*, 85.

Biblical and theological support offered for the covenant of works[88]

The Bible does not explicitly state in Genesis 1–3 that God established a pre-fall covenant of works with Adam. Nevertheless, classical covenant theology presents various biblical and theological arguments for a covenant of works.

First, God superimposed the structure of a covenant of works upon created reality when he voluntarily condescended and commanded Adam and Eve not to eat of the fruit of the tree of the knowledge of good and evil. This command is generally referred to as the "probationary" command. The implication is that God created them as morally responsible beings who could know and obey his law and who would know that disobedience to God's law is sin and would make them guilty before God. This moral responsibility continues after the fall into sin.

Establishing a covenant in this manner, with a command, entails that this covenant is essentially a legal/ethical relationship with God. Moreover, because humanity remains morally responsible to God after the fall into sin, the covenant of works ensures the stability of God's law.

Second, when God established this covenant by commanding Adam and Eve not to eat of the tree of the knowledge of good and evil, he promised them the reward of the eschatological inheritance of eternal life. Personal obedience would lead to that reward in a *quid pro quo* manner (Gen 2:16–17). The reward is not according to God's strict standard of justice, as if their obedience in itself was worthy of the reward (condign merit), but rather was *ex pacto*, that is, a reward that God freely grants because of his covenantal promise. If Adam and Eve would be personally disobedient, however, they and their posterity would forfeit the reward and instead suffer the curse of the covenant of works, namely, death.

Thus, this covenant of works not only determines the destiny of humanity; it also means that humanity's foundational relationship with God and creation is characterized by earning God's blessings through obedience or meriting his curse through disobedience in a *quid pro quo* manner. This covenant of command and reward (or punishment) is the primary covenantal relationship between God and humanity and only later, in response to man's sin, does God establish a covenant of grace in which there is mercy and forgiveness. The covenant of works implies,

---

88. For this section, I made use of Burger, "Theology without a Covenant of Works"; "'Theirs Are the Covenants'" ; "Story of God's Covenants"; Irons, "Redefining Merit."

then, that God is primarily a God of law and justice and only then of mercy and grace.

Third, as the federal or covenantal head of the human race, Adam represented humanity in his obedience to this law principle of inheritance. When Adam, by his disobedience, failed to fulfill the covenant of works, Christ, as the head of the covenant of grace, represented the elect and fulfilled the covenant of works by his obedience (Rom 5:12–21; 1 Cor 15:21–22, 44b–49). The parallels and contrast between Adam and Christ in terms of the requirement of obedience, then, are seen as support for understanding the covenant with Adam as a covenant of works. In this way, the concept of the covenantal headship of Christ in the new covenant is incorporated into the covenant of works, so that humanity does not exist as unrelated individuals but rather exists in solidarity, as an organic or covenantal unity in Adam, its covenantal head. As such, all humanity is included in Adam's disobedience and its consequences.

Fourth, some proponents of a covenant of works also look to Hosea 6:7 ("like Adam, they transgressed the covenant") and Jeremiah 33:20–21 ("my covenant with the day and my covenant with the night") as support for a pre-fall covenant with Adam and with creation. Others look to God's covenants with Noah, Abraham, and Israel and see these as "anchored in" and "fulfilling . . . God's creative purposes."[89]

What distinguishes Horton's understanding of the covenant of works from mainstream classical covenant theology are the following elements.

First, on Horton's view, the covenant of works is not an additional structure superimposed upon created reality but instead is part of created reality itself. God constituted Adam and Eve as covenant beings by voluntarily creating them in his image with the commission to lead all of creation into the eschatological reward of God's Sabbath rest following "God's own pattern of creating and enthronement."[90]

Second, as the image of God, Adam did not need any grace to be able to obey God and fulfill his covenant commission, since he had been created with a transcendent ethical consciousness because the law of God was written on his heart. Since human beings are constituted as covenant beings with the ability to respond to God, the covenant of works is not an expression of God's voluntary condescension toward humanity after

---

89. Bartholomew, "Covenant and Creation," 28–30.

90. Horton, *Christian Faith*, 386; see also 381, 384, 421, 425, 440–42, 688; *God of Promise*, 10, 83–84.

he had created them, but rather a revelation of his justice and goodness toward them in creating them.

Consequently, Adam and Eve's obedience would not earn the reward as a result of God's free acceptance of their obedience on the basis of his covenantal promise (*meritum ex pacto*) but instead as a result of his strict justice toward them, having constituted them as covenant beings created in his image. In this way, the legal and meritorious character of the covenant of creation is protected from a confusion or conflation of law and grace.[91]

Third, Horton uses the law-gospel distinction dogmatically as a hermeneutical lens to interpret all biblical passages that contain obligations or in which eternal life is conditional in some sense on the believer's obedience or perseverance as law and not gospel.[92]

Fourth, Horton believes that incorporating the covenantal headship of Christ into the covenant works is necessary to uphold the doctrine of the imputation of Christ's active and passive obedience.[93] The doctrine of the imputation of Christ's active obedience implies that Christ had to *merit* (strict justice) our salvation, which in turn implies that for there to be a covenant of grace he had to fulfill a covenant requiring works, and since he is the last Adam, the parallel indicates that Adam too was in such a covenant.

Fifth, Horton considers the Mosaic covenant at Mount Sinai in some sense a republication of the covenant of works God made with Adam in the Garden. After all, the conditional language of this law-performance covenant is illustrated by the constant reminder that if Israel would do what God commanded, it would live, but if it failed to do this, it would.[94] "You shall therefore keep my statutes and my rules; if a person does them, he shall live by them" (Lev 18:5). Keeping the covenant would bring blessings; failing to keep it would bring curse (Deut 28).[95]

---

91. Horton, *Christian Faith*, 411, 424; *Lord and Servant*, 83–84, 94, 100; *God of Promise*, 54, 84, 89, 91–93, 100; "Post-Reformation Reformed Anthropology," 49; "Obedience Is Better Than Sacrifice," 316.

92. Horton, *Christian Faith*, 137; "Calvin and the Law-Gospel Hermeneutic," 27–42.

93. Horton, *God of Promise*, 87, 89; *Christian Faith*, 632.

94. Horton, *Covenant and Eschatology*, 133; *Lord and Servant*, 120–21, 151, 159; *God of Promise*, 32–33, 97; *Covenant and Salvation*, 13–15, 17, 97; *Christian Faith*, 420, 541, 712, 77.

95. Because the majority of covenant theologians considered the Mosaic covenant to be "simply an administration of the one covenant of grace while others viewed it as a distinct covenant" (Caughey, *Puritan Responses*, 31; Jones, "The 'Old' Covenant,"

Sixth, the covenant of works is still in effect today, and humanity can know the reality of it because the law is written on their consciences.[96]

Evaluation of the main biblical and theological support offered for the covenant of works

There are several questions that arise in connection with the arguments offered as support for a covenant of works.

First, did God make a covenant with Adam and Eve of any kind before the fall into sin? The answer to this question depends upon one's definition of "covenant." Because covenant theology—including Horton's—considers divine-human covenants to be synonymous with divine-human relationships, it considers God's relationship with Adam and Eve before the fall to be covenantal, whether God added the covenant after creation or whether Adam was created in covenant with God.[97]

189–99), I am including Horton's understanding of the Mosaic covenant as in some sense a republication of the covenant of works in this evaluation of covenant theology in general. Because of "the legal and conditional character of the Mosaic covenant with its blessings of long life in the land of Canaan offered for obedience, and its curse of captivity and slavery threatened for disobedience," the Mosaic covenant was considered by the minority to be a republication in some sense of the covenant of works (Caughey, *Puritan Responses*, 31; Letham, "Not a Covenant of Works," 169; Venema, "Mosaic Covenant," 93–94). Jones refers to these two positions as the dichotomist and the trichotomist views (Jones, "The 'Old' Covenant," 189–99; see also Reid, "Mosaic Covenant," 149–52). For a taxonomy of the various positions highlighting the difference nuances, see Ferry, "Works in the Mosaic Covenant," 76–105; Golding, *Covenant Theology*, 164–73; Karlberg, *Covenant Theology in Reformed Perspective*, 17–57.

96. Horton, *Christian Faith*, 138, 140–42, 387, 979; *God of Promise*, 92–93, 118, 191; *Covenant and Salvation*, 35, 88, 92; *Christless Christianity*, 125, 209; "In Praise of the Profanity," 261; *Gospel-Driven Life*, 253; *Gospel Commission*, 237; *Core Christianity*, 84–85, 90; *Justification*, 1:62, 295; 2:63, 75, 136–37.

97. Karl Barth understands creation to be the external basis or context within which God enters into a covenant of grace with humanity. Thus, Barth's theology has no room for a pre-fall covenant of works that is distinct from a covenant of grace (Barth, *Church Dogmatics* III/1, 94–228; cf. 229–339). Barth's perspective has influenced others to criticize covenant theology's twofold distinction between a meritorious covenant of works and a non-meritorious covenant of grace. For a criticism of Barth's covenant theology, see McGowan, *Adam, Christ, and Covenant*, 22–40. For criticism of the Scottish theologians T. F. Torrance and J. B. Torrance who fundamentally shared Barth's perspective on covenant theology, see McGowan, *Adam, Christ, and Covenant*, 40–45. For Berkouwer's, De Graaf's, and Hoeksema's understanding of a pre-fall covenant that was not a covenant of works, see Berkouwer, *Sin*, 206–9; De Graaf, *Promise and Deliverance*, 1:37; *True Faith*, 23–24; Hoeksema, *Reformed Dogmatics*, 308–12. For a thorough summary of De Graaf's doctrine of the covenant that also documents how De Graaf went from understanding the pre-fall covenant as a covenant of works in which Adam

But, as we have seen above, covenant (*běrît*) and relationship are not synonymous. A covenant is a redemptive instrument that secures and guarantees God's missional intent for humanity and creation, often during times of uncertainty. But there is no indication in Scripture that God's relationship with Adam and Eve before the fall entailed a covenant.

Some argue that, even though the term "covenant" is not used in Genesis 1 and 2, nevertheless there is a relationship that can be described as covenantal because it shares common features with later biblical covenants. This argument, nevertheless, still depends on taking *běrît* as referring to a relationship. Moreover, it attempts to interpret Genesis 1 and 2 by deriving a concept of covenant from elsewhere in Scripture and then superimposing it upon the narrative of Genesis.[98]

Second, did God promise to reward Adam and Eve with eternal life for their obedience in a *quid pro quo* manner?[99] Genesis 2:17–18 does not promise the reward of eternal life. In fact, it makes no promise at all. It only warns that the sanction for disobedience would be death.[100] Instead of implying a promise that Adam and Eve could earn their eternal destiny by personal obedience, the sanction "marked the path to the loss of the state Adam already enjoyed."[101] Thus, "Genesis does not tell us of

---

had to obtain eternal life to understanding this covenant as a covenant of God's favour in which he would inherit eternal life, see Wendt, *S. G. De Graaf*, 81–109; Dijkstra-Algra, *Geschiedenis als verbondsgeschiedenis*, 11–12; For Frame's, Hoekema's, Murray's, and Williams's understanding of the pre-fall arrangement between God and humanity, see Frame, *Systematic Theology*, 62–66; Hoekema, *Created in God's Image*, 117–21; Murray, "The Adamic Administration," 47–59; Williams, *Far as the Curse Is Found*, 46, 51, 62, 72–74. For a thorough summary of Murray's response to covenant theology, see Jeon, *Covenant Theology*, 103–90. For Klaas Schilder's emphasis on the unity of the covenant and his defence of the covenant with Adam in paradise see Strauss, *"Alles of Niks,"* 66–98, 112, 201; "Schilder on the Covenant," 23–24; Veldhuizen, *God en mens onderweg*, 104–5. For the legacy of covenant theology in the Reformed Churches Liberated, see Burger, *Verder met het verbond*, 109–26. For different ways of understanding grace regarding the covenant of works, see Ward, *God and Adam*, 117–23.

98. In this regard, Leder helpfully writes, "Biblical theological topics in GK [Genesis-Kings] emerge in terms of the narrative development of the theological problem, not as a conclusion from the examination and comparison of a variety of texts. Its theology of covenant does not begin with a summary of features typical of a covenant and drawn from any and all biblical texts without regard to the text's narrative shape" (Leder, "Divine Presence, Part 3," 694).

99. For a brief discussion of the debate among seventeenth-century theologians about the nature of Adam's reward and whether it was the reward of heaven or continued life in the garden, see Jones, "(Gracious?) Covenant of Works."

100. Burger, "Story of God's Covenants," 277; Williamson, *Sealed with an Oath*, 54.

101. McComiskey, *Covenants of Promise*, 217.

PARTICIPATION AND COVENANT

earning life by obedience and good works, but rather of *making good use of given possibilities and not losing them.*"[102]

Third, does the Bible teach that unfallen man could earn or merit anything from God in strict justice? As we have seen earlier, while some forms of the covenant of works concept deny that Adam's obedience could have earned anything from God in strict justice but instead merited life *ex pacto*, simply because God voluntarily chose to reward his obedience with life, Horton's view of the covenant of works does involve Adam and Eve meriting eternal life as a matter of strict justice.

In this connection, Jelle Faber writes, "But the question must arise: Can man ever earn anything in relation to God? The Belgic Confession states in Article 24, speaking about man's sanctification and good works: Therefore we do good works, but not to merit by them (for what can we merit?); nay, we are indebted to God for the good works we do, and not He to us, since it is He who *worketh in us both to will and to work, for His good pleasure.*"

He then adds, "Would this confession be valid only for the life in the covenant of God's grace and not also for the covenant in the Paradise situation? The question 'For what can we merit?' is a strong and striking rhetorical statement concerning the basic structure of the relation between God and man, Creator and creature. Each and every breath was a gift of God of life, and the creation of man as the image of God was fruit of God's favour."[103]

Fourth, did Adam and Eve's relationship with God need to be regulated by law? We saw above that covenant theology assumes that since there can be no "natural" (i.e., inherently compatible) communion between God and humanity on account of their ontological distance, God voluntarily condescends and secures his relationship with them by way of a covenant of works. We also saw that covenant theology can best be understood against the background of late medieval nominalist covenant theology, which makes use of the distinction between *potentia absoluta* (what God can theoretically do because of his absolute power) and *potentia ordinata* (what God in actual fact does and will do because he has ordained it and has revealed that he will act in a certain manner). Accordingly, on this view, God's ordained and revealed will is not

---

102. Burger, "Story of God's Covenants," 278; see also "'Theirs Are the Covenants,'" 9.

103. Faber, "Covenant of Works," 90–91.

a manifestation of his justice and goodness, but simply a matter of his sovereign good pleasure.

But because God really is good and just, his sovereign good pleasure is a manifestation of his goodness and justice, and therefore creation, by its very nature, is also a manifestation of his goodness and justice.

Thus, it would appear that God's relationship with Adam and Eve before the fall did not need to be secured by a covenant of law or works, either as an additional structure superimposed upon created reality or as an aspect of God's creation of Adam and Eve as covenant beings in his image, with his law written on their hearts as a manifestation of his justice.

Instead, God's justice was manifested simply by the fact that being created according to their kind had moral implications. In this light, according to Burger, "we can understand God's wrath and judgment over a sinful world in Romans 1 and 2 without any law or covenant. Law and covenant enlarge the problem of sin and God's wrath, as the Jewish people have experienced. But justice exists before the law or the covenant."[104]

This also implies that Horton's dogmatic law-gospel distinction and his assertion that the covenant of works is still in effect today is not warranted by Scripture. It is not the case that all commands in Scripture are "law," let alone a manifestation of the covenant of works principle, while "gospel" refers to all promises of salvation by grace through faith.[105] In fact, both law and gospel include promises and commands.[106] When

---

104. Burger, "Theology without a Covenant of Works," 342; see also van Bruggen, "Hoe kunnen Gods wetten."

105. *Contra* Horton, *Law of Perfect Freedom*, 21; *Christian Faith*, 665. Failing to see and adhere to this law-gospel hermeneutic is not a confusing of law and gospel (*contra* Horton, *Christless Christianity*, 107–19, 122, 124, 157, 247, 250; *Gospel-Driven Life*, 35, 210; *Christian Faith*, 439; *Putting Amazing Back into Grace*, 159, 214, 226, 260; *Gospel Commission, Gospel Commission*, 227; *Core Christianity*, 129; *Justification*, 2:94, 97). Furthermore, failing to see and adhere to this law-gospel hermeneutic also does not confuse what God has done and what we do. Consequently, speaking to others about living, doing, and being the gospel is also not a confusing of law and gospel (*contra* Horton, *Christless Christianity*, 18, 152, 240; cf. 124–48; "Reflections on Gospel Theology," 77; "Enduring Power," 35–38; *Gospel Commission*, 27; "Why Are We Celebrating?," 27–32).

106. McGraw, "Threats of the Gospel," 79–111. The Canons of Dort, for instance, "highlights the imperative force of the gospel: 'And as it hath pleased God by the preaching of the gospel, to begin this work of grace in us, so He preserves, continues, and perfects it by the hearing and reading of His Word, by meditation thereon, and by the exhortations, threatenings, and promises thereof, as well as by the use of the sacraments' (5.14)" (see Beeke and Jones, *Puritan Theology*, 323; McGraw, "Threats of the Gospel," 83).

Horton asserts that the law alone tells us that we are sinners, while the gospel alone tells us that we are pardoned and saved,[107] he forgets that the gospel also tells us that we are sinners (1 Cor 15:3) and that the New Testament can speak of obeying the gospel (Rom 10:16; 2 Thess 1:8; 1 Pet 4:17).

It is a mistake, then, to identify all commandments with law and law with a covenant of works principle. Nor ought we to conclude from the presence of a commandment in the Garden that God's relationship was characterized by law and merit rather than by grace, love, favor, and inheritance.[108]

Fifth, did Adam and Eve not need God's grace in order to be able to obey God and fulfill their covenant commission? Horton says they did not, because they were created with a transcendent ethical consciousness because the law of God was written on their hearts.

But the answer to this question depends on one's definition of "grace." In Horton's theology, grace is given only to sinners and so Adam and Eve did not need grace. Saying they did would imply that they were sinners. Moreover, as God's image, they did not need any supplemental grace to obey God since they did have his law written on their hearts.

But if "grace" is not restricted to forgiving grace—God's favor in the presence of sin—but includes God's "condescending" grace and supplemental grace, as this has been understood by much of covenant theology,[109] then Adam and Eve did receive grace in the Garden for the fulfillment of their commission, just as the second Adam received grace for the fulfillment of his (Isa 42:1; Luke 2:40, 52).

In this connection, Jones says, "Divine grace is a perfection of God's nature, and thus a characteristic of how he relates to finite creatures, even apart from sin. In the garden, the grace of God was upon Adam; in the 'wilderness,' the grace of God is upon his Son, the second Adam. God's graciousness may be summarized simply as what he is in and of himself."[110]

Moreover, because "the true human who bears God's image is inconceivable even for a moment without the indwelling of the Holy Spirit,"

---

107. See Keller, Response to Michael Horton, 96.

108. Barth, *Church Dogmatics* III/1, 231–32; Burger, "Theology without a Covenant of Works," 336; De Graaf, *Promise and Deliverance*, 1:37; Torrance, "Covenant or Contract?," 67.

109. Strange, *Imputation*, 123.

110. Jones, "Can Humans Merit (2 of 2)"; see also Kevan, *Grace of Law*, 112.

it is incorrect to assert that as the image of God, Adam did not need any supplemental grace to be able to obey God simply because he had the law of God written on his heart.[111]

Furthermore, the law written on Adam's heart simply was not enough for Adam to be able to obey God. He also received special revelation, without which he would not have known that the tree of the knowledge of good and evil was forbidden.

Sixth, does the concept of covenantal headship need to be incorporated into the covenant of works? The answer to this question is twofold. First, if there is no covenant of works that Christ had to fulfill with his obedience because man by disobedience failed to do so, then the concept of covenantal headship *cannot* be incorporated into a covenant of works. Second, the parallel between Adam and Christ does not *need* to be put into a covenantal structure.[112]

Burger rightly notes that "the idea of Adam's headship is crucial to understand the influence of sin. Nevertheless, the idea of headship is not sufficient to understand our participation in Christ. The mystical union with Christ implies a renewed indwelling in Christ and transcends the idea of headship."[113]

It is therefore not necessary to incorporate the concept of covenantal headship into the covenant of works in order to uphold a doctrine of the imputation of Christ's active and passive obedience. Put the other way around, one can hold to the imputation of Christ's active and passive obedience without arguing by way of parallels between Adam and Christ as covenant heads back to a pre-fall covenant in which Adam was required to merit God's blessing by his obedience.

---

111. Bavinck, *Reformed Dogmatics*, 3:292; see also 2:558–59; Jones, "Can Humans Merit (2 of 2)"; Leithart, "Adam the Catholic?," 170–71, 187–91; McGowan, "In Defense of 'Headship Theology,'" 191–98.

112. Leder, "Divine Presence, Part 3," 694; McGowan, "In Defense of 'Headship Theology,'" 178–99; *Adam, Christ, and Covenant*, 111–203; Murray, "The Adamic Administration," 47–59; *contra* Horton, *God of Promise*, 87, 89; *Christian Faith*, 632; Bolt, "Why the Covenant of Works," 181, 185; Schreiner, *Covenant and God's Purpose*, 22.

113. Burger, "Theology without a Covenant of Works," 342. Regarding covenant theology's use of the analogy of Adam and Christ in which Christ solves the problem Adam created, Leder writes, "Federal theology reads GK [Genesis-Kings] from the point of view of the Pauline Adam-Christ analogy. From the point of view of GK, however, Adam plays a minor role; Abraham is the character with and through whom God begins to solve the problem of exile from the Garden presence when divine instruction excises him from the scatteredness of Babel to direct him to 'the land,' the place where God would dwell in the midst of Abraham's descendants" ("Divine Presence, Part 3," 691).

Seventh, was the Mosaic covenant in some sense a republication of the covenant of works?[114] Again, the answer is twofold. First, if there was no covenant of works, there can be no republication of it. Second, if Adam and Eve's relationship with God did not need to be regulated by law, then Scripture gives no warrant for taking the Mosaic covenant as, in some sense, a republication of the covenant of works in which Israel's primary function was to reveal just how sinful humanity was. If there was no law in the Garden, but only a command, then the presence of law in the Mosaic covenant does not make it a republication of Adam's relationship with God.

Moreover, Horton's restriction of the works principle in the Mosaic covenant to Israel's remaining in the land as a nation and enjoying God's temporal blessings as typological of the eschatological Paradise of God and salvation in Christ suffers from a serious problem, which Letham exposes: "Let us suppose for a moment that this was so. If this argument is correct, the archetypal blessings of salvation in Christ would be received by grace through faith . . . but Israel would receive the typological blessings, such as Canaan, by meritorious law-keeping according to the works principle. These . . . are two alternative, antithetical ways of inheritance."

He adds, "But a type corresponds to the antitype. If the one is a type of the other, we conclude either that the blessings of the covenant of grace are received by law-keeping on the part of the recipients—in which case there is no gospel—or the temporal blessings of the Mosaic covenant were to be received by grace, which undermines [Horton's] argument."[115] He concludes, "The only other possibilities are either that law and grace work together, in distinct ways, or that the typical relationship is untenable; in both cases the argument is undermined.[116]

Furthermore, Horton's distinction between Old Testament believers being individually justified by faith according to the Abrahamic covenant and remaining the land corporately as a nation by works is also seriously problematic.[117] As Letham points out, "if the Mosaic covenant had been based on a works principle an unavoidably schizoid character would

---

114. For the position of the Orthodox Presbyterian Church on republication, see The Orthodox Presbyterian Church, "Report of the Committee to Study Republication."

115. Letham is writing about Kline, but since Horton follows Kline here, what Letham says also applies to Horton.

116. Letham, "Not a Covenant of Works," 170–71; *Systematic Theology*, 459.

117. Huijgen says, "The dichotomy between collective and individual . . . is indicative of present day post-Enlightenment philosophy rather than characteristic for the times of the Bible" ("Covenant Theology as Trinitarian Theology," 310).

have dogged the rest of the OT—which aspect was Abrahamic and which Mosaic?"[118]

Appeal is often made to Leviticus 18:5 ("You shall therefore keep my statutes and my rules; if a person does them, he shall live by them: I am the Lord") in support of the idea that the Mosaic covenant was a republication of the covenant of works, with the understanding that this text teaches a works-righteousness as a way to life.[119]

But instead, this text teaches a faith-righteousness, that is, the obedience of faith that leads to life.[120] According to Davies, "This is the constant and repeated dynamic of faith and obedience to which the O.T. bears witness (Deut. 5.33; 30.16; 32.46f.; Neh. 9.29; Ps. 119.93; Prov. 4.4, 22; 8.35; 19.16; 21.21; Ezek. 18.21; 20.11, 20.13, 20.21; Amos 5.14; cf. Luke 10:28)."[121]

Because faith characterizes obedience in both the old and the new covenant, Galatians 4:21–31 is not contrasting works-righteousness and faith-righteousness as two opposing ways to life.[122] Nor is Paul making a timeless, abstract comparison between the old covenant and new covenant in general. Rather, he is making a contemporary, concrete comparison between the old covenant that has rejected the Christ (i.e., present day Jerusalem, v. 25) and the new covenant that has acknowledged him as its redeemer in particular.[123]

Eighth, do Hosea 6:7 and Jeremiah 33:20–21, 25–26 provide exegetical support for a pre-fall covenant? The translation of Hosea 6:7 is strongly debated. Some translate k^e'$ādām$ in a personal sense ("like Adam"), while others translate k^e'$ādām$ in a geographical sense ("at Adam"; cf. Josh. 3:16).[124] Because of the difficulty of translation and therefore of interpretation, Hosea 6:7 does not provide conclusive exegetical support for a covenant of works.[125]

---

118. Letham, "Not a Covenant of Works," 148; see also Elam, and Van Kooten, Bergquist, *Merit and Moses*, 125–29, 142; Gaffin, "Covenant and Salvation"; Turretin, *Institutes*, 2:265; cf. Dennison, Sanborn, and Swinburnson, "Merit or 'Entitlement,'" 81.

119. E.g., Estelle, "Leviticus 18:5 and Deuteronomy 30:1–14," 109–46.

120. Letham, "Not a Covenant of Works," 147; Shepherd, Foreword to Boersema, *Not of Works*, xx–xxii; van Bruggen, *Romeinen*, 149–50; Williams, *Far as the Curse Is Found*, 150–52.

121. Davies, *Faith and Obedience*, 192; cf. 177–204.

122. McGowan, *Adam, Christ, and Covenant*, 75–76.

123. Van Bruggen, *Galaten*, 131–32.

124. The Septuagint translated k^e'$ādām$ as ὡς ἄνθρωπος, "like mankind."

125. Dumbrell, *Covenant and Creation*, 45–46; McComiskey, *Covenants of Promise*,

While Jeremiah 33:20–21, 25–26 does refer to a covenant with creation, this is probably an allusion to God's covenant with Noah and creation (Gen 9).[126] Moreover, there is no reference here to a covenant with humanity.

Ninth, are God's post-fall covenants anchored in God's pre-fall covenant and do they then fulfill God's creational purpose for this pre-fall covenant? First, if there is no pre-fall covenant, then post-fall covenants cannot be anchored in it or fulfill its purpose. It is not legitimate to argue that there must have been a pre-fall covenant because the post-fall covenants need it to have existed.

Granted, some post-fall covenants may contain terminology that alludes to the pre-fall narrative. But the use of this language does not mean that God's pre-fall relationship with Adam must be understood as a covenant.[127]

While some have asserted that Genesis 6:18 and 9:9, 11, 17 speak about "establishing" a covenant (*hēqîm bĕrît*) instead of "cutting" a covenant (*kāraṯ bĕrît*), this terminology does not necessarily imply that Genesis 6 and 9 are speaking about confirming an already existing covenant. The phrase *hēqîm bĕrît* can also refer to initiating a covenant (Ezek 16:60–62), and the context of Genesis 6:18 makes this interpretation quite likely here too.[128]

Thus, a fourth systemic problem with Horton's covenant theology is that it operates with a covenant of works for which there is no Scriptural warrant.

The covenant of grace[129]

In addition to a pretemporal covenant of redemption and a pre-fall covenant of meritorious works, covenant theology also operates with a

---

214–16; Williamson, *Sealed with an Oath*, 55–56; *contra* Allen, *Reformed Theology*, 41; Bavinck, *Reformed Dogmatics*, 2:656; Curtis, "Hosea 6:7," 170–209; Robertson, *Christ of the Covenants*, 22–24; Williams, *Far as the Curse Is Found*, 47.

126. Williamson, *Sealed with an Oath*, 66, 71, 74; *contra* Beale, *New Testament Biblical Theology*, 43; Robertson, *Christ of the Covenants*, 19–21; Schreiner, *Covenant and God's Purpose*, 20–21.

127. *Contra* Bartholomew, "Covenant and Creation," 28–30; cf. 13–14, 18, 21–29.

128. Burger, "Story of God's Covenants," 279–80; *contra* Gentry and Wellum, *Kingdom through Covenant*, 187–95, 213, 587, 667.

129. For this section, I made use of Burger, "Theology without a Covenant of Works"; "'Theirs Are the Covenants'"; "Story of God's Covenants."

supra-historical or meta-covenant of grace that includes and holds together all the post-fall historical covenants and continues to advance, through the new covenant, toward its fulfillment in the new creation.[130] Horton is no exception.[131]

But is there exegetical, biblical-theological, and systematic-theological support for such a construct? Would it not be better to seek the unity and continuity between the covenants in the unity and continuity of God's purpose to bring creation and a new humanity into the eternal Sabbath rest, where God is all in all?[132]

The main biblical and theological support offered for the covenant of grace

In our discussion of the covenant of redemption, we saw that this covenant involved the Son voluntarily agreeing to become the representative head and guarantor of elect sinners, taking upon himself the responsibility not only to meet their legal obligations but also to pay for their sins and purchase their salvation by his death on the cross. The Holy Spirit, too, voluntarily agreed to apply these purchased benefits of salvation to the elect so that they can inherit the eternal life that the Son earned for them by his faithful obedience. These purposes, determined upon in the

---

130. Covenant theology's understanding of this overarching covenant of grace is not monolithic. Our discussion will focus on what might be called the mainstream approach. See Allen, *Reformed Theology*, 42–43; Bavinck, *Reformed Dogmatics*, 3:193–232; Beeke and Jones, *Puritan Theology*, 259–78; Belcher, *Fulfillment of the Promises*, 37–46; Berkhof, *Systematic Theology*, 272–301; Cocceius, *Doctrine of the Covenant*, 68–169; Currid, "Adam and the Beginning," 99–109; De Graaf, *True Faith*, 21–23, 34, 45, 53, 59, 64, 67, 72, 85, 111, 115, 121, 187, 189, 192, 196–97, 216–17, 228, 263, 282, 292; Frame, *Systematic Theology*, 66–67; Gentry and Wellum, *Kingdom through Covenant*, 84–94, 666; Grudem, *Systematic Theology*, 519–22; Hodge, *Systematic Theology*, 354–77; Kamphuis, *Aantekeningen bij J.A. Heyns dogmatiek*, 64–65; Kline, *Kingdom Prologue*, 138–153; Muller, "Divine Covenants," 11–56; Letham, *Systematic Theology*, 440–63; Macleod, *Faith to Live By*, 128–31; Murray, *Covenant of Grace*; Packer, *Concise Theology*, 87; Robertson, *Christ of the Covenants*, 93–300; Shepherd, *Call of Grace*, 11–63; Spykman, *Reformational Theology*, 263–64; Stam, *Covenant of Love*, 61–64; cf. 65–118; Turretin, *Institutes*, 2:169–89; Van Genderen and Velema, *Reformed Dogmatics*, 539–72; Vos, "Doctrine of the Covenant," 252–67; Vos, *Anthropology*, 76–84, 92–137; Waltke, "Kingdom of God," 76; Witsius, *Economy of the Covenants*, 3:104–355).

131. Horton, *God of Promise*, 104–7; *Christian Faith*, 138, 152–53, 157, 196, 203–4, 250, 420, 446, 487, 575, 609, 612, 615–16, 644–45, 682, 716–17, 733, 772, 779, 781, 789, 791, 795, 797, 818, 851, 854, 866.

132. Williamson, *Sealed with an Oath*, 30–31, 48–49.

pretemporal covenant of redemption, thus drive the economy of salvation in the covenant of grace, giving it stability and unity.

The result is a Christocentric view of history, where history is interpreted in the light of the covenant of redemption and the gospel is communicated from this perspective. Thus, Bavinck says, "It is a false perception that God first made his covenant with Adam and Noah, with Abraham and Israel, and only finally with Christ; the covenant of grace was ready-made from all eternity in the pact of salvation of the three persons and was realized by Christ from the moment the fall occurred."[133]

Thus, when God announces the promise of redemption or the so-called *protevangelium* (Gen 3:15) to Adam and Eve immediately after their fall into sin, promising to make all things new through a human being who would crush the serpent's head, this was the historical inauguration of the covenant of grace, even though the term "covenant" does not appear in Genesis 3. This promise is then formally ratified—now using the term "covenant"—by God with Abraham, through whom God wants to bless all the nations of the earth by giving them faith to accept this promise of redemption and to have this redemption realized in their lives (Gen 15; cf. 12:1–3).

Even though this covenant of grace is unilateral in origin—God takes the initiative to establish it—it is bilateral in its continuation or realization (Gen 17; 22). Thus, to enjoy the promised blessings of the covenant of grace, the recipients of the promises need to respond to those promises with faith and obedience. Because Abraham believed the promises of God, he is considered the father of believers (Rom 4; Gal 3).

The covenant with Abraham is then renewed with Israel as a nation to whom God gives the law as a guide to help them to be a holy nation and a kingdom of priests and as a guardian to lead them to Christ for salvation (Exod 19:5–6; 24; 32; Gal 3:24). Thus, both old covenant and new, law and gospel, become two administrations of the one covenant of grace, and old covenant Israel has a typological function so that it "prefigures in an imperfect way what will be given perfectly in Christ."[134] As a result, Israel essentially has a pedagogical function as a means to an end in the history of redemption, namely, preparing the church for the coming of Christ.[135]

---

133. Bavinck, *Reformed Dogmatics*, 3:215; cf. 228; Burger, "'Theirs Are the Covenants,'" 6.

134. Burger, "Theirs Are the Covenants," 2.

135. Bavinck, *Reformed Dogmatics*, 1:376; cf. Burger, "'Theirs Are the Covenants,'" 4.

This covenant with Israel is then renewed with David, to whom God promises an eternal kingship if his sons are faithful to him (2 Sam 7; 1 Chr 17; Pss 89, 132; 1 Kgs 2:4). These promises made to Adam and Eve, Abraham, Israel, and David are then fulfilled in a new covenant that God makes with all believers (Jer 31–33; Ezek 36–37).

The covenant of redemption drives the economy of salvation within the covenant of grace, providing it stability and unity. But the covenant of works also informs it.

As the head and mediator of the covenant of grace, Christ comes under and fulfills the conditions of the covenant of works for elect sinners. In his active obedience, he perfectly fulfills the demands of the law under this covenant. In his passive obedience, he deals with the sanction of the covenant of works by bearing the curse of the law and satisfying God's justice for these elect sinners (Gal 3:10–14; Heb 8, 10).

As a result, he earned substantivized benefits of salvation for elect sinners, which the Holy Spirit then applies to them in a particular order (*ordo salutis*) when they believe in Christ (Rom 3:21–26; 8:30; 1 Cor 1:30). Typically, that order is election, effectual calling, regeneration, faith, justification, sanctification, perseverance, and redemption/glorification.[136] In particular, when they believe in Christ, both his active and passive obedience are imputed to them (Rom 4; Gal 3).

In addition, with the inauguration of the new covenant, Israel's typological and pedagogical function comes to an end, and so do God's dealings with Israel.

Horton's view of the covenant of grace does differ from mainstream classical covenant theology at some points.

First, drawing on ancient Near Eastern parallels, Horton considers the covenant of grace to be an unconditional promissory land covenant made with Abraham, comparable to ancient Near Eastern royal grant or gift covenants where the vassals are the beneficiaries of an inheritance because of a victory of the suzerain.[137]

But because the Mosaic covenant is in some sense a republication of the covenant of works, based on a law-merit principle, Israel, on the one hand, has the conditional promise of corporately staying in the land as a nation and enjoying God's temporal blessings on the basis of obedience

---

136. Burger, *Life in Christ*, 174.
137. Horton, *Christian Faith*, 537, 779.

to this covenant of works and, on the other hand, has the unconditional promise of individual salvation in Christ through faith alone.

Second, because the Mosaic covenant is in some sense a republication of the covenant of works, Israel's corporate history is an interlude or parenthesis in the history of redemption and primarily has the function of revealing our human sinfulness.[138] But because individual Israelite believers were justified by faith, Israel's history also has a secondary pedagogical function of prefiguring salvation in Christ.[139]

After Israel has served these temporary typological and pedagogical functions, however, God's dealing with Israel as a nation becomes unclear. On the one hand, the church does not replace Israel but is the fulfillment of God's promise to Abraham that in him all the families of the earth will be blessed.[140] On the other hand, Israel has no distinct place in Horton's ecclesiology, even though he thinks Romans 11 seems to argue for an extensive ingrafting of Jews into the church.[141]

Third, in Horton's view, the new covenant is both unconditional and conditional. It is unconditional in its essence: Members of the new covenant are freed from obeying the law for their justification. But it is conditional in its administration: Obedience to the law is needed for final salvation, though this obedience is the fruit of having received a new heart in regeneration.[142]

Evaluation of the main biblical and theological support offered for the covenant of grace

There are several questions that arise in connection with the arguments offered as support for this view of an overarching covenant of grace that stretches from Adam after the fall through the various covenants to the new covenant and beyond to the final consummation.

---

138. Horton, *Christian Faith*, 440–43; cf. 152–53, 337, 384, 420, 448, 493, 528, 537, 539, 959, 986; *God of Promise*, 47, 69; *Justification*, 2:81.

139. Horton, *God of Promise*, 74; Burger, "'Theirs Are the Covenants,'" 6. Here Horton's view overlaps with mainstream covenant theology.

140. Horton, *Christian Faith*, 730.

141. Horton, *Christian Faith*, 945–50; *God of Promise*, 132; cf. Burger, "Theirs Are the Covenants," 5–6.

142. Horton, *God of Promise*, 182; cf. 173–94; *Christian Faith*, 575–86, 615–19, 653–80; *Putting Amazing Back into Grace*, 150–54, 156–60; *Gospel Commission*, 152; cf. 150–53; *Covenant and Salvation*, 148–52, 263–66; "Obedience Is Better," 330–36.

First, did God announce an overarching covenant of grace to Adam and Eve in Genesis 3:15? In fact, we find no such announcement in Genesis 3. What we do read is God's promise to make all things new through a human being who would deal with the problem of the devil by crushing his head.

Read in the light of the rest of Scripture, the promise—in the form of a threat to the serpent—affirms God's commitment to the creational purpose of his mission for his glory and his intention to bring creation and humanity into the Sabbath rest of the fullness of his loving presence in Christ, through the Spirit, in his coming kingdom, the new heavens and new earth where he will be all in all.[143] But what we don't read about here is a covenant.

Second, did God ratify this overarching covenant of grace with Abraham and then renew it with Israel, with David, and then in the new covenant? Nowhere do we read in Scripture that God did so. What we do read is that God formally regulated his existing relationship with Abraham, with Israel at Sinai and on the plains of Moab, and with David by way of individual covenants and that he promised to formally regulate his relationship with Israel in a new covenant. Each of these covenants builds upon the former and strengthens it.

Third, is God's history with Israel merely an interlude or parenthesis in the history of redemption that came to an end with the coming of Christ that now has only a typological and pedagogical function, showing us human sinfulness and giving typological glimpses of the salvation we have in Christ?

Certainly, God's history with Israel does have those functions. But instead of the new covenant setting aside Israel, marking an end to that parenthetical history and returning to the main story, the new covenant is in fact not a new covenant with the New Testament church as such but precisely God's new covenant with Israel in its representative Messiah.

In fact, covenant theology's emphasis on the unity of the covenant of grace with its canonical narrative of creation, fall, redemption, and consummation and its reduction of Israel's function in the history of redemption to a typological and pedagogical role has a supercessionist tendency that does not take seriously the dynamics of the history of

---

143. This theme will be developed further in the next chapter.

redemption in which God enters into multiple covenants with Israel, Israel's kings, and Israel's fathers.[144]

Fourth, did Christ, in his active obedience, fulfill the conditions of the covenant of works for elect sinners by perfectly fulfilling the law obedience required of Adam in this covenant? If there was no covenant of works, as I have argued above, Christ would not have been required to fulfill its conditions.

Instead, Christ was Israel's representative, sent to fulfill Israel's role to be a blessing for the nations, to be the true Israel in the way Israel was meant to be. Since Israel was the priestly nation, representing the world and appointed to bring about blessing for the nations instead of the curse that Adam brought upon the world, Christ—as the true Israel—was also the last Adam, in whom we receive our new humanity. Christ's obedience was the obedience of faith in a loving Father with whom he lived in close communion.[145]

In fact, the distinction between Christ's active obedience and his passive obedience introduces a bifurcation into the obedience of Christ that Scripture considers of one piece. Carson helpfully points this out when he writes, "A passage like the so-called Christ-hymn in Philippians 2 seems to depict Christ's obedience as all of a piece, including his willingness to become a human being and his progressive self-humiliation, climaxing in his obedience on the cross itself." He adds, "By virtue of all of this obedience Christ was vindicated and his people are saved."[146]

Fifth, did Christ, in his passive obedience, bear the curse of the law for elect sinners and satisfy God's justice for them? While we do read in Scripture that Christ represented those who were elected from all eternity (John 6:44; 17:2, 6, 9, 24; Rev 7), we also read that he represented all humanity (John 1:29; 3:16–17; 12:47; 1 John 2:2; 4:14), as well as Israel in particular (Gal 3:10–14; 4:4–5).

Moreover, the phrase "the curse of the law" refers specifically to the Mosaic law. Only Israel was under the law and therefore only Israel was under the curse of the law. "The curse of the law" thus pertains not to humanity in general, but to Israel alone.[147] Salvation from the curse of

---

144. Burger, "'Theirs Are the Covenants,'" 4, 8–9, 18; "Story of God's Covenants," 271; Soulen, *God of Israel*, 12–17; Westerman, *Learning Messiah*, loc. 363, 506.

145. This theme will be developed further in the next chapter.

146. Carson, "Systematic Theology and Biblical Theology," 55.

147. Wright, *Climax of the Covenant*, 137–56; *Paul and the Faithfulness of God*, 526–27.

the law through the satisfaction of God's justice, then, would also pertain specifically to Israel in connection with their failure to keep the law.

Christ came to be Israel's representative, sent to fulfill Israel's role to be a blessing to the nations. By his obedience, he rescued Israel from the curse of the law by becoming a curse for them and, in doing so, he satisfied God's justice for them (Gal 3:10–13). But having rescued Israel from the curse of the law, as Israel's representative and Abraham's seed, he also then fulfills Israel's calling to bring Abraham's blessing to the nations.[148]

"The curse of the law," says Burger, "has to be understood not as the problem of humanity, but of Israel solely. The law was given to Israel as Israel's prerogative and problem, as Paul makes clear in Galatians 3 and Romans 2–3. Having solved the problem of Israel, however, Jesus was able to fulfil Israel's role as well and to solve Adam's problem, as Paul makes clear in Galatians 3 and Romans 2–3."[149] In this regard, Van Bruggen writes, "If it can be said at all that the Gentiles also have been redeemed from the curse of the law, then it happened before that curse could reach them."[150]

This understanding prevents us from developing a narrowed, individualistic understanding of salvation that "leav[es] out the breadth of creation, neglecting the role of Israel, forgetting Jesus' gospel of the Kingdom of God, without any missionary drive."[151]

Sixth, did Christ earn or purchase substantivized benefits of salvation with his death on the cross, which the Holy Spirit then applies to elect sinners when they appropriate them through faith in Christ? In fact, nowhere does the New Testament speak this way. It speaks about Christ ransoming people (Mark 10:45; Rev 5:9; 14:4).

Moreover, the twofold soteriological structure wherein Christ purchases benefits and the Holy Spirit applies these benefits leads to an extrinsic appropriationist understanding of salvation, where salvation "no longer is 'in Christ' but rather 'on the basis of what Christ has done.'"[152] This, in turn, can lead to a Christian discipleship that is

148. Van Bruggen, *Paul*, 199–201; O'Donovan, *Resurrection and Moral Order*, 123–30, 134, 141; Wright, *Knowing Jesus*, 22, 44, 62–63, 125–35, 153–74, 182; Wright, *Mission of God*, 65–66, 325, 342–44; Wright, *Paul and the Faithfulness of God*, 495–537; cf. Burger, "Theology without a Covenant of Works," 343; "'Theirs Are the Covenants,'" 15.

149. Burger, "Theology without a Covenant of Works," 343.

150. Van Bruggen, *Paul*, 199; Burger, "'Theirs Are the Covenants,'" 15.

151. Burger, "Clothed with Christ," 3.

152. Evans, "Calvin's Doctrine of the Lord's Supper," 24; *Imputation and Impartation*, 264.

"functionally Christless" or in which Christ is "not personally involved in [one's] obedience."[153]

Furthermore, disconnecting the benefits of Christ from participation in the person of Christ can leave Christians thrown back on themselves, wondering whether these benefits are for them or not.[154] Instead of recognizing that they are in Christ and therefore have everything in him, regardless of how they feel or what they seem to be experiencing, they begin to look for evidence in themselves that they possess his benefits, that the Spirit really has bestowed those benefits on them.

Van den Brink and Van der Kooi write, "The danger of overemphasizing the subject is that the reality of salvation becomes completely determined by our human appropriation. God's acts seem to become real and present only when, through the Spirit, the believer touches that reality and is enabled to appropriate it as his or her own. Or in theological language, the work of Christ is completely absorbed in the work of the Spirit." They add, "When the objective aspect . . . is absorbed by the subjective aspect . . . the human subject begins to revolve around its own axis."[155]

According to Scripture, however, instead of participating in the salvation Christ has purchased for us by the Holy Spirit applying the benefits of Christ's work to us, we participate in Christ himself through our ontological union with him through faith. Consequently, our Christian identity is relocated and reconstituted so that we live ex-centrally in Christ and can say with Paul that it is no longer we who live, but Christ who lives in us (Gal 2:20; see John 15:5).[156]

The typical Reformed order of salvation, which presents images of salvation as benefits that believers receive in a certain order, "does not help to do justice to the use of these biblical images in the New Testament," Burger says. "It seems more fruitful to me to disconnect these biblical images from the moments in the order of salvation, and no longer use them as if they were dogmatic concepts, with each representing a benefit of salvation as identified in the order of salvation." He adds, "It seems to make more sense to me, on the one hand, to allow these images

---

153. Macaskill, *Living in Union with Christ*, viii; cf. vii–xi; Burger, "Clothed with Christ," 3; see also Canlis, *Calvin's Ladder*, 155–57.

154. Burger, *Life in Christ*, 11, 17-18.

155. Van den Brink and Van der Kooi, *Christian Dogmatics*, 504.

156. See Macaskill, *Living in Union with Christ*, 1–10; O'Donovan, *Resurrection and Moral Order*, 22, 25, 76–97, 247–48; *Finding and Seeking*, 14, 40–41.

to speak for themselves, as images that each have something to say about Jesus' significance for healing and restoration; but, on the other hand, to describe the moments in the order of salvation with words that are different from these biblical images."[157] Elsewhere, he writes, "Each image highlights different aspects of the entire process."[158]

Accordingly, Burger proposes the following reformulation of the order of salvation: "1. God's eternal love in Christ. 2. The gift of Christ for those who believe the good news of Christ. 3. The transformation of our lives through the effect of Christ in our lives. 4. The completion of this at his second coming, when we will be conformed to Christ."[159]

Seventh, are the active and passive obedience of Christ imputed to us when we believe in Christ? This question assumes a theology in which Christ, by his active and passive obedience, purchased certain benefits of salvation that are disconnected from him and bestowed on believers as part of the order of salvation. But, as we saw above, the New Testament nowhere speaks about Christ purchasing benefits of salvation. Rather, it talks about Christ ransoming *people*. And therefore his active and passive obedience cannot be imputed to us.

There is, moreover, no need to use the language of imputation. When Romans 4 and Galatians 3 use the language of imputation, they do so in connection with their citation of Genesis 15:6, which speaks about faith being imputed to Abraham as righteousness. There is no mention in Genesis 15 of the imputation of the righteousness of Christ. When Paul does speak about the relationship between Christ and our justification, he no longer uses the language of imputation because it is no longer needed. Nor, for that matter, does Paul use the expression "righteousness of Christ."[160]

When we clothe ourselves with Christ through faith, we participate in Christ's obedience, resurrection, and justification and we are given

---

157. Burger, *Life in Christ*, 173, 176.

158. Burger, *Being in Christ*, 544; cf. 545; cf. Gaffin, *Resurrection and Redemption*, 127, 130–31, 138; McGowan, "Justification and the *Ordo Salutis*," 160–63; Seifrid, *Christ, Our Righteousness*, 174.

159. Burger, *Life in Christ*, 176.

160. Burger, *Being in Christ*, 247–48; Burger, "Clothed with Christ," 8. Even though there is no need to use the language of imputation, this does not mean that it cannot be used. Canlis rightly observes that "[s]trictly speaking, 'imputation' involves the 'gifted' character of our righteousness, underscoring that it comes only from God and not from ourselves. . . . [This imputation] can also occur through union with Christ" (*Calvin's Ladder*, 139–40).

him as our righteousness and new life. Furthermore, we share in Christ's identity as Son of God (1 Cor 1:30; Rom 4:25; Gal 3:27; Eph 2:10).[161]

Eighth, is the twofold scheme of unconditional and conditional covenants warranted by Scripture? No, it is not.[162]

To assert that the Abrahamic covenant is unconditional does not do justice to the fact that there are both conditional and unconditional aspects to that covenant. God's covenant in Genesis 15 has a strongly unconditional aspect in that it makes no explicit mention of Abram's responsibilities. Nevertheless, it must assume those responsibilities. If Abram had no responsibilities, then God would not have made a second covenant with Abraham in Genesis 17 after he and Sarai tried to realize the fulfillment of the covenant promise on their own terms and not God's.[163] Moreover, this second covenant had conditional aspects—walking before God and being blameless—which were to find concrete expression in the condition of circumcision.

Because Horton considers the Abrahamic covenant to be unconditional, he is constrained to describe the obligation to circumcise not as a condition of the covenant but as a sign of this covenant, comparable to the rainbow as a sign of God's covenant with Noah and creation.[164] But Horton fails to see that the condition of circumcision "served as a synecdoche for the covenantal requirement of a blameless life."[165]

Moreover, when Horton considers the fulfillment of the stipulations of the Abrahamic covenant not to be necessary for Abraham to enjoy the salvific blessings of this covenant but views them only as a means through which these blessings would come to Abraham's heirs

---

161. Bird, "Incorporated Righteousness," 253–75; Burger, *Being in Christ*, 248–50; Burger, "Clothed with Christ," 7–9; Gaffin, *Resurrection and Redemption*, 122–24; Gundry, "Nonimputation of Christ's Righteousness," 17–45; Han, *Raised for Our Justification*, 231–39; Seifrid, *Christ, Our Righteousness*, 173–75. Instead of teaching that our union with Christ in his resurrection includes our justification, Horton interprets Romans 4:25 to mean that because with the resurrection of Christ the age to come has broken into this age, the future verdict of our justification has been brought forward into the present (*Justification*, 2:257, 275; *Covenant and Salvation*, 300; *Christian Faith*, 709).

162. Burger, "Story of God's Covenants," 299; Garcia, Response to Horton's "Law and Gospel," 174; Gentry and Wellum, *Kingdom through Covenant*, 662–66, 693–94; Kwakkel, "Verplichting of relatie," 130; "Conditional Dynastic Promise."

163. Pratt, "God of Covenant," 8–9; Wright, *Mission of God*, 205–6.

164. Horton, *God of Promise*, 33; *Covenant and Salvation*, 15.

165. Pratt, "God of Covenant," 8, 10.

and as typological of the obedience of Christ,[166] he is operating with a false dichotomy. Kim explains: "If the stipulations only pertain to the *extension* of the Abrahamic covenant and the prefiguring of the Messiah's obedience how does this align with Paul's quotation of Genesis 15:6 in Romans 4:3 and Galatians 3:6 in regards to Abraham's faith (both verses written in the context of *personal* salvation)?" He concludes, "It is more appropriate to maintain, based on the biblical evidence, that faith (which, if genuine, is expressed in obedience to God) is also the necessary means for an individual to enjoy the *salvific* blessings of the covenant (cf. James 2:22–23)."[167]

The same is true with the Davidic covenant. While God makes an unconditional dynastic promise to David in 2 Samuel 7, this unconditional promise contains an implicit condition, indicated by God's statement that he will discipline David's son if he is disloyal (2 Sam 7:14b). This implicit condition is made explicit in 1 Kings 2:4 where God's dynastic promise to David is conditional upon his sons' loyalty to God (cf. 1 Kgs 9:4–5).

Based on a comparison with 1 Samuel 2:30, Kwakkel writes, "From this text onward, readers of Samuel and Kings know that YHWH reserves the right to cancel a promise if the behavior of its recipients runs counter to his expectations. Apparently, he did not think it necessary to stipulate explicitly things that could be considered self-evident at all times."[168] Elsewhere, he writes, "When God speaks, he always appeals to the listener, even when he makes an unconditional promise (as in Gen. 9:8–17 and 15:18–21). Precisely the unconditional aspect implies a strong call to a faithful trusting response."[169]

So, too, when Horton considers the new covenant to be unconditional in its essence but conditional in its administration,[170] he is imposing a distinction upon biblical covenants that is foreign to their nature.

Ninth, is it wise to use extrabiblical material, such as the Hittite international treaties, as a template to interpret biblical covenants, as Horton does?[171]

---

166. Horton, *God of Promise*, 45.
167. Kim, *Michael Horton's Covenant Theology*, 176.
168. Kwakkel, "Conditional Dynastic Promise," 86.
169. Kwakkel, "Verplichting of relatie," 130.
170. Horton, *God of Promise*, 182; cf. 173–94.
171. Horton, *God of Promise*, 29; cf. 23–34; *Covenant and Salvation*, 13; *Christian Faith*, 44, 151, 424, 782–83.

Horton himself makes the following concession: "It is probably unwise to make the law-covenant/promise-covenant too heavily dependent on formal similarities with ancient Near Eastern treaties. Regardless of parallels, only the exegesis of particular covenants in Scripture can determine its basis and terms."[172]

But this concession rings hollow in the light of Horton's actual use of these parallels. For instance, Hittite suzerainty law treaties form the structural template for interpreting biblical covenants in his introduction to covenant theology (*God of Promise*). After asserting that God adapted these treaties for his relationship with his people, he then deals with the Mosaic covenant before the Abrahamic covenant so that "he effectively sets up a system where law comes before grace."[173]

In spite of whatever similarities one may detect between biblical covenants and extrabiblical covenants, Horton's grounding of his distinction between conditional and unconditional covenants on the distinction between conditional suzerain-vassal law covenants, on the one hand, and unconditional promissory royal grant covenants, on the other, lacks warrant—and not just Scriptural warrant.

The view that promissory royal grant covenants were unconditional, it turns out, was based on early research that more recent research has called into question. Knoppers, for instance, has concluded that because land grants were always dependent on loyalty to the king, even when this was not explicitly mentioned, these land grants were predominantly conditional.[174] Moreover, the making of treaties or covenants in the ancient Near East was a diverse and complex matter. The claim that covenants fell into these two categories—one conditional and the other unconditional—does not do justice to the complexity of the data.[175]

Thus, a fifth systemic problem in Horton's covenant theology is that it operates with an overarching covenant of grace that does not have Scriptural warrant.

---

172. Horton, *Christian Faith*, 45.

173. McGowan, *Adam, Christ, and Covenant*, 73; cf. 72–76

174. Knoppers, "Ancient Near Eastern Royal Grants," 670–97.

175. Weeks, *Admonition and Curse*, 6–10, 139, 163; Letham, *Systematic Theology*, 460–61; van Bekkum, "Biblical Covenants"; Burger, "Story of God's Covenants," 275–76.

The essence-energies distinction

As we have seen, Horton's covenant theology operates with the distinction between God's essence and his energies. This distinction is "the necessary metaphysical underpinning of many ideas and doctrines" in Horton's covenant theology.[176]

Horton's understanding of the essence-energies distinction

First, Horton appropriates the Eastern Orthodox essence-energies distinction because he wants to maintain the Creator-creature distinction and yet acknowledge that communion with God is possible and real without any fusion of persons or essences.[177] Following Gregory Palamas, he compares the essence of God to the sun and the energies of God to the rays of the sun.[178]

Second, although God's attributes are identical with his essence, they do not reveal this essence, but only his energies.[179] While God is immutable in his essence, there is real change in his activity or his energies in the history of redemption.[180] Although God's essence is impassible and thus cannot feel, will, act, or be affected by creatures, the persons of the Trinity are passable and can be affected by creatures because they can feel, will, and act. While God does not communicate his essence to us when he speaks, he does communicate his energies when he creates, sustains, governs, redeems, and reveals himself through his speech.[181]

Although we cannot be united to Christ's essence, we can be united to his energies. In this way, we participate in the fellowship of the Trinity and become partakers of the divine nature.[182] While the Lord's Supper

---

176. Bintsarovskyi, *Hidden and Revealed*, 26; cf. Horton, *Christian Faith*, 612.

177. Horton, *Christian Faith*, 602–5, 611, 691, 736–37, 818, 851, 910; *Covenant and Salvation*, 143–46, 268–69, 274–75, 281–83, 285, 302–7.

178. Horton, *Christian Faith*, 130; cf. 52, 228, 237, 613, 690, 817; *Covenant and Salvation*, 212, 268, 270.

179. Horton, *Christian Faith*, 131, 228, 237, 255, 265, 267, 269, 332, 556, 603, 694, 698; *Covenant and Salvation*, 282.

180. Horton, *Christian Faith*, 235–42; *Pilgrim Theology*, 77–79; *Lord and Servant*, 46–48, 49; *Thomas Goodwin*, 31–34.

181. Horton, *Christian Faith*, 130–31, 136, 154, 159, 164, 166, 181, 237, 331–34, 360, 574, 612, 751, 753; *Lord and Servant*, 69–70, 85; *Covenant and Salvation*, 302–3; *People and Place*, 101, 137; *Rediscovering the Holy Spirit*, 4, 58, 64, 93, 120.

182. Horton, *Covenant and Salvation*, 186, 285, 302; *Christian Faith*, 603, 612–15,

does not communicate the essence of Christ's life-giving flesh to us, it does communicate the energies of his life-giving flesh.[183] Although we cannot partake of the divine essence and be deified, we can partake of the divine energies of God that emanate from his essence but are distinguished from it as the rays of the sun are from the essence of the sun itself.[184]

Third, Horton considers the essence-energies distinction comparable to what Reformed theology teaches about the incomprehensibility of God[185] and about our ability to know God, not in his essence, but in his works,[186] as well as to the Reformed epistemological distinction between archetypal and ectypal theology and between a theology of glory and a theology of the cross.[187]

Fourth, because Reformed theology teaches that even in our glorified state we will know God only in his works, Horton considers that there is overlap between the Western doctrine of glorification and the Eastern doctrine of *theosis*.[188] Thus, Horton claims that Reformed theology, while not explicitly mentioning the essence-energies distinction, presupposes it.

Fifth, Horton believes that the essence-energies distinction safeguards the Creator-creature difference better than Western theology against pantheistic tendencies in Western mysticism.[189]

690–91, 694, 698–700.

183. Horton, *Covenant and Salvation*, 202–3, 285, 302; *People and Place*, 137; *Christian Faith*, 700, 816–18, 843; *Rediscovering the Holy Spirit*, 272.

184. Horton, *Christian Faith*, 689–92, 694, 698–700; *Rediscovering the Holy Spirit*, 285–86; cf. *Covenant and Salvation*, 267–307.

185. *Christian Faith*, 49–53, 113, 129, 223, 263, 689, 698.

186. Horton, *Christian Faith*, 130, 574, 690; *Covenant and Salvation*, 212, 231, 274–75.

187. Horton, *Covenant and Eschatology*, 7–9, 184–91; *Lord and Servant*, 16–18; *Covenant and Salvation*, 272, 282; *Christian Faith*, 54, 77–79, 128–29, 131, 210.

188. Horton, *Christian Faith*, 688, 689; cf. 688–710; *Pilgrim Theology*, 325–41; "Kingdom of God," 390; *Rediscovering the Holy Spirit*, 45, 284–88, 488–93; *Covenant and Salvation*, 267–307.

189. Horton, *Christian Faith*, 52, 237, 615.

Evaluation of Horton's understanding of the essence-energies distinction

There are several questions that arise in connection with Horton's approach to and use of the essence-energies distinction.

First, is the essence-energies distinction as it applies to the unknowability of God's essence comparable to what Reformed theology teaches about the incomprehensibility of God? When Reformed theology talks about the incomprehensibility of God, it means that the finite cannot contain the infinite. Our knowledge of God is never exhaustive knowledge but is always partial and limited. Moreover, our knowledge of God is always cloaked in mystery.[190]

Nevertheless, we do know God. The partial, limited knowledge we have of him is knowledge of him. He is not unknowable. In this regard, Bavinck rightly says, "God's incomprehensibility, so far from canceling out God's knowability, rather presupposes and affirms it."[191]

Second, is the distinction between God being unknowable in his essence but knowable in his energies comparable to what Reformed theology teaches about our ability to know God in his works but not in his essence?

In fact, when Reformed theology teaches that we know God not in his essence but in his works, it does not mean that when God reveals himself in his works, he is not revealing his essence. Rather, it means that God reveals his essence through his works.

Consequently, Bavinck writes, "The 'ontological' Trinity is mirrored in the 'economic' Trinity."[192] According to Reformed theology, there is a unity between God's being and his works.[193] When God reveals himself, he is revealing his essence or nature. This is especially the case when God reveals himself in Jesus Christ.[194] Knowing Jesus is knowing the Father; seeing Jesus is seeing the Father (John 14:7, 9).

Furthermore, as Bintsarovskyi notes, "Horton's formulation presents a false dilemma. The issue is not whether we know God from

---

190. Bavinck, *Reformed Dogmatics*, 2:28, 40, 48; Beeke and Smalley, *Revelation and God*, 69–70; Frame, *Systematic Theology*, 702–4; Letham, *Systematic Theology*, 167–68.

191. Bavinck, *Reformed Dogmatics*, 2:56.

192. Bavinck, *Reformed Dogmatics*, 2:318.

193. Torrance, *Christian Doctrine of God*, 87.

194. Huijgen, *Divine Accommodation*, 183–84; Bintsarovskyi, *Hidden and Revealed*, 17.

his essence or his acts. The real issue is whether we know God's essence from his acts, or whether it remains shrouded despite God's revelatory activity."[195] Furthermore, this formulation "drive[s] a wedge between the inner Life of God and his saving activity in history or between the ontological Trinity and the economic Trinity."[196]

Third, is the essence-energies distinction comparable to the distinction between archetypal and ectypal theology, the Reformed epistemological concept of analogical knowledge, and the contrast between a theology of glory and a theology of the cross?

The distinction between archetypal and ectypal theology is intended to distinguish between God's self-knowledge and the knowledge that he gives of himself to creatures by his revelation. It does not, however, imply that the ectypal revelatory knowledge is not in any way a revelation of God's archetypal knowledge. Instead, it implies that our knowledge of God is not separated from God's own self-knowledge and is always partial and limited.[197]

When Reformed theology speaks of the analogical knowledge of God, it means that our knowledge of God is "shaped by analogy to what can be discerned of God in his creatures, having as its object not God himself in his knowable essence, but God in his revelation, his relation to us, in the things that pertain to his nature, in his habitual disposition to his creatures. Accordingly, this knowledge is only a finite image, a faint likeness and creaturely impression of the perfect knowledge that God has of himself."[198] Thus, analogical knowledge of God means that there is similarity and dissimilarity between us and God, that we can receive true but imperfect knowledge of God's essence.[199]

---

195. Bintsarovskyi, *Hidden and Revealed*, 319.

196. Torrance, *Christian Doctrine of God*, 187; see also Bintsarovskyi, *Hidden and Revealed*, 319–24; Zorgdrager, "On the Fullness of Salvation," 374, 380.

197. Bavinck, *Reformed Dogmatics*, 1:214.

198. Bavinck, *Reformed Dogmatics*, 2:110.

199. Bavinck, *Reformed Dogmatics*, 2:33, 99, 110, 128, 136–37, 342; Bintsarovskyi, *Hidden and Revealed*, 134–37. However, Bavinck does not always consistently maintain that we can have imperfect, but true knowledge of God's essence. Occasionally, he writes that we cannot know God in his essence (e.g., *Reformed Dogmatics*, 2:36). However, when he does so, he means that God "cannot be known perfectly, that is, in his essence" (*Reformed Dogmatics*, 2:190; cf. 36). Moreover, when Bavinck asserts that God cannot be known in his essence, he is combating speculative knowledge of God apart from God's revelation of himself in Christ (*Reformed Dogmatics*, 1:110–11; cf. Bintsarovskyi, *Hidden and Revealed*, 75).

Instead of using the Reformed concept of analogy in a positive manner like this, however, Horton uses it in a negative sense. For him, analogical knowledge of God means that we can never have any knowledge of God's essence. This becomes very clear when Horton speaks about God's essential attributes,[200] which are identical with his essence or existence.[201] He writes, "However, according to the analogical account, *all* the passages that disclose God's being and character are accommodated to our capacity rather than predicates that obtain univocally between God and creatures."[202] Consequently, Bintsarovskyi concludes, "Horton seems to believe that the essence is not simply a set of attributes, but a sort of interior substantiality that requires strictly univocal predication in order to be known."[203] Similarly, Frame says, "There is a certain picture of God lurking behind Horton's expressions. In this picture, God has a periphery and a dark center. The periphery contains his goodness, omnipotence, wisdom, the things revealed to us in his word. We can know this periphery by God's revelation. But the center is entirely unknown to us. It is like a black hole, from which no light escapes."[204]

According to Horton, "theology of the cross" is a "phrase used by Protestant Reformer Martin Luther (1483–1546) to emphasize that human knowledge and experience must be based on the foolishness of the cross, not human abilities or human ascent to God (theology of glory)." "Theology of glory" is a "phrase used by Protestant Reformer Martin Luther (1483–1546) to criticize medieval theologians who sought direct access to God without the need of mediation."[205]

Horton writes, "At the heart of all theologies of glory, Luther warned, is the desire to ascend to God and strip off his self-chosen masks so that we are no longer restricted to his back but can behold his inner essence—the blinding glory of his face."[206]

Certainly, we do not ascend on our own to discover who God is. But when God reveals himself, he is not wearing a mask. More pointedly, Jesus is not a mask that God wears that conceals who he really is. When God reveals himself, he is not hiding his essence. He is always giving

---

200. Horton, *Christian Faith*, 255, 267, 286, 288, 290, 303, 336.
201. Horton, *Christian Faith*, 245, 265.
202. Horton, *Christian Faith*, 257.
203. Bintsarovskyi, *Hidden and Revealed*, 28.
204. Frame, *Escondido Theology*, 214.
205. Horton, *Christian Faith*, 1001–2.
206. Horton, *Christian Faith*, 250.

some knowledge of his being. The essence-energies distinction, with its implication that we cannot know God's essence, does not correspond to the contrast between the theology of glory and the theology of the cross or to the distinction between archetypal and ectypal theology or to the Reformed emphasis on analogical knowledge of God. These are not ways of saying the same thing, nor do these distinctions mean that Reformed theology somehow presupposes the essence-energies distinction.

Fourth, is there overlap between the Western doctrine of glorification and the Eastern doctrine of *theosis* ("deification") or participating in the divine nature? The answer to this question is both yes and no.

If *theosis* is taken to mean that participating in the divine nature entails a participation in the energies of God and not in the essence or being of God, then there is no overlap with the Western doctrine of glorification. The essence-energies distinction, as we have seen, it itself incompatible with Reformed theology.

But there is overlap between the Western doctrine of glorification and the Eastern doctrine of *theosis* if participation in the divine nature is understood as a real participation in God in which our humanity reaches its destiny by being completely transformed into the image of Christ through the Holy Spirit. This real participation in God is not a participation only in the energies of God but a participation in the being of God in Christ by the Spirit.[207]

Fifth, does comparing the essence-energies distinction to the distinction between the sun and its rays prove what Horton is attempting to prove? In fact, it does not, because the rays of the sun always manifest something about the essence of the sun. Thus, the metaphor actually proves what Horton denies.

Bintsarovskyi aptly formulates the problem for Horton in this manner: "While it is true, of course, that we do not know the sun directly, it is equally true that the rays communicate some knowledge of the sun rather than leaving us totally ignorant about it." He adds, "The metaphor of the sun and its rays fits well in analogical reasoning . . . because the properties of heat and light communicated by the rays presuppose that

---

207. This understanding of glorification and *theosis* will be developed further in the next two chapters. On this subject, see also Billings, "John Calvin"; *Calvin, Participation, and the Gift*, 51–61, 96, 190, 193, 196; Canlis, "Calvin, Osiander and Participation"; *Calvin's Ladder*, 188–91, 236–38; Fairbairn, "Patristic Soteriology"; *Life in the Trinity*, 6–12, 33–35; Finlan, "Peter's Notion"; "Can We Speak of *Theosis*"; Habets, "Reforming *Theosis*"; "Reformed *Theosis*?"; *Theosis in the Theology*; Letham, *Systematic Theology*, 769–88; *Union with Christ*, 91–102, 123–28; Mosser, "Greatest Possible Blessing."

the sun itself possesses these properties, albeit in a different measure—with greater temperature and luminosity. Thus, the metaphor illustrates that while we do not know God's essence directly, we do know it in some measure based on its 'operations.'"[208]

Thus, a sixth systemic problem with Horton's covenant theology is that it operates with an essence-energies distinction that misunderstands Reformed theology and has no warrant in Scripture.

Justification as the engine that drives the ordo salutis

As we have seen in the previous chapter, Horton sees justification as the engine that drives the *ordo salutis*. Everything else in the order of salvation follows from justification.

First, Horton identifies and attempts to solve what he sees as a problem in the way Protestants often present soteriology.

When Protestant soteriology distinguishes regeneration from effectual calling through the Word, it uses a forensic ontology in answering the problem of our guilt and a participatory ontology (e.g., regeneration, infused habits) in answering the problem of our corruption, so that these two events are like two trains running of parallel tracks.[209] Moreover, if we say that intrinsic transformative change through the infusion of habits occurs before justification, that obscures the *extra nos* basis of our justification.[210]

To get these two trains running on the same track and to secure the *extra nos* basis of our justification, then, Horton makes God's judicial verdict of justification, announced through the effectual call, the generative source of the whole *ordo salutis* or order of salvation so that justification is "the engine that pulls adoption, new birth, sanctification, and glorification in tow."[211]

Second, while union with Christ is the matrix or proper habitat of the *ordo salutis*, justification is the forensic basis of this union.[212]

---

208. Bintsarovskyi, *Hidden and Revealed*, 322.

209. Horton, *Covenant and Salvation*, 301–2; cf. 216, 236.

210. Horton, *Covenant and Salvation*, 176, 261.

211. Horton, *Christian Faith*, 708; cf. 588, 597, 610–12, 677, 706, 710, 708; *Covenant and Salvation*, 129, 138–39, 143, 147–48, 198, 201, 203, 216–17, 247, 264, 292–93; "Calvin's Theology of Union," 91, 93; "Covenant and Justification," 184; *Justification*, 1:209, 219, 273; 2:361, 470–71, 493.

212. Horton, *Covenant and Salvation*, 129, 143, 174; *Christian Faith*, 620; "Calvin's

Third, drawing on the work of Kevin Vanhoozer and speech act theory, Horton asserts that this judicial verdict of justification, announced in the effectual call, occurs when the Father speaks in the Son through the Spirit or—to use the language of speech act theory—when God's illocutionary act of justification is combined with the perlocutionary work of the Holy Spirit, issuing forth into repentance and faith. In other words, God's declaration creates the reality it declares and is constitutive of what it declares.[213]

Fourth, although God's declaration of righteousness is a judicial verdict that generates transformative change, the transformative change is not part of that declaration of righteousness.[214] To illustrate the difference between primary and secondary causality, Horton compares God's effectual calling to a speech act analogous both to the initiating act of creation *ex nihilo*—as God said, "Let there be light!" he now says "Let there be righteousness!"—and to the Spirit's action within creation, so that as God said, "Let the earth bring forth" and so the Spirit brings forth the transformative effect of God's declarative speech act.[215]

Moreover, since God's declaration of righteousness is a judicial verdict that generates transformative change, the charge that a Protestant doctrine of justification by faith is a legal fiction—God justifying someone who is not, in fact, righteous—no longer applies.

Fifth, because God's judicial verdict of justification, announced in the effectual call, is the generative source of the whole *ordo salutis*, Horton distinguishes between what he considers the "gospel" and the "effects of the gospel," typically using the word "gospel" to refer to our justification through faith and "effects of the gospel" to refer to the transformation that follows from our justification by faith.

Sixth, in asserting that God's declaration creates the reality it declares and is constitutive of what it declares, Horton dispenses with the concept of the infusion of habits. Instead, he makes regeneration and effectual calling synonymous.[216]

Theology of Union," 91; *Justification*, 2:285, 470.

213. Horton, *Covenant and Salvation*, 135, 138, 166, 198, 201–3, 218, 220–30, 240; *Christian Faith*, 567, 610–11, 645, 649, 892; *Justification*, 2:361.

214. Horton, *Covenant and Salvation*, 139, 203, 250.

215. Horton, "Calvin's Theology of Union," 91; cf. *Covenant and Salvation*, 203; *Christian Faith*, 159, 326, 575, 611, 621, 645, 662–63, 753; "Let the Earth Bring Forth . . . ," 127–49.

216. Horton, *Covenant and Salvation*, 197; cf. 195–204; 240–42; cf. 232–39; *Christian Faith*, 610; cf. 608–12, 669–70; 573; cf. 572–75.

Seventh, Horton considers his covenant ontology, with justification as the engine that drives the *ordo salutis* as the core of this ontology, to be a rival paradigm to a participatory ontology and superior to it because it deals better with the common charge that the Protestant doctrine of justification by faith is a legal fiction—God justifying someone who is not, in fact, righteous. On Horton's view, since God's declaration of righteousness is a judicial verdict that generates transformative change, this charge no longer applies.[217]

Evaluation of Horton's understanding of justification as the engine that drives the *ordo salutis*

There are several questions that can be raised with regard to Horton's approach to justification.

First, is justification the forensic basis of union with Christ?[218] Scripture does not present justification this way. As we saw earlier, justification is not grounded on the imputation of Christ's active and passive obedience to us when we believe in Christ. Rather, when we clothe ourselves with Christ through faith, we share in Christ's resurrection and justification and are given him as our righteousness and new life. Justification is not the basis of our union with Christ, but rather is included in this union. This is what we read in the New Testament. Because the historical resurrection of Christ was his justification (Rom 1:3–4; 4:23–25; 1 Tim 3:16) and we share in the redemptive life history of Christ (Rom 6:1–11; 2 Cor 5:14; Col 3:1–4), we are justified through union with him (Rom 4:25).[219]

---

217. Horton, *Covenant and Salvation*, 201.

218. While this is Horton's default position, he sometimes makes union with Christ precede justification (Horton, *Christian Faith*, 587, 622; *Justification*, 2:470–71). This leads to a lack of conceptual clarity as well as confusion (McGraw, "Threats of the Gospel," 255–56; Michelson, "Covenantal History and Participatory Metaphysics," 399–400).

219. See Burger, *Being in Christ*, 186, 193, 248, 250–51; Burger, "Clothed with Christ"; Evans, *Imputation and Impartation*, 264–65; Gaffin, *Resurrection and Redemption*, 122–24; Miller, "Debate over the *Ordo Salutis*," 55–62; Seifrid, *Christ, Our Righteousness*, 47, 174–75; Tipton, "Union with Christ," 23–38; Vos, *Pauline Eschatology*, 149–5. For a discussion of the debate between members of Westminster Theological Seminary (Philadelphia) and Westminster Seminary California (Escondido), see Miller, "Debate over the *Ordo Salutis*."

Thus, it is not the doctrine of justification as Horton formulates it but rather the doctrine of union with Christ that keeps the Reformed soteriological train from running on two separate sets of tracks.

Furthermore, that our justification is an aspect of our union with Christ implies that the word "gospel" includes both what Christ has done for us and what Christ does in us.

Second, if God's judicial verdict of justification is the forensic basic of our union with Christ, as Horton says, what is the forensic basis for that verdict?

We just saw that the historical resurrection of Christ is the legal basis of our justification because we are united to him and share in his redemptive life history. In other words, the redemptive-historical justification of Christ that was his resurrection is the forensic basis for God's judicial verdict of justification—or his justifying speech act—for those who are in Christ.

But because Horton makes God's justifying speech act to be the forensic basis of our union with Christ, he essentially has no forensic basis for God's verdict of justification. Michelson writes, "Yet on what basis are sinners declared to be 'in the right'? If the justifying declaration is prior to the single covenantal and ontological relation of the believer with Christ, then the declaration of justification is baseless. This is worse than a legal fiction, for we have no relation to Christ whatsoever by which we are considered to be in solidarity with him."[220]

Third, is God's declaration of righteousness a judicial verdict that creates what it declares or generates transformative change? No, it is not. Scripture does not indicate that justification transforms us.[221] Rather, the transformative change occurs because what Christ has done *for* us in his death and resurrection and in which we share in our union with him, he also does *in* us by the Spirit who joins us to him, having us put him on by faith, so that it is now no longer we who live but Christ who lives in us (Gal 2:20). When we include what Christ does *in* us in the content of the

---

220. Michelson, "Covenantal History and Participatory Metaphysics," 400; see also Hoglund, *Called by Triune Grace*, 72.

221. When Horton asserts that Paul compares God's justifying speech act to his *ex nihilo* fiat in creation in Romans 4:17 (*Christian Faith*, 611, 645, 753; *Justification*, 2:300, 361), he fails to see that this text refers to God creating descendants of Abraham through his effectual call (Hoglund, *Called by Triune Grace*, 72–73).

gospel, then, we are not confusing the fruit or effects of the gospel with the gospel itself, as Horton charges.[222]

Because God's declaration that we are righteous is thus included in his justification of Christ through our union with him, it essentially "affirms an already existing reality." Thus, instead of God's verdict generating transformative change, it is "just a stamp that officially creates the new status."[223] This is how the charge that a Protestant doctrine of justification is a legal fiction is properly defused.[224]

A participatory ontology, then, not only answers the legal fiction charge better than Horton's covenant ontology. It also does not overload justification by making it do more than Scripture says. Michelson writes, "A 'covenantal ontology' represents an overinflation of the doctrine of justification by faith alone, as justification is extracted from its setting within the economy of redemption and given a task—i.e., funding an all-encompassing ontology—which is not native to its constrained, yet crucial role in a more balanced *ordo salutis*."[225]

Fourth, do infused habits involve the infusion of a divine substance leading to a fusion of the divine and the creature? No, they do not. When Christ does in us what he has done for us, this does not infuse into us a divine substance that somehow fuses us with the divine. Rather, it involves Christ infusing his inherent righteousness in us as he lives his life in us through the Spirit.

Lindbeck aptly captures this when he writes, "Inherent righteousness is simply the effect in human beings of incorporation into Christ and of the indwelling of the Holy Spirit. It is not a quasi-independent external product of God's efficient causality. . . . Insistence on infused created grace becomes a way of saying that union with Christ is genuinely transformative of the human person." He concludes, "Thus it can be argued that when Aristotelian categories are given a participationist interpretation, they can no longer be as easily misused."[226]

---

222. Horton, "Law and the Gospel"; "Reflections on Gospel Theology," 76–79.

223. Burger, "Clothed with Christ," 11. This was only an option, not a settled opinion for Burger in 2014. Later, however, writing about God's declaration of justification generating transformative change, he writes, "Justification language in the New Testament, however, does not go that far. You are still too close to the Augustinian idea of justification, which understood justification as the 'engine' of the entire Christian life" (*Life in Christ*, 184).

224. Michelson, "Covenantal History and Participatory Metaphysics," 401–8.

225. Michelson, "Covenantal History and Participatory Metaphysics," 393.

226. Lindbeck, "Question of Compatibility," 238; Michelson, "Covenantal History

Horton on occasion contrasts the infusion of supernatural habits with the role of the Holy Spirit, suggesting that the latter can take over the function performed by the former.[227] "Yet as Lindbeck suggests," says Michelson, "the notion of infused habits interpreted along participatory lines provides the metaphysical density to describe the Spirit's work in the redeemed individual in conforming them to Christ. The Spirit's continuing agency in bringing about this act of intrinsic participation in Christ is indispensable, but the remaining question is whether an account which dispenses with habitual grace altogether can adequately denote the intrinsic change enacted by the Spirit's ongoing work in the believer."[228]

Fifth, should the terminology of infused habits be abandoned because it opens the door for a non-forensic source of justification that obscures the *extra nos* basis of justification? No. Any infused habits prior to our justification cannot obscure its *extra nos* basis because they never meet the standard of perfection needed for justification.[229]

What does obscure the *extra nos* basis of justification, however, is Horton's assertion that God's declaration of justification generates transformative change—thereby rebutting the legal fiction charge—while not making a firm distinction between the declaration and the transformative change it generates, since the transformation, on Horton's view, is the effect of a *single* speech act announced in the effectual call. Because the forensic is the ontological, God's single justifying speech act is implicitly transformative, making us righteous and thereby obscuring the *extra nos* basis of justification.[230]

Thus, a seventh systemic problem in Horton's covenant theology is that it operates with an understanding of the relationship between justification and the *ordo salutis* that misunderstands how Scripture speaks about this relationship and thus finds no warrant in Scripture.

---

and Participatory Metaphysics," 404–5.

227. Horton, *Covenant and Salvation*, 146, 185.

228. Michelson, "Covenantal History and Participatory Metaphysics," 405.

229. Michelson, "Covenantal History and Participatory Metaphysics," 406–7.

230. Michelson, "Covenantal History and Participatory Metaphysics," 399–400. When Horton compares God's effectual call to both the initiating act of creation *ex nihilo* ("Let there be righteousness") and to the Spirit's act in creation of making the earth bring forth fruit, he is no longer speaking about the transformative effect of a single speech act but has introduced a second speech act into the comparison. Hoglund hints at this when he asserts that Horton's reference to God's justifying verdict as being both a "forensic verdict" as well as a "summons" are in fact "two different speech acts" (*Called by Triune Grace*, 72).

Two-kingdom theology

Horton's two kingdom theology can be characterized as follows.

First, while he understands the expression "the kingdom of God" to refer to the eschatological kingdom, he takes the use of this expression in Scripture to refer primarily to the kingship or rule of God in the Garden of Eden, in Israel, and in the church.[231] He also distinguishes this rule from the way God rules in the world.

He bases this distinction on the difference between the cultural mandate and the Great Commission, as well as on his dogmatic understanding of law and gospel. The cultural mandate was given to all humanity in the covenant of creation and is directed by God's general revelation or natural law and enabled by common grace. The Great Commission or cultic mandate, on the other hand, was given to the church in the covenant of grace, is directed by Scripture, and is enabled by special grace.[232]

Second, God unconditionally promises to uphold creation by his common grace in his covenant with Noah, his descendants, and all living creatures. However, this is not a redemptive covenant but a covenant of law that enables believers and unbelievers to fulfill the cultural mandate and engage in cultural activity.[233]

Third, since the fall into sin, the cultural activity mandated in Genesis 1 belongs to the common or secular realm and pertains to the temporal, not the eternal, while the cultic mandate belongs to the sacred realm and pertains to the eternal. These two realms or kingdoms exist independently, parallel to or alongside each other.[234] As a result, Christians are dual citizens, fulfilling their cultural vocation in the common kingdom in a common way, like unbelievers, with the natural law as their source of revelation, and fulfilling their cultic vocation in the sacred kingdom in a special way, with Scripture as their source of revelation.

"There is no difference between Christians and non-Christians with respect to their vocations," Horton writes, referring here to the cultural vocation, to the jobs or tasks people perform in the world. "If Christians

---

231. Horton, *Christian Faith*, 539; cf. 537–47, 720, 754; "Kingdom of God," 363–74, 381–9.

232. Horton, *God of Promise*, 111–26; *Christian Faith*, 712–15, 719, 728; *Gospel-Driven Life*, 161–65; *Gospel Commission*, 62–64.

233. Horton, *God of Promise*, 115–28; *Christian Faith*, 364–68, 712–15, 925–27; "Time Between," 45–65; *Gospel-Driven Life*, 245–66; *Gospel Commission*, 210–46, 282.

234. Horton, *God of Promise*, 114–15; "In Praise of the Profanity," 252–66; *Where in the World*, passim.

as well as non-Christians participate in the common curse and common grace of this age in secular affairs, then there is no 'Christian politics' or 'Christian art' or 'Christian literature,' any more than there is 'Christian plumbing.'"[235]

That was in 2006. In a 2011 blog post, responding to criticisms by Tim Keller, Horton wrote, "Nothing in the 2K view entails that 'Christians do not, then, pursue their vocation in a "distinctively Christian way"' or 'that neither the church nor individual Christians should be in the business of changing the world or society.'" If the church is doing its job, then "there will be Christians who reflect their Christian faith in their daily living." Nevertheless, the power by which they do their daily work is not the power of the gospel, nor is their daily work "ushering in Christ's redemptive kingdom." While the gospel does transform ordinary lives, Horton concludes, "Our goal should not be to change the world, but to maintain a faithful presence in the world as 'salt' and 'light.'"[236]

Later still, in 2011, Horton wrote, "There is no such thing as Christian farming, holy medicine, kingdom art, even though believers engaged in these callings alongside unbelievers are holy citizens of his kingdom. The service that a janitor, homemaker, doctor, or business person provides is part of God's providential care of his creatures. It requires no further justification."[237]

On Horton's view, then, a Christian will be an honest businessman. He will not embezzle money from the company or cheat his employees. He will not attempt to seduce his secretary. He will do his business in a "distinctively Christian way." But his work is not Christian work or "kingdom work," referring to "Christ's redemptive kingdom." It is common work, the same work unbelievers do, carried out in the secular realm just as theirs is.

Similarly, a Christian may be involved in politics. He may vote for people that he believes will carry out the task well. He may even get elected himself. He may understand from Scripture that abortion is sin and work to have it made illegal. Horton speaks highly of Wilberforce who, shaped by John Newton's ministry, "committed his life to the extirpation of the slave trade."[238] Nevertheless, there is no "Christian politics," Horton insists. Politics is secular, in the realm of common grace and natural

---
235. Horton, "How the Kingdom Comes."
236. Horton, "Christ and Culture Once More."
237. Horton, *Calvin on the Christian Life*, 228.
238. Horton, "Christ and Culture Once More."

law." Discipleship "never transforms the kingdoms of this age into the kingdom of Christ." The two-kingdoms remain separate, even when a Christian—discipled by the Word—engages in work or politics in the world.[239]

Fourth, because our vocations outside the church have bearing only on the temporal, they are considered "creation" work (non-redemptive) and not kingdom work (redemptive).[240] Consequently, the church should not try to apply the gospel to social issues, not least because "Christianity is not a culture [but] a system of truth claims."[241] To apply the gospel to social issues would not only lead to a confusion of kingdoms, of Christ and culture, of general and special revelation, and of law and gospel; it would also trivialize the gospel.[242]

Fifth, since the marks of the church are the mission of the church, such that the church fulfills its mission in the world by opening and shutting the kingdom of heaven by the keys of the kingdom and by the faithful execution of the marks of the church, the church should also not try to make disciples by being a people who are active in the world, endeavoring to embody the gospel. In Horton's view, this approach easily distracts from the church as a place where Christ is the active party, forgiving and renewing sinners.[243]

Evaluation of Horton's two-kingdom theology

Horton's two-kingdom theology raises several questions.

First, is Horton's two-kingdom theology simply the teaching of Augustine and the Reformers?

The language of "two kingdoms" is not unique to Horton, of course. It found its way into theological discourse via Augustine's use of the concept of two cities. Luther and Calvin both speak of two kingdoms. But the

---

239. Horton, "Christ and Culture Once More."

240. Horton, "Transforming Culture."

241. Horton, *Beyond Culture Wars*, 26. For Horton's critique of the idea of Christendom, see Horton, *Beyond Culture Wars*, 83–106.

242. Horton, *Where in the World*, 90–91; *Beyond Culture Wars*, 35, 83; *God of Promise*, 17, 121–28; *Christless Christianity*, 114, 124, 157, 206; *Gospel-Driven Life*, 253–54, 263; cf. 245–66; *Gospel Commission*, 84, 86, 100, 118, 212, 226–28, 238, 248, 271, 286.

243. Horton, *Gospel Commission*, 266–90; *Christless Christianity*, passim; *Gospel-Driven Life*, passim.

only two kingdoms that Scripture speaks about are the kingdom of God and the kingdom of Satan.[244]

When Horton asserts that Augustine taught the two-kingdoms approach when he wrote about the two cities—the city of God and the city of man—he spatializes Augustine's city of man into a common realm or earthly domain.[245] But for Augustine, "the earthly city is a systemic—and disordered—configuration of creaturely life" that manifests itself in a love for self and a lust for power *within* human society.[246]

When Horton implies that his two-kingdom approach is comparable to Luther's,[247] he overlooks the fact that Luther's two kingdoms are primarily "two realms within human existence corresponding to humanity's two natures," with the invisible spiritual realm referring to "the human person before God alone (*coram Deo*)," where God governs invisibly and directly through his Word, and the visible physical or earthly realm referring to the human person in the eyes of men and the world (*coram hominibus* or *coram mundo*), where God governs visibly through external means.[248]

When Horton implies that his two-kingdom approach is comparable to Calvin's,[249] he fails to understand that for Calvin talk about two kingdoms "does not so much refer to two separate realms or worlds as to a twofold government of God over the conduct of believers who are being renewed after his image and are subject to his rule."[250]

When Horton criticizes Augustine, Luther, and Calvin for not being consistent with their two-kingdom theology,[251] what Crouse writes about VanDrunen also applies to Horton: "Not once does VanDrunen allow that what he calls 'inconsistencies' may actually be practices consistent with a theory that he has misinterpreted."[252]

---

244. Scheuers, "Dual Citizenship, Dual Ethic?," 275.

245. Horton, *Beyond Culture Wars*, 88–92; *God of Promise*, 120–22; *Gospel-Driven Life*, 250; *Christian Faith*, 924.

246. Smith, *Awaiting the King*, 46; Bourke, *Essential Augustine*, 200–202.

247. Horton, *Beyond Culture Wars*, 93–94; *God of Promise*, 120; *Christian Faith*, 924; *Gospel Commission*, *Gospel Commission*, 245.

248. Crouse, *Two Kingdoms*, 5–6; cf. 1–34; Littlejohn, *Two Kingdoms*, 12–29.

249. Horton, *Beyond Culture Wars*, 94–98; *God of Promise*, 120, 126; *Christian Faith*, 924; *Gospel Commission*, 245.

250. Venema, "Restoration of All Things," 14; cf. 3–32; Calvin, *Institutes*, 3.19.15.

251. Horton, *God of Promise*, 120, *Christian Faith*, 924.

252. Crouse, *Two Kingdoms*, 100.

Second, and more importantly, what is the relationship between "the rule of the king" and "the realm of the king" when Jesus uses the expression "the kingdom of God"?

While the word "kingdom" (βασιλεία) refers to both the reign of the king and the realm of the king, when Jesus uses the expression "kingdom of God," he is not referring to the reality of Christ's reign of grace here and now, in which Christ applies the benefits of his redemptive work to believers by the Spirit to create a new covenant community or church. Rather, he is speaking of the reality of the realm of the Sabbath rest of the fullness of God's loving presence in Christ, by the Spirit, in the coming new heavens and new earth, where God will be all in all.[253]

Van Bruggen articulates this as follows: "The Greek word *basileia*, like the Hebrew word *malkut*, means both kingly *rule* and kingly *territory*. These meanings reflect different aspects of the word but are not mutually exclusive. The word *basileia* is not an abstract term for king*ship* (which exists apart from the recognition of such a status); it is rather a concrete reference to 'kingly dominion' (the acknowledged and exercised royal power in a particular territory)."[254]

This *basileia* is a realm that we will inherit (1 Cor 6:9–10; 15:50; Gal 5:21; Eph 5:5) and into which we must enter (Matt 5:20; 18:3; John 13:5) "in which everything is subject to him [i.e., God]."[255] Accordingly, Jesus can say that his kingdom is not of *this* world (John 18:36).

Thus, when Horton uses the nomenclature of "two kingdoms" to refer to the two different ways in which Christ rules the world and the church, he is using the word "kingdom" in a different way than Jesus when he spoke of the "kingdom of God."

Third, does the cultural mandate belong to the covenant of works (or creation) and the Great Commission belong to the covenant of grace? Horton's approach depends on this distinction, but we have seen already in this chapter that Scripture does not teach a pre-fall covenant

---

253. The reality of this dominion acknowledged and exercised in a particular territory was promised in the so-called *protevangelium* or promise of redemption (Gen 3:15), promised to Abraham (Gen 12:3), prophesied by Daniel (Dan 2:44; 7:11–14), and proclaimed by John the Baptist, Jesus, and the apostles. This theme will be developed further in the next chapter.

254. Van Bruggen, *Jesus the Son of God*, 76; cf. 73–82; "Evangelie van het koninkrijk"; "Hoe is het hemelrijk nabij?" God intended this reality to be prefigured in his relationship with Israel and the land in the Old Testament, see de Bruijne, "Niet van deze wereld," 371; cf. 370–76.

255. Van Bruggen, *Jesus the Son of God*, 76.

of works nor an overarching covenant of grace. Furthermore, since faith characterizes obedience in both the Old and New Testament, the cultural mandate and the Great Commission are both to be carried out through the obedience of faith. Scripture never suggests that the cultural mandate was to be carried out by works apart from faith.

Fourth, is the dichotomizing of two sources of revelation—the enlightening by common grace and natural law on the one hand and the enlightening by special grace and Scripture on the other—warranted by Scripture?

According to Horton, "It is a fact that the law of God which we call the [written] moral law is nothing else than a testimony of natural law and of that conscience which God has engraved on the minds of men."[256]

But when Horton asserts that the law is written on the hearts of every human being, he overlooks the fact that Romans 2:15 speaks about "the work of the law" written on their hearts. Because the law Paul is referring to is the Mosaic law, he means that when Gentiles spontaneously—"by nature"—do what the law requires, they do so because somehow the influence of the written law of God makes itself felt in their lives. Stob expresses this well when he writes, "Paul is here declaring that in the consciousness of the unregenerate an effect of the law's 'operation' is registered."[257]

This implies that God's general revelation through conscience is intrinsically tied to his special revelation in Scripture and thus is not an independent source of revelation alongside Scripture. Kloosterman aptly captures this intrinsic relationship when he writes, "From Paul's argument, however, it seems clear that, for him, 'nature' is not the source of any moral norms, of which then the law was supposedly the objectification. Rather, precisely the reverse was the case: this doing 'by nature' . . . what the law requires indeed demonstrates the power of the [written] law."[258]

Moreover, Genesis 1:28 and 2:16–17 show that before the fall into sin, God kept general and special revelation together.[259] He has

---

256. Horton, *Gospel-Driven Life*, 253.

257. Stob, "Natural Law Ethics," 63; Kloosterman, "Biblical Case."

258. Kloosterman, "Biblical Case"; Bavinck, *Reformed Dogmatics*, 1:87; Scheuers, "Dual Citizenship, Dual Ethic?," 135; Waddington, "Duplex in Homine Regimen," 193.

259. Frame, *Escondido Theology*, 325–26; Vos, *Biblical Theology*, 27–40; Waddington, "Duplex in Homine Regimen," 192–93; "Westminster Seminary California Distinctives?," 191–92; see also Poythress, *Lordship of Christ*, 193–96, 205.

throughout history, and this will continue to be the case in the eschatological kingdom.

In fact, when Horton separates general and special revelation into two parallel realms, he forgets that "moral consensus between Christians and non-Christians does not originate in general revelation, as is often assumed, but rather originates in a mixture of general and special revelation. What is often taken as evidence of general revelation, natural law, and common grace in our Western culture may actually be rather the historical influence of special revelation, biblical law, and the gospel."[260] Moreover, as Paas writes, "Who will say where God's saving grace begins? I myself have talked to enough people for whom the way of God's peace began with a dream, an experience in nature, the desire to give their children something more than money and career, an inexplicable coincidence, or just with experiences of failure—a divorce, bankruptcy or imprisonment."[261]

Furthermore, as Frame points out, "Scripture never suggests that pagan governments are not responsible to God's special revelation. Indeed, Israelite prophets brought God's special revelation to bear against Babylon, Assyria, Moab, Cush, Egypt, Tyre, and Sidon, as well as Israel (as in Isa. 13–23) and against Rome (the Book of Revelation)."[262]

When Horton asserts that God rules the world in general through common grace and by natural law but empowers and guides the church by special grace and Scripture, he is operating with an artificial duality that has never existed and that has no basis in Scripture.[263]

Fifth, is general revelation sufficient to fund a parallel ethic in the common kingdom alongside an ethic in the sacred kingdom? No, it is not.

As we saw in the introduction, humanity is no longer open and receptive to living in the presence of God and each other because, when

---

260. Strange, "Not Ashamed!," 253. Leithart calls this mixture "middle grace" ("Did Plato Read Moses?," 4–5). Furthermore, the separation of two sources of revelation, enlightenment by common grace and enlightenment by special grace, implies that a secular state can be religiously neutral. However, this is "a 'myth,' a confused, compromised, and unstable state of affairs, and a fruit of the Enlightenment rather than the Reformation" (Strange, "Not Ashamed!," 248; cf. Keller, *Center Church*, 211).

261. Paas, *Vrede op aarde*, 367–68. All translations from Dutch to English are mine unless otherwise noted.

262. Frame, *Escondido Theology*, 322.

263. Ouweneel roots two-kingdom dichotomizing in the scholastic nature-grace dualism (*The World Is Christ's*, 9, 34–35, 185, 228, 233, 235, 261, 287, 289, 297–98).

they fell into sin, they closed themselves off to this possibility and became turned in on themselves and self-enclosed—with consequences for our inner orientation or mindset. As a result of sin, our understanding became futile and darkened (Rom 1:21, 28). Our will suppresses the truth that God reveals in his general revelation (Rom 1:18–20). Thus, both epistemologically and ethically, general revelation is insufficient to fund an ethic in the common kingdom, parallel to the ethic in the special kingdom.[264]

Sixth, is God's covenant with Noah a common grace non-redemptive law covenant? This is not the case. The distinction between redemptive and non-redemptive covenants is based on Horton's dogmatic law-gospel distinction or hermeneutic, which is not warranted by Scripture. Divine-human covenants are redemptive instruments that secure and guarantee God's missional intent for humanity and creation, often during times of uncertainty. Consequently, there is no such thing as a non-redemptive covenant: all God's covenants are redemptive.

Moreover, asserting that God's covenant with Noah is a non-redemptive covenant dichotomizes God's work in creation and God's work in redemption, which Scripture presents as a unity (e.g., 1 Pet 3:20).[265]

Seventh, is it true that Christianity is not a culture but rather a system of truth claims? This is a false dilemma that further dichotomizes creation and redemption and compartmentalizes the Christian life. Christianity is both a system of truth claims and a culture. The truth claims give direction for clearly communicating the gospel in our secular culture and properly shaping our Christian identity and practice.

Moreover, the Spirit uses the gospel to create the culture of the new creation of Christ's resurrection life, to which the members of the church bear witness as they perform what is in Christ by putting on Christ and clothing themselves with him so that they act out the perfection of God's eternal life and do heaven on earth. Therefore, applying the gospel to social issues does not trivialize the gospel, nor should we be prohibited from using the adjective "Christian" for our vocations, as if our vocations

---

264. Frame, *Escondido Theology*, 325–32; Keller, *Center Church*, 210; Kloosterman, "Biblical Case"; O'Donovan, *Resurrection and Moral Order*, 81–82; Poythress, *Lordship of Christ*, 193–94, 207; Stob, "Natural Law Ethics," 62; Strange, "Not Ashamed!," 250–52; Venema, "Restoration of All Things," 21–23.

265. Venema, "One Kingdom or Two?," 117–18; cf. 114–20; "Christ's Kingship," 13–19; *contra* Van Pelt, "Noahic Covenant," 111–32.

outside the church are functionally secular because they have bearing only on the temporal.[266]

In Horton's view, the idea of Christendom is a Christian capitulation to a worldly status quo. But when Horton asserts that, he forgets that "the core idea of Christendom is . . . intimately bound up with the church's mission . . . not as a *project* of the church's mission, . . . [but as a] *response* to mission, and as such a sign that God has blessed it. It is constituted not by the church's seizing alien power, but by alien power's becoming attentive to the church."[267]

Being a missional church that makes disciples by being a people who are active in the world, endeavoring to embody the gospel and developing a Christian culture, a Christendom, does not distract from the church as a place where Christ is the active party, forgiving and renewing sinners. Rather, this activity in the world should attract people to this place—the church—because that is the place where Christians are not only forgiven but empowered and directed to be the interactive theater of the gospel that bears witness to the reality of God in this world and that embodies the Christian hope for the world.

Thus, an eighth systemic problem in Horton's covenant theology is that it operates with a two-kingdom theology that finds no warrant in Scripture.

---

266. For an essay on the Christian witness as redeemed culture, see McIhenny, *Kingdoms Apart*, 251–74. McIhenny, with a nod to Wolters, rightfully observes that when two-kingdom advocates resist using the adjective "Christian" for the vocations of Christians and institutions because these things are functionally secular, they ignore the useful distinction between the structure and direction of creation (*Kingdoms Apart*, 68–69, 265–70; see also Wolters, *Creation Regained*, 49–52, 72–95). For a balanced view of the relationship between the church and culture that does not dichotomize Christ's redemptive and creational rule, see Carson, *Christ and Culture Revisited*; Keller, *Center Church*; Leithart, *Theopolitan Vision*; O'Donovan, *Desire of the Nations*; Schilder, *Christ and Culture*; Smith, *Awaiting the King*; Venema, "Christ's Kingship." For the impact of Christianity on the development of Western civilization, see Holland, *Dominion*. For reckoning with this fact in ethical decision-making, see de Bruijne, "Gij geheel anders. Of toch niet?"

267. O'Donovan, *Desire of the Nations*:195; see also Leithart, *Against Christianity*, 135–57.

IMPLICATIONS OF THE SYSTEMIC PROBLEMS IN HORTON'S COVENANT THEOLOGY[268]

Having identified these systemic problems in Horton's covenant theology, I will now draw out some implications they have for the communication of the gospel and for the shaping of our Christian identity and practice.

First, Horton asserts that humanity needed to be created in a covenant relationship because there could be no "natural" (i.e., inherently compatible) communion between God and humanity, due to the metaphysical distance between Creator and creature. As a result, he does not consider the possibility that there can be a "natural" communion between God and humanity that nevertheless does maintain the Creator-creature distinction, such as an ontology of love in Christ through the Holy Spirit. His view, in turn, appears to drive his strident opposition to any form of a "natural" participation in the life of God and his embrace of a rival covenant theology in which we have only a legal/ethical union with God.

Second, finding the unity of salvation in a pretemporal intratrinitarian covenant of redemption between the Father and the Son and the Holy Spirit apparently leads Horton to understand the covenant of grace as being governed by God's decretal election. This, in turn, seems to lead him to consider the new covenant as unconditional in its essence but conditional in its administration, and it may be the reason why he considers those who have been baptized but have not yet been united to Christ to be only *externally* related to the covenant. Nevertheless, because Horton does not collapse the covenant of redemption and the covenant of grace into one covenant, made only with those predestined to glory with Christ, his covenant theology does not lead to a soteriological determinism that fails to do justice "to what the Bible says about God's interaction in time with all those with whom he concludes the covenant of grace."[269]

Third, asserting that to demonstrate God's holiness and justice and to protect the integrity of the doctrine of justification there must be a sharp distinction between law and gospel does not allow Horton to

---

268. While this section focuses primarily on negative consequences of Horton's covenant, there are positive consequences as well. For instance, together with mainstream covenant theology, his theology communicates a gospel that embraces the five *solas* of the Reformation. However, the fact that these fives *solas* are also embraced by those who do not hold to covenant theology means that they are not intrinsic to covenant theology.

269. Van Genderen and Velema, *Reformed Dogmatics*, 207; Van Asselt, "Covenant Theology as Relational Theology," 81–82.

consider that God's foundational relationship with humanity could be a relationship that is first determined by love and then by law.

As a result, Horton considers Adam's relationship with God and creation to be such that he was required to earn God's blessing through obedience or merit his curse through disobedience in a *quid pro quo* manner. The law-gospel distinction also leads Horton to view God's covenant with Israel as in some sense a republication of the covenant of works and indeed to think that the covenant of works is still in effect today for all those who do not believe in Christ. Man's fundamental relationship with God, on Horton's view, is one in which he is required to render perfect obedience in order to enter into God's blessings.

All of this seems to lead to a communication of the gospel in which God is first viewed as a God of law and justice and only then as a God of mercy and grace. On this view, we must always first be confronted with the law—which condemns us because we cannot obey it perfectly to merit God's blessings—and only then with the gospel. As Horton says, the law alone tells us that we are sinners, while the gospel alone tells us that we are pardoned and saved. This view, then, also affects our self-image, so that our fundamental understanding of our identity is legal and ethical: Do we measure up to God's standards?

Fourth, asserting that God works out his plan of salvation in one overarching covenant of grace with a canonical narrative of creation, fall, redemption, and consummation does not allow Horton to take seriously the dynamics of the history of redemption in which God enters into a plurality of covenants with Israel, Israel's king, and Israel's fathers. This view, in turn, appears to lead him to consider God's history with Israel to be an interlude or parenthesis for typological and pedagogical reasons.

That Horton considers the Mosaic covenant to be, in some sense, a republication of the covenant of works in which Israel primarily functions to reveal our human sinfulness seems to confirm this understanding of the implications of his view. But this approach, then, can lead to a communication of the gospel in which God's concrete dealings with Israel have no place.

When Horton makes the doctrine of justification, which deals with the problem of our guilt, the heart of the economy of redemption and considers God's justification of sinners through faith to be, essentially, the gospel, it can lead to an individualizing communication of the gospel, narrowing the gospel to the forgiveness of sins and the declaration that an individual sinner is right with God. Again, it shapes our self-image in terms of law and ethics, so that our view of ourselves is primarily concerned with whether we have a right legal standing before God.

When Horton claims that Christ, as the head and mediator of the covenant of grace, fulfills the conditions of the covenant of works for elect sinners by perfectly carrying out the obedience of the law required in the covenant of works (active obedience) and dealing with the sanction of the covenant of works by bearing the curse of the law and satisfying God's justice for them by his suffering and death (passive obedience) and that by this obedience Christ purchased benefits of salvation for these elect sinners, which the Holy Spirit then applies to them in a particular order when they believe in Christ, the result is a communication of the gospel with a twofold soteriological structure—purchasing and applying—and an extrinsic appropriationist understanding of salvation.

The proclamation of the gospel, on this view, leaves the sinner, in a sense, at arm's length from Christ. Christ purchased benefits, which the Spirit then bestows on the elect believer. But you can receive a gift from someone without any real union with the giver. Nor is Jesus, on this view, personally involved in one's obedience of faith. Moreover, there is a danger that Christians are thrown back on themselves, wondering whether the benefits of salvation are really for them or not.

Fifth, Horton's use of the distinction between God's essence and energies and the claim that we can never know God in his essence, which undergirds his assertion that humanity needed a covenantal relationship to bridge the metaphysical gap between Creator and creature, appears to lead to a communication of the gospel that brings us to a knowledge of God's works and his energies but never to a knowledge of God's being. Moreover, this distinction affects our understanding of our Christian identity, as well, so that we seem to have only an outward or extrinsic union with Christ.

Sixth, the assertion that God's declaration of justification is the forensic basis of our union with Christ leaves us with a communication of the gospel in which justification itself has no forensic basis. Moreover, Horton's assertion that God's declaration of justification is the generative source of the transformative aspects of our union with Christ appears to lead to an approach to the shaping of our Christian identity and practice that requires us to constantly look to our justification rather than to Christ and our union with him as the source of and power for transformation.

It appears, too, that this view of justification is the reason Horton restricts the use of the term "gospel" to what Christ has done *for* us and does not include what Christ does *in* us. If Christ's work in us is not the gospel, that may be why Horton sees the practice of spiritual formation through spiritual disciplines of contemplative spirituality, pursued as a means of cultivating our participation in God's covenantal counterdrama of redemption, as a distraction from the gospel.[270]

Seventh, Horton's assertion that the culture mandate was given to all humanity, is directed by general revelation or natural law, and enabled by common grace, while the Great Commission or cultic mandate was given to the church, is directed by Scripture, and enabled by special grace, so that Christ rules in the world through general revelation and in the church through special revelation, separates what Scripture holds together. This two-kingdoms theology also affects Christian practice, artificially dichotomizing all of a Christian's activities into sacred and secular.[271]

CONCLUSION

The negative consequences that Horton's covenant theology have for our communication of the gospel and for the shaping of our Christian identity and practice invite us to reframe our understanding of divine-human

---

270. Comparing a covenant ontology and an ontology of participating in God's loving presence in Christ through the Holy Spirit reminded me that the structural design of Heidelberg Catechism—a catechism I grew up with and have learned to love very much—has as a consequence a limited presentation of the gospel. Having analyzed the structure of the Heidelberg Catechism with the use of Thorsten Latzel's foundational study (*Theologische grundzüge des Heidelberger Katechismus*), Burger concludes that "the main question to which the Heidelberg Catechism is an answer [is]: how am I righteous before God?" ("Gospel Presentation and the Structure of the Heidelberg Catechism," 273). This is understandable because of the theological and pastoral questions the Catechism is giving a contextual and pastorally sensitive answer to. However, "[it] fosters ... a spirituality that focuses on juridical and individual issues. In the 21st century, it is important to see the limitations of the Catechism, especially in churches heavily influenced by it. It is only partly helpful in understanding communion with and participation in Christ which is spiritually so important. Its replotting of the story of the Bible might lead to a neglect of notions such as the kingdom of God and the mission of the church." Burger concludes, "Finally, it does not do enough to prevent an image of God that gives God's punishment too prominent a place. We need other presentations of the gospel to explain its significance. The gospel is richer than we can see in the perspective of the Heidelberg Catechism" ("Gospel Presentation and the Structure of the Heidelberg Catechism," 277–78).

271. I sent a copy of my dissertation to Michael Horton in January 2022 for feedback, but I have not yet received a response.

covenants, incorporating into it an ontology that has participation in the life of God as its integrative center. To that task I turn in the next chapter.

4

Participation in the Life of God and Divine-human Covenants: The Drama of God's Mission for His Glory

THE PREVIOUS TWO CHAPTERS have shown how the design of Horton's theology depends upon his covenant theology. This chapter sketches the contours of a theodramatic biblical narrative that has participation in the life of God as its integrative center, incorporates a reframed understanding of divine-human covenants in five acts, and has the unifying theme of the drama of God's mission for his glory. The following chapter, then, will deal with how the contours of this theodramatic biblical narrative gives rise to the contours of a theodramatic systematic theology.

BEFORE THE CURTAIN RISES

The unifying theme of the drama: God's mission for his glory

As I showed in chapter 1, God's communicative activity in the economic Trinity bears witness to his communicative activity in the immanent Trinity.[1] When Jesus glorifies or makes known the glory of the Father and the Father and Spirit glorify or make known the glory of the Son (John 8:54; 12:28; 14:13; 16:14; 17:1, 5), this activity bears witness to the communicative activity of mutual glorification in the immanent Trinity.

---

1. But note that "the economic Trinity corresponds to but does not exhaust or encompass the reality of the immanent Trinity" (Vanhoozer, *Remythologizing Theology*, 203).

Moreover, when Jesus glorifies the Father by a listening and thankful filial spirit characterized by the openness and responsiveness of faith (John 5:30; 6:38; 7:16; 8:26; 12:49; 14:10; 15:15; 17:8), this bears witness to the Son's openness and responsiveness to the Father in the immanent Trinity (John 5:19; 2 Cor 4:6; Col 1:15; Heb 1:3).

It is this communicative activity of mutual glorification—making the glory of each other known—that is the heart of the drama that God enacts in his mission for his glory when he creates the world and humanity and has them participate in and bear witness to him, on earth as in heaven, in Christ by the Holy Spirit.[2]

On earth as in heaven! The persons of the Trinity freely determined the plot of this drama of God's mission for his glory (John 6:39; 17:4, 6, 24; Eph 1:3–14), which Paul refers to as "a plan for the fullness of time, to unite all things in him, things in heaven and things on earth" (Eph 1:10).[3]

The terminology used in describing the plot

If we want to understand the plot of the drama of God's mission for his glory, we need to understand the terminology used in the description of that plot.

God's glory

God's glory is the splendor of his perfect life.[4] Bavinck, for instance, says, "The 'glory of the Lord' is the splendor and brilliance that is inseparably associated with all of God's attributes and his self-revelation in nature

---

2. Vanhoozer, *Remythologizing Theology*, 241–94; *Faith Speaking Understanding*, 73–77, 80–82; "At Play," 14–17; *Biblical Authority after Babel*, 50–53; Webster, "God's Perfect Life," 143–52.

3. *Contra* Vanhoozer and Edwards who see this free self-determination as the covenant of redemption or the *pactum salutis* (Vanhoozer, *Remythologizing Theology*, 258–59; Vanhoozer, *Faith Speaking Understanding*, 77–80; Vanhoozer, "At Play," 17–19; Edwards, *Observations*).

4. "Splendor" is an attempt to translate the idea of "weight" or "heaviness" associated with the Hebrew word *kabod* (כָּבוֹד). *Kabod* is translated with *doxa* (δόξα) in the Septuagint (LXX). Kittel writes, "The LXX word receives its distinctive force from the fact that it is used for כָּבוֹד. We find in it the meanings of כָּבוֹד, and we do not find in the LXX term the meanings of the Greek δόξα. It has become identical with כָּבוֹד" (Kittel, "δόξα," 242).

and grace, the glorious form in which he everywhere appears to his creatures."[5]

This splendor of God's perfect life is like "a many-faceted gem, which reflect and refracts light in ever-new, ever-unexpected ways as it is admired."[6] This splendor is associated with God's light, as the visible manifestation of God's presence (Isa 58:8; 60:1–3).[7] Moreover, it is closely associated or interchangeable with God's presence and God's name. The former is the visible and active manifestation or presentation of God's glory (Exod 16:7; 33:12–22; Lev 9:23–24; Deut 5:24; 1 Sam 4:21–22; Ps 19:1; Isa 6:3).[8] The latter describes God's glory (Exod 33:18–19; 34:6–7).[9] When Moses asks to see God's glory, God says that he will make all of his goodness pass before him. In doing so, he proclaims his name to Moses. This implies that as the name of the Lord is a description of God's glory, so it is also a description of his goodness. Thus, God's glory and God's goodness appear to be used synonymously.

Rose compares listening to texts to listening to music. Accordingly, he hears the melody of God's glory not only in the word *kabod* or one of its synonyms, but also in the melody of superlatives, such as, "The Lord is high above all nations, and his glory above the heavens!" (Ps 113:4; cf. Pss 96:3–4; 72:19; 145:11–12; Exod 18:11; Deut 10:17), the melody of being incomparable, such as, "Who is like the Lord our God" (Ps 113:5; cf. Jer 10:6; Isa 45:14; Pss 88:8; 89:7–9; Deut 6:4), and the melody of simultaneously being above and below, such as, "Who is like the Lord our God, who is seated on high, who looks far down on the heavens and the earth? (Pss 113:5–6; 36:6–7; Isa 44:6, 8).[10]

Since love is the bond of perfection (Col 3:14; cf. Matt 22:37–40; Rom 13:8, 10), God's love binds the splendor of his perfect life together in perfect unity. Performing and bearing witness to the glory of God's perfect life in Christ through the Holy Spirit on earth as in heaven, then, involves acting out and making God's glory known, so that God is

---

5. Bavinck, *Reformed Dogmatics*, 2:252; see VanDrunen, *God's Glory Alone*, 32; see also Ashford and Bartholomew, *Doctrine of Creation*, 113.

6. Hamilton, *God's Glory*, 59.

7. Dodd, *Interpretation of the Fourth Gospel*, 206; Vanhoozer, *Remythologizing Theology*, 250.

8. Gaffin, "Glory," 508; Fairbairn, *Life in the Trinity*, 17–19; Vriezen, *Outline of Old Testament Theology*, 207–9.

9. Hamilton, *God's Glory*, 56–59; van der Woude, "Shem (name)," 1363.

10. Rose, *Hij is goed*, 285–93.

recognized and acknowledged for who he is in the splendor of his perfect life.[11] This, in turn, will evoke praise for God from others.[12]

Participation

Participating in the life of God in Christ through the Holy Spirit is partaking of the divine nature (2 Pet 1:14) by living in God's loving presence and sharing in the Son's status of sonship and his communion of love with the Father through the Spirit.

This participation is not limited to the future; it is a present reality. Starr writes, "The consensus view that 2 Peter writes solely of the future, of an eschatological entry into a state of divine incorruption, fails to take seriously the juxtaposition of the divine attribute of virtue mentioned in 1:3 and the exhortation for the readers to enter into virtue *now* (1:5–7). The readers have already now been given everything that is necessary for piety and therefore are no longer subject to the tyranny of passionate desire." He concludes, "The interpretation that 2 Peter envisions something belonging solely to the future cannot be supported from the immediate context and suggests mistakenly that a departure from the physical world is requisite for participation in the divine nature."[13]

Letham correctly notes that our partaking of the divine nature occurs through our union with the person of Christ. He writes, "This [partaking of the divine nature] goes beyond communion. It entails union. It is more than participation in the communicable attributes of God. It is not to be restricted to union with righteousness, goodness, holiness, or truth, neither is it union with the benefits of Christ, as if it were union with the doctrine of sanctification. It is union with *Christ*."[14]

Burger is hesitant to speak about participating in God, because we do not directly participate in the unique relationship of the Father and the Son. As a result, he prefers to restrict the use of the word "participation"

---

11. Vanhoozer, *Remythologizing Theology*, 249; *Faith Speaking Understanding*, passim; "At Play," 16, 20. For the connection between God's mission for his glory and God wanting to be known for who he is, see Wright, *Mission of God*.

12. Von Rad, "כָּבוֹד in the OT," 238; Kilner, *Dignity and Destiny*, 63; Longman, "Glory of God," 78.

13. Starr, "2 Peter 1:4," 83; *contra* Bauckham, *Jude, 2 Peter*, 181–82; Kelly, *Peter and Jude*, 301–3; van Houwelingen, *2 Petrus en Judas*, 33–34.

14. Letham, *Systematic Theology*, 788; *Union with Christ*, 127; *contra* Beale, *Union with the Resurrected Christ*, 421–33; Frame, *Systematic Theology*, 1011–12.

to participation in Christ.[15] I understand that we do not want to suggest that participating in the life of God entails becoming part of the Trinity, but I fail to see how the language of "participating in the life of God" suggests such a thing when it is clear that this participation or dwelling in the life of God is the result of our indirect, mediated participation in Christ by the Spirit (John 17:21; 1 John 3:24; 4:15-16; 5:20). As Canlis says in analyzing Calvin's view, it is a Christological participation in God or communion (*koinonia*) with God.[16]

Since the Son glorifies the Father by being open and responsive to him, listening to him and thankfully doing his will, participating in the Son's communion of love with the Father involves sharing in this same openness and responsiveness, this listening and thankful filial spirit.[17] Faith joins us to Christ so that we are now objectively relocated in this risen and ascended Christ and it is no longer we who live, but Christ Jesus who lives in us (Gal 2:20), and so this participation in Christ by the Holy Spirit is an ontological participation in the life of God.[18]

Drawing on Calvin, Billings refers to this as a "substantial" participation, because through faith we participate in the substance of Christ.[19] Canlis thinks the term "substantial" can hinder more than help and thus prefers to speak about a "pneumatological" or "non-substantial" participation, but she believes that she and Billings are saying the same thing, since they both ground their theology of participation in the Spirit.[20]

---

15. Burger, "Hart en wezen," 344-48; *Being in Christ*, 325, 350, 352-54; *Life in Christ*, 114.

16. Canlis, *Calvin's Ladder*, 278; cf. 14-17, 53-58, 138, 142, 145. Evans refers to this as "pneumatological-incarnational realism" ("Three Current Reformed Models," 27-30). Whether we should call our participation in the divine nature "glorification" or "*theosis*" or "deification" is essentially "just a matter of words" (Burger, *Being in Christ*, 543). Macaskill cautions against using the word "*theosis*" because it is both "under-determined" and "over-determined." It is "under-determined" because "the terminology of *theosis* can be applied to a broad range of theological accounts that vary in significant ways." It is "over-determined" because "the modern doctrine, with all its varieties, has come to operate within a certain conceptual framework that may not be directly mapped onto that of the New Testament writers" (Macaskill, *Union with Christ*, 75).

17. Canlis, *Calvin's Ladder*, 3-5, 43-44, 47-51; Fairbairn, *Life in the Trinity*, 13-37; Torrance, *Mediation of Christ*, 73-98.

18. Billings, "John Calvin"; *Calvin, Participation, and the Gift*, 61-65; Evans, "Three Current Reformed Models," 27-30; Fairbairn, "Patristic Soteriology"; *Life in the Trinity*, 6-12, 33-35; Letham, *Union with Christ*, 85-128; *Systematic Theology*, 768-88.

19. Billings, *Calvin, Participation, and the Gift*, 53-65.

20. Canlis, *Calvin's Ladder*, 14; Billings, *Calvin, Participation, and the Gift*, 62-63.

Letham writes, "Strictly speaking, we are united to [Christ's] humanity, but his humanity is inseparable from his deity, due to the hypostatic union. Thus, union with his humanity is union with his person. Moreover, since the person of Christ is that of the eternal Son, we are united to God." He adds, "This does not mean any blurring of the Creator-creature distinction, any more than the assumption of humanity by the Son in the incarnation does. His humanity remains his humanity (without confusion, without mixture). So, we remain creatures."[21]

Covenant

A divine-human *covenant* is an expression of God's commitment to secure and guarantee his creational purpose[22] in the drama of his mission for his glory.

God intends to bring creation and humanity into the Sabbath rest of the fullness of his loving presence in Christ, through the Spirit, in his coming kingdom, the new heavens and new earth where he will be all in all. But because sin and unbelief often threaten the fulfillment of this creational goal and thus lead to uncertainty in God's relationship with his people, he regulates this existing relationship and rescues the mission for his glory by making covenants with his people.[23] As such, covenants are manifestations of God's faithfulness to his creational purpose and to his people.

Divine-human covenants are thus "redemptive instruments" with missional intent. Leder sums up this redemptive function of covenants: "Theologically, covenants are redemptive instruments by which God manages human life in exile from his presence until that problem is solved (Rev. 21:3–4)." He adds, "Until then, God's priestly people are

---

21. Letham, *Holy Trinity*, 468.

22. For the relationship between God's creational purpose and his covenants with creation and humanity, see Williamson, *Sealed with an Oath*, 44–58.

23. For regulating an existing relationship in order to deal with a problem of uncertainty by making covenants with his people to secure and guarantee the fulfillment of God's purposes, see Burger, "Story of God's Covenants," 274–75, 283; "Verder met het verbond," 124; Goldingay, *Israel's Gospel*, 181; *Israel's Faith*, 182–84; Leder, "Presence, Part 1," 180, 182; "Divine Presence, Part 2," 208, 211–18; "Divine Presence, Part 3," 686, 694–96; Noort, "Overlijden en overleven," 7–32; Stek, "'Covenant' Overload," 25, 37–41; *contra* Bartholomew, "Covenant and Creation," 23–26. For understanding the reason for making covenants as a rescue operation, see Burger, "'Theirs Are the Covenants,'" 14; Wright, *Paul and the Faithfulness of God*, 504.

bound to God (Ex. 19-24; Gen. 17), within the framework of a divine commitment to Abraham and his descendants (Gen. 15; cf. Gal. 3), which in itself is a particular outworking of his divine commitment to creatures in his presence."[24]

Wright describes the missional intent of God's covenants, speaking here of Israel: "As the people of YHWH they would have the historical task of bringing the knowledge of God to the nations, and bringing the nations to the means of atonement with God." He adds, "The Abrahamic task of being a means of blessing to the nations also puts them in the role of priests in the midst of the nations. Just as it was the role of the priests to bless the Israelites, so it would be the role of Israel as a whole ultimately to be a blessing to the nations."[25]

The eschatological orientation of the plot[26]

The plot of the drama of God's mission for his glory is oriented toward the future. We see this eschatological orientation primarily in the following five features.

First, the end of the narrative plot, as depicted in Revelation 21-22, shows us the ultimate fulfillment of the drama of God's mission for his glory, depicting a new creation where heaven and earth are united and, together with God's people, participate in the glory of God's perfect life.

This fulfillment of the plot is depicted in the imagery of a new creation as a new Jerusalem, a new temple, and a new Paradise that echoes the imagery of Genesis 1 and 2. Consequently, this eschatological depiction of the telos of the narrative plot functions as a template or lens

---

24. Leder, "Divine Presence, Part 3," 695-96.

25. Wright, *Mission of God*, 331; cf. Bauckham, *Bible and Mission*, 1-54; Booth, *Tabernacling Presence*, location 1181; Burger, "Story of God's Covenants," 298; Gentry and Wellum, *Kingdom through Covenant*, 653, 654-55; *God's Kingdom*, 245-46; Goheen, *Light to the Nations*, 23-48; *Introducing Christian Mission Today*, 40-48; Goheen and Wright, "Mission and Theological Interpretation"; Goheen and Mullins, *Symphony of Mission*, 13-30; Wielenga, *Verbond en Zending*, 190-224.

26. This study has a synchronic, not a diachronic approach to reading Scripture. About these two approaches, Williamson writes, "A diachronic approach looks at how the shape of the text may have developed through time, whereas a synchronic analysis looks at the shape of the text at a single point in time: namely, the final or canonical form of the text" (*Sealed with an Oath*, 85).

through which to read the whole story.[27] Horton is correct when he says that "eschatology should be a lens and not merely a locus."[28]

Second, the end of the narrative plot shows us Christ being glorified with the glory he had with the Father before all time and forever (John 17:5; Jude 25). The glorified Christ is the image of God for whom humanity was created (Col 1:15–16; 2 Cor 4:4, 6; Heb 1:3). As the image of God, Christ is also the last (*eschatos*) Adam, whose eschatological image redeemed humanity will one day bear (1 Cor 15:45). This eschatological Adam is the Son of God into whose image redeemed humanity is predestined to be conformed (Rom 8:29). This eschatological depiction of redeemed humanity in the glorified image of Christ serves as a lens to interpret the creation of humanity in God's image in Genesis 1.[29]

As Grenz writes, "When the nature of the human person is assumed to emerge solely from creation—i.e., apart from Christ—and when Christ is cast as, above all, the divine antidote to human sin, not only is anthropology cut loose from any Christological grounding, but Christology is also made dependent on anthropology. We might say that the first Adam thereby becomes the measuring rod for the Second."

Grenz goes on: "Furthermore, the linear approach [i.e., Christology reduced to merely the third topic of systematic theology] endangers the cosmic dimension of Christology. It suggests that Christ's connection to the wider creation story is mediated through the story of the fall of humankind rather than arising directly out of Jesus' vocation in the divine program."

He concludes: "The result is an anthropocentric, rather than a theocentric, doctrine of creation. Creation becomes the background or stage for the drama of the fall and subsequent restoration of humankind,

---

27. Alexander, *From Eden to the New Jerusalem*, 13–73, 131–32; Alexander, *City of God*, 18–28; Alexander, "The Story of Israel," 12; Beale, "Final Vision," 191–209; *Temple and the Church's Mission*, 66–80, 365–73; *New Testament Biblical Theology*, 15–24; "End Starts at the Beginning," 3–14; Beale and Kim, *God Dwells Among Us*, 15–16; Dumbrell, *End of the Beginning*, 1–78, 165–96; Lister, *Presence of God*, 63–69, 79–81.

28. Horton, *Covenant and Eschatology*, 5.

29. Behr, "Promise of the Image," 27; Boer, *Ember Still Glowing*, 160; Fairbairn, *Life in the Trinity*, 59–64; Grenz, "Jesus as the *Imago Dei*," 626; Holmes, "Image of God," 319; Hughes, "Christology of Hebrews," 20; Kline, "Creation in the Image," 261, 266; *Kingdom Prologue*, 92–93; Letham, *Union with Christ*, 13–14; Ridderbos, *Paul*, 73; Tanner, *Christ the Key*, 12–14; Vorster, *Created in the Image*, 4, 16; cf. Kilner, *Dignity and Destiny*, 60–69, 79–82.

rather than an area in which Christ is Lord and as Lord completes the human vocation to be the *imago Dei*."[30]

Vorster writes, "The Genesis version of the *imago Dei* offers a broad framework to understand the nature of humankind's relationship with God, but at the same time gives the concept an open meaning which makes further theological reflection possible. A theological anthropology should therefore not be limited to a protological understanding of the *imago Dei*. The Christological foundation that the New Testament ascribes to the concept is of crucial importance for the further understanding of the concept, specifically with regard to the destination of the human."[31]

Third, Hebrews 4:9 tells us that "there remains a Sabbath rest for the people of God." This future Sabbath rest is the eschatological goal of God's work of creation, the new creation in which heaven and earth are united and share with God's people in the glory of God's perfect life. As such, this goal serves as a lens to help us interpret why God rested from his work of creation on the seventh day (Gen 1–2) and why he instituted the Sabbath as a sign of the Mosaic covenant (Exod 16; 31:16; Neh 9:14).[32]

In this connection, Vos writes, "The Sabbath is an expression of the eschatological principle on which the life of humanity has been constructed. There is to be to the world-process a finale, as there was an overture, and these two belong inseparably together."[33] Westermann says, "What is peculiar to the holy day in the course of everyday happenings is that it points to the goal of the creature which God has created in his image. The world which has been laid on man is not his goal. His goal is the eternal rest which has been suggested by the rest of the seventh day."[34] Because God's goal is the eternal Sabbath, Moltmann refers to the Sabbath as that "which completes and crowns creation."[35]

Fourth, the life, death, and resurrection of Christ and the outpouring of the Spirit launched the penultimate fulfillment of God's creational

---

30. Grenz, "Jesus as the *Imago Dei*," 626.

31. Vorster, *Created in the Image*, 16.

32. Dumbrell, *Covenant and Creation*, 34–36; *Search for Order*, 22–23; Kline, *Kingdom Prologue*, 33–38; Horton, *Lord and Servant*, 79–80; *God of Promise*, 106; *Christian Faith*, 386, 403–4, 419–20, 441, 906; *Pilgrim Theology*, 122–23, 138, 145–46, 446, 452–58; Vos, *Biblical Theology*, 140–41; Westermann, *Creation*, 65.

33. Vos, *Biblical Theology*, 140.

34. Westermann, *Creation*, 65; cf. Dumbrell, *Covenant and Creation*, 35.

35. Moltmann, *God in Creation*, 6; cf. Van den Brink and Van der Kooi, *Christian Dogmatics*, 231.

purpose as an already, but not yet, fulfillment that is available to those who put on Jesus Christ through faith. This means that with Jesus' life, death, and resurrection and the outpouring of the Spirit, the future glory of God's eschatological new creation breaks forth into the present.[36]

Beale writes, "The NT transformation of the storyline of the OT that I propose is this: *Jesus' life, trials, death for sinners, and especially resurrection by the Spirit have launched the fulfilment of the eschatological already-not yet new-creational reign, bestowed by grace through faith and resulting in worldwide commission to the faithful to advance this new-creational reign and resulting in judgment for the unbelieving, unto the triune God's glory.*"[37]

Writing about the possibility that Israel could continue to be able to bring the blessing of Abraham to the nations during this already and not yet period ushered in by Jesus' resurrection, Jenson writes, "By Jesus' Resurrection occurring 'first,' a sort of *hole* opens *in* the event of the End, a space for something like what used to be history, for the church and its mission."[38]

Fifth, within this penultimate fulfillment of God's creational purpose, Christ's outpouring of the Holy Spirit plays a central role, as was predicted with the promise of the new covenant (Jer 31:33; Ezek 36:26–27). This is the same Spirit through whom Christ was conceived and who enabled him to faithfully fulfill his ministry on earth in the listening and thankful filial spirit of openness and responsiveness to his Father. The climax of this ministry is his outpouring of this same Spirit upon his church as the down payment (*arrabon*) of the incorruptible and immortal life that awaits in the Sabbath rest in the eschatological new creation. With

---

36. Beale, *Temple and the Church's Mission*, 25; *New Testament Biblical Theology*, 15–16, 19; Beale and Kim, *God Dwells Among Us*, 17–28, 135–40; cf. Alexander, *From Eden to the New Jerusalem*; Alexander, *City of God*; Horton, *Covenant and Eschatology*, 116.

37. Beale, *New Testament Biblical Theology*, 16, italics his.

38. Jenson, *Systematic Theology*, 1:85; Burger, *Being in Christ*, 526.

the outpouring of the Spirit, the future of the glorified or transfigured[39] eschatological new creation already breaks forth into the present.[40]

"As the consequence of Christ's Spirit conception and Spirit filling," Macchia writes, "his resurrection is an overflow of the Spirit that is poured out beyond Christ at Pentecost.... Christ was always meant to overflow so that he could take others into union with himself.... His entire journey, from his incarnation to his crucifixion and resurrection, creates the means by which he incorporates all flesh into his life in the Spirit, his life with the Father." He concludes, "Mediating a river of the Spirit for others on behalf of the Father reveals Christ's identity and mission."[41]

THE DRAMA OF GOD'S MISSION FOR HIS GLORY

Just as most lengthy dramas are divided into various acts, so too the theodrama of Scripture has various acts. "In the context of theater," Vanhoozer writes, "an act is a major division of a play that signals a change of

---

39. "Glorified" or "transfigured" can be synonymous with created life undergoing *theosis* or deification. The New Testament links "glory" and "image" (Rom 8:30; 1 Cor 11:7; 2 Cor 3:18; 4:4, 6; Heb 2:5–10). Mathews writes, "Peter likewise speaks of Christ as the valued Son who received 'honor and glory from God the Father' (2 Pet 1:17) at the mount of transfiguration, where the disciples witnessed the 'glory' of the kingdom to come (Matt 17:1–8). It is this 'glory' for which redeemed humanity in Christ is destined who himself is the 'glory' of God (John 1:14, 18; 17:4)" (*Genesis 1:1–11:26*, 171).

40. Billings, "John Calvin"; *Calvin, Participation, and the Gift*, 51–61, 96, 190, 193, 196; Canlis, "Calvin, Osiander and Participation"; *Calvin's Ladder*, 188–91, 236–38; Fairbairn, "Patristic Soteriology"; *Life in the Trinity*, 6–12, 33–35; Habets, "Reforming Theosis"; "Reformed *Theosis*?"; Horton, *Covenant and Salvation*, 267–69, 272, 284, 302, 306, 308; *Christian Faith*, 386; *Rediscovering the Holy Spirit*, 285–86; *Justification*, 1:49, 52, 208, 250, 364; 2:488–93; Letham, *Systematic Theology*, 769–88; *Union with Christ*, 91–102, 123–28; Macchia, *Jesus the Spirit Baptizer*, *passim*; Mosser, "Greatest Possible Blessing."
This eschatological orientation of the plot of the drama of God's mission for his glory implies an eschatological ontology in which "God is the eternal God [who] [c]oming from the eschaton, . . . is already present from the beginning" (Burger, "Quadriga without Platonism," 10). Burger's whole essay provides a helpful analysis and comparison of an eschatological ontology that "takes the dynamics of the history of salvation with its tensions, disappointments, hopes, surprises and all its unexpected newness" seriously with a version of a Christian-Platonist participatory ontology that ignores these dynamics because "reality is perceived as a cyclic movement from eternal unity to temporal plurality and back to eternal unity" or an "'ecstatic and self-gathering movement of being'" (Burger, "Quadriga without Platonism," 10). See also Huijgen, "Allegory within the Bounds," 82–84.

41. Macchia, *Jesus the Spirit Baptizer*, 27.

time and/or place and is susceptible of being further divided into various scenes. In the context of theology, however, it is better to think of each act as a vital ingredient in the historical outworking (i.e., economy) of the divine decree. As such, each act is 'according to the definite plan and foreknowledge of God' (Acts 2:23). What we need is a way of marking the historical progression of a single unified action."[42]

Elsewhere, Vanhoozer writes, "Correctly identifying the number of acts in the theodrama . . . helps us better to understand the unity and diversity of Scripture (i.e., one play with many acts); second, it helps disciples to understand better where they are in the story." He adds, "The most important thing is to do justice to the story line of Scripture. To omit something essential to the story is to risk compromising the logic of the gospel. We can call this first criterion 'canonical comprehensiveness.'"

On the other hand, he says, "for the sake of explanatory power, it is important to focus on essential developments only. The goal here is to find the simplest yet also most powerful outline, the story line that can account for the integrity of the whole plot in the least amount of moves. We can call this second criterion 'theodramatic loveliness,' lovely because it provides the most understanding in the briefest compass."[43]

I mentioned several ways authors have divided the narrative of Scripture and history into acts in the introduction. Particularly well known is N. T. Wright's suggestion that the theodrama of Scripture is divided into five acts: (1) Creation, (2) Fall, (3) Israel, (4) Jesus, and (5) Church.[44] As the church, we are familiar with the first four acts of the drama, as well as the beginning of the fifth act at Pentecost, but the church needs now to faithfully and creatively bring the fifth act to completion by immersing itself in those earlier acts and scenes and improve appropriately.

Sam Wells agrees that this model has tremendous potential, but he disagrees with Wright's version of the drama. Since the drama begins and ends with God, it should not end with the church but with the eschaton or end of the drama. Moreover, since Jesus is the goal to which creation pointed forward and the eschaton points back, he ought to be in the middle of the drama. Furthermore, making the fall the beginning of a new act implies that the fall is an act of God and not the result of

---

42. Vanhoozer, *Remythologizing Theology*, 97.

43. Vanhoozer, *Faith Speaking Understanding*, 96. For an overview of the various proposals that have been offered, see *Faith Speaking Understanding*, 95–98.

44. Wright, "How Can the Bible Be Authoritative?," 7–32; *New Testament and the People of God*, 140–43.

humanity's misuse of the freedom God created them with. Thus, the fall should be part of Act One, dealing with creation. Wells, then, amends Wright's five-act play as follows: (1) Creation, (2) Israel, (3) Jesus, (4) Church, and (5) Eschaton.

Following Wells, I will now sketch the unfolding of the plot of the theodrama in these five acts, incorporating a reframed understanding of divine-human covenants. The first act is creation: the stage of the theodrama. The second act is the election of Israel. The third is the sending of God's Son. The fourth is the outpouring of the Holy Spirit on the church. And the fifth is the return of Christ.

In sketching the unfolding of this plot, I will read the narrative of Scripture backwards and forwards, allowing the Old Testament to shed light of the New and the New to shed light on the Old.[45] While the final resolution of the plot is known from the beginning, this method of reconstructing the plot nevertheless respects the dramatic unfolding of the plot with its tensions and questions.

Act one: the drama of creation as the stage of the theodrama

The first act of the drama of God's mission for his glory is the creation of the stage for the theodrama, which includes both heaven and earth.[46] At the same time, while creation can be called the stage of the theodrama— it is the place where the drama occurs—it also participates in the theodrama (e.g., Pss 19, 98, 148; Rom 8:22–25).[47]

Scene one portrays the creation of the visible stage of the theodrama, the world as a holy temple. Scene two shows the creation of humanity in the image of God, participating in his life through the listening and thankful filial spirit of the openness and responsiveness of faith. Scene three presents the antagonist introducing sin and death onto the stage of the theodrama. Scene four reveals God's prediction that humanity will solve the problem that humanity created. Scene five shows us God securing and guaranteeing his commitment to his mission for his glory with his covenants with Noah and with creation.

---

45. Cf. Hays, *Echoes of Scripture*, 26–33; "Reading Scripture," 216–38; see also the discussion of biblical interpretation in chapter 1.
46. Balthasar, *Theo-Drama*, 2:173–88.
47. Cf. Vander Lugt, *Living Theodrama*, 189–91.

Scene one: the creation of the world as a holy temple

The persons of the Trinity make their intratrinitarian mutual glorification present in time by creating the world as a holy temple in which they act out and bear witness to the life of heaven on earth, making the world a place where heaven and earth meet.[48] On earth as in heaven! That is God's goal.

That the world is a cosmic holy temple is implied by the fact that the end of the narrative plot, as depicted in Revelation 21–22, portrays God's new creation as a temple (Rev 21:16; cf. 21:10–27). On the one hand, John says there will be no temple on the new earth (Rev 21:22). On the other, he describes the New Jerusalem with temple imagery. Thus, he appears to assimilate the temple and the city, implying that "God's presence does not dwell in one place like the temple of old, but fills the whole of the new creation."[49]

Furthermore, Scripture uses temple imagery to describe creation (e.g., Pss 78:69; 104:1–2; Isa 66:1), and there are parallels between features of the Garden of Eden and those of the Tabernacle and Temple.[50]

---

48. For the expression "heaven and earth meeting," see Wright, *Day the Revolution Began*, 76, 340; see also Vanhoozer, "At Play," 75.

49. Lister, *Presence of God*, 74.

50. Alexander, *From Eden to the New Jerusalem*, 37–42; Beale, "Final Vision," 191–209; *Temple and the Church's Mission*, 31–38, 66–76; *New Testament Biblical Theology*, 617–48; Gentry and Wellum, *Kingdom through Covenant*, 246–53; Gladd, *From Adam and Israel*, 6–7; Hamilton, *God's Glory*, 73–74; Horton, *Christian Faith*, 401; Kline, *Images of the Spirit*, 35–42; *Kingdom Prologue*, 47–49; Middleton, *Liberating Image*, 81–88; Smith, *Priestly Vision*, 14–17, 27–32, 36–37; van Bekkum, *Verdreven uit de hof*, 27–28; Walton, *Lost World of Genesis One*, 78–86; Wenham, "Sanctuary Symbolism," 399–404; Wright, *The Great Story*, 113–15.

For ancient Near Eastern parallels, see Beale, "Final Vision," 195–97; *Temple and the Church's Mission*, 50–60, 76–80; Walton, *Lost World of Genesis One*, 78–92. Because of these parallels, it has been suggested that, while the world is a cosmic temple, Eden could be compared to the holy of holies in the temple (Beale, *Temple and the Church's Mission*, 74; *New Testament Biblical Theology*, 620). Block has challenged the view that Eden is a cosmic temple. He has a fundamental hermeneutical difficulty with reading Genesis 1–3 as "temple-building texts": "The question is, should we read Gen 1–3 in the light of the later texts, or should we read later texts in the light of these? . . . The fact that Israel's sanctuaries were Edenic does not make Eden into a sacred shrine. At best this is a nonreciprocating equation" ("Eden," 21). However, Garvey writes, "It is utterly plausible that Moses was simultaneously made aware both of a cosmic pattern of creation, and of an architectural plan that was to imitate it in the form of the tabernacle. Or else it is possible that later, his inspired reflection on the divinely appointed structure of the tabernacle led him to the understanding of the cosmos that inspired Genesis 1. . . . So whichever insight came first, it is likely to be the same prophetic mind that gave us both the pattern of the tabernacle, and the temple imagery of the creation narrative."

As the author of the theodrama, the Father speaks the creation of the world into existence through Christ[51] as the eternal Word, who is life itself, in whom and for whom all things were created and in whom all things hold together (John 1:3-5; 5:26; Col 1:16-17).[52] "Not only are believers, therefore, in Christ," writes Van Eck. "All of creation is 'in Him.'"[53] "Creation is Christ-shaped," Macleod writes. "The space-time curve is Christ-shaped."[54]

Letham puts it this way: "Creation was made *in Christ*. In turn, the cosmos has a purpose. It is held together by the Son. He sustains it at every moment and directs it toward the end he intends for it. That end is himself. All things were created and are sustained *for Christ*. The reason the universe exists is for the glory of Christ, the Son of God. The goal toward which it is heading is conformity to him."[55]

Not only does the Father create the world in and through and for Christ. He forms and fills his formless and empty creation into "a hospitable home for the plant world, animal kingdom, and, as the crown of creation, the human race" by the Holy Spirit (Gen 1:2; Ps 104:30).[56] This hospitable home is beautiful and corresponds to God's intentions for it (Gen 1:31).[57]

Regarding the beauty of creation, Brueggemann writes, "In Gen 1:31, at the conclusion of the sixth day of creation, Yahweh exclaimed, 'It

---

He adds, "Each therefore informs the other, making it foolish to ask if the tabernacle is a representation of the cosmos, or that the description of the cosmos is derived from the tabernacle. As described in the *Torah*, they are both simply macrocosmic and microcosmic representations of God's relationship to the world" (*Generations of Heaven and Earth*, loc. 5105-17; see also Braun, *God's Praise and God's Presence*, 186-87).

51. Referring to the eternal Word as Christ before he was Christ has scriptural warrant (Phil 2:5-6). Sanders writes, "Paul may be using the kind of shorthand we use when we say, 'The sixteenth president of the United States was born in this cabin'" (*Deep Things of God*, 91).

52. Because Paul uses both *en* and *dia* in Col 1:16, it is better to translate *en* as "in" and not "through." Otherwise, there is no difference (Van Eck, *Kolossenzen en Filemon*, 83).

53. Van Eck, *Kolossenzen en Filemon*, 83.

54. Macleod, *Faith to Live By*, 93.

55. Letham, *Union with Christ*, 13.

56. Allison and Köstenberger, *Holy Spirit*, 297. For a comparison of the Genesis account of creation with other accounts, see Hamilton, *God's Glory*, 70-72. Hamilton writes, "Contrasting what Genesis says with other accounts of the origin of all things will help us see more clearly how Genesis 1 and 2 proclaim the glory of God" (*God's Glory*, 70).

57. Allison and Köstenberger, *Holy Spirit*, 300-301.

was very good.' Most probably this is an aesthetic judgment and response to a brilliant act of creation. The sense of beauty, or loveliness evokes on Yahweh's part a doxological response to the created order, a sense of satisfaction on the part of the artist, a glad acknowledgment of success. Here and in some other places a glad affirmation of creation is moved more by awe and delight than by ethical insistence or command. Thus Prov 8:30–31, in speaking of creation, culminates in a statement of 'delight' and 'rejoicing.'"[58]

Because the Father is present in this hospitable home in Christ (Heb 1:3) and through the Holy Spirit (Ps 104:30), as they act out and bear witness to their trinitarian life of mutual glorification, creation has a "natural" relationship with God. While distinct from God, creation is inherently compatible with God. "This compatibility," Letham writes, "is demonstrably at the heart of God's intentions for his creation *and for man himself.*"[59] Elsewhere, he says, "Since the Son found it possible to live as man, we must conclude that God made humanity in such a manner as to be capable of union with him in Christ."[60]

From the beginning, the world was created to live in God's loving presence and to participate in his life by living and moving and having its being in God (Acts 17:28). Participating in the life of God in Christ by the Spirit makes the world a place for communion in the life of God.[61] As such, created reality is able to participate in God's trinitarian act of mutual glorification.

After six days of creation, God rested from his work of creating on the seventh day because he had reached the goal for which he had created. He had arrived at the Sabbath rest.[62] This Sabbath rest was meant to last forever, as is evident from the fact that the narrator does not mention the evening and the morning of this day as he had with the other six days.[63] However, the glory of this Sabbath rest at creation would be elevated in the life of the new creation, for in the new creation there will

---

58. Brueggemann, *Theology of the Old Testament*, 339; cf. Allison and Köstenberger, *Holy Spirit*, 300.

59. Letham, *Union with Christ*, 16.

60. Letham, *Systematic Theology*, 475.

61. Canlis, *Calvin's Ladder*, 53–61, 70–74.

62. Dumbrell, *Covenant and Creation*, 34–36; *Search for Order*, 22–23; Letham, *Union with Christ*, 10; Westermann, *Creation*, 64–65. For ancient Near-Eastern parallels to divine rest after creating a temple, see Beale, *Temple and the Church's Mission*, 60–66; Walton, *Lost World of Genesis One*, 72–77.

63. Dumbrell, *Covenant and Creation*, 22; Letham, *Union with Christ*, 10.

be no sun, moon, or stars because it will bask directly in the light of the glory of God and the Lord Jesus Christ (Rev 21:23; 22:5).[64]

In this regard, Horton rightfully says, "Creation was the stage—the 'beautiful theater'—for God's drama, not an end in itself. Life in the garden was not intended to simply go on in perpetuity but was merely the point of departure for the great march of creation behind God's vice-regent into the everlasting life of God's own Sabbath-rest."[65]

Scene two: the creation of humanity in the image of God

Having made their intratrinitarian mutual glorification present in time by creating a world as a holy temple in which they would act out and bear witness to the life of heaven on earth, so that the world is a place where heaven and earth meet and a place for communion in the life of God, the persons of the Trinity now create humanity in their image and after their likeness (Gen 1:26).

Since the glorified Christ is the image of God for whom humanity was created (Col 1:15–16; 2 Cor 4:4; Heb 1:3) and since the Son is characterized by a listening and thankful filial spirit, open and responsive to the Father, creating humanity in his image and after his likeness[66] would entail creating them to be partakers of the divine nature by participating in the Son's status of sonship and his communion of love with the Father through the Spirit.

This is confirmed by the fact that "in" (*be*) and "according to" (*ke*) refer to a model in which humanity is created. Accordingly, being created

---

64. While the glory of the Sabbath rest of creation will be transfigured and elevated in the eternal Sabbath rest, this does not mean that the precise nature of this transfigured and elevated Sabbath rest was *determined* by the beginning. Thus, God's love gives more than we could ever predict.

65. Horton, *Christian Faith*, 386. Letham writes, "At the end comes the unfinished seventh day, when God enters his rest, which he made to share with man, his partner, whom he made in his own image. There is an implicit invitation for us to follow" (*Union with Christ*, 10). Van Bekkum suggests that one of the ways we can do this is that, when we rest from our weekly work, we should focus our attention on God's creation and celebrate it with him as he did when he rested from his work (*Verdreven uit de hof*, 22–23, 59).

66. Not only are the terms "image" (*tselem*) and "likeness" (*demuth*) a form of Hebrew parallelism (Smail, "In the Image," 25); the terms are also more or less synonymous and interchangeable (Berkhof, *Systematic Theology*, 203; Fairbairn, *Life in the Trinity*, 60; Horton, *Christian Faith*, 391; Kilner, *Dignity and Destiny*, 124–33).

in God's image entails being created "according to" the model of God's image.⁶⁷

Letham writes, "The text of Genesis states that the man and his wife were created *in* the image of God. The image of God itself is identified for us in the NT. Paul points out that it is Christ who *is* the image of God (2 Cor 4:4). . . . Christ as the second Adam *is* the image of God. Adam was created *in* Christ."⁶⁸ This runs parallel to the world being created *in* Christ. If the world being created in Christ implies that the world is Christ-shaped, then Adam and Eve, created in the image of Christ, are also Christ-shaped.

Similarly, Smail says, "We can say that the doctrine of the *imago Dei* has both a protological and an eschatological dimension. It describes the basic constitution, and indeed the ontology of our humanity, as well as its ultimate destiny. If Adam is made in the image of God, so is Christ, the *eschatos Adam*, the ultimate human being, who is the possibility, the actuality and the promise of a human life that images the life of God."⁶⁹

Since, as the image of the Father, Christ represented the Father and bore witness to his glorious presence on earth so that he was a person where heaven and earth met (John 14:9–10; 12:28; 13:31–32; 17:1, 4), it follows that, participating in the Son's status and communion of love with the Father through the Spirit, humanity is designed to represent God and bear witness to his glorious presence so that the Father becomes visible on earth as heaven and earth meet in humanity.⁷⁰ As such, humanity is

---

67. Brown, Driver, Briggs, *Hebrew and English Lexicon*, 90; Koehler and Baumgartner, *Hebrew and Aramaic Lexicon*, 104; Kilner, *Dignity and Destiny*, 90. Regarding being created in the image of God entailing being created according to the image of God as a model or standard, Kilner writes, "This meaning is confirmed by the corresponding use of *kata* (normally 'according to') in the New Testament. In fact, the Greek Old Testament, the Septuagint, most often uses *kata* to translate both *be* and *ke*; the Latin Vulgate always uses *ad* (toward) for both" (*Dignity and Destiny*, 91).

68. Letham, *Union with Christ*, 14.

69. Smail, "In the Image," 22–23.

70. For ancient Near Eastern background of kings embodying the presence of a god, see Beale, *New Testament Biblical Theology*, 31; Middleton, *Liberating Image*, 121. When Gen 1 considers humanity as such to be created in the image of God to represent him by embodying his presence, this is "a genuine democratization of ancient Near Eastern royal ideology" (Middleton, *Liberating Image*, 121). For ancient Near East background of images representing rulers who are physically absent and establishing their presence and rule, see Beale, *New Testament Biblical Theology*, 31; Clines, "Image of God," 87–88; Kilner, *Dignity and Destiny*, 55–58; Middleton, *Liberating Image*, 104–8.

PARTICIPATION IN THE LIFE OF GOD

designed to become a participant in the drama of God's mission for his glory.[71]

God energizes humanity to carry out this mission by breathing into Adam the breath of life so that he becomes a living being (Gen 2:7; cf. Job 33:4). "What is not being said is that the infusion of breath into life into Adam is an impartation of the Holy Spirit," Allison and Köstenberger say, but they add, "Though the two are distinct, they are not unconnected, in that the Holy Spirit as 'the Lord and Giver of life,' gives the spark of life to the previously formed 'dust of the ground,' and Adam becomes a living creature."[72]

Created in the image of God and energized by the same Spirit through whom he lives with Christ in the Father, Adam is given the mission of acting out or performing his ontological identity as the image and son of God. As Christ was the model according to whose image humanity was created, so Christ is the model for humanity's mission (Heb 2:9). As the image of the Father, Christ's mission involves "carrying out the Father's will throughout creation and [the] sustaining of the universe (See Jn 1:1–5; Col 1:15–20; Heb 1:1–3)."[73]

What this looks like we see when the Son of God becomes incarnate. As the incarnate Son of God, Christ loves creation (John 3:16), has compassion on it (Matt 9:36; 14:14; 15:32; 20:34; Mark 6:34), and restores

---

71. For being created in the image of God as an ontological status and destiny, see Kilner, *Dignity and Destiny*, passim. For having been created in the image of God as an ontological reality, see Strachan, *Reenchanting Humanity*, 29–31. Regarding the connection between image of God and sonship, Mathews writes, "Genesis 5:1–3 clearly echoes 1:26–28 and demonstrates that the 'likeness' (dĕmût) of God that stamped Adam was perpetuated by his offspring. Adam fathered a 'son' in his own 'likeness' and 'image' (5:3), which showed that the Adamic family continued the *imago Dei* and also the divine blessing first received by Adam (5:3–31)" (*Genesis 1:1–11:26*, 169). Mathews adds, "The motif of sonship is also taken up in Luke's Gospel, where he appeals to Genesis 5 in reciting Jesus' genealogy and rightly infers that Adam is 'the son of God'" (3:38) (*Genesis 1:1–11:26*, 169; see also Crouch, "Genesis 1:26–27," 1–15; Dempster, *Dominion and Dynasty*, 58; Kline, *Kingdom Prologue*, 45–46; Van Genderen and Velema, *Reformed Dogmatics*, 321–23). For an overview and refutation of understanding the image of God as the attributes of reason, righteousness, or relationality, and the function of rulership, as well as how these attributes and function flow from being created in the image of God, see Kilner, *Dignity and Destiny*, 177–230. For examples of importing theological and cultural ideas into one's interpretation of being created into the image of God, see Kilner, *Dignity and Destiny*, 43–51.

72. Allison and Köstenberger, *Holy Spirit*, 334–35. Macchia writes, "Adam and Eve were created to be the dwelling place of God in the Spirit (implicitly) in the image of the Word by which all things were created (Gen. 2:7)" (*Jesus the Spirit Baptizer*, 189).

73. Fairbairn, *Life in the Trinity*, 61.

and heals it. Moreover, as the mediator of creation, he cares for the sparrows (Matt 10:29), feeds the birds of the air (Matt 12:24), and clothes the flowers and grass of the field (Matt 6:28–30). Furthermore, after having fed the five thousand, he commands the leftovers to be gathered up so that nothing would be wasted (John 6:12).[74]

When God creates humanity in Christ's image, he intends them to share Christ's filial spirit as they participate in the mission for his glory. Genesis describes this mission: "Then God said, 'Let us make mankind in our image, in our likeness, *so that* they may rule over the fish in the sea and the birds in the sky, over the livestock and all the wild animals, and over all the creatures that move along the ground'" (Gen 1:26 NIV, emphasis mine).[75]

It goes on: "God blessed them and said to them, 'Be fruitful and increase in number; fill the earth and subdue it. Rule over the fish in the sea and the birds in the sky and over every living creature that moves on the ground'" (Gen 1:28). "Here again," Van Bekkum writes, "the powerful activity of God's speaking comes first: God blesses and in the uttering of that blessing he effects their being fruitful and becoming numerous."[76]

In the next chapter, the narrator further describes this mission: "The Lord God took the man and put him in the Garden of Eden to work it and take care of it" (Gen 2:15). Beale writes, "Adam's commission to 'cultivate' (with connotations of 'serving') and 'guard' in Gen. 2:15 . . . is probably part of the commission given in 1:26–28."[77]

Since "ruling" (*radah*) has royal overtones and "to work" (*abad*) and "take care" (*shamar*) have priestly overtones,[78] God intends humanity

---

74. Cf. Moo and Moo, *Creation Care*, 120–22.

75. Kilner writes, "Some translations use 'and' to render the conjunction between the statements about image and rule. But this Hebrew conjunction (*we*), connecting a cohortative verb like 'let us make' with a jussive verb, typically expresses a more purposeful 'so that'—here, 'so that they may rule'" (*Dignity and Destiny*, 207; see also Middleton, *Liberating Image*, 53). Interestingly, the Dutch *Nieuwe Vertaling* also translates with "so that" (*opdat*) (Middleton, *Liberating Image*, 53).

76. Van Bekkum, *Verdreven uit de hof*, 22.

77. Beale, *New Testament Biblical Theology*, 32.

78. Wenham writes, "Here is added that man's job in the garden is 'to till it and guard it.' עבד 'to serve, till' is a very common verb and is often used of cultivating the soil (2:5; 3:23; 4:2, 12, etc.). The word is commonly used in a religious sense of serving God (e.g., Deut 4:19), and in priestly texts, especially of the tabernacle duties of the Levites (Num 3:7–8; 4:23–24, 26, etc.)." He adds, "Similarly, שמר 'to guard, to keep' has the simple profane sense of 'guard' (4:9; 30:31), but it is even more commonly used in legal texts of observing religious commands and duties (17:9; Lev 18:5) and particularly of the

to participate in the drama as kings and priests, participating in, performing, and bearing witness to Christ's kingly rule and priestly care for creation through "fill[ing] up the earth, tak[ing] possession of it, and tak[ing] control of it."[79]

As a king, Adam would be involved in "the work of forming culture or developing civilization" as a good steward of creation.[80] As a priest, he would be one who "takes the world in his hands to refer [i.e., consecrate] it to God and who, in return, brings God's blessing to what he refers [i.e., consecrates] to God. Through this act, creation is brought into communion with God himself."[81] Adam's task, then, is "to extend the geographical boundaries of the garden till Eden covers the whole earth."[82]

If Adam and Eve would participate in this drama faithfully—with the filial spirit that characterizes Christ—they would enter into the fullness of God's eternal Sabbath rest and live forever, as the tree of life in the center of the Garden of Eden symbolized (Gen 2:9). Because Adam is the representative head of humanity (Rom 5:12-21; 1 Cor 15:21-22, 45-49), so would his posterity.

But if they would not participate in this drama with that faithful and filial spirit, they would lose what they already enjoyed, as the sanction attached to the command not to eat from the tree of the knowledge of good and evil indicates (Gen 2:16-17),[83] and so would their posterity.

Whereas living in communion with God and participating in his life in a lush and abundant Garden was meant to draw Adam and Eve into an ever-deeper communion with God through a posture of thankfulness

---

Levitical responsibility for guarding the tabernacle from intruders (Num 1:53; 3:7-8)" (*Genesis 1-15*, 67; cf. Alexander, *City of God*, 22-23, 26; Beale, *Temple and the Church's Mission*, 66-70; *New Testament Biblical Theology*, 32-33; Leder, "Divine Presence, Part 2," 210-11).

79. Barr, "Man and Nature," 22; Kilner, *Dignity and Destiny*, 208-9. "Subdue" (*kabash*) also has priestly overtones (Smith, *Priestly Vision*, 101-2). About "subdue" (*kabash*), Barr writes, "I doubt whether more is intended here than the basic needs of settlement and agriculture . . . Basically what is intended is tilling; it corresponds with the 'working' or 'tilling' of the ground in the J story, Genesis ii.5, 15" ("Man and Nature," 22).

80. Middleton, *Liberating Image*, 89.

81. Zizioulas, "Proprietors or Priests of Creation,"4; cf. Burger, *Hoop voor een zuchtende schepping*, 20-21.

82. Beale, *Temple and the Church's Mission*, 81-82; Burger, *Hoop voor een zuchtende schepping*, 21; Hamilton, *God's Glory*, 73; Kline, *Kingdom Prologue*, 68-70; Moo and Moo, *Creation Care*, 77.

83. McComiskey, *Covenants of Promise*, 217; Burger, "Story of God's Covenants," 278; "'Theirs Are the Covenants,'" 9.

to God, the prohibition on eating from the tree of the knowledge of good and evil was meant to draw them into this communion through a posture of trustfully listening to God.[84]

Scene three: the antagonist introduces sin and death into the drama

Using a serpent, Satan (Rev 12:9), the antagonist, introduces sin and death onto the stage of God's mission for his glory. Through the serpent, he attacks Adam and Eve's thankful and trustful listening posture with the suggestion that God has withheld something from them and that what God has said to them cannot be trusted (Gen 3:1–5).[85] They allow themselves to be driven by their own agenda and standards, independent of God and unreceptive to his voice. In doing so, they become self-enclosed or curved in on themselves.[86]

Instead of enhancing their lives, this curved-in way of living diminishes their lives because they no longer live in communion with God in Christ through the Holy Spirit and no longer bear witness to God's intratrinitarian mutual glorification as they have been designed to do. Instead, they bear witness to just how estranged and destabilized their lives have become as a result of not participating in the life of God as they were created to.

---

84. Gerrish, "Mirror of God's Goodness," 218; Canlis, *Calvin's Ladder*, 84. Van Bekkum indicates something similar when he writes, "By forbidding humanity to eat from this tree, God does not so much put a brake on the development of knowledge and skill, but prioritizes trust in Him" (*Verdreven uit de hof*, 27).

85. Van Bekkum writes, "The cosmic battle between good and evil is first and foremost a battle for humanity and its devotion to God" (*Verdreven uit de hof*, 33–34). For the interpretation of "you will be like God knowing good and evil" as wisdom apart from God or moral autonomy, see Dumbrell, *Search for Order*, 27; Kidner, *Genesis*, 63; Mathews, *Genesis 1:1–11:26*, 206; Sailhamer, *Pentateuch as Narrative*, 104; van Bekkum, *Verdreven uit de hof*, 31; Waltke, *Old Testament Theology*, 258; Wenham, *Genesis 1–15*, 63–64; Williamson, *Sealed with an Oath*, 50). Beale writes, "Adam did not guard the Garden but allowed entrance to a foul snake that brought sin, chaos and disorder into the sanctuary and into Adam and Eve's lives. He allowed the Serpent to 'rule over' him rather than 'ruling over' it and casting it out of the Garden" (*Temple and the Church's Mission*, 87; cf. Hamilton, *God's Glory*, 75; Horton, *Christian Faith*, 410; Waltke, *Old Testament Theology*, 259).

86. For understanding sin as being curved in on oneself or *homo incurvatus in se*, see Luther, *Lectures on Romans*, 245, 291, 313, 345–46, 513; Burger, "Theologische hermeneutiek," 38; O'Donovan, *Finding and Seeking*, 14–23; Balthasar, *Theo-Drama*, 4:165; cf. 4:137–201; see also Jenson, *Gravity of Sin*.

They are ashamed of themselves and of being in each other's presence (Gen 3:7). They are ashamed to be in God's presence (Gen 3:8). They are afraid to tell the whole truth when God questions them (Gen 3:10, 12). Instead of lovingly and uninhibitedly living for the other—for God, each other, and creation—they selfishly and fearfully live for themselves.[87]

When God comes in judgment, their self-enclosed, destabilized existence becomes even more weakened. They no longer are allowed to live in God's presence in the Garden of Eden, but are condemned to live outside (Gen 3:23–24). Moreover, God pronounces a curse on their relationship with creation (Gen 3:17–19).[88] Childbearing will become hard work and painful for women (Gen 3:16a). Wives will desire to control and dominate their husbands. However, rather than being controlled and dominated, husbands will resist this desire by ruling over their wives (Gen 3:16b).[89] Working the land will become hard work and painful for men (Gen 3:17–19).[90]

Furthermore, they are no longer allowed to eat from the tree of life (Gen 3:22). Whereas before their fall into sin death was a possibility,[91] now it is inevitable because of God's judgment (Gen 3:19). As a result of their sin, God subjects creation to futility so that it does not function as it was designed to but is instead in bondage to decay (Rom 8:20–21).[92]

---

87. Burger, *Hoop voor een zuchtende schepping*, 23.

88. Burger, *Hoop voor een zuchtende schepping*, 15, 23–24; Moo and Moo, *Creation Care*, 103.

89. Regarding "desire" and "rule," Mathews points to "the explanation suggested by Gen 4:7b, where 'desire' and 'rule' [*māšal*] are found again in tandem: 'It desires to have you, but you must master [*māšal*] it.' In chap. 4 'sin' is like an animal that when stirred up will assault Cain; it 'desires' to overcome Cain, but the challenge God puts to Cain is to exercise 'rule' or 'mastery' over that unruly desire." He concludes, "If we are to take the lexical and structural similarities as intentional, we must read the verses in concert. This recommends that 3:16b also describes a struggle for mastery between the sexes" (*Genesis 1:1–11:26*, 251).

90. Mathews, *Genesis 1:1–11:26*, 249.

91. Burger, *Hoop voor een zuchtende schepping*, 23; van Bekkum, *Verdreven uit de hof*, 30.

92. Dunn, *Romans 1–8*, 470; Van Bruggen, *Romeinen*, 122. Dunn writes, "God subjected all things to Adam, and that included subjecting creation to fallen Adam, to share in his fallenness" (*Romans 1–8*, 471).

Consequently, creation mourns (e.g., Hos 4:3; Jer 4:28; 12:4, 11; Isa 24:4)[93] and groans (Rom 8:22–23).[94]

Because Christ is the model according to whose image humanity is created, with their fall into sin Adam and Eve did not lose their status of being in the image of God nor was the model of this image damaged.[95] Rather, their humanity is damaged in the sense that it is now curved in on itself. Because Adam is the representative head of the human race, this has consequences for his posterity. Due to Adam's fall into sin, every human being is conceived and born in sin. Every human being by nature is self-enclosed and curved in on himself with a natural tendency to unthankfulness and an unresponsive posture toward God. This in turn has harmful consequences for humanity's mission of performing and bearing witness to Christ's kingly and priestly care for creation. As Burger says, "Where our task as human beings was to govern, sanctify and bless the rest of creation in the name of God, people and the rest of creation are now a mutual threat to each other."[96]

Scene four: God predicts that humanity will deal with the problem it created

When God manifested or performed his glory in his judgment on Adam and Eve because of their fall into sin, he also judged the serpent and Satan (Rev 12:9). First, God curses the serpent that Satan used to introduce sin and death. While all animals would experience the curse of humanity's fall into sin, the serpent would experience this curse the most because God cursed it "above all livestock and all animals" (Gen 3:14). Because "eating the dust" symbolizes total defeat (Isa 25:12; 65:25; Mic 7:17) as well as humiliation (Pss 44:25; 72:9), its crawling on its belly and eating dust will be a perpetual reminder of its—and Satan's—humiliation and ultimate defeat.[97]

---

93. Moo and Moo, *Creation Care*, 103–7.

94. Moo and Moo, *Creation Care*, 107–10; see also Burger, *Hoop voor een zuchtende schepping*, passim.

95. For an overview and refutation of those who assert that the image of God is completely lost, virtually lost, partly lost, or appears to be lost, see Kilner, *Dignity and Destiny*, 159–76.

96. Burger, *Hoop voor een zuchtende schepping*, 24.

97. Sailhamer, *Pentateuch as Narrative*, 106–7; Waltke, *Genesis*, 93. Sailhamer writes, "This curse does not necessarily suggest that the snake had previously walked with feet

This ultimate defeat is further spelled out when God declares, "I will put enmity between you and the woman, and between your offspring and her offspring; he shall bruise your head, and you shall bruise his heel" (Gen 3:15). With this declaration, God rescues the drama of the mission for his glory by "break[ing] up the unholy alliance between Satan and the woman. Instead of Satan and humanity being pitted against God, God says he will draw the battle lines differently."[98]

Moreover, God predicts that humanity will deal with the problem humanity created.[99] In doing so, God gives humanity "literally a seed of hope."[100] However, the drama will entail a lifelong conflict or warfare between Satan and his seed—those who bear witness to him and his way (John 8:44; 1 John 3:8, 12)—on the one hand, and the woman and her seed—those who bear witness to Christ and his ways (Rev 12:17; 14:12; cf. Rom 4:13, 16–18; Gal 3:8)—on the other.

Thus, there will be a history-long struggle between good and evil.[101] But the promise is that through this conflict God's drama will become a redemptive drama in which God redeems creation and humanity from Satan, as the god of this world (Matt 4:8, 9; John 12:31; 14:30; 16:11; 2 Cor 4:4; Eph 2:2; 6:12; 1 John 5:19), and restores them to their role in his drama and into his loving presence (Isa 65:17; Rev 21–22). As Leder says, "The entire biblical narrative, then, develops the problem of humanity's refusal of divine instruction and exile from the presence of God and emplots a sequence of events, complications, and conflicts that bring about life in God's presence again."[102]

This redemption and restoration will be accomplished by humanity crushing Satan's head with his heel and receiving damage to his own heel

---

and legs as the other land animals" (*Pentateuch as Narrative*, 106).

98. Greidanus, *Preaching Christ from Genesis*, 83–84. Even though there is a crisis here and God comes to the rescue of the drama, it does not entail the making of a covenant.

99. This implies that God is committing himself to his creational purpose.

100. Dempster, *Dominion and Dynasty*, 68. This has rightly been called the *protevangelium*, i.e., the first mention of the Father's good news of salvation. For an innerbiblical interpretation of Gen 3:15, see Hamilton, "Skull Crushing Seed," 3–34. For an exploration of the connection between Gen 3:15 and Johannine theology, see Köstenberger, "Cosmic Drama," 264–84. For serpents and dragons being symbols of spiritual opposition and supernatural forces, see Williamson, "Snakes and Dragons," 332–52.

101. Ross, *Creation and Blessing*, 145.

102. Leder, *Waiting for the Land*, 25.

in the process. However, the question is whether humanity will succeed in crushing Satan's head.[103]

Scene five: God promises to preserve humanity and creation

God declared that the drama of his mission for his glory would entail a history-long conflict or warfare between Satan and his seed and the woman and her seed and we see this struggle coming to a head in the days of Noah in the maturing of sin.

In Noah's days, "the Lord saw how great the wickedness of the human race had become on the earth, and that every inclination of the thoughts of the human heart was only evil all the time." As a result, "the Lord regretted that he had made human beings on the earth, and his heart was deeply troubled."

Consequently, he decided that he would manifest his glory by coming in wrath[104] to administer his judgment and "wipe from the face of the earth the human race [he had] created—and with them the animals, the birds and the creatures that move along the ground" (Gen 6:5–7).[105]

Because "Noah found favor in the eyes of the Lord" (Gen 6:5–8), God communicates to him his decision to destroy all of life on the earth. At the same time, he tells him that he is going to establish his covenant with him (Gen 6:18).[106]

---

103. I am aware that crushing Satan's head will ultimately be accomplished by the seed of the woman, that is, by Christ striking a mortal blow to Satan's head. Moreover, this victory will be attained at the cost of his own life, for Satan will strike a mortal blow to Christ's heel. Thus, this redemption and restoration will be accomplished through Christ's death on the cross (John 19:30; Matt 27:51; Greidanus, *Preaching Christ from Genesis*, 84) and his return in glory (Heb 2:14; Rom 16:20; Williamson, *Sealed with an Oath*, 51). However, because all that we know at this time in Genesis is that humanity will crush Satan's head with his heel and have its heel damaged in the process, I ask whether humanity—the woman's seed—will succeed in crushing Satan's head. This has the benefit of keeping the dramatic tension in the narrative.

104. The reality of God's wrath in judgment has been described as his offended holy love (Vriezen, *Outline of Old Testament Theology*, 306; Peels, *Wij is als gij?*, 110).

105. Leder writes, "Adam and Eve's descendants now relate to God as defiled and defiling priests on the earthly plane of the heaven-and-earth-sanctuary.... Humanity's continuing and increasing defilement of God's presence is the narrative occasion for the flood..." ("Divine Presence, Part 2," 211).

106. There is no need to understand this covenant as a confirmation of a covenant God supposedly made at creation because "establish" (*heqim*) not only refers to the confirmation of a covenant (Lev 26:9; Deut 8:18), but also to the initiation of a covenant (Exod 6:4; Kwakkel, "Verplichting of relatie," 120–21; *contra* Dumbrell, *Covenant and*

This covenant functions as a rescue operation in which God deals with the problem of uncertainty by bearing witness to or performing[107] his faithfulness to his purpose. Here, God's destruction of all life on the earth except for Noah and his family because of sin and unbelief has led to the uncertainty about the prediction made in Genesis 3:15 that humanity would solve the problem it created. But God secures and guarantees this prediction by making his covenant with Noah.[108] Noah can fully place his trust in God because God will make sure that his prediction will be fulfilled.

At the same time, God's covenant with Noah secures and guarantees God's promise that Noah and his family will survive the waters of the flood if Noah builds an ark for himself, his family, and the animals God commanded him to put in the ark. And Noah can—and must—also firmly place his trust in this promise.[109] God's promise of survival was unconditional—God did not require Noah to meet certain conditions before he made the promise—but his covenant with Noah was not: "When God speaks, he always appeals to the listener, even when he makes an unconditional promise.... Precisely the unconditional aspect implies a strong call to a faithful, trusting response."[110]

After the waters of the flood subside, Noah offers a sacrifice to God (Gen 8:20). When God smells the pleasing aroma of the sacrifice, he determines never to destroy all of life on the earth by a flood, even though humanity's sinful nature has not changed (Gen 8:21).

Then, God updates his covenant with Noah with another covenant (Gen 9:8–17),[111] this time a covenant with Noah and all of creation. As God's first covenant with Noah was necessary because sin and unbelief

---

Creation, 24, 25–26).

107. Because God's attributes are attributes of his being in communicative activity or divine doing, I speak about God performing his attributes. This will be further developed in the next chapter.

108. With the expression "my covenant" (Gen 6:18), God highlights "the absolute character of God's assignment and promise (Kwakkel, "Verplichting of relatie," 121; "Eerste verbondsword," 176).

109. Kwakkel, "Verplichting of relatie," 120–21; "Eerste verbondsword," 176; see also Burger, "Story of God's Covenants," 280–81.

110. Kwakkel, "Verplichting of relatie," 130.

111. Burger, "Story of God's Covenants," 282. God's covenants with his people are not independent and unrelated to each other but are "interrelated and mutually dependent" (Gentry and Wellum, *Kingdom through Covenant*, 656; *God's Kingdom*, 252). Thus, "the same relationship can be regulated by different successive *bĕrîts*" (Burger, "Story of God's Covenants," 274).

threatened the fulfillment of God's prediction that humanity would solve the problem it created, leading to uncertainty between God and his people, so also this second covenant is necessary because human nature is still the same after the flood.[112] By this covenant God guarantees his commitment to his promises—and to his original creational purpose—in spite of man's sin.[113]

Furthermore, God seals this commitment with the sign of the rainbow. Every time the rainbow appears in the clouds, God will remember his commitment never to destroy all of life on the earth with the waters of a flood.[114]

---

112. Leder, "Divine Presence, Part 2," 211; Williamson, *Sealed with an Oath*, 61. Whereas in Gen 6:5, humanity's depravity is the ground for God's judgment, in Gen 8:21, it is grounds for God's mercy. Wenham aptly writes, "were it not for the changed logic of God, in that he now cites man's depravity as a ground for his mercy rather than for his judgment, the descendants of Noah would be heading for extinction in another deluge" (*Genesis 1–15*, 206; Williamson, *Sealed with an Oath*, 61).

113. For God's covenant with Noah and creation guaranteeing his commitment to creation, see Burger, "Story of God's Covenants," 282; Dumbrell, *Covenant and Creation*, 43; *Search for Order*, 31; Gentry and Wellum, *Kingdom through Covenant*, 204–208; Kwakkel, "Verplichting of relatie," 121–123; Williamson, *Sealed with an Oath*, 68; Wright, *Mission of God*, 326–27; see also Belcher, *Fulfillment of the Promises*, 51–55. Kwakkel writes, "It is customary to speak of God's covenant with Noah or the Noahic covenant. Usually this means not only the promise of Gen 9:8–17 but also the obligations described in 9:1–7. In other words, it is a covenant of mutual obligations and to that extent also a relationship. There is nothing wrong with that, as long as one distinguishes this nomenclature from the meaning of the Hebrew word *běrît* in 9:8–17. That *běrît* has the character of an unconditional commitment" ("Verplichting of relatie," 123).

114. Turner writes, "The majority of exegetes understand the bow (*qeset*) in the clouds to maintain its military connotations and thus to represent, in one way or another, God's war bow." He says, "I suggest that a plausible explanation for the use of the rainbow as a sign of the covenant, in this context, can be found not in the suggestions outlined above [the war bow thesis], but in the Genesis cosmology itself, set out in some detail in ch. 1. Gen. i.6–8 recounts God's creation of the "firmament" (*raqiah*), to act as a barrier between the 'waters above' and the 'waters below'" ("Rainbow as a Sign," 120). Thus, Turner sees the rainbow as symbolizing a domelike barrier that holds back the waters above the dome (Williamson, *Sealed with an Oath*, 64).

Act two: the drama of the election of Israel as the theater of the theodrama (1)[115]

The second act of the drama of God's mission for his glory concerns the election of Israel as the theater of the theodrama. This act will be sketched in five scenes.

Scene one depicts God continuing the drama by electing Abraham (and Israel)[116] to be the theater in and through whom God would display his communicative activity of mutual glorification and bear witness to the splendor of his perfect life and spreading its blessing throughout the world. God's election of Abraham and Israel for the sake of the world implies that the world is the audience of the theodrama, which continues to be the case even when Gentiles become believing participants in it.[117] The drama of God's mission is an interactive drama of redemption, and so it is performed not only before the audience but among the audience so that they may be incorporated into it.[118]

The following scenes show God committing himself to use Abraham and Israel to spread the blessing of living in his loving presence and participating in his life in Christ through the Spirit throughout the world by making covenants with Abraham (scene two), with Israel (scene three), and with David (scene four). Scene five portrays God committing himself to use Israel to spread that blessing by promising to make a new covenant with Israel after the exile.

Scene one: the election of Abraham (and Israel)

Just as humanity before the flood failed to participate faithfully in the drama, so too after the flood humanity unthankfully allowed itself to be

---

115. "Theater" reconceptualizes the biblical notion of "holy temple." For Calvin on creation being a theater, see, e.g., Calvin, *Institutes*, 1.5.1, 8; 6.2; 14.20; 2.6.1; 3.9.2. For his use of "theater" for the church, see, e.g. Calvin, *Institutes*, 3.20.23. While act one also includes a theater of God's drama, viz. humanity and creation, act two focuses intentionally on the election of a specific people to be the theater of God's drama. Because Jesus, the church, and the new heaven and the new earth are also the theater of God's drama, I placed a number behind this act and each of the following acts in the drama of God's mission for his glory.

116. Since Abraham is the father of Israel, Israel is elected in Abraham's election.

117. Vander Lugt, *Living Theodrama*, 163.

118. Vander Lugt, *Living Theodrama*, 126, 137, 161–78; Vanhoozer, *Drama of Doctrine*, 414–17.

driven by its own agenda and standards, independent of God and unreceptive to his voice. And so, when they decided to make a name for themselves by building a city with a tower reaching to the heavens and to remain together instead of spreading out over the earth, God confused humanity's language and dispersed them (Gen 11:1–9).

But God does not give up on his intention to make all things new in a world where his people and creation could dwell in his loving presence. God rescues his drama and makes a new beginning, albeit without a covenant this time.[119] He calls Abram and Sarai to be a blessing for the world and to be the theater of the drama. He wants to use them as a new Adam and Eve to deal with the problem caused by Adam and Eve's sin (Gen 3:15),[120] to subdue the chaos and disorder caused by sin and invite humanity and creation into his Sabbath rest.[121] But will Abram and Sarai succeed in dealing with the problem and, in so doing, crush Satan's head?[122]

To accomplish this goal, God calls Abram to make a complete break with his past and leave behind everything dear to him—his country, his distant relatives, his immediate family—and go to the land that God would show him (Gen 12:1).[123] To encourage Abram, God promises that he will bless him and make his name great by making a great nation of

---

119. Even though there is a crisis and a rescue operation here, Gen 12:1–3 does not contain a covenant (*contra* Dumbrell, *Covenant and Creation*, 55–72; cf. Bartholomew, "Covenant and Creation," 23; Stek, "'Covenant' Overload," 28; cf. Burger, "Story of God's Covenants," 284).

120. Bartholomew and Goheen, *Drama of Scripture*, 55; Burger, "Story of God's Covenants," 283; Gentry and Wellum, *Kingdom through Covenant*, 260–64; *God's Kingdom*, 94–97; Leder, *Waiting for the Land*, 27, 79; "Divine Presence, Part 2," 212; Wright, *Mission of God*, 194–95; Wright, *New Testament and the People of God*, 216, 262.

121. Williamson describes the significance of Gen 12:1–3 as follows, "[Gen 12:1–3] has been well described as the Bible's Magna Carta. Here we find a synopsis of the divine agenda in which God's rescue plan for humanity is revealed. . . . It has been hinted at in the previous chapters but here is disclosed most fully. As the apostle Paul puts it [Gal 3:8], here God announced the gospel in advance to Abraham" (*Sealed with an Oath*, 77).

122. I am aware that ultimately Abraham's great Son will deal with the problem caused by Adam and Eve's sin and crush Satan's head, but at this point in the narrative, we do not know this. Thus, to keep the dramatic tension in the narrative, I ask: will Abram and Sarai succeed in dealing with the problem caused by Adam and Eve's sin and, in doing so, crush Satan's head?

123. Waltke writes, "The past perfect tense [i.e., "had said," e.g., NIV and NKJV] is used because God calls Abraham in Ur before his father dies, not in Haran (see 12:28, 31; 15:7; Acts 7:4)." He adds, "Or does God call Abraham a second time as he does with Jeremiah (1:4–19; 15:19–21)?" (*Genesis*, 204).

him (Gen 12:2).[124] Moreover, he promises that he will not only be "the recipient of [national] blessing," but will also be "the mediator of [international] blessing" for "in [him] all the families of the earth will be blessed" (Gen 12:3).[125]

This last promise would not be fulfilled automatically. Its fulfillment would depend on the nations' attitude to Abram. Those who would be on good terms with him and identify with him and his God, God would bless. But those who would be hostile to him and treat him lightly, God would curse. Nevertheless, God's overriding concern was that in Abram all the families of the earth would be blessed. God blessed Abram to be a blessing by living for the other, willing the good of the other, namely, the nations of the world (Gen 12:3).[126]

Scene two: God's covenants with Abraham

As God made covenants with Noah to deal with the uncertainty caused by man's sin and unbelief before and after the flood and manifest his faithfulness to his purposes, so God also makes two covenants with Abram/Abraham.

Even though God had promised Abram that he would bless him and make his name great by making a great nation of him, he doubted this promise because God had not given him any offspring (Gen 15:2-3). God tells him not to be afraid and reiterates his promise to make him into a great nation (Gen 15:4-5). Abram trusts God's promise, and God accepts this response to his promise—this listening and thankful filial spirit, characterized by the openness and responsiveness of faith—as an

---

124. Williamson understands the threefold promise of verse 2 to center on the promise of nationhood. He writes, "The 'great nation' and the 'great name' appear to define more precisely the nature of the anticipated 'blessing.'" He adds, "The prospect of a 'great name' likewise relates to the overarching promise of nationhood." He sees this suggested "by the implicit contrast with the failed aspirations of the tower-builders of Babel (cf. Gen. 11:4), whose attempts at civil organization (nationhood) had been thwarted by divine judgment" (*Sealed with an Oath*, 82-83).

125. Williamson, *Sealed with an Oath*, 82. The niphal form of *brk* can have either a passive sense ("in you shall all the families of the earth be blessed"), a reflexive sense ("by you all the families of the earth shall bless themselves"), or a middle sense ("all the families of the earth will find blessing in you"). While the passive sense is the most natural in the context (Mathews, *Genesis 1:1-11:26*, 117), the reflexive and middle senses each have a passive implication (Wright, *Mission of God*, 217).

126. Williamson, *Sealed with an Oath*, 83-84.

act of righteousness (Gen 15:6), that is, "a response that now fits with what he expects from him."[127]

When God rewards this posture of faith with a repeated promise of the gift of the land of Canaan (Gen 15:7; cf. 12:7; 13:14–17), Abram asks how he can know that he will possess the land (Gen 15:8).[128] To secure and guarantee the fulfillment of these two promises, which both pertain to the fulfillment of his creational purpose, God makes a covenant with Abram according to the custom of those days, where covenant partners cut animals in half and then walked between them, thereby guaranteeing their commitment to the covenant that they have made or, literally, "cut."[129] But in this case, only God walks between the bloody carcasses of the animals in the signs of a smoking fire pot and a flaming torch. In doing so, he is swearing an oath: "May I be cut in half if I do not fulfill my promise of giving you and your descendants the land of Canaan" (see Gen 15:9–21; cf. Jer 34:18–20).[130]

As God updated his first covenant with Noah by making a second one to deal with uncertainty in a new situation, so he updates this first covenant with Abram by making a new covenant with Abram in Genesis 17 (cf. Num 25:12)[131] to deal with uncertainty in a new situation.

Abram and Sarai have tried to bring about the fulfillment of God's promise on their own—by being curved in on themselves instead of responding with filial faith in God's promise—and as a result, Abram has

---

127. Kwakkel, *Gerechtigheid van Abram*, 48.

128. Kwakkel writes, "The new element in 15:18–21 is the broader description of the land and the way in which God records his promise, namely in the form of a *bĕrît*" ("Verplichting of relatie," 123). Moreover, if Abram is going to become a great nation, this nation will need to possess land.

129. For the making of this covenant in order to deal with Abram's uncertainties, see Burger, "Story of God's Covenants," 284: Leder, "Divine Presence, Part 2," 213.

130. Gentry and Wellum, *Kingdom through Covenant*, 287, 292; *God's Kingdom*, 110–11; Kwakkel, "Verplichting of relatie," 124; Robertson, *Christ of the Covenants*, 131–37; Ross, *Creation and Blessing*, 212; Waltke, *Genesis*, 244–45; Williamson, *Sealed with an Oath*, 86. Because God unconditionally guarantees the fulfillment of his promises in this covenant, it is usually compared with ancient Near Eastern royal grant or gift covenants (Burger, "Story of God's Covenants," 284; Stek, "'Covenant' Overload," 29; Williamson, *Sealed with an Oath*, 86). However, in the previous chapter, I observed that these land grants were predominantly conditional (see Knoppers, "Ancient Near Eastern Royal Grants," 670–97).

131. Burger, "Story of God's Covenants," 285–86; Kwakkel, "Verplichting of relatie," 124–27; Williamson, *Sealed with an Oath*, 84–91; *contra* Belcher, *Fulfillment of the Promises*, 66–69; Gentry and Wellum, *Kingdom through Covenant*, 299–305, 312–18; *God's Kingdom*, 117–19; Redd, "Abrahamic Covenant," 141–43.

fathered a son through Sarai's maidservant, Hagar (Gen 15:6). But doing so has led to uncertainty about whether God can still use Abram and Sarai in his mission for his glory.[132]

To deal with the problem of this uncertainty, God offers to make a covenant with Abram, if he walks before him and is blameless.[133] While God's promises in the first covenant with Abram were unconditional, his promises in this second covenant are conditional (cf. Gen 17:9). In other words, if God is going to be able to use Abram and Sarai in the drama of the mission for his glory, if they are going to represent him and bear witness to his glorious presence so that he becomes visible on earth through his people, they will have to faithfully and wholeheartedly live in his loving presence, in the openness and responsiveness of faith, with a listening and thankful filial spirit, rather than allowing themselves to be driven by their own agenda.[134]

This faithful response to God would include the practice of the rite of circumcision as a sign of God's covenant, intended to visibly remind them of their status and the obligations of belonging to God's covenant community (Gen 17:9–14). Circumcision thus "served as a synecdoche for the covenantal requirement of a blameless life."[135]

While God's first covenant with Abraham focused only on the national blessing of nationhood, this second covenant focuses on both national and international blessing, with the emphasis being on Abraham's

---

132. Leder writes, "Sarah's attempt to overcome her barrenness (= death) forms the narrative occasion for God's securing the promise by means of another covenant" ("Divine Presence, Part 2," 214; "Divine Presence, Part 3," 695; Burger, "Story of God's Covenants," 285).

133. Leder writes, "The cohortative after the two imperatives expresses intended result" ("Divine Presence, Part 2," 214). Consequently, Williamson suggests the following translation, "Walk before me and be blameless *so that* I may establish my covenant with both you and your descendants" (*Sealed with an Oath*, 87).

134. Leder writes, "The covenant offer makes clear that, by binding himself to God as a vassal to a suzerain, Abraham and his descendants are committed by self-maledictory oath to God's way and time of fulfilling the promise of an heir" ("Divine Presence, Part 2," 214). God's continual use of the expression "my covenant" (verses 2, 4, 7, 9, 10, 13, 14) illustrates the same point. Burger writes, "God remarkably and consistently refers in this chapter to his covenant with Abraham as 'my covenant.' On the one hand, such references emphasize the decisive role of God in this covenant, which is a relief to Abram given his own clumsy efforts to help God realize his promise. On the other hand, by means of such references God indicates subtly that he is God, which itself creates obligations on Abraham" ("Story of God's Covenants," 285).

135. Pratt, "God of Covenant," 8, 10.

international significance.[136] Abraham will become "the father of a multitude of nations," a promise God enshrines in the changing of his name from Abram to Abraham (Gen 17:4–5) and which would include him being the spiritual father of many nations, that is, "the spiritual benefactor" "mediating divine blessing to them" (cf. Gen 45:8; Rom 4:16–17).[137] This will occur through God giving Abraham the land and his descendants, including kings, becoming a great nation.

God's covenant with Abraham would be an everlasting covenant. The heart of his covenant is that God would be God to them (Gen 17:6–8). In other words, there will always be descendants of Abraham who will live in God's loving presence and be a blessing for the world.

Sometime after God fulfilled his promise by providing Abraham with a son, Isaac, God tests Abraham's faith by commanding him to take the son for whose birth he had waited for twenty-five years and sacrifice him as a burnt offering, much as Canaanites sacrificed their children as an offering (Gen 22:1). Because Abraham has the filial spirit of open and responsive faith, he is ready to sacrifice Isaac and he passes God's test (cf. Heb 11:17–19). God intervenes and calls the sacrifice of Isaac off. Instead, he provides a ram with its horns caught in a thicket, and Abraham sacrifices the ram instead of Isaac (Gen 22:13).

God rewards his posture of faith by promising him under oath that he will surely bless him by making him into a great nation, through whom all the nations of the earth will be blessed (Gen 22:15–18).[138] God

---

136. Williamson, *Sealed with an Oath*, 87–88.

137. Williamson, *Sealed with an Oath*, 89, 88; Dumbrell, *Covenant and Creation*, 73. Williamson writes, "Moreover, in every other place where the precise grammatical construction found here is employed (i.e., the inseparable preposition *le* [to/for] joined to the noun *ab* [father] in a 'resultative sense'), a non-physical concept of fatherhood is undeniably in view" (*Sealed with an Oath*, 88).

138. Burger rightly notes, "The word *berit* is not used in Genesis 22, but the divine oath again gives an unconditional character to the promises attached to the covenants of Genesis 15 and 17. As such, we find here the climax of the story of God's covenant with Abraham" ("Story of God's Covenants," 287). According to Hahn, "oaths always contain both a blessing and a curse element . . . [The] self-curse may be expressed in either the verbal declaration or the ritual enactment. . . . Since there is no curse element in [God's] verbal declaration, it is proper to suppose that it is symbolically contained in the ritual enactment. Since the only ritual act is Abraham's sacrificial 'offering' of Isaac, it emerges as *the* sign of [God's] self-malediction." He then concludes, "The net effect of God's self-maledictory oath, then, is that God has now assumed sole and complete responsibility to bless the nations through Abraham's seed, even if that means bearing the curse in order to remove whatever might impede its fulfillment" (*Kinship by Covenant*, 127; cf. Burger, "Story of God's Covenants," 287).

will indeed use Abraham and his descendants as the theater of the drama of his mission for his glory, to represent him and to bear witness to his glorious presence by being people and places where heaven and earth meet. On earth as in heaven!

Scene three: God's covenants with Israel

When God made his first covenant with Abraham, he had said, "Know for certain that your offspring will be sojourners in a land that is not theirs and will be servants there, and they will be afflicted for four hundred years. But I will bring judgment on the nation that they serve, and afterward they shall come out with great possessions" (Gen 15:13–14).

After the four hundred years, God remembered his covenant with Abraham and revealed his name to Moses (Exod 3:14). Accordingly, he led his people Israel—his son (Exod 4:22–23; Isa 63:16; 64:8; Jer 31:9; Hos 11:1; Rom 9:4)—out of Egypt to himself at Mount Sinai, where he made his first covenant with them (Exod 19–24).

Whereas God demonstrated his faithfulness to his creational purpose and his love for creation and humanity by establishing covenants with Noah and with Abraham in response to a crisis that caused uncertainty about whether this creational purpose would be fulfilled, there is no crisis causing uncertainty when he makes his first covenant with Israel at Mount Sinai.[139] But God's covenants with his people are not independent and unrelated to each other but instead update previous covenants for new situations, and here God's first covenant with Israel updates his two covenants with Abraham for the new situation in which Abraham's descendants have become a nation (Exod 24:8).[140] Accordingly, Anderson writes, "In the final form of the Pentateuch (Torah), the Mosaic covenant is subordinate to the Abrahamic. In this canonical context the Abrahamic covenant, which guarantees the promise of land and posterity, is the overarching theme within which the Mosaic covenant of law is embraced."[141]

---

139. Burger, "Story of God's Covenants," 298. Leder considers God's covenant with Israel to be a "response to the threat of the nations to annihilate the promised seed" ("Divine Presence, Part 2," 216). However, God had dealt with this threat by delivering Israel out of Egypt.

140. Burger, "Story of God's Covenants," 288.

141. Anderson, *Contours of Old Testament Theology*, 137; Williamson, *Sealed with an Oath*, 96.

Before God makes his covenant with his son Israel as a nation,[142] he explains what kind of nation Israel will be if they keep his covenant in the openness and responsiveness of faith (Exod 19:5–6). They will be his "treasured possession [*sĕgullâ*][143] among all people." That is, they will be a people with whom he has a valued and special relationship for the sake of the other people in the world.[144]

They will function as "a kingdom of priests." That is, they will mediate the presence of God to the nations, bearing witness to the splendor of his presence and participating in his life. "As the people of YHWH," Wright says, "they would have the historical task of bringing the knowledge of God to the nations, and bringing the nations to the means of atonement with God. The Abrahamic task of being a means of blessing to the nations also put them in the role of priests in the midst of the nations. Just as it was the role of the priests to bless the Israelites, so it would be the role of Israel as a whole ultimately to be a blessing to the nations."[145]

They will also function as "a holy nation," that is, a nation that is set apart from the other nations and consecrated to God as the theater of God's drama of his mission for his glory. Dumbrell puts it this way: "Israel as a 'holy people' then represents a third dimension of what it means to be committed in faith to Yahweh: they are to be a people set apart, different from all other people by what they are and are becoming—a display-people, a showcase to the world of how being in covenant with Yahweh changes a people."[146]

---

142. For Israel as God's son, see Exod 4:22–23; Hos 11:1. As Adam had the status of God's son, so Israel has the status of God's son. As Adam was given the mission to represent this status by making it visible on earth, so Israel is given the mission to represent their status by making it visible on earth.

143. Durham writes, "The image presented is that of the unique and exclusive possession, and that image is expanded by what appears to be an addition ('for to me belongs the whole earth') to suggest the 'crown jewel' of a large collection, the masterwork, the one-of-a-kind piece" (*Exodus*, 262).

144. Williamson, *Sealed with an Oath*, 96–97; Wright, *Mission of God*, 255–56.

145. Wright, *Mission of God*, 331. While Kwakkel does not consider Wright's interpretation to be the primary interpretation of Israel being a kingdom of priests, he does allow for it as a secondary interpretation ("Sinaitic Covenant," 29–31). Commenting on Israel being God's treasured possession "for [*ki*] all the earth is mine," Dumbrell writes, "Israel is called because the whole world ('earth') is the object of Yahweh's care" (*Search for Order*, 45; see also Williamson, *Sealed with an Oath*, 97; *contra* Kwakkel, "Sinaitic Covenant," 29).

146. Durham, *Exodus*, 263.

As God's treasured possession, a kingdom of priests and a holy nation, Israel is to bring the blessing of Abraham to the nations (Gen 12:3). They are to function, as Scripture says elsewhere, as the servant of the Lord who would be a light to the nations by bringing his justice to them (Isa 42:1, 6; 49:6). God wants to use them to deal with the problem caused by Adam and Eve's sin and crush Satan's head. Will Israel succeed?

Israel agrees to keep God's covenant with them (Exod 19:8). But doing so will involve keeping God's commandments and statutes (Exod 20–23).[147] To impress upon the people his holiness and the holiness required to live in his presence, God presents himself to them in a powerful display of his majesty (Exod 19:16–25). When Israel keeps God's covenant faithfully, it will not only increasingly learn what participating in God's mission for his glory entails, but it will also bear witness of it to the surrounding nations.[148] Essentially, it involves a life of love (*agape*), living for the other and willing the good of the other, as God himself does (Matt 22:37–40).

The covenant agreed to (Exod 19:8) is then formally ratified (24:1–8). After Moses tells the people all of God's commandments and statutes, the people agree to keep them (24:3–4, 7). Having offered sacrifices to God (24:5), Moses throws some of the blood of the sacrifices on the altar, which symbolizes God's presence, and some on the people, symbolizing their consecration to God.[149] The people again repeat their commitment to be God's treasured possession by being a kingdom of priests and a holy nation through keeping God's covenant (24:6–8).[150]

---

147. For the difference between God's commands (Exod 20) and his statutes (Exod 21–23), see Williamson, *Sealed with an Oath*, 98.

148. About the revelatory function of God's commandments and statutes, Williamson writes, "Just as Yahweh had made himself known to Pharaoh (cf. Exod. 5:2) and the Egyptians (as well as the surrounding nations) through the deliverance of the exodus, so he would further make himself known to Israel and the nations through the covenant relationship established at Sinai" (*Sealed with an Oath*, 98–99).

149. About some of the blood being thrown on the altar, Kwakkel writes, "As for the sprinkling of the blood of the animals on the altar, this blood represented the life of the animal (see Gen 9:4; Lev 17:11, 14). When the blood was sprinkled on the altar, the life of the animal was given to God. This shows once more that Moses' offerings were a symbolic expression of the people's willingness to dedicate their lives to God." He adds, "Viewed from this perspective, the ritual act of sprinkling the other half of the blood on the people is very meaningful. The fact that Israel's involvement in the covenant was confirmed by this blood showed that the covenant was forever bound up with their willingness to dedicate their lives to God" ("Sinaitic Covenant," 33).

150. Dumbrell, *Covenant and Creation*, 98; Durham, *Exodus*, 343; Kwakkel, "Sinaitic Covenant," 33; Nicholson, *God and His People*, 172–74; Williamson, *Sealed with an*

A few days later, however, God's son Israel violates the second commandment by having Aaron make a golden calf and worshiping it (32:1–6). Consequently, God no longer considers Israel his people (32:7). He wants to destroy them and make a great nation out of Moses (32:10).[151] Moses intercedes for the people, invoking God's unconditional promise to make Abraham into a great nation, and God decides not to destroy Israel (32:14). When God decides to send an angel with Israel instead of going himself (32:34; 33:2), Moses intercedes again (33:12–16) and God has compassion on his people and forgives them (34:6–7; cf. 33:19; 34:9). Moreover, he commits to personally accompanying his people with his presence (33:17).

Because of the crisis and uncertainty Israel's violation of God's covenant with them has caused, God acts in faithfulness and rescues the drama of the mission for his glory by formalizing his commitment to his creational purpose and to his intention to have Israel be the theater for this drama by making another covenant that updates his first covenant with them for the new situation that has arisen as a result of Israel's breaking of that covenant (34:10).[152]

Oath, 100. Nicholson writes, "Thus, what is set out in a programmatic manner in Exodus 19:3b–8 is finally completed in 24:3–8 where Israel gives its pledge of obedience to the words of the covenant and is then, as the author of Exodus 19:3b–8 took it, constituted as Yahweh's 'kingdom of priests and a holy nation'" (*God and His People*, 173).

151. Williamson writes, "Clearly, Israel's special status as the people of God is called into question: Yahweh describes them to Moses as 'Your people whom you brought up' and 'this people' (Exod. 32:7, 9)" (*Sealed with an Oath*, 106).

152. Burger, "Story of God's Covenants," 289, 292; Dumbrell, *Covenant and Creation*, 105–107; Kwakkel, "Sinaitic Covenant," 34–38; Williamson, *Sealed with an Oath*, 106–8; *contra* Gentry and Wellum, *Kingdom through Covenant*, 435–37; *God's Kingdom*, 179–80.

It is noteworthy that the violation of the second commandment with the making and worship of the golden calf is immediately preceded and followed by the Sabbath command. Enns writes, "The framing of the rebellion narrative by the Sabbath law indicates that although God's plan has almost been destroyed, it is now proceeding undiminished. God will be with his people, no matter what happens" (*Exodus*, 149; cf. Williamson, *Sealed with an Oath*, 108). The fact that the Sabbath functioned as a weekly reminder of God entering his rest after six days of creation and the people's calling to increasingly enter into this Sabbath rest by being God's holy people (Exod 31:13, 16–17), emphasizes this same point (cf. Williamson, *Sealed with an Oath*, 102–3). The same can be said about the instructions for the construction of the tabernacle and the actual construction that bracket Israel's violation of the second commandment. About the covenantal significance of the tabernacle, Williamson writes, "The tabernacle (signifying Yahweh's kingly presence in the midst of his people . . .) vouchsafed Israel's enjoyment of 'rest' in the Promised Land—itself a foretaste of the ultimate restoration of God's creation intention for humankind" (*Sealed with an Oath*, 103).

This second covenant, however, is different from the previous one because it is first a covenant with Moses and then, in Moses, a covenant with Israel (34:27).[153] This second covenant is a *mediated* covenant.[154] Because Moses has found favor in the sight of God (33:12–13, 16–17; 34:9), God has compassion on his people and forgives them. This "special position of Moses distinguishes the covenant of Exodus 34 from the covenant in Exodus 24." As such, Israel's participation in or performance of God's drama can only be based on "the wonders to which [God's] name testifies; that is, his undeserved mercy, compassion, grace, love, faithfulness, and willingness to forgive (Exod 33:19; 34:6–7)."[155]

153. Burger, "Story of God's Covenants," 289. That this second covenant is made with Moses and in him with Israel can also be seen in the use of the singular pronoun "you" in Exod 34:10-28. Kwakkel writes, "However, in Exod 34:10 the second person singular refers only to Moses, since he is distinguished from the other Israelites, who are denoted as 'your people' and 'the people you live among'. If, then, in the next verse God continues to use the second person singular by saying, 'Obey what I command you today', the most logical interpretation is that he is addressing Moses in this and the following verses." He adds, "All the Israelites had to obey [cf. v. 13], but the second person singular pronoun in this chapter shows that Moses bore primary responsibility for their obedience" ("Sinaitic Covenant," 37).

154. Dumbrell, *Covenant and Creation*, 110. Commenting on Moses meeting face to face with God in the Tent of Meeting and wearing a veil when he speaks with the people, Dumbrell writes, "The conjecture is that as a result of the national apostasy of Exod. 32, an apostasy of the kind which continued to trouble Israel right to the end of its history, the full significance of the Sinai covenant is now veiled in her experience." He adds, "This situation would continue for Israel until the veil would be removed in Christ and through the Spirit Israel would be placed in the Mosaic position (and indeed in the Exod. 19 position. Never again in the Old Testament does Israel return to its original Sinai position or realise its Sinai potential" (*Covenant and Creation*, 110).

155. Kwakkel, "Sinaitic Covenant," 38. Burger writes, "The sons of Aaron take over the priestly role of the people as a whole, and the Levites will serve in the tabernacle. . . . Israel is no longer a kingdom of *priests*" ("Story of God's Covenants," 289–90). However, when God gave Israel the status of being a kingdom of priests, Israel already had special priests (Exod 19:22, 24). Moreover, before God made his second covenant with Israel, he had already given instruction for the special priesthood (Exod 28–29; 30:30). Thus, I fail to see how "the sons of Aaron take over the priestly role of the people as a whole . . . [and] Israel is no longer a kingdom of *priests*." The claim that Israel must no longer be a kingdom of priests because, when Israel is on the Plains of Moab, God continues to call them "his treasured possession" (Deut 7:6) and "a people holy to the Lord," but not "a kingdom of priests" (Deut 29:16; Burger, "Story of God's Covenants," 290; Duncan, "Curious Silence," 83), depends on an argument from silence, which is generally considered to be weak or even fallacious. What can be said is that "the priests facilitated the maintenance of the divine-human relationship between Yahweh and Abraham's descendants" (Williamson, *Sealed with an Oath*, 105; see also Burger, "Story of God's Covenants," 289). Moreover, Burger rightly notes that "The covenant with Levi serves as a reinforcing supplement to the covenant with Israel (Num. 3:11–31; 8:16–19)" ("Story of God's Covenants," 289). God's covenant with Phinehas (Num 25:12-13)

After forty years in the wilderness, a new generation of the people of Israel stands on the threshold of the Promised Land. But this new generation is no better than the previous generation (Ezek 20:18–26; Num 25:1–13).[156] Both generations have rebelled against the Holy Spirit (Ps 106:33), grieved the Spirit (Isa 63:10; cf. 63:11–14), and resisted him (Acts 7:51).

This leads to uncertainty about whether God can use this new generation in the mission for his glory. Moreover, in addition to having Joshua lead them instead of Moses, the new generation's situation in the Promised Land will be different from their situation in the wilderness. In response, God once again is faithful to his purposes and comes to the rescue by making a third covenant with his son, Israel (Deut 29:1; cf. 8:5; 14:1).[157]

But because this new generation is no better than the previous one with its uncircumcised hearts (Deut 10:12–22) and because the commandments God gave them could not give them life (Ezek 20:25), this new generation too will not be able to keep this new covenant which promised them a blessed life in the Promised Land if they kept it[158] and a cursed life if they failed to do so, the ultimate curse being exile from the land (Deut 28; 31:16, 20).[159] Yet precisely because God is faithful, he offers his people hope by promising that he will one day—beyond the curse of exile—bring his people to repentance by circumcising their hearts and restoring them to the Promised Land (Deut 30:1–10).[160] On earth as in heaven!

Scene four: God's covenant with David

Israel's failure to keep the covenant, which God had predicted on the Plains of Moab, soon became a reality in the Promised Land. Not only

---

should be seen within this context.

156. Burger, "Story of God's Covenants," 290–91.

157. Burger, "Story of God's Covenants," 290; "Verder met het verbond," 124.

158. For the Promised Land as a recapture of Eden, see Dumbrell, *Covenant and Creation*, 119–23, 126.

159. Burger writes, "The external character of the law means it is not enough to solve the problems of humanity, and not even enough to secure a good life in the Promised Land. Covenantal nomism is only an intermediate solution (cf. Gal. 3)" ("Story of God's Covenants," 291).

160. Burger, "Story of God's Covenants," 291; Williamson, *Sealed with an Oath*, 112–13.

did Israel fail to drive out all the Canaanites (Josh 13:13; 16:10; 17:11–13; 15:63; Judg 1:21, 27–36; 2:1–5), but its own life soon also resembled the life of the Canaanites (Judg 2:11–13, 19–20; 3:7, 12; 4:1; 6:1, 25; 8:33; 10:6; Pss 78:56–64; 106:34–39). By the end of the book of Judges, Israel has become like the nations and the inhabitants of Sodom and Gomorrah.[161]

We continue to see this failure to keep God's covenant when Israel demands a king like all the nations (2 Sam 8:5, 20). When God had made his second covenant with Abraham, he had promised that kings would come forth from his descendants (Gen 17:6, 16), but when Israel demands a king, they are rejecting God as their king (1 Sam 8:7). God grants Israel Saul as its first king, but then Saul, like Israel, rejects God as his king (1 Sam 10:19; 15:23, 26) and God then rejects him as king (1 Sam 15:23, 26; 16:1, 7).

Israel's second king, however, is a man after God's own heart. As Wright explains, "The phrase does not mean (as it may sound in English) a special favorite of God. Rather since the heart is the seat of the will and intentions in Hebrew, the phrase simply means that David will be the one who will carry out the purposes of God."[162] David will be a king who is willing to live with a listening and thankful filial spirit, a king who, in faith, is open and responsive to God (1 Sam 13:14; Acts 13:22).

After David has been anointed king of all Israel (2 Sam 5:1–12), has brought rest to Israel by defeating Israel's enemies, and has brought the ark of God up to Jerusalem (2 Sam 6; Ps 132:5, 8), he wants to build a house for the ark (2 Sam 7:1–2). But instead of having David build him a house, God promises that he will build a house for David by establishing his throne forever (2 Sam 7:16).

The narrator in 2 Samuel 7 does not refer to this promise of a Davidic dynasty as a covenant, but Scripture does elsewhere (Pss 89:3–4, 28, 34, 39; 132:11–12). When we consider that Israel's continued apostasy led to uncertainty as to whether God could continue to use Israel in his mission for his glory and that God's covenant with David is a covenant *within* God's three covenants with Israel, then we see that with this covenant God is once again acting in faithfulness to his mission and to his love for creation and humanity by coming to the rescue of the drama (2 Sam 7:24; 1 Chr 17:22). The covenant with David is meant to give stability to his three covenants with Israel, so that Israel could be his treasured

---

161. De Jong, *Van oud naar nieuw*, 88.
162. Wright, *Mission of God*, 344.

possession, functioning as a kingdom of priests and a holy nation in order to bring the blessing of Abraham to the nations (Ps 89:19–20;[163] Jer 30:21–22; Ezek 34:23–24; Luke 1:68–75; Isa 55:3b–4[164]).[165] But will God's covenant with David's house bring this stability? Will it enable Israel to deal with the problem caused by Adam and Eve's sin and to crush Satan's head?

In the previous chapter, I noted that God's covenant with David has both unconditional and conditional aspects (2 Sam 7:14; 1 Kgs 2:4; 9:4–5; Ps 132:11–12; cf. 1 Sam 2:30).[166] This mixture of unconditional and conditional aspects has to do with the connection between God's covenant with David and his choice of Zion/Jerusalem as the place for his dwelling (Ps 132:13, 17–18). As God's covenant with David is meant to give stability to his covenants with Israel, so his choice of Zion/Jerusalem as the place of his dwelling is meant to give stability to his covenant with David.

If David and his sons are to participate in God's drama for his glory by sharing in Christ's status of sonship and his communion of love with the Father through the Spirit and are to represent Christ on earth so that God becomes visible and Israel is a place where heaven and earth meet, they will need to find their source of strength in God's dwelling in Zion/Jerusalem.[167]

163. Most Hebrew manuscripts speak of "godly ones," not "godly one." Tate writes, "A number of Heb. mss have the singular, 'your loyal-one,' probably with Nathan and 2 Sam 7 in mind. LXX has 'your sons' (τοῖς υἱός σου = בָּנֶיךָ)" (*Psalms 51–100*, 410). See also de Jong, *Van oud naar nieuw*, 96–97.

164. De Jong interprets the parallel position of "with you an everlasting covenant" and "my steadfast, sure love for David" as follows: "I think it's better to stick to the reality of both of them [i.e., both covenants] and imagine that the covenant with the people gets the usual Davidic upgrading. God remains faithful to his covenant with his people, but the manifestation of that faithfulness is shown by what the Lord God does in and to the house of David" (*Van oud naar nieuw*, 97).

165. De Jong, *Van oud naar nieuw*, 87–89, 92–97; Burger, "Story of God's Covenants," 293.

166. Kwakkel, "Conditional Dynastic Promise," 86; "Verplichting of relatie," 130.

167. De Jong, *Van oud naar nieuw*, 37. With regard to the unconditional form of promise that one of his sons would always be on his throne, de Jong writes, "What should not escape us is that this promise was made to David in connection with the building of the temple" (*Van oud naar nieuw*, 29; cf. Robertson, *Christ of the Covenants*, 232–33). Commenting on the connection between God's promise to David and his choice of Zion in Ps 132, de Jong points to the significance of the preposition "for" (*ki*) connecting verses 11–12 and verses 13–18: "If we want to take the word 'because' with which this sentence begins seriously, we have to explain this verse in such a way that the choice of Zion is placed under the promise to David as its solid ground" (*Van oud*

But even if they fail to do so and consequently fail to keep the conditional form of God's covenant, God will still keep the unconditional form of his promise because of his choice of Zion/Jerusalem (Ps 132:12-13; Isa 14:32). As De Jong says, "Thus, the election of Zion reinforces the unconditional promise in order to protect it from damage inherent in its conditional form."[168] Moreover, out of Zion/Jerusalem, God will make "a horn sprout for David" and "a lamp for [his] anointed" (Ps 132:17; cf. 89:24; Luke 1:69), who will one day perform and bear witness to God's glorious presence on earth and bring the blessing of Abraham to the nations because he himself will be a place and a person where heaven and earth meet.[169] On earth as in heaven!

Scene five: the new covenant

When God made his third covenant with Israel on the Plains of Moab, he predicted that, because of their constitutional incorrigibility, they would fail to keep his covenant and be sent into exile (Deut 28:36, 54-68; 30:1).[170] What God had predicted also happened (Jer 11:10; Ezek 16:59; 2 Kgs 17:7-23; 24:10—25:11). Yet, God also offered his people hope by promising that he would one day bring his people Israel to repentance by circumcising their hearts and restore them to the Promised Land (Deut 30:1-10).

Because the exile created uncertainty about the fulfillment of God's purposes, he rescued the drama of the mission for his glory by encouraging his people in exile with the promise of a new covenant (Jer 31:31-34; Ezek 36:22-28; Isa 54:1-10).[171]

With this new covenant, God will achieve his ideal: a theater of his theodrama, made up of actors who bear witness to the intratrinitarian mutual glorification by sharing in Christ's status of sonship and his

---

naar nieuw, 31).

168. De Jong, *Van oud naar nieuw*, 32; see also Williamson, *Sealed with an Oath*, 138–39.

169. Cf. de Jong, *Van oud naar nieuw*, 32; Burger, "Story of God's Covenants," 293.

170. Williamson, *Sealed with an Oath*, 112.

171. About the newness of the new covenant, Dumbrell writes, "In short, the 'new' will be its irrefragability. It will not be new because of new conditions which Yahweh will attach to it, nor because it is the product of a new historical epoch, nor because it will contain different promises, for indeed those attached to the Sinai covenant could hardly have been more comprehensive, but what will make it new is that in the new age *both* partners will keep it" (*Covenant and Creation*, 178).

communion of love with the Father through the Spirit and whose lives, characterized by a listening and thankful filial spirit and the openness and responsiveness of faith, make God visible on earth—actors who are themselves a people and place where heaven and earth meet.

God will achieve this purpose by circumcising his people's hearts (Deut 30:6). He will give them a new heart and a new spirit—that is, he will make them into new creations by changing them so that instead of being curved in on themselves and self-enclosed, driven by their own agenda and standards, independent of God and unreceptive to his voice, they will now respond in faith (Ezek 36:26–27).[172]

Consequently, they will not live in the flesh, but in the Spirit of the Father and the Son, with the law written on their hearts, performing and bearing witness to the life of heaven on earth (Ezek 36:27, 33; Jer 31:33; cf. Isa 32:15; 44:3; Joel 2:28–29; Ezek 37:14; Zech 12:10). As such, they will be born of God and live in God (1 John 2:29; 3:9; 4:7; 5:1, 4, 18; cf. 1 John 4:15, 16). This Spirit will not depart from them (Isa 59:21). Moreover, God will cleanse them of their sins—that is, he will forgive them their sins and spiritually cleanse them from sin's effects (Ezek 26:25; Jer 31:34).[173]

Furthermore, he will have his people return to the Promised Land, where they will live under a Davidic king as one people and he will be their God and they will be his people (Ezek 34:23; 36:28; 28:25; 37:15–28; 39:28; Jer 30:22, 24; 31:33; 32:38; 50:4). The temple will be restored (Ezek 40–48). The nations will be incorporated into this covenant, as promised to Abraham (Ezek 36:36; 37:28; Jer 33:9; Isa 42:6; 49:6; 55:3–5; 56:4–8; 66:18–24). And the land/creation will enjoy an abundant fruitfulness comparable to the Garden of Eden (Ezek 36:34–35; Isa 51:3). This will be nothing less than a resurrection from the dead and a new creation (Ezek 37:1–14; 36:33–38). God will do this for the sake of his name (Ezek 36:20–23).[174]

Because this covenant is eternal (Jer 32:40; 50:5; Ezek 37:26; Isa 55:3; 61:8), it is also God's last covenant with Israel and will achieve what God always wanted in the drama of his mission for his glory—on earth as in heaven.[175]

---

172. Thomas, *God Strengthens*, 238.

173. Allen, *Ezekiel 20–48*, 179; Thomas, *God Strengthens*, 237–38.

174. Wright observes that God wants to be known and worshiped for who he is: the creator, the ruler, the judge, and the savior of the world (*Mission of God*, 71–188).

175. Robertson writes, "Because it [i.e., the new covenant] shall bring to full fruition

Thus, "while the restoration of the Jews in the Promised Land marked the beginning of the fulfillment of the new covenant promises, this was merely the beginning. The best was yet to come when the 'rest' foreshadowed in Joshua would find its ultimate consummation in the new heavens and the new earth."[176]

Act three: the drama of the sending of God's Son as the theater of the theodrama (2)

The third act of the drama of God's mission for his glory is the sending of his Son as Israel's representative and substitute to be the theater of the theodrama.

This act will be sketched in six scenes. Scene one depicts the incarnation of the Son of God through the power of the Holy Spirit. Scene two portrays the baptism of the Son of God with water and the Spirit. Scene three shows the Son of God offering the Father the sacrifice of his life through the Holy Spirit. Scene four depicts the Son of God offering the Father the sacrifice of his death through the Holy Spirit. Scene five portrays the Son of God arising from the dead and being vindicated as the Son of God through the Holy Spirit. And scene six shows us the Son of God ascending into heaven through the Holy Spirit and becoming the head and mediator of the new covenant and lord of the universe.

---

that which God intends in redemption, it never shall be superseded by a subsequent covenant." He adds, "God's previous covenants may be regarded as 'everlasting' only insofar as they find their realization in the new covenant" (*Christ of the Covenants*, 277–78).

176. Williamson, *Sealed with an Oath*, 180; Robertson, *Christ of the Covenants*, 299–300. Regarding continuity between the old and new covenant, see Burger, "'Theirs Are the Covenants,'" 14–18; "Story of God's Covenants," 295–96, 298; Dumbrell, *Covenant and Creation*, 177–78; Gentry and Wellum, *Kingdom through Covenant*, 547–62, 705–12; *God's Kingdom*, 229–36; Robertson, *Christ of the Covenants*, 280–300; Waltke, "Kingdom of God," 91–92; Williamson, *Sealed with an Oath*, 180.

When Gentry and Wellum assert that the old covenant was made up of believers and unbelievers while the new covenant is made up of only believers (*Kingdom through Covenant*, 555–56, 707–8; *God's Kingdom*, 233–34), they forget that "the reality of the new covenant partly has a hidden and contested character, and is open to further eschatological realization in the future. This aspect is important when discussing the partly hidden character of Christ's reign, the restoration of Israel, the (im)perfection of the church, and the (im)perfection of Christian holiness." Moreover, they forget that "the church is a mixed community because not all church members are regenerate or remain faithful until the end, and the process of the writing of the law on the heart is unfinished, and the consequences and effects of sin are still felt notwithstanding the promise of complete forgiveness" (Burger, "Story of God's Covenants," 296).

Scene one: the incarnation of the Son of God through the Spirit

God began to fulfill the promises of the new covenant by having his son Israel return to the Promised Land. But because, by and large, he did not circumcise their hearts, the generation that returned was no better than the generation that had been sent into exile (e.g., Isa 56:9–12; 57:1–13; 58:1–14; 59:1–13). Because they too resisted the Holy Spirit (Acts 7:51), they were not a theater of his theodrama that bore faithful witness to him and made him visible on earth.

But God maintains his faithfulness to his creational purpose and to his loving promise of a new covenant, a covenant in which he would make Israel a new creation by circumcising their hearts and filling them with the Holy Spirit, who would make them receptive to his voice, writing the law on their hearts so that they would listen to and do his will and bear witness to the life of heaven on earth—and he does it by sending his own Son in our flesh as Israel's substitute and representative, so that he will be the theater of the theodrama.

To accomplish this goal, the Son needed to be conceived and born through the Holy Spirit. For even though the Son possesses the Spirit as the eternal Son of the Father, for him to fill or baptize Israel with the Spirit he also needed to possess the Spirit as a human being. It is as the holy, incarnate Son of God that he would baptize Israel (Acts 2:33).

Accordingly, the Son of God took on the flesh of an Israelite through the Holy Spirit, as announced by an angel to Joseph and Mary (Matt 1:18, 20; Luke 1:35).[177] At the same time, when he took on our flesh by the Spirit, he identified with us and united himself with our human nature forever (Phil 2:6–7). Now "we can become one with him because he first became one with us."[178]

---

177. Macchia, *Jesus the Spirit Baptizer*, 3, 37, 158–66, 185; Torrance, *Worship*, 31. Macchia writes, "He is conceived by the Spirit to be the Spirit baptizer, to bear flesh that will incorporate in itself all flesh. The incorporation of all peoples into himself as his own body by the Spirit has its embryo in the Son's uniting himself by the Spirit to flesh at the virginal conception." Moreover, "The mediation of the Spirit at the incarnation is sanctifying, for Jesus is conceived as the holy Son of God (Luke 1:35)" (*Jesus the Spirit Baptizer*, 163).

178. Letham, *Union with Christ*, 21.

Scene two: the Son of God baptized with water and the Spirit

Having been conceived and born by the Spirit, Jesus grows and becomes strong in the Spirit (Luke 2:40, 42; cf. 1:80) as he spends time in the Scriptures (Luke 2:46-47, 49) and in prayer (Matt 26:36, 39, 42, 44; Mark 1:35; 6:46; Luke 5:16; 6:12; 9:18, 28, 29; 11:1; John 11:41-42; 17; Heb 5:7). Then, as an adult, Jesus is baptized by John in the Jordan.

As God's son (Exod 4:22-23; Isa 63:16; 64:8; Jer 31:9; Hos 11:1; Rom 9:4), Israel would have been God's treasured possession among the nations, chosen to mediate God's presence to the nations, if they had kept God's covenant. Because Israel failed, John calls Israel to repent and be baptized with a baptism of repentance "to make ready for the Lord a people prepared" (Luke 1:17) or else face the fire of God's coming judgment (Matt 3:2-3, 7-12).

Christ, however, identifies with Israel and is baptized just like Israel in order to fulfill all righteousness, even though he as the true Israel does not need a baptism of repentance (Matt 3:13-17). In submitting to baptism, as God's beloved Son, he publicly and officially becomes Israel's substitute and representative, "so that Israel can be freed from the curse of the law and . . . can finally fulfill its role: remove the curse of sin so that God's blessing can reach the nations (cf. Galatians 3,6-14)."[179]

Having identified with Israel in his baptism by John in the Jordan, Jesus is then also baptized or anointed with the Spirit when he rises from the water of his baptism. Whereas being anointed with oil in the Old Testament symbolized being publicly consecrated for being a prophet, priest, or king (Exod 30:30; Num 3:3; 1 Sam 10:1; 15:17; 16:13; 2 Sam 2:4; 1 Kgs 1:39; 19:16) and being empowered for these tasks by the Holy Spirit (1 Sam 16:13; Zech 4:1-6), Jesus is publicly consecrated and empowered for his task as Israel's prophet (Deut 18:15, 17-19; John 7:16; 8:28; 12:49-50; 14:24; Acts 3:22-23), priest (Ps 110:4; Heb 4:14-16; 5:1-10; 7:11-28; 9:11-14; 10:8-12, 19-22; 1 Tim 2:5), and king (Ps 110:1-2; Matt 22:42; Luke 1:31-33; Rev 1:5; 19:16) directly by the Holy Spirit (Matt 3:16). Accordingly, Jesus will fulfill his mission in the power of the Holy Spirit (Isa 61:1-2; Luke 4:18).

However, Jesus is not only baptized with the Spirit to be empowered for his mission as Israel's true prophet, priest, and king. He is also baptized with the Spirit because he will himself baptize Israel with the Spirit on Pentecost, since he permanently possesses the Spirit "without

---

179. Burger, *Life in Christ*, 67; cf. "Hoe vergeeft God?," 167.

measure," that is, fully (John 3:34; 1:33; 7:38–39; 20:22; Acts 1:5; 2:17, 33; 10:44–47; Col 1:19).[180] When he performs this baptism, God's ideal will begin to be fulfilled. He will have a theater of the theodrama made up of actors who bear witness to his intratrinitarian mutual glorification, who share Christ's status and filial spirit, and who make God visible on earth. Thus, Jesus' baptism with the Spirit at the Jordan ties together his conception by the Spirit and his baptizing with the Spirit as the climax of his ministry and the fulfillment of Israel's hope of the promise of the new covenant.[181]

Scene three: the Son of God offering the Father the sacrifice of his life through the Spirit

Having identified with Israel when he was baptized by John in the Jordan and having been anointed or baptized by the Spirit when he rose from the water of his baptism, Jesus continues to identify with Israel by offering the Father the sacrifice of his life through the Holy Spirit as Israel's representative and substitute in order to deal with the problem of sin, death, and the devil.

This begins with his being led by the Spirit into the desert for forty days, where he is tempted by the devil with regard to his relationship with himself, the world, and God (Luke 4:1–13).[182] Where Adam and Eve and Israel failed, Jesus, as the faithful Adam and true Israel, resists the devil's temptations in the power of the Spirit.

Then, as a prophet, like John the Baptist before him, Christ begins his ministry by calling Israel to faith and repentance in the power of the Spirit and summoning Israel to believe the good news that the kingdom of heaven has come near[183] in order "to make ready for the Lord a

---

180. Macchia, *Jesus the Spirit Baptizer*, 184–85; Burger, *Life in Christ*, 156.

181. Macchia, *Jesus the Spirit Baptizer*, 242. Macchia writes, "Though impressive patristic evidence can be mustered from the fourth and fifth centuries granting the reception of the Spirit at the Jordan a significant role to play, the classic creeds of the church (Apostles' Creed, Nicene Creed, and the Chalcedonian Definition) do not mention it, nor Christ's bestowal of the Spirit at Pentecost, for that matter." He adds, "The creeds focus theologically on the eternal Son's taking on flesh at the incarnation in order to die and rise again. While this confession is orthodox as far as it goes (cf. Heb. 2:14), it does not go far enough" (*Jesus the Spirit Baptizer*, 190). Wright comes to the same conclusion in what he calls "The Missing Middle" (*Day the Revolution Began*, 3–24).

182. Van Bruggen, *Lucas*, 116.

183. With regard to the kingdom of heaven being near, Van Bruggen writes, "The

people prepared" (Luke 1:17) or else face the fire of God's coming judgment (Matt 4:17; Mark 1:14-15; cf. Luke 4:18; Isa 61:1-2; Matt 7:13-27; 11:24-30; 18:23-25; 20:1-16; 21:18-27, 33-44; 22:1-14; 24:1—25:46; Luke 13:1-8, 22-30; 16:1-31; 18:1-8).

This kingdom had been prophesied by Daniel, who said that a day would come when God would destroy the kingdoms of this world and set up a kingdom that would never be destroyed (Dan 2:44; 7:11-14; cf. Rev 11:15). It had been proclaimed by John the Baptist as well, when he called people to repent and be baptized with a baptism of repentance (Matt 3:1-12; Mark 1:3-8; Luke 3:2-27).

Because this kingdom of heaven is a realm that one will inherit (1 Cor 6:9-10; 15:50; Gal 5:21; Eph 5:5) and into which one must enter (Matt 5:20; 7:13-14; 18:3; John 3:5), Israel needs to repent and believe the Father's good news of this coming kingdom by being born again and believing in Jesus Christ as their substitute and representative (Matt 5:3, 20; 7:21; 18:3; 19:24; 25:34; Mark 9:47; John 3:3, 5; Rom 14:17; 1 Cor 6:9-10;

---

proximity [of the kingdom] does not primarily refer to time ('it's almost there'), but to spatial proximity ('it's close by').... John knew that the Messiah would come directly after him: He was already born and was near (as near as the distance from Nazareth to the Jordan River)! When the Lord Jesus begins to preach, He is near Israel.... And now the kingdom of heaven is as close to the people as the King walking in their streets." He adds, "Today that Savior is in heaven, but that is not far away. Heaven (invisible to us) is as close as the palace adjacent to the forecourt. In faith we see Him there at Father's right hand.... With Jesus' coming, the kingdom of heaven has come near. That is not the same as 'having come.'" He concludes, "Precisely the preaching of the nearness [of the kingdom] makes clear that it is not a question of 'is it here or not?' The real question is: 'Are *we* ready to believe in that kingdom of Jesus and to expect it?' Good news: the kingdom is already near. Now the question: Where are you staying?" ("Hoe is het hemelrijk nabij?"). *Contra* those who understand the kingdom primarily as the expansion of God's rule in Christ and thus being already here (e.g., Allison, "Kingdom of God," 183-87; Bartholomew and Goheen, *Drama of Scripture*, 129-35; Beale, *New Testament Biblical Theology*, 428-37; Duvall and Hays, *God's Relational Presence*, 172-73; Gentry and Wellum, *God's Kingdom*, 243-52; *Kingdom through Covenant*, 648-54; Goldsworthy, "Kingdom of God," 615-20; Ladd, *Presence of the Future*; Perrin, *Kingdom of God*, 23-98, 152-68; Ridderbos, *Coming of the Kingdom*; Schreiner, *New Testament Theology*, 41-79; Vos, *Biblical Theology*, 372-86; Waltke, "Kingdom of God," 49-71; Wright, *Jesus and the Victory of God*, 172, 191-96; Wright, *The Great Story*, 28, 71); Yarbrough, "Kingdom of God," 95-123). About this expansion of the rule of God in Christ, Van Bruggen writes, "So when the gospel of the kingdom of God resounds from John the Baptist, it is not about *expanding* the power of God on earth: He is and always has been the Almighty on earth and always will be! That is reality, not nearness" ("Evangelie van het koninkrijk der hemelen"). While the proximity of the kingdom does not refer primarily to time, it does also refer to time when we consider that Scripture uses the same word (*eggizo*) for the kingdom being near and the end being near (Luke 21:31; Rom 13:12; Heb 10:25; Jas 5:8; 1 Pet 4:7).

Gal 5:19–21; Eph 5:5; Jas 2:5). When they do, he forgives them their sins so that they can enter the kingdom of heaven (Matt 9:2, 6; Luke 7:47–48, 50; cf. Mic 7:18–19). Moreover, they will be able to call God their Father because they participate in Jesus' status and communion of love with the Father (Matt 5:16, 45, 48; 6:1, 8, 9, 14, 26, 32; 7:11; 18:14; Luke 11:13; cf. Rom 8:14–17; 2 Cor 6:18; 1 John 3:1).

Christ not only proclaims the Father's good news of the nearness of the kingdom of heaven in the power of the Spirit. He also demonstrates it by healing the sick in the power of the Spirit (Luke 4:14; 5:17). His preaching of the good news of the coming kingdom of heaven goes "hand in hand with his 'healing every disease and sickness among the people' (Matt. 4:23–24; 9:35; Mark 1:39)."[184]

In the coming kingdom of heaven, we will be immortal and incorruptible (1 Cor 15:49–50). There will be no death, mourning, crying, or pain (Rev 21:4). To demonstrate the nearness of that coming kingdom, Jesus heals the sick who are brought to him and who place their faith in him.[185] He even raises the dead in the power of the Spirit (Mark 5:35–42; Luke 7:11–17; John 11:37–44; Matt 27:51–53). What is more, he even casts out demons in the power of the Spirit to demonstrate that the kingdom of heaven, in which Satan will have been crushed, has come near (Matt 4:24; 8:16–17; 10:1; Luke 6:18).[186]

---

184. Van Bruggen, *Jesus the Son of God*, 83. Van Bruggen writes, "These healings are part of a program of *preaching* and must not be isolated from it. The miracles *show* that the kingdom of heaven is really around the corner. Its blessings are already being felt!" (*Jesus the Son of God*, 83).

185. Van Bruggen writes, "Jesus demands *faith* when he heals. People must have faith in him if they are to be healed. When that faith is absent, he cannot do signs and wonders (as in Nazareth, Mark 6:5–6), not because his power is inadequate, but because the gifts of heaven are sent only through him, and only to believers" (*Jesus the Son of God*, 84).

186. Concerning Matthew 12:28 where Jesus says, "But if it is by the Spirit of God that I cast out demons, then the kingdom of God has come upon you," Van Bruggen writes, "Every time he drives out evil spirits by the power of the Holy Spirit, the kingdom of heaven has come to earth and touches people (Matt. 12:28). These exorcisms are like invading troops landing in hostile territory" (*Jesus the Son of God*, 86). Elsewhere he says, "It is not Jesus' intention to make a statement about whether God's kingdom has already been fully established, or is in the process of advancing. The expression *ephthasen eph' humas* means that God's kingdom has now 'come to you' or 'reached you.'" He adds, "The discussion, however, is not about how exactly that kingdom will become reality, but about whether one is currently dealing with phenomena of *God's* kingdom or *Satan's* kingdom. Jesus states that the reality of the casting out of these demons is a presentation of *God's* kingdom and of the arrival of this new messianic reign in Israel. This verse does not deal with the further course of events concerning

In successfully resisting the devil's temptations, proclaiming the Father's good news of the coming kingdom of heaven, and demonstrating that good news by healing the sick, casting out demons, and raising the dead—all in the power of the Spirit—Jesus, as a priest, was surrendering his life to his Father and thankfully offering him the sacrifice of his life through the Spirit as Israel's representative and substitute.[187] He continues to do this by perfectly keeping the law of love that Israel failed to keep (Matt 3:15; 5:17; Rom 5:19; 1 Cor 1:30; Gal 4:4–5; Phil 2:8; 3:9). What he preaches about the lifestyle that leads to the coming kingdom of heaven (Matt 5–7), he also practices himself, even when people disappoint him, oppose him, want to kill him, and betray him.[188] He is poor in spirit, meek, merciful, and pure in heart. He never has any unrighteous anger or impurity in his heart. He never retaliates or is anxious. He loves his enemies, prays for them, and even lays down his life for them (Luke 23:34; Rom 5:6–8; 1 Pet 2:22–23).

Scene four: the Son of God offering the Father the sacrifice of his death through the Spirit

When God gave Adam and Eve the mission to fill the earth and subdue it and spread the life of the Garden of Eden over the whole world, they failed to do so and instead spread over the earth a life of sin and death, with the devil as the god of this world. God called Abram and Sarai to be a new Adam and Eve who would deal with the problem caused by their sin and be a blessing for the nations. When he made his first covenant with Israel at Sinai, he wanted to use them in the same way, to make them his treasured possession, a kingdom of priests and a holy nation, to mediate the presence of God to the nations and to be a light to the nations.

---

the establishment of that kingdom" (*Matteüs*, 227–28). Thus, he writes, "In Matthew 12:28 (compare Luke 11:20), we read that *in the person of Jesus* the kingdom of God is presented to his contemporaries. It reaches them through Jesus. Those who do not want to seek it through him will fail to find it" (*Jesus the Son of God*, 81). This is also Van Bruggen's interpretation of Luke 17:21 where Jesus says, "Behold, the kingdom of God is in the midst of you." He writes, "The presentation of the kingdom is so humble and modest that mocking Pharisees can ask just *when* it is coming—failing to notice that it is already in their midst (Luke 17:21)" (*Lucas*, 320–21).

187. Torrance writes, "Jesus comes to be the priest of creation to do for us, men and women, what we failed to do, to offer to the Father the worship and the praise we failed to offer, to glorify God by a life of perfect love and obedience, to be the one true servant of the Lord" (*Worship*, 14).

188. Burger, *Life in Christ*, 66–67; "Hoe vergeeft God?," 160–61.

But Israel, even under the leadership of the house of David, failed in that task. Not only did they not deal with the problem caused by Adam and Eve's sin and bring blessing to the nations; they also called down upon themselves the curse of the law, the ultimate curse being the condemnation of death (Deut 27:26; Jer 11:3; Ezek 18:4; Rom 6:23; Gal 3:10).

But God comes to the rescue of the drama of his mission for his glory. He maintains his faithfulness to his promise of a new covenant and his love for creation and humanity by having Christ identify with Israel—not only in the sacrifice of his life as their representative and substitute, but also with the sacrifice of his death. His death reveals "what happens when God approaches the world with his salvation."[189]

Jesus is not only opposed and ridiculed; he also needs to be eliminated (Luke 20:9–18). In the process, he becomes the victim of horrible injustice as he, though innocent, is condemned to death as a blasphemer and crucified as a political threat. Thus, "at its core, the suffering of Jesus is the result of the violence, dishonesty, cowardice, and treason of the people towards him. . . . People got rid of Jesus because he was in their way."[190] Yet, God uses this terrible injustice done to Jesus so that his suffering and death deal with the problem of sin, death, and the devil and bring the blessing of Abraham to the nations (Acts 2:23).[191]

Accordingly, knowing why he had taken on human flesh, Jesus predicts his death (and resurrection) several times beforehand (Matt 16:21; 17:22–23; 20:18–19; Mark 8:31; 10:33; Luke 9:22, 44; 18:32–33). On one occasion, he indicates that he must suffer and die (Matt 16:21; Mark 8:31; 9:31; Luke 9:22). This ultimately referred to the fact that he had come "to give his life as a ransom for many" (Matt 20:28; Mark 10:45).[192]

Because Jesus knows he has to go to Jerusalem to suffer and die, "he signed his own death sentence by entering Jerusalem on a donkey" as Israel's king "and bringing the temple service to a halt" (Matt 21:1–17; Mark 11:1–11, 15–18; Luke 19:29–40, 45–46; John 12:12–19).[193] Shortly thereafter, he celebrates the Passover with his disciples and gives the

---

189. Van den Brink and Van der Kooi, *Christian Dogmatics*, 478.

190. Van den Brink and Van der Kooi, *Christian Dogmatics*, 479.

191. I am aware that the distinction between the sacrifice of Jesus' life and the sacrifice of his death is not an absolute distinction since the sacrifice of his death is, strictly speaking, still part of the sacrifice of his life. However, I am using this distinction primarily as a *theological* distinction.

192. Burger, *Life in Christ*, 66.

193. Burger, *Life in Christ*, 67.

elements of bread and wine a new interpretation, interpreting the bread as his body and the wine as his blood of the new covenant, clearly alluding to the blood of the old covenant (Luke 22:19-20; Exod 24:8; Matt 26:26-28; Mark 14:22-24). Moreover, he asserts that he will not drink of the fruit of the vine until he drinks it new in the kingdom of his Father (Matt 26:29; Mark 14:25). In interpreting the elements of bread and wine in this manner, Jesus is interpreting his imminent death as the means that will bring about a new exodus that will deal with the problem of sin, death, and the devil once and for all.[194]

After fighting an intense spiritual battle with regard to doing the will of his heavenly Father and drinking the cup of his wrath (Matt 26:36-46; Mark 14:32-42; Luke 22:40-46), Jesus is betrayed and arrested (Matt 26:47-56; Mark 14:43-50; Luke 22:47-53). He is led before the Sanhedrin, who condemn him to death as a blasphemer (Matt 26:57-68; Mark 14:53-65; John 18:12-13, 19-24), and then before Pilate, the governor, who condemns him to death by crucifixion for claiming to be a king (Matt 27:11-26; Mark 15:2-15; Luke 23:2-3, 18-25). In being condemned to death, though innocent, Jesus not only continues to identify with Israel; he also identifies with victims of injustice.[195]

Scene five: the Son of God vindicated as the Son of God through the Spirit

God promised that a son of Adam and Eve would deal with the problem of sin, death, and the devil caused by their rebellion (Gen 3:15). He promised that a son of Abraham would deal with the problem caused by their sin and bring blessing to the nations instead of curse (Gen 12:3). He promised that a son of David would rule Israel so that she would truly mediate the presence of God to the nations (Exod 19:5, 6; 2 Sam 7:12-16). And when God promised to make a new covenant with Israel, it was compared to the resurrection from the dead and a new creation (Ezek 37:1-14; 36:33-38). Accordingly, many Jews believed in a future bodily resurrection from the dead, when God would intervene in history and set things right, renewing creation, destroying Israel's enemies, and restoring Israel as the true people of God.[196]

---

194. Cf. Burger, *Life in Christ*, 67; Wright, *Matthew for Everyone*, 155-56.
195. Burger, *Life in Christ*, 56, 59, 161.
196. Wright, *New Testament and the People of God*, 321-32; *Jesus and the Victory of*

When the Holy Spirit raises Jesus from the dead, God begins to do this. Jesus had not only predicted his death; he had also announced that he would rise from the dead (Matt 16:21; 17:22–23; 20:18–19; Mark 8:31; 10:33–34; Luke 9:22; 18:32–33). In doing so, he linked his resurrection to his death. When he does rise from the dead, he rises with a glorified resurrection body, as the first fruits of God's new creation in fulfillment of the promise of a new covenant (John 11:25–26; Acts 2:24; Rom 6:9; 1 Cor 15:20–23; Col 1:18; Rev 1:5, 18; cf. Ezek 37:1–14; 36:33–38). Thus, when the Spirit raises him from the dead, he vindicates Jesus as the Son of God.

Scene six: the Son of God ascends into heaven through the Spirit

Even though many Jews believed in a bodily resurrection from the dead when God would intervene in history and set things right, they did not believe that the Messiah would have to die to achieve that goal (Luke 24:1–49; John 20:24–29). Even though Jesus had announced his resurrection from the dead in advance, none of Jesus' followers initially believed that he had arisen (Matt 28:1–10; John 20:11–18; cf. Matt 16:22; Luke 9:45; 18:34). And even though Jesus appeared to some of his followers after his resurrection from the dead (Matt 28:9; Luke 24:13–30, 34, 36–49, 50–53; John 20:16, 19–29; 21:1–14; Acts 1:1–11; 1 Cor 15:5–7), no one had been present when he arose, giving the resurrection "the character of a miraculous mystery . . . the beginning of something new that still remains unknown to us . . . the beginning of a new creation, in which death is conquered and sin defeated. What that really means for us at this time is still unimaginable."[197]

Forty days after his resurrection from the dead, Jesus ascends into heaven through the power of the Holy Spirit, where he inherits the glory of God, as he is glorified with the glory that he had in his Father's presence before the world existed (Luke 24:50–53; Acts 1:9–11; John 17:5, 24).[198]

God, 126–27, 255–56; *Surprised by Hope*, 46–47; Burger, *Life in Christ*, 31.

197. Burger, *Life in Christ*, 50; cf. 50–51; cf. Luke 24:31, 36; John 20:19; Rom 8:17–25; 1 Cor 15:35–44; 1 John 3:2.

198. Burger, *Being in Christ*, 532. The ascension through the power of the Holy Spirit can be seen also in 1 Pet 3:18–19, 22. Having been made alive through the Spirit, Christ also ascended into heaven through the same Spirit. The very fact of his ascension was a proclamation to the spirits in prison of his victory over his adversaries (Van

PARTICIPATION IN THE LIFE OF GOD

The disciples who are present at his ascension only see him ascending, however; they do not see him entering heaven, because "a cloud took him out of their sight" (Acts 1:9). Consequently, the two angels who are also present need to tell them that Jesus has ascended into heaven (Acts 1:11). While a cloud often reveals God's glory or his presence (Exod 40:34-38; 1 Kgs 8:10; Luke 9:34-35; 21:27), it also conceals his glorious presence (Exod 40:35; 1 Kgs 8:11-12). Thus, as the resurrection has a hidden character, so too the ascension has a hidden character: it conceals Christ's glorious presence, since he is now hidden in the glory of God (Col 3:3).[199]

Moreover, those who have been made alive together with Christ through faith participate in Christ's hiddenness in the glory of the Father. Their life is hidden with Christ in God because they are seated with him in the heavenly places (Col 3:3; Eph 2:5-6). Accordingly, their life too has a hidden and mysterious character, like Christ's life.[200]

Having triumphantly ascended into heaven, Christ is rewarded for his obedience by being given "the name that is above every name, so that at the name of Jesus every knee should bow," in fulfillment of Psalm 110 (Phil 2:9-10; Mark 12:35-37).[201] From heaven, Christ continues to participate in the drama of his Father's mission for his glory through filial openness and responsiveness, so that "he might fill all things" (Eph 4:10).

Houwelingen, *1 Petrus*, 130-38; see also Kistemaker, *Peter and Jude*, 141, 150). Allison and Köstenberger argue that Jesus' ascension into heaven through the Spirit is an implication of his descent into Mary's womb through the Holy Spirit. They write, "God the Father sends God the Son on his earthly mission which begins with the Holy Spirit effecting the incarnation and ends with the Spirit's effecting the ascension.... As the Holy Spirit works the descent of the Son into the earthly womb of the virgin Mary, so the Spirit works the ascent of the Son to the heavenly throne room. From heaven to earth and back again: the work of the Holy Spirit" (*Holy Spirit*, 360-61).

199. Burger, *Life in Christ*, 51; Kamphuis, *Verborgen in God*, 9-11. The fact that Jesus' ascension conceals his glory has implications for understanding the so-called states of Christ, i.e., his humiliation and his exaltation. Instead of understanding these states in terms of a rigid, historical progression, we must also view them in a dialectical manner. Thus, Horton correctly writes, "So, we see not simply a progression from the state of humiliation to that of exaltation, or from prophet to priest and finally king, but a dialectic of cross and glory" (*Lord and Servant*, 258). Kamphuis adds, "Humiliation continues in his exaltation. For he is hidden. He can still be misunderstood and mocked. Even his sufferings are filled up in the suffering of his own" (*Verborgen in God*, 11).

200. Burger, *Life in Christ*, 51; Kamphuis, *Verborgen in God*, 16-17.

201. Burger, *Life in Christ*, 52.

Act four: the drama of the outpouring of the Holy Spirit on the church as a theater of the theodrama (3)

The fourth act of the drama of God's mission for his glory entails the outpouring of the Holy Spirit on the church so that the church can be the theater of the theodrama. Because the new covenant is made with Israel in Christ, its representative, the church on which the Spirit is poured is the reconstitution and expansion of Israel.[202]

This act will be sketched in two scenes. Scene one depicts the outpouring of the Spirit on the church. Scene two portrays the church performing and bearing witness to what is in Christ by the power of the Spirit.

Scene one: the outpouring of the Holy Spirit on the church

Having been conceived by the Holy Spirit and anointed or baptized with the Spirit at the Jordan, having offered up to the Father the sacrifice of his life and of his death through the Spirit, having been vindicated in his resurrection by the Spirit, and having ascended into heaven by the Spirit's power, to be exalted at the right hand of his Father, Jesus receives from his Father the promise of the new covenant Spirit and pours the Spirit out on the church on the day of Pentecost as the climax of Israel's history and the history of his life (Acts 2:33).[203]

When the day of Pentecost arrives,[204] a group of about 120 people, including the disciples, are all in one place (Acts 2:1). Suddenly, they are

---

202. Cf. Burger, "Story of God's Covenants," 294-95, 298; Wright, *Paul and the Faithfulness of God*, 774-1042.

203. *Contra* Burger, who refers to the resurrection as the climax of Israel's history and the history of Jesus' life (*Life in Christ*, 35, 49); see also Wright, who falls short of seeing the outpouring of the Holy Spirit as the climax of Israel's history and the history of Jesus' life (*How God Became King*, passim; *Day the Revolution Began*, 205, 208, 312, 357).

204. The day of Pentecost had agricultural associations because it celebrated the beginning of the grain harvest. Accordingly, it was also called the Feast of Weeks and celebrated the first fruits of the wheat harvest (Exod 34:22; Lev 23:15-17; Num 28:26; Stott, *Spirit*, 612-62; Wright, *Acts for Everyone*, 21). Pentecost also had historical associations because it celebrated the giving of the law at Mount Sinai which was considered to have occurred fifty days after the exodus from Egypt (Stott, *Spirit*, 62; Wright, *Acts for Everyone*, 21). These two associations could symbolize the gift of the Spirit as the first-fruits (Rom 8:23) of God's eschatological future (Rom 8:23; Van Eck, *Handelingen*, 55) and the Spirit writing the law on the hearts of members of the new covenant (Jer 31:33; Stott, *Spirit*, 62) so that Israel would be able to fulfill its mission of bringing the

PARTICIPATION IN THE LIFE OF GOD

baptized with the Holy Spirit (2:2). As a result, they begin to proclaim the mighty works of God in different languages, as the Spirit enables them (2:4–11), symbolizing the incorporation of the nations into Israel.[205]

Participating in Christ's prophetic ministry from heaven, Peter, in response to the people's confusion (Acts 2:13), explains that what is happening is the fulfillment of the promise of the new covenant that in the last days God would pour out his Spirit on all flesh.[206] Peter then goes on to preach the history of Jesus' life, death, resurrection, and ascension to encourage his audience to call upon the name of the Lord (Acts 2:22–36).

When many in the audience ask what they should do, because the Spirit has convicted them of sin (cf. John 16:8–9), Peter calls them to repent and be baptized in the name of Jesus, symbolizing their dying with Christ to their old life and their rising with Christ to a new life (Rom 6:3–11; Col 2:11–12). When they do, they will receive the forgiveness of their sins. Moreover, they will receive the gift of the Holy Spirit, as a fulfillment of God's promise in the new covenant (Jer 31:33; Isa 32:15; 44:3; 59:21; Ezek 36:27; 37:14; 39:29; Joel 2:28–29).

Furthermore, this promise of receiving the Spirit will also be fulfilled for "all those who are far off, everyone whom the Lord our God calls to himself," that is, those Jews living in the dispersion further away from Jerusalem and the nations among whom they live (Acts 2:39; Gal 3:14).[207] In this way, God will fulfill his promise to Abraham that in him all the families of the earth will be blessed (Gen 12:3).

---

blessing of Abraham to the nations (cf. Wright, *Acts for Everyone*, 21).

205. Stott writes that the speaking of other languages symbolizes the universality of the church (*Spirit*, 63). Moreover, the curse of the tower of Babel is reversed, even though the languages remain.

206. For the expression "last days" or similar ones, see also 2 Tim 3:1; Heb 1:1; 1 Pet 1:20; 2 Pet 3:3; Jude 18; 1 John 2:18. These expressions do not refer to the future, but to the time in which people lived, that is, the time between Jesus' ascension and his return (Van Eck, *Handelingen*, 65). The expression "all flesh" applies, in the first place, to the 120 people gathered together in the house. As such, these 120 represent all Israel (Van Eck, *Handelingen*, 65–66; cf. 47). The Spirit being poured out on all Israel is an initial fulfillment of Num 13:29 (Van Eck, *Handelingen*, 66).

207. Van Eck, *Handelingen*, 79–80.

Scene two: the church performing and bearing witness to what is in Christ

Because Christ surrendered his life to his Father and offered him the sacrifice of his life through the power of the Spirit, not only as Israel's substitute but also as its representative, Israel participated in that sacrifice and was sanctified in him. In his death on the cross, Christ made atonement for Israel's sin, expiating it or removing it from God's sight and propitiating or stilling his wrath, so that in him Israel is reconciled to God and freed from the curse of the law and the power of the devil. Because Jesus rose from the dead as Israel's representative and was thereby vindicated or justified, Israel shared in that resurrection and was justified in him and has new life in him. What is in Christ, Israel's representative, can be summed up as the resurrection life of God's new creation (Gal 6:15; Eph 2:15; 2 Cor 5:17; Rev 21:5).[208]

But if God would achieve his goal—having Israel be the theater of his theodrama, made up of actors who live out and bear witness to his intratrinitarian mutual glorification by sharing in Christ's status of sonship and his communion of love with the Father by the Spirit and his filial spirit, trustfully listening to and doing his will, so that God becomes visible on earth—he would have to do more than have Christ do things *for* Israel. He would also need to have Christ do things *in* the hearts of the people of his new covenant community by his Holy Spirit.[209]

Christ would have to circumcise or regenerate their hearts and make them into new creations by changing them from being curved in on themselves, self-enclosed, driven by their own agenda and standards, independent of God and unreceptive to his voice. He would have to give them a spirit of filial openness and responsiveness so that they listen to and obey his will in faith by baptizing them with the Holy Spirit and increasingly incorporating them into his communion of love with the Father. He would have to work by the Spirit so that they would bear witness

---

208. O'Donovan, *Resurrection and Moral Order*, passim.

209. While Scripture does not teach a twofold soteriological structure where Christ purchases benefits of salvation and the Holy Spirit applies these benefits, the point that Calvin makes about this structure can be applied to our distinction between what Christ has done *for* us and what he also needs to do *in* us by his Spirit. Calvin says that "we must understand that as long as Christ remains outside of us, and we are separated from him, all that he has suffered and done for the salvation of the human race remains useless and of no value for us. Therefore, to share with us what he has received from the Father, he had to become ours and to dwell within us" (Calvin, *Institutes*, 3.1.1)

to what is in him by putting on Christ through faith and clothing themselves with him and sharing in the mind of Christ (John 1:12-13; 3:4-5; 4:13-14; 6:35, 53-58; 7:37-39; 8:31-32; 10:3, 27; 14:19, 21; 15:4-5, 7-8, 10-12, 16; 17:11, 20-23, 26; 20:21; Rom 8:9-10; 12:5; 13:14; 15:3, 5; 1 Cor 3:11, 16; 6:17, 19; 10:16; 11:1; 12:27; Gal 3:1-5, 27; 4:6; Eph 1:22-23; 2:21-22; 4:10, 13; 5:2; Col 1:18; 2:9-10, 19; 3:12; 1 Pet 1:23; 2:21; 4:1; 1 John 2:6; 4:15-16; 5:20; cf. 1 Cor 2:16).[210]

Being the theater of God's drama by living out the resurrection life of God's new creation in the power of the Holy Spirit is an incarnational life because it manifests our being joined to the glorified human Christ in heaven, through the bond of the Spirit, as members of his body (Rom 12:4-5; Eph 1:23; 4:12; 5:23, 30; 1 Cor 12:12, 14-20, 27). Of course, the incarnation as such was a one-time event at Jesus' conception and is unrepeatable, but this incarnational life is a participatory life through union with Christ.[211] It involves being the anointed presence of Jesus on earth, looking at those in need with the compassionate eyes of Jesus (Luke 7:13), listening to those in need with the merciful ears of Jesus (Matt 9:27-31), speaking into the lives of the lost with the prophetic mouth of Jesus (Matt 9:35-38), giving to the hungry with the loving hands of Jesus (Matt 14:13-21), and going to those in need with the ministering feet of Jesus (Acts 10:38).

It is also a cruciform life because it manifests our having died and been buried together with Christ (Rom 6:3-11; Gal 2:20; Col 2:11-13). This cruciform life entails daily putting off our old self in Adam (Eph 4:22, 24; Col 3:9). It requires denying ourselves, taking up our cross, and

---

210. Most of these Scripture references come from Burger's illuminating chapter on images for union with Christ (Burger, *Life in Christ*, 96-136). In a summary statement about our union with Christ through faith and the Spirit, he writes, "When we come to faith, we discover: we are in Christ and he is in us. Union with Christ is given through faith in Christ. Those who do not believe can read about this union, but do not know this union from personal experience." He adds, "Nevertheless, union with Christ remains a deep mystery for those who believe. Nowhere does the Bible give a description of that union or of the creation of that union. Many images are used to indicate that union and to clarify it, as we have seen in 6.2 and 6.3: the true bread that we eat, the good shepherd and his sheep, the vine and the branches, clothing we put on, a body, a body with a head, a marriage, a building or a temple with Christ as its cornerstone or as a foundation." He concludes, "All these images show something, but at the same time it is clear how difficult it is to adequately describe the position of Christ with these images. If—as Christians believe—there is union with Christ, then it is a divine reality. And wherever we encounter a divine reality, we discover something bigger than we can comprehend, but therefore all the more real" (*Life in Christ*, 128-29).

211. See Billings, *Union with Christ*, 123-65.

following Jesus (Matt 10:38; 16:24; Mark 8:34; Luke 9:23; 14:27; Gal 2:20; 1 John 3:16).[212] In losing our lives in this manner and following Jesus, we paradoxically find our lives in his death and resurrection (Matt 10:39; 16:25; Mark 8:35; Luke 9:24; 17:33; John 12:25–26; 2 Tim 2:11–13; 4:6–8; Rev 2:10–11; 7:14–17; 12:11).

Putting off our old self in Adam also involves no longer being a slave to sin (Rom 6:2, 7, 11, 15–23; 8:12–13; 12:17, 19, 21; 13:13–14; Gal 5:19–21, 24; Eph 2:3; 4:25–31; 5:3–7, 11–12, 18; Col 2:20; 3:5–9; 1 Cor 6:9–10, 12–19; 2 Cor 12:20–21; 1 Thess 4:3–6; 5:22; 1 Tim 5:22; Titus 2:12; 3:3; Jas 3:14–16; 4:1; 1 Pet 2:11, 24; 4:1–4; 1 John 3:4, 8–9).

Putting off our old self also entails leading a counter-cultural life (Rom 12:2; 1 Cor 1:26–28; 3:19; 4:19, 13; 5:9–11; 7:28, 31, 33–34; 11:32; 2 Cor 7:10; Gal 4:3, 9; 6:14; Eph 2:2; Phil 2:15; Col 2:8, 20; 2 Tim 4:9; Titus 2:12; Jas 1:27; 4:4; 2 Pet 1:4; 2:20; 1 John 2:15–17; 3:2, 13; 4:4–6; 5:4–5, 19).[213]

At the same time, this incarnational and cruciform life is also an *anastiform* or resurrectional life,[214] because it manifests our having arisen together with Christ. This resurrectional life entails daily putting on our new self in Christ (Eph 4:22, 24; Col 3:9). It involves having Christ form himself in us as he lives the resurrection life of God's new creation in and through us (John 6:57; 15:1–17; Gal 2:20; 4:19; 5:22–23; Eph 1:19–20; 2:5, 10; 3:16–17; Phil 1:21; 2:13; 4:13; Col 2:6–7, 10). This resurrection life of God's new creation is a manifestation of the wholeness of the different facets of a life of love for God and one's neighbor (Matt 5–7; Rom 6:12–14, 16–18, 22; 8:1–11; 9:11–21; 13:1–10, 14; 14:1–23; 15:1–7; 1 Cor 3:16–17; 6:1–20; 7:1–40; 8:1–13; 9:4–6, 12, 15, 18; 10:23–33; 11:1–34; 13:1–13; 16:1–2; 2 Cor 1:5–11; 6:14–18; 8:1–14; 9:6–15; Gal 6:1–10; Eph 4:25, 28–29, 32; 5:1, 15–33; 6:1–20; Phil 1:9–11, 27; 2:1–5, 14–18; 3:17; 4:1–9; Col 3:10–25; 4:1–6; 1 Thess 4:9–12; 5:12–18; 2 Thess 2:15;

---

212. "How complete our self-denial needs to be can be seen in the other expression Jesus uses for it: taking up his cross. The cross is a Roman means of execution. Whoever takes up the cross is going to die" (Van Bruggen, *Marcus*, 190).

213. About this cruciform counter-cultural life, Burger writes, "Pentecost gives perseverance and hope to live a cruciform life: to be present at the place of the cross and to share in Christ's suffering: where I am confronted with my own sin, with brokenness and pain, with the social and ecological injustice in the world, with persecution and temptation, with the experience of being forsaken by God. Expectantly, we may look forward to the Spirit of God's love, who, through our efforts, overcomes evil through his goodness" ("Gedachten over Pinksteren").

214. For the term and concept of "resurrectional," see Gorman, *Participating in Christ*, 53–76.

3:5, 13-15; 1 Tim 5:1—6:2, 11-21; 2 Tim 1:3-14; 2:1-26; 4:1-5; Titus 2:1—3:11; Philem 17-18; Heb 4:1-11; 10:22-25; 12:1-17; 13:1-19; Jas 1:1-5:20; 1 Pet 1:13-25; 2:13—3:7; 4:7-11; 1 John 4:12, 15-16; Rev 2-3).

This cruciform and yet resurrectional life involves spiritual warfare (2 Cor 10:3-5; Rom 8:37; Eph 6:10-20; 2 Thess 3:3; Jas 4:7; 1 Pet 5:8-9; Rev 12:13-17) and a participation in the sufferings and death of Christ (Matt 5:10-12; 10:18-22, 25; 24:9; John 15:18-25; Acts 5:41; Rom 8:17-23; 2 Cor 1:5; 2:16; 4:9-12, 16-18; 5:14-17; 12:9-10; Gal 2:19-20; Phil 1:29; 3:10; 2 Tim 2:3, 9; Heb 10:32; Jas 5:10, 13; 1 Pet 2:19-20; 3:14, 17; 4:13-16).[215] Through these sufferings, the crucified Christ is increasingly formed in us (Rom 8:29; Gal 4:19; cf. 2:20), so that these sufferings "fill up what is lacking in Christ's afflictions" (Col 1:24) and "are not worth comparing with the glory that is to be revealed to us" (Rom 8:18).[216]

But this is also an ascensional life, because it manifests our having been seated with Christ in the heavenly realms (Eph 1:20; 2:7; Col 1:13).[217] This ascension life of daily putting on our ascensional self and living out what is in Christ involves participating in the drama of

---

215. About "filling up what is lacking in Christ's afflictions," Van Eck, pointing his readers to Acts 4:24 and Rev 6:11, writes, "The thought behind this is that Christ only bore part of the suffering that one has to endure for his name in this world. The remainder is for his followers. Paul sees the imprisonment he is now undergoing for the cause of Christ and his congregation as part of this suffering that is still lacking" (*Kolossenzen en Filemon*, 121). About the word "suffering," Burger writes, "The word that is used for 'suffering' in the Greek, however, is never used in connection with the dying of Christ for our sins. It about suffering that belongs to the end time, all kinds of trouble or oppression, but not to deal with the problem of our sin. In other words, it's not about participating in Christ's suffering and death for our sin" (*Life in Christ*, 146-47).

216. Van Bruggen writes, "The 'sufferings of this present time' are not limited to persecution. It is all suffering related to the time in which we live. This time is characterized by the reign of Sin resulting in death (5:12-21)." He adds, "The sufferings of this present time include the degeneration of society as outlined in 1:24-32. This suffering is thus closely related to the reality of people who experience the reality of Sin (5:12). Precisely Christians, like Lot in Sodom, will suffer injustice and sin in this world. In this injustice and sin, Christ's kingship is not acknowledged. Those who are of Christ suffer this with him in this time" (*Romeinen*, 121; see also Burger, *Life in Christ*, 146-47, 158-59).

217. About "transferred us to the kingdom of his beloved Son," Van Bruggen writes, "When Paul says that 'God has brought us into the kingdom of the Son he loves' (Col. 1:13), he does not mean that this kingdom is the Christian community. Rather, he is speaking about the indissoluble tie that already exists with the kingdom of heaven. Thus, he also says concerning people who are still living on the earth: 'God raised us up with Christ and seated us with him in the heavenly realms in Christ Jesus' (Eph. 2:6)" (*Jesus the Son of God*, 82).

Christ as priest, "the mediator of worship,"[218] and glorifying the Father in heavenly worship when we come to worship together on earth (Heb 2:12; 8:2; 12:22–24). On earth as in heaven!

As such, the drama of our worship on earth is "the echo" of the drama of worship taking place in heaven.[219] We share in the drama of his prayers in heaven (Luke 22:31–32; John 17:9–21; Rom 8:34; Heb 4:13–16; 6:20; 7:25—8:6; 9:24; 1 John 2:1–2; cf. Rom 8:26–27), prayers not only for ourselves but also prayers for the world (Exod 19:6; 1 Pet 2:9; 1 Tim 2:1–4).[220] Of foremost importance is the petition for the gift and filling of the Holy Spirit (Luke 11:13; John 3:34; 4:10; 7:37–39; 14:16–17; Acts 4:31; 8:15; Eph 3:14–19; 5:18)[221] so that we can, in union with Christ as priest, offer God the priestly sacrifice of our lives (Rom 12:1; 1 Pet 2:5, 9).[222]

Putting on our ascensional self also involves participating in the drama of Christ's prophetic ministry of preaching the Father's good news of the coming kingdom and calling people to repentance to "make ready for the Lord a people prepared" (Luke 1:17) or face the fire of God's coming judgment (Matt 3:9–10; 11:10–24; Luke 12:47–48; Rom 2:4–5, 9; 1 Cor 11:32; 2 Cor 7:9–10; Heb 12:24–25; 1 Pet 4:17; Rev 2:5, 21–22; 3:3, 19).

It also involves participating in the drama of Christ's kingly ministry of forgiving people their sins and exercising church discipline (Matt 16:19; 18:15–20; 1 Cor 5:1–5), administering the sacraments (Matt 26:26–29; 28:18–19; 1 Cor 11:17–31), and sharing in the gifts of the Spirit Christ gives from heaven as the ascended king (Rom 12:6–8; 1 Cor 7:7; 12:1–31; 14:1–40; Eph 4:9–16; 1 Pet 4:10–11).[223]

---

218. Torrance, *Worship*, 43–67.

219. Torrance, *Worship*, 14.

220. Burger, *Life in Christ*, 164; *Being in Christ*, 535–38.

221. Burger, *Life in Christ*, 164–65.

222. Burger, *Life in Christ*, 164. About our response of faith, Torrance rightly writes, "Our response in faith and obedience is a response to the response already made for us by Christ to the Father's holy love, a response we are summoned to make in union with Christ" (*Worship*, 53–54). In the same vein, Burger writes, "Whoever puts on Christ can participate in good practices that are, as it were, prepared beforehand: we are, says Paul, 'created in Christ Jesus for good works, which God prepared beforehand, that we should walk in them' (Ephesians 2:10)" (*Life in Christ*, 119).

223. Burger, *Life in Christ*, 163. In 1 Corinthians 13:8–10, Paul writes, "As for prophecies, they will pass away; as for tongues, they will cease; as for knowledge, it will pass away. For we know in part and we prophesy in part, but when the perfect comes, the partial will pass away." Since this "perfect" refers to the eschaton when we will no longer

Living this cruciform, resurrectional, and ascensional life is the only fitting response to God's mercy in the life of God's new covenant community and is meant to arouse ethnic Jews who do not believe in Christ to jealousy (Rom 11:17-24, 30-32; 12:1-2). The more non-Christian ethnic Jews are able to see how the Christian church presents its life to God as an innovative and creative sacrifice by thankfully participating in the drama of God's mission for his glory, the more the Holy Spirit can use this sacrifice to arouse them to jealousy and graft them back into reconstituted Israel through faith in Jesus Christ.[224]

Because the outpouring of the Holy Spirit is the first fruits or the down payment of the resurrection life of God's new creation (Rom 8:23; 2 Cor 1:22; 5:5; Eph 1:14), our participation in or performance of the drama by our incarnational, cruciform, resurrectional, and ascensional life is incomplete.[225] Burger says, "You can see the incompleteness in the use of the expression 'in Christ.' On the one hand, this expression reminds us that Christ is our substitute: representative and inclusive. We can be in him." He adds, "On the other hand, this expression is necessary when we still participate incompletely in Christ. It has only happened to the substitute; there is still something to be done to us—'in Christ' always calls attention to this incompleteness. The tension between what has already happened and what has not yet happened—but will happen—is part of the expression 'in Christ.'"[226]

Accordingly, we are still eagerly awaiting the redemption of our bodies (Rom 8:23-25). This brings us to the last act of God's drama of his mission for his glory.

Act five: the drama of the return of Christ and the theater of the theodrama (4)

The fifth act of the drama of God's mission for his glory will be the theater of God's glory in the way he always wanted. The persons of the Trinity will make their intratrinitarian mutual glorification present in time in a new creation where they, humanity, and creation will act out and bear

---

see in a mirror dimly, but face to face, it is exegetically untenable to consider the so-called special gifts of the Spirit to have ceased after the time of the apostolic church (De Bruijne, "Tiende zegen"; cf. Fee, *First Epistle to the Corinthians*, 645-46).

224. De Bruijne, "Christelijke ethiek," 141-45.
225. Burger, *Life in Christ*, 143, 145, 148, 149, 153, 164, 166.
226. Burger, *Life in Christ*, 153.

witness to the life of heaven on earth, making the world a place where heaven and earth meet.

This act will be sketched in two scenes. Scene one depicts the return of Christ to judge the living and the dead. Scene two portrays the ushering in of a new heaven and new earth, a new holy temple, where creation and humanity live in God's loving presence, participating in life, and reflect his glory by doing heaven on earth for all eternity.

Scene one: the return of Christ as judge

In act three, scene two, John the Baptist called Israel to repent and be baptized with a baptism of repentance or face the fire of God's coming judgment. John said that the one coming after him would baptize with the Holy Spirit and fire (Matt 3:11; Luke 3:16)—that is, the fire of God's judgment. In the next scene of that act, Christ, as a prophet, called Israel to faith and repentance in the power of the Spirit and summoned them to believe the good news that the kingdom of heaven had come near, again with the alternative of the fire of God's coming judgment (Matt 5:22; 7:19; 13:40, 42, 50; 18:8–9; 25:41; Mark 9:43, 45, 47; Luke 12:49; John 15:6).[227]

Because only the Father knows when the Lord Jesus Christ, the son of David, will return (Mark 13:32), Jesus and the apostles after him urge the people to wait and be watchful in order to be prepared for his return (Matt 24:42, 44; 25:10, 13; Mark 13:35–37; Luke 12:40; 1 Thess 5:6; Jas 5:9; 2 Pet 3:12; Rev 19:7; 22:14). His return will be preceded by the birth pangs of God's new creation (Matt 24:1–31; Mark 13:3–27; Luke 17:5–28; Rom 8:22), so that "the community of Christ is living during the last days under a constellation that tells them that 'it is near, right at the door'" (Mark 13:29).[228]

There will be many antichrists, incited by the spirit of antichrist, the devil, who will oppose and deny that Jesus is the Christ (1 John 2:18, 22–23; 4:3; 2 John 7; cf. John 8:12–20, 25–30, 44–47, 54–58; 1 Pet 5:8; 1

---

227. Van Bruggen, *Jesus the Son of God*, 232–33. "Already in the Old Testament, fire is a symbol of God's purifying and cleansing activity. This fire is not an uncontrollable, irrational natural disaster in which a great deal of value is lost, but a carefully planned trash incineration project to purify and preserve the environment of God's world" (Van Bruggen, *Jesus the Son of God*, 233).

228. Van Bruggen, *Jesus the Son of God*, 235.

John 5:18).[229] There will be an increase in lawlessness, during which time many will fall away from the faith (Matt 24:12; Luke 17:26–30; 21:24–27; 2 Thess 2:1–12; 2 Tim 3:1–4; 2 Pet 2:5–10; Jude 7).[230] In addition, there will be precursors of God's final judgment (1 Cor 11:22; Heb 12:5–11; 1 Pet 4:17; Rev 3:19; 6:1–8; 8:6–12; 9:1–21; 16:1–16).[231]

When the time the Father has allotted for this lawlessness is finished, the Lord Jesus Christ will suddenly and unexpectedly appear on the clouds of heaven, the graves will give up their dead, those who died in Christ and the living in Christ who are instantaneously transfigured will meet him in the air, and the final judgment will take place (Matt 24:27, 29–30; 1 Thess 4:13–18; 2 Thess 2:8; 2 Pet 3:10; Rev 19:11–21).[232] Then the Lord Jesus will be publicly vindicated and acknowledged as Lord to the glory of the Father (Phil 2:10–11).

On the day of judgment, God will manifest his glory by showing no partiality. Whether one is an Israelite or not will make no difference (Rom 2:11; 1 Pet 1:17). When God opens the books, he will judge everyone by what they have done (Matt 12:36–37; 16:27; Rom 2:6–16; 2 Cor 5:10; 1 Pet 1:17; Rev 20:12–13; 22:12). For some, this judgment will be more tolerable than for others (Luke 10:12, 14; 12:47–48).

---

229. Van Bruggen, *Geheim van Jezus' Namen*, 95–109.

230. About "the man of lawlessness," Van Bruggen writes, "It is not very plausible that we should think of this 'man of lawlessness' as a human person. It is a summarizing characterization, a personification like we can also speak of 'the modern man.' There will come a time when the God-fearing man will be repressed by the godless man" (*Geheim van Jezus' namen*, 114). Because 2 Thess 2 speaks about lawlessness and 1 and 2 John speak about denial that Jesus is the Christ, the antichrists and the man of lawlessness are not the same. However, they are related because they both are incited by Satan (*Geheim van Jezus' namen*, 114–15). Rev 13 depicts this satanic relationship between the man of lawlessness and the antichrists as the relation between the beast rising from the sea and the beast rising from the earth. Satan uses both to deceive and reinforce each other (cf. Rev 20:10) (*Geheim van Jezus' namen*, 116).

231. Because God's judgment is meant to remove the curse of sin from this world, his fatherly discipline is also a form of God's judgment. Burger writes, "God can punish us from a pedagogical point of view to train and encourage us to purge our lives of evil. Thus, punishment and judgment can have a positive effect: not condemning and negative, but educational and encouraging" (*Life in Christ*, 186).

232. Van Bruggen, *Geheim van Jezus' Namen*, 111–27. About the word "appearance" (*parousia*), Van Bruggen writes, "The word for his appearance (*parousia*) actually means 'presence.' It stands in contrast to 'absence' (cf. Phil. 2:12). To be present somewhere, people often have to travel and arrive somewhere. This does not play a role in the appearance of the Lord of Lords. There is no distance to be bridged. With Him it is as if a curtain is pulled back and we suddenly see His presence when He appears on the clouds" (*Geheim van Jezus' namen*, 128).

Those who did not participate in God's mission for his glory with a listening and thankful filial spirit, characterized by the openness and responsiveness of faith, will be condemned to hell (Matt 5:29–30; 10:28; 13:42, 50; 18:9; 25:46; Mark 9:43; 1 Cor 6:9; Gal 5:21; Eph 5:5; 2 Thess 1:9; 2 Pet 2:4; Jude 7; Rev 21:8).[233] But those who did participate in the drama of God's mission for his glory in this way will be acquitted and vindicated and will "inherit the kingdom prepared for [them] from the foundation of the world" (Matt 25:34; cf. 13:43; 19:29; 20:23; Luke 12:32; 22:29; John 3:16; 14:2–3; Rom 8:1, 17; 1 Cor 2:9; Eph 1:11; Col 3:24; 2 Tim 2:12; Titus 3:7; Heb 11:16; 12:28; Jas 2:5; 1 Pet 1:4–5; 2 Pet 1:11).[234] Moreover, because they have put on Christ, borne witness to what is in him, and are

---

233. About those who have never heard of Christ, Van Bruggen writes, "It is difficult for human beings to make definitive statements about God's dealings with those who have never heard of Christ. What was true in the circle of the disciples is even more true now. There the question was asked, 'Lord, what about him?' (John 21:21). Jesus answered, 'If I want him to remain alive until I return what is that to you? You must follow me' (John 21:22)" (*Jesus the Son of God*, 235). However, Paul does write, "For when Gentiles, who do not have the law, by nature do what the law requires, they are a law to themselves, even though they do not have the law. They show that the work of the law is written on their hearts, while their conscience also bears witness, and their conflicting thoughts accuse or even excuse them on that day when, according to my gospel, God judges the secrets of men by Christ Jesus" (Rom 2:14–16). In the previous chapter, we saw that because the law Paul is referring to is the Mosaic law, he means that when Gentiles by nature or spontaneously do what the law requires, they do so because somehow the influence of the written law of God makes itself felt in their lives. Moreover, Paul also writes, "For the wrath of God is revealed from heaven against all ungodliness and unrighteousness of men, who by their unrighteousness suppress the truth. For what can be known about God is plain to them, because God has shown it to them. For his invisible attributes, namely, his eternal power and divine nature, have been clearly perceived, ever since the creation of the world, in the things that have been made. So they are without excuse" (Rom 1:18–20). Thus, every human being has an innate sense of God, which Calvin referred to as the *sensus divinitatis* or *semen religionis*. Calvin writes, "And they who in other aspects of life seem least to differ from brutes still continue to retain some seed of religion" (*Institutes*, 1.3.1). Heppe writes, "The most essential content of natural religion is given by Riissen thus (I,7): '(1) that God is, (2) and that he must be worshipped, (3) that we must live good lives, (4) that the soul is immortal, (5) that a reward is due to virtue, punishment to wickedness" (*Reformed Dogmatics*, 1–2). Regarding this sense of punishment, see Rom 1:32. Because of the noetic effects of sin, the *sensus divinitatis* does not work properly in every human being (Plantinga, *Warranted Christian Belief*, 213–16).

234. This acquittal and vindication were already received in faith when they were justified through faith. This acquittal and vindication of our life as a totality does not preclude the condemnation, exposure, and purification by fire of parts of our life (1 Cor 3:10–15; 4:5). Thus, Burger writes, "Knowing that you are freed from condemnation and that you will escape God's wrath (Romans 5:9) does not rule out that the filter of God's corrective judgment can painfully affect your life" (*Life in Christ*, 186).

heirs together with him, they will be rewarded for their good works by participating in his reward (Matt 25:21; Luke 14:14; 22:29–30; Rom 8:17; 1 Cor 3:14; 4:5; 2 Tim 4:8; Rev 3:21; 11:18; 21:7).[235]

On this day of judgment, God will also manifest his glory by crushing Satan under his feet and throwing him into the lake of fire and sulfur (Rom 16:20; Rev 20:10). Moreover, he will throw death and the grave into that lake (1 Cor 15:26; Rev 20:14; 21:4). In doing so, he will fulfill the first part of his promise to rescue the drama of his mission for his glory by removing sin, death, and the devil from this world (Gen 3:15).

Scene two: the new heaven and the new earth

To fulfill the second part of his promise by making all things new, God ushers in a new stage for the drama, a new heaven and new earth, a new holy temple, where creation and humanity live in the Sabbath rest of his loving presence, participating in his life in Christ through the Holy Spirit and reflecting the glory of this life by witnessing to all that is in Christ, that is, the resurrection life of his new creation (Rev 21–22).

First, God dismantles the old stage with a cosmic fire that destroys the old heavens, with the sun, moon, and stars, and the old earth with all its unrighteous works (2 Pet 3:10, 12).[236] Then he ushers in a new stage, a new heaven and earth, according to his promise, where righteousness will dwell (2 Pet 3:13). Thus, the continuity between the old stage of the drama and the new stage lies in God's faithfulness to his promise to continue the drama by making all things new (Gen 3:15; Isa 65:17; Rev 21:3–5).[237]

---

235. Burger, *Life in Christ*, 187.

236. *Contra* Wolters who rejects "a cosmic annihilation, a complete destruction or abolition of the created order" ("Worldview and Textual Criticism," 408). Wolters writes, "Against this we shall argue that the author of 2 Peter . . . pictures the day of judgement as a smelting process from which the world will emerge purified" ("Worldview and Textual Criticism," 408; see also Wright, *The Great Story*, 35, 134-36). Van Houwelingen disagrees: "In this way, however, justice is not done to the words 'pass away,' 'burned up,' 'loosed' and 'dissolved.' The terms Peter uses are so strong that the concept of purging is insufficient" (*2 Petrus en Judas*, 91). Concerning the text critical issue of εὑρίσκω ("be exposed" or "be found") or κατακαίω ("be burned up") in verse 10, he opts for κατακαίω because he considers this to be the more difficult reading. He writes, "Because of the enormous consequences for today's world, substantially the reading *katakaesetai* is undoubtedly the most difficult!" (*2 Petrus en Judas*, 94; *contra* Wolters, "Worldview and Textual Criticism," 410).

237. See also Van Houwelingen, *2 Petrus en Judas*, 93, 96

On this new stage, we will receive our inheritance together with Christ as we live in the Sabbath rest of God's loving presence and reflect the glory of his presence. All things will have been summed up in Christ, God will be all in all, and redeemed humanity will completely participate in the divine nature. This will include fully sharing in the Son's status of sonship and his communion of love with the Father through the Spirit (John 14:23; 17:21–24), being glorified or transfigured into "the measure of the stature of the fullness of Christ" (Eph 4:13; Matt 13:34; Rom 8:29–30; 2 Cor 3:18; 4:4, 17; Col 3:4; 2 Tim 2:10; Heb 2:10; 1 Pet 5:1, 19; 2 Pet 1:4; 1 John 3:2), and having incorruptible and immortal spiritual bodies—bodies completely indwelt and controlled by the Spirit of God (1 Cor 15:26, 42–44, 50, 53–54; Luke 20:36; Rom 8:21; Heb 2:14–15; 1 Pet 1:4; Rev 20:14; 21:4; 22:3).[238] It will also involve the termination of marital life so that humanity will be completely oriented toward God and one another as the angels are (Matt 22:30).[239]

The drama of God's mission for his glory, which began with the creation of the world and humanity, will then continue for all eternity as humanity bears continual witness of the mutual glorification of the immanent Trinity by participating fully in the Son's listening and thankful spirit and in the openness and responsiveness of faith and sharing in his kingly rule and priestly care for creation. On earth as in heaven!

---

238. About the spiritual body, Gaffin writes, "The somatic aspect of resurrection, even more than what has already been experienced, will disclose the full dimension of the Holy Spirit's work in the believer" (*Resurrection and Redemption*, 68). Kistemaker writes in a similar vein, "The resurrected body will be completely filled with the Spirit of glory" (*First Epistle to the Corinthians*, 573). Macchia prefers to refer to the spiritual body as a "Spirit body" in which our mortal existence has been "'swallowed up' (or baptized) into immortal life (2 Cor. 5:4)" (*Jesus the Spirit Baptizer*, 188). Later, he writes, "A translation better than *spiritual* here might be 'pneumatic'—or even 'Spiritful'—*body*" (*Jesus the Spirit Baptizer*, 296).

239. Van Bruggen writes, "Jesus does not say that one *cannot* marry anymore. He also does not say anything about the possibilities of angels. The situation of the heavenly angels (the fallen angels are left out of the picture) is such that they praise God and are focused on His service. The male/female orientation is transcended and sublimated to a complete orientation toward God, which does not exclude one's fellow man, but does end the special marriage relationship with one specific person" (*Marcus*, 269).

5

Outlining a Theodramatic Framework

IN THE PREVIOUS CHAPTER, I traced the theodrama through its five acts from creation to consummation. Now I turn from history—from the theodrama itself, as it is presented to us in Scripture—to the systematic theology that it gives rise to, a theology that has participation in the life of God as its integrative center, that incorporates a reframed understanding of divine-human covenants, and that appeals to our imagination, invites us into the drama of God's mission for his glory, and gives us direction for communicating the gospel clearly and for shaping our Christian identity and practice.

BEFORE THE CURTAIN RISES[1]

When I outlined the design features of a theodramatic framework in chapter 1, I said that there are at least five reasons for comparing doctrine to drama. First, Scripture is dramatic both in its form and its content. Second, both doctrine and God's relationship with humanity are essentially

---

1. This section recaps two design features of a theodramatic framework outlined in chapter 1. That chapter, which also included reflection on the nature of Scripture and hermeneutics, dealt with themes normally dealt with in the prolegomena of a systematic theology. For topics that are dealt with in the prolegomena of systematic theologies, see Barth, *CD*, I/1:3–44; Bavinck, *Reformed Dogmatics*, 1:25–621; Beeke and Smalley, *Revelation and God*, 25–173; Frame, *Systematic Theology*, 3–117; Grenz, *Theology for the Community of God*, 1–25; Horton, *Christian Faith*, 35–219; Jones, *Grammar of Christian Faith*, 1–148; Letham, *Systematic Theology*, 66–96; Spykman, *Reformational Theology*, 3–136; Van den Brink and Van der Kooi, *Christian Dogmatics*, 1–74; Van Genderen and Velema, *Reformed Dogmatics*, 1–19.

dialogical. Third, doctrine as drama appeals to the imagination.[2] Fourth, comparing doctrine to drama is a constant reminder that the Christian life is filled with tension and urgency. And fifth, comparing doctrine to drama bridges the gap between theory and practice by reminding us that reading and interpreting Scripture redemptive-historically includes not only the text of Scripture but also the reader of Scripture, for it shows how he figures in the story and is related to Christ in the history of redemption.

Doctrine reconceptualizes the speech acts of Scripture into "thought-acts" or "mental habits," through which we interpret and experience God's speech acts in Scripture and in Jesus Christ in terms of theodramatic imagination and action. As such, doctrine functions as the grammar[3] of the church's practice and performance of the biblical narrative.

Moreover, a theodramatic systematic theology is the result of reflection upon the theodramatic nature of Scripture, appealing to our imagination to creatively improvise and perform the dramatic transcript of Scripture in new situations. Doctrine is meant to give direction to our imagination and action so that we participate in the drama in a way that fits with the whole theodrama of redemption communicated to us in its script, transcript, and prescript and fittingly extend the meaning of the canonical text, developing the dramatic action in new situations and reincorporating those new situations into the theodrama. Thus, doctrine as grammar and as direction for our theodramatic imagination makes ontological truth claims about reality.

The structure of a theodramatic systematic theology, as I showed in chapter 1, is the intentional pedagogical form that is given to our communication of the gospel and the shaping of our Christian identity and practice.[4] As such, a theodramatic systematic theology should be

2. In chapter 1, citing Vanhoozer on theodramatic imagination, I wrote, "While imagination as such is 'the power of forming mental images of what is not really present,' theodramatic imagination 'is the ability to form mental images of what is *really* present . . . even though it cannot be perceived empirically with the senses' (*Drama of Doctrine*, 416). It is 'the power of synoptic vision: the ability to synthesize heterogeneous elements into a unified whole. . . . [It] is the ability to discover connections' (*Drama of Doctrine*, 416, 281; *Pictures at a Theological Exhibition*, 23–27, 133, 165, 177, 232; *Doers and Hearers*, 56, 108).

3. As the grammar of the church's practice and performance of the biblical narrative, doctrine attempts to make clear "*how Christian discourses have sense-making and life-shaping power for their users*" (Jones, *Grammar of Christian Faith*, 9).

4. "Themes are selected, these themes are put together in a certain order, relations

designed to train us more in wisdom and life with God than in abstract truth.

OUTLINING A THEODRAMATIC FRAMEWORK

Participation in the life of God and the drama of God as Trinity

The drama of God as Trinity

As Kasper rightly remarks, the doctrine of the Trinity is the "grammar and summation of the entire Christian mystery of salvation."[5] Van den Brink and Van der Kooi refer to the Trinity as "the Gateway to the Doctrine of God."[6] It is fitting for theological reflection on the doctrine of God to begin with reflection on the Trinity.[7]

---

are made between these themes.... This is what we always do when we explain the gospel to someone else ... in a way that communicates the message effectively." He adds, "We do the same in education, but also in systematic theology ... putting theological themes together in a certain structured way.... We always have a certain point of view from which we select and order theological themes, choosing words and images that fit our purposes. This is done in response to certain questions, which are being asked in our context" (Burger, "Gospel Presentation," 269).

5. Kasper, *God of Jesus Christ*, 311; cf. 310-14; Lash, "Considering the Trinity," 183, 188, 192, 193, 194; Burger, "Hart en wezen," 341-42.

6. Van den Brink and Van der Kooi, *Christian Dogmatics*, 76.

7. Others who begin their doctrine of God with the doctrine of the Trinity include Barth (*Church Dogmatics* I/1:293-489), Grenz (*Theology for the Community of God*, 53-76), Jones (*Grammar of Christian Faith*, 149-232), Kärkkäinen (*Trinity and Revelation*, 250-82), Letham (*Systematic Theology*, 66-154), Pannenberg (*Systematic Theology*, 259-336), and Van Genderen and Velema (*Reformed Dogmatics*, 143-64).

For a cartography of the renaissance of trinitarian theology, see Grenz, *Rediscovering the Triune God*; Kärkkäinen, *The Trinity*, 67-380. For further scriptural warrant for understanding God as Trinity, see Barth, *Church Dogmatics* I/1, 384-489; Bavinck, *Reformed Dogmatics*, 2:261-64, 269-79; Beeke and Smalley, *Revelation and God*, 876-80; Berkhof, *Systematic Theology*, 85-86; Calvin, *Institutes*, 1.13.16-20; Frame, *Systematic Theology*, 433-43; Grenz, *Theology for the Community of God*, 53-56; Horton, *Christian Faith*, 273-78; Kärkkäinen, *The Trinity*, 3-15; Letham, *Systematic Theology*, 66-96; Macleod, *Faith to Live By*, 49-59; Van den Brink and Van der Kooi, *Christian Dogmatics*, 81-86; Van Genderen and Velema, *Reformed Dogmatics*, 143-46; see also Swain, *The Trinity*, 25-51. For a defense that the oneness of God in Deut 6:4 refers to qualitative uniqueness and not quantitative oneness as well as Paul's rephrasing of it in 1 Cor 8:6, see Huijgen and Versluis, "'Our God Is One,'" 213-25. For the historical development of the doctrine of the Trinity, see Beeke and Smalley, *Revelation and God*, 902-8; Berkhof, *Systematic Theology*, 82-83; Grenz, *Theology for the Community of God*, 56-64; Horton, *Christian Faith*, 278-306; Kärkkäinen, *The Trinity*, 19-64; Letham, *Systematic Theology*, 97-125; Van den Brink and Van der Kooi, *Christian Dogmatics*, 90-104. For von

The doctrine of the Trinity is generated by the theodramatic biblical narrative outlined in the previous chapter.[8] "If we follow the order of knowledge," says Kasper, "we must begin with the missions as they occur in the history of salvation and with the revelation of these in words, and then come to know the eternal processions via the missions as their ground and presupposition."[9]

Grammatically reconceptualizing the speech acts of the drama of God as Trinity in terms of theodramatic imagination and action entails the following. First, within the immanent or internal life of God, there are eternal relationships or processions of Father, Son, and Holy Spirit.[10]

Second, these eternal relationships of Father, Son, and Spirit include relationships of origin.[11] The Father eternally generates or begets the Son in the spiration of the Holy Spirit. The Son is eternally generated or begotten by the Father in the spiration of the Spirit (*spiritusque*).[12] Moreover, the Spirit simultaneously proceeds from the Father and the Son (*filioque*).[13] These eternal relations of origin that subsist within the one being of God are what is meant by the "persons" of the Trinity.

Balthasar on the Trinity, see Balthasar, *Theo-Drama*, 3:505–35. For how the biblical figure of the Trinity rhythms and patterns our understanding of ultimate reality, see Watkin, *Biblical Critical Theory*, 33-52.

8. Horton writes, "Doctrine grows out of the biblical *drama*. . . the drama yields specific *doctrine*. . . doctrines are rooted in the drama" (*Core Christianity*, 17). Vanhoozer writes that doctrine can be considered "the conceptual elaboration of *divine action*." As such, it is "a by-product of God's prior communicative action" (*Remythologizing Theology*, 272, cf. 274). Thus, the biblical drama is foundational for doctrine.

9. Kasper, *God of Jesus Christ*, 277; see also Vanhoozer, *Remythologizing Theology*, 148

10. The immanent or internal life of God is also referred to as the immanent, ontological or essential Trinity (Sanders, *Deep Things of God*, 95).

11. Pannenberg correctly writes, "The Father does not merely beget the Son. He also hands over his kingdom to him and receives it back from him. The Son is not merely begotten of the Father. He is also obedient to him. . . . The Spirit is not just breathed. He also fills the Son. . . . The persons cannot be identical simply with any one relation. Each is a catalyst of many relations" (*Systematic Theology*, 320; Vanhoozer, *Remythologizing Theology*, 148).

12. For the Father begetting the Son in or through the Spirit, see Weinandy, *The Father's Spirit of Sonship*.

13. Habets, *Anointed Son*, 223–27. "The word *filioque* was never intended to say that the Spirit proceeds from the Father and from the Son as from two different sources (such a 'double procession' would undermine the unity of God). Rather, it intended to convey the idea that the Spirit proceeded in a flowing movement from the Father and the Son, as from one source" (Van den Brink and Van der Kooi, *Christian Dogmatics*, 103).

Accordingly, "it is not as though the relations *exist between* the three persons... Rather the persons *are* the relations."[14]

Third, the eternal relationships of Father, Son, and Spirit include not only generative relations but also communicative relations.[15] Since God speaks or communicates light to creation and humanity in Christ through the Spirit in history, the three persons speak or communicate light to each other in Christ through the Spirit (John 1:4, 9; 1 John 1:5). Since God shares life with creation and humanity in Christ through the Spirit, the Father, Son, and Spirit share life in Christ through the Spirit (John 5:26; 6:63; 14:6; Acts 3:15). Since Christ was always open and responsive to the Father by trustfully listening to and doing his will through the Spirit in time, he is always open and responsive to the Father by trustfully listening to and doing his will through the Spirit in eternity (John 5:19).[16] Since the Father, Son, and Spirit act together in the

---

14. Allison and Köstenberger, *Holy Spirit*, 255–56; see also Vanhoozer, *Remythologizing Theology*, 146–47. This is not to say that the divine persons are "nothing but relations," but that "their distinct personal *identities* are relational" (Vanhoozer, *Remythologizing Theology*, 144).

15. Vanhoozer gives the following definition of communication: "To communicate (Lat. *communicare*) is to 'share' or 'make common.'" Moreover, it "carries connotations of 'communion' and 'communicant'" (*Remythologizing Theology*, 206, 212).

The fact that God communicates or makes common implies the drama of revelation. For the drama of God's revelation in Scripture, see chapter 1. Because the drama of revelation is implied, it will not be further developed in this chapter. However, the drama of revelation in Scripture will be further developed in connection with the drama of the Holy Spirit. For systematic theological overviews of the drama of revelation, see Balthasar, *Glory of the Lord*, 1:429–683; Barth, *Church Dogmatics* I/1, 45–489; I/2, 1–537; Bavinck, *Reformed Dogmatics*, 1:281–494; Beeke and Smalley, *Revelation and God*, 177–480; Berkhof, *Systematic Theology*, 34–39; Calvin, *Institutes*, 1.1–9; Frame, *Systematic Theology*, 519–693; Grenz, *Theology for the Community of God*, 133–39; Horton, *Christian Faith*, 113–85; Jones, *Grammar of Christian Faith*, 57–109; Kärkkäinen, *Trinity and Revelation*, 7–178; Letham, *Systematic Theology*, 52–65; Van den Brink and Van der Kooi, *Christian Dogmatics*, 157–99; Van Genderen and Velema, *Reformed Dogmatics*, 20–116. In chapter 1, I concluded that because in our communication of the gospel we are creatures limited by time and history, body and finitude, the design of a theodramatic framework for communicating the gospel needs to highlight that our understanding will always be a subjective and limited interpretation of reality. Van den Brink and Van der Kooi come to the same conclusion regarding revelation when they assert that, because revelation is always mediated indirectly through our earthly sensory perception, it will never give us a God's eye view but will always be a partial knowledge that is multi-interpretable (*Christian Dogmatics*, 167–71).

16. The eternal filial responsiveness of the Son to the Father implies an eternal hypostatic subordination, but not a substantial subordination (Boyer, "Articulating Order," 271). Eternal hypostatic subordination does not lead to the Son having a different will from the Father because the Father and the Son (and Spirit) possess a common or

economy of creation and redemption, with each person fulfilling his task in his specific manner, the three persons act together in the immanent Trinity.[17] This is all the more the case since they live in each other (John 14:10; 17:21).[18] Since the Son glorifies the Father, and the Father and the Son and the Spirit glorify each other in time, they glorify each other in eternity (John 17:5, 24). Thus, the economic Trinity reveals or communicates the immanent Trinity.[19]

---

shared will which they each hold properly or distinctively as Father and Son (and Spirit) internal to the indivisible fullness of their being. See Swain and Allen, "Obedience of the Eternal Son," 122–23, 126–31; Allen, *Justification and the Gospel*, 83–89; Boyer, "Articulating Order," 264–67; Muller, *Triunity of God*, 324–32; Vanhoozer, "At Play," 19.

17. Augustine formulated this concept as follows: "God's works *ad extra* are indivisible, though the order and distinction of the persons is preserved" (cited in Bavinck, *Reformed Dogmatics*, 3:318). Bavinck adds, "The Father works *of* himself *through* the Son *in* the Spirit. Scripture marks these distinctions very clearly in the so-called 'differentiating prepositions' ἐκ (out of), διὰ (through), and ἐν (in) (1 Cor. 8:6; John 1:3, 14)" (Bavinck, *Reformed Dogmatics*, 3:319). Burger correctly notes, "However, this choice does not do justice to the fact that the New Testament shows a greater diversity in the use of prepositions. God acts through (*dia*) but also in (*en*) Christ. When we participate in Christ the Bible speaks of with (*sun*) Him. God acts in (*en*) but also through (*hupo* or *dia*) the Spirit." He offers a suggestion: "In order not to hinder one's reading of the Bible, I would rather not give three prepositions precedence over others, but look for the specific nature of the work of the three persons." Drawing on Basil, one of the Cappadocian fathers, he suggests that this can be done by speaking about the Father initiating an act, the Son effecting the act, and the Spirit perfecting the act ("Hart en wezen," 337). Concerning the interior works, Van den Brink and Van der Kooi write, "Only the interior works (*ad intra*), which are between the person of the Trinity, are divided. Only in this realm is it true that what the Father does differs from what the Son does; and the same is true for the relationship of the Spirit to the other two (*Christian Dogmatics*, 97).

18. This is often referred to as *perichoresis* (Clark and Johnson, *Incarnation of God*, 64–67). For a critique of taking the concept of *perichoresis* to imply that God is a sort of ontotheological, open, social society who has an ontological, perichoretic, dependent relationship with the world, see Vanhoozer, *Remythologizing Theology*, 81–177. For a redefinition of social trinitarianism that takes into account justified objections, see Van den Brink, "Social Trinitarianism," 431–50; see also Horrell, "Eternal God," 44–79. For a defense of a social aspect to the doctrine of the Trinity, drawing on the Gospel of John, see Burger, "Hart en wezen," 345–48. For a sustained critique of any form of social trinitarianism, see Dolezal, *All That Is in God*. For an argument that perichoresis has nothing to do with dancing, see Perkins, "The Dance Is Not PERICHŌRĒSIS."

19. As Vanhoozer says, "the economic Trinity corresponds to but does not exhaust or encompass the reality of the immanent Trinity" (*Remythologizing Theology*, 203). See also Gunton, *Act and Being*, 76–93; Van den Brink and Van der Kooi, *Christian Dogmatics*, 87–89. The thesis that the economic Trinity reveals or communicates the immanent Trinity is a helpful improvement to Rahner's thesis: "The 'economic' Trinity is the 'immanent' Trinity, and the 'immanent' Trinity is the 'economic' Trinity" (*The Trinity*, 22). This has become known as "Rahner's rule." Gunton's version of Rahner's rule is "God is what he does and he does what he is" (*Act and Being*, 76). For the background

Fourth, the generative and communicative acts of Father, Son, and Spirit in time reveal the generative and communicative activity of the three persons in eternity and imply that God's being is not static but active.[20] Because the Father initiates divine acts, he is the author or playwright of the theodrama.[21] As such, "his will, plan, and purpose for the theodrama precede its actualization on the world stage."[22] Because the Son effects divine acts, he is the protagonist in the theodrama. As such, he "mak[es] his embodied entrance onto the world stage in order to play the most important role and bring the theodrama to its climax." Accordingly, "every person and event in the theodrama either sets the stage for his performance or results from the role he plays."[23] Because the Holy Spirit perfects divine acts, he is the producer and director of the theodrama. As such, "the Spirit *produce[s]* the theodrama of God the playwright *through* Jesus the protagonist and other players to the world

---

and origin of Rahner's rule, see Sanders, *Image of the Immanent Trinity*, 47–82.

20. In discussing modes of divine activity, Dalferth considers activity to be a universal property that is actualized in particular acts or events (*Becoming Present*, 145–47; cf. Vanhoozer, *Remythologizing Theology*, 219). Drawing on Aquinas (God's being is an active presence) and Barth (God's being is his act), Vanhoozer proposes a post-Barthian Thomism of the drama of God as "being-in-communicative-act" (*Remythologizing Theology*, 222). By post-Barthian he means that his proposal "include[es] other instances of divine speaking and acting alongside the Incarnation" (*Remythologizing Theology*, 207). Regarding the difference between Aquinas and Barth, Vanhoozer writes, "The key differences are two: (1) Aquinas employs a single conceptual scheme, that of Aristotle, while Barth is more eclectic; (2) Aquinas asks what God the creator must be given the existence of creation while Barth asks what God must be given the history of Jesus Christ" (*Remythologizing Theology*, 221). For a helpful introduction of Jonathan Edwards's understanding of God as a communicative being, see Schweitzer, *God Is a Communicative Being*. For the communicative nature of God within the Trinity, see Schweitzer, *God Is a Communicative Being*, 11–30.

21. For this theodramatic triad, see also Vanhoozer, *Drama of Doctrine*, 102, 106–7, 117, 177, 189, 193, 243–44, 249, 272, 448; Balthasar, *Theo-Drama*, 1:268–305. Vanhoozer outlines the involvement of the Trinity in the theodrama as follows: "The Father is the playwright and producer of the action; the Son is the climax and summation of the action; the Spirit, as the one who unites us to Christ, is the dresser who clothes us with Christ's righteousness, the prompter who helps us remember our biblical lines, and the prop master who gives gifts (accessories) to each church member, equipping us to play our parts" (*Drama of Doctrine*, 448).

22. Vander Lugt, *Living Theodrama*, 65. He adds, "Human participants have a genuine role to play in the theodrama, but God still maintains his sovereignty" (*Living Theodrama*, 65). Because the Father, Son, and Spirit always work together because they are in one another, the Father also acts in the theodrama he authors.

23. Vander Lugt, *Living Theodrama*, 71.

audience *in terms of the theodrama.*" Accordingly, he can be called the "improvisation of God."[24]

The drama of God as God

The theodramatic biblical narrative outlined in the previous chapter generates the drama of God as God. Grammatically reconceptualizing the speech acts of the drama of God as God in terms of the theodramatic imagination and action entails the following.

First, there is a connection between God's communicative acts and his communicative or performative attributes or properties.[25] When God performs the splendor of his perfect life as the God who communicatively acts in a compassionate, gracious, faithful, loving manner, then this implies that God is these performative attributes.[26] The same is true when he justly punishes the guilty; he is a communicatively holy and just God.

---

24. Vander Lugt, *Living Theodrama*, 80. He adds, "While responsible for the entire production of the theodrama, the Spirit is also intimately involved in directing the theodrama, prompting the actors, equipping them with gifts, and empowering their performance." He concludes that "it may be best to identify the Spirit as the producer-director, with the freedom of using these titles interchangeably and in a complementary fashion" (*Living Theodrama*, 80). About the Spirit's role in the theodrama, von Balthasar writes, "The Father entrusts his play to him to be translated into real life . . . ; the Son entrusts himself to the Spirit's guidance, and, above all, the Church must entrust herself to him if her mission to proclaim the word, administer the sacraments and shepherd souls is to succeed" (Balthasar, *Theo-Drama*, 3:534; Vander Lugt, *Living Theodrama*, 80). Because Scripture depicts God's being in generative and communicative theodramatic activity, Vanhoozer writes, "Scripture depicts the life of the Father, Son, and Spirit as a 'perfect drama': a doing than which nothing greater can be conceived; a ceaseless activity of communication that yields consummate communion" (*Remythologizing Theology*, 243; Vanhoozer, *Biblical Authority After Babel*, 52).

25. Because God's attributes are attributes of his being in communicative activity or divine doing, Vanhoozer suggests that we could speak of them as "theatricals" (*Remythologizing Theology*, 277; *Faith Speaking Understanding*, 39). Speaking of God's performative attributes tries to capture the notion of theatrical.

26. Van den Brink and Van der Kooi speak appreciatively about Krötke's suggestion to refer to God's attributes as "God's transparencies" (*Christian Dogmatics*, 149). Together with Krötke, they believe all God's properties or transparencies are connected to God's glory (*Christian Dogmatics*, 149, 153). Moreover, they add, "The attributes that God has form his being; in that sense God 'is' his attributes. Each of them offers a certain perspective on what God is in the essence of his being" (*Christian Dogmatics*, 153). They relate this to the simplicity of God. Rejecting the scholastic definition of the simplicity of God—that he is not composed of parts—because this definition is based on the Greek philosophical "premise that anything composite must be defective and imperfect," they choose the definition that God is a unity or "of one piece" and thus completely trustworthy (*Christian Dogmatics*, 151). This entails that "his properties

Second, because love binds everything together in perfect harmony (Col 3:14; cf. Matt 22:37-40; Rom 13:8, 10), love also binds the splendor of all of God's communicative attributes together in perfect performative harmony. Accordingly, the most fundamental thing that can be said about God is that he is love (*agape*)—that is, that he lives for the other and desires communion with the other (1 John 4:8, 16; cf. John 3:35; 5:20; 15:9, 13; 17:23-24, 26; Rom 5:8; 1 John 3:16).²⁷

Third, when God comes in the wrath of his holy judgment, this holy justice is not an independent attribute, separate from and alongside his love, but a manifestation of his offended love and thus intrinsically connected to it.²⁸

Fourth, as God's love and holiness and justice should not be placed side by side as distinct, separate attributes, because they are intrinsically connected in the drama of God as God, so God's immanence and transcendence should not be placed side by side either. They too are intrinsically connected in the drama. Because God is immanently

---

cannot be played off against each other and that he is utterly serious about his merciful turning toward us" (*Christian Dogmatics*, 146). They have the same difficulty with the Greek philosophical baggage put into God's impassibility. Instead of impassibility meaning that God is unable to suffer and thus is invulnerable, they understand it to mean that "God is not derailed by evil and misery" because he is "in charge of history and in that sense stands above it. He does not become one of its many victims" (*Christian Dogmatics*, 152). In speaking about God, we must remember that we speak analogically—that is, taking God as the prime referent, there is a partial commonality between God and humanity. The touchstone for this analogy is God's revelation in Scripture. Thus, it is an analogy of faith (*analogia fidei*) before it is an analogy of creation (*analogia entis*) (*Christian Dogmatics*, 135-40; see also Spencer, *Analogy of Faith*).

27. Gunton, *Christian Faith*, 186-87. Gunton writes, "To say that God is love means, first, that God is constituted, made up without reminder, of a personal structure of giving and receiving. Internally, God is a fellowship of *persons* whose orientation is entirely to the other." He adds, "The second is that the orientation of this God, his inner drive, we might say, is not to remain content with his eternal ordering as eternal love, but to move outwards to create a world which he loves and wishes to bring into relation with himself" (*Christian Faith*, 86-187). Commenting on 1 John 4:8, 16, Van den Brink and Van der Kooi write, "Ultimately, this is the most fundamental statement that can be made about God" (*Christian Dogmatics*, 128). However, they nuance this statement by asserting that God's other attributes should not be subsumed under his love because "all God's properties are equally essential" (*Christian Dogmatics*, 150).

28. Vriezen, *Outline of Old Testament Theology*, 306; Peels, *Wij is als gij?*, 110; Van den Brink and Van der Kooi, *Christian Dogmatics*, 143-44. Since there is no wrath within the immanent Trinity, the wrath of God is not an essential attribute of God (Ferguson, *Some Pastors and Teachers*, 454). As God's offended love, however, it is a manifestation of God's essential attribute of love. Lane sums up this idea as follows, "Wrath is not an attribute of God in the way that his love or holiness is. His wrath is his response to something outside of himself" ("Wrath of God," 146).

present and involved in the life of Israel as Father, Son, and Holy Spirit, our knowledge of the drama of God as God takes its starting point in his immanently turning toward Israel. Thus, our knowledge of him "is embedded in the relationship that God has initiated with us." We cannot know God in a detached, objectified way, but only as a participant, that is, in a relational manner.[29] However, because God is also transcendently present and involved in the life of Israel, his transcendence qualifies the manner in which he is immanently present and involved.[30]

Participation in the life of God and the drama of creation

The drama of the creation of the heavenly stage of the theodrama[31]

The theodramatic biblical narrative generates the drama of the creation of the heavenly stage of the theodrama. Grammatically reconceptualizing

---

29. Van den Brink and Van der Kooi, *Christian Dogmatics*, 115. Calvin sums up this idea as follows, "Nearly all the wisdom we possess, that is to say, true and sound wisdom, consists of two parts: the knowledge of God and of ourselves. But, while joined by many bonds, which one precedes and brings forth the other is not easy to discern" (Calvin, *Institutes*, 1.1.1; Van den Brink and Van der Kooi, *Christian Dogmatics*, 114–16).

30. Van den Brink and Van der Kooi, *Christian Dogmatics*, 141–44. Because the distinction between incommunicable and communicable attributes can lead to unfruitful discussions as to whether God can communicate an attribute or the fact that the so-called incommunicable attribute of immortality is communicated to angels, Van den Brink and Van der Kooi prefer to speak of "the attributes of divine transcendence and the attributes pertaining to God's condescension, or turning towards us" (*Christian Dogmatics*, 140). For how beginning with and placing a one-sided emphasis on the transcendent attributes of God can lead to an imbalanced view of God, see Van den Brink and Van der Kooi, *Christian Dogmatics*, 133–35, 142. For systematic theological overviews of the attributes of God, see Barth, *Church Dogmatics* II/1, 322–677; Bavinck, *Reformed Dogmatics*, 2:95–255; Beeke and Smalley, *Revelation and God*, 518–875; Frame, *Systematic Theology*, 231–420; Grenz, *Theology for the Community of God*, 88–97; Horton, *Christian Faith*, 223–72; Jones, *Grammar of Christian Faith*, 215–32; Kärkkäinen, *Trinity and Revelation*, 283–309; Letham, *Systematic Theology*, 155–81; Van den Brink and Van der Kooi, *Christian Dogmatics*, 113–56; Van Genderen and Velema, *Reformed Dogmatics*, 132–43, 164–92; see also Gunton, *Act and Being*; Holmes, "Attributes of God," 54–71.

31. For systematic theological overviews of the drama of the creation of the heavenly stage of the theodrama, see Balthasar, *Theo-Drama*, 3:465–501; Barth, *Church Dogmatics* III/3, 369–531; Bavinck, *Reformed Dogmatics*, 2:443–72; *Reformed Dogmatics*, 3:35–36; Berkhof, *Systematic Theology*, 141–49; Beeke and Smalley, *Revelation and God*, 1109–57; Calvin, *Institutes*, 1.14.3–19; Frame, *Systematic Theology*, 771–80; Grenz, *Theology for the Community of God*, 213–42; Van den Brink and Van der Kooi, *Christian Dogmatics*, 332–35; Van Genderen and Velema, *Reformed Dogmatics*, 276–80.

OUTLINING A THEODRAMATIC FRAMEWORK

the speech acts of this drama in terms of theodramatic imagination and action entails the following.

First, because the Father, as the author of the theodrama, initiates divine acts, the Son, as the protagonist in the theodrama, effects divine acts, and the Holy Spirit, as the producer and director of the theodrama, perfects divine acts, the Father voluntarily[32] creates the heavenly stage of their theodrama in Christ through the Holy Spirit (Col 1:16; cf. Gen 1:2; Ps 104:30) to live in their loving presence and participate in their intratrinitarian act of mutual glorification. This heavenly stage can be compared to "a multi-dimensional space that surrounds and permeates our earthly reality from all sides."[33]

Second, they create angels who live in their loving presence and share in their mutual glorification through continuous heavenly worship (Job 38:7; Isa 6; Ps 103:20; 148:2; Rev 5:11) and also through participation in the history of redemption (e.g., Gen 3:24; 18–19; 28:12; 32:1; 2 Kgs 6:15–17; 19:35; Dan 10:13, 20; Gal 3:19),[34] serving as supporting actors who give interpretive clues by communicating God's intention through "announc[ing] what God is doing, will do, or may do" (cf. Heb 1:14).[35] Van Houwelingen describes them as "travel guides" who accompany us on our journey to the kingdom of heaven.[36] This makes heaven a place for communion in the life of God in Christ through the Holy Spirit, where God's will is done in a listening and thankful spirit of openness and responsiveness (Ps 103:21; Matt 6:10).

Third, because living in the Spirit entails being involved in spiritual warfare with the powers of darkness and because Jesus' return will be preceded by the appearance of many antichrists who oppose Jesus and deny that Jesus is the Christ, incited by the spirit of antichrist, who is the devil—the same devil who used a serpent to introduce sin and death onto the stage of the drama of God's mission for his glory—there must have been a fall into sin on the heavenly stage so that God's will is no

---

32. Since God exists in himself, he did not need to create and thus intentionally chose to create as an act of his love (Jones, *Grammar of Christian Faith*, 244–46; Van den Brink and Van der Kooi, *Christian Dogmatics*, 207–10).

33. Van Houwelingen, *Hemelse reisbegeleiding*, 19.

34. Bavinck, *Reformed Dogmatics*, 2:463–64. This twofold angelic ministry can be referred to as a liturgical and diaconal service (Van Houwelingen, *Hemelse reisbegeleiding*, 11)

35. Vanhoozer, *Remythologizing Theology*, 229.

36. Van Houwelingen, *Hemelse reisbegeleiding*, 7, 13–14.

longer done. This fall appears to have been led by one angel, whom we know as the devil and Satan.[37]

Fourth, as "the father of lies" in whom "there is no truth" (John 8:44), Satan intentionally corrupts the communicative agency God had created him with and becomes the chief antagonist in God's drama as he subverts and opposes the playwright's theodramatic intention by manipulating humanity not to participate in God's mission for his glory with a listening and thankful, open and responsive filial spirit.[38]

Fifth, because the Father is the author of his theodrama, he has authorial determination over Satan. This does not mean, however, that Satan does not determine his own self-enclosed and unresponsive response to the divine author's dialogical interaction with him. Because God created Satan as a communicative, dialogical being, he incorporated a relative freedom into his playwright's design for Satan to freely determine his response to God.[39]

Sixth, because angels participate in the drama and Satan and his fallen angels are antagonists in this drama, the drama of God's mission

---

37. About this fall, Frame writes, "Scripture does not narrate the fall of Satan and his angels, but Isaiah 14:3–21 and Ezekiel 28:2–19 deal with the defeat of the kings of Babylon and Tyre, respectively, using imagery suggesting analogies with the fall of Satan" (*Systematic Theology*, 775). Bavinck writes, "All the power of sin on earth is connected with a kingdom of darkness in the world of spirits. There, too, a fall has occurred." He adds, "And Jude (v. 6) speaks of 'the angels that did not keep their own position, but left their proper dwelling,' that is, of angels who did not hold onto their principle, origin, or even rule, and left the dwelling place assigned to them. Clearly implied here is that many angels were not content with the state in which God had placed them. Pride took possession of them to make them strive for another and higher position" (*Reformed Dogmatics*, 3:35–36).

38. Vanhoozer writes, "A lie is a misbegotten communicative act whose birth in words (what one claims as true) contradicts what one conceives (what one knows as false) and consequently misleads the one who hears it" (*Remythologizing Theology*, 343). He adds, "One should no more dismiss Satan's pathological communicative agency, however, than ignore evil. For though it lacks positive being, nevertheless it is (paradoxically) there. For Satan's power is precisely the power of non-being and nothingness, the power of delusion, the means by which Satan works his diabolical version of dialogical consummation. The darkness, death, and hatred in the world are the spawn of Satanic delusion (Rom. 1:28–32)" (*Remythologizing Theology*, 343–44). Because "God is the ultimate person who, as the Giver of life, makes us into persons, into responsive and responding beings," Van den Brink and Van der Kooi write, "the figure of Satan falls far short of this concept of personhood. The devil stands for disintegration, estrangement, emptiness, and curse, and he is therefore the opposite of God as a person. The devil is in the service of *depersonalization*. . . . The devil is 'unperson' or 'antiperson'" (*Christian Dogmatics*, 333–34).

39. Vanhoozer, *Remythologizing Theology*, 334–37.

for his glory is porous to action that is initiated on the heavenly stage of the theodrama. Consequently, God's drama is an enchanted drama, suffused with the supernatural—and this supernatural suffusion is part of its interpretative framework.[40]

The drama of the creation of the earthly stage of the theodrama[41]

The theodramatic biblical narrative generates the drama of the creation of the earthly stage of the theodrama. Grammatically reconceptualizing the speech acts of this drama in terms of theodramatic imagination and action entails the following.

First, because the Father initiates divine acts, the Son effects divine acts, and the Holy Spirit perfects divine acts, the Father voluntarily creates[42] or authors the earthly stage of their theodrama in Christ, the protagonist of the drama, through the Holy Spirit, the producer and director of the drama (Col 1:16; cf. Gen 1:2; Pss 33:6; 104:30).[43]

Second, because the Father authors or speaks the world into existence in Christ as the eternal Word (Pss 33:6; 148:5; Isa 48:13; John

---

40. For more on porosity and enchantment, see Taylor, *Secular Age*, 25-43.

41. For systematic theological overviews of the drama of the creation of the earthly stage of the theodrama, see Balthasar, *Theo-Drama*, 2:173-88; Barth, *Church Dogmatics* III/1, 1-414; Bavinck, *Reformed Dogmatics*, 2:406-39, 473-506; Berkhof, *Systematic Theology*, 126-40, 150-64; Calvin, *Institutes*, 1.14.1-2, 20-22; Frame, *Systematic Theology*, 184-206; Grenz, *Theology for the Community of God*, 98-112; Jones, *Grammar of Christian Faith*, 233-59; Kärkkäinen, *Creation and Humanity*, 9-163; Letham, *Systematic Theology*, 271-91; Macleod, *Faith to Live By*, 81-93; Van den Brink and Van der Kooi, *Christian Dogmatics*, 200-233; Van Genderen and Velema, *Reformed Dogmatics*, 246-76. For how the biblical figure of creation having a beginning rhythms and patterns our understanding of how things are, see Watkin, *Biblical Critical Theory*, 53-81

42. While *creatio ex nihilo* is not explicitly mentioned in Scripture, it is implied. See Rom 4:17; Heb 11:3; Rev 4:11; Van den Brink and Van der Kooi, *Christian Dogmatics*, 212-13; see also Gunton, *Christian Faith*, 17; Van Bekkum, *Verdreven uit de hof*, 19. For an overview of the historical development of *creatio ex nihilo*, see Gunton, *Triune Creator*, 65-96. Because God voluntarily creates, his act of creation can be considered an act of grace. Vanhoozer says that "grace is the gift of God's beneficent presence and activity—that is the communication of God's own light, life, and love to those who have neither the right to them nor a claim on God. . . . Grace is the economic Trinity, the means by which God extends himself toward others, first in creation and later in redemption. Put simply, grace is the Triune God—God sharing his Fatherly love for creation in the Son through the Spirit" (*Biblical Authority after Babel*, 53).

43. While God's drama of his mission for his glory takes place on the planet earth, the earthly stage of his theodrama includes the whole universe (Gen 1:1; Pss 24; 90; 104; 148; Job 38-41; Isa 40-44).

1:3; 1 Cor 8:6; Col 1:16; Heb 1:2), Christ is the ontological mediator of creation.[44]

Third, because the Father is ontologically present in his creation in Christ (Heb 1:3) and through the Holy Spirit (Ps 104:30), creation has a "natural"—that is, inherently compatible—relationship with God, entailing living and moving and having its being in God (Acts 17:28).[45] Because creation is the dwelling place of God in Christ through the Spirit, it is porous to God and to good and bad angels. It is enchanted.[46] Consequently, created reality can ontologically participate in God's intratrinitarian mutual glorification and be a theater of God's glory (Pss 8; 19:1–6; 29; 65:9–13; 69:34; 96:11–12; 104; 148:1–4; Isa 44:23; 49:13; 55:12).[47]

---

44. Calvin defines Christ as ontological mediator of creation as follows, "In what pertains to the matter at hand we must first see what the word mediator means. Certainly, the eternal λόγος was already mediator from the beginning, before Adam's fall and the alienation and separation of the human race from God. In this sense, unless we are mistaken, he is also called by Paul the first-born of all creatures; and when John says that life was in him, he indicates the mode of communication from which otherwise hidden source, the grace of God flowed to men." He adds, "It is the proper function of the mediator to unite us to God" (Tylenda, "Controversy," 147, 148; see also Tylenda, "Christ the Mediator"; Canlis, *Calvin's Ladder*, 53–88; Edmonson, *Calvin's Christology*, 4–39; Cumin, *Christ at the Crux*, 96–125). About the world being created *in* Christ, Macleod writes, "Creation is Christ-shaped. The space-time curve is Christ-shaped" (*Faith to Live By*, 93).

45. Cosmologically participating in Christ is not the same as redemptively participating in Christ. For this distinction, see Vanhoozer, *Remythologizing Theology*, 156, 281.

46. Because creation is the sacred dwelling place of God in Christ through the Spirit, it can also be considered to be ontologically sacramental, i.e., it mediates or communicates the presence or glory of God. As such, creation is an icon or a window through which we perceive God (Letham, *Systematic Theology*, 282–83). There is no need to understand a sacramental ontology in a Platonic sense where Christ as the mediator of creation is identified with the Platonic forms or ideas (*contra* Boersma, *Nouvelle théologie*; *Heavenly Participation*; cf. Billings, *Remembrance, Communion, and Hope*, 86–93; Burger, "Quadriga without Platonism"; Huijgen, *Lezen en laten lezen*, 82–84; Provan, *Reformation*, 416–23).

47. Thus, creation is not only the stage of the theodrama, but also participates in this drama. For Calvin on creation being a theater, see, e.g., Calvin, *Institutes*, 1.5.1–6, 8; 1.6.2; 1.14.20; 2.6.1; 3.9.2). About how Christians should deal with evolution, see Van Bruggen, "Blind Man," 4–7. Van Bruggen argues that there is an invisible aspect to created reality, and therefore we should remember that scientific conclusions are tentative because they are based on incomplete information and limited to natural causes. However, as such, they may be useful as computational models. For instance, "The computational models that are released on strata may be useful for exploratory drilling, without thereby requiring that the mathematical models of processes lasting millions of years be deemed also historically accurate." And, "A theory of evolution may be a

Fourth, because God reached the goal toward which he had created on the seventh day,[48] the eschatological goal of creation is the eternal Sabbath rest where creation will rest in the fullness of God's loving presence in Christ through the Spirit and God will be all in all.

The drama of providence[49]

The theodramatic biblical narrative generates the drama of providence.[50] Grammatically reconceptualizing the speech acts of this drama in terms of theodramatic imagination and action entails the following.

First, the drama of providence communicates that, after having created, God continues to be involved with creation by providing for it.

---

useful model for organizing everything we observe in the world of fossils and animals, but it does not have to be at the same time a statement of historical nature" ("Blind Man," 7; see also Van Bekkum and Kwakkel, "Veilige leefwereld," 333–34). McGrath writes that because of the limits of science and human rationality, we should not "force reality into a Procrustean mould predetermined by the limits of our reason" (*Territories of Human Reason*, 202).

48. When Kline undergirds his framework hypothesis by asserting that "the divine author has employed the imagery of an ordinary week to provide a figurative chronological framework for the account of his creative acts" ("Because It Had Not Rained," 156), this statement does not do justice to the fact that Exod 20:11 and 31:17 seem to indicate that "the Israelite week is derived from God's creation week and not the other way around" (Van Bekkum and Kwakkel, "Veilige leefwereld," 329).

49. For systematic theological overviews of the drama of providence, see Barth, *Church Dogmatics* III/3, 3–368; Bavinck, *Reformed Dogmatics*, 2:591–619; Berkhof, *Systematic Theology*, 165–78; Calvin, *Institutes*, 1.16–18; Frame, *Systematic Theology*, 141–83; Grenz, *Theology for the Community of God*, 112–23; Jones, *Grammar of Christian Faith*, 259–92; Kärkkäinen, *Creation and Humanity*, 164–93; Letham, *Systematic Theology*, 292–311; Van den Brink and Van der Kooi, *Christian Dogmatics*, 233–44; Van Genderen and Velema, *Reformed Dogmatics*, 283–313.

50. God's providence entails conservation (*conservatio* or *preservatio*), concurrence (*concursus* or *cooperatio*), and governance (*gubernatio*) (Frame, *Systematic Theology*, 172–82; Van den Brink and Van der Kooi, *Christian Dogmatics*, 239–44). Barth refers to concursus as "divine accompanying" (*Church Dogmatics* III/3, 67–102). Because we live and move and have our being in God (Acts 17:28), God participates in what we do (Phil 2:12–13). This includes that "1. God equips people to act and gives them space to act independently and effectively. 2. People are and remain absolutely dependent on God's all-encompassing and decisive action" (Van den Brink and Van der Kooi, *Christian Dogmatics*, 242). Concerning *concursus* and the responsibility for sin, "God is minimally present in human sin only in the sense that he creates the conditions that enable us to sin. God wanted people who would be able to sin, but did not want the sin itself" (Van den Brink and Van der Kooi, *Christian Dogmatics*, 242–43).

Second, the drama of providence is a trinitarian,[51] communicative,[52] gracious[53] activity with the Father initiating divine acts, the Son effecting divine acts, and the Holy Spirit perfecting divine acts.

Third, that the Father has authorial determination over Satan does not mean that Satan does not himself determine his response to the divine author's dialogical interaction with him. When the divine author created Satan as a communicative, dialogical being, he incorporated a relative freedom in his playwright's design so that he could freely determine his response. So also, the Father's providential determination over humanity does not mean that humanity does not determine their response to the divine author's dialogical interaction with them. As with Satan, so with people: When the divine author created them as communicative, dialogical beings, he incorporated a relative freedom in his design so that they could determine their response.[54]

Fourth, because the drama of God's providence is not self-evident, it must be embraced with "the framework of faith."[55]

Fifth, as with the drama of the Trinity and of creation, the drama of providence implies that creation is ontologically permeated with—and thus enchanted with—the presence of God.

---

51. "Divine providence is less a matter of God's 'strong hand' than of the Father's *two* hands (i.e.,Son and Spirit)—in a word, triune authorship" (Vanhoozer, *Remythologizing Theology*, 367). Lord's Day 9 of the Heidelberg Catechism captures this well when it begins its answer to the question "What do you believe when you say, 'I believe in God, the Father almighty, creator of heaven and earth'?" with "That the eternal Father of our Lord Jesus Christ, who out of nothing created heaven and earth and everything in them who still upholds and rules them by his eternal counsel and providence, is my God and Father because of Christ the Son" (*Trinity Psalter Hymnal*, 876). What Lord's Day 10 confesses about the providence of God needs to be seen within this context (Van den Brink and Van der Kooi, *Christian Dogmatics*, 238–39; see also Vanhoozer, *Remythologizing Theology*, 369–70).

52. Because the Father exercises his authorial providence through his two hands—Son/Word and Spirit—the drama of his providence is best understood in personal communicative terms rather than in impersonal causal terms (Vanhoozer, *Remythologizing Theology*, 370).

53. The drama of providence involves God's special grace to the church as well as his common grace to those outside his church. Common grace includes the restraint of sin, God's wrath, and God's gift of temporal blessings, enabling unregenerate people to do good, know the truth, and experience some blessings of the Holy Spirit (Frame, *Systematic Theology*, 246–48; see also Horton, *Christian Faith*, 364–68).

54. Vanhoozer, *Remythologizing Theology*, 334–37; see also Kwakkel, *Uitgekozen*, 72, 78–79.

55. Van den Brink and Van der Kooi, *Christian Dogmatics*, 237.

The drama of the creation of humanity[56]

The theodramatic biblical narrative generates the drama of the creation of humanity. Grammatically reconceptualizing the speech acts of this drama in terms of theodramatic imagination and action entails the following.

First, because the Father initiates divine acts, the Son effects them, and the Holy Spirit perfects them, the Father voluntarily creates or authors humanity in Christ, the protagonist of the theodrama, through the Holy Spirit, the producer and director of it, in their image and likeness as communicative agents who are able to bear witness to the communicative act of mutual glorification in the immanent Trinity as they share in Christ's filial spirit of faith, and who will one day share in the eschatological destiny of Christ.[57]

Second, humanity can carry out this role because human beings are created as an anthropological duality, with a soul and a body that function as a psychosomatic unity (Matt 10:28; 2 Cor 4:16; 5:8).[58] This soul is a porous, spiritual, ontological reality distinct from the physical body. It is essentially a receptive and affective reality that functions like a sounding board through which we experience the resonances or vibrations of ourselves and others, such as God, other human beings, and the world in

---

56. For systematic theological overviews of the drama of the creation of humanity, see Balthasar, *Theo-Drama*, 2:335–429; *Glory of the Lord*, 6:31–211; Barth, *Church Dogmatics* III/2, 1–640; Bavinck, *Reformed Dogmatics*, 2:509–88; Beeke and Smalley, *Man and Christ*, 125–321; Berkhof, *Systematic Theology*, 179–218; Calvin, *Institutes*, 1.15; Frame, *Systematic Theology*, 783–844; Grenz, *Theology for the Community of God*, 125–32, 139–80; Horton, *Christian Faith*, 373–407; Jones, *Grammar of Christian Faith*, 293–343; Kärkkäinen, *Creation and Humanity*, 233–386, 426–68; Letham, *Systematic Theology*, 315–65; Macleod, *Faith to Live By*, 107–17; Van den Brink and Van der Kooi, *Christian Dogmatics*, 247–92; Van Genderen and Velema, *Reformed Dogmatics*, 314–84. For how the biblical figure of being created in the image of God rhythms and patterns our understanding of who we are, see Watkin, *Biblical Critical Theory*, 83-106.

57. Humanity is created as male and female (Gen 1:27). About the significance of having been created as sexual beings, see Grenz, *Theology for the Community of God*, 269–303; Van den Brink and Van der Kooi, *Christian Dogmatics*, 280–87. For a defense of Adam and Eve being the first biological parents of the whole human race, see Beeke and Smalley, *Man and Christ*, 143–78; Frame, 803–6; Grenz, *Theology for the Community of God*, 146–48; Macleod, *Faith to Live By*, 92–92; Van Dam, *In the Beginning*, 215–18, 285–86; *contra* Kärkkäinen, *Creation and Humanity*, 245–68; Van den Brink and Van der Kooi, *Christian Dogmatics*, 302; Van den Brink, *Reformed Theology and Evolutionary Theory*, 165–80.

58. Duality is not the same as dualism. The latter thinks of the distinction hierarchically.

which we live. Our souls respond rationally, affectively, and volitionally to the resonances they receive.[59] As a receiving and responding spiritual reality, the soul can be equated with our subjectivity or personhood.[60]

Third, because the Father is ontologically present in his creation in Christ (Heb 1:3) and through the Holy Spirit (Ps 104:30), humanity has a "natural" (inherently compatible) relationship with God, entailing living in his loving presence and participating in his life, living and moving and having their being in God (Acts 17:28).[61] Accordingly, like the rest of creation, the ontological structure of humanity is porous to God and to good and bad angels.

Fourth, because creating humanity in the image of Father, Son, and Spirit and after their likeness refers to creating them according to the model or standard of Christ—that is, as sons of God who participate in Christ's status of sonship and his communion of love with the Father through the Spirit[62]—humanity's calling to represent this status and communion as kings and priests who share in and bear witness to Christ's kingly rule and priestly care for creation does not constitute their being created in God's image and likeness but flows forth from it.[63] Since

---

59. Huijgen, *Lezen en laten lezen*, 130–37. About the soul being essentially a receptive reality, Huijgen writes, "Knowledge starts with experience and is a form of perception. . . . Reason receives . . . before it starts producing, and that receptivity precedes conscious, reasoning thought." He adds, "In this context, it is striking that the German word reason (*Vernunft*) involves perceiving (*vernehmen*)" (*Lezen en laten lezen*, 132). About the soul being essentially an affective reality, Huijgen writes, "Affective, because experience (rather than thought) is primary" (*Lezen en laten lezen*, 133).

60. See Oldhoff, *Kijk op de ziel*; Van den Brink and Van der Kooi, *Christian Dogmatics*, 267–74; Waaijman, *Spirituality*, 435–46.

61. What I wrote about Christ being the ontological mediator of creation also applies to humanity. Thus, Canlis, drawing on Calvin, writes, "Even in the Garden of Eden, Adam received life not from God *simpliciter*, but from Christ. 'He was the midpoint [*medium*] between God and creatures, so that the life which was otherwise hidden in God would flow from him'" (*Calvin's Ladder*, 59).

62. As we noted earlier, cosmologically participating in Christ is not the same as redemptively participating in Christ.

63. Kilner, *Dignity and Destiny*, 94–105, 199–210; *contra* Beale, *Temple and the Church's Mission*, 83; *New Testament Biblical Theology*, 30–33; Horton, *Lord and Servant*, 105; *Christian Faith*, 397–400. Just as humanity's royal rule and priestly care flow from their having been created in the image of God, so also human attributes that resemble God's attributes flow from their having been created in the image of God (Kilner, *Dignity and Destiny*, 104, 189–99, 227–30). The same can be said about humanity having relational capacity (Kilner, *Dignity and Destiny*, 210–27; *contra* Jones, *Grammar of Christian Faith*, 322–36; Van den Brink and Van der Kooi, *Christian Dogmatics*, 264–66; see also Horton, *Christian Faith*, 387–93).

the model of Christ cannot be lost or damaged, the image of God cannot either,[64] though it can fail to function and thus damage humanity and creation.[65]

Fifth, because Adam's obedience or disobedience has consequences not only for Adam and Eve but also for their posterity, he is a public person who is the natural representative head of humanity.[66]

Sixth, because God created Adam and Eve as communicative, dialogical beings (Gen 1:28; 2:16–17), he incorporated a relative freedom into his playwright's design for humanity to freely determine their response to him.[67] This relative freedom to determine their own response entails that their actions have moral implications (Gen 2:16–17). This, in turn, is a manifestation of God's justice.[68]

---

64. For an overview and refutation of those who assert that the image of God is completely lost, virtually lost, partly lost, or appears to be lost, see Kilner, *Dignity and Destiny*, 159–76.

65. When Paul speaks about having "put on the new self, which is being renewed in knowledge after the image of its creator" (Col 3:10; Eph 4:24), he is not referring to the image being renewed, but to humanity being renewed according to the image. Kilner writes, "Although the passage in Colossians indicates that the person is changing, and that the unchanging standard according to which the person is changing is the 'image of its creator,' many mistakenly read the passage to be saying that the image itself is changing" (*Dignity and Destiny*, 192).

66. McGowan, "In Defense of 'Headship Theology,'" 189–98; *Adam, Christ, and Covenant*, 126–28.

67. Vanhoozer, *Remythologizing Theology*, 334–37. Vanhoozer asserts, "The Author's and hero's activities ultimately exist on different levels. The Author is not, therefore, the hero's antagonist. On the contrary, the hero is concerned with the 'effort to exist' and the 'desire to be' on the horizontal plane of earthly existence, the very thing the Author enables." He adds, "My capacity for self-determination therefore has its ground not in my own (monological) existence but rather in the potentially infinite dialogue with the Author God who alone calls me into being and who consummates my life and gives it meaning. It is in response to the dialogical situations that comprise my life, especially my dialogical relation to God, that I exercise the freedom to realize my own voice-idea" (*Remythologizing Theology*, 336). About the nature of the will, Van Raalte writes, "Our wills, by definition, make free choices, or they are not wills" ("Free Will?," 559). Van den Brink and Van der Kooi write something similar when they assert that our freedom of choice belongs to "our anthropological structure" (*Christian Dogmatics*, 277). Philosophically, this freedom of choice is referred to as compatibilism because is compatible with our desires and compatible with determinism (Frame, *Systematic Theology*, 824–25).

68. Burger, "Theology without a Covenant of Works," 341–42; van Bruggen, "Hoe kunnen Gods wetten."

The drama of the fall into sin[69]

The theodramatic biblical narrative generates the drama of the fall into sin. Grammatically reconceptualizing the speech acts of this part of this drama in terms of theodramatic imagination and action entails the following.

First, since the antagonist introduced sin onto the stage of God's drama of his mission for his glory after humanity had been created in the image of God, sin "does not belong to the ontological structure of our humanness."[70]

Second, even though the playwright creates the conditions that enable Satan to subvert and oppose the playwright's theodramatic intention by manipulating humanity to turn away from God and not participate in God's mission in faith, humanity freely determine their own response by allowing themselves to be driven by their own agenda instead of God's.[71] Thus, humanly speaking, humanity is responsible for bringing sin onto the earthly stage of the theodrama.

Third, since God wants humanity to participate in and reveal the intratrinitarian mutual glorification by sharing Christ's filial spirit of listening, trustful, open, and responsive faith, the essence of sin is rebelliously and unthankfully turning away from God and refusing to take part in the drama of his mission for his glory, rejecting his divine instruction, and becoming autonomously self-enclosed and unresponsive

---

69. For systematic theological overviews of the drama of the fall into sin, see Barth, *Church Dogmatics* IV/1, 358–513; IV/2, 378–498; IV/3a, 368–478; Bavinck, *Reformed Dogmatics*, 3:23–190; Beeke and Smalley, *Man and Christ*, 325–496; Berkhof, *Systematic Theology*, 219–61; Calvin, *Institutes*, 2.1–5; Frame, *Systematic Theology*, 845–73; Grenz, *Theology for the Community of God*, 181–212; Horton, *Christian Faith*, 408–43; Jones, *Grammar of Christian Faith*, 343–64; Kärkkäinen, *Creation and Humanity*, 387–425; Letham, *Systematic Theology*, 366–401; Macleod, *Faith to Live By*, 107–17; Van den Brink and Van der Kooi, *Christian Dogmatics*, 293–337; Van Genderen and Velema, *Reformed Dogmatics*, 385–436. For how the biblical figure of the fall into sin rhythms and patterns our analysis and engagement with culture, see Watkin, *Biblical Critical Theory*, 107-221.

70. Van den Brink and Van der Kooi, *Christian Dogmatics*, 301.

71. Regarding how evil, sin, and suffering can be harmonized with God's goodness and justice, "we *can* and *may* say that God, in choosing this creation with its possibilities and limitations, has chosen a reality that is vulnerable. . . . This quality allows us to say that suffering (including suffering that is not inflicted upon us by other people) does not happen outside the will of God. But we *absolutely may not* say that God actually wants evil, let alone sin" (Van den Brink and Van der Kooi, *Christian Dogmatics*, 330–31).

to the playwright's dialogical interaction.⁷² In doing so, humanity lives in the flesh and not in the Spirit (Rom 8:5-9). As a result, they lost the glory they once possessed and fell short of the glory that was promised them (Rom 3:23).⁷³ This, in turn, had an impact on all of creation (Rom 8:18-25).⁷⁴

Fourth, because Adam was the natural representative head of humanity (Rom 5:12-19; 1 Cor 15:21-22), all of humanity participated in his distrustful rebellion and its consequences.⁷⁵ As a result, every human is conceived and born in sin. Every human being by nature is self-enclosed, curved in on itself, with a natural tendency to be unthankful, estranged from God, and driven by his own agenda and standards,

---

72. Calvin considers unfaithfulness to be the essence of sin (Calvin, *Institutes*, 2.1.4). Gerrish, however, writes, "But it is crucial to note that, for him [Calvin], the essence of infidelity is *not listening to God*" ("Mirror of God's Goodness," 218; cf. Canlis, *Calvin's Ladder*, 84). For an overview of how pride, concupiscence, sloth, and falsehood flow forth from unbelief or unfaithfulness, see Jones, *Grammar of Christian Faith*, 356-61. For understanding sin as being curved in on oneself or *homo incurvatus in se*, see Luther, *Lectures on Romans*, 245, 291, 313, 345-46, 513; Burger, "Theologische hermeneutiek," 38; O'Donovan, *Finding and Seeking*, 14-23; Balthasar, *Theo-Drama*, 4:165; cf. 4:137-201; see also Jenson, *Gravity of Sin*.

73. Dunn, *Romans 1-8*, 168.

74. Since scientific conclusions are tentative because they are based on incomplete information and limited to natural causes, I see no need to recontextualize the fall into sin along evolutionary biological lines as Van den Brink and Van der Kooi do, even though they want to maintain a historical fall into sin by the first "true" human beings (*Christian Dogmatics*, 302; Van den Brink, *Reformed Theology and Evolutionary Theory*, 187-95; also *contra* Kärkkäinen, *Creation and Humanity*, 400-404).

75. Moo, *Romans*, 344-56; Murray, *Romans*, 180-86; McGowan, *Adam, Christ, and Covenant*, 119-21. Because of the parallel between verse 12 and verses 15-19, Murray writes, "We must conclude that the 'all sinned' of verse 12 and the one trespass of the one man of verses 15-19 must refer to the same fact or event, that the one fact can be expressed in terms of both singularity and plurality, as the sin of one and the sin of all." He adds, "And the only solution is that there must be some kind of solidarity existing between the 'one' and 'the all' with the result that the sin of the one may at the same time and with equal relevance be regarded as the sin of all" (*Romans*, 1:186). Moo comes to a similar conclusion when he writes, "The point is . . . that the sin here attributed to the 'all' is to be understood, in the light of vv. 12a-c and 15-19, as a sin that in some manner is identical to the sin committed by Adam. Paul can therefore say both 'all die because all sin' and 'all die because Adam sinned' with no hint of conflict because the sin of Adam *is* the sin of all" (*Romans*, 354, see also Van Genderen and Velema, *Reformed Dogmatics*, 408-10).

independent of God and unreceptive to his voice.[76] Moreover, every human being is subject to death.[77]

Fifth, when God predicts that humanity will deal with the problem it created through a lifelong conflict with Satan and his followers, through which he will redeem creation and humanity from Satan and restore them into his loving presence again, he is maintaining his faithfulness to his creational purpose and his love for creation and humanity. The human being who strikes a mortal blow to Satan's head at the cost of his own life is the protagonist of the theodrama, through whom the playwright effects all of his divine acts.

---

76. Scriptural support for being conceived and born with a sinful nature can be adduced from, e.g., 1 Kgs 8:46; Pss 51:5; 130:3; Job 14:4; John 3:3–5; see Van Genderen and Velema, *Reformed Dogmatics*, 407.

77. Being conceived and born with a sinful nature and being subject to death because humanity participated in Adam's sin is referred to as original sin. For a confessional description of original sin, see article 15 of the Belgic Confession (*Trinity Psalter Hymnal*, 860). Because article 15 states that original sin "is enough to condemn the human race," it implies that original sin includes original guilt (see also Calvin, *Institutes*, 2.1.8; Canons of Dort, III/IV.2–3; Van Genderen and Velema, *Reformed Dogmatics*, 409–10). However, original guilt can also simply be the result of participation in the sinful act of the natural representative head (Rom 5:18–19; Eph 2:3; cf. McGowan, *Adam, Christ, and Covenant*, 126–28).

Johnson uses the "Christological realism" of the nature of our singular, realistic union with Christ with the dual implications of legal and transformative effects to shed light on our singular, realistic union with Adam. Accordingly, he writes, "If we take this understanding of the implications of being in Christ and apply it to the implications of being in Adam, we derive the following assertion: by virtue of our singular, realistic union with Adam, we experience both the guilt and condemnation of his primal trespass, as well as the corrupt condition into which he fell. Guilt and pollution are distinguishable but inseparable dilemmas that issue forth from our union with Adam" (*One with Christ*, 75–76; cf. 69–77; see also Ashford and Bartholomew, *Doctrine of Creation*, 233–35). For original sin implying total depravity, see Frame, *Systematic Theology*, 860–63. About the transmission of original sin, Bavinck writes, "How original sin is propagated remains somewhat mysterious. It is not something physical—transmitted by propagation—but a moral quality of the person who lacks the communion with God that one should and does possess by virtue of one's original nature" (*Reformed Dogmatics*, 3:364).

Participation in the life of God and the drama of the election of Israel and the covenants

The theodramatic biblical narrative generates the drama of the election of Israel and the establishment of God's covenants. Grammatically reconceptualizing the speech acts of this drama in terms of theodramatic imagination and action entails the following.

First, because God chose Israel to deal with the problem caused by Adam and Eve's sin by bringing the blessing of Abraham to the nations through bearing witness to what is in Christ, Israel's function in the drama of God's mission for his glory is not simply typological and pedagogical—not simply to perform actions that in some way foreshadow Christ or that teach us a lesson about sin or salvation or morality—but rather is essential for the salvation of the world. It is as Israel's representative and substitute that Christ is also Adam's representative and substitute who bears the world's existence in their place and on their behalf, enabling them to participate in his history and destiny.[78]

Second, because God's new covenant is a covenant with Israel in its representative Messiah, God's covenant with Israel is not an interlude or parenthesis in God's drama that can simply be skipped over now that the new covenant has been inaugurated. Rather, Israel continues to have an abiding place in God's drama (Rom 11:28). Instead of Israel being replaced with the new covenant, it is reconstituted in Christ. However, whereas Israel was to be a blessing to the Gentiles, now the Gentile church is called to be a blessing for ethnic Jews by arousing them to jealousy so that they can be regrafted into reconstituted Israel (Rom 11:11–24).

Third, because God chose Israel to be the theater of the drama of his mission for his glory, the drama of election begins with God's election

---

78. Cf. Burger, *Life in Christ*, 55–56.

of Israel.[79] What God enacts in the election of Israel in history is the outworking of his plan of salvation in Christ from eternity (Eph 1:11).[80]

---

79. About two kinds of election, see de Jong, *Van oud naar nieuw*, 165–349; Calvin, *Institutes*, 3.21.5–7; see also Barach, "Covenant and Election," 149–56. For an overview of discussions and developments within the Reformed Churches in The Netherlands (Liberated) regarding the relationship between covenant and election, see de Boer, "Unfinished Homework," 107–36; see also de Jong, *Van oud naar nieuw*, 165–71.

God's special election unto eternal salvation will be dealt with in the drama of the Holy Spirit. Within his election of Israel, we also see God electing the older to serve the younger (Rom 9:11–12; cf. vv. 7–8 with regard to Isaac and Ishmael). Van Bruggen writes, "Later, what is written in these verses have repeatedly been thought to refer to *eternal* election. However, the primary concern here is the designation of a place in time and the acceptance of that designation or calling. There is a place for Ishmael, but not the first place in God's history. The same is true for Esau: there is a place for him, but subservient to his younger brother. In both cases, God's direction and speaking is decisive" (*Romeinen*, 138).

We see something similar with the dynamics of God's dealing with Pharaoh and Israel when God wanted Pharaoh, as the superior, to step aside and serve Israel, as the inferior. However, he did not want to do this (Rom 9:17–18). Van Bruggen writes, "Pharaoh could have immediately stepped aside for Moses and God. That's what God wanted. Nothing else. Then Pharaoh would have saved Egypt, because the superior (Pharaoh and his people) had served the inferior (the slave people) at God's direction." He adds, "However, when Pharaoh resisted God's command, he and all his subjects burned themselves on the fire of God's mercy upon whom he wills (in this case: Israel). Thus, Pharaoh was awakened [or "raised up'] to demonstrate God's power. Either through cooperation or helpless resistance" (*Romeinen*, 140). Because of his resistance, Pharaoh evoked God's wrath and prepared himself (cf. middle voice) for destruction (Rom 9:22).

Van Bruggen writes, "There is an expression in 9:22 that seems to indicate that with the vessels of wrath, God never wanted anything but their destruction ('prepared for destruction'). . . . If Paul wants us to think of being predestined for destruction, however, there is no longer room for 'wrath.' Why should a vessel made to be thrown away be able to evoke wrath? However, the Greek word order makes it clear that 'wrath' *precedes* the preparation for destruction because of their unwillingness and hardening" (*Romeinen*, 143).

This is also why God hated Esau/Edom (Rom 9:13; Mal 1:3). Van Bruggen writes, "Because Edom resisted that choice [the older will serve the younger] and continually was an enemy of Israel, Edom has become the object of God's hatred. God has an abiding wrath against this area of wickedness (Ml. 1:4)" (*Romeinen*, 138). What Paul writes about vessels of wrath preparing themselves for destruction because of their unbelief parallels what he wrote in Rom 1:18–32 and 2:1–13 (*Romeinen*, 143). Thus, there is no eternal hatred or wrath in God (Douma, *Common Grace*, 326–33).

80. In Rom 9–11, Paul describes this reconstitution as a cutting of hardened Jews off Israel, the olive tree, and a grafting in of Christian Gentiles into Israel (Rom 11:17–24). Whether Paul, in Rom 11:25–26a indicates that the elect Jews will be grafted in (e.g., Bavinck, *Reformed Dogmatics*, 4:668–72; Hendriksen, *Romans*, 381; Hoekema, *Bible and the Future*, 139–47) or is speaking of a large conversion of the Jewish people (e.g., Bruce, *Romans*, 209; Cranfield, *Romans*, 282; Dunn, *Romans 9-16*, 681; Greijdanus, *Brief*, 2:515–16; Murray, *Romans*, 2:98; Van den Brink and Van der Kooi, *Christian*

Fourth, while God's election of Israel is the performance of his unconditional love (Deut 7:6–8; 9:4–6), it is conditional upon Israel's obedience of faith (Exod 19:5–6; cf. 2 Pet 2:10–11).

Fifth, because God makes covenants with Noah, Abraham, Israel, and David mostly to deal with problems of uncertainty regarding the fulfillment of his creational purpose and his promises, covenants are redemptive instruments with missional intent through which God rescues the drama of the mission for his glory and moves it forward to its eschatological fulfillment.[81]

Dogmatics, 356; Van Houwelingen, "Redemptive-Historical Dynamics," 305–13; Venema, "In This Way," 35–40; Vos, *Pauline Eschatology*, 89) is difficult to determine. Because both lines of thought are present in the context of verses 25–26a and have a bearing on its interpretation, Van Bruggen speaks about "an exegetical stalemate" (*Romeinen*, 172). Because the word "Israel" in Rom 9–11 always refers to ethnic Jews, it is highly unlikely that "all Israel" refers to the church, the Israel of God, made up of believing Jews and Gentiles (*contra* Calvin, *Romans*, 437; Barth, *Romans*, 416; Wright, *Climax of the Covenant*, 249–50; *Romans, Part 1*, 61–62; *Paul and the Faithfulness of God*, 1244–52).

81. Leder, "Divine Presence, Part 3," 695–96; Wright, *Mission of God*, 331. For a systematic theological overview of the drama of Israel and covenant, see Berkhof, *Christian Faith*, 221–65; Van den Brink and Van der Kooi, *Christian Dogmatics*, 338–80. For how the biblical figure of God making and keeping his promises rhythms and patterns our understanding of the universe, see Watkin, *Biblical Critical Theory*, 223-58.

Participation in the life of God and the drama of Christ

The drama of the person of Christ[82]

The theodramatic biblical narrative generates the drama of the person of Christ.[83] Grammatically reconceptualizing the speech acts of this drama in terms of theodramatic imagination and action entails the following.

First, the Son of God, who is sent by the Father, takes on humanity's frail human flesh, and represents the Father on earth, bearing witness to his glorious presence, is the second person of the Trinity who eternally and perichoretically subsists in the generative and communicative being of God with his personal identity, communicatively effecting divine acts in time as the protagonist of God's drama of his mission for his glory (Matt 1:23).

Second, when Christ takes on human flesh, he unites our human nature to his divine person so that he has both a divine and a human nature.[84] In having a human nature, Christ laid the indispensable foundation for our redemption. Our redemption takes place in him. He must obediently participate in the drama with a listening and thankful filial spirit, in the openness and responsiveness of faith, as a human being.

---

82. For systematic theological overviews of the drama of the person of Christ, see Balthasar, *Theo-Drama*, 3:149–282; *Theo-Logic*, 2:13–361; 3:17–60; Barth, *Church Dogmatics* I/2, 1–202; Bavinck, *Reformed Dogmatics*, 3:233–319; Beeke and Smalley, *Man and Christ*, 721–865; Berkhof, *Systematic Theology*, 303–30; Calvin, *Institutes*, 2.12–14; Frame, *Systematic Theology*, 877–98; Grenz, *Theology for the Community of God*, 243–339; Horton, *Christian Faith*, 446–82; Jones, *Grammar of Christian Faith*, 365–426; Kärkkäinen, *Christ and Reconciliation*, 35–290; Letham, *Systematic Theology*, 471–544; Macleod, *Faith to Live By*, 133–44; Van den Brink and Van der Kooi, *Christian Dogmatics*, 381–431; Van Genderen and Velema, *Reformed Dogmatics*, 437–62. For how the biblical figure of the incarnation rhythms and patterns our understanding of ultimate reality, see Watkin, *Biblical Critical Theory*, 341-70. For the implications of the incarnation for a holistic soteriology, see Paas, *Vrede op aarde*, 103-08, 145-51, 266-68, 332, 335-401. However, see also Rietkerk, "In het heil voor de mens is er geen vrede zonder redding."

83. "Christology and soteriology are two-in-one; person and work, Christology and soteriology, cannot be separated. In what Jesus does we detect who he is, and who he is becomes clear from the course of his life and his exaltation by God . . . Thus, the sequence of dealing with the person of Christ before the work of Christ is arbitrary and might just as easily have been reversed" (Van den Brink and Van der Kooi, *Christian Dogmatics*, 385; see also Jones, *Grammar of Christian Faith*, 366).

84. On the different understanding of the *communicatio idiomatum* or communication of attributes between the Lutheran and the Reformed, see Davidson, "Christ," 454–555. About Christ's divinity not being restricted by his humanity, but also being outside (*ex*) of it, see Davidson, "Christ," 461–63.

OUTLINING A THEODRAMATIC FRAMEWORK

Moreover, because Israel and humanity called the wrath of God's judgment down upon themselves through their intentional disobedience, a human being must still this wrath and bear this judgment.[85] Furthermore, for Israel and humanity to rise from the dead as a glorified new creation, transfigured by the Holy Spirit, a human being must rise from the dead in this glory.

Third, in being conceived and born by the Holy Spirit and uniting himself to our flesh, Christ is the promised son of Adam and Eve, the human being who would deal with the problem of sin, death, and the devil caused by their sin, the promised son of Abraham who would invite humanity and creation into God's Sabbath rest by sharing in his life by the Spirit, and the promised son of David who would rule Israel as God's treasured possession and mediate God's presence to the nations. In short, he is the promised Messiah and the authentic human being.

Fourth, as such, Christ is Israel's representative and substitute,[86] who bears their existence in their place and on their behalf, enabling them to participate in his history and destiny. Because God wanted to use Israel to bring the blessing of Abraham to the nations, by being

---

85. When speaking about the redemption Christ achieves, we need to remember that we have redemption in spite of and because of Christ. We have redemption "in spite of" Christ because his death is the result of his being violently eliminated as a blasphemer and a political threat. Accordingly, "[at] its core the suffering of Jesus is the result of the violence, dishonesty, cowardice, and treason of the people toward him.... People got rid of Jesus because he got in their way. We cannot dress up this rejection in nice soteriological terms, for it manifests no saving or redeeming aspects" (Van den Brink and Van der Kooi, *Christian Dogmatics*, 479). We have redemption "because of" Christ because, as the sovereign Lord of history, God uses this terrible injustice done to Jesus so that his suffering and death deal with the problem of sin, death, and the devil and bring the blessing of Abraham to the nations (Ac 2:23). Thus, "God absorbs the acts of people in his own acts" (Van den Brink and Van der Kooi, *Christian Dogmatics*, 480).

86. Substitution is the exclusive element of our relationship with Christ. Burger writes, "Jesus Christ takes our place and remains permanently exclusive in this: *exclusive*, in the sense of unique and irreplaceable. With this moment, it is about him taking our place and taking over our role.... What he is, we are not. What he experiences, we do not need to experience. What he does, we cannot do" (*Life in Christ*, 61). Representation is the inclusive element in our relationship with Christ. Burger writes, "Jesus Christ is our representative. Thus, he is called the 'last Adam' (1 Corinthians 15:45). Unlike substitution (taking our place), representation is inclusive and thus open in the direction of . . . participation.... We can participate in his story to a certain extent and experience what he experienced. As he is, we may become. What he experienced we can also experience. What he does, we can do. Representation and participation, therefore, belong together" (*Life in Christ*, 62).

Israel's representative and substitute, Christ is also Adam's representative and substitute as well.[87]

Fifth, in taking on our weak and frail human flesh and uniting himself to our human nature, Christ enabled the love the Father has for him in eternity to enter into time so that our humanity can participate in this eternal Father-Son love by becoming children of God who are joined to the Son and born of God and who share in Christ's filial spirit, responding to God in faith, by the Spirit of God.[88]

Sixth, because Christ is the image of the Father who represented the Father and bore witness to his glorious presence on earth, "God's identity is definitively and irreversibly defined by Jesus."[89]

The drama of the work of Christ[90]

The theodramatic biblical narrative generates the drama of the work of Christ. Grammatically reconceptualizing the speech acts of this drama in terms of theodramatic imagination and action entails the following.

First, by offering the Father the sacrifice of his life through the Holy Spirit as Israel's representative and substitute,[91] Christ was the theater of

---

87. Cf. Burger, *Life in Christ*, 55.

88. Cf. Clark and Johnson, *Incarnation of God*, 58; Fairbairn, *Life in the Trinity*, 131–39.

89. Van den Brink and Van der Kooi, *Christian Dogmatics*, 383; see also Clark and Johnson, *Incarnation of God*, 79–82.

90. For systematic theological overviews of the drama of the work of Christ, see Balthasar, *Theo-Drama*, 4:205–423; Barth, *Church Dogmatics* IV/1, 3–356; IV/2, 3–498; IV/3a, 3–367; Bavinck, *Reformed Dogmatics*, 3:323–482; Beeke and Smalley, *Man and Christ*, 869–1180; Berkhof, *Systematic Theology*, 331–411; Calvin, *Institutes*, 2.15–17; Frame, *Systematic Theology*, 899–920; Grenz, *Theology for the Community of God*, 339–56; cf. 256–60; Horton, *Christian Faith*, 483–547; Jones, *Grammar of Christian Faith*, 427–82; Kärkkäinen, *Christ and Reconciliation*, 291–403; Letham, *Systematic Theology*, 545–94; Macleod, *Faith to Live By*, 145–55; Van den Brink and Van der Kooi, *Christian Dogmatics*, 432–88; Van Genderen and Velema, *Reformed Dogmatics*, 462–538; see also Vanhoozer, "Redemption Accomplished," 473–96). For how the biblical figures of the life, death, and resurrection of Christ rhythms and patterns understanding our engagement with culture, see Watkin, *Biblical Critical Theory*, 371–458.

91. While we do read in Scripture that Christ represented those who were elected from all eternity (John 6:44; 17:2, 6, 9, 24; Rev 7), we also read that Christ represented all humanity (John 1:29; 3:16–17; 12:47; 1 John 2.2; 4:14) as well as Israel in particular (Gal 3:10–14; 4:4–5).

Instead of pressing these different perspectives into a theological system, Burger suggests that we formulate rules to help us understand the rhetorical intent or grammar of the speech acts in Scripture in the various situations in which these speech acts occur

God's mission for his glory, performing and bearing witness to the communicative activity of mutual glorification in the immanent Trinity by being open and responsive to his Father, trustfully listening to and doing his will, with the loving intent to redeem Israel and creation from the powers of evil: sin, death, and the devil.[92] Consequently, he called Israel to repent and believe the good news of the coming kingdom of heaven.

Second, when Christ offered the Father the sacrifice of his life through the Holy Spirit as Israel's representative and substitute, Israel participated in this sacrifice and was sanctified in him (John 17:19; 1 Cor 1:30). Because Christ offered the Father the sacrifice of his life through the Spirit as *Israel's* representative and substitute, there is no need to formulate that sacrifice as a fulfillment of a covenant of works. Because God wanted to use Israel to bring the blessing of Abraham to the nations, the world also participated in Christ's history and is sanctified in him.[93]

---

so that we can give a pastoral answer when one wonders who Christ represented. If one wonders whether he has been represented by Christ, then it is fitting to give the inviting answer that Christ represented all humanity. If one thinks that simply belonging to humanity is sufficient to be represented by Christ, then it is fitting to give the descriptive answer that Christ represented his church, i.e., believers and their children. If one does not want to believe because he trusts in his own capacities, then it is fitting to give the confronting answer that Christ represented only those whom the Father draws to himself, i.e., the decretal elect. This last answer can also be considered a doxological answer that gives praise to God (cf. Burger, *Being in Christ*, 545–46; *Life in Christ*, 208–9).

Thus, I agree with the confessional formulation of the doctrine of limited atonement found in the Canons of Dort II.8: "It was God's will that Christ . . . should effectively redeem . . . only those who were chosen from eternity for salvation and given to him by the Father" (*Trinity Psalter Hymnal*, 904). The pastoral context of this answer is the Remonstrants' assertion that Christ only made salvation possible for humanity and that it is up to humanity to make this a reality in their lives. However, I consider this to be only one perspective on the death of Christ that should be given as a confrontational and doxological answer. It could also be given as an eschatic-descriptive answer that is given in the life hereafter (Burger, *Being in Christ*, 456).

That this confessional formulation of the Canons of Dort is only one possible confession formulation can be seen in the fact that the Belgic Confession in article 34 gives the descriptive answer—Christ represented the church, that is, believers and their children—when it says, "And truly, Christ has shed his blood no less for washing the little children of believers than he did for adults" (*Trinity Psalter Hymnal*, 868). The pastoral context of this answer has to do with the Anabaptists, who asserted that children were not members of the covenant and therefore not in Christ. This same descriptive answer to the question of who Christ represented is found in the historic Form for the Baptism of Infants (*Liturgical Forms and Prayers of the URCNA*, 9–15).

92. The word "redemption" "points to a broad spectrum of total deliverance (atonement, inner healing, sanctification, glorification) in Christ and emphasizes the unity of these aspects" (Van den Brink and Van der Kooi, *Christian Dogmatics*, 444).

93. Cf. Burger, *Being in Christ*, 546. For being sanctified by the Spirit, see the drama

Accordingly, as the true Israel Christ is also the last Adam in whom humanity receives its new humanity (Eph 2:15; 4:24; 2 Cor 5:17; Col 3:10; cf. 1 Cor 15:45).

Third, when Christ offered the Father the sacrifice of his death through the Holy Spirit, as Israel's representative and substitute, he continued to be the theater of God's drama, revealing the intratrinitarian mutual glorification by trustfully listening to and obeying the Father's will in order to redeem Israel and creation from the powers of evil. Again, because Jesus acts as *Israel's* representative and substitute, there is no need to formulate the sacrifice of his death as a fulfillment of the covenant of works.

Fourth, Israel participated in Christ's sacrifice of his death through the Spirit as Israel's representative and substitute and so was redeemed in him (Rom 3:24; 1 Cor 1:30; Eph 1:7; Col 1:14; Titus 2:14; Heb 9:12; 1 Pet 1:18–19; Rev 5:9; 14:4).

Fifth, through the sacrifice of his death as Israel's representative and substitute, Christ defeated the powers of evil: sin, death, and the devil (Luke 10:18; John 12:31; 1 Cor 15:55; Col 2:15; 2 Tim 1:10; Heb 2:14–15; 1 John 3:8; Rev 1:18; 21:4). He defeated sin by making atonement for it as priest to redeem Israel from it. His sacrificial death expiates sin or removes it from God's sight and also propitiates or stills God's wrath (Rom 3:25; Heb 2:17; 1 John 2:2; 4:10).[94] He did not purchase benefits by his death, which would then be applied later to believers; rather, by his death he ransomed Israel from the evil of sin.[95]

As priest, he reconciled Israel to God (Rom 3:24–26; Col 2:14), and as king, he freed them from the curse of the law and the power of the

---

of the Holy Spirit below.

94. Expiation and propitiation are intrinsically tied together. You cannot have one without the other. Macleod writes, "The expiation has meaning and value only as a means of propitiation. . . . To speak here of an expiation which does not propitiate would be meaningless." He adds, "In saying this, however, we have always to keep in mind that, in Christian terms, the expiation is offered to the God who is love, who already, indeed, loves sinners and is altogether predisposed to welcome the expiation offered to him" (*Christ Crucified*, 147; cf. 101–50; Burger, *Hoop voor een zuchtende schepping*, 168–69; see also Packer, *Knowing God*, 161–80).

95. Thus, the work of Christ does not have a twofold soteriological structure where Christ purchased substantivized benefits of salvation which the Holy Spirit then applies to those who believe so that salvation is no longer in Christ (1 Cor 1:30). For an overview of the historical background of how this twofold soteriological structure developed, see Burger, *Life in Christ*, 11-19.

devil (Isa 43:5–6; Matt 20:28; Mark 10:45;[96] Rom 5:15–19; Gal 3:13; Heb 2:14–15; John 16:11; Col 1:13; 2:15), so that Israel can bring the blessing of Abraham to the nations by bearing witness to all that is in Christ (Gal 3:14),[97] and doing so before the curse of the law could reach them.[98] Moreover, he freed them from absolute separation from God in hell.[99] And in addition, he purified their conscience from dead works and sanctified them (Heb 9:14; 10:1–18).[100]

In this way, he laid the soteriological basis for the new covenant, enabling them to participate in the divine nature by living in the Father's presence and sharing in his filial status and communion of love with his Father (Heb 8:1–13). As a result, he brought about a new exodus.

In defeating sin by making atonement for Israel's sin, God demonstrated his righteousness and condemned sin in the flesh of Christ. In doing so, he demonstrated his faithfulness to his covenant with Israel by having a true Israelite deal with the problem of sin, death, and the devil, so that the blessing of Abraham—redemption in Christ—flows to the nations, but he also demonstrated his faithfulness to his law, the law that demanded that sin be punished with death (Gen 2:17; Rom 3:5–7, 21–26; 6:23).[101] As a result, God's justice was satisfied.[102] Indeed, the whole of Christ's work of redemption was according to the plan of God (Isa 53:10; Luke 22:22; 24:26; Acts 2:23; Eph 1:3–11).

---

96. About the metaphor of "ransom," Macchia writes, "He [i.e., Jesus] used the metaphor of a *ransom* (Mark 10:45), which meant a payment or offering made to deliver someone from captivity. The point of the ransom metaphor is not so much the payment, as though God needs to be paid off to show humanity mercy. Instead, the point is that the self-offering of Christ in the fulfillment of the Father's will frees humanity from its captivity to sin and death" (*Jesus the Spirit Baptizer*, 263; see also Burger, *Hoop voor een zuchtende schepping*, 161, 170, 172).

97. Burger, "Hoe vergeeft God?," 167; Macchia, *Jesus the Spirit Baptizer*, 249–50.

98. Van Bruggen, *Paul*, 199; cf. *Jesus the Son of God*, 201; O'Donovan, *Resurrection and Moral Order*, 123–30, 134, 141; Wright, *Knowing Jesus*, 22, 44, 62–63, 125–35, 153–74, 182; *Mission of God*, 65–66, 325, 342–44; Wright, *Paul and the Faithfulness of God*, 495–537; cf. Burger, "Theology without a Covenant of Works," 343; "'Theirs Are the Covenants,'" 15.

99. When Christ was forsaken by his Father, this was not just his subjective experience, but an absolute reality (Van den Brink and Van der Kooi, *Christian Dogmatics*, 479–80).

100. Burger, "Tussen atomisering en samenklontering," 76–77.

101. Burger, "Hoe vergeeft God?," 171; *Hoop voor een zuchtende schepping*, 169; Wright, *Romans, Part 1*, 51–59; *Paul and the Faithfulness of God*, 835–46; *Day the Revolution Began*, 295–351.

102. Burger, "Hoe vergeeft God?," 176.

Because God wanted to use Israel to bring the blessing of Abraham to the nations, the world also participated in the history of Israel's representative and is ransomed and reconciled in him (John 1:29;[103] 2 Cor 5:19;[104] 1 John 2:2;[105] 4:14[106]).[107]

103. "As God's lamb, Jesus takes upon himself the sin not merely of Israel, but of the entire world (cf. 1:10). . . . John makes clear that Jesus came to save the entire world (John 3:17; 1 John 2:2) and that he is the Savior of the world, not merely Israel (John 4:42; 1 John 4:14)" (Köstenberger, *John*, 67–68).

104. Martin writes, "The periphrastic tense (participle + verb ἦν, "was") denotes an element of contingency that, although the reconciliation is complete from God's side, there is the possibility that some people may not accept it . . . or that, with an eye on his readers, they may not have entered into the full experience of reconciliation" (*2 Corinthians*, 154). Van Spanje writes, "The fact that Christ died on behalf of and in place of all not only means that all died (verse 14), but also has as goal (cf. *hina*) that humanity will live for the other [like Christ]! However, this only becomes a reality in believers: those who live in Christ (indicated by *hoi zoontes*), also live for Christ" (van Spanje, *2 Korintiërs*, 158–59). Commenting on 2 Cor 5:18–21, he adds, "If people do not accept God's [universal] act of reconciliation (cf. 2 Cor 5:20), the reconciliation remains incomplete in some respects" (*2 Korintiërs*, 163; cf. 167–68). O'Donovan articulates the same idea when he says, "The question that is asked of us, in our time is not: shall all mankind then be saved in Christ?—for that question has been answered by him in his time, and does not need the living of our lives to answer it further. The question is this: shall we ourselves be saved with all mankind in Christ?" (*On the Thirty-Nine Articles*, 125; see Burger, *Being in Christ*, 461). Accordingly, Smits says, "We thus distinguish between the Christological and the pneumatological moment of the reality of reconciliation. The former involves the reality of reconciliation *extra nos*, the latter the reality of reconciliation *in nobis*, that is, here and now" (*Plaatsbereiding*, 15).

105. Smalley writes, "As in the Gospel of John, the scope of divine salvation is ultimately regarded as all-inclusive. The fourth evangelist describes Jesus as the 'Savior of the world' (4:42; cf. 3:16); and here John refers to him as the one whose 'atoning sacrifice' relates to the sins of 'the whole world.'" He adds, "The adjective 'whole' (περὶ) ὅλου, is intensive. The sacrificial offering of Christ is effective not just for the sins of the 'world' (which could refer to a section of it), and still less for 'our' sins (those of John's immediate circle) alone; it embraces the sins of the *whole* world" (*1, 2, 3 John*, 40).

106. "The writer maintains that Jesus the Son is 'savior of the world' (τοῦ κόσμου). The 'world' in this context means not only mankind in general, as the theater of salvation . . . but also the world in *opposition* to God (5:19), in need of redemption. . . . In both cases the thought of the scope of salvation is potentially universal" (Smalley, *1, 2, 3 John*, 253).

107. See Burger, *Being in Christ*, 546; O'Donovan, *Resurrection and Moral Order*, 15; O'Donovan, *Desire of the Nations*, 130, 136–37, 141–42.

The world participating in the history of Israel's representative and having its salvation in him could be considered a form of hypothetical universalism, which holds that "the work of Christ is universal in its sufficiency but applied to an elect number less than the total number of fallen humanity; hence *hypothetical* universalism" (Crisp, *Deviant Calvinism*, 176; cf. 175–209; Moore, "Extent of the Atonement," 124–61).

This distinction between the extent and the application of the work of Christ draws on the sufficiency/efficiency distinction first formulated by Peter Lombard

Moreover, when Christ defeated death by his death on the cross, he not only redeemed humanity from the fear of death (Heb 2:15; 1 Cor 15:15; Rev 1:18; 21:4); he also enabled them to participate in the incorruptibility of his divine nature (2 Pet 1:4). By defeating the devil through his death, he bound the devil, mortally wounding him and curtailing his

(1096–1160). Lombard wrote, "He offered himself on the altar of the cross not to the devil, but to the triune God, and he did so for all with regard to the sufficiency of the price, but only for the elect with regard to its efficacy, because he brought about salvation only for the predestined" (cited by Allen, *Extent of the Atonement*, 27). Allen writes, "Historically this statement indicated that Christ's death paid the price for the sins of the world but that the benefits of the atonement were only applied to the elect (those who believe)" (*Extent of the Atonement*, 27). He adds, "The [sufficient/efficient] *concept*, however, is *at least* as old as Ambrose (AD 338–397)." This extrinsic sufficiency was modified and narrowed by later Reformers to an intrinsic sufficiency or intrinsic value of the sacrifice of Christ so that his death "'could have been' (instead of 'was') a ransom for the sins of all people" (*Extent of the Atonement*, 27, cf. 27–31).

Hypothetical universalism has always been part of the Reformed tradition. Muller writes, "Given that there was a significant hypothetical universalist trajectory in the Reformed tradition from its beginnings, it is arguably less than useful to describe its continuance as a softening of the tradition." He adds, "More importantly, the presence of various forms of hypothetical universalism as well as various approaches to a more particularistic definition renders it rather problematic to describe the tradition as 'on the whole' particularistic and thereby to identify hypothetical universalism as a dissident, subordinate stream of the tradition, rather than as one significant stream (or, perhaps two!) among others, having equal claim to confessional orthodoxy" (Muller, "Diversity in the Reformed Tradition," 25; *Calvin and the Reformed Tradition*, 126–60; Crisp, *Deviant Calvinism*, 178). It should be noted that "hypothetical universal has never been repudiated by a Reformed synod or council" (Crisp, *Deviant Calvinism*, 178). For a refutation of the double payment objection, see Crisp, "Anglican Hypothetical Universalism," 35–38.

For how "the position of English Hypothetical Universalism ... was brought to bear powerfully upon the deliberations and final formulations of the Synod to the extent that the British Delegation were able to subscribe to the resulting Canons shortly before returning to England," see Moore, "Extent of the Atonement," 145; cf. 144–48; Lynch, *John Davenant's Hypothetical Universalism*, 85–98; cf. 70–100. On options available at the Synod of Dort, see Thomas, *Extent of the Atonement*, 128–59. On the Canons of Dort representing "a balanced compromise statement of the Reformed doctrine of the extent of the atonement which accommodated the considerable varieties of thought on that subject within the international Reformed community," see Godfrey, "Reformed Thought," 171; Gattis, "Abundant Sufficiency," 156.

Regarding the interpretation of universalist-sounding and particularist-sounding texts in Scripture, Crisp writes, "Those defending the definite-atonement position think that the particularist passages are somehow theologically more fundamental than the universalist-sounding ones. The latter should be understood in the light of the former, for God's purposes are not confounded by creaturely actions and God accomplishes all God set out to do in creation." He adds, "Hypothetical universalism presents readers of the biblical texts with a different way of thinking about the same material. Rather than privileging one set of passages over another, why not let them stand in tension?" (*Deviant Calvinism*, 197–98).

power (Gen 3:15; Luke 10:18; John 12:31; Col 2:15; 2 Tim 1:10; Heb 2:14; 1 John 3:8; Rev 20:2–3).

Christ's work of redemption by the sacrifice of his life and the sacrifice of his death is meant to evoke our response of faith (Luke 7:47; Acts 2:37; 2 Cor 5:19–21; John 13:15; Eph 5:2; Phil 2:5; Heb 12:1–2; 1 Pet 2:21; 1 John 2:6; 3:16).[108]

Sixth, when Christ was raised from the dead by the Holy Spirit and vindicated as God's—and Israel's—true Messiah (Rom 1:4; 1 Tim 3:16), God reversed the miscarriage of justice that had taken place when Jesus was condemned to death, though innocent. His resurrection is also proof that, as king, he had defeated Israel's and our real enemies—sin, death, and the devil—and that our redemption is already realized and complete in him, even though it still has a hidden quality. When he rose from the dead with a glorified body, he was the first fruits of God's hidden, eschatological, incorruptible new creation in fulfillment of the promise of a new covenant (John 11:25–26; Acts 2:24; Rom 6:9; 1 Cor 15:20–23; Col 1:18; Rev 1:5, 18; cf. Ezek 37:1–14; 36:33–38). Furthermore, by rising from the dead through the Holy Spirit, Christ could pour forth the Spirit.[109]

Since Jesus rose from the dead as Israel's representative, Israel participated in his resurrection and was justified in him and has its new life in him (Rom 4:25; 1 Cor 1:2, 39; John 17:19).[110] Victims of injustice have

---

108. See Van den Brink and Van der Kooi, *Christian Dogmatics*, 467–70. The various models of atonement—through victory, satisfaction, and transformation—are complementary. For an overview of the three models, see Aulén, *Christus Victor*; Boersma, *Violence, Hospitality, and the Cross*, 99–201; Van den Brink and Van der Kooi, *Christian Dogmatics*, 453–70. For the sacrament of penance being the background of the satisfaction model, see Burger, "Gospel Presentation," 273–74; *Life in Christ*, 12; "Foundation or Perspective?," 75–76. For how the satisfaction model can isolate the cross from the rest of the history of Jesus Christ, including his resurrection, the history of Israel, the kingdom of God, and eschatology, as well as our participation in the death of Christ, see Burger, *Life in Christ*, 13–14; cf. 67–102, 135–39; *Hoop voor een zuchtende schepping*, 159–62. The three models should be tied together with the concept of Christ as Israel's substitute and representative (cf. Burger, "Tussen atomisering en samenklontering," 63; *Hoop voor een zuchtende schepping* 158, 165). For a similar integrative concept, see Hastings, *Total Atonement*. For an overview of the different biblical images for salvation forming one story of salvation, see Burger, *Life in Christ*, 173-209; "Foundation or Perspective?," 61–79.

109. Macchia, *Jesus the Spirit Baptizer*, 248.

110. For more on being justified by faith and being made alive in the Spirit, see the discussion of the drama of the Holy Spirit below.

their vindication in him as well (Rom 4:25).[111] And because God wanted to use Israel to bring the blessing of Abraham to the nations and because, as Israel's representative, Christ is also the representative head of creation and humanity, the world also participated in his resurrection and has new life in him.[112]

Seventh, when Christ ascended into heaven through the power of the Holy Spirit, his life was hidden in the glory of the Father. From there, he continues to participate in the drama of his Father's mission for his glory as the head and mediator of the new covenant and lord of the universe (Acts 2:33; Eph 1:20–22; 4:15; 5:23; Col 1:18; 2:10; Heb 8:6; 9:15; 12:4; 1 Tim 2:5).

By his ascension, he inaugurated the last days (Acts 2:17; 2 Tim 3:1; Heb 1:1; 1 Pet 1:20; 2 Pet 3:3; Jude 18; 1 John 2:18).

As king, he rules as the last Adam (1 Cor 15:45) and the great son of David (Luke 1:32–33; Acts 2:34–35; Heb 1:13), upholding and governing his body, the church (Matt 18:20; 28:20; John 16:13; Eph 4:8; Rev 2–3) and leading history to its ultimate fulfillment in the coming kingdom of God by his Word and Spirit (Rev 1:8; 21:6; 22:13). As priest, he intercedes for his people (Rom 8:34; Heb 2:16–18; 4:14–16; 7:25; 1 Tim 2:5; 1 John 2:1–2) and blesses them (Luke 24:51; Eph 1:3). As prophet, he continues to confront Israel and the nations with the Father's good news of the nearness of the kingdom of heaven, urging them to repent and believe this good news or else face the fire of God's wrath in his coming judgment and be excluded from the kingdom (John 10:11; Acts 8:12; 14:22; 19:8; 20:25; 28:23, 30–31; Rom 14:17; 1 Cor 4:20; Gal 5:21; Eph 5:5; 1 Thess 2:12; 2 Tim 4:1; Heb 12:28; 2 Pet 1:11; Jas 2:5; Rev 11:15).

---

111. Burger, *Life in Christ*, 19, 161.

112. Burger, *Being in Christ*, 546; O'Donovan, *Resurrection and Moral Order*, 13–15, 31, 57; *Desire of the Nations*, 142.

Participation in the life of God and the drama of the Holy Spirit[113]

The drama of the Holy Spirit as the giver of life[114]

The theodramatic biblical narrative generates the drama of the Holy Spirit as the giver of life. Grammatically reconceptualizing the speech acts of this drama in terms of theodramatic imagination and action entails the following.

First, the Spirit who gives life is the third person of the Trinity, who eternally and perichoretically subsists in the generative and communicative being of God with his personal identity, perfecting divine acts in time as the producer and director of God's drama of his mission for his glory.

Second, because God preserves his creation through the Spirit, the Spirit also works in human culture and history. This work has generally been referred to as God's common grace.[115]

Third, as the giver of life, the Spirit has a threefold relationship with Christ. Because the Father eternally generates or begets the Son in the spiration of the Holy Spirit, Christ *proceeds* from the Spirit. Because the Spirit rests on Jesus, Christ is also the *bearer* of the Spirit. Because the Spirit is distributed by the Father and the Son, the Father and Christ also *send* the Spirit.

---

113. Formally, I am following Van den Brink and Van der Kooi who outline their pneumatology as the Holy Spirit, Giver of Life, the Book of God and of Humans, Renewal of God's Community, and Renewal of the Human Being (*Christian Dogmatics*, 489–710). They also include eschatology in their pneumatology as the renewal of God's world (*Christian Dogmatics*, 711–59).

114. For systematic theological overviews of the drama of the Spirit as the giver of life, see Barth, *Church Dogmatics* I/1, 448–66; IV/1, 740–79; Bavinck, *Reformed Dogmatics*, 4:29–95; Beeke and Smalley, *Revelation and God*, 366–68, 940–44, 1065; Berkhof, *Systematic Theology*, 95–99; Calvin, *Institutes*, 1.13.14–15; 3.1; Frame, *Systematic Theology*, 477–79, 923–63; Grenz, *Theology for the Community of God*, 105–6, 357–78, 405–22; Horton, *Christian Faith*, 551–86; *Rediscovering the Holy Spirit*, 29–40; Jones, *Grammar of Christian Faith*, 497–501; Kärkkäinen, *Spirit and Salvation*, 43–118, 263–311; Letham, *Systematic Theology*, 86–91; Macleod, *Faith to Live By*, 197–207; Van den Brink and Van der Kooi, *Christian Dogmatics*, 489–532; Van Genderen and Velema, *Reformed Dogmatics*, 294–97, 578–89.

115. Douma gives a summary description of Kuyper's understanding of common grace: "Common grace is that favor of God which as *common* grace is not universal and found in everyone by nature, but is a conferred good within the circle of humanity, common to elect and non-elect; and which as common *grace* is not salvific, but only arrests sin and its consequences (and therefore the execution of Gen. 2:17)" (*Common Grace*, 7).

This threefold relationship between Christ and the Spirit entails that the Spirit, as the giver of life, is the one who draws us into the life of God, enabling us to participate in this life and partake of the divine nature by uniting us to Christ, having us put him on through faith and clothe ourselves with him. It also entails that Christ cannot be separated from the Spirit or the Spirit from Christ.[116]

Fourth, as the giver of life, the Spirit is not only a person; he is also a gift. More precisely, he is the promised eschatological gift of the new covenant who empowers God's new covenant community to be a theater of the drama of his mission for his glory, made up of actors who bear witness to the communicative activity of mutual glorification in the immanent Trinity. As such, the gift of the Holy Spirit is the future of God's glorified eschatological new creation breaking forth into the present.

The drama of the Holy Spirit as the communicator of direction[117]

The theodramatic biblical narrative generates the drama of the Holy Spirit as the giver of direction. Grammatically reconceptualizing the speech acts of this drama in terms of theodramatic imagination and action entails the following.

First, because God's being is a dynamic communicative activity between the Father, Son, and Spirit and because God's communicative activity in the economic Trinity reveals his activity in the immanent Trinity, God is also communicatively present in this world, encountering us in Christ through the Holy Spirit through a variety of means in order to draw us into his divine life.[118]

---

116. Van den Brink and Van der Kooi, *Christian Dogmatics*, 498, 505–6.

117. For systematic theological overviews of the drama of the Spirit as the communicator of direction, see Balthasar, *Theo-Drama*, 2:102–15; 3:61–104; Barth, *Church Dogmatics* I/1, 88–186; I/2, 203–79; Bavinck, *Reformed Dogmatics*, 1:283–494; Beeke and Smalley, *Revelation and God*, 177–480; Berkhof, *Systematic Theology*, 34–40; Calvin, *Institutes*, 1.1–9; Frame, *Systematic Theology*, 519–693; Grenz, *Theology for the Community of God*, 132–39, 379–404; Horton, *Christian Faith*, 151–219; Jones, *Grammar of Christian Faith*, 57–148; Kärkkäinen, *Spirit and Salvation*, 7–178; Letham, *Systematic Theology*, 52–65, 185–267; Macleod, *Faith to Live By*, 9–36; Van den Brink and Van der Kooi, *Christian Dogmatics*, 157–99; 533–71; Van Genderen and Velema, *Reformed Dogmatics*, 20–116; see also Treier, "Holy Scripture," 546–61.

118. For Calvin on God's accommodation in his revelation, see Huijgen, *Divine Accommodation*. For an analysis and evaluation of various models of revelation, see Van den Brink and Van der Kooi, *Christian Dogmatics*, 171–81. For Horton's understanding of general revelation as an independent source of revelation alongside special revelation, see chapter 3.

Second, God sends his Son into this world to embody his communicative action in order to draw people into the new covenant community and have them participate in his divine life in Christ.

Third, Scripture is God's communicative agent, addressing and engaging those who hear and read it through a wide variety of divine communicative acts, drawing them into an ever-deeper communion with himself in Christ.[119] This gives to God's communicative action a mystagogical orientation—that is, it is intended to guide and draw believers into the mystery of their participation in the divine nature by uniting them to Christ, having them put him on by faith and clothe themselves with him, so that they participate in the Son's status of sonship and his communion of love with the Father.[120]

Fourth, because Scripture is the inspired script, transcript, and prescript that witnesses to the unfolding drama of God's mission for his glory in Christ through the Holy Spirit, it is a reliable and authoritative means by which he dialogically engages Israel and humanity with his speech acts and prompts them to participate faithfully and fittingly[121] in the theodrama that is being played out in the history of this world and the history of their lives.[122]

---

119. Vanhoozer, *First Theology*, 35; cf. 9–13, 202, 291–92; cf. Huijgen, *Lezen en laten lezen*, 24–31.

120. Billings writes, "Interpreting Scripture cannot be reduced to method or technique, because it is nothing less than a part of our life of participation in Christ through the Spirit, a means by which God nurtures our love of God and neighbor" (Billings, *Word of God*, 195). On the fourfold sense in connection with reading Scripture and how this fourfold sense can be reconfigured to give a fourfold perspective on how the reader is included in the theodrama of Scripture, see chapter 1.

121. For fitting participation involving creative improvisation in new situations, see chapter 1. As I noted there, in addition to having Scripture directing the church to creatively improvise in new situations so that it wisely meets new challenges and deals with new problems in a way that is faithful to the authorial intent of God's divine discourse in Scripture, the church has the "classic productions" or "masterpiece theater" of the ecumenical councils and the "classic productions" or "regional theater" of the confessional theology of their own denomination and those of other denominations (Vanhoozer, *Drama of Doctrine*, 449–53; Vanhoozer, "Drama-of-Redemption Model," 174–75; Vanhoozer, *Faith Speaking Understanding*, 147–49). These masterpiece and regional theatrical productions have relative authority in the church.

122. The "Bible has authority in the church because it testifies to the saving acts of God in Israel, in Jesus Christ, and in the Spirit. . . . The authority of the Bible therefore rests on the salvific character of its content. It is soteriologically determined. If we can say that God is spoken of in the history of Israel and the history of Jesus and the Spirit, then the Bible is the book in which this speaking is reduced to a written form" (Van den Brink and Van der Kooi, *Christian Dogmatics*, 564–65). Because Christ is the foundation of our Christian faith, the Bible is foundational in a secondary sense (cf. 2 Cor

Fifth, because God sent Scripture on a mission to verbalize his communicative action to draw Israel and the nations into his new covenant community and have them participate in his divine life in Christ, as he sent his Son on a mission to achieve that same goal, Scripture is located in the drama of redemption. As God's communicative action in Christ was accompanied by the Spirit and required the Spirit, so too his action in and through Scripture is accompanied by and requires the work of the Spirit.[123]

Sixth, because Scripture contains the unified speech act of a single speaker through the speech acts of different human authors, Scripture is not only a trustworthy witness to God's revelation but is itself also a trustworthy revelation.[124] This entails that meaning is stable in Scripture.

Seventh, because the Word of God was embodied in Jesus Christ in the New Testament and because of the continuity of God's acts in his Word, later revelations can be typologically prefigured in earlier texts. Moreover, because of the close relationship between Christ, the incarnate Word of God, in whose image God wants to transform us, and the Scriptures as the Word of God, the Spirit can use the written Word to transform us into the image of Christ, for the more we see the glory of Christ in Scripture, the more we can be transformed into his image. In this way, the Spirit directs and forms the readers and interpreters of Scripture into actors who share in Christ's filial spirit, listening to the Father and responding in faith, and so participating in the drama of God's intratrinitarian mutual glorification that he is enacting on the stage of his creation.[125]

1:19–20). For more on Christ being the foundation as opposed to different forms of foundationalism, see chapter 1.

123. Vanhoozer, *Drama of Doctrine*, 60, 70–71, 228. Because Scripture is located in the drama of redemption, it is located within the drama of the Holy Spirit. See also Grenz, *Theology for the Community of God*, 379–404; Van den Brink and Van der Kooi, *Christian Dogmatics*, 533–71.

124. Vanhoozer, *Drama of Doctrine*, 38, 147, 267, 276. The canon developed around the testimony of God's saving acts in Scripture. "The authority of the Bible is grounded in its recognition by the church. *The acceptance of this list of books in the fourth century was a matter of taking stock of the actual situation, of the pattern of practice that had developed in the reading and liturgical use of these writings*" (Van den Brink and Van der Kooi, *Christian Dogmatics*, 564).

125. Cf. Vanhoozer, "Ascending the Mountain," 797; Burger, "Tussen atomisering en samenklontering," 59–60.

The drama of the Spirit as the creator of a new community[126]

The theodramatic biblical narrative generates the drama of the Holy Spirit as the creator of a new community. Grammatically reconceptualizing the speech acts of this drama in terms of theodramatic imagination and action entails the following.

First, the church is the preliminary or provisional[127] visible form of God's eschatological new creation, created by the Holy Spirit and formed by putting on Christ through faith and clothing ourselves with him, so that it is no longer we who live but Christ Jesus who lives in us (2 Cor 5:17; Gal 2:20; 4:19; 6:15; Eph 2:15; Rev 21:5).[128]

Second, as God's eschatological community, created by the Spirit and formed in union with Christ through faith, the church is God's new covenant community or reconstituted Israel that bears the Spirit in order to bring the blessing of Abraham to the nations. When Gentiles come to faith in Christ and are grafted into this reconstituted Israel, the Spirit wants to use the beauty of God's eschatological creation to arouse jealousy in non-Christian Jews and bring them to faith in Christ (Rom 11).

Third, because the church as God's new creation is formed in union with Christ through faith, the essence of church membership is being

---

126. For systematic theological overviews of the drama of the Spirit as the creator of a new community, see Balthasar, *Glory of the Lord*, 6:225–416; 7:33–543; *Theo-Drama*, 3:361–446; 4:453–69; *Theo-Logic*, 3:255–411; Barth, *Church Dogmatics* I/2, 741–884; IV/1, 643–739; IV/2, 614–840; IV/3b, 681–901; IV/4, 1–212; Bavinck, *Reformed Dogmatics*, 4:271–585; Berkhof, *Systematic Theology*, 551–658; Calvin, *Institutes*, 4.1–20; Frame, *Systematic Theology*, 1017–72; Grenz, *Theology for the Community of God*, 461–570; Horton, *Christian Faith*, 711–903; Jones, *Grammar of Christian Faith*, 593–688; Kärkkäinen, *Hope and Community*, 233–483; Letham, *Systematic Theology*, 612–47, 705–23; Macleod, *Faith to Live By*, 243–85; Van den Brink and Van der Kooi, *Christian Dogmatics*, 572–644; Van Genderen and Velema, *Reformed Dogmatics*, 677–818; see also Moore-Keish, "Sacraments," 528–45; Pauw, "Church," 514–27. For how the biblical figure of the church as a new community rhythms and patterns our being in the world, see Watkin, *Biblical Critical Theory*, 459–508.

127. For the expression "preliminary" and "provisional," see Van den Brink and Van der Kooi, *Christian Dogmatics*, 582, 593; see also Pauw, "Church," 526.

128. As Burger notes, "the reality of the new covenant partly has a hidden and contested character and is open to further eschatological realization in the future." As a result, "the church is a mixed community because not all church members are regenerate or remain faithful until the end, and the process of the writing of the law on the heart is unfinished, and the consequences and effects of sin are still felt notwithstanding the promise of complete forgiveness" (Burger, "Story of God's Covenants," 296). For an overview of conceptually understanding union with Christ, see Campbell, *Paul and Union with Christ*; Macaskill, *Union with Christ*; Thate, Vanhoozer, and Campbell, eds., "*In Christ*" *in Paul*.

a partaker of the divine nature by putting on Christ through faith and participating in his status of sonship and his communion of love with the Father as we share his filial spirit. The Holy Spirit has joined us, as the church, to Christ. And this implies that the church's essence is hidden with Christ in God (John 17:21, 23; Col 3:3; 1 John 3:2). Thus, the essence and identity of the church is "not in institutional forms, organization, and offices, nor in active and engaged persons, but in the action that issues from God himself."[129]

Fourth, because the church is a partaker of the divine nature in Christ by the Spirit, the church is dependent upon Christ through the Spirit, as certain metaphors for the church indicate (John 15:1–8; 1 Cor 3:9–10, 16; 12:27; Eph 2:19–22; 5:23–32; 1 Pet 2:5).[130]

Fifth, Christ himself cultivates and nurtures our becoming partakers of the divine nature in him in his new creation by his Word and Spirit. As Van den Brink and Van der Kooi note, "This phrasing does not mean that God directs *either* through the Word *or* through the Spirit, but that Word and Spirit are closely related. The Word proceeds from the work of the Spirit, and the Spirit brings that Word to us."[131]

For this task, Christ primarily uses the drama of the proclamation of the Word and the drama of the administration of the sacraments,[132] through which he rescripts his new creation by giving it his mindset[133] for fitting participation in or performance of the drama of the mission

---

129. Van den Brink and Van der Kooi, *Christian Dogmatics*, 593.

130. Van den Brink and Van der Kooi, *Christian Dogmatics*, 581; cf. 573–80.

131. Van den Brink and Van der Kooi, *Christian Dogmatics*, 596. "Word" should not be limited to a thought, but "is address and communication in the fullest sense; it may be a gesture or a way of looking at someone. This broad meaning of Word becomes immediately clear when we look at John 1:14. There we read that Jesus Christ is the incarnate Word" (Van den Brink and Van der Kooi, *Christian Dogmatics*, 594; cf. 597). Barth speaks about the threefold form of the Word of God: the Word of God preached, the Word of God written, and the Word of God revealed (Barth, *Church Dogmatics* I/1, 88–120).

132. Even though Christ is sacramentally present everywhere, there is an intensification of his sacramental presence in his new covenant community in general and in the means of grace in particular.

133. De Bruijne writes, "The church as a whole receives a new collective 'mentality,' just as . . . the church is said to be a new creation not of individuals but of the church. God does not transform a collection of loose individuals but a people called into the world as a body. Therefore, knowledge of God's will can only arise and grow in the context of the Christian congregation" (De Bruijne, "Christelijke ethiek," 141).

for his glory that is being played out in history—world history and the history of the lives of the members of God's new creation (Rom 12:2).[134]

The Spirit uses the drama of the proclamation of the Word by enabling people to hear the voice of God addressing them to form and transform them.

The Spirit uses the drama of the sacrament of baptism by visibly proclaiming their incorporation into God's new covenant community by symbolically performing their participation in the drama of the history of Christ's death and resurrection as they are sprinkled with or immersed in water, emphasizing the rescripting of their lives because they have died to their old identity, derived from Adam, and have risen to their new "*ex-centric* [identity], derived from Christ, [their] new life-center."[135]

The Spirit uses the sacrament of the Lord's Supper by proclaiming their being forgiven and sanctified as members of God's new exodus community by symbolically performing their participation in the drama of the history of Christ's death and resurrection as they eat bread and drink wine together, emphasizing their intent to seek their identity eccentrically—outside themselves—in Christ, allowing his death and resurrection to rescript their lives on their journey to the Sabbath rest of the kingdom of God.

Because the proclamation of the Word and the administration of the sacraments are intended to guide and draw members of God's new creation into the mystery of their participation in the divine nature so that their lives will be rescripted by it, both the proclamation of the Word and the administration of the sacraments have a mystagogical orientation.

Sixth, the Holy Spirit also equips God's new covenant community for its task by pouring out gifts (*charismata*) on it (Rom 12:3–8; 1 Cor 12–14; 1 Pet 4:10–11). These gifts include the offices Christ gives to his church for the sake of the upbuilding of the church and the salvation of the world by keeping its members connected to Christ and maturing in him (Eph 4:11–16).

---

134. While the drama of the proclamation of the Word and the drama of the administration of the sacraments are the primary means of grace through which Christ cultivates and nurtures our becoming partakers of the divine nature in him through the Spirit in his new creation, he also uses other means. Through the Spirit, Christ also uses "counseling, governing, the services of the diaconate, prayer and intercession, brotherly love, the interaction of the charismata, praise, and song and music" (Van den Brink and Van der Kooi, *Christian Dogmatics*, 593; cf. 624–25).

135. Van den Brink and Van der Kooi, *Christian Dogmatics*, 604.

Seventh, as the preliminary visible form of God's eschatological new creation, the church is a pilgrim community on its way to the Sabbath rest of the kingdom of God (Heb 11:16; 1 Pet 1:1).[136] On its journey, it bears witness to the resurrection life of God's new creation that has its unity and holiness in Christ (John 17:11, 21-23; Eph 4:4-6; John 17:19; 1 Cor 1:30; Eph 2:10; 5:26), creatively and imaginatively extending the meaning of the script, transcript, and prescript of God's drama in ways that develop the theodramatic action in new situations and reincorporate the new situation into the theodrama.

In doing so, the church participates in Christ's office of prophet, priest, and king, performing its prophetic task,[137] enacting its priestly life of love, and bearing witness to its royal eschatological hope by being "grounded in heaven"[138] while living its life here on the stage of this creation that is busy passing away (1 Cor 7:31), always watchful and ready for the return of the Lord Jesus Christ (Matt 24:42; 25:13; Luke 12:37-40; Rom 13:12; 1 Cor 16:13; 1 Thess 5:6; Heb 10:25; 1 Pet 4:7; Rev 16:15) and calling others to be watchful and ready as well or else face the fire of God's coming judgment and exclusion from the Sabbath rest of the coming kingdom of heaven.[139]

The drama of the Spirit as the renewer of our humanity[140]

The theodramatic biblical narrative generates the drama of the Holy Spirit as the renewer of humanity. Grammatically reconceptualizing the

---

136. For the church as a pilgrim community, see Horton, *Christian Faith*, 11, 32, 47, 75, 91, 111, 535-36, 736; Clapp, *Peculiar People*; *New Creation*; Pauw, "Church," 526.

137. For an example of prophetically speaking into our Western culture, see Van Noppen, et al., "Christenen praten over hoop." The authors entitle their article "Christians talk about hope, but not about repentance, and that conversation is urgently needed."

138. See Allen, *Grounded in Heaven*.

139. For more on the relationship between Christ and culture, see chapter 3.

140. For systematic theological overviews of the drama the Spirit as the renewer of our humanity, see Balthasar, *Glory of the Lord*, 1:131-425; *Theo-Drama*, 3:447-61; Barth, *Church Dogmatics* IV/1, 514-642; 740-79; IV/2, 499-613; IV/3b, 902-42; IV/4, 3-40; Bavinck, *Reformed Dogmatics*, 3:27-270; cf. 2:337-405; Berkhof, *Systematic Theology*, 413-549; cf. 100-125; Calvin, *Institutes*, 3.1-24; Frame, *Systematic Theology*, 923-1014; cf. 216-30; Grenz, *Theology for the Community of God*, 432-60; Horton, *Christian Faith*, 551-710; cf. 309-23; Jones, *Grammar of Christian Faith*, 511-91; Kärkkäinen, *Spirit and Salvation*, 201-415; Letham, *Systematic Theology*, 597-616, 648-705, 724-50, 768-89; Macleod, *Faith to Live By*, 157-242; Van den Brink and Van der Kooi,

speech acts of this drama in terms of theodramatic imagination and action entails the following.

First, because God's being is a dynamic communicative activity between the Father, Son, and Spirit and because God's communicative activity in the economic Trinity reveals his activity in the immanent Trinity, God draws humanity into his intratrinitarian life, making people partakers of his divine nature, by effectually addressing and engaging humanity with his Word and Spirit, uniting them to Christ through faith, declaring them to be righteous, and renewing their lives in him.[141]

Second, the Spirit does this by working in and through our humanity and personhood by opening and illuminating our hearts,[142] enabling us to hear and understand[143] the Word that is spoken to us, persuading[144] us from within that it is Christ's voice we are hearing and writing the

---

Christian Dogmatics, 645–710; Van Genderen and Velema, *Reformed Dogmatics*, 573–676; see also Billings, "Redemption Applied," 497–51.

141. Regarding the primacy of God in his dialogical interaction with humanity, Vanhoozer writes, "The effectual call is the Spirit's ministering the word in such a way that hearers freely and willingly answer God by responding with faith" (*Remythologizing Theology*, 374–75).

142. Regarding the Spirit opening our hearts, Hoglund writes, "I contend . . . that when one considers how Luke uses the term 'opening' in Luke 24:31–32 for the giving of hermeneutic understanding of Jesus' identity in the Old Testament, the divine action to 'open' Lydia's heart in Acts 16:14 can be understood as both necessary and sufficient. The opening of her heart resulted inevitably in her paying attention to Paul's message." He adds, "Like the disciples on the road to Emmaus and the Twelve later that evening, the Lord 'opened' Lydia's heart within the process of discernment and understanding" (*Called by Triune Grace*, 207).

143. Understanding is middle-voiced and thus something we come to experience from the inside as Christ gives himself to us through the Spirit. Vanhoozer writes, "In the context of grammar, 'voice' indicates the relation of a subject to the action of the verb." Moreover, "The middle voice is neither a *doing* nor a *being-done-to* but a being caught up in a process—or in the case of soteriology, a person (Christ)—in which one is nevertheless active." Thus, "to say 'I understand,' for example, is to say that one is neither simply active ('doer') nor simply passive ('done to') but rather that one is both active and caught up in a larger process: understanding is both a (mental) 'doing' and a 'happening.'" Accordingly, "God bring[s] about change in a person's heart and mind [dialogically] *precisely by bringing about understanding*" (*Remythologizing Theology*, 76, 283, 426, 373).

144. I am aware that "the Synod of Dort denies that regeneration comes about 'by moral suasion' (*morale suasionem*), which it defines as a mode of operating that, 'after God has done his work, it remains in man's power whether or not to be reborn or converted'" (Hoglund, *Called by Triune Grace*, 186). Thus, "only God persuades, but he does so through discourse" (Hoglund, *Called by Triune Grace*, 187). For Calvin on the inner testimony of the Holy Spirit, see Calvin, *Institutes*, 1.7.4.

Word that is spoken into our hearts (Luke 24:45; John 6:44-45; 10:3, 27; Acts 16:14; 2 Cor 3:14-16; 4:6; Eph 1:17-18; cf. Jer 31:33).[145]

Third, by drawing humanity into his intratrinitarian life, making us partakers of his divine nature, he breaks open our enclosed selves and relocates[146] us in the risen and ascended Christ and subjectively renews our understanding by giving us the *nous* or mind of Christ, enabling us to discern "what is the will of God, what is good and acceptable and perfect" (Rom 12:2).[147] This implies that the effectual call and regeneration are two sides of one coin.[148]

Fourth, because the Spirit relocates us in the risen and ascended Christ, our Christian self is constituted by Christ, by the Holy Spirit, living his moral life in and through us as "the principal moral agent" in our lives (John 15:5; Gal 2:20).[149]

Fifth, because our Christian life is constituted by Christ living his moral life in and through us, our union with Christ in his death and resurrection is the source of our renewal, through forgiveness and transformation (Rom 4:25; Gal 2:20).

---

145. Regarding the possibility of God dialogically engaging those who are spiritually dead, Hoglund writes, "Reformed theology means by passivity that humans are radically dependent for the first and decisive act of God, yet has sought to leave room for the continued use of human reason and consciousness. Spiritually dead does not mean the same thing as Lazarus's deadness." He adds, "A communicative approach to the effectual call agrees that there is dependence on God for the first moment of new spiritual life (and every subsequent moment), but this must be understood to mean that no living person is passive in every sense." He concludes, "God the Spirit takes up a person's activity and channels or directs it to appropriate ends by means of a convincing and transforming encounter with the divine word of witness. The Spirit bridges the hermeneutic gap in converting change. This is unmediated in the sense that no independent entity stands in between, but it takes place within the medium of speaking, hearing and coming to understand" (*Called by Triune Grace*, 164).

146. About the use of the verb *pisteuō* plus the preposition *eis* in the Gospel of John, Morris writes, "Faith, for John, is an activity which takes men right out of themselves and makes them one with Christ." He adds, "While believing and abiding are not connected in so many words (though cf. 12:46) they clearly mean much the same" (Morris, *Gospel of John*, 336).

147. When the Holy Spirit subjectively renews our understanding by giving us the mind of Christ, we need to remember what I wrote earlier that knowledge of God's will can arise and grow only in the context of the Christian congregation to whom the Holy Spirit also gives the mind of Christ. For hermeneutics and the mind of Christ, see also chapter 1.

148. Hoglund, *Called by Triune Grace*; Horton, *Covenant and Salvation*, 220-42; Vanhoozer, *Remythologizing Theology*, 370-77.

149. Macaskill, *Living in Union with Christ*, 2.

Sixth, because the Holy Spirit unites us to Christ as the source of our renewal, through forgiveness and transformation, there is no need to formulate an order of salvation in which the Holy Spirit applies the so-called benefits of Christ in a certain order, such as election, effectual calling, regeneration, faith, justification, sanctification, perseverance, and glorification.

Instead, this order can be reformulated along the lines of "God's eternal love for us in Christ," the "gift of Christ for those who believe the good news of Christ," the "transformation of our lives through the effect of Christ in our lives," and the "completion of this at the second coming, when we will be conformed to Christ."[150] This order of salvation does justice to the organic unity of salvation: our complete salvation is communicated at once through union with Christ, who is clothed with his benefits.

Seventh, putting on Christ and clothing ourselves with him through faith involves seeking our salvation outside of ourselves and entrusting ourselves completely to Christ, so that we are drawn into the life of God in Christ and become partakers of the divine nature in him through the Holy Spirit.

Eighth, the Holy Spirit enables those who have been drawn into the life of God through faith to persevere[151] and be conformed unto the image of Christ because God has elected them to eternal salvation in Christ, according to the good pleasure of his will (Eph 1:3–6; Rom 8:29–30).[152]

---

150. Burger, *Life in Christ*, 176.

151. Because of the risk of apostasy, Scripture calls us to be faithful and persevere (Matt 24:13; Rom 11:20; 1 Cor 10:11–12; Gal 5:4; Heb 3:7–19; 4:11; 6:4–8; 10:26–31; 2 Pet 2:18–22; Rev 2:10, 17, 25–26). About the warning passages in Hebrews, Van Bruggen writes, "The setting of the statements in Hebrews about being permanently lost upon the abandonment of faith is one of exhortation and warning. These statements are primarily intended to sharpen the readers' grasp of the seriousness of faith and the gospel *so that* they will continue to believe in Jesus" ("Volhouden op de weg," 261; see also Fanning, "Classical Reformed View," 218–19).

152. "From the ontic [i.e., referring to time and space] angle God's election precedes all history, or rather it comprises all history, just as God's eternity comprises our time. Seen from a noetic perspective, 'election' comes to mind only as the final word. That is, the doctrine of election is not the main element in our thinking but an important auxiliary that ensures that grace remains grace and that we always realize how we owe our salvation from beginning to end to the triune God" (Van den Brink and Van der Kooi, *Christian Dogmatics*, 702). For placing the drama of eternal election near the end of the drama of renewal, see also Calvin, *Institutes*, 3.21–24). Horton places the drama of predestination before the God who creates (Horton, *Christian Faith*, 309–23). He also operates with a covenant of grace that is governed by the doctrine of election (see chapter 3).

This implies that, also according to the good pleasure of his will, God passes by those to whom he does not give faith and leaves them in their sin, for which they are justly condemned (1 Pet 2:8).[153]

Ninth, the goal of being elected to put on Christ through faith and share in the divine nature in Christ by the Spirit is to participate faithfully and fittingly in the intratrinitarian act of mutual glorification that is being performed on the stage of the world and in the history of our lives by bearing witness to the eschatological resurrection life of God's new creation in a cruciform, resurrectional, and ascensional manner, as Christ performs in us what he has performed for us. When the stage of the world is completely dismantled, those who have been effectively drawn into the life of God through faith will continue to participate in God's intratrinitarian mutual glorification on the stage of a new creation.

Participation in the life of God and the drama of the return of Christ in glory[154]

The theodramatic biblical narrative generates, finally, the drama of the return of Christ in glory. Grammatically reconceptualizing the speech acts of this last phase of the drama in terms of theodramatic imagination and action entails the following.

First, because the goal of God's creation is the elevated life of creation and humanity participating in the incorruptibility and immortality of God in Christ through the Holy Spirit in the kingdom of God, the

---

153. Regarding the good pleasure of God and human responsibility with regard to reprobation, Douma writes, "That the reprobate are *rejected* takes account of their sin and guilt; that *they* are rejected (and not also others) rests entirely in God's good pleasure" (*Common Grace*, 326). Thus, while there is a parallelism between election and reprobation regarding the good pleasure of God, there is no parallelism with regard to the origin of faith and unbelief. While God is the source of faith, unbelief has its own source in the sinful human heart.

154. For systematic theological overviews of the drama of the return of Christ, see Balthasar, *Theo-Drama*, 5:19–521; Bavinck, *Reformed Dogmatics*, 4:587–729; Berkhof, *Systematic Theology*, 659–738; Calvin, *Institutes*, 3.25; Frame, *Systematic Theology*, 1075–97; Grenz, *Theology for the Community of God*, 571–659; Horton, *Christian Faith*, 906–90; Jones, *Grammar of Christian Faith*, 689–748; Kärkkäinen, *Hope and Community*, 1–230; Letham, *Systematic Theology*, 817–907; Macleod, *Faith to Live By*, 287–333; Van den Brink and Van der Kooi, *Christian Dogmatics*, 711–59; Van Genderen and Velema, *Reformed Dogmatics*, 819–86; see also Holmes, "Last Things," 609–20. For understanding how the biblical figures of eschatology and the book of Revelation rhythm and pattern understanding our social imaginary, time, identity, and culture, see Watkin, *Biblical Critical Theory*, 529–99.

drama of the return of Christ in glory is meant to bring about the consummation of this goal.

Second, the consummation of this goal includes the beatific vision. Because humanity has been drawn into the divine life in Christ, this beatific vision is a mediated vision of God (Matt 5:8; John 1:14, 18; 10:38; 14:7, 9–10; 17:22–24; 1 Cor 13:12; 2 Cor 3:18; 4:6; 1 Tim 1:17; 6:16; Heb 1:2–3; 1 John 3:2; Rev 22:4).[155] However, the fact that the vision is mediated does not mean that we will not see the essence of God, because when God reveals himself, he reveals his essence or nature.[156] This is especially the case when he reveals himself essentially in Jesus Christ.[157]

Third, because humanity needs to repent and believe in order to inherit this life or else face the fire of God's coming judgment and be excluded from this kingdom, the delay of the return of Christ in glory is a time in which God is patient because he does not wish that "any should perish, but that all should reach repentance" (2 Pet 3:9). The binding of Satan so that he should not deceive the nations (Rev 20:2–3) is also a manifestation of this same patience.[158]

Fourth, because Christ urged his church to wait and be watchful, to be prepared for his return, the time between the first and second coming

155. Bavinck, *Reformed Dogmatics*, 4:685; Boersma, *Seeing God*, 409–20. For Calvin's ambiguity on whether the beatific vision is mediated through Christ, see Billings, *Union with Christ*, 80–86.

156. Because for Horton, participation in the divine nature is not a participation in the essence or being of God, but only in his energies, the beatific vision would not be a vision of the essence of God in Christ, but only of his energies. See chapter 3.

157. Huijgen, *Divine Accommodation*, 183–84; Bintsarovskyi, *Hidden and Revealed*, 17. Because seeing the essence of God in Christ is a vision accommodated to our human finiteness, seeing the essence of God in Christ does not entail plumbing the depth of God's essence.

158. Christ's defeat of the devil on the cross is depicted in Revelation as the binding of the devil for a thousand years "so that he might not deceive the nations any longer, until the thousand years were ended" (Rev 20:3). After the thousand years are over, "he will be released for a little while" (Rev 20:3). About the thousand years, Morris writes, "We should take this symbolically. One thousand is the cube of ten, the number of completeness. We have seen it used over and over again in this book [i.e., Revelation] to denote completeness of some sort and John is surely saying here that Satan is bound for the complete time that God has determined" (*Revelation*, 229). About the binding of Satan, he writes, "Here he says specifically that Satan was restrained, not from all evil, but from *deceiving the nations* during *the thousand years*. From verse 8 we see that this means that Satan cannot gather the nations for the final cataclysm" (*Revelation*, 229; see also Van de Kamp, *Openbaring*, 437). About Satan being released for a little while, Morris writes, "The period of restraint will end, for Satan *must* (*dei*) be loosed, though only *for a short time*. This is God's way of bringing on the End and because it is God's plan Satan *must* be released" (*Revelation*, 229–30).

of Christ ought to be marked by a readiness to meet Christ (Matt 25:1–13) through prayer for his return (Rev 22:17). We must be faithful and wise servants who creatively and innovatively make something beautiful of what Christ has entrusted to our care (Matt 25:14–30; cf. vv. 31–46).

Fifth, because the time preceding the return of Christ in glory will be characterized by the appearance of many antichrists and an increase in lawlessness and because many will fall away from the faith during this time, the church is involved in an intense spiritual battle against the forces of evil (Eph 6:10–12). While Christ in principle defeated the devil with his death on the cross (D-Day), the church will not be able to celebrate V-Day until Christ returns in glory and God crushes the head of the serpent.[159]

Sixth, when Christ returns in glory, he will impartially judge the living and the dead according to what they have done. Therefore, members of God's new covenant community need to abide in Christ through faith so that Christ can generate his own life of the obedience of faith in them through the Holy Spirit. In this way, when Christ rewards us according to our works, he rewards his own work in us.[160]

Seventh, when Christ condemns those who did not participate in the drama of God's mission for his glory and refused to respond to him in filial faith, they will experience what appears to be "the endless dissolution of the personality by a condemning conscience,"[161] "the agonizing awareness of God's displeasure,"[162] "the loss, not merely of God, but of all good, and everything that made life seem worth living,"[163] and

---

159. For the analogy of D-Day and V-Day, see Cullmann, *Christ and Time*, 84.

160. For Paul, there is no theological tension or paradox between being justified by faith and judged according to works because for him the contrast is not faith and works, but faith and not having faith. Accordingly, Yinger writes, "This [lack of tension between justification by faith and being judged by works] is easily explainable when one realizes that the apostle Paul has inherited a way of speaking and thinking about divine judgment according to deeds which itself felt no such tension." He adds, "Those who had already been justified by grace through faith in Christ were expected (by God's grace and the Holy Spirit, of course) to live righteous lives as well. That is, their righteousness by faith would manifest itself in obedience, in works; though not necessarily in sinless perfection" (*Paul, Judaism and Judgment*, 290; cf. Van Bruggen, *Romeinen*, 51). While Yinger does not want to call this judgment of our works a second justification, others have (e.g., Calvin, *Institutes*, 3.17.8; see also Beale, *Union with the Resurrected Christ*, 365–71).

161. "Their worm does not die" (Mark 9:48).

162. "The fire is not quenched" (Mark 9:43, 48; Luke 16:24).

163. "Outer darkness" (Matt 8:12; 22:13; 25:30).

"self-condemnation and self-loathing,"[164] which they themselves have chosen (Matt 16:24-27; John 3:18-19).[165]

Eighth, when Christ acquits and vindicates those who did participate in the drama of God's mission for his glory in a listening and thankful filial spirit, characterized by the openness and responsiveness of faith, they will reach the goal for which they were created by being the theater of God's drama made up of actors who bear witness to the intratrinitarian mutual glorification, sharing in Christ's status of sonship and his communion of love with the Father through the Spirit. In them, God will become visible on earth, because they will be a people where heaven and earth meet.

---

164. "Weeping and gnashing of teeth" (Matt 8:12; 13:42, 50; 24:51).

165. Packer, *Knowing God*, 138–39. Packer writes, "These things are, no doubt, unimaginably dreadful, though those who have been convicted of sin know a little of their nature. But they are not arbitrary inflictions; they represent rather, a conscious growing into the state in which one has chosen to be. The unbeliever has chosen to be by himself, without God, defying God, having God against him, and he shall have his preference." He adds "Nobody stands under the wrath of God save those who have chosen to do so. The essence of God's action in wrath is to *give men what they choose*, in all its implications: nothing more, and equally nothing less" (*Knowing God*, 138–39). About those who have never heard of Christ, when Gentiles by nature or spontaneously do what the law requires (Rom 2:14–16), they do so because somehow the influence of the written law of God makes itself felt in their lives. Because every human being has an innate sense of God, no one is without excuse (Rom 1:18–20); every human being even has a sense that punishment is due to sin (Rom 1:32). About the need to speak more about hell in church and society, see Huijgen, *Waarom de wereld een hel nodig heeft*; see also Stolk, "Prof. Huijgen: Mens kiest zelf voor de hel."

6

Communicating the Gospel and Shaping our Christian Identity and Practice

SCRIPTURE IS THE SCRIPT, transcript, and prescript of God's theodrama, which we are to participate in, creatively and imaginatively—but also faithfully and fittingly—living out the drama in our new situations to the glory of God. Theology reconceptualizes the biblical narrative, providing us with dramatic direction.

Now, in this chapter, we see how this theodramatic framework of Scripture and theology outlined in the previous chapters equips us to communicate the gospel effectively—even in our secular culture—and shapes our Christian identity and practice so that we become fitting participants in the life of God.

THE SOCIAL IMAGINARY OF OUR SECULAR CULTURE

In the introduction, I outlined certain features of our secular culture and certain characteristics of the church within this culture.[1]

Our secular culture is a *disenchanted* culture in which people live as enclosed, individual, "buffered" selves, within an immanent frame of life, in a natural and material world that has lost contact with the transcendent beyond themselves. It is an *expressive* culture, in which people pursue authenticity by following their own desires and defining for

---

1. As noted in the introduction, the features of the social imaginary of our secular culture are not monolithic.

themselves what it means to be human. It is an *experiential* culture that seeks its sources of morality and truth within itself through experience. Story or narrative is central in the experience of the personal and the expression and explanation of these personal experiences. Our secular culture is a *distracted* culture because it is a technological culture. It is also a *pluralistic* culture, in which any ultimate belief—including belief in God—is one option among others and thus contestable and contested because of the change in the social imaginary and plausibility structures of society. But even so, it has not yet forgotten its experience of the transcendent. Accordingly, it experiences the cross-pressures of "openings to transcendence" and "the closure of immanence" in its search for meaning, significance, and fullness.

As for the church within our secular culture, many have a faith that could be described as "Moralistic Therapeutic Deism." They perceive the God of the Christian faith as a God who is not involved in their lives, but who wants them to be good so that they will feel good. Christians often live with a partial Jesus, who determines their past and their future but not their present. Because many in the Christian church have difficulty perceiving their world in biblical terms, they experience a disconnect between the world they live in and the world depicted in Scripture. Consequently, many are more formed by the social imaginary of the secular culture they live in than by the imaginary of Scripture. They do not use this biblical imaginary as their main plausibility structure to understand their life in this world.

THE IMAGINATION AND OUR PLAUSIBILITY STRUCTURE

If we want to communicate the gospel effectively in our secular culture, it is of the utmost importance that we appeal to the imagination. As we saw in chapter 1, the imagination is a cognitive faculty through which we perceive and make sense of our lives in this world. As such, it functions as a wholistic integrative organ of meaning that can perceive and explore possible ways of being in the world and be captivated by these possibilities.[2]

---

2. While Horton does believe that the Christian faith as an unfolding drama "captivates the heart and imagination, animating and motivating our action in the world" (Horton, *Christian Faith*, 19), I have not found in his writings any explicit treatment of the imagination as a holistic integrative organ of meaning that can perceive and explore

Moreover, as we saw in chapter 1, one of the main reasons it was natural for most premodern people to believe in God was the way they imagined their social surroundings, while many postmodern secular people today consider belief in God to be merely an epistemological option because of the way they imagine their social surroundings. A change in the social imaginary led to a change in the plausibility structures or what people consider believable.

Thus, appealing to the imagination is crucial for effectively communicating the gospel in our secular culture in a way that resonates with its social imaginary.[3] As Bailey puts it, appealing to the imagination does not secure an "epistemic *obligation*" to believe, but it does give "epistemic *permission*" to believe.[4]

It is specifically the theodramatic imagination to which we must appeal. As we saw in chapter 1, the theodramatic imagination allows us to see that God is carrying out a mission—performing a drama—of his intratrinitarian glorification on earth as it is heaven and that, in union with Christ by the Spirit and through faith, we participate in or perform this drama.

But the theodrama does not just appeal to the secular unbeliever's imagination, inviting him to recognize the reality of God's drama and to join in. It also appeals to the imagination of believers who, too often, are more formed by the secular imaginary of the culture they live in than the imaginary of Scripture, which may be one of the reasons many in the Christian church often live with a partial Jesus who determines their past, but not their present.

Secularity, Bailey says, drawing on Taylor, is "an imaginative crisis and an imaginative opportunity." To be able to take advantage of the opportunity and communicate the gospel effectively, it is vitally important to encourage Christians to use their theodramatic imagination, to learn

---

possible ways of being in the world.

3. In the previous chapter, I wrote that the soul "is essentially a receptive and affective reality that functions like a sounding board through which we experience the resonances or vibrations of ourselves and others, such as God, other human beings, and the world in which we live." For the importance of resonance as a point of contact between religious expressions and reality, see Thiessen, *Having a Critical Faith*. For the importance of resonance in communicating with our secular culture, see Rosa, *Resonance*; Root, *Congregation in a Secular Age*, 151–262.

4. Bailey, *Reimagining Apologetics*, 7.

the script of Scripture and to heed the theatrical direction that doctrine provides.[5]

REIMAGINING APOLOGETICS

Since it is of utmost importance for us to appeal to the imagination if we want to communicate the gospel effectively, it will be beneficial for us to reimagine apologetics. Bailey writes,

> By *reimagining apologetics*, I mean simply an approach that takes the imaginative context of belief seriously. Such an approach prepares the way for Christian faith by provoking desire, exploring possibility, and casting an inhabitable Christian vision. When successful, it enables outsiders to inhabit the Christian faith from the inside, feeling their way in before attempting to criticize it by foreign standards. Whether a person ultimately embraces the vision that is being portrayed, imaginative engagement cultivates empathy. It enables a glimpse, even if just for a moment, of the possibilities that Christian faith facilitates for our life in the world.[6]

Regarding the Christian faith, Bailey writes,

> By *Christian faith*, I mean a holistic pattern of life. This includes the embedded practices that make belief intelligible (prayer, worship, hospitality, peacemaking, creation care, etc.), as well as the felt sense of what belief means for everyday life. In other words, to be a Christian is not simply to believe a list of propositions but also to experience the world through the lens of a meaningful vision. This vision is a theodrama in which the world of meaning has been gifted to our perception, and ultimate reality is personal, revealed most fully in Jesus Christ. Intellectual assent remains an essential part of the mix. The personal and relational does not exclude its propositional character. But beliefs should not be extracted from the imaginative context in which they become believable. Indeed, it is impossible to separate my faith (what I believe and in whom I trust) from my desire (what I love and what I wish to be the case) and my imagination (what I feel is possible), as well as from

---

5. Bailey, *Reimagining Apologetics*, 54.
6. Bailey, *Reimagining Apologetics*, 4.

my concrete, lived reality (the way that my faith is tested and maintained in the course of everyday life).[7]

In what follows, I assume this integrated approach to apologetics.[8]

DIRECTIONS FOR EFFECTIVELY COMMUNICATING THE GOSPEL[9]

Emphasize that the gospel concerns the drama of God's mission for his glory and our participation in it

If we want to communicate the gospel effectively in our secular culture, we need to emphasize that the gospel concerns the drama of God's mission for his glory and our participation in or performance of this drama. It is important to emphasize this because our secular culture is a disenchanted culture, where people seek the meaning, significance, and fullness of their lives in a natural and material world that has lost contact with the transcendent beyond themselves. However, because they do not have an overarching narrative beyond the narrative of human flourishing within a natural and material world, they often suffer from a sense of malaise because the ordinary can feel so flat and empty.

---

7. Bailey, *Reimagining Apologetics*, 4–5. What Bailey says here corresponds to what Thiselton writes about belief: "Belief, then, is *action-oriented, situation-related*, and embedded in the *particularities and contingencies* of everyday living." Drawing on Wittgenstein, he writes, "Wittgenstein would call this relationship between belief, life, and action one of 'internal' grammar. *Action, contingency, particularity*, and the *public world of embodied life* constitute part of the very grammar of what it is to *believe*" (*Hermeneutics of Doctrine*, 21; see also Bailey, *Reimagining Apologetics*, 5).

8. About this integrated apologetic approach, Bailey writes, "I want to make it clear that in proposing an imaginative approach I am not arguing that all other apologetic models be replaced. Still less am I calling for apologetics to end. I am offering what I hope will be a supplement to other forms of apologetics...." (*Reimagining Apologetics*, 5). For C.S. Lewis on a similar approach, see Williams, *C. S. Lewis*. For an overview of traditional apologetics, see Boa and Bowman, *Faith Has Its Reasons*.

9. The order of the directions here goes from the drama of God, the drama of creation, the drama of Israel and the divine-human covenants, the drama of Christ, the drama of the Holy Spirit, and the drama of the return of Christ. The directions given concern the central elements in each drama and how they can resonate with our secular culture. As Burger says, "Theology is critical reflection on the practice of the church aimed at helping to communicate the gospel of Jesus Christ as clearly as possible and to enable the members of the church to live in Christ and in the Spirit in communion with God and with each other to the glory of God" (*Being in Christ*, 7).

At the same time, however, our secular culture is a pluralistic culture, where every ultimate belief, including belief in God, is just one option among many. As a result, it has not forgotten its experience of the transcendent. Consequently, it experiences the cross-pressures of "openings to transcendence" and "the closure of immanence" in its search for meaning, significance, and fullness.

It is possible for the gospel to resonate[10] with this search in a culture that can feel flat and empty, on the one hand, and experience openings to transcendence, on the other. The drama of God reminds us that the gospel concerns God enacting his eternal generative and communicative life of intratrinitarian mutual glorification on the stage of this world as the unfolding drama of his mission for his glory—on earth as in heaven! As such, the Father initiates divine acts as the playwright or author of the drama, the Son effects these acts as the protagonist of the drama, and the Spirit perfects them as the producer or director of the drama—and by the Spirit, in Christ, we can be caught up in this drama and participate in it.

Accentuate that God is a God of love who desires communion with the other

If we want to communicate the gospel effectively in our secular culture, we must accentuate that God is a God of love who desires communion with the other. Our secular culture is an individualistic culture in which people want to do their own thing and discover and define for themselves what it means to be human. But this individualism results in a loss of communion and in loneliness and the fragmentation of their lives.

The church has not escaped the influence of this individualistic culture. Many in the Christian church experience their faith in an individualized consumeristic manner because they embrace a sort of moralistic therapeutic deism, in which God is not viewed as being involved in their lives but only wants them to be good so that they will feel good.[11]

But it is possible for the gospel to resonate in this loneliness, loss of communion, and fragmentation, as well as in this individualized, consumerist, moralistic, therapeutic, deistic experience of the Christian

---

10. By speaking of the gospel resonating, I refer to how the *structure* of the contours of my theodramatic systematic theology facilitates the gospel resonating with how humanity experiences its secular culture. Determining the perlocutionary effect would require field research.

11. Smith and Denton, *Soul Searching*.

faith. The drama of God reminds us that God is a God of love who desires communion with the other and whose love binds all of his communicative attributes together in perfect performative harmony so that he is immanently and transcendently present and involved in the life of this world as the three persons of the Trinity enact their perfect life on earth as it is in heaven. The Holy Spirit draws us into this divine communion of love, enabling us ontologically to participate in this communion by uniting us to Christ so that we share in his sonship, in the Father's love, and in his ministry of love in this world as members of his body.

Assert that creation is enchanted and suffused with the presence of God and angels

If we want to communicate the gospel effectively in our secular culture, we need to assert that creation is enchanted and suffused with the presence of God and angels. Our secular culture is a culture in which people live as enclosed, individual, rational, buffered selves within an immanent frame of life. As such, they imagine a boundary between their inner self and their external world that enables them to block out divine and demonic influences that might impinge upon their lives. They consider the world and themselves to be innately self-sufficient. Furthermore, they no longer consider meaning to be embedded in the external world; instead it is found within themselves, something they create for themselves and from within themselves.

At the same time, however, many in our secular culture experience the immanent frame of life to be haunted with memories of the transcendent and it is possible for the gospel to resonate with these memories. The drama of creation reminds us that the Father voluntarily created a heavenly and an earthly stage for his theodrama and continues to be communicatively involved with both stages in Christ by the Spirit. Both stages have a "natural" (i.e., inherently compatible) porous relationship with God. Moreover, the Father, Son, and Holy Spirit created angels to live in their loving presence and participate in the drama not only in heaven but on earth.

Highlight that God's election of Israel and his divine-human covenants are meant to deal with the problem caused by humanity's pursuit of authenticity

If we want to communicate the gospel effectively in our secular culture, we need to highlight that God's election of Israel and his divine-human covenants are meant to deal with the problem caused by humanity's pursuit of authenticity. When people in our *expressive* secular culture view themselves as enclosed, buffered selves and see meaning as created from within themselves rather than embedded in the external world, it leads to a pursuit of authenticity in which people follow their own desires to be authentic, to be true to themselves instead of obedient to external norms, institutions, and values.[12]

But the gospel can resonate with this expressive, individualistic pursuit of authenticity by the buffered self. The drama of the fall into sin reminds us that the devil subverted and opposed the playwright's theo-dramatic intention by manipulating Adam and Eve to freely turn away from God, so that instead of participating in the drama of the intratrinitarian glorification in a thankful and listening spirit, they were driven by their own agenda instead of God's.

In doing so, they intentionally rejected living in a porous relationship with God in the openness and responsiveness of faith so that the splendor of God's perfect life would become visible on earth as it is in heaven. Instead, they became autonomous buffered selves, unresponsive to the playwright's dialogical interaction. They incurred God's wrath, lost the glory they once possessed, and became subject to death.

Because all of humanity participated in Adam's distrustful rebellion and its consequences, every human being by nature is self-enclosed and curved in on themselves, with a natural tendency to be estranged from God, driven by their own agenda and standards, independent of God, unthankful, unreceptive to his voice, and subject to death.

But the drama of the election of Israel reminds us that God chose Israel to deal with the problem of brokenness caused by humanity's pursuit of authenticity. Israel's history is not just typological and pedagogical. Israel was to bring the blessing of Abraham to the nations by being the theater of the drama of God's intratrinitarian mutual glorification.

---

12. Douma writes, "By the way, have you ever noticed how much authentic people look alike? And that they all seem to have roughly the same personal desires? How authentic is that really?" (Douma, *Zin in bidden*, 52).

Israel, as God's firstborn son, was to bear witness to all that is in Christ by exhibiting his listening and thankful filial spirit. In this way, they would also show the nations what authentic humanity looks like. Israel continues to have an abiding place in the theater of God's drama because God's new covenant is a covenant with Israel in its representative Messiah, by whom Israel does accomplish its mission and bring the blessing of Abraham to the nations.

The drama of the divine-human covenants reminds us that covenants are redemptive instruments with missional intent, through which God rescues the theodrama in the face of his people's uncertainty and fear and moves it forward to its eschatological fulfillment.

Point out that Jesus is the only authentic human being, who dealt with the problem caused by humanity's pursuit of authenticity as humanity's representative and substitute

If we want to communicate the gospel effectively in our secular culture, we need to point out that Jesus is the only authentic human being, who dealt with the problem caused by humanity's pursuit of authenticity as humanity's representative and substitute. It is important to point this out because the brokenness of our world and of the people in this world is the result of humanity imagining that they can pursue authenticity by following their own desires instead of being obedient to an external norm.

The gospel can resonate with this brokenness that results from this attempted pursuit of authenticity. Though God elected Israel to deal with the problem humanity created and to bring the blessing of Abraham to the nations, Israel failed in this calling and, in so doing, failed to manifest to the nations what authentic humanity looks like.

The drama of Christ, however, reminds us that Israel's failure was not the failure of God's theodrama. God sent his own Son to deal with the problem of sin and brokenness as the authentic human being who is Israel's and humanity's representative and substitute. He offered to the Father the sacrifice of his life and of his death in the openness and responsiveness of faith. And as a result, the world has its justification and sanctification in Christ. Our redemption has a single soteriological structure: it is located completely in him as the only authentic human being.[13]

13. For Horton's twofold soteriological structure and an extrinsic appropriationist

Accentuate that Jesus is the authentic human being who identified with victims of injustice and perpetrators of injustice

If we want to communicate the gospel effectively in our secular culture, we need to accentuate that Jesus is the authentic human being who identified with both the victims and the perpetrators of injustice.

Injustice—social, economic, political, religious, environmental, or of any other sort—is one of the manifestations of the brokenness that results from an expressive, individualistic pursuit of authenticity. But Jesus is the authentic human being who identified with victims of injustice.

The drama of Christ reminds us that when the Father sent Christ into the world with the loving intent to redeem Israel and creation from the powers of evil, he was not only opposed and ridiculed but was also eliminated. He became the victim of horrendous injustice when he, though innocent, was condemned to death as a blasphemer and crucified as a political threat. In this suffering, he identified with victims of injustice. But God reversed the miscarriage of justice, vindicating Jesus by raising him from the dead and vindicating humanity in him, so that not only the victims but even perpetrators of injustice have their vindication in Christ through faith.[14]

Affirm that the gift of the Holy Spirit is the future of God's glorified eschatological new creation breaking forth into the present

If we want to communicate the gospel effectively in our secular culture, we need to affirm that the gift of the Holy Spirit is the future of God's glorified eschatological new creation breaking forth into the present.

In our secular culture, people have no other goals than human flourishing exclusively within a natural and material world. But at the same time, our culture feels haunted in some ways by transcendence. The gospel can resonate with this quest for human flourishing.

The drama of Christ reminds us that because Christ was conceived and born through the Holy Spirit and anointed with the Holy Spirit, he is the bearer of the eschatological Spirit, through whom he will bring God's

---

understanding of salvation, see chapter 3.

14. It is, of course, good news for the victims of injustice that unconverted perpetrators will be judged and condemned.

drama of intratrinitarian mutual glorification to fulfillment and cause humanity and creation to flourish by filling them with his Spirit.

Furthermore, Christ baptized the church with his Spirit as the climax of his ministry and the fulfillment of Israel's hope of the promise of the new covenant where creation and humanity would flourish according to God's ideal. As such, the Holy Spirit is the promised eschatological gift of the new covenant who empowers God's new covenant community to be the theater of the drama of his mission for his glory, made up of actors who bear witness to all that is in Christ. The Holy Spirit creates this community, communicates direction to it, and increasingly transforms its members by drawing them into God's intratrinitarian life in Christ so that they partake in his divine nature and their humanity flourishes as God intended it to flourish.

Stress that when Christ returns, he will judge the living and the dead according to what they have done, as well as usher in the goal of creation, where God will be all in all in the glorification of humanity and creation

If we want to communicate the gospel effectively in our secular culture, we need to stress that when Christ returns, he will judge the living and the dead according to what they have done, as well as usher in the goal of creation, where God will be all in all in the glorification of humanity and creation.

Again, our secular culture focuses on human flourishing exclusively within a natural and materialistic world, while being haunted in some ways by transcendence. The gospel can resonate with this haunted quest for human flourishing in an exclusively immanent frame.

The drama of God reminds us that the three persons of the Trinity enact their perfect life on earth as it is in heaven, making this world a place where heaven and earth meet.

The drama of creation reminds us that God created the world and humanity to live in his loving presence, to be inherently compatible with him, capable of having a relationship with him in Christ through the Holy Spirit. It reminds us, too, that God created humanity with an innate sense of God that includes a sense of God's judgment.

The drama of the return of Christ reminds us that when Christ returns, he will judge the living and the dead according to what they have done. Moreover, he will usher in a new heaven and a new earth where humanity and creation will be glorified and participate in God's intratrinitarian mutual glorification in Christ through the Spirit for all eternity.

DIRECTIONS FOR PROPERLY SHAPING OUR CHRISTIAN IDENTITY[15]

The theodramatic framework of Scripture and theology equips us to communicate the gospel effectively, but it also shapes our Christian identity and practice—in spite of the influence of our secular culture—so that we become fitting participants in the life of God.

Emphasize that the essence of our humanity is participation in the life of God in a listening and thankful filial spirit of the openness and responsiveness of faith

If we want our Christian identity shaped so that we become fitting participants in God's life, we must emphasize that such participation in a listening and thankful filial spirit of the openness and responsiveness of faith is the essence, not just of our Christian life, but of our humanity.

Our secular culture, which influences us as Christians too, sees the essence of humanity as autonomy—being self-enclosed, unthankful, and unresponsive to God. But the buffer of the autonomous self has cracks in it that allow the gospel to resonate—and to appeal to the imagination—in spite of the spirit of rebellion.

The drama of creation reminds us that the Father, Son, and Holy Spirit created human beings to live in their loving presence and participate in the drama of their intratrinitarian activity of mutual glorification so that heaven and earth become a place for an ontological porous communion in the life of God in Christ by the Spirit.

It reminds us that we were created according to the model or standard of Christ, as sons of God who share in Christ's status of sonship, his communion of love with the Father through the Spirit, and his ministry of love in this world by the Spirit. As such, we are called to represent

---

15. The directions here move from directions concerning humanity in general (including the church) to directions concerning the church in particular, and they concern central elements in the drama that resonate with elements in our secular culture.

Christ by enacting our identity in the openness and responsiveness of faith as kings and priests who take part in and bear witness to Christ's kingly rule and priestly care for creation. This is the essence of being human,[16] and it is this understanding of our humanity that must capture our imagination and shape us to take up our role and share in the life of God.[17]

Accentuate that the essence of our humanity is hidden with Christ in God

If we want our Christian identity shaped so that we become fitting participants in God's life, we must accentuate that the essence of our humanity is hidden with Christ in God. Our secular culture, which influences us as Christians, imagines the essence of humanity to be located in an immanent frame that has lost contact with the transcendent. But even so, there are echoes of transcendence within that immanent frame that allow the gospel to resonate.

The drama of Christ reminds us that when Jesus rose from the dead as the first fruits of God's new creation, this resurrection life had a hidden and mysterious quality. When Jesus ascended into heaven, a cloud concealed him from his disciples' sight, symbolizing that his life as the ascended Christ is hidden in the glory of the Father.

Because the church, as God's new covenant community, rose from the dead with Christ and ascended with him into heaven to be seated in heavenly places (Eph 2:6), our life has a hidden quality. Our life too is hidden with Christ in God (Col 3:3). Moreover, the drama of the Holy Spirit reminds us that because the church, as God's new creation, is formed in union with Christ, the essence of the church is being a partaker of the divine nature (2 Pet 1:4).

The shaping of our Christian identity requires us to recognize that there is a hiddenness to our life as Christians, that there is more to who

---

16. For Christianity as the true humanism, see Howard and Packer, *Christianity: The True Humanism*; Zimmermann, *Incarnational Humanism*. For faith in a Person and not in a book, see Webber, *Ancient Future Faith*; see also Webber, *Divine Embrace*.

17. Contrast this understanding of our identity as humans and particularly as Christians with Horton's presentation of our Christian self-image first and foremost legal and ethical and our union with Christ and our Christian identity as only outward or extrinsic (see chapters 2 and 3).

we are than we can see, more than just what is evident or experienced in the immanent frame.

Assert that the generative source of our authentic humanity is union with Christ through faith

If we want our Christian identity shaped so that we become fitting participants in God's life, we must assert that the generative source of our authentic humanity is union with Christ through faith.

Instead of seeing the internal self and the external world as interdependent, the secular buffered self imagines that there is a boundary between the two and that it can control and manipulate the external world by its instrumental reason. Accordingly, humanity considers itself to be self-sufficient in its pursuit of human flourishing within a strictly immanent frame of life.

Even our ecclesiastical culture often imagines a partial Jesus, a Jesus who deals with the past and future—forgiving sins and securing heaven when we die—but who does not have much to do with life in the present.

But the drama of Christ reminds us that when Jesus offered the Father the sacrifice of his life and of his death by the Holy Spirit as Israel's and humanity's representative and substitute, Israel and all of humanity participated in this sacrifice and was redeemed in him. The drama of the Holy Spirit reminds us that when the Spirit draws Israel and humanity into God's intratrinitarian life, uniting them to Christ through faith, God makes them partakers of his divine nature. In doing so, he breaks open their enclosed selves, relocates their subject in the risen and ascended Christ, and renews their understanding by giving them the mind of Christ. As a result, the Christian self is constituted by Christ living his moral life in and through them *in the present* by the Spirit.

Highlight that the core of our humanity is our receptive and responsive soul

If we want our Christian identity shaped so that we become fitting participants in God's life, we must highlight that the core of our humanity is our receptive and responsive soul. When people imagine that the material world in which they exclusively seek meaning, significance, and fullness in human flourishing is the only world there is, a side effect can be that they imagine themselves to be exclusively material beings. Accordingly, they imagine that "all our acts can be reduced to brain functions that cease when we die."[18]

But there are cracks in the buffer of the materialistic self, and the gospel can resonate with this imagined disappearance of the soul. The drama of creation reminds us that the three persons of the Trinity created humanity in their image and likeness, as communicative agents who can bear witness to the communicative activity in the immanent Trinity. We are able to do so because we are created with a porous soul that is an ontological spiritual reality distinct from the physical body.[19] This soul is essentially a receptive and affective reality through which we experience the resonances of ourselves and others, such as God, other human beings, and the world in which we live. Our souls respond affectively, rationally, and volitionally to the resonances they receive.

Point out that our corporate identity as church is inherently missional

If we want our Christian identity shaped so that we become fitting participants in God's life, we must point out that our corporate identity as the church is inherently missional.

The immanent frame of our secular culture is characterized by the cross-pressures of the malaise of immanence and the memory of transcendence. As such, people experience both "openings to transcendence" and "the closure of immanence" in their search for meaning, significance, and fullness. But precisely because there are these cross-pressures, the gospel can resonate with the memory of transcendence.

The drama of the Spirit reminds us that the church is the preliminary or provisional visible form of God's eschatological new creation, created by the Holy Spirit and formed in union with Christ. As such, the church is God's new covenant community, a reconstituted Israel that bears the Spirit in order to bring the blessing of Abraham to the nations by being the theater of the drama of God's mission for his glory and by performing and bearing witness to what is in Christ.

---

18. Van den Brink and Van der Kooi, *Christian Dogmatics*, 270

19. In chapter 5, I spoke about humanity being an anthropological duality, not a dualism, because the latter implies a hierarchy between body and soul.

DIRECTIONS FOR PROPERLY SHAPING OUR CHRISTIAN PRACTICE[20]

Our Christian practice must also be shaped so that we may communicate the gospel effectively in our secular culture and live out our identity as participants in the life of God. This shaping of our practice is of paramount importance because there are many in our culture—and sometimes in the church—who consider themselves to be spiritual, but not religious,[21] because our secular culture is a technologically distracted culture that tends to foster a superficial experience of beliefs,[22] and because belief formation often occurs through belonging, behaving, and believing.[23]

---

20. The order of the directions goes from directions concerning practices of the church in general as a creature of the Word (*creatura verbi divini*) and the mystagogical nature of preaching, the sacraments, and the reading of Scripture to directions concerning practices of the church in particular. The directions given concern central elements in each drama and how they can resonate with our secular culture.

21. "The phrase 'spiritual but not religious' is the contemporary way of trying to explain some sort of connection to God, separate from, in tension with, or in opposition to religious institutions" (Bass, *Christianity after Religion*, 87).

22. Because the church lives in a technologically distracted secular culture, it does not escape this influence. However, because of the formative power of habit, the practices of the church structurally facilitate a deeper experience of belief. For evangelism that stresses taking one's place within the body of Christ, see Webber, *Ancient-Future Evangelism*.

23. Bass, *Christianity after Religion*, 102–214. Bass writes, "Long ago, before the last half millennium, Christians understood that faith was a matter of community first, practices second, and belief as a result of the first two" (*Christianity after Religion*, 203). This is not to say that the Spirit cannot mix up the order in his own way, should he please to do so. However, Bass unnecessarily plays belief-centered faith and experience-centered faith off against each other (*Christianity after Religion*, 109–11, 120–28, 210–14). The price she is willing to pay for this is her dream of an interfaith awakening where Protestants, Catholics, Jews, Muslims, Hindus, and Buddhists have the freedom to experience God on their own terms and in their own ways. She writes, "On the stage of awakening, I imagine Christians carrying high the cross, all the different varieties with their Bibles, prayer books, icons, and rosary beads; Jews holding the Torah; Muslims bearing the Qur'an; Buddhists with their Dharma wheel; Native peoples beating their drums; and so on, each group cheering its own flag.... But when the time comes [Isa 2:2–4], we will all be one in communion with God, in harmony with the cosmos, loving each other" (*Christianity after Religion*, 268).

Emphasize the practice of theodramatic worship

If we want our Christian practice shaped so that we become effective communicators of the gospel in our secular culture, we need to emphasize the practice of theodramatic worship. This is important because our secular culture is an expressive, experiential culture in which story or narrative is central in the experience of the personal and in the expression and explanation of these personal experiences because we have a narrative identity. The gospel can resonate with this expressive, experiential narrative identity.[24]

The drama of Christ reminds us that, after his ascension into heaven, Christ continues to participate in the drama of his Father's mission for his glory by his filial openness and responsiveness as the head and mediator of the new covenant. As such, he upholds and governs his church as king, intercedes for his people and blesses them as priest, and continues to confront them with the Father's good news of the coming kingdom of heaven as prophet, urging them to repent and believe.

The drama of the Holy Spirit reminds us that Christ carries out his threefold office of prophet, priest, and king primarily through his Word and Spirit in the drama of the proclamation of the Word and the drama of the administration of the sacraments. By these means, he rescripts his new creation by giving it his mindset for fitting participation in or performance of the drama of his mission for his glory that is being played out in the history of this world and in the history of the lives of the members of God's new creation.

Because we are seated with Christ in heaven, we participate in the drama of Christ as the priestly mediator of worship, glorifying the Father in heavenly worship—joining in the prayer and song of heaven—when we come to worship together on earth.

For our Christian practice to be properly shaped, then, we must appeal to the imagination so that we recognize what is happening and what we are doing in our worship. This practice can be cultivated by imagining that worship is a theodramatic activity in which we are being "touched by the sacred."[25] Ultimately, theodramatic worship is cultivated by the Holy

---

24. On the importance of narrative for apologetics, see McGrath, *Mere Apologetics*, 138–48. He writes, "Stories can give answers to what philosopher Karl Popper calls 'ultimate questions' . . . [such as] 'Who am I?' What is the point of life? What can I do to make a difference?'" (*Mere Apologetics*, 139).

25. Immink, *Touch of the Sacred*.

Spirit who forms Christ in us by joining us to Christ's worship in heaven as we abide in him through faith.[26]

Even those who are not Christians may experience the practice of theodramatic worship for themselves—with its appeal to their imagination—in the community of faith. As Burger reminds us, though, "Participation in these practices [i.e., the liturgy of the church] is useless when we are not born again of water and the Spirit. The Spirit has to blow on these practices to make them salutary. At the same time, the Word of God is the seed of regeneration, and the Holy Spirit works with and through the Word." He adds, "Hence, the best someone can do to receive formation as someone with a new perspective is conversion to participation in the Christian life with the prayer that the Spirit will give new life in those forms. Participation in Christian practice will lead to participation in Christ and to sharing in his perspective."[27]

Accentuate the practice of mystagogical preaching

If we want our Christian practice shaped so that we become effective communicators of the gospel in our secular culture, we need to accentuate the practice of mystagogical preaching. This sort of preaching is important in our secular culture. At one time, people imagined the ontological structure of creation to be enchanted and suffused with the presence of God and angels, having a "natural" (i.e., inherently compatible) porous and open relationship with God so that they were vulnerable to his presence and the presence of angels, either good or bad. In spite of

---

26. For the eschatological nature of worship, see Saliers, *Worship as Theology*. For enchanted worship, see Boersma, "Liturgical Medium"; de Ruijter, *Hemel op aarde*; Schmemann, *For the Life of the World*. For worship ordered by the pattern of Christ's life, death, resurrection, ascension, and return, see Webber, *Ancient-Future Time*. For an analysis of what our enactment of the liturgy says about the God we worship, see Wolterstorff, *God We Worship*. For an analysis of the relationship between human and divine agency in the enactment of the liturgy, see Wolterstorff, *Acting Liturgically*. For a liturgical analysis of "the social imaginary embedded in Christian worship," see Smith, *Desiring the Kingdom*, 155–213. For how liturgical practices form our imagination and sanctify our perception by "re-story-ing our being-in-the- world," see Smith, *Imagining the Kingdom*, 161; cf. 101–92; see also Saliers, "Liturgy and Ethics." Interacting with Smith, Vanhoozer helpfully writes, "Yet, we become disciples not simply by participating in Christian liturgical practices but by participating in—living into and acting out—Scripture's canonical practices and, yes, Christian doctrine (see 1 Tim 4:16)" (Vanhoozer, *Doers and Hearers*, 56).

27. Burger, "Foundation or Perspective?," 70.

its rejection of this understanding of the world, in spite of its emphasis on an immanent frame, in spite of its materialism, our culture is still haunted by these memories of transcendence and the gospel can resonate with them.

The drama of the Holy Spirit reminds us that we must seek our salvation outside of ourselves by entrusting ourselves completely to Christ and then, when we do, we are drawn into the life of God in Christ and become partakers of the divine nature in him by the Spirit. It reminds us also that God brings this about by effectually addressing and engaging us with his Word and Spirit, not only uniting us to Christ but renewing our lives in him. And it reminds us that Christ guides and draws us into the mystery of our participation in the divine nature primarily through the proclamation of the Word. In doing so, he relocates our subject in him and subjectively renews our understanding by giving us his mind so that he lives his life in and through us. He is the main actor in our lives.

Mystagogical preaching—preaching that reveals and draws us into the mystery of our participation in the divine nature in Christ by the Spirit[28]—resonates with the sense even secular people have of something more than the material, something that transcends the immanent frame.

This practice of mystagogical preaching entails preaching not only what Christ has done *for* us, but also what he does *in* us as we put him on through faith and clothe ourselves with him, so that it is no longer we who live, but Christ Jesus who lives in us.[29] This practice of faith is ultimately cultivated by the Holy Spirit who forms Christ in us by generating his own participation or dwelling in the life of God in us as we abide in him through faith.[30]

28. Thus, the expression "mystagogical preaching" is not limited to preaching on the sacraments to initiate people into the life of the church after their baptism. For the latter, see Satterlee, *Ambrose of Milan's Method*.

29. For the drama of the proclamation of the Word, see Childers, *Performing the Word*; Horton, *Better Way*, 33–92; see also Webber, *Ancient-Future Worship*. For a biblical-theological approach to preaching God's drama, see Lee, *Preaching God's Drama*. For sacramental preaching, see Boersma, *Sacramental Preaching*. For preaching as listening to the voice of God, see De Ruijter, *Horen naar de stem*. For a comprehensive model for transformational preaching, see Anderson, *Integrative Preaching*. For a spiritual homiletic and spiritual formation, see Douma, "Preken met het oog." For the meaning of meditation for the homiletic process, see Douma, *Veni Creator Spiritus*. For determining the purpose or fallen condition focus of a text, see Chapell, *Christ-Centered Preaching*, 48–52. For religious involvement in hearing sermons, see Pleizier, *Religious Involvement*. For preaching Christ to the heart, see Keller, *Preaching*, 157–87.

30. What is said here about preaching is not meant to downplay the importance of the rest of the liturgy. There is danger in a one-sided emphasis on the sermon in a

Stress the practice of a mystagogical understanding of the sacraments

If we want our Christian practice shaped so that we become effective communicators of the gospel in our secular culture, we need to stress the practice of a mystagogical understanding of the sacraments. In this way, too, the gospel can resonate with the memories of transcendence that haunt our secular society.

The drama of the Holy Spirit reminds us that Christ, by the Spirit, uses not only the proclamation of the Word but also the administration of the sacraments to cultivate and nurture us to become partakers of the divine nature. Through the sacraments, he rescripts his new creation, giving it his mindset for fitting participation in or performance of the drama of God's mission for his glory.

Christ, by the Spirit, uses the drama of baptism to visibly incorporate believers and their children into God's new covenant community by symbolically performing their participation in the drama of the history of Christ's death and resurrection. By immersing them in or sprinkling them with water, he emphasizes that they have died to their old identity in Adam and have arisen to their new identity in Christ. This dramatic rescripting of their lives highlights that their new identity now lies ex-centrally, outside of themselves and in Christ as the new center of their humanity.

The Holy Spirit uses the drama of the Lord's Supper to cultivate and nurture the members of God's new covenant community by visibly and tangibly proclaiming that they are forgiven and sanctified as they symbolically perform their participation in the drama of Christ's death and resurrection by eating bread and drinking wine together. In partaking of the Lord's Supper in faith, believers proclaim their intent to seek their identity outside of themselves in Christ, who is really present at the

---

worship service. De Bruijne writes, "In the church service, it [is] no longer the sermon that [should] receive all the emphasis. Every church service . . . is at its core praise and should, therefore, as a rule, include the celebration of the Lord's Supper. . . .You do not come to church first of all to get something but to bring something." He adds, "You are only truly human when you put God first. And the human activities in which you do and practice that par excellence are prayer and praise. In these, you renounce yourself and give yourself with Christ as an offering to God." He concludes, "God-centered praise detaches you from the idols of spiritual need-fulfillment and spiritual market mechanisms. You learn to shed your consumer attitude in church because you didn't come here first of all to get something. You came to bring yourself" ("Eenzijdige nadruk").

celebration by the Spirit doing in them what he has done for them, allowing his death and resurrection to rescript their lives on their journey to the Sabbath rest of the kingdom of God.[31]

The physicality of the Lord's Supper is important in relation to our secular culture. The sacraments do not direct us away from immanence to transcendence or away from the material to the spiritual. It is not one or the other; it is both. Burger writes, "Humans are material beings and physicality is essential to who we are. The sacrament is necessary in connection with that physicality." Rejecting the notion that God is not sacramentally present in impersonal things so that we should turn our eyes away from the elements of bread and wine, he suggests that we should actually turn our eyes towards them in faith. Thus, he writes, "The physical and material is good and necessary. The challenge is to see Christ not above or behind the material signs, but rather in bread and wine."[32]

Highlight the practice of the mystagogical reading of Scripture

If we want our Christian practice shaped so that we become effective communicators of the gospel in our secular culture, we need to highlight the practice of the mystagogical reading of Scripture. Again, this is important because our secular culture is cross-pressured between "openings to transcendence" and the "closure of immanence."

The drama of the Holy Spirit reminds us that Scripture is located in the drama of redemption. It is God's communicative action, in and through which he is present in Christ, by the Spirit, drawing us into an ever-deeper communion with himself in Christ as he increasingly forms

---

31. When Jesus commands his followers to celebrate the Lord's Supper in remembrance of him, he uses the term *anamnesis*. "Much more than just the idea of recalling, *anamnesis* reflects the Hebrew word *zkr*, which is usually translated 'remember' and specifically implies that we live in the present and behave in the present in light of our memory.... This act of remembrance is one in which the past shapes, informs, and penetrates the present... We live now ... as a people for whom everything has altered" (Smith, *Holy Meal*, 38–39; see also Moore-Keish, "Sacraments," 537–38). Vander Zee writes, "It [*anamnesis*] is not just a call to historical memory, but a call to present participation in the saving events of history" (Vander Zee, *Christ, Baptism, and the Lord's Supper*, 210). Billings rightfully observes that this remembrance is part of "broader framework—one in which [we] are hungry for Christ and need to be nourished by Christ via the Spirit" (Billings, *Remembrance, Communion, and Hope*, 17). Regarding the mystery of the hidden but real presence of Christ at the celebration of the Lord's Supper, see Calvin, *Institutes*, 4.17.3-33.

32. Burger, "Avondmaal is juist nodig."

Christ in us. Scripture is the reliable script, transcript, and prescript by which God dialogically engages us with his speech acts and prompts us to participate faithfully and fittingly as actors in the drama of his intratrinitarian activity of mutual glorification who enact his life on earth as it is in heaven. Accordingly, God's communicative action in and through Scripture does not end with Scripture, but in us.[33]

The practice of mystagogical reading of Scripture can be cultivated through the use of *lectio divina*[34] and the spiritual reading of Scripture.[35] But ultimately, it is cultivated by the Holy Spirit who forms Christ in us by generating Christ's own reading of the Scriptures in our lives as we abide in him through faith.

Stress the practice of praying to be filled with the Holy Spirit

If we want our Christian practice shaped so that we become effective communicators of the gospel in our secular culture, we need to stress the practice of praying to be filled with the Holy Spirit. This is important to emphasize in our secular culture, which sees itself as self-enclosed, buffered, impermeable to transcendent influence, and yet haunted by transcendence.

The drama of the Holy Spirit reminds us that, as the giver of life, the Spirit is the promised eschatological gift of the new covenant who empowers God's new covenant community to be a theater of the drama of his mission for his glory. He draws us into the life of God, enabling us to participate in this life and partake of the divine nature, living in God's loving presence and sharing in the Son's status of sonship, his communion of love with the Father, and his ministry of love in this world.

---

33. In an interview, Eugene Peterson says, "When we approach the biblical text, instead of asking, 'What does it mean?'—which is what people usually do—we should ask, 'What is it doing? How do I enter into this? How does it enter into me?'" He adds, "You know, it's surprising: We have Jesus as the centerpiece of what we're doing, but he almost never talked in terms of explaining. He was always using enigmatic stories and difficult metaphors. He was always pulling people into some kind of participation. It's essential for us to develop an imagination that is participatory" (Overstreet, "Cultivating the Imagination").

34. See Bianchi, *Praying the Word*; Boersma, *Pierced by Love*; Douma and Grün et al., *Samen luisteren*; Douma and Kroon et al., *Kijken en luisteren*; Foster, *Reading with God*; Stinissen, *Nourished by the Word*.

35. See Boersma, *Scripture as Real Presence*; Foster and Helmers, *Life with God*; Huijgen, *Lezen and Laten Lezen*; Peterson, *Eat This Book*.

As the communicator of direction, the Spirit dialogically engages and prompts us to participate faithfully and fittingly in the theodrama that is being played out in the history of this world and the history of our lives. As the creator of the new community, the Spirit sustains the church in Christ. As the renewer of our humanity, the Spirit unites us to Christ through faith and renews our lives in him.

Our need for the Spirit corresponds with our secular culture's openness to transcendence and its need for the Spirit to permeate its buffers, designed rebelliously to maintain autonomy but with cracks that leave people longing for something more than materialism and the immanent frame. Believers pray for the filling of the Spirit, but even those who are not Christians may experience this practice of praying to be filled with the Spirit themselves in the community of faith in answer to their longings for transcendence.

This practice can be cultivated through a spirituality of receptivity.[36] But it is ultimately cultivated as the Spirit forms Christ in us by generating Jesus' own being filled with the Spirit in us as we abide in him through faith.

Focus on the practice of putting on Christ through faith and clothing ourselves with him

If we want our Christian practice shaped so that we become effective communicators of the gospel in our secular culture, we need to focus on the practice of putting on Christ through faith and clothing ourselves with him. This practice is important because our secular culture is an expressive, experiential culture. We have a narrative identity, and story or narrative is central in the experience of the personal and the expression and explanation of these personal experiences. But it is important also because many Christians live with a partial Jesus, a Jesus who determines the past and future—sins forgiven, heaven when we die—but not their life in the present.

The drama of the creation of humanity reminds us that being created in the image of God entailed humanity's participation in the divine nature by sharing in Christ's status of sonship and his communion of love with the Father. As we saw, this issued forth in humanity representing

---

36. Troost, *Spiritualiteit*.

God by performing their ontological identity through a listening and thankful filial spirit in the openness and responsiveness of faith.

The drama of the election of Israel and the divine-human covenants reminds us that God chose Israel to be the theater of the drama of his mission for his glory. They were to perform and bear witness to the intratrinitarian communicative activity of mutual glorification by that filial spirit.

The drama of the Spirit reminds us that the church is God's new covenant community that bears the Spirit for the sake of bringing the blessing of Abraham to the nations again, by that same spirit of sonship.

This filial spirit, characterized by the openness and responsiveness of faith, involves seeking our salvation outside of ourselves and entrusting ourselves completely to Christ so that we are drawn into the life of God in him and partake in the divine nature in him by the Spirit. When we put Christ on by faith and clothe ourselves with him, we receive his mind as Christ does in us what he has done for us, so that we now can bear witness to what is in him.

The practice of being the church is the practice of putting on Christ. It appeals to the imagination of our secular culture because it involves entering into the story and experience of Christ. And it cultivates living with a whole Jesus—a Jesus who has not just dealt with the past or prepared a future for us but who lives in us and us in him in the present.

This practice of faith can be cultivated through a spirituality of receptivity[37] and by accentuating Christian virtues and character formation in the life of Christian discipleship.[38] But ultimately this practice of faith is cultivated by the Spirit who forms Christ in us by generating Jesus' own faith and character in us as we abide in him (Matt 27:43; John 5:30; Heb 2:13).[39]

Affirm the practice of the fear of the Lord

If we want our Christian practice shaped so that we become effective communicators of the gospel in our secular culture, we need to affirm the practice of the fear of the Lord. People in our secular culture have

---

37. Troost, *Spiritualiteit*; see also Peterson, *Practice Resurrection*.

38. De Bruijne, "Christelijk leven"; Vos, "Christelijke Deugden in de Gemeente"; Wright, *After You Believe*.

39. Allen, *Justification and the Gospel*, 83–89; Macaskill, *Union with Christ*, 187.

not forgotten that at one time people imagined the ontological structure of creation to be enchanted and suffused with the presence of God and angels, having a "natural" (i.e., inherently compatible) porous or open relationship with God so that they were vulnerable to his presence and the presence of angels, either good or bad. Because they have not forgotten, our secular culture is still haunted by these memories of transcendence, and the gospel can resonate with them.

The drama of God reminds us that he is a God of love who desires communion with the other. This God is the Lord who performs the splendor of his perfect life, acting communicatively in a compassionate, gracious, faithful, and loving manner but also in a just and holy manner by punishing the guilty.

The drama of creation reminds us that the Father voluntarily created the earthly stage of his theodrama in Christ by the Spirit so that it has a "natural" (inherently compatible) porous relationship with him. It is designed for life in his loving presence and for participation in his life, for in him all people live and move and have their being (Acts 17:28).

The drama of the Holy Spirit reminds us that the Spirit gives life to creation and humanity, communicates direction to humanity, creates a new community, and renews humanity.

The fear of the Lord fits in this context as a reverent and attentive filial spirit evoked by living in the glorious and sacred presence of God. It can be synonymous with the obedience of faith.[40] The practice of the fear of the Lord can be cultivated by attentively practicing the presence of God,[41] as well as by the practice of Sabbath keeping.[42] Ultimately, it is

---

40. Peterson writes, "The fact that fear-of-the-Lord cannot be precisely defined is one of its glories—we are dealing with something that we cannot pin down, we inhabit mystery, we can't be cocksure about anything, we cultivate an attentive and reverent expectation before every person, event, rock, and tree. Presumption recedes, attentiveness increases, expectancy heightens." He adds, "Fear-of-the-Lord . . . turns everything we do into a life of 'breathing God'" (*Christ Plays in Ten Thousand Places*, 44). De Bruijne writes, "In my view, this [i.e., the fear of the Lord] is the fundamental affect of faith in Christian spirituality. Whoever knows the fear of the Lord responds to the real presence of God himself" ("Affect and Effect," 69; see also "Besef van God," 44–47). Waltke writes, "What notes are to music and the alphabet is to reading, the fear of *I AM* is to attaining wisdom" (*Old Testament Theology*, 160; see also "Fear of the Lord," 17–33). See also Reeves, *Rejoice and Tremble*.

41. Booram and Booram, *When Faith Becomes Sight*; Lawrence, *Practice of the Presence*; Troost, *Mindful met Jezus*; *Gewoon God*; *Energie van de Geest*; Warren, *Liturgy of the Ordinary*; Wilson, *God in All Things*.

42. Peterson, *Christ Plays in Ten Thousand Places*, 109–18; see also Bass, "Christian Formation."

cultivated by the Spirit who forms Christ in us by generating in our lives Jesus' own fear of the Lord (Isa 11:2).

Emphasize the practice of solitude and the conversational life of prayer

If we want our Christian practice shaped so that we become effective communicators of the gospel in our secular culture, we need to emphasize the practice of solitude and a conversational life of prayer. Our secular culture is both expressive and individualistic, but because of the cracks in the buffer of these self-enclosed people, the gospel can resonate with this expressive individualism.

The drama of Christ reminds us that Jesus increasingly became strong in the Spirit through the practice of prayer and solitude. Jesus often spent time alone with his Father in private prayer. He also publicly prayed with and for his disciples, as well as for his enemies. When Jesus ascended into heaven, he continued—and continues—his life of prayer, interceding for his people. This life of prayer is the expression of his listening and thankful filial spirit, characterized by the openness and responsiveness of faith.

The church, too, is shaped and strengthened by the Spirit through these practices. This life of prayer and solitude can be described as the practice of a conversational relationship with God and can be cultivated through a life of contemplative prayer,[43] including the meditative practice of mindfulness. This practice is ultimately cultivated by the Spirit who forms Christ in us by generating in our lives Jesus' own conversational life of prayer.[44]

Conversational prayer and solitude—being away from other people but close to God—resonates with the echoes of transcendence experienced within the cross-pressures of the immanent frame of our secular culture that is searching for meaning, significance, and fullness. But it also facilitates speaking into and connecting with a church culture that

---

43. Johnson, *When the Soul Listens*; Willard, *Hearing God*; contra Horton's discouragement of the practice of spiritual formation through spiritual disciplines of contemplative spirituality.

44. Root writes, "In a theological sense, no person prays directly to God; no human words and actions can penetrate the very relationship that is God. But in the mystery of the hypostatic union, the mystery where Jesus is *the* person who shares completely in the divine and human, this Jesus prays our prayers" (Root, *Relational Pastor*, 176).

perceives God as uninvolved in people's lives or as a God who wants people to be good so that they will feel good.

Stress the practice of being a community of love

If we want our Christian practice shaped so that we become effective communicators of the gospel in our secular culture, we need to stress the practice of being a community of love, a community where life flourishes as each lives for the other. Our secular culture's only goal is the human flourishing of life within an immanent frame and it recognizes that the pursuit of human flourishing does include living for the other. But because this same culture is also an expressive individualistic culture, in which people follow their own desires to be authentic and true to themselves instead of being obedient to external norms, institutions, and values, it has no adequate moral sources to determine what authentically living for the other looks like.

The drama of the Holy Spirit reminds us that the church is the preliminary or provisional visible form of God's eschatological new creation, created by the Holy Spirit and formed in union with Christ, in which life begins to flourish the way God meant it to. The church is God's new covenant community, the reconstituted Israel that bears the Spirit in order to bring the blessing of Abraham to the nations by being the theater of the drama of his mission for his glory, performing and bearing witness to what is in Christ by living for the other as God lives for the other in Christ. As such, the church is the eyes, ears, mouth, hands, and feet of Christ in the world.

Moreover, the drama of the Spirit reminds us that when Gentiles come to faith in Christ and are grafted into the reconstituted Israel, the Spirit uses the beauty of the human flourishing of God's eschatological creation to draw non-Christian ethnic Jews to jealousy and bring them to faith in Christ as well.

Furthermore, the drama of the Spirit reminds us that the church is a pilgrim community on its way to the Sabbath rest of the kingdom of God and that, as this community, the church creatively and imaginatively extends the meaning of the script, transcript, and prescript of God's drama of his mission for his glory in ways that develop the theodramatic action in new situations and reincorporate the new situation into the theodrama.

This practice of love—living for the other—is not yet perfect. "This side of the eschaton, even as the church's sanctification takes place, it remains, like the wider world, besieged and entangled by vices and weakness."[45] But nevertheless, as this practice is cultivated in the church, it can resonate with a culture that wants human flourishing but has no moral source to guide it.

Living for the other involves being a community of hospitality,[46] truth,[47] political engagement,[48] communion,[49] forgiveness,[50] goodness,[51] and generosity.[52] Love makes us a community of cultural agents.[53] It can be cultivated also by the practice of Sabbath keeping.[54] Ultimately, love is cultivated by the Spirit who forms Christ in us, generating his own life of love—living for the other—as we abide in him by faith.

---

45. Boulton, *Life in God*, 220.

46. Butterfield, *Gospel Comes with a House Key*; Pohl, *Making Room*.

47. Noble, *Disruptive Witness*, points out that, in being a community of truth, the church bears a disruptive witness. Van de Beek uses stronger language when he speaks about prophetically unmasking the lies of our secular culture (Van de Beek, *Ontmaskering*).

48. De Bruijne, "Niet van deze wereld"; de Jong, *Church Is the Means*; O'Donovan, *Desire of the Nations*. Being a community of political engagement includes prophetically addressing current political issues, unmasking the so-called political gospels as counterfeit gospels, encouraging authorities to honor God, seeking the wellbeing of the community with words and deeds (De Bruijne, "Niet van deze wereld," 383–87). De Bruijne writes that addressing current political issues is not done to "reform existing society into a kingdom form [but for the sake of] a missionary appeal" ("Niet van deze wereld," 384). With regard to what political engagement concretely looks like, he writes, "The church already speaks publicly in its assembly where God is 'publicly called upon' (Lord's Day 38 HC). Pastors can use encounters and write letters. Christians can frequent opinion pages or websites and engage missionally in public debate. Theologians can practice public theology. Missionaries can protest against injustice. Local church councils can raise issues with their municipal councils" ("Niet van deze wereld," 385–86; see also de Jong, *Church Is the Means*, 19).

49. Bonhoeffer, *Life Together*; Dawn, *Truly the Community*; Pohl, *Living into Community*; Smith and Pattison, *Slow Church*.

50. Jones, *Embodying Forgiveness*; McKnight, *Community Called Atonement*; Volf, *Exclusion and Embrace*.

51. McKnight and Barringer, *Church Called Tov*.

52. Berlin, *Generous Church*; Millard, *Gratitude Path*.

53. Vanhoozer, "What Is Everyday Theology?," 15–60; *conta* Horton's compartmentalization of the Christian life which drives a wedge between activities in the common realm and activities in the sacred realm (see chapters 2 and 3).

54. Brueggemann, *Sabbath as Resistance*; Dawn, *Keeping Sabbath Wholly*; *Sense of the Call*; Swoboda, *Subversive Sabbath*; Wirzba, *Living the Sabbath*.

Accentuate the practice of the kingly rule and priestly care of creation

If we want our Christian practice shaped so that we become effective communicators of the gospel in our secular culture, we need to accentuate the practice of the kingly and priestly care of creation. Through this creation care the gospel can resonate with our secular culture, whose goal of human flourishing within an immanent frame of life includes a heightened concern for the preservation of this planet.

The drama of creation reminds us that all things were created in Christ and that all things hold together in him. Because creation is the porous dwelling place of God in Christ through the Spirit, created reality can ontologically participate in God's intratrinitarian mutual glorification and be a theater of God's glory.

Moreover, humanity's creation according to the image of Christ issues forth in its calling to represent this ontological status as kings and priests who participate in and bear witness to Christ's kingly rule and priestly care for creation as they cultivate creation and consecrate it to God. But the drama of creation reminds us, too, that humanity refused to do this, being driven by their own agenda and standards, which led to the breakdown and degradation of creation.

The drama of Christ reminds us that Jesus dealt with the problem of sin, death, and the devil by the sacrifice of his life and the sacrifice of his death and thereby redeemed creation from the powers of evil. When he rose from the dead with his glorified resurrection body, he did so as the first fruits of God's hidden and incorruptible eschatological new creation in fulfillment of the promise of a new covenant. Accordingly, there is hope for creation.

The drama of the Holy Spirit reminds us that when the Spirit renews humanity by giving them the mind of Christ, they can once more take part in and bear witness to Christ's kingly rule and priestly care for creation as they were meant to.

The drama of the return of Christ in glory reminds us that creation and humanity will experience the goal for which they were created by participating in the incorruptibility and immortality of God in Christ through the Spirit in the Sabbath rest of the kingdom of God.

The practice of creation care as kings and priests in Christ can be cultivated by a renewed sense of gratitude for the blessing and gift of the world we are allowed to live in, as well as a renewed sense of the responsibility we have within God's creation.[55] It can be cultivated, too, by reappropriating the drama of creation as the theater in which Father, Son, and Spirit glorify each other and in which we participate, in union with Christ, as faithful, patient, and hopeful stewards of creation.[56] Ultimately, this practice is cultivated by the Holy Spirit who forms Christ in us by generating his own kingly rule and priestly care for creation in us as we abide in him by faith.

Give prominence to the practice of being a watchful and waiting community

If we want our Christian practice shaped so that we become effective communicators of the gospel in our secular culture, we need to give prominence to the practice of being a watchful and waiting community. Our secular culture experiences echoes of transcendence within the cross-pressures of its immanent frame, and the gospel hope can resonate with these echoes.

The drama of creation reminds us that God's goal in creation is the elevated life of creation and humanity participating in Christ in his incorruptibility and immortality by the Spirit in the kingdom of God.

The drama of Christ reminds us that Christ called Israel to repent and believe the good news of the nearness of the kingdom of heaven or else face the fire of God's coming judgment and be excluded from this kingdom. But it also reminds us that after Christ ascended into heaven, he continued to confront Israel and the nations with this good news to make ready a people to meet him when he returns.

The drama of the Spirit reminds us that as the preliminary visible form of God's eschatological new creation formed around Christ by the Spirit, the church is a pilgrim community on its way to the Sabbath rest of the kingdom of God.

The drama of the return of Christ in glory reminds us that God is going to consummate his creational goal of a glorified humanity and a glorified creation that participate in the drama of his mission for his

---

55. Wirzba, *From Nature to Creation*; Francis, "Laudate Deum"; *Laudato Si'*; *Our Mother Earth*; see also Burger, *Hoop voor een zuchtende schepping*; "Wat ik leerde van de paus"; Zizioulas, "Proprietors or Priests of Creation"; Zizioulas, "Priest of Creation."

56. Cf. Wilson, *God's Good World*. For ecological repentance, see Paas, *Vrede op aarde*, 314-24. About the danger of environmental moralism, see de Bruijne, "Er zit milieumoralism."

glory and that bear witness to the mutual glorification of the Father, Son, and Spirit.

To become this watchful and waiting community, the church can emphasize that the nearness of the kingdom is not ultimately a matter of whether it is present here or not but whether we are prepared to enter the kingdom when Christ returns.[57] Watchfulness can be cultivated by regular prayer for the coming of the kingdom. But ultimately being a watchful and waiting community is cultivated by the Spirit who generated in us Christ's own prayer for the coming of the kingdom.

---

57. Van Bruggen, "Hoe is het hemelrijk nabij?"

Conclusion

WHAT SHOULD THE STRUCTURE of our systematic theology look like?

The question may, at first, seem uninteresting. What sometimes is called "theological encyclopedia"—the discussion of theological methodology and structure—is not a hot topic. Why spend time on it when we could plunge into theology itself? Surely there are much more interesting things to discuss in the realm of theology than how to do theology.

But the framework within which we consider theological topics—the way we think these topics relate to each other—does affect the conclusions we come to with regard to those topics themselves. The structure of our systematic theology affects the way we theologize.

Even more importantly, it affects our lives and the lives of those around us—in the church and, just as importantly, outside the church. It affects how we communicate the gospel in our secular culture. And it affects our own understanding of and growth in our Christian identity and practice.

In the preceding chapters, I have outlined a theological framework that has participation in the life of God in Christ through the Spirit as its integrative center. In doing so, I entered into conversation with covenant or federal theology, particularly as it has been presented by Michael Horton, in which the integrative center is the concept of the covenant.

I have argued that God's fundamental relationship with humanity does not entail a covenant ontology—a fundamentally legal and ethical relationship to God, as we find in Horton's presentation—but rather an ontology of participating in God's loving presence in Christ through the Holy Spirit. For this relationship we were created and this participation is therefore natural to us. And to this relationship we are restored in Christ and by the Spirit.

Accordingly, a theodramatic framework that incorporates a reframed understanding of divine-human covenants and that has participation in the life of God in Christ by the Spirit as its integrative center is better able to give direction for clearly communicating the gospel in our secular culture and for properly shaping our Christian identity and practice—in the face of the secularism that affects the church, too—than Horton's framework of covenant theology.

It is my prayer that this study of theological structure would not remain in the study—let alone in an ivory tower or on a dusty shelf—but that it would spark a renewed theologizing within this theodramatic framework, a theologizing that would capture our imagination as Christians so that we recognize more clearly who we are in Christ and become fitting participants in God's life. Moreover, it is my prayer that this study would also capture the imagination of those outside of Christ through unbelief whose secular immanent framework has cracks in it and who are haunted by and longing for something more, something better—the relationship for which they were created, which they can enjoy through faith in Christ, and to which God is calling them by the Spirit through us.

Bibliography

Adams, Marilyn McCord. "Eucharistic Drama: Rehearsal for a Revolution." In *Theatrical Theology: Explorations in Performing the Faith*, edited by Wesley Vander Lugt and Trevor A. Hart, 203–23. Eugene, OR: Cascade, 2014.
Alexander, T. Desmond. *The City of God and the Goal of Creation: An Introduction to the Biblical Theology of the City of God*. Short Studies in Biblical Theology. Wheaton: Crossway, 2018.
———. *From Eden to the New Jerusalem: An Introduction to Biblical Theology*. Nottingham: Inter-Varsity, 2008.
———. "The Story of Israel." In *Salvation to the Ends of the Earth: A Biblical Theology*, edited by Andreas Köstenberger, 11–37. 2nd ed. New Studies in Biblical Theology 53. Downers Grove: InterVarsity, 2020.
Allen, David L. *The Extent of the Atonement: A Historical and Critical Review*. Nashville: B&H Academic, 2016.
Allen, Leslie C. *Ezekiel 20–48*. Word Biblical Commentary 29. Dallas: Word, 1990.
Allen, Michael. *Grounded in Heaven: Recentering Christian Hope and Life on God*. Grand Rapids: Eerdmans, 2018.
Allen, R. Michael. *Justification and the Gospel: Understanding the Contexts and Controversies*. Grand Rapids: Baker Academic, 2013.
———. *Reformed Theology*. Doing Theology. London: T. & T. Clark, 2010.
Allison, Gregg R. "The Kingdom of God." In *The Kingdom of God*, edited by Christopher W. Morgan and Robert A. Peterson, 179–205. Theology in Community. Wheaton: Crossway, 2012.
Allison, Gregg R., and Andreas J. Köstenberger. *The Holy Spirit*. Theology for the People of God. Nashville: B&H Academic, 2020.
Anderson, Bernhard W. *Contours of Old Testament Theology*. Minneapolis: Fortress, 1999.
Anderson, Kenton C. *Integrative Preaching: A Comprehensive Model for Transformational Proclamation*. Grand Rapids: Baker Academic, 2017.
Andrews, Alan, ed. *The Kingdom Life: A Practical Theology of Discipleship and Spiritual Formation*. Carol Stream: NavPress, 2016.
Ashford, Bruce Riley, and Craig G. Bartholomew. *The Doctrine of Creation: A Constructive Kuyperian Approach*. Downers Grove: IVP Academic, 2020.
Augustine. *On Christian Doctrine*. Translated by D. W. Robertson Jr. Upper Saddle River: Prentice Hall, 1997.

Aulén, Gustaf. *Christus Victor: A Historical Study of the Three Main Types of the Idea of Atonement*. Reprint, Eugene, OR: Wipf & Stock, 2003.
Austin, J. L. *How to Do Things with Words*. Oxford: Clarendon, 1962.
Bailey, Justin Ariel. *Reimagining Apologetics: The Beauty of Faith in a Secular Age*. Downers Grove: IVP Academic, 2020.
Balthasar, Hans Urs von. *The Action*. Vol. 4 of *Theo-Drama: Theological Dramatic Theory*. Translated by Graham Harrison. San Francisco: Ignatius, 1994.
———. *Dramatis Personae: Man in God*. Vol. 2 of *Theo-Drama: Theological Dramatic Theory*. Translated by Graham Harrison. San Francisco: Ignatius, 1990.
———. *Dramatis Personae: Persons in Christ*. Vol. 3 of *Theo-Drama: Theological Dramatic Theory*. Translated by Graham Harrison. San Francisco, Ignatius, 1993.
———. *The Last Act*. Vol. 5 of *Theo-Drama: Theological Dramatic Theory*. Translated by Graham Harrison. San Francisco: Ignatius, 1998.
———. *Prolegomena*. Vol. 1 of *Theo-Drama: Theological Dramatic Theory*. Translated by Graham Harrison. San Francisco: Ignatius, 1988.
———. *The Realm of Metaphysics in Antiquity*. Vol. 4 of *The Glory of the Lord: A Theological Aesthetics*. Edited by John Riches. Translated by Oliver Davies et al. San Francisco: Ignatius, 1989.
———. *The Realm of Metaphysics in the Modern Age*. Vol. 5 of *The Glory of the Lord: A Theological Aesthetics*. Edited by Brian McNeil and John Riches. Translated by Oliver Davies et al. San Francisco: Ignatius, 1991.
———. *Seeing the Form*. Vol. 1 of *The Glory of the Lord: A Theological Aesthetics*. Edited by John Riches. Translated by Erasmo Leiva-Merikakis. San Francisco: Ignatius, 1982.
———. *The Spirit of the Truth*. Vol. 3 of *Theo-Logic: Theological Logical Theory*. Translated by Graham Harrison. San Francisco: Ignatius, 2005.
———. *Studies in Theological Style: Clerical Styles*. Vol. 2 of *The Glory of the Lord: A Theological Aesthetics*. Edited by John Riches. Translated by Andrew Louth et al. San Francisco: Ignatius, 1984.
———. *Theology: The New Covenant*. Vol. 7 of *The Glory of the Lord: A Theological Aesthetics*. Edited by John Riches. Translated by Brian McNeil. San Francisco: Ignatius, 1990.
———. *Theology: The Old Covenant*. Vol. 6 of *The Glory of the Lord: A Theological Aesthetics*. Edited by John Riches. Translated by Brian McNeil and Erasmo Leiva-Merikakis. San Francisco: Ignatius, 1991.
———. *Truth of God*. Vol. 2 of *Theo-Logic: Theological Logical Theory*. Translated by Adrian J. Walker. San Francisco: Ignatius, 2004.
Barach, John. "Covenant and Election." In *The Auburn Avenue Theology, Pros and Cons: Debating the Federal Vision: The Knox Theological Seminary Colloquium on the Federal Vision, August 11–13, 2003*, edited by E. Calvin Beisner, 149–56. Fort Lauderdale: Knox Theological Seminary, 2004.
Barr, James. "Man and Nature: The Ecological Controversy and the Old Testament." *Bulletin of the John Rylands Library* 55, no. 1 (1972) 9–32.
———. "Some Semantic Notes on the Covenant." In *Beiträge zur alttestamentlichen Theologie: Festschrift für Walther Zimmerli zum 70 Geburtstag*, edited by H. Donner et al., 23–38. Göttingen: Vanderhoeck and Ruprecht, 1977.

BIBLIOGRAPHY

Barth, Karl. *Church Dogmatics*. Vol. I/1. 2nd ed. Edited by Geoffrey W. Bromiley and Thomas F. Torrance. Translated by T. H. L. Parker, et al. London: T. & T. Clark, 1975.

———. *Church Dogmatics* Vol. I/2. Edited by Geoffrey W. Bromiley and Thomas F. Torrance. Translated by G. T. Tomson and H. Knight. London: T. & T. Clark, 1956.

———. *Church Dogmatics*. Vol. II/1. Edited by Geoffrey W. Bromiley and Thomas F. Torrance. Translated by T. H. L. Parker, et al. London: T. & T. Clark, 1957.

———. *Church Dogmatics*. Vol. III/1. Edited by Geoffrey W. Bromiley and Thomas F. Torrance. Translated by J. W. Edwards, O. Bussey, and H. Knight. London: T. & T. Clark, 1958.

———. *Church Dogmatics*. Vol III/2. Edited by Geoffrey W. Bromiley and Thomas F. Torrance. Translated by H. Knight, et al. London: T. & T. Clark, 1960.

———. *Church Dogmatics*. Vol. III/3. Edited by Geoffrey W. Bromiley and Thomas F. Torrance. Translated by Geoffrey W. Bromiley and R. J. Ehrlich. London: T. & T. Clark, 1960.

———. *Church Dogmatics*. Vol. IV/1. Edited by Geoffrey W. Bromiley and Thomas F. Torrance. Translated by Geoffrey W. Bromiley. London: T. & T. Clark, 1956.

———. *Church Dogmatics*. Vol. IV/2. Edited by Geoffrey W. Bromiley and Thomas F. Torrance. Translated by Geoffrey W. Bromiley. London: T. & T. Clark, 1958.

———. *Church Dogmatics*. Vol. IV/3a. Edited by Geoffrey W. Bromiley and Thomas F. Torrance. Translated by Geoffrey W. Bromiley. London: T. & T. Clark, 1961.

———. *Church Dogmatics*. Vol. IV/3b. Edited by Geoffrey W. Bromiley and Thomas F. Torrance. Translated by Geoffrey W. Bromiley. London: T. & T. Clark, 1961.

———. *Church Dogmatics*. Vol. IV/4. Edited by Geoffrey W. Bromiley and Thomas F. Torrance. Translated by Geoffrey W. Bromiley. London: T. & T. Clark, 1969.

———. *The Epistle to the Romans*. Oxford: Oxford University Press, 1968.

Barth, Marcus. *Justification: Pauline Texts Interpreted in the Light of the Old and New Testaments*. Translated by A. M. Woodruff III. Eugene, OR: Wipf & Stock, 2006.

Bartholomew, Craig G. "Covenant and Creation: Covenant Overload or Covenant Deconstruction." *Calvin Theological Journal* 30 (1995) 11–33.

———. *Introducing Biblical Hermeneutics: A Comprehensive Framework for Hearing God in Scripture*. Grand Rapids: Baker Academic, 2015.

Bartholomew, Craig G., and Michael W. Goheen, *The Drama of Scripture: Finding Our Place in the Biblical Story*. Grand Rapids: Baker Academic, 2004.

Bartholomew, Craig G., and Heath A. Thomas, eds. *A Manifesto for Theological Interpretation*. Grand Rapids: Baker Academic, 2016.

Bass, Diana Butler. *Christianity after Religion: The End of Church and the Birth of a New Spiritual Awakening*. New York: HarperCollins, 2013.

Bass, Dorothy C. "Christian Formation in and for Sabbath Rest." *Interpretation* 59, no. 1 (2005) 25–37.

Bauckham, Richard J. *Bible and Mission: Christian Witness in a Postmodern World*. Grand Rapids: Baker Academic, 2003.

———. *Jude, 2 Peter*. Word Biblical Commentary 50. Dallas: Word, 1983.

Baugh, S. M. "Galatians 3:20 and the Covenant of Redemption." *Westminster Theological Journal* 66 (2004) 49–70.

Bavinck, Herman. *Reformed Dogmatics*. 4 vols. Translated by John Vriend. Grand Rapids: Baker Academic, 2003–2008.

Beach, J. Mark. "The Doctrine of the *Pactum Salutis* in the Covenant Theology of Herman Witsius." *Mid-America Journal of Theology* 13 (2002) 101–42.

Beale, G. K. "The End Starts at the Beginning." In *Making All Things New: Inaugurated Eschatology for the Life of the Church*, edited by Benjamin L. Gladd and Matthew S. Harmon, 7–20. Grand Rapids: Baker Academic, 2016.

———. "The Final Vision of the Apocalypse and Its Implications for a Biblical Theology of the Temple." In *Heaven on Earth: The Temple in Biblical Theology*, edited by T. Desmond Alexander and Simon Gathercole, 191–209. Carlisle: Paternoster, 2004.

———. *Handbook on the New Testament Use of the Old Testament: Exegesis and Interpretation*. Grand Rapids: Baker, 2012.

———. *A New Testament Biblical Theology: The Unfolding of the Old Testament in the New*. Grand Rapids: Baker Academic, 2011.

———. *The Temple and the Church's Mission: A Biblical Theology of the Dwelling Place of God*. New Studies in Biblical Theology 17. Downers Grove: IVP Academic, 2004.

———. *Union with the Resurrected Christ: Eschatological New Creation and New Testament Theology*. Grand Rapids: Baker Academic, 2023.

Beale, G. K., and Mitchell Kim. *God Dwells Among Us: Expanding Eden to the Ends of the Earth*. Downers Grove: IVP, 2014.

Beeke, Joel R., and Mark Jones. *A Puritan Theology: Doctrine for Life*. Grand Rapids: Reformation Heritage, 2012.

Beeke, Joel R., and Paul M. Smalley. *Man and Christ*. Vol. 2 of *Reformed Systematic Theology*. Wheaton: Crossway, 2020.

———. *Revelation and God*. Vol. 1 of *Reformed Systematic Theology*. Wheaton: Crossway, 2019.

Behm, J. "Nous." In *Theological Dictionary of the New Testament*, vol. 4, edited and translated by Geoffrey W. Bromiley, 951–60. Grand Rapids: Eerdmans, 1967.

Behr, John. "The Promise of the Image." In *Imago Dei: Human Dignity in Ecumenical Perspective*, edited by Thomas Albert Howard, 15–37. Washington: Catholic University of America Press, 2013.

Belcher, Richard P., Jr. "The Covenant of Works in the Old Testament." In *Covenant Theology: Biblical, Theological, and Historical Perspectives*, edited by Guy P. Waters et al., 63–78. Wheaton: Crossway, 2020.

———. *The Fulfillment of the Promises of God: An Explanation of Covenant Theology*. Fearn: Mentor, 2020.

Berkhof, Hendrikus. *Christian Faith: An Introduction to the Study of Faith*. Translated by Sierd Woudstra. Grand Rapids: Eerdmans, 1979.

Berkhof, Louis. *Systematic Theology*. Grand Rapids: Eerdmans, 1996.

Berkouwer, G. C. *Sin*. Studies in Dogmatics. Translated by Philip C. Holtrop. Grand Rapids: Eerdmans, 1971.

Berlin, Tom. *The Generous Church: A Guide for Pastors*. Nashville: Abingdon, 2016.

Bianchi, Enzo. *Praying the Word: An Introduction to* Lectio Divina. Translated by James W. Zona. Kalamazoo: Cistercian, 1998.

Billings, J. Todd. *Calvin, Participation, and the Gift: The Activity of Believers in Union with Christ*. Changing Paradigms in Historical and Systematic Theology. Oxford: Oxford University Press, 2007.

———. "John Calvin: United to God through Christ." *Harvard Theological Review* 98 (2005) 315–35.

———. "Redemption Applied: Union with Christ." In *The Oxford Handbook of Reformed Theology*, edited by Michael Allen and Scott Swain, 497–513. Oxford: Oxford University Press, 2020.

———. *Remembrance, Communion, and Hope: Rediscovering the Gospel at the Lord's Table*. Grand Rapids: Eerdmans, 2018.

———. *Union with Christ: Reframing Theology and Ministry for the Church*. Grand Rapids: Baker Academic, 2011.

———. *The Word of God for the People of God: An Entryway to the Theological Interpretation of Scripture*. Grand Rapids: Eerdmans, 2010.

Bintsarovskyi, Dmytro. *Hidden and Revealed: The Doctrine of God in the Reformed and Eastern Orthodox Traditions*. Studies in Historical and Systematic Theology. Bellingham, WA: Lexham, 2021.

Bird, Michael F. "Incorporated Righteousness: A Response to Recent Evangelical Discussion Concerning the Imputation of Christ's Righteousness in Justification." *Journal of the Evangelical Theological Society* 47 (2004) 253–75.

Block, Daniel I. "Eden: A Temple? A Reassessment of the Biblical Evidence." In *From Creation to New Creation: Biblical Theology and Exegesis: Essays in Honor of G. K. Beale*, edited by Daniel M. Gurtner and Benjamin L. Gladd, 3–29. Peabody: Hendrickson, 2013.

Boa, Kenneth D. *Conformed to His Image: Biblical, Practical Approaches to Spiritual Formation*. Rev. ed. Grand Rapids: Zondervan Academic, 2020.

———. *Life in the Presence of God: Practices for Living in the Light of Eternity*. Downers Grove: IVP, 2017.

Boa, Kenneth D., and Robert M. Bowman Jr. *Faith Has Its Reasons: Integrative Approaches to Defending the Christian Faith*. 2nd ed. Downers Grove: IVP, 2006.

Boer, Harry R. *An Ember Still Glowing: Humankind as the Image of God*. Grand Rapids: Eerdmans, 1990.

Boersma, Hans. *Heavenly Participation: The Weaving of a Sacramental Tapestry*. Grand Rapids: Eerdmans, 2011.

———. "The Liturgical Medium Is the Message." *First Things*, May 3, 2021.

———. *Nouvelle Théologie and Sacramental Ontology: A Return to Mystery*. Oxford: Oxford University Press, 2009.

———. *Pierced by Love: Divine Reading with the Christian Tradition*. Bellingham, WA: Lexham, 2023.

———. *Sacramental Preaching: Sermons on the Hidden Presence of Christ*. Grand Rapids: Baker Academic, 2016.

———. *Scripture as Real Presence: Sacramental Exegesis in the Early Church*. Grand Rapids: Baker, 2018.

———. *Seeing God: The Beatific Vision in Christian Tradition*. Grand Rapids: Eerdmans, 2018.

———. *Violence, Hospitality, and the Cross: Reappropriating the Atonement Tradition*. Grand Rapids: Baker Academic, 2004.

Bolt, John. "Why the Covenant of Works Is a Necessary Doctrine: Revisiting the Objections to a Venerable Reformed Doctrine." In *By Faith Alone: Answering the Challenges to the Doctrine of Justification*, edited by Gary L. W. Johnson and Guy P. Waters, 171–89. Wheaton: Crossway, 2006.

Bonhoeffer, Dietrich. *Life Together*. 5th ed. Translated by John W. Doberstein. London: SCM, 2012.

Booram, Beth A., and David Booram. *When Faith Becomes Sight: Opening Your Eyes to God's Presence All Around You*. Downers Grove: IVP, 2019.

Booth, Susan Maxwell. *The Tabernacling Presence of God: Mission and Gospel Witness*. Eugene, OR: Wipf & Stock, 2015.

Borg, Marcus J., and N. T. Wright. *The Meaning of Jesus: Two Visions*. San Francisco: Harper, 1999.

Boulton, Matthew Myer. *Life in God: John Calvin, Practical Formation, and the Future of Protestant Theology*. Grand Rapids: Eerdmans, 2011.

Bourke, Vernon J. *The Essential Augustine*. 2nd ed. Indianapolis: Hackett, 1974.

Bowald, Mark Alan. *Rendering the Word in Theological Hermeneutics: Mapping Divine and Human Agency*. Studies in Historical and Systematic Theology. Bellingham, WA: Lexham, 2015.

Bowsher, Clive, *Life in the Son: Exploring Participation and Union with Christ in John's Gospel and Letters*. Downers Grove: IVP Academic, 2023.

Boyer, Steven D. "Articulating Order: Trinitarian Discourse in an Egalitarian Age." *Pro Ecclesia* 18 (2009) 255–72.

Bradshaw, David. *Aristotle East and West: Metaphysics and the Division of Christendom*. Cambridge: Cambridge University Press, 2004.

———. "The Concept of Divine Energies." In *Divine Essence and Divine Energies: Ecumenical Reflections on the Presence of God in Eastern Orthodoxy*, edited by C. Athanasopoulos and C. Schneider, Location 544–1214. Cambridge: James Clarke, 2013 [kindle edition].

Braun, Gabriele G. *God's Praise and God's Presence: A Biblical-Theological Study*. Eugene, OR: Wipf & Stock, 2020.

Brown, F., S. R. Driver, and C. A. Briggs. *A Hebrew and English Lexicon of the Old Testament*. Oxford: Oxford University Press, 1973.

Brown, Michael G., and Zach Keele. *Sacred Bond: Covenant Theology Explored*. 2nd ed. Grand Rapids: Reformed Fellowship, 2017.

Browning, Don S. *A Fundamental Practical Theology: Descriptive and Strategic Proposals*. Minneapolis: Fortress, 1991.

Bruce, F. F. *Romans*. Rev. ed. Tyndale New Testament Commentaries. Grand Rapids: Eerdmans, 1987.

Brueggemann, Walter. *Sabbath as Resistance: Saying No to the Culture of Now*. Louisville: Westminster John Knox, 2017.

———. *Theology of the Old Testament: Testimony, Dispute, Advocacy*. Minneapolis: Fortress, 1997.

Burger, Hans. "Het avondmaal is juist nodig vanwege het lichamelijke." *Nederlands Dagblad*, March 9, 2021. https://www.nd.nl/geloof/geloof/1023907/het-avondmaal-is-juist-nodig-vanwege-het-lichamelijke.

———. *Being in Christ: A Biblical and Systematic Investigation in a Reformed Perspective*. Eugene, OR: Wipf & Stock, 2008.

———. "Clothed with Christ, Our Righteousness." Lezing conferentie Tom Wright and Our Justification. Kampen, October 31, 2014. https://www.academia.edu/9064386/Clothed_with_Christ_our_righteousness.

———. "Foundation or Perspective? On the Usefulness of Formation and Epistemology." In *Sola Scriptura: Biblical and Theological Perspectives on Scripture, Authority, and Hermeneutics*, edited by Hans Burger et al., 56–78. Studies in Reformed Theology 32. Leiden: Brill, 2017.

———. "Gedachten over Pinksteren: leert de Geest ons 'kruisdragen' of in de 'overwinning staan'?" *Nederlands Dagblad*, May 18, 2021.

———. "God spreekt: Wolterstorff over het word van God." In *Denken om shalom: de praktische filosofie van Nicholas Wolterstorff*, edited by R. van Putten et al., 139–54. Amsterdam: Buijten & Schipperheijn, 2017.

———. "Gospel Presentation and the Structure of the Heidelberg Catechism." In *The Spirituality of the Heidelberg Catechism: Papers of the International Conference on the Heidelberg Catechism Held in Apeldoorn 2013*, edited by A. Huijgen, 268–79. Refo500 Academic Studies 24. Göttingen: Vandenhoeck & Ruprecht, 2015.

———. "'Het hart en wezen der christelijke religie zelve': over de praktische relevantie van de triniteitsleer." *Theologia Reformata* 55 (2012) 333–49.

———. "Hoe vergeeft God? Hoe overwint God het kwaad." In *Hoe kan Jezus' kruisdood ons verlossen? Christus victor en verzoening in verleden en heden*, edited by W. den Boer, 157–76. Amsterdam: Buijten & Schipperheijn, 2020.

———. *Hoop voor en zuchtende schepping: reflecties over lijden en ecologie bij Romeinen 8*. Baarn: Willem de Zwijgerstichting, 2020.

———. *Life in Christ: The Signficance of Jesus' Story*. Edited by Jane de Glint-Sneep. Translated by Dick Moes. Eugene, OR: Cascade, 2023.

———. "Quadriga without Platonism: In Search for the Usefulness of the Fourfold Sense of Scripture in Dialogue with Hans Boersma." Paper presented at the online workshop Scripture and Hermeneutics, part of the 2020 Conference of the European Academy of Religion, July 3, 2020. https://www.academia.edu/43417498/Quadriga_without_Platonism_In_search_for_the_usefulness_of_the_fourfold_sense_of_Scripture_in_dialogue_with_Hans_Boersma.

———. "Receiving the Mind of Christ: Epistemological and Hermeneutical Implications of Participation in Christ according to Oliver O'Donovan." *Journal of Reformed Theology* 10 (2016) 52–71.

———. "A Soteriological Perspective on Our Understanding." In *Correctly Handling the Word of Truth: Reformed Hermeneutics Today*, edited by M. te Velde and G. H. Visscher, 195–206. Eugene, OR: Wipf & Stock, 2014.

———. "The Story of God's Covenants: A Biblical-Theological Investigation with Systematic Consequence." *Calvin Theological Journal* 54 (2019) 267–99.

———. "'Theirs Are the Covenants': Israel and the Covenant of Grace." Paper presented at the BEST Study Day on Israel as a Theological Challenge, Kampen, March 21 and 22, 2018.

———. "Theologie: een hermeneutisch model." In *Gereformeerde hermeneutiek vandaag: theologische perspectieven*, edited by A. de Bruijne and Hans Burger, 263–83. Barneveld: De Vuurbaak, 2017.

———. "Theologische hermeneutiek in soteriologische perspectief." In *Gereformeerde hermeneutiek vandaag: theologische perspectieven*, edited by A. de Bruijne and Hans Burger, 35–65. Barneveld: De Vuurbaak, 2017.

———. "Theology without a Covenant of Works: A Thought Experiment." In *Covenant: A Vital Element of Reformed Theology: Biblical, Historical and Systematic-Theological Perspectives*, edited by Hans Burger et al., 325–48. Leiden: Brill, 2022.

———. "Transformatie door de vernieuwing van het denken." In *Verhalen om te delen: bij het afscheid van Peter van de Kamp*, edited by H. Schaeffer and G. Tamminga-Van Dijk, 95–101. TU Bezinningsreeks 21. Amsterdam: Buijten & Schipperheijn, 2018.

———. "Tussen atomisering en samenklontering: op zoek naar Bijbels-theologische samenhang van beelden voor verzoening." In *Schuld en vrijheid: opstellen aangeboden aan prof. dr. G. C. den Hertog*, edited by A. Huijgen et al., 61–79. Zoetermeer: Boekencentrum, 2017.

———. "Verder met het verbond: de erfenis van de vrijgemaakte verbondstheologie." In *Gereformeerde theologie stroomopwaarts: terugkijkem op 75 jaar Vrijmaking*, edited by E. de Boer et al., 109–26. Amsterdam: Buijten & Schipperheijn, 2021.

———. "Voorbij de offerkritiek: het beeld van het offer." In *Cruciaal: de verassende betekenis van Jezus' kruisiging*, edited by J. M. Burger and R. Sonneveld, 51–65. Amsterdam: Buijten & Schipperheijn, 2014.

———. "Wat ik leerde van de paus: 'Ons gemeenschappelijk huis is er niet alleen voor rijke westerlingen.'" *Nederlands Dagblad*, October 10, 2023. https://www.nd.nl/opinie/opinie/1195009/wat-ik-leerde-van-de-paus-ons-gemeenschappelijk-huis-is-er-ni.

Burger, Hans, and G. J. Spijker, eds. *Open voor God: Charles Taylor en christen-zijn in een seculiere tijd*. TU bezinningsreeks 14. Barneveld: De Vuurbaak, 2014.

Butterfield, Rosaria. *The Gospel Comes with a House Key: Practicing Radically Ordinary Hospitality in Our Post-Christian World*. Wheaton: Crossway, 2018.

Calhoun, Adele Ahlberg. *Spiritual Disciplines Handbook: Practices That Transform Us*. Downers Grove: IVP, 2005.

Calvin, John. *Commentary on the Epistle of Paul the Apostle to the Romans*. Edited by Henry Beveridge. Calvin's Commentaries 19. Reprint, Grand Rapids: Baker, 1989.

———. *The Institutes of the Christian Religion*. Edited by J. T. McNeill. Translated by Ford Lewis Battles. 2 vols. Philadelphia: Westminster, 1960.

Campbell, Constantine R. *Paul and Union with Christ: An Exegetical and Theological Study*. Grand Rapids: Zondervan, 2012.

Canlis, Julie. "Calvin, Osiander and Participation in God." *International Journal of Systematic Theology* 6 (2004) 169–84.

———. *Calvin's Ladder: A Spiritual Theology of Ascent and Ascension*. Grand Rapids: Eerdmans, 2010.

Carson, D. A. *Christ and Culture Revisited*. Grand Rapids: Eerdmans, 2012.

———. "Systematic Theology and Biblical Theology." In *New Dictionary of Biblical Theology*, edited by T. Desmond Alexander et al., 89–104. 2nd ed. Downers Grove: InterVarsity, 2000.

Caughey, Christopher Earle. *Puritan Responses to Antinomianism in the Context of Reformed Covenant Theology: 1630–1696*. PhD diss., Trinity College Dublin, 2013.

Chandler, Diane J. *Christian Spiritual Formation: An Integrated Approach for Personal and Relational Wholeness*. Downers Grove: IVP Academic, 2014.

Chapell, Bryan. *Christ-Centered Preaching: Redeeming the Expository Sermon*. Grand Rapids: Baker Academic, 2005.

Charry, Ellen T. *By the Renewing of Your Minds: The Pastoral Function of Christian Doctrine*. Oxford: Oxford University Press, 1997.

Chatraw, Joshua D. *Telling a Better Story: How to Talk about God in a Skeptical Age*. Grand Rapids: Zondervan, 2020.

Childers, Jana. *Performing the Word: Preaching as Theater*. Nashville: Abingdon, 1999.

Childs, Brevard S. *Biblical Theology of the Old and New Testaments: Theological Reflections on the Christian Bible*. London: SCM, 1992.

Church of Scotland. *The Confession of Faith, the Larger Catechism and Shorter Catechism with the Scripture Proofs at Large, Together with the Sum of Saving Knowledge*. Glasgow: Free Presbyterian Publications, 1973.

Clapp, Rodney. *New Creation: A Primer on Living in the Time between the Times*. Eugene, OR: Cascade, 2018.

———. *A Peculiar People: The Church as Culture in a Post-Christian Society*. Reprint, Eugene, OR: Wipf & Stock, 1996.

Clark, John C., and Marcus Peter Johnson. *The Incarnation of God: The Mystery of the Gospel as the Foundation of Evangelical Theology*. Wheaton: Crossway, 2015.

Clark, R. Scott. "'Do This and Live': Christ's Active Obedience as the Ground of Justification." In *Covenant, Justification, and Pastoral Ministry: Essays by the Faculty of Westminster Seminary California*, edited by R. Scott Clark, 229–65. Phillipsburg: P&R, 2007.

Clines, D. J. A. "The Image of God in Man." *Tyndale Bulletin* 19 (1968) 53–103.

Cocceius, Johannes. *The Doctrine of the Covenant and Testament of God*. Translated by Casey Carmichael. Classic Reformed Theology. Grand Rapids: Reformation Heritage, 2016.

Collins, Jack. "A Syntactical Note (Genesis 3:15): Is the Woman's Seed Singular or Plural?" *Tyndale Bulletin* 48 (1997) 139–48.

Colorado, Carlos D., and Justin D. Klassen, eds. *Aspiring to Fullness in a Secular Age: Essays on Religion and Theology in the Work of Charles Taylor*. Notre Dame: University of Notre Dame Press, 2014.

Courtenay, W. J. "Covenant and Causality in Pierre d'Ailly." *Speculum* 46 (1971) 94–119.

Cranfield, C. E. B. *Romans: A Shorter Commentary*. Grand Rapids: Eerdmans, 2018.

Crisp, Oliver D. "Anglican Hypothetical Universalism." In *Unlimited Atonement: Amyraldism and Reformed Theology*, edited by Michael F. Bird and Scott Harrower, 23–42. Grand Rapids: Kregel Academic, 2023.

———. *Deviant Calvinism: Broadening Reformed Theology*. Minneapolis: Fortress, 2014.

Crouch, C. L. "Genesis 1:26–27 as a Statement of Humanity's Divine Parentage." *Journal of Theological Studies* 61 (2010) 1–15.

Crouse, Robert C. *Two Kingdoms & Two Cities: Mapping Theological Traditions of Church, Culture, and Civil Order*. Emerging Scholars. Minneapolis: Fortress, 2017.

Cullmann, Oscar. *Christ and Time: The Primitive Christian Conception of Time and History*. 2nd ed. Translated by Floyd V. Filson. Philadelphia: Westminster, 1964.

Cumin, Paul. *Christ at the Crux: The Mediation of God and Creation in Christological Perspective*. Eugene, OR: Pickwick, 2014.

Currid, John D. "Adam and the Beginning of the Covenant of Grace." In *Covenant Theology: Biblical, Theological, and Historical Perspectives*, edited by Guy Prentiss Waters et al., 99–109. Wheaton: Crossway, 2020.

Curtis, Byron G. "Hosea 6:7 and Covenant-breaking Like/at Adam." In *The Law Is Not of Faith: Essays on Works and Grace in the Mosaic Covenant*, edited by Bryan D. Estelle et al., 170–209. Phillipsburg: P&R, 2009.

Dalferth, Ingolf U. *Becoming Present: An Inquiry into the Christian Sense of the Presence of God*. Leuven: Peeters, 2006.

———. *Theology and Philosophy*. Oxford: Basil Blackwell, 1988.

Davidson, Ivor J. "Christ." In *The Oxford Handbook of Reformed Theology*, edited by Michael Allen and Scott R. Swain, 446–72. Oxford: Oxford University Press, 2020.

Davies, Glenn. *Faith and Obedience in Romans: A Study in Romans 1–4*. Sheffield: Sheffield Academic, 1990.

Dawkins, Richard. *The God Delusion*. Boston: Houghton Mifflin Harcourt, 2008.

Dawn, Marva J. *Keeping the Sabbath Wholly: Ceasing, Resting, Embracing, Feasting*. Grand Rapids: Eerdmans, 1989.

———. *The Sense of the Call: A Sabbath Way of Life for Those Who Serve God, the Church, and the World*. Grand Rapids: Eerdmans, 2006.

———. *Truly the Community: Romans 12 and How to Be the Church*. Grand Rapids: Eerdmans, 1992.

Dean, Kenda Creasy. *Almost Christian: What the Faith of Our Teenagers is Telling the American Church*. Oxford: Oxford University Press, 2010.

De Boer, Erik. "Unfinished Homework: Charting the Influence of B. Holwerda with Respect to the Doctrine of Election." Translated with introduction and epilogue by Nelson D. Kloosterman. *Mid-America Journal of Theology* 18 (2007) 107–36.

De Bruijne, A. "Affect and Effect: The Significance of Biblical Spirituality for Christian Ethics in a Secular Age." *Lux Mundi* 30, no. 3 (2011) 66–71.

———. "'A Banner That Flies Across This Land': An Interpretation and Evaluation of Dutch Evangelical Political Awareness Since the End of the Twentieth Century." In *Evangelical Theology in Transition: Essays Under the Auspices of the Center of Evangelical and Reformation Theology (CERT)*, edited by C. van der Kooi et al., 86–130. Amsterdam: VU University Press, 2012.

———. "Besef van God in een spirituele tijd." In *Proeven van spiritualiteit: bijdragen ter gelegenheid van 160 jaar Theologische Universiteit Kampen*, edited by P. Niemeijer and H. de Wolf, 42–56. Barneveld: De Vuurbaak, 2014.

———. "Christelijke ethiek tussen wet, schepping en gemeenschap: een positionering naar aanleiding van Romeinen 12, 1 en 2." *Radix* 27, no. 2/3 (2001) 116–48.

———. "Christelijk leven: gaan lijken op Jezus." In *Oefenen in discipleschap: de gemeente als groeiplaats van het goede leven*, edited by James Kennedy and Pieter Vos, 15–26 Zoetermeer: Boekencentrum, 2015.

———. "De eenzijdige nadruk op de preek in de kerkdienst, maakt van kerkganger een consument." *Nederlands Dagblad*, July 12, 2019. https://www.nd.nl/opinie/columns/523918/column-de-eenzijdige-nadruk-op-de-preek-in-een-kerkdienst-maakt-van-kerkganger-een-consument.

———. "Er zit milieumoralism in de lucht." *Nederlands Dagblad*, November 9, 2019. https://www.nd.nl/opinie/columns/939818/column-ad-de-bruijne-er-zit-milieumoralisme-in-de-lucht.

———. "Gij geheel anders. Of toch niet? 'Veel christenen ervoeren de westerse cultuur als heel christelijk.'" *Nederlands Dagblad*, September 25, 2023. https://www.nd.nl/opinie/columns/1192810/gij-geheel-anders-of-toch-niet-veel-christenen-ervoeren-de-we.

———. "De kunst van het verstaan: hermeneutiek in Kampen." In *Gereformeerde hermeneutiek vandaag: theologische perspectieven*, edited by A. de Bruijne and Hans Burger, 13–34. Barneveld: De Vuurbaak, 2017.

———. "Niet van deze wereld: de hedendaagse Gereformeerde publieke theologie en de 'doperse optie.'" *Theologica Reformata* 54 (2011) 366–90.

———. "De tiende zegen: een aanzet tot evaluatie van de huidige charismatische interesse in gereformeerde kringen." *Kontekstueel* 21, no. 1 (2006). https://www.kontekstueel.nl/archief-kontekstueel/35-algemene-artikelen/590-nr6-2008-luisteroefeningen-reactie-v15-590.

De Graaf, S. G. *Promise and Deliverance*. 4 vols. Translated by H. Evan Runner and Elisabeth Wichers Runner. St. Catherines: Paideia, 1977.

———. *The True Faith: Commentary on the Heidelberg Catechism Lord's Day 1–22*. Translated by Richard Stienstra. https://spindleworks.com/library/DeGraaf/DeGraafTheTrueFaith.pdf.

De Jong, H. *Van oud naar nieuw: de ontwikkelingsgang van het Oude naar het Nieuwe Testament*. Kampen: Kok, 2002.

De Jong, J. M. *The Church Is the Means, the World Is the End: The Development of Klaas Schilder's Thought on the Relationship between the Church and the World*. Ede: GVO, 2019.

Dempster, Stephen G. "The Canon and Theological Interpretation." In *A Manifesto for Theological Interpretation*, edited by Craig G. Bartholomew and Heath A. Thomas, 131–48 Grand Rapids: Baker Academic, 2016.

———. *Dominion and Dynasty: A Theology of the Hebrew Bible*. New Studies in Biblical Theology 15. Downers Grove: IVP Academic, 2003.

Dennison, James T., Jr., Scott F. Sanborn, and Benjamin W. Swinburnson. "Merit or 'Entitlement' in Reformed Covenant Theology: A Review." *Kerux* 24, no. 3 (2009) 3–152.

DeYoung, Kevin. "Why Covenant Theology?" In *Covenant Theology: Biblical, Theological, and Historical Perspectives*, edited by Guy Prentiss Waters et al., 589–98. Wheaton: Crossway, 2020.

Dijkstra-Algra, N.. *Geschiedenis als verbondsgeschiedenis: een onderzoek naar de visie van Simon Gerrit de Graaf (1889–1955) op de zin deer geschiedenis*. MTh thesis, Vrije Universiteit, 1982.

Dodd, C. H. *The Interpretation of the Fourth Gospel*. Cambridge: Cambridge University Press, 1953.

Doede, Robert. "Transhumanism, Technology, and the Future: Posthumanity Emerging or Subhumanity Descending?" *Appraisal* 7, no. 3 (2009) 39–54.

Dolezal, James E. *All That Is in God: Evangelical Theology and the Challenge of Classical Theism*. Grand Rapids: Reformation Heritage, 2017.

Dooley, Kate. "From Penance to Confession: The Celtic Contribution." *Bijdragen: International Journal for Philosophy and Theology* 43 (1982) 390–411.

Douma, J. *Common Grace in Kuyper, Schilder, and Calvin: Exposition, Comparison, and Evaluation*. Edited by William Helder. Translated by A. H. Oosterhoff. Hamilton: Lucerna, 2017.

Douma, Jos. *Beholding the Glory of the Lord: Being Changed by His Beauty*. Translated by Dick Moes. Bloomington: iUniverse, 2012.

———. "Preken met het oog op Christusgelijkvoormigheid: over spirituele homiletiek en spirituele vorming." In *Instemmend luistern: studies voor Kees de Ruijter*, edited by M. Beute and P. Van der Kamp, 66–78. Utrecht: Kok, 2014.

———. *Veni Creator Spiritus: de meditatie en het preekproces*. Kampen: Kok, 2000.

———. *Zin in bidden*. Amsterdam: Ark Media, 2017.

Douma, Jos, et al. *Kijken en luisteren naar Jezus:40 keer lectio divina*. Heerenveen: Ark Media, 2010.

———. *Samen luisteren in de stilte: lectio divina met 40 oefeningen*. Heerenveen: Royal Jongbloed, 2019.

Dumbrell, William J. *Covenant and Creation: An Old Testament Covenant Theology*. Milton Keynes: Paternoster, 1984.

———. *The End of the Beginning: Revelation 21-22 and the Old Testament.* Eugene, OR: Wipf & Stock, 1985.

———. *The Search for Order: Biblical Eschatology in Focus.* Eugene, OR: Wipf & Stock, 1994.

Duncan, Mike. "The Curious Silence of the Dog and Paul of Tarsus: Revisiting the Argument from Silence." *Informal Logic* 32, no. 1 (2012) 83-97.

Dunn, James D. G. *Romans 1-8.* Word Biblical Commentary 38A. Dallas. Word, 1988.

———. *Romans 9-16.* Word Biblical Commentary 38B. Dallas. Word, 1988.

Durham, J. I. *Exodus.* Word Biblical Commentary 3. Dallas. Word, 1987.

Duvall, J. Scott, and J. Daniel Hays. *God's Relational Presence: The Cohesive Center of Biblical Theology.* Grand Rapids: Baker Academic, 2019.

Edmondson, Stephen. *Calvin's Christology.* Cambridge: Cambridge University Press, 2004.

Edwards, Jonathan. *Observations Concerning the Scripture Economy of the Trinity and Covenant of Redemption.* New York: Charles Scribner's Sons, 1880.

Egan, Kieran. *Imagination in Teaching & Learning: The Middle School Years.* London: Althouse, 1992.

Elam, Andrew M, Robert C. van Kooten, and Randall A. Bergquist. *Merit and Moses: A Critique of the Klinean Doctrine of Republication.* Leopold Classic Library. Eugene, OR: Wipf & Stock, 2014.

Enns, Peter. "Exodus." In *New Dictionary of Biblical Theology*, edited by T. Desmond Alexander et al., 146-52. 2nd ed. Downers Grove: InterVarsity, 2000.

Estelle, Bryan D. "The Covenant of Works in Moses and Paul." In *Covenant, Justification, and Pastoral Ministry: Essays by the Faculty of Westminster Seminary California*, edited by R. Scott Clark, 89-135. Phillipsburg: P&R, 2007.

———. "Leviticus 18:5 and Deuteronomy 30:1-14 in Biblical Theological Development: Entitlement to Heaven Foreclosed and Proffered." In *The Law Is Not of Faith: Essays on Works and Grace in the Mosaic Covenant*, edited by Bryan D. Estelle et al., 109-46. Phillipsburg: P&R, 2009.

Evans, C. Stephen. "Methodological Naturalism in Historical Biblical Scholarship." In *Jesus and the Restoration of Israel: A Critical Assessment of N. T. Wright's Jesus and the Victory of God*, edited by Carey C. Newman, 180-205. Downers Grove: InterVarsity, 1999.

Evans, William B. "Calvin's Doctrine of the Lord's Supper and its Relevance for Today" Foundations 68, no. 1 (2015) 3-25.

———. *Imputation and Impartation: Union with Christ in American Reformed Theology.* Studies in Christian History and Thought. Eugene, OR: Wipf & Stock, 2009.

———. "Three Current Reformed Models of Union with Christ." *Presbyterion* 41, no. 1-2 (2015) 12-30.

Faber, Jelle. "The Covenant of Works." *Clarion* 31 (1982) 90-91. http://www.spindleworks.com/library/faber/cov_works.htm.

Fairbairn, Donald. *Life in the Trinity: An Introduction to Theology with the Help of the Church Fathers.* Downers Grove: IVP Academic, 2009.

———. "Patristic Soteriology: Three Trajectories." *Journal of the Evangelical Theological Society* 50 (2007) 289-310.

Fanning, Buist M. "A Classical Reformed View." In *Four Views on the Warning Passages in Hebrews*, edited by Herbert W. Bateman IV, 172-219. Grand Rapids: Kregel, 2007.

Farlow, Matthew S. *The Dramatizing of Theology: Humanity's Participation in God's Drama*. Eugene, OR: Pickwick, 2017.

Fee, Gordon D. *The First Epistle to the Corinthians*. New International Commentary on the New Testament. Grand Rapids: Eerdmans, 1987.

Ferguson, Sinclair B. *Some Pastors and Teachers: Reflecting a Biblical Vision of What Every Minister Is Called To Be*. Edinburgh: Banner of Truth, 2017.

Ferry, Brenton C. "Works in the Mosaic Covenant: A Reformed Taxonomy." In *The Law Is Not of Faith: Essays on Works and Grace in the Mosaic Covenant*, edited by Bryan D. Estelle et al., 76–108. Phillipsburg: P&R, 2009.

Fesko, J. V. *The Covenant of Redemption: Origins, Development, and Reception*. Reformed Historical Theology 25. Göttingen: Vandenhoeck & Ruprecht, 2016.

———. "On the Antiquity of Biblical Theology." In *Resurrection and Eschatology: Theology in Service of the Church: Essays in Honor of Richard B. Gaffin Jr.*, edited by Lane G. Tipton and Jeffrey C. Waddington, 443–77. Phillipsburg: P&R, 2008.

———. *The Theology of the Westminster Standards: Historical Context and Theological Insights*. Wheaton: Crossway, 2014.

———. *The Trinity and the Covenant of Redemption*. Fearn: Christian Focus, 2016.

Finlan, Stephen. "Can We Speak of *Theosis* in Paul?" In *Partakers of the Divine Nature: The History and Development of Deification in the Christian Traditions*, edited by Michael J. Christenson and Jeffrey A. Wittung, 68–80. Grand Rapids: Baker Academic, 2007.

———. "Peter's Notion of Divine Participation." In *Theosis: Deification in Christian Theology*, edited by Stephen Finlan and Vladimir Kharlamov, 32–50. Eugene, OR: Pickwick, 2006.

Foster, David. *Reading with God: Lectio Divina*. London: Continuum, 2006.

Foster, Richard J. *Celebration of Discipline: The Pathway to Spiritual Growth*. San Francisco: HarperSanFrancisco, 1978.

———. *Streams of Living Water: Celebrating the Great Traditions of Christian Faith*. San Francisco: HarperSanFrancisco, 1998.

Foster, Richard J., and Kathryn A. Helmers. *Life with God: Reading the Bible for Spiritual Formation*. San Francisco: HarperOne, 2008.

Fowl, Stephen E. *Theological Interpretation of Scripture*. Cascade Companions. Eugene, OR: Cascade, 2009.

Frame, John M. *The Doctrine of the Knowledge of God*. A Theology of Lordship. Grand Rapids: Baker, 1987.

———. *The Escondido Theology: A Reformed Response to Two Kingdom Theology*. Lakeland, FL: Whitefield Media, 2011.

———. *Systematic Theology: An Introduction to Christian Belief*. Phillipsburg: P&R, 2013.

Francis. "Laudate Deum: To All People of Good Will on the Climate Crisis." Vatican: 2023. https://www.vatican.va/content/francesco/en/apost_exhortations/documents/20231004-laudate-deum.html.

———. *Laudato Si': On Care for Our Common Home*. Huntington: Our Sunday Visitor, 2015.

———. *Our Mother Earth: A Christian Reading of the Challenge of the Environment*. Huntington: Our Sunday Visitor, 2020.

Frei, Hans. *The Eclipse of Biblical Narrative: A Study in Eighteenth and Nineteenth Century Hermeneutics*. New Haven: Yale University Press, 1974.

Gadamer, Hans-Georg. *Truth and Method*. Translated by Joel Weinsheimer and Donald G. Marshall. 2nd ed. New York: Bloomsbury Academic, 2004.

Gaffin, Richard B., Jr. *By Faith, Not by Sight: Paul and the Order of Salvation*. Milton Keynes: Paternoster, 2006.

———. "Covenant and Salvation: A Review Article." *Ordained Servant*, March 2009. https://opc.org/os.html?article_id=141.

———. "Glory." In *New Dictionary of Biblical Theology*, edited by T. Desmond Alexander et al., 507–11. 2nd ed.. Downers Grove: InterVarsity, 2000.

———. *Resurrection and Redemption: A Study in Paul's Soteriology*. Phillipsburg: P&R, 1987.

Garcia, Mark A. "A Response to Michael S. Horton's 'Law and Gospel.'" *The Confessional Presbyterian* 8 (2012) 170–76.

Garvey, Jon. *The Generations of Heaven and Earth: Adam, the Ancient World, and Biblical Theology*. Eugene, OR: Wipf & Stock, 2020.

Gattis, Lee. "Abundant Sufficiency and Intentional Efficacy: Particular Redemption at the Synod of Dort." *Unio cum Christo* 4 (2018) 145–61.

Gentry, Peter J., and Stephen J. Wellum. *God's Kingdom through God's Covenants: A Concise Biblical Theology*. Wheaton: Crossway, 2015.

———. *Kingdom through Covenant: A Biblical-theological Understanding of the Covenants*. 2nd edition. Wheaton: Crossway, 2018.

Gerrish, B. A. "The Mirror of God's Goodness: Man in the Theology of Calvin." *Concordia Theological Quarterly* 45 (1981) 211–22.

Gladd, Benjamin L. *From Adam and Israel to the Church: A Biblical Theology of the People of God*. Downers Grove: InterVarsity, 2019.

Godfrey, W. Robert. "Reformed Thought on the Extent of the Atonement to 1618." *Westminster Theological Journal* 37 (1975) 133–71.

Goheen, Michael W. *Introducing Christian Mission Today: Scripture, History and Issues*. Downers Grove: InterVarsity, 2014.

———. *A Light to the Nations: The Missional Church and the Biblical Story*. Grand Rapids: Baker Academic, 2011.

Goheen, Michael W., and Jim Mullins. *The Symphony of Mission: Playing Your Part in God's Work in the World*. Grand Rapids: Baker Academic, 2019.

Goheen, Michael W., and Christopher J. H. Wright. "Mission and Theological Interpretation." In *A Manifesto for Theological Interpretation*, edited by Craig G. Bartholomew and Heath A. Thomas, 171–96. Grand Rapids: Baker Academic, 2016.

Golding, Peter. *Covenant Theology: The Key of Theology in Reformed Thought and Tradition*. Fearn: Christian Focus, 2004.

Goldingay, J. *Israel's Faith*. Vol. 2 of *Old Testament Theology*. Downers Grove: InterVarsity, 2006.

———. *Israel's Gospel*. Vol. 1 of *Old Testament Theology*. Downers Grove: InterVarsity, 2003.

Goldsworthy, Graeme. *According to Plan: The Unfolding Revelation of God in the Bible*. Downers Grove: IVP Academic, 2002.

———. "The Kingdom of God." In *New Dictionary of Biblical Theology*, edited by T. Desmond Alexander et al., 615–20. 2nd ed. Downers Grove: InterVarsity, 2000.

Gorman, Michael J. *Participating in Christ: Explorations in Paul's Theology and Spirituality*. Grand Rapids: Baker Academic, 2019.

BIBLIOGRAPHY

Gould, Paul M. *Cultural Apologetics: Renewing the Christian Voice, Conscience, and Imagination in a Disenchanted World*. Grand Rapids: Zondervan, 2019.

Green, Joel B. *Practicing Theological Interpretation: Engaging Biblical Texts for Faith and Formation*. Theological Explorations for the Church Catholic. Grand Rapids: Baker Academic, 2011.

Greenman, Jeffrey P., and George Kalantzis, eds. *Life in the Spirit: Spiritual Formation in Theological Perspective*. Downers Grove: IVP Academic, 2010.

Greidanus, Sidney. *Preaching Christ from Genesis: Foundations for Expository Sermons*. Grand Rapids: Eerdmans, 2007.

Greijdanus, S. *De brief van den apostle Paulus aan de gemeente te Rome*. 2 vols. Amsterdam: Bottenburg, 1933.

Grenz. Stanley J. "Jesus as the *Imago Dei*: Image-of-God Christology and the Non-linear Linearity of Theology." *Journal of the Evangelical Theological Society* 47 (2004) 617–28.

———. *A Primer on Postmodernism*. Grand Rapids: Eerdmans, 1996.

———. *Rediscovering the Triune God: The Trinity in Contemporary Theology*. Minneapolis: Fortress, 2004.

———. *Theology for the Community of God*. Grand Rapids: Eerdmans, 1994.

Grenz, Stanley J., and John R. Franke. *Beyond Foundationalism: Shaping Theology in a Postmodern Context*. Louisville: Westminster John Knox, 2001.

Grudem, Wayne A. *Systematic Theology: An Introduction to Biblical Doctrine*. Downers Grove: InterVarsity, 1994.

Gumbel, Nicky. *Questions of Life: A Practical Introduction to the Christian Faith*. Colorado Springs: David C. Cook, 1996.

Gundry, Robert H. "The Nonimputation of Christ's Righteousness." In *Justification: What's at Stake in the Current Debates*, edited by Mark Husbands and Daniel J. Treier, 17–45 Downers Grove: InterVarsity, 2004.

Gunton, Colin E. *Act and Being: Toward a Theology of Divine Attributes*. London: SCM, 2002.

———. *The Christian Faith: An Introduction to Christian Doctrine*. Oxford: Blackwell, 2002.

———. *The Triune Creator: A Historical and Systematic Study*. Edinburgh Studies in Constructive Theology. Grand Rapids: Eerdmans, 1998.

Habets, Myk. *The Anointed Son: A Trinitarian Spirit Christology*. Eugene, OR: Pickwick, 2010.

———. "Reformed *Theosis*?: A Response to Gannon Murphey." *Theology Today* 65 (2009) 489–98.

———. "Reforming *Theosis*." In *Theosis: Deification in Christian Theology*, edited by Stephen Finlan and Vladimir Kharlamov, 146–67. Eugene, OR: Pickwick, 2006.

———. *Theosis in the Theology of Thomas Torrance*. Routledge New Critical Thinking in Religion, Theology, and Biblical Studies. Abingdon: Routledge, 2009.

Hahn, Scott W. *Kinship by Covenant: A Canonical Approach to the Fulfillment of God's Saving Promises*. New Haven: Yale University Press, 2009.

Hamilton, James M., Jr. *God's Glory in Salvation through Judgment: A Biblical Theology*. Wheaton: Crossway, 2010.

———. "The Skull-Crushing Seed of the Woman: Inner-biblical Interpretation of Genesis 3:15." In *The Seed of Promise: The Suffering and Glory of the Messiah:*

Essays in Honor of T. Desmond Alexander, edited by Paul R. Williamson and Rita F. Cefalu, 3–34. Wilmore: GlossaHouse, 2020.

Hansen, Collin, ed. *Our Secular Age: Ten Years of Reading and Applying Charles Taylor*. Deerfield: The Gospel Coalition, 2017.

Harris, Max. *Theater and Incarnation*. Grand Rapids: Eerdmans, 2005.

Hart, Trevor A., and Steven R. Guthrie, eds. *Faithful Performances: Enacting Christian Tradition*. Routledge Studies in Theology, Imagination and the Arts. New York: Routledge, 2007.

Hastie, P. "Christians and Culture: An Interview with Michael Horton." *The Briefing*, November 1, 2008. https://matthiasmedia.com/briefing/2008/11/christians-and-culture-an-interview-with-michael-horton/.

Hastings, W. Ross. *Total Atonement: Trinitarian Participation in the Reconciliation of Humanity and Creation*. Lanham: Lexington, 2019.

Hauerwas, Stanley, and William H. Willimon. *Resident Aliens: Life in the Christian Colony*. Nashville: Abingdon, 1989.

Hays, Richard B. *Echoes of Scripture in the Letters of Paul*. New Haven: Yale University Press, 1989.

———. "Knowing Jesus: Story, History and the Question of Truth." In *Jesus, Paul and the People of God: A Theological Dialogue with N. T. Wright*, edited by Nicholas Perrin and Richard B. Hays, 41–61. Downers Grove: IVP Academic, 2011.

———. *Reading Backwards: Figural Christology and the Fourfold Gospel Witness*. Waco: Baylor University Press, 2014.

———. "Reading Scripture in the Light of the Resurrection." In *The Art of Reading Scripture*, edited by Ellen F. Davis and Richard B. Hays, 216–38. Grand Rapids: Eerdmans, 2003.

Heide, Gale. *Timeless Truth in the Hands of History: A Short History of System in Theology*. Princeton Theological Monograph Series 178. Eugene, OR: Pickwick, 2012.

Heidegger, Martin. *Being and Time*. Translated by Joan Stambaugh and Dennis J. Schmidt. Albany: State University of New York Press, 2010.

Helm, Paul. *John Calvin's Ideas*. Oxford: Oxford University Press, 2004.

Hendriksen, William. *Exposition of Paul's Epistle to the Romans*. New Testament Commentary. Grand Rapids: Baker, 1981.

Heppe, Heinrich. *Reformed Dogmatics*. Edited by E. Bizer. Translated by G. T. Thomson. Eugene, OR: Wipf & Stock, 2007.

Hiestand, Gerald. "Not 'Just Forgiven': How Athanasius Overcomes the Under-realized Eschatology of Evangelicalism." *Evangelical Quarterly* 84, no 1 (2012) 47–66.

Hitchens, Christopher. *God Is Not Great: How Religion Poisons Everything*. Toronto: Emblem, 2007.

Hodge, Charles. *Systematic Theology*. Vol. 2. Grand Rapids: Eerdmans, 1952.

Hoekema, Anthony A. *The Bible and the Future*. Grand Rapids: Eerdmans, 1994.

———. *Created in God's Image*. Grand Rapids: Eerdmans, 1986.

Hoeksema, Herman. *Reformed Dogmatics*. Jenison: Reformed Free, 2004.

———. *The Triple Knowledge: An Exposition of the Heidelberg Catechism*. 3 vols. Jenison, MI: Reformed Free, 1976.

Hoglund, Jonathan. *Called by Triune Grace: Divine Rhetoric and the Effectual Call*. Studies in Christian Doctrine and Scripture. Downers Grove: IVP Academic, 2016.

Holland, Tom. *Dominion: The Making of the Western Mind*. Boston: Little, Brown Book Group, 2019.

Holland, Tom. *Tom Wright and the Search for Truth: A Theological Evaluation*. 2nd ed. London: Apiary, 2020.

Holmes, Christopher R. J. "Last Things." In *The Oxford Handbook of Reformed Theology*, edited by Michael Allen and Scott R. Swain, 609–20. Oxford: Oxford University Press, 2020.

Holmes, Stephen R. "The Attributes of God." In *The Oxford Handbook of Systematic Theology*, edited by John B. Webster et al., 54–71. Oxford: Oxford University Press, 2007.

———. "Image of God." In *Dictionary for Theological Interpretation of the Bible*, edited by Kevin J. Vanhoozer, 318–19. Grand Rapids: Baker, 2005.

Holt, Robby, and Aubrey Spears. "The Ecclesia as Primary Context for the Reception of the Bible." In *A Manifesto for Theological Interpretation*, edited by Craig G. Bartholomew and Heath A. Thomas, 72–93. Grand Rapids: Baker Academic, 2016.

Holwerda, B. "The History of Redemption in Preaching the Gospel." Translated by P. Y. de Jong. https://spindleworks.com/library/holwerda/holwerda.htm.

Horrell, J. Scott. "The Eternal God in the Social Trinity." In *Jesus in Trinitarian Perspective*, edited by Fred Sanders and Klaus Issler, 44–79. Nashville: B&H, 2007.

Horton, Michael S. "Are Eastern Orthodoxy and Evangelicalism Compatible? No." In *Three Views on Eastern Orthodoxy and Evangelicalism*, edited by J. J. Stamoolis, 115–43. Counterpoints: Bible and Theology. Grand Rapids: Zondervan, 2004.

———. "Better Homes and Gardens." In *The Church in Emerging Culture: Five Perspectives*, edited by Leonard Sweet, 105–38. Grand Rapids: Zondervan, 2003.

———. *A Better Way: Rediscovering the Drama of God-centered Worship*. Grand Rapids: Baker, 2002.

———. "Beyond Culture Wars." *Modern Reformation*, May/June 1993 1–26.

———. *Beyond Culture Wars: Is America a Mission Field or Battlefield?* Chicago: Moody, 1994.

———. "Calvin and the Law-Gospel Hermeneutic." *Pro Ecclesia* 6, no. 1 (1997) 27–42.

———. *Calvin on the Christian Life: Glorifying and Enjoying God Forever*. Wheaton: Crossway, 2014.

———. "Calvin's Theology of Union with Christ and the Double Grace: Modern Reception." In *Calvin's Theology and Its Reception: Disputes, Developments, and New Possibilities*, edited by J. Todd Billings and I. John Hesselink, 72–94. Louisville: Westminster John Knox, 2012.

———. "Christ and Culture Once More." *The White Horse Inn*, December 17, 2011. https://www.whitehorseinn.org/2011/12/christ-and-culture-once-more/.

———. *The Christian Faith: A Systematic Theology for Pilgrims on the Way*. Grand Rapids: Zondervan, 2011.

———. *Christless Christianity: The Alternative Gospel of the American Church*. Grand Rapids: Baker, 2008.

———. "The Church." In *Christian Dogmatics: Reformed Theology for the Church Catholic*, edited by Michael Allen and Scott R. Swain, 311–38. Grand Rapids: Baker Academic, 2016.

———. "A Classical Calvinist View." In *Four Views on Eternal Security*, edited by J. Matthew Pinson, 21–42. Grand Rapids: Zondervan, 2002.

———. *Core Christianity: Finding Yourself in God's Story*. Grand Rapids: Zondervan, 2016.

———. *Covenant and Eschatology: The Divine Drama*. Louisville: Westminster John Knox, 2002.

———. "Covenant and Justification: Engaging N.T. Wright and John Piper." In *Justified: Essays on the Doctrine of Justification*, edited by Ryan Glomsrud and Michael S. Horton, 11–32. 2nd ed. Charleston: Createspace Independent, 2013.

———. *Covenant and Salvation: Union with Christ*. Louisville: Westminster John Knox, 2007.

———. "The Enduring Power of the Christian Story: Reformation Theology for a Secular Age." In *Our Secular Age: Ten Years of Reading and Applying Charles Taylor*, edited by Collin Hansen, 23–38. Deerfield: The Gospel Coalition, 2017.

———. *For Calvinism*. Grand Rapids: Zondervan, 2011.

———. "Gathered, Protected, and Preserved: The Church in the Heidelberg Catechism." In *A Faith Worth Teaching: The Heidelberg Catechism's Enduring Legacy*, edited by Jon D. Payne and Sebastian Heck, 127–48. Grand Rapids: Reformation Heritage, 2013.

———. *God of Promise: Introducing Covenant Theology*. Grand Rapids: Baker, 2006.

———. *The Gospel Commission: Recovering God's Strategy for Making Disciples*. Grand Rapids: Baker, 2011.

———. *The Gospel-Driven Life: Being Good News People in a Bad News World*. Grand Rapids: Baker, 2009.

———. "How the Kingdom Comes." *Christianity Today* 50, no. 1 (2006). https://www.christianitytoday.com/ct/2006/january/2.43.html.

———. "In Praise of the Profanity: A Theological Defense of the Secular." In *Evangelicals and Empire: Christian Alternatives to the Political Status Quo*, edited by Bruce Ellis Benson and Peter Goodwin Heltzel, 252–66. Grand Rapids: Brazos, 2008.

———. *In the Face of God: The Dangers and Delights of Spiritual Intimacy*. Nashville: Thomas Nelson, 1996.

———. *Justification*. 2 vols. New Studies in Dogmatics. Grand Rapids: Zondervan, 2018.

———. "Kingdom of God." In *Christian Dogmatics: Reformed Theology for the Church Catholic*, edited by Michael Allen and Scott R. Swain, 363–91. Grand Rapids: Baker Academic, 2016.

———. "The Law and the Gospel." https://www.hopereformedrcus.com/the-law-the-gospel/. Previously at http://www.whitehorseinn.org/free-articles/the-law-the-gospel-by-michael-horton.html.

———. *The Law of Perfect Freedom: Relating to God and Others through the Ten Commandments*. Chicago: Moody, 1993.

———. "'Let the Earth Bring Forth . . .': The Spirit and Human Agency in Sanctification." In *Sanctification: Explorations in Theology and Practice*, edited by Kelly M. Kapic, 127–49. Downers Grove: IVP Academic, 2014.

———. *Made in America: The Shaping of Modern American Evangelicalism*. Grand Rapids: Baker, 1991.

———. *Mission Accomplished: What Today's Christian Must Know about God and Salvation*. Nashville: Thomas Nelson, 1986.

———. "Obedience Is Better Than Sacrifice." In *The Law Is Not of Faith: Essays on Works and Grace in the Mosaic Covenant*, edited by Bryan D. Estelle et al., 315–36. Phillipsburg: P&R, 2009.

———. *Ordinary: Sustainable Faith in a Radical, Restless World*. Grand Rapids: Zondervan, 2014.

———. "Participation and Covenant." In *Radical Orthodoxy and the Reformed Tradition: Creation, Covenant, and Participation*, edited by James K. A. Smith and James Olthuis, 107–32. Grand Rapids: Baker Academic, 2005.

———. *People and Place: A Covenant Ecclesiology*. Louisville: Westminster John Knox, 2008.

———. *Pilgrim Theology: Core Doctrines for Christian Disciples*. Grand Rapids: Zondervan, 2011.

———. *A Place for Weakness: Preparing Yourself for Suffering*. Grand Rapids: Zondervan, 2010.

———. "Post-Reformation Reformed Anthropology." In *Personal Identity in Theological Perspective*, edited by Richard Lints et al., 45–69. Grand Rapids: Eerdmans, 2006.

———. *Putting Amazing Back into Grace*. 2nd ed. Grand Rapids: Baker, 2011.

———. *Rediscovering the Holy Spirit: God's Perfecting Presence in Creation, Redemption, and Everyday Life*. Grand Rapids: Zondervan, 2017.

———. "Reflections on Gospel Theology." In *Shaped by the Gospel: Doing Balanced, Gospel-centered Ministry in Your City*, edited by Timothy Keller, 75–90. Grand Rapids: Zondervan, 2016.

———. "The Subject of Contemporary Relevance." In *Power Religion: The Selling Out of the Evangelical Church?*, edited by Michael S. Horton, 327–53. Chicago: Moody, 1992.

———. *Thomas Goodwin and the Puritan Doctrine of Assurance: Continuity and Discontinuity in the Reformed Tradition, 1600-1680*. PhD thesis, Coventry University, 1998.

———. "The Time Between: Redefining the 'Secular' in Contemporary Debate." In *After Modernity: Secularity, Globalization, and the Re-enchantment of the World*, edited by James K. A. Smith, 45–65. Waco: Baylor University Press, 2008.

———. *Too Good to Be True: Finding Hope in a World of Hype*. Grand Rapids: Zondervan, 2006.

———. "Toward a Second Reformation." In *The Agony of Deceit: What Some TV Preachers Are Really Teaching*, edited by Michael S. Horton, 243–51. Chicago: Moody, 1990.

———. "Traditional Reformed." In *Justification: Five Views*, edited by James K. Beilby and Paul Rhodes Eddy, 83–111. Spectrum Multiview. Downers Grove: IVP Academic, 2011.

———. "Traditional View." In *Five Views on the Extent of the Atonement*, edited by Adam J. Johnson, 112–36. Grand Rapids: Zondervan, 2019.

———. "Transforming Culture with a Messiah Complex." *9 Marks Journal*, February 26, 2010. https://www.9marks.org/article/transforming-culture-messiah-complex/.

———. "The T.V. Gospel." In *The Agony of Deceit: What Some TV Preachers Are Really Teaching*, edited by Michael S. Horton, 123–50. Chicago: Moody, 1990.

———. "Union with Christ." In *Christ the Lord: The Reformation and Lordship Salvation*, edited by Michael S. Horton, 107–15. Grand Rapids: Baker, 1992.

———. *We Believe: Recovering the Essentials of the Apostles' Creed*. Nashville: Thomas Nelson, 1998.

———. *Where in the World Is the Church? A Christian View of Culture and Your Role in It*. Chicago: Moody, 1995.

———. "Which Covenant Theology?" In *Covenant, Justification, and Pastoral Ministry: Essays by the Faculty of Westminster Seminary California*, edited by R. Scott Clark, 197–227. Phillipsburg: P&R, 2007.

———. "Why Are We Celebrating? Taking Stock after Five Centuries." In *Reformation Theology: A Systematic Summary*, edited by Matthew Barrett, 13–36. Wheaton: Crossway, 2017.

———. "Yale Postliberalism: Back to the Bible?" In *A Confessing Theology for Postmodern Times*, edited by Michael S. Horton, 183–216. Wheaton: Crossway, 2000.

Houston, James M., and Jens Zimmermann, eds. *Sources of the Christian Self: A Cultural History of Christian Identity*. Grand Rapids: Eerdmans, 2018.

Howard, Thomas, and J. I. Packer. *Christianity: The True Humanism*. Vancouver: Regent College Publishing, 1984.

Hugenberger, Gordon P. *Marriage as a Covenant: A Study of Biblical Law and Ethics Governing Marriage Developed from the Perspective of Malachi*. Supplements to Vetus Testamentum 52. Leiden: Brill, 1994.

Hughes, Philip Edgcumbe. "The Christology of Hebrews." *Southwestern Journal of Theology* 28, no. 1 (1985) 19–27.

Huijgen, Arnold. "Allegory within the Bounds of the Letter: Towards a Pneumatological Reorientation of Protestant Interpretations of the Old Testament." In *The Spirit Is Moving: New Pathways in Pneumatology: Studies Presented to Professor Cornelis van der Kooi on the Occasion of His Retirement*, edited by Gijsbert van den Brink et al., 77–90. Leiden: Brill, 2019.

———. "Covenant Theology as Trinitarian Theology: A Discussion of the Contributions of Michael S. Horton, Scott W. Hahn, and N.T. Wright." In *Covenant: A Vital Element of Reformed Theology: Biblical, Historical and Systematic-Theological Perspectives*, edited by Hans Burger et al., 301–24. Leiden: Brill, 2022.

———. *Divine Accommodation in John Calvin's Theology: Analysis and Assessment*. Reformed Historical Theology 16. Göttingen: Vandenhoeck & Ruprecht, 2011.

———. *Lezen en laten lezen: gelovig omgaan met de Bijbel*. Utrecht: KokBoekencentrum, 2019.

———. *Waarom de wereld een hel nodig heeft*. Utrecht: KokBoekencentrum, 2023.

Huijgen, A., and A. Versluis. "'Our God is One': The Unity of YHWH and the Trinity in the Interplay between Biblical Exegesis and Systematic Theology." In *Reading and Listening: Meeting One God in Many Texts: Festschrift for Eric Peels on the Occasion of His 25th Jubilee as Professor of Old Testament Studies*, edited by J. Dekker and G. Kwakkel, 213–25. Amsterdamse Cahiers Supplement Series 16. Bergambacht: 2VM, 2018.

Huttinga, Wolter. *Participation and Communicability: Herman Bavinck and John Milbank on the Relation between God and Creation*. Amsterdam: Buijten & Schipperheijn Motief, 2014.

Hyde, Daniel R. *Welcome to a Reformed Church: A Guide for Pilgrims*. Sanford: Reformation Trust, 2012.

BIBLIOGRAPHY

Immink, F. Gerrit. *The Touch of the Sacred: The Practice, Theology, and Tradition of Christian Worship*. Translated by Reinder Bruinsma. Grand Rapids: Eerdmans, 2014.

Irenaeus. *Irenaeus Against Heresies*. In *The Ante-Nicene Fathers: Translations of the Writings of the Fathers Down to A.D. 325*. Edited by Alexander Roberts and James Donaldson. Vol. 1. Reprint, Peabody: Hendrickson, 1996.

Irons, Lee. "Redefining Merit: An Examination of Medieval Presuppositions in Covenant Theology." In *Creator, Redeemer, Consummator: A Festschrift for Meredith G. Kline*, edited by Howard Griffith and John R. Muether, 253–69. Eugene, OR: Wipf & Stock, 2007.

Jenson, Matt. *The Gravity of Sin: Augustine, Luther and Barth on* Homo Incurvatus in Se. London: T. & T. Clark, 2006.

Jenson, Robert W. *The Triune God*. Vol. 1 of *Systematic Theology*. Oxford: Oxford University Press, 2001.

Jeon, Jeong Koo. *Covenant Theology: John Murray's and Meredith G. Kline's Response to the Historical Development of Federal Theology in Reformed Thought*. Lanham: University Press of America, 1999.

Johnson, Jan. *When the Soul Listens: Finding Rest and Direction in Contemplative Prayer*. Carol Stream: NavPress, 2017.

Johnson, Marcus Peter. *One with Christ: An Evangelical Theology of Salvation*. Wheaton: Crossway, 2013.

Jones, Beth Felker. *Practicing Christian Doctrine: An Introduction to Thinking and Living Theologically*. Grand Rapids: Baker Academic, 2014.

Jones, Joe R. *A Grammar of Christian Faith: Systematic Explorations in Christian Life and Doctrine*. 2 vols. Lanham: Rowman & Littlefield, 2002.

Jones, L. Gregory. *Embodying Forgiveness: A Theological Analysis*. Grand Rapids: Eerdmans, 1995.

Jones, Mark. "Can Humans Merit before God? (1 of 2)." *reformation21*, April 21, 2015. https://www.reformation21.org/blogs/merit-could-adam-merit-anythin.php.

———. "Can Humans Merit before God? (2 of 2)." *reformation21*, April 21, 2015. https://www.reformation21.org/blogs/can-humans-merit-before-god-2.php.

———. "The (Gracious?) Covenant of Works (Again). *reformation21*, 13 September 13, 2014. https://www.reformation21.org/blogs/the-gracious-covenant-of-works-1.php.

———. "In What Sense? Review of Estelle, Bryan D., Fesko, J. V. and VanDrunen, David,, eds. *The Law Is Not of Faith: Essays on Works and Grace in the Mosaic Covenant*." *Ordained Servant Online* (April 2010). https://www.opc.org/os.html?article_id=199.

———. *Living for God: A Short Introduction to the Christian Faith*. Wheaton: Crossway, 2019.

———. "The 'Old' Covenant." In *Drawn into Controversie: Reformed Theological Diversity and Debates within Seventeenth-Century British Puritanism*, edited by Michael A. G. Haykin and Mark Jones, 183–203. Göttingen: Vandenhoek & Ruprecht, 2011.

Kalluveettil, Paul. *Declaration and Covenant: A Comprehensive Review of Covenant Formulae from the Old Testament and the Ancient Near East*. Rome: Biblical Institute Press, 1982.

Kamphuis, B. *Verborgen in God: Christologie na de hemelvaart*. Kampen: Theologische Universiteit, 2015.

Kamphuis, J. *Aantekeningen bij J.A. Heyns dogmatiek*. Kampen: van den Berg, 1982.
Kärkkäinen, Veli-Matti. *Christ and Reconciliation. A Constructive Christian Theology for the Pluralistic World* 1. Grand Rapids: Eerdmans, 2013.
———. *Creation and Humanity. A Constructive Christian Theology for the Pluralistic World* 3. Grand Rapids: Eerdmans, 2015.
———. *Hope and Community. A Constructive Christian Theology for the Pluralistic World* 5. Grand Rapids: Eerdmans, 2017.
———. *Spirit and Salvation. A Constructive Christian Theology for the Pluralistic World* 4. Grand Rapids: Eerdmans, 2016.
———. *The Trinity: Global Perspectives*. Louisville: Westminster John Knox, 2007.
———. *Trinity and Revelation. A Constructive Christian Theology for the Pluralistic World* 2. Grand Rapids: Eerdmans, 2014.
Karlberg, Mark W. *Covenant Theology in Reformed Perspective: Collected Essays and Book Reviews in Historical, Biblical, and Systematic Theology*. Eugene, OR: Wipf & Stock, 2000.
Kasper, Walter. *The God of Jesus Christ*. 2nd ed. London: T. & T. Clark, 2012.
Keller, Timothy. *Center Church: Doing Balanced, Gospel-centered Ministry in Your Church*. Grand Rapids: Zondervan, 2012.
———. *Preaching: Communicating Faith in an Age of Skepticism*. New York: Viking, 2015.
———. "Response to Michael Horton." In *Shaped by the Gospel: Doing Balanced, Gospel-centered Ministry in Your City*, 91–98. Grand Rapids: Zondervan.
Kelly, J. N. D. *The Epistles of Peter and of Jude*. London: A & C Black, 1969.
Kersten, G. H. *Reformed Dogmatics: A Systematic Treatment of Reformed Doctrine Explained for the Congregations*. Translated by Joel R. Beeke and Jan C. Weststrate. Vol. 1 Sioux Center: Netherlands Reformed Book and Publishing Committee, 1980.
Kevan, Ernest F. 1964. *The Grace of Law: A Study in Puritan Theology*. London: Carey Kingsgate, 1964.
Kidner, Derek. *Genesis: An Introduction and Commentary*. Tyndale Old Testament Commentary. Downers Grove: InterVarsity, 1967.
Kilner, John F. *Dignity and Destiny: Humanity in the Image of God*. Grand Rapids: Eerdmans, 2015.
Kim, Mark. *Michael Horton's Covenant Theology as a Defense of Reformation Theology in the Context of Current Discussions*. ThD thesis, Wycliffe College, 2013. https://tspace.library.utoronto.ca/bitstream/1807/35527/1/Kim_Mark_201305_ThD_thesis.pdf.
Kinzer, Mark S. *Jerusalem Crucified, Jerusalem Risen: The Resurrected Messiah, the Jewish People, and the Land of Promise*. Eugene, OR: Cascade, 2018.
———. *Post-missionary Messianic Judaism: Redefining Christian Engagement with the Jewish People*. Grand Rapids: Brazos, 2005.
Kistemaker, Simon J.. *Exposition of the First Epistle to the Corinthians*. New Testament Commentary. Grand Rapids: Baker, 1993.
Kittel, G. "δόξα in the LXX and Hellenistic Apocrypha." In *Theological Dictionary of the New Testament*. Vol. 2, edited by G. Kittel. Translated by G. W. Bromiley, 242–45. Grand Rapids: Eerdmans, 1964.
Kline, Meredith G. "Because It Had Not Rained." *Westminster Theological Journal* 20 (1958) 146–57.

———. "Covenant Theology Under Attack." *New Horizons*, February 1994. https://opc.org/new_horizons/Kline_cov_theo.html.

———. "Creation in the Image of the Glory-Spirit." *Westminster Theological Journal* 39 (1977) 250–72.

———. *Glory in Our Midst: A Biblical-theological Reading of Zechariah's Night Visions.* Eugene, OR: Wipf & Stock, 2001.

———. *Images of the Spirit.* Reprint, Eugene, OR: Wipf & Stock, 1999.

———. *Kingdom Prologue: Genesis Foundations for a Covenantal Worldview.* Eugene, OR: Wipf & Stock, 2006.

Klink, Edward W., III, and Darian R. Lockett. *Understanding Biblical Theology: A Comparison of Theory and Practice.* Grand Rapids: Zondervan, 2012.

Kloosterman, Nelson D. "A Biblical Case for Natural Law: A Response Essay." Ordained Servant Online, December 2007. https://opc.org/os.html?article_id=77.

Knoppers, Gary N. "Ancient Near Eastern Royal Grants and the Davidic Covenant: A Parallel?" *Journal of the American Oriental Society* 116 (1996) 670–97.

Koehler, Ludwig, and Walter Baumgartner. *The Hebrew and Aramaic Lexicon of the Old Testament.* Revised by W. Baumgartner and Johann Stamm. Translated by M. E. J. Richardson. Leiden: Brill, 2001.

Köstenberger, Andreas J. "The Cosmic Drama and the Seed of the Serpent: An Exploration of the Connection between Gen. 3:15 and Johannine Theology." In *The Seed of Promise: The Suffering and Glory of the Messiah: Essays in Honor of T. Desmond Alexander*, edited by Paul R. Williamson and Rita F. Cefalu, 264–84. Wilmore: GlossaHouse, 2020.

———. *John.* Baker Exegetical Commentary on the New Testament. Grand Rapids: Baker Academic, 2004.

Köstenberger, Andreas J., and Scott R. Swain. *Father, Son, and Spirit: The Trinity and John's Gospel.* New Studies in Biblical Theology 24. Downers Grove: InterVarsity, 2008.

Kuhrt, Stephen. *Tom Wright for Everyone: Putting the Theology of N. T. Wright into Practice in the Local Church.* London: SPCK, 2011.

Kutsch. E. "Berit." In *Theological Lexicon of the Old Testament*, edited by Ernst Jenni and Claus Westermann, 256–65. Peabody: Hendrickson, 1997.

Kwakkel, G. "The Conditional Dynastic Promise in 1 Kings 2,4." In *Reading and Listening: Meeting One God in Many Texts. Festschrift for Eric Peels on the Occasion of his 25th Jubilee as Professor of Old Testament Studies*, edited by J. Dekker and G. Kwakkel, 79–89. Bergambacht: 2VM, 2018.

———. "Het eerste verbondswoord." *Nader Bekeken* 26, no. 6 (2019) 175–76.

———. *De gerechtigheid van Abram: exegese van Genesis 15:6.* Barneveld: De Vuurbaak, 1996.

———. "Kun je wel zeggen: 'Dit is wat de Bijbel leert'?" *Nederlands Dagblad*, February 11, 2020. https://www.nd.nl/geloof/geloof/953654/kun-je-wel-zeggen-dit-is-wat-de-bijbel-leert-.

———. "The Sinaitic Covenant in the Narrative of the Book of Exodus." In *Living Waters from Ancient Springs: Essays in Honor of Cornelis Van Dam*, edited by J. van Vliet, 27–40. Eugene, OR: Pickwick, 2014.

———. *Uitgekozen: de bijbel over vragen rond de uitverkiezing.* Barneveld: De Vuurbaak, 1990.

———. "Verplichting of relatie: verbonden in Genesis. Henk de Jong en zijn visie op het verbond." In *Verrassend vertrouwd: een halve eeuw verkondiging en theologie van Henk de Jong*, edited by J. Bouma et al., 117–30. Franeker: Van Wijnen, 2009.

Ladd, George Eldon. *The Presence of the Future: The Eschatology of Biblical Realism*. Grand Rapids: Eerdmans, 1974.

Lane, Tony. "The Wrath of God as an Aspect of the Love of God." In *Nothing Greater, Nothing Better: Theological Essays on the Love of God*, edited by Kevin J. Vanhoozer, 138–67. Grand Rapids: Eerdmans, 2001.

Lash, Nicholas. "Considering the Trinity. "*Modern Theology* 2 (1986) 183–96.

———. *Theology on the Way to Emmaus*. London: SCM, 2005.

Latzel, T. *Theologische grundzüge des Heidelberger Katechismus: Eine fundamentaltheologische Untersuchung seines Ansatzes zur Glabuenskommunikation*. Marburg: N.G. Elwert Verlag. 2004.

Lawrence, Brother. *The Practice of the Presence of God*. Translated by John J. Delaney. New York: Doubleday, 1977.

Leder, Arie C. "Divine Presence, Then the Covenants: An Essay on Narrative and Theological Precedence (Part Two). *Nederduitse Gereformeerde Teologiese Tydskrif* 54 (2013) 207–20.

———. "Divine Presence, Then the Covenants: An Essay on Narrative and Theological Precedence (Part Three). *Nederduitse Gereformeerde Teologiese Tydskrif* 55 (2014) 685–99.

———. "Presence, Then the Covenants: An Essay on Narrative and Theological Precedence (Part One)." *Nederduitse Gereformeerde Teologiese Tydskrif* 53 (2012) 179–93.

———. *Waiting for the Land: The Storyline of the Pentateuch*. Phillipsburg: P&R, 2010.

Lee, Amhi. *Preaching God's Drama: A Biblical-theological Approach*. Grand Rapids: Baker Academic, 2019.

Lehrer, Steve. *New Covenant Theology: Questions Answered*. Steve Lehrer, 2006.

Leithart, Peter J. "Adam the Catholic? Faith and Life in the Adamic Covenant." In *A Faith That Is Never Alone: A Response to Westminster Seminary California*, edited by P. Andrew Sandlin, 163–91. La Grange: Kerygma, 2007.

———. *Against Christianity*. Moscow: Canon, 2003

———. "Did Plato Read Moses? Middle Grace and Moral Consensus." Biblical Horizons Occasional Paper 23. Niceville: Biblical Horizons, 1995.

———. *The Theopolitan Vision*. West Monroe: Athanasius, 2019.

Letham, Robert. *The Holy Trinity: In Scripture, History, and Worship*. Phillipsburg: P&R, 2004.

———. "'Not a Covenant of Works in Disguise' (Herman Bavinck): The Place of the Mosaic Covenant in Redemptive History." *Mid-America Journal of Theology* 24 (2013) 685–99.

———. *Systematic Theology*. Wheaton: Crossway, 2019.

———. *Union with Christ: In Scripture, History, and Theology*. Phillipsburg: P&R, 2011.

Levering, Matthew. *Participatory Biblical Exegesis: A Theology of Biblical Interpretation*. Notre Dame: University of Notre Dame Press, 2008.

Lewis, C. S. "Bluspels and Flalansferes: A Semantic Nightmare." In *Selected Literary Essays*, edited by Walter Hooper, 251–65. Cambridge: Cambridge University Press, 1969.

BIBLIOGRAPHY

Lewis, Gordon R., and Bruce A. Demarest. *Integrative Theology: Historical, Biblical, Systematic, Apologetic, Practical.* 3 vols in one. Grand Rapids: Zondervan, 1996.

Lillback, Peter A. *The Binding of God: Calvin's Role in the Development of Covenant Theology.* Grand Rapids: Baker, 2001.

Lindbeck, George A. "Atonement and the Hermeneutics of Intratextual Social Embodiment." In *The Nature of Confession*, edited by Timothy R. Phillips and Dennis L. Okholm, 221–40. Downers Grove: InterVarsity, 1996.

———. *The Nature of Doctrine: Religion and Theology in a Post-liberal Age.* Louisville: Westminster John Knox, 1984.

———. "Postcritical Canonical Interpretation: Three Modes of Retrieval." In *Theological Exegesis: Essays in Honor of Brevard S. Childs*, edited by Christopher Seitz and Kathryn Green-McCreight, 26–51. Grand Rapids: Eerdmans, 1998.

———. "A Question of Compatibility: A Lutheran Reflects on Trent." In *Justification by Faith*, edited by H. George Anderson et al., 230–40. Minneapolis: Augsburg, 1985.

Lister, J. Ryan. *The Presence of God: Its Place in the Storyline of Scripture and the Story of Our Lives.* Wheaton: Crossway, 2015.

Littlejohn, W. Bradford. *The Two Kingdoms: A Guide for the Perplexed.* Davenant Guides 2. Burford: Davenant, 2017.

Longman, Tremper W., III. "The Glory of God in the Old Testament." In *The Glory of God*, edited by Christopher W. Morgan and Robert A. Peterson, 47–78. Theology in Community. Wheaton: Crossway, 2010.

Loonstra, B. *Verkiezing, verzoening, verbond: beschrijving en beoordeling van de leer van het pactum salutis in de gereformeerde theologie.* 's-Gravenhage: Boekencentrum, 1990.

Luther, Martin. *Commentary on the Epistle to the Galatians.* Translated by Theodore Graebner. Scotts Valley: Amazon Digital Services, 2018.

———. *Luther's Works.* Vol. 25. Edited by Hilton C. Oswald. St. Louis: Concordia, 1972.

———. *Martin Luther's Basic Theological Writings.* 2nd ed. Minneapolis: Fortress, 2005.

Lynch, Michael J. *John Davenant's Hypothetical Universalism: A Defense of Catholic and Reformed Orthodoxy.* Oxford Studies in Historical Theology. Oxford: Oxford University Press, 2021.

Macaskill, Grant. *Living in Union with Christ: Paul's Gospel and Christian Moral Identity.* Grand Rapids: Baker Academic, 2019.

———. *Union with Christ in the New Testament.* Oxford: Oxford University Press, 2013.

Macchia, Frank D. *Jesus the Spirit Baptizer: Christology in Light of Pentecost.* Grand Rapids: Eerdmans, 2018.

MacIntyre, Alasdair. *After Virtue: A Study in Moral Theory.* 3rd ed. Notre Dame: University of Notre Dame, 2007.

Macleod, Donald. *Christ Crucified: Understanding the Atonement.* Downers Grove: InterVarsity, 2014.

———. "Covenant Theology." In *The Dictionary of Scottish Church History and Theology*, edited by Nigel M. de S. Cameron et al., 214–18. Downers Grove: InterVarsity, 1993.

———. *A Faith to Live By: Understanding Christian Doctrine.* Fearn: Mentor, 2002.

Magee, Bryan. *The Great Philosophers: An Introduction to Western Philosophy.* Oxford: Oxford University Press, 1987.

Martin, Ralph P. *2 Corinthians.* Word Biblical Commentary 40. Dallas: Word, 1986.

Mathews, Kenneth A. *Genesis 1:1–11:26.* New American Commentary 1A. Nashville: Broadman & Holman, 1996.

McCarthy, Dennis J. *Treaty and Covenant: A Study in Form in the Ancient Oriental Documents and in the Old Testament.* New ed. Rome. Biblical Institute Press, 1981.

McComiskey, Thomas E. *The Covenants of Promise: A Theology of the Old Testament Covenants.* Grand Rapids: Baker, 1985.

McConville, J. Gordon. "Berit." In *New International Dictionary of Old Testament Theology and Exegesis,* edited by Willem A. VanGemeren, vol. 1, 747–55. Carlisle: Paternoster, 1997.

McCormack, Bruce L. "What's at Stake in Current Debates over Justification? The Crisis of Protestantism in the West." In *Justification: What's at Stake in the Current Debates,* edited by Mark Husbands and Daniel J. Treier, 81–117. Downers Grove: InterVarsity, 2004.

McGowan, A. T. B. *Adam, Christ and Covenant: Exploring Headship Theology.* London: Apollos, 2016.

———. "In Defence of 'Headship Theology.'" In *The God of Covenant: Biblical, Theological and Contemporary Perspectives,* edited by Jamie A. Grant and Alistair I. Wilson, 178–99. Nottingham: Apollos, 2005.

———. "Justification and the *Ordo Salutis.*" In *Justification in Perspective: Historical Developments and Contemporary Challenges,* edited by Bruce L. McCormack, 147–63. Grand Rapids: Baker Academic, 2006.

McGrath, Alister. *Christian Theology: An Introduction.* 5th ed. Hoboken: Wiley-Blackwell, 2011.

———. *The Genesis of Doctrine: A Study in the Foundation of Doctrinal Criticism.* Grand Rapids: Eerdmans, 1990.

———. *Iustitia Dei.* Cambridge: Cambridge University Press, 2005.

———. *Mere Apologetics: How to Help Seekers and Skeptics Find Faith.* Grand Rapids: Baker, 2012.

———. *The Territories of Human Reason: Science and Theology in an Age of Multiple Rationalities.* Oxford: Oxford University Press, 2019.

———. *Why God Won't Go Away: Is the New Atheism Running on Empty?* Nashville: Thomas Nelson, 2011.

McGrath, Alister, and Joanna Collicut McGrath. *The Dawkins Delusion? Atheist Fundamentalism and the Denial of the Divine.* Downers Grove: IVP, 2010.

McGraw, Ryan M. "The Threats of the Gospel: John Owen on What the Law/Gospel Distinction Is Not." *Calvin Theological Journal* 51 (2016) 79–111.

McKenzie, Steven L. *Covenant.* Understanding Biblical Themes. St. Louis: Chalice, 2000.

McKnight, Scot. *A Community Called Atonement.* Living Theology. Nashville: Abingdon, 2007.

McKnight, Scot, and Laura Barringer. *A Church Called Tov: Forming a Goodness Culture That Resists Abuses of Power and Promotes Healing.* Carol Stream: Tyndale, 2020.

McWilliams, David B. "The Covenant Theology of the Westminster Confession of Faith and Recent Criticism." *Westminster Theological Journal* 53 (1991) 109–24.

Melanchthon, Philip. *Commonplaces: Loci Communes 1521.* Translated by Christian Press. St. Louis: Concordia, 2014.

Michel, Jen Pollock. *A Habit Called Faith: 40 Days in the Bible to Find and Follow Jesus.* Grand Rapids: Baker, 2021.

Michelson, Jared. "Covenantal History and Participatory Metaphysics: Formulating a Reformed Response to the Charge of Legal Fiction." *Scottish Journal of Theology* 71 (2018) 391–410.

Middleton, J. Richard. *The Liberating Image: The Imago Dei in Genesis One.* Grand Rapids: Brazos, 2005.

Millar, J. Gary. *Changed into His Likeness: A Biblical Theology of Personal Transformation.* New Studies in Biblical Theology 55. Downers Grove: IVP Academic, 2021.

Millard, Kent. *The Gratitude Path: Leading Your Church to Generosity.* Nashville: Abingdon, 2015.

Miller, Timothy. "The Debate over the *Ordo Salutis* in American Reformed Theology." *Detroit Baptist Theological Journal* 18 (2013) 44–66.

Moes, Dick. *Cultivating a God-Generated Life: Being Embedded with Christ in the Father through the Advance Installment of the Holy Spirit.* http://www.godgeneratedlife.com/.

Moltmann, Jürgen. *God in Creation: A New Theology of Creation and the Spirit of God.* Translated by Margaret Kohl. San Francisco: Harper & Row, 1985.

Moo, Douglas J. *The Letter to the Romans.* 2nd ed. New International Commentary on the New Testament. Grand Rapids: Eerdmans, 2018.

Moo, Douglas J., and Jonathan A. Moo. *Creation Care: A Biblical Theology of the Natural World.* Biblical Theology for Life. Grand Rapids: Zondervan, 2018.

Moore, Jonathan D. "The Extent of the Atonement: English Hypothetical Universalism Versus Particular Redemption." In *Drawn into Controversie: Reformed Theological Diversity and Debates within Seventeenth-Century British Puritanism,* edited by Michael A. G. Haykin and Mark Jones, 124–61. Göttingen: Vandenhoek & Ruprecht, 2011.

Moore-Keish, Martha. "Sacraments." In *The Oxford Handbook of Reformed Theology,* edited by Michael Allen and Scott R. Swain, 528–45. Oxford: Oxford University Press, 2020.

Morris, Leon. *The Gospel of John.* New International Commentary on the New Testament. Grand Rapids: Eerdmans, 1971.

———. *Revelation.* 2nd ed. Tyndale New Testament Commentaries. Grand Rapids: Eerdmans, 1987.

Mosser, Carl. "The Greatest Possible Blessing: Calvin and Deification." *Scottish Journal of Theology* 55 (2002) 36–57.

Muether, John R. "An Annotated Bibliography of Reformed Reflection on the Covenant." In *Covenant Theology: Biblical, Theological, and Historical Perspectives,* edited by Guy Prentiss Waters et al., 599–622. Wheaton: Crossway, 2020.

Muller, Richard A. *Calvin and the Reformed Tradition: On the Work of Christ and the Order of Salvation.* Grand Rapids: Baker, 2012.

———. "Diversity in the Reformed Tradition: A Historiographical Introduction." In *Drawn into Controversie: Reformed Theological Diversity and Debates within Seventeenth-Century British Puritanism,* edited by Michael A. G. Haykin and Mark Jones, 11–30. Göttingen: Vandenhoek & Ruprecht, 2011.

———. "Divine Covenants, Absolute and Conditional: John Cameron and the Early Orthodox Developments of Reformed Covenant Theology." *Mid-America Journal of Theology* 17 (2006) 11–56.

———. "Toward the *Pactum Salutis*: Locating the Origins of a Concept." *Mid-America Journal of Theology* 18 (2007) 11–65.

———. *The Triunity of God*. Vol. 4 of *Post-Reformation Reformed Dogmatics: The Rise and Development of Reformed Orthodoxy, ca. 1520 to 1725*. 2nd ed. Grand Rapids: Baker Academic, 2003.

Murphy, Nancey. "Epistemology." In *Dictionary for Theological Interpretation of the Bible*, edited by Kevin J. Vanhoozer, 191–94. Grand Rapids: Baker Academic, 2005.

Murray, John. "The Adamic Administration." In *Collected Writings of John Murray*, vol. 2, 47–59. Edinburgh: Banner of Truth, 1977.

———. *The Epistle to the Romans*. New International Commentary on the New Testament. Grand Rapids: Eerdmans, 1968.

———. "Systematic Theology." In *Collected Writings of John Murray*, vol. 4, 1–21. Edinburgh: Banner of Truth, 1982.

Newell, Roger. "Participation and Atonement." In *Christ in Our Place: The Humanity of God in Christ for the Reconciliation of the World*, edited by Trevor A. Hart and Daniel Thimell, 92–101. Exeter: Paternoster, 1989.

Nichols, Aiden. *A Key to Balthasar: Hans Urs von Balthasar on Beauty, Goodness, and Truth*. Grand Rapids: Baker Academic, 2011.

———. *No Bloodless Myth: A Guide through Balthasar's Dramatics*. Washington: Catholic University of America Press, 2000.

———. *The Word Has Been Abroad: A Guide Through Balthasar's Aesthetics*. Washington: Catholic University of America Press, 1998.

Nicholson, Ernest W. *God and His People: Covenant and Theology in the Old Testament*. Oxford: Oxford University Press, 1986.

Noble, Alan. *Disruptive Witness: Speaking Truth in a Disruptive Age*. Downers Grove: IVP, 2018.

Noort, E. "Overlijden en overleven: de verbondsvoorstellingen van de deuteronomistische scholen." In *Sleutelen aan het verbond*, edited by E. Noort et al, 7–32. Boxtel: KBS/Tabor, 1989.

Nouwen, Henri J. M. *The Only Necessary Thing: Living a Prayerful Life*. Edited by Wendy Wilson Greer. New York: Crossroad, 1999.

———. *The Selfless Way of Christ: Downward Mobility and the Spiritual Life*. Maryknoll: Orbis, 2012.

O'Donnell, Laurence. "Not Subtle Enough: An Assessment of Modern Scholarship on Herman Bavinck's Reformulation of the *Pactum Salutis* Contra 'Scholastic Subtlety.'" *Mid-America Journal of Theology* 22 (2011) 89–106.

O'Donovan, Oliver. *The Desire of the Nations: Rediscovering the Roots of Political Theory*. Cambridge: Cambridge University Press, 1996.

———. *Finding and Seeking*. Vol. 2 of *Ethics as Theology*. Grand Rapids: Eerdmans, 2014.

———. *On the Thirty-Nine Articles: A Conversation with Tudor Christianity*. Exeter: Paternoster, 1986.

———. *Resurrection and Moral Order: An Outline for Evangelical Ethics*. 2nd ed. Grand Rapids: Eerdmans, 1994.

———. *Self, World and Time*. Vol. 1 of *Ethics as Theology*. Grand Rapids: Eerdmans, 2013.

Oldhoff, M. *Kijk op de ziel*. Utrecht: KokBoekencentrum, 2020.

Oliphint, K. Scott. *God with Us: Divine Condescension and the Attributes of God*. Wheaton: Crossway, 2011.

Ordway, Holly. *Apologetics and the Christian Imagination: An Integrated Approach to Defending the Faith*. Steubenville: Emmaus Road, 2017.

Origen. *De principiis*. In *The Ante-Nicene Fathers: Translations of the Writings of the Fathers Down to A.D. 325*, edited by Alexander Roberts and James Donaldson, vol. 4, 221–384. Rept., Edinburgh: T. & T. Clark, 1994.

Orthodox Presbyterian Church. Report of the Committee to Study Republication Presented to the Eighty-Third (2016) General Assembly of the Orthodox Presbyterian Church. https://opc.org/GA/republication.html.

Osborne, Grant R. *The Hermeneutical Spiral: A Comprehensive Introduction to Biblical Interpretation*. 2nd ed. Downers Grove: InterVarsity, 2006.

Osterhaven, M. E. "Covenant Theology." In *Evangelical Dictionary of Theology*, edited by Walter A. Elwell, 279–80. Grand Rapids: Baker, 1984.

Ouweneel, Willem. *The World Is Christ's: A Critique of Two Kingdoms Theology*. Toronto: Ezra, 2017.

Overstreet, Jeffrey. "Cultivating the Imagination: A Conversation with Eugene Peterson." *SPU Stories*, October 22, 2018. https://spu.edu/stories/articles/cultivating-imagination-conversation-with-eugene-peterson/.

Paas, S. *Vrede op aarde: Over heil en redding in deze tijd*. Utrecht: KokBoekencentrum, 2023.

Packer, J. I. *Concise Theology: A Guide to Historic Christian Beliefs*. Wheaton: Tyndale, 1993.

———. *Knowing God*. Downers Grove: InterVarsity, 1973.

Paddison, Angus. "The History and Reemergence of Theological Interpretation." In *A Manifesto for Theological Interpretation*, edited by Craig G. Bartholomew and Heath A. Thomas, 27–47. Grand Rapids: Baker Academic, 2016.

Pannenberg, Wolfhart. *Systematic Theology*. Vol. 1. Translated by Geoffrey W. Bromiley. Grand Rapids: Eerdmans, 1991.

Parsons, Burk. "An Interview with Dr. Michael Horton." November 30, 2009. https://www.ligonier.org/blog/interview-dr-michael-horton/.

Pauw, Amy Plantinga. "Church." In *The Oxford Handbook of Reformed Theology*, edited by Michael Allen and Scott R. Swain, 514–27. Oxford: Oxford University Press, 2020.

Peels, H. G. L. *Wie is als gij? schaduwkanten van het oudtestamentische Godsbeeld*. Zoetermeer: Boekencentrum, 2007.

Pelikan, Jaroslav. *The Emergency of the Catholic Tradition (100–600)*. Vol. 1 of *The Christian Tradition: A History of the Development of Doctrine*. Chicago: University of Chicago Press, 1975.

———. *The Growth of Medieval Theology (600–1300)*. Vol. 3 of *The Christian Tradition: A History of the Development of Doctrine*. Chicago: University of Chicago Press, 1978.

Perkins, Larry. "The Dance Is Not PERICHŌRĒSIS." http://moments.nbseminary.com/archives/182-the-dance-is-not-perichoresis/.

Perrin, Nicholas. *The Kingdom of God: A Biblical Theology*. Biblical Theology for Life. Grand Rapids: Zondervan, 2019.

Peterson, Eugene H. *Christ Plays in Ten Thousand Places*. Grand Rapids: Eerdmans, 2005.

———. *Eat This Book: A Conversation in the Art of Spiritual Reading*. Grand Rapids: Eerdmans, 2006.

———. *Practice Resurrection: A Conversation about Growing Up in Christ*. Grand Rapids: Eerdmans, 2010.

Peterson, Jonathan. "Ordinary Spiritual Growth: An Interview with Michael Horton." https://www.biblegateway.com/blog/2014/10/ordinary-spiritual-growth-an-interview-with-michael-horton.

Plantinga, Alvin. *Knowledge and Christian Belief*. Grand Rapids: Eerdmans, 2015.

———. "Reason and Belief in God." In *Faith and Rationality: Reason and Belief in God*, edited by Alvin Plantinga and Nicholas Wolterstorff, 16–93. Notre Dame: University of Notre Dame, 1983.

———. *Warranted Christian Belief*. Oxford: Oxford University Press, 2000.

Pleizier, T. *Religious Involvement in Hearing Sermons*. Delft: Eburon Academic, 2010.

Plummer, Robert. *40 Questions about Interpreting the Bible*. Grand Rapids: Kregel Academic, 2010.

Pohl, Christine D. *Living into Community: Cultivating Practices That Sustain Us*. Grand Rapids: Eerdmans, 2011.

———. *Making Room: Recovering Hospitality as a Christian Tradition*. Grand Rapids: Eerdmans, 1999.

Poythress, Vern S. *The Lordship of Christ: Serving Our Savior All the Time, in All of Life, with All of Our Hearts*. Wheaton: Crossway, 2016.

Pratt, Richard, Jr. "God of Covenant." *Reformed Perspectives* 10 (2008) 1–23. https://thirdmill.org/newfiles/ric_pratt/ric_pratt.Covenant.ab_david.html.

Provan, Iain. *The Reformation and the Right Reading of Scripture*. Waco: Baylor University Press, 2017.

Rad, Gerhard von. "כָּבוֹד in the OT." In *Theological Dictionary of the New Testament*, vol. 2, edited by G. Kittel, translated by Geoffrey W. Bromiley, 238–42. Grand Rapids: Eerdmans, 1964.

Rae, Murray. "Theological Interpretation and Historical Criticism." In *A Manifesto for Theological Interpretation*, edited by Craig G. Bartholomew and Heath A. Thomas, 94–109 Grand Rapids: Baker Academic, 2016.

Rahner, Karl. *The Trinity*. Translated by Joseph Donceel. New York: Crossroad, 1997.

Redd, John Scott. "The Abrahamic Covenant." In *Covenant Theology: Biblical, Theological, and Historical Perspectives*, edited by Guy Prentiss Waters et al., 133–47. Wheaton: Crossway, 2020.

Reeling Brouwer, Rinse H. "Adam als koopman—over het 'verbond' in de theologie van Johannes Coccejus en het 'contract' in het vroegkapitalism." In *Debharim: opstellen aangeboden aan Frans Breukelman ter gelegenenheid van zijn zevenstigste verjaardag*, edited by N. T. Bakker et al., 161–73. Kampen: Kok, 1986.

———. *Grondvormen van theologische systematiek*. Vught: Skandalon, 2009.

———. "Karl Barth's Encounter with the Federal Theology of Johannes Coccejus: Prejudices, Criticisms, Outcomes and Open Questions." *Zeitschrift für Dialektische Theologie* 4 (2010) 160–208.

Reeves, Michael. *Rejoice and Tremble: The Surprising Good News of the Fear of the Lord*. Wheaton: Crossway, 2021.

Reid, J. Nicholas. "The Mosaic Covenant." In *Covenant Theology: Biblical, Theological, and Historical Perspectives*, edited by Guy Prentiss Waters et al., 149–71. Wheaton: Crossway, 2020.

Renihan, Samuel D. *From Shadow to Substance: The Federal Theology of the English Particular Baptists (1642–1704)*. Oxford: Center for Baptist History and Heritage, 2018.

Rhodes, Jonty. *Covenants Made Simple: Understanding God's Unfolding Promises to His People*. Phillipsburg: P&R, 2014.

Richard, Guy M. "The Covenant of Redemption." In *Covenant Theology: Biblical, Theological, and Historical Perspectives*, edited by Guy Prentiss Waters et al., 43–62. Wheaton: Crossway, 2020.

Ricoeur, Paul. *The Conflict of Interpretations: Essays in Hermeneutics*. Edited by Don Ihde. Evanston: Northwestern University Press, 2007.

———. *Hermeneutics and the Human Sciences: Essays on Language, Action and Interpretation*. Translated by John B. Thompson. Cambridge: Cambridge University Press, 19981.

———. *Interpretation Theory: Discourse and the Surplus of Meaning*. Fort Worth: Texas Christian University Press, 1977.

———. "Narrative Identity." In *On Paul Ricoeur: Narrative and Interpretation*, edited by David Wood, 188–99. London: Routledge, 1991.

———. *Oneself as Another*. Translated by Kathleen Blamey. Chicago: University of Chicago Press, 1992.e

———. *Time and Narrative*. Translated by Kathleen McLaughlin and David Pallauer. Vol. 1. Chicago: University of Chicago Press, 1984.

Ridderbos, Herman. *The Coming of the Kingdom*. Phillipsburg: Presbyterian and Reformed, 1962.

———. *Paul: An Outline of His Theology*. Translated by John Richard de Witt. Grand Rapids: Eerdmans, 1975.

Rietkerk, W. "In het heil voor de mens is er geen vrede zonder redding. Maar versmal dat nooit tot hemel en hel." *Nederlands Dagblad*, 23 October 2023.

Rishmawy, Derek. "Millennial Belief in the Super-Nova." In *Our Secular Age: Ten Years of Reading and Applying Charles Taylor*, edited by Collin Hansen, 49–62. Deerfield: The Gospel Coalition, 2010.

Robertson, O. Palmer. *The Christ of the Covenants*. Phillipsburg: Presbyterian and Reformed, 1980.

Root, Andrew. *The Congregation in a Secular Age: Keeping Sacred Time Against the Speed of Modern Life*. Ministry in a Secular Age 3. Grand Rapids: Baker Academic, 2021.

———. *Faith Formation in a Secular Age: Responding to the Church's Obsession with Youthfulness*. Grand Rapids: Baker Academic, 2017.

———. *The Relational Pastor: Sharing in Christ by Sharing Ourselves*. Downers Grove: IVP, 2013.

Rosa, Hartmut. *Resonance: A Sociology of Our Relationship to the World*. Translated by James C. Wagner. Medford: Polity, 2019.

Rose, Wolter. *Hij is goed, hij is koning: de profeet Zacharia, de Hebreeuwse taal, het evangelie en God's glorie*. Franeker: Van Wijnen 2020.

Ross, Allen P. *Creation and blessing.* Grand Rapids: Baker, 1988.
Ruijter, C. J. de. *De hemel op aarde: liturgie voor kerkgangers.* Utrecht: KokBoekencentrum, 2021.
———. *Horen naar de stem van God: theologie en methode van de preek.* Zoetermeer: Boekencemtrum, 2013.
Sailhamer, John H. *The Pentateuch as Narrative: A Biblical-Theological Commentary.* Grand Rapids: Zondervan, 1992.
Saliers, Don E. "Liturgy and Ethics: Some New Beginnings." In *Liturgy and the Moral Self: Humanity at Full Stretch Before God*, edited by E. Byron Anderson and Bruce T. Morrill, 15–35. Collegeville: Liturgical, 1998.
———. *Worship as Theology: Foretaste of Glory Divine.* Nashville: Abingdon, 1994.
Sanders, Fred. *The Deep Things of God: How the Trinity Changes Everything.* 2nd ed. Wheaton: Crossway, 2017.
———. *The Image of the Immanent Trinity: Rahner's Rule and the Theological Interpretation of Scripture.* New York: Peter Lang, 2005.
Sandlin, P. Andrew. "The Gospel of Law and the Law of Gospel: An Assessment of the Antithetical Gospel-Law Paradigm." In *A Faith That Is Never Alone: A Response to Westminster Seminary California*, edited by P. Andrew Sandlin, 193–247. La Grange: Kerygma, 2007.
Santoso, Audy. *Union with God: An Assessment of Deification (Theosis) in the Theologies of Robert Jenson and John Calvin.* Reformed Historical Theology 69. Göttingen: Vandenhoeck and Ruprecht, 2021.
Sarot, Marcel. "Christian Fundamentalism as a Reaction to the Enlightenment." In *Orthodoxy, Liberalism, and Adaptation: Essays on Ways of Worldmaking in Times of Change from Biblical, Historical and Systematic Perspectives*, edited by Bob Becking, 249–67. Leiden: Brill, 2011.
Satterlee, Craig A. *Ambrose of Milan's Method of Mystagogical Preaching.* Collegeville: Liturgical, 2002.
Sayers, Dorothy L. *Creed or Chaos: Why Christians Must Choose Either Dogma or Disaster (Or, Why It Really Does Matter What You Believe).* Manchester: Sophia Institute, 1995.
———. *Letters to a Diminished Church: Passionate Arguments for the Relevance of Christian Doctrine.* Nashville: Thomas Nelson, 2004.
Scheuers, Timothy R. "Dual Citizenship, Dual Ethic? Evaluating the Two Kingdoms Perspective on the Christian in Culture." In *Kingdoms Apart: Engaging the Two Kingdoms Perspective*, edited by Ryan McIlhenny, 125–55. Phillipsburg: P&R, 2012.
Schilder, K. *Heaven: What Is It?* Translated by Marion Schooland. Grand Rapids: Eerdmans, 1950.
———. *Heidelbergse Catechismus: Zondag 1–4.* Goes: Oosterbaan & Le Cointre, 1947.
———. *Looze kalk: een wederwoord over de (zedelijke) crisis in de "Gereformeerde Kerken in Nederland".* Groningen: de Jager, 1946.
———. "The Main Points of the Doctrine of the Covenant." Translated by T. van Laar. http://spindleworks.com/library/schilder/covenant.htm.
———. *Wat is de hel?* 3rd ed. Kampen: Kok, 1932.
———. *Wat is de hemel?* Kampen: Kok, 1935.
Schmemann, Alexander. *For the Life of the World.* Yonkers: St Vladimir's Seminary Press, 2018.

Schreiner, Thomas R. *Covenant and God's Purpose for the World.* Short Studies in Biblical Theology. Wheaton: Crossway, 2017.

———. *New Testament Theology: Magnifying God in Christ.* Grand Rapids: Baker, 2008.

Schweitzer, William M. *God Is a Communicative Being: Divine Communicativeness and Harmony in the Theology of Jonathan Edwards.* T. & T. Clark Studies in Systematic Theology 14. London: T. & T. Clark International, 2012.

Searle, Alison. *The Eyes of Your Heart: Literary and Theological Trajectories of Imagining Biblically.* Paternoster Theological Monographs. Eugene, OR: Wipf & Stock, 2008.

Searle, John R. *Expression and Meaning: Studies in the Theory of Speech Acts.* Cambridge: Cambridge University Press, 1979.

———. *Speech Acts: An Essay in the Philosophy of Language.* Cambridge: Cambridge University Press, 1969.

———. "A Taxonomy of Illocutionary Acts." In *Language, Mind, and Knowledge,* edited by Keith Gunderson, 344–69. Minnesota Studies in the Philosophy of Science 7. Minneapolis: University of Minnesota Press, 1975.

Seifrid, Mark A. *Christ, Our Righteousness: Paul's Theology of Justification.* New Studies in Biblical Theology 9. Downers Grove: Apollos/InterVarsity, 2000.

Seitz, Christopher R. *The Character of Christian Scripture: The Significance of a Two-Testament Bible.* Studies in Theological Interpretation. Grand Rapids: Baker Academic, 2011.

Shepherd, Norman. *The Call of Grace: How Covenant Illuminates Salvation and Evangelism.* Phillipsburg: Presbyterian and Reformed, 2000.

———. Foreword. In *Not of Works: Norman Shepherd and His Critics* by Ralph F. Boersema, vii–xxiii. Minneapolis: NextStep Resources, 2012.

Smail, Thomas A. "In the Image of the Triune God." *International Journal of Systematic Theology* 5 (2003) 22–33.

Smalley, Stephen S. *1, 2, 3 John.* Word Biblical Commentary 51. Dallas: Word, 1984.

Smith, C. Christopher, and John Pattison. *Slow Church: Cultivating Community in the Patient Way of Jesus.* Downers Grove: IVP, 2014.

Smith, Christian, and Melina Lundquist Denton. *Soul Searching: The Religious and Spiritual Lives of American Teenagers.* New York: Oxford University Press, 2005.

Smith, Gordon T. *A Holy Meal: The Lord's Supper in the Life of the Church.* Grand Rapids: Baker Academic, 2005.

Smith, James K. A. *Awaiting the King: Reforming Public Theology.* Grand Rapids: Baker Academic, 2017.

———. *Desiring the Kingdom: Worship, Worldview, and Cultural Formation.* Grand Rapids: Baker Academic, 2009.

———. *How (Not) To Be Secular: Reading Charles Taylor.* Grand Rapids: Eerdmans, 2014.

———. *Imagining the Kingdom: How Worship Works.* Grand Rapids: Baker Academic, 2013.

———. "Who's Afraid of Postmodernism? A Respond to the 'Biola School.'" In *Christianity and the Postmodern Turn,* edited by Myron Penner, 215–28. Grand Rapids: Brazos, 2005.

———. *You Are What You Love: The Spiritual Power of Habit.* Grand Rapids: Brazos, 2016.

Smith, Mark S. *The Priestly Vision of Genesis 1.* Minneapolis: Fortress, 2010.

Smith, Ralph A. *Eternal Covenant: How the Trinity Reshapes Covenant Theology.* Moscow: Canon, 2003.
Smits, Cees-Jan. *Plaatsbereiding: verzoening in Christus bij Hans Joachim Iwand en Eberhard Jüngel.* Utrecht: Eburon, 2021.
Soulen, R. Kendall. *The God of Israel and Christian Theology.* Minneapolis: Fortress, 1996.
Spanje, T. E. van. *2 Korintiërs: profiel van een evangeliedienaar.* Commentaar op het Nieuwe Testament. Kampen: Kok, 2009.
Spencer, Archie J. *The Analogy of Faith: The Quest for God's Speakability.* Downers Grove: IVP Academic, 2015.
Spykman, Gordon J. *Reformational Theology: A New Paradigm for Doing Dogmatics.* Grand Rapids: Eerdmans, 1992.
Stam, Clarence. *The Covenant of Love: Exploring Our Relationship with God.* Winnipeg: Premier 1999.
Stanislavski, Constantin. *An Actor Prepares.* Translated by Elizabeth Reynolds Hapgood. New York: Theatre Arts, 1948.
———. *Building a Character.* Translated by Elizabeth Reynolds Hapgood. New York: Theatre Arts, 1949.
Starr, James. "Does 2 Peter 1:4 Speak of Deification?" In *Partakers of the Divine Nature: The History and Development of Deification in the Christian Tradition*, edited by Michael J. Christensen and Jeffery A. Wittung, 81–92. Grand Rapids: Baker Academic, 2007.
Stek, John H. "'Covenant' Overload in Reformed Theology". *Calvin Theological Journal* 29 (1994) 12–41.
Stinissen, Wilfrid. *Nourished by the Word: Reading the Bible Contemplatively.* Translated by Joseph W. Board. Missouri: Liguori, 1999.
Stob, Henry. "Natural Law Ethics: An Appraisal." *Calvin Theological Journal* 20 (1985) 58–68.
Stolk, Maarten. "Prof. Huijgen: Mens kiest zelf voor de hel." *Reformatorisch Dagblad*, 26 October 2023. https://www.rd.nl/artikel/1039497-prof-huijgen-mens-kiest-zelf-voor-de-hel
Storer, Kevin. *Reading Scripture to Hear God: Kevin Vanhoozer and Henri de Lubac on God's Use of Scripture in the Economy of Redemption.* Eugene, OR: Pickwick, 2014.
Stott, John R. W. *The Spirit, the Church, and the World: The Message of Acts.* Downers Grove: InterVarsity, 1990.
Strachan, Owen. *Reenchanting Humanity: A Theology of Mankind.* Fearn: Mentor, 2019.
Strange, Alan D. *Imputation and the Active Obedience of Christ in the Westminster Standards.* Explorations in Reformed Confessional Theology. Grand Rapids: Reformation Heritage, 2019.
Strange, Alan D., and Derrick J. Vander Meulen, eds. *Trinity Psalter Hymnal.* Willow Grove: The Committee on Christian Education of the Orthodox Presbyterian Church and the Psalter Hymnal Committee of the United Reformed Churches in North America, 2018.
Strange, Dan. "Not Ashamed! The Sufficiency of Scripture for Public Theology." *Themelios* 36 (2011) 238–60.
Strauss, S.A. 1986. *"Alles of niks". K. Schilder oor die verbond.* Bloemfontein: DUO-drukkers, 1986.

———. "Schilder on the Covenant." In *Always Obedient: Essays on the Teachings of Dr. Klaas Schilder*, edited by J. Geertsema, 81–92. Phillipsburg: P&R, 1995.
Strehle, Stephen. *Calvinism, Federalism, and Scholasticism: A Study of the Reformed Doctrine of Covenant*. Bern: Peter Lang, 1988.
Stroup, George W. *The Promise of Narrative Theology: Recovering the Gospel in the Church*. Atlanta: John Knox, 1981.
Swain, Scott R. "Covenant of Redemption." In *Christian Dogmatics: Reformed Theology for the Church Catholic*, edited by Michael Allen and Scott R. Swain, 107–25. Grand Rapids: Baker Academic, 2016.
———. *The Trinity: An Introduction*. Short Studies in Systematic Theology. Wheaton: Crossway, 2020.
———. *Trinity, Revelation, and Reading: A Theological Introduction to the Bible and Its Interpretation*. London: T. & T. Clark, 2011.
Swain, Scott R., and Michael Allen. "The Obedience of the Eternal Son." *International Journal of Systematic Theology* 15 (2013) 114–34.
Swoboda, A.J. *Subversive Sabbath: The Surprising Power of Rest in a Nonstop World*. Grand Rapids: Brazos, 2018.
Tanner, Kathryn. *Christ the Key*. Current Issues in Theology. Cambridge: Cambridge University Press, 2010.
Tate, Marvin E. *Psalms 51–100*. Word Biblical Commentary 20. Dallas: Word, 1998.
Taylor, Charles. "Charles Taylor's Response to a Roundtable Discussion of His Book *A Secular Age*." *Political Theology* 11 (2010) 299–300.
———. *Dilemmas and Connections: Selected Essays*. Cambridge: Belknap, 2011.
———. *The Ethics of Authenticity*. Cambridge: Harvard University Press, 1991.
———. *The Language Animal: The Full Shape of Human Linguistic Capacity*. Cambridge: Belknap, 2016.
———. *Modern Social Imaginaries*. Durham: Duke University Press, 2004.
———. *The Secular Age*. Cambridge: Belknap, 2007.
———. *Sources of the Self: The Making of the Modern Identity*. Cambridge: Harvard University Press, 1989.
———. *Varieties of Religion Today: William James Revisited*. Cambridge: Harvard University Press, 2002.
Terlouw, I. *Real Faith: Performativity and Materiality in the Personal Relationship with Jesus of Evangelical Protestants*. Delft: Eburon, 2015.
Thate, Michael J., et al., eds. *"In Christ" in Paul: Explorations in Paul's Theology of Union and Participation*. Grand Rapids: Eerdmans, 2018.
Thiessen, Gerd. *On Having a Critical Faith*. Translated by John Bowdon. London: SCM, 2012.
Thiselton, Anthony C. *The Hermeneutics of Doctrine*. Grand Rapids: Eerdmans, 2007.
Thomas, Derek. *God Strengthens: Ezekiel Simply Explained*. Darlington: Evangelical, 1993.
Thomas, Heath A. "The Telos (Goal) of Theological Interpretation." In *A Manifesto for Theological Interpretation*, edited by Craig G. Bartholomew and Heath A. Thomas, 197–217. Grand Rapids: Baker Academic, 2016.
Thomas, Michael G. *The Extent of the Atonement: A Dilemma for Reformed Theology from Calvin to the Consensus (1536–1675)*. Studies in Christian History and Thought. Eugene, OR: Wipf & Stock, 2006.

Tipton, Lane G. "Union with Christ and Justification." In *Justified in Christ: God's Plan for Us in Justification*, edited by K. Scott Oliphint, 23–49. Fearn: Mentor, 2007.

Torrance, James B. "Covenant or Contract? A Study of the Theological of Worship in Seventeenth-Century Scotland." *Scottish Journal of Theology* 23 (1970) 51–76.

———. *Worship, Community, and the Triune God of Grace*. Downers Grove: InterVarsity, 1996.

Torrance, Thomas F. *The Christian Doctrine of God: One Being, Three Persons*. London: Bloomsbury T. & T. Clark, 2016.

———. *Incarnation: The Person and Life of Christ*. Edited by Robert T. Walker. Downers Grove: IVP Academic, 2008.

———. *The Mediation of Christ*. Colorado Springs: Helmers & Howard, 1992.

Treier, Daniel J. "Holy Scripture." In *The Oxford Handbook of Reformed Theology*, edited by Michael Allen and Scott R. Swain, 546–61. Oxford: Oxford University Press, 2020.

———. *Introducing Theological Interpretation of Scripture: Recovering a Christian Practice*. Grand Rapids: Baker Academic, 2008.

Troost, P. *Energie van de Geest: het vergeten geheim van een vitaal geloof*. Utrecht: KokBoekencentrum, 2019.

———. *Gewoon God: 40 zoekwoorden om God te vinden in het allerdaagse*. Utrecht: Kok, 2017.

———. *Mindful met Jezus: inwezig leven*. Kampen: Kok, 2013.

———. *Spiritualiteit van ontvankelijkheid*. Kampen: VCL/West-Friesland, 2008.

Trueman, Carl R. *The Rise and Triumph of the Modern Self: Cultural Amnesia, Expressive Individualism, and the Road to Sexual Revolution*. Wheaton: Crossway, 2020.

Turner, Laurence A. "The Rainbow as the Sign of the Covenant in Genesis ix 11–13." *Vetus Testamentum* 43 (1993) 119–24.

Turretin, Francis. *Institutes of Elenctic Theology*. Edited by James T. Dennison Jr. Translated by George Musgrave Giger. 3 vols. Phillipsburg: Presbyterian and Reformed, 1992–1997.

Tylenda, Joseph N. "Christ the Mediator: Calvin versus Stancaro." *Calvin Theological Journal* 8 (1973) 5–16.

———. "The Controversy on Christ the Mediator: Calvin's Second Reply to Stancaro." *Calvin Theological Journal* 8 (1973) 131–57.

Tyson, Paul. *Seven Brief Lessons on Magic*. Eugene, OR: Cascade, 2019.

U.S. Catholic Church. *Catechism of the Catholic Church*. New York: Doubleday, 1995.

United Reformed Churches in North America. *Liturgical Forms and Prayers of the URCNA*. Wellandport: United Reformed Churches in North America, 2018.

Van Asselt, W. J. "Covenant Theology as Relational Theology: The Contributions of Johannes Cocceius (1603) and John Owen (1618–1683) to a Living Reformed Theology." In *The Ashgate Research Companion to John Owen's Theology*, edited by Kelly M. Kapic and Mark Jones, 65–84. Farnham: Ashgate, 2012.

Van Bekkum, Koert. "Biblical Covenants in Their Ancient Near Eastern Context: A Methodological, Historical and Theological Reassessment." In *Covenant: A Vital Element of Reformed Theology: Biblical, Historical and Systematic-Theological Perspectives*, edited by Hans Burger et al., 43–78. Leiden: Brill, 2022.

———. *Verdreven uit de hof, levend uit de belofte: mens en wereld in het licht van Genesis 1–11*. Baarn: Willem de Zwijgerstichting, 2020.

BIBLIOGRAPHY

Van Bekkum, Koert, and G. Kwakkel. "Een veilige leefwereld voor de mens in dienst van God: overwegingen bij alternatieve lezingen van het begin van Genesis." *Theologia Reformata* 53, no. 4 (2010) 318–35.

Van Bruggen, Jakob. "The Blind Man Sat by the Road and He Cried: About Seeing and Not Seeing." *Lux Mundi* 34, no. 1 (2015) 4–7.

———. "Het evangelie van het koninkrijk der hemelen (Algemene inleiding)." https://www.bijbelstudiesnt.nl/bijlagen/bijlagen-bij-bijbelstudies/99-2013-12-23-08-55-45.

———. *Galaten: het goed recht van gelovige Kelten*. Commentaar op het Nieuwe Testament. Kampen: Kok, 2004.

———. *Het geheim van Jezus' namen*. Kampen: Kok, 2016.

———. "Hoe is het hemelrijk nabij?" https://www.bijbelstudiesnt.nl/bijlagen/bijlagen-bij-bijbelstudies/100-2013-12-23-09-00-38.

———. "Hoe kunnen Gods wetten voor christenen goed zijn? 2. Bijbelse wetten zijn vloeiend: ze veranderen immers met tijd en cultuur?" https://www.bijbelstudiesnt.nl/bijlagen/bijlagen-bij-bijbelstudies/130-sd.

———. "Kingdom of God or Justification of the Sinner? Paul between Jesus and Luther." *Lux Mundi* 27, no. 1 (2008) 5–12.

———. *Jesus the Son of God: The Gospel Narratives as Message*. Translated by Nancy Forrest-Flier. Grand Rapids: Baker, 1999.

———. *Lucas: het evangelie als voorgeschiedenis*. Commentaar op het Nieuwe Testament. Kok: Kampen, 1991.

———. *Marcus: het evangelie volgens Petrus*. Commentaar op het Nieuwe Testament. Kampen: Kok, 1988.

———. *Matteüs: het evangelie voor Israel*. Commentaar op het Nieuwe Testament. Kampen: Kok, 1990.

———. *Paul: Pioneer for Israel's Messiah*. Translated by Ed M. van der Maas. Phillipsburg: P&R, 2005.

———. *Romeinen: Christenen tussen stad en synagoge*. Commentaar op het Nieuwe Testament. Kampen: Kok, 2006.

———. "Volhouden op de weg naar het hemelse Sion (Hebreeën 10, 19–13,25)." In *Hebreeën: geloven is volhouden*, by H. R. van de Kamp, 249–321. Commentaar op het Nieuwe Testament. Kampen: Kok, 2010.

Van Dam, Cornelis. *In the Beginning: Listening to Genesis 1 and 2*. Grand Rapids: Reformation Heritage, 2021.

Van de Beek, A. *Ontmaskering: Christelijk geloof en cultuur*. Zoetermeer: Meinema, 2001.

Van de Kamp, H. *Openbaring: profetie vanaf Patmos*. Commentaar op het Nieuwe Testament. Kampen: Kok, 2000.

Van den Brink, Gijsbert. *Reformed Theology and Evolutionary Theory*. Grand Rapids: Eerdmans, 2020.

———. "Social Trinitarianism: A Discussion of Some Recent Theological Criticisms." *International Journal of Systematic Theology* 16 (2014) 431–50.

Van den Brink, Gijsbert, and Cornelis van der Kooi. *Christian Dogmatics: An Introduction*. Translated by Reinder Bruinsma with James D. Bratt. Grand Rapids: Eerdmans, 2017.

Vander Lugt. Wesley. *Living Theodrama: Reimagining Theological Ethics*. Routledge Studies in Theology, Imagination and the Arts. Abingdon: Routledge, 2014.

Van der Woude, A. S. "Shem (Name)." In *Theological Lexicon of the Old Testament*, edited by Ernst Jenni and Claus Westermann, translated by Mark E. Biddle, 1348–66. Peabody: Hendrickson, 1997.

Vander Zee, Leonard J. *Christ, Baptism, and the Lord's Supper: Rediscovering the Sacraments for Evangelical Worship*. Downers Grove: InterVarsity, 2004.

VanDrunen, David. *Divine Covenants and Moral Order: A Biblical Theology of Natural Law*. Grand Rapids: Eerdmans, 2014.

———. *God's Glory Alone—The Majestic Heart of Christian Faith and Life*. Grand Rapids: Zondervan 2015.

———. "Where We Are: Justification under Fire in the Contemporary Scene." In *Covenant, Justification, and Pastoral Ministry: Essays by the Faculty of Westminster Seminary California*, edited by R. Scott Clark, 25–57. Phillipsburg: Presbyterian and Reformed, 2007.

VanDrunen, David, and R. Scott Clark. "The Covenant before the Covenants." In *Covenant, Justification, and Pastoral Ministry: Essays by the Faculty of Westminster Seminary California*, edited by R. Scott Clark, 167–96. Phillipsburg: Presbyterian and Reformed, 2007.

Van Dusseldorp, K. *Preken tussen de verhalen: een homiletische doordenking van narrativiteit*. Kok: Kampen, 2012.

Van Eck, J. *Handelingen: de wereld in het geding*. Commentaar op het Nieuwe Testaement. Kampen: Kok, 2003.

———. *Kolossenzen en Filemon: waarheid en recht*. Commentaar op het Nieuwe Testament. Kampen: Kok, 2007.

Van Genderen, J., and W. H. Velema. *Reformed Dogmatics*. Translated by Gerrit Bilkes and Ed M. van der Maas. Phillipsburg, P&R, 2008.

Vanhoozer, Kevin J. "Ascending the Mountain, Singing the Rock: Biblical Interpretation Earthed, Typed, and Transfigured." *Modern Theology* 28 (2012) 781–803.

———. "At Play in the Theodrama of the Lord: The Triune God of the Gospel." In *Theatrical Theology: Explorations in Performing the Faith*, edited by Wesley Vander Lugt, 1–29. Eugene, OR: Cascade, 2014.

———. *Biblical Authority after Babel: Retrieving the Solas in the Spirit of Mere Protestant Christianity*. Grand Rapids: Brazos, 2016.

———. *Doers & Hearers: A Pastor's Guide to Making Disciples through Scripture*. Bellingham: Lexham, 2019.

———. *The Drama of Doctrine: A Canonical Linguistic Approach to Christian Theology*. Louisville: Westminster John Knox, 2005.

———. "A Drama-of-Redemption Model: Always Performing?" In *Four Views on Moving beyond the Bible to Theology*, edited by Gary T. Meadors, 151–98. Grand Rapids: Zondervan, 2009.

———. *Faith Speaking Understanding: Performing the Drama of Doctrine*. Louisville: Westminster John Knox, 2014.

———. "Imprisoned or Free? Text, Status, and Theological Interpretation in the Master/Slave Discourse in Philemon." In *Reading Scripture with the Church: Toward a Hermeneutic for Theological Interpretation* by A. K. M. Adam et al., 51–93. Grand Rapids, 2006.

———. "In Bright Shadow: C. S. Lewis on the Imagination for Theology and Discipleship." In *The Romantic Rationalist: God, Life, and Imagination in the*

Work of C. S. Lewis, edited by John Piper and David Mathis, 81–104. Wheaton: Crossway, 2014.

———. *Is There a Meaning in This Text? The Bible, the Reader, and the Morality of Literary Knowledge*. Grand Rapids: Zondervan, 1998.

———. *Pictures at a Theological Exhibition: Scenes of the Church's Worship, Witness and Wisdom*. Downers Grove: IVP Academic, 2016.

———. "Putting on Christ: Spiritual Formation and the Drama of Discipleship." *Journal of Spiritual Formation and Soul Care* 8 (2015) 147–71.

———. "Redemption Accomplished: Atonement." In *The Oxford Handbook of Reformed Theology*, edited by Michael Allen and Scott R. Swain, 473–96. Oxford: Oxford University Press, 2020.

———. *Remythologizing Theology: Divine Action, Passion, and Authorship*. Cambridge Studies in Christian Doctrine. Cambridge: Cambridge University Press, 2010.

———. "The Voice and the Actor: A Dramatic Proposal about the Ministry and Minstrelsy of Theology." In *Evangelical Futures: A Conversation on Theological Method*, edited by John G. Stackhouse Jr., 61–106. Grand Rapids: Baker, 2000.

———. "What is Everyday Theology? How and Why Christians Should Read Culture." In *Everyday Theology: How to Read Cultural Texts and Interpret Trends*, edited by Kevin J. Vanhoozer et al., 15–60. Grand Rapids: Baker Academic, 2007.

Van Houwelingen, P. H. R. *2 Petrus en Judas: testament in tweevoud*. Commentaar op het Nieuwe Testament. Kampen: Kok, 1993.

———. *Hemelse reisbegeleiding: sporen van engelen in het Nieuwe Testament*. Utrecht: Kokboekencentrum, 2021.

———. *Johannes: het evangelie van het woord*. Commentaar op het Nieuwe Testament. Kampen: Kok, 1997.

———. "The Redemptive-historical Dynamics of the Salvation of 'All Israel' (Rom. 11:26a)." *Calvin Theological Journal* 46 (2011) 301–14.

Van Noppen, Koos, et al. "Christenen praten over hoop, maar niet over inkeer en dat gesprek is dringend nodig." *Nederlands Dagblad*, 7 July 2020. https://www.nd.nl/opinie/opinie/981430/christenen-praten-over-hoop-maar-niet-over-inkeer-en-dat-gesprek-.

Van Pelt, Miles V. "The Noahic Covenant of the Covenant of Grace." In *Covenant Theology: Biblical, Theological, and Historical Perspectives*, edited by Guy Prentiss Waters et al., 111–32. Wheaton: Crossway, 2020.

Van Raalte, Theodore G. "'Free Will'? Augustine and Dordt." *Clarion* 67 (2018) 558–60.

Van Til, Cornelius. "Covenant Theology." In *New 20th Century Encyclopedia of Religious Knowledge*, edited by J. D. Douglas, 240–41. 2nd ed. Grand Rapids: Eerdmans, 1991.

Velde, D. te. "De hemel is niet boven maar kan bij wijze van spreken om de hoek zijn." *Nederlands Dagblad*, May 11, 2021. https://www.nd.nl/opinie/opinie/1034217/de-hemel-is-niet-boven-maar-kan-bij-wijze-van-spreken-om-de-hoe.

Veldhuizen, P. *God en mens onderweg: hoofdmomenten uit de theologische geschiedenisbeschowing van Klaas Schilder*. Leiden: Groen en Zoon, 1995.

Venema, Cornelis P. "Christ's Kingship in All of Life: Butchers, Bakers, and Candlestick-Makers in the Service of Christ." *Mid-America Journal of Theology* 25 (2014) 7–33.

———. "'In This Way All Israel Will Be Saved': A Study of Romans 11:26." *Mid-America Journal of Theology* 22 (2011) 19–40.

———. "The Mosaic Covenant: A 'Republication' of the Covenant of Works? A Review Article: *The Law Is Not of Faith: Essays on Works and Grace in the Mosaic Covenant*." *Mid-America Journal of Theology* 21 (2010) 35–101.

———. "One Kingdom or Two? An Evaluation of the 'Two Kingdoms' Doctrine as an Alternative to Neo-Calvinism." *Mid-America Journal of Theology* 23 (2012) 77–129.

———. "The Restoration of All Things to Proper Order: An Assessment of the 'Two Kingdoms/Natural Law' Interpretation of Calvin's Public Theology." In *Kingdoms Apart: Engaging the Two Kingdoms Perspective*, edited by Ryan McIlhenny, 3–32 Phillipsburg: P&R, 2012.

Vlach, Michael J. "New Covenant Theology Compared with Covenantalism." *The Master's Seminary Journal* 18 (2007) 201–19.

Volf, Miroslav. *Exclusion and Embrace: A Theological Exploration of Identity, Otherness, and Forgiveness*. 2nd ed. Nashville: Abingdon, 2019.

Vorster, Nicolaas. *Created in the Image of God*. Eugene, OR: Pickwick, 2011.

Vos, Geerhardus. *Anthropology*. Vol. 2 of *Reformed Dogmatics*. Translated by Richard B. Gaffin Jr. Bellingham: Lexham, 2014.

———. *Biblical Theology: Old and New Testaments*. Grand Rapids: Eerdmans, 1948.

———. "The Doctrine of the Covenant in Reformed Theology." In *Redemptive History and Biblical Interpretation*, edited by Richard B. Gaffin Jr., 234–67. Phillipsburg: Presbyterian and Reformed, 1980.

———. *The Pauline Eschatology*. Phillipsburg: P&R, 1994.

Vos, P. "Christelijke deugden in de gemeente." In *Oefenen in discipelschap: de gemeente als groeiplaats van het goede leven*, edited by James Kennedy and P. Vos, 27–49. Zoetermeer: Boekncentrum, 2015.

Vriezen, Th. C. *An Outline of Old Testament Theology*. 2nd ed. Newton: Charles T. Branford, 1970.

Waaijman, Kees. *Spirituality: Forms, Foundations, Methods*. Translated by John Vriend. Lueven: Peeters, 2002.

Waddington, Jeffrey C. "*Duplex in homine regimen*: A Response to David VanDrunen's 'The Reformed Two Kingdoms Doctrine: An Explanation and Defense.'" *The Confessional Presbyterian* 8 (2012) 191–96.

Waltke, Bruce K. "The Fear of the Lord: The Foundation for a Relationship with God." In *Alive to God: Studies in Spirituality Presented to James Houston*, edited by J. I. Packer and Loren Wilkinson, 17–33. Downers Grove: InterVarsity, 1992.

———. *Genesis: A Commentary*. Grand Rapids: Zondervan, 2001.

———. "The Kingdom of God in the Old Testament: The Covenants." In *The Kingdom of God*, edited by Christopher W. Morgan and Robert A. Peterson, 73–93. Theology in Community. Wheaton: Crossway, 2012.

———. *An Old Testament Theology: An Exegetical, Canonical, and Thematic Approach*. Grand Rapids: Zondervan, 2007.

Walton, John H. *The Lost World of Genesis One: Ancient Cosmology and the Origins Debate*. Downers Grove: InterVarsity, 2009.

Ward, Roland S. *God and Adam: Reformed Theology and the Creation Covenant*. Wantirna: New Melbourne, 2003.

Warner, Michael, et al., eds. *Varieties of Secularism in a Secular Age*. Cambridge: Harvard University Press, 2010.

Warren, Tish Harrison. *Liturgy of the Ordinary: Sacred Practices in Everyday Life*. Downers Grove: IVP, 2016.

Waters, Guy Prentiss. "The Covenant of Works in the New Testament." In *Covenant Theology: Biblical, Theological, and Historical Perspectives*, edited by Guy Prentiss Waters et al., 79–97. Wheaton: Crossway, 2020.

Waters, Guy Prentiss, et al., eds. *Covenant Theology: Biblical, Theological, and Historical Perspectives*. Wheaton: Crossway, 2020.

Watkin, Christopher. *Biblical Critical Theory: How the Bible's Unfolding Story Makes Sense of Modern Life and Culture*. Grand Rapids: Zondervan Academic: 2022.

Watkins, Eric Brian. *The Drama of Preaching: Participating with God in the History of Redemption*. Eugene, OR: Wipf & Stock, 2016.

Webber, Robert E. *Ancient-Future Evangelism: Making Your Church a Faith-forming Community*. Grand Rapids: Baker, 2003.

———. *Ancient-Future Faith: Rethinking Evangelism for a Postmodern World*. Grand Rapids: Baker, 1999.

———. *Ancient-Future Time: Forming Spirituality through the Christian Year*. Grand Rapids: Baker, 2004.

———. *Ancient-Future Worship: Proclaiming and Enacting God's Narrative*. Grand Rapids: Baker, 2008.

———. *The Divine Embrace: Recovering the Passionate Spiritual Life*. Grand Rapids: Baker, 2006.

Webster, John. "God's Perfect Life." In *God's Life in Trinity*, edited by Miroslav Wolf and Michael Welker, 143–52. Minneapolis: Fortress, 2006.

Weeks, Noel. *Admonition and Curse: The Ancient Near Eastern Treaty/Covenant Form as a Problem in Inter-cultural Relationships*. London: Bloomsbury: T. & T. Clark, 2004.

Weinandy, Thomas. *The Father's Spirit of Sonship: Reconceiving the Trinity*. Edinburgh: T. & T. Clark, 1995.

Weir, David A. *The Origins of the Federal Theology in Sixteenth-Century Reformation Thought*. New York: Oxford University Press, 1990.

Wells, Samuel. *Improvisation: The Drama of Christian Ethics*. Grand Rapids: Brazos, 2004.

Wendt, H. T. *S. G. de Graaf: Life, Influences, Theology: A Preliminary Study*. Neerlandia: Inheritance, 2020.

Wenham, Gordon J. *Genesis 1–15*. Word Biblical Commentary 1. Dallas: Word, 1987.

———. "Sanctuary Symbolism in the Garden of Eden Story." In *"I Studied Inscriptions from before the Flood": Ancient Near Eastern, Literary, and Linguistic Approaches to Genesis 1–11*, edited by Richard S. Hess and David T. Tsumura, 399–404. Winona Lake: Eisenbrauns, 1994.

Westerman, Edjan. *Learning Messiah: Israel and the Nations: Learning to Read God's Way Anew*. Eugene, OR: Wipf & Stock 2018.

Westermann, Claus. *Creation*. Translated by John Scallion. Minneapolis: Fortress, 1974.

Wielenga, B. *Verbond en zending: een verbondsmatige benadering van zending*. PhD thesis, University of South Africa, 1997. http://uir.unisa.ac.za/bitstream/handle/10500/16473/thesis_weilenga_b.pdf.

Wigley, Stephen. *Balthasar's Trilogy*. London: T. & T. Clark, 2010.

Willard, Dallas. *Hearing God: Developing a Conversational Relationship with God*. Downers Grove: IVP, 2012.

———. *Renovation of the Heart: Putting on the Character of Christ.* Carol Streams: NavPress, 2002.

———. *The Spirit of the Disciplines: Understanding How God Changes Lives.* San Francisco: HarperSanFrancisco, 1991.

Williams, Brian M. *C. S. Lewis: Pre-Evangelism for a Post-Christian World: Why Narnia Might Be More Real Than We Think.* Cambridge, OH: Christian Publishing, 2021.

Williams, Michael. *Far as the Curse Is Found: The Covenant Story of Redemption.* Phillipsburg: P&R, 2005.

Williamson, Paul R. "The *Pactum Salutis*: A Scriptural Concept or Scholastic Mythology?" *Tyndale Bulletin* 69 (2018) 259–81.

———. *Sealed with an Oath: Covenant in God's Unfolding Purpose.* New Studies in Biblical Theology 23. Downers Grove: InterVarsity, 2007.

———. "Snakes and Dragons: A Neglected Theological Trajectory of Genesis 3:15 in Scripture." In *The Seed of Promise: The Suffering and Glory of the Messiah: Essays in Honor of T. Desmond Alexander*, edited by Paul R. Williamson and Rita F. Cefalu, 332–52. Wilmore: GlossaHouse, 2020.

Wilson, Andrew. *God in All Things: Rediscovering the Sacred in an Everyday World.* Grand Rapids: Zondervan, 2021.

Wilson, Jonathan R. *God's Good World: Reclaiming the Doctrine of Creation.* Grand Rapids: Baker, 2013.

Wirzba, Norman. *From Nature to Creation: A Christian Vision for Understanding and Loving Our World.* The Church and Postmodern Culture. Grand Rapids: Baker Academic, 2015.

———. *Living the Sabbath: Discovering the Rhythms of Rest and Delight.* Grand Rapids: Brazos, 2006.

Witsius, Herman. *The Economy of the Covenants between God and Man: Comprehending a Complete Body of Divinity.* Translated by William Crookshank. 2 vols. Kingsburg: Den Dulk Christian Foundation, 1990.

Wittgenstein, Ludwig. *Philosophical Investigation.* Translated by G. E. M. Anscombe. 3rd ed. Malden: Blackwell, 2001.

Wolters, Al. "Worldview and Textual Criticism in 2 Peter 3:10." *Westminster Theological Journal* 49 (1987) 405–13.

Wolterstorff, Nicholas. *Acting Liturgically: Philosophical Reflections on Religious Practice.* Oxford: Oxford University Press, 2018.

———. *Divine Discourse: Philosophical Reflections on the Claim That God Speaks.* Cambridge: Cambridge University Press, 1995.

———. *The God We Worship: An Exploration in Liturgical Theology.* Grand Rapids: Eerdmans, 2015.

———. Introduction to *Faith and Rationality: Reason and Belief in God.* Edited by Alvin Plantinga and Nicholas Wolterstorff. Notre Dame: University of Notre Dame Press, 1983.

———. *Reason within the Bounds of Religion.* 2nd ed. Grand Rapids: Eerdmans, 1984.

Woo, B. Hoon. *The Promise of the Trinity: The Covenant of Redemption in the Theologies of Witsius, Owen, Dickson, Goodwin, and Cocceius.* Reformed Historical Theology 48. Göttingen: Vandenhoeck and Ruprecht, 2018.

Wood, W. Jay. *Epistemology: Becoming Intellectually Virtuous.* Contours of Christian Philosophy. Downers Grove: InterVarsity, 1998.

Woolsey, Andrew A. *Unity and Continuity in Covenantal Thought: A Study in the Reformed Tradition to the Westminster Assembly*. Grand Rapids: Reformation Heritage, 2012.
Wright, Christopher J. H. *The Great Story and the Great Commission: Participating in the Biblical Drama of Mission*. Grand Rapids: Baker Academic, 2023.
———. *Knowing Jesus through the Old Testament*. Downers Grove: InterVarsity, 1992.
———. "Mission as a Matrix for Hermeneutics and Biblical Theology." In *Out of Egypt: Biblical Theology and Biblical Interpretation*, edited by Craig Bartholomew et al., 104–42. Grand Rapids: Zondervan, 2004.
———. *The Mission of God: Unlocking the Bible's Grand Narrative*. Downers Grove: IVP Academic, 2006.
Wright, N. T. *Acts for Everyone. Part 1: Chapters 1–12*. London: SPCK, 2008.
———. *After You Believe: Why Christian Character Matters*. San Francisco: HarperOne, 2010.
———. *The Challenge of Jesus: Rediscovering Who Jesus Was and Is*. Downers Grove: InterVarsity, 1999.
———. *The Climax of the Covenant: Christ and the Law in Pauline Theology*. Minneapolis: Fortress, 1993.
———. *The Day the Revolution Began: Reconsidering the Meaning of Jesus' Crucifixion*. New York: HarperOne, 2016.
———. "How Can the Bible Be Authoritative?" *Vox Evangelica* 21 (1991) 7–32.
———. *How God Became King: The Forgotten Story of the Gospels*. San Francisco: HarperOne, 2012.
———. *Jesus and the Victory of God*. Christian Origins and the Question of God 2. Minneapolis: Fortress, 1996.
———. *Matthew for Everyone. Part 2: Chapters 16–28*. London: SPCK, 2002.
———. *The New Testament and the People of God*. Christian Origins and the Question of God 1. Minneapolis: Fortress, 1992.
———. *Paul and the Faithfulness of God*. Christian Origins and the Question of God 4. Minneapolis: Fortress, 2013.
———. *Paul for Everyone. Romans. Part 1: Chapters 9–16*. London: SPCK, 2004.
———. *The Resurrection of the Son of God*. Christian Origins and the Question of God 3. Minneapolis: Fortress, 2003.
———. *Surprised by Hope: Rethinking Heaven, the Resurrection, and the Mission of the Church*. New York: HarperCollins, 2008.
Wright, Shawn D. "Covenant Theology." In *God's Glory Revealed in Christ: Essays on Biblical Theology in Honor of Thomas R. Schreiner*, edited by James M. Hamilton et al., 33–44. Nashville: B&H Academic, 2019.
Yarbrough, Robert W. "The Kingdom of God in the New Testament." In *The Kingdom of God*, edited by Christopher W. Morgan and Robert A. Peterson, 95–123. Theology in Community. Wheaton: Crossway, 2012.
Yinger, Kurt L. *Paul, Judaism, and Judgment According to Deeds*. Cambridge: Cambridge University Press, 1999.
Young, Frances. *The Art of Performance: Towards a Theology of Holy Scripture*. London: Longman and Todd, 1990.
Zimmermann, Jens. *Hermeneutics: A Very Short Introduction*. Oxford: Oxford University Press, 2015.

———. *Incarnational Humanism: A Philosophy of Culture for the Church in the World.* Downers Grove: IVP Academic, 2012.

Zizioulas, John. "Priest of Creation." In *Environmental Stewardship: Critical Perspectives—Past and Present*, edited by R. J. Berry, 273–90. London: T. & T. Clark, 2006.

———. Proprietors or Priests of Creation [Blog post]. http://www.orth-transfiguration.org/proprietors-or-priests-of-creation/.

Zorgdrager, H. E. "On the Fullness of Salvation: Tracking *Theosis* in Reformed Theology." *Journal of Reformed Theology* 8 (2014) 357–81.

Subject Index

accommodation, 90, 93, 167, 293n118, 304n157
allegory, 26, 40n108
analogical mode, 90, 91, 93, 109, 166–68, 265n26
anamnesis, 327n31
anastasiform life, 248
angels, 8, 256, 266n30, 267–69, 270, 274, 313, 324, 331
anthropology, 120n5, 121, 196–97. See also humanity; image of God.
apologetics, 310–11
apostasy, 302n151
art, Christian, 176
ascensional life, 33, 82, 249–51, 303
atheism, 72–73, 108
atonement, 195, 224, 246, 285n292, 286, 287
    extent of, 285, 288n107
    limited, 285
    models of, 290n108
authenticity, 8–9, 307, 314–16, 320, 333

baptism, 85, 86–87, 96, 106, 136, 137, 298, 325n28, 326
    Jesus', 233, 235–36
    John's, 235, 237, 252
    with Spirit, 235–36, 244, 245, 317
beatific vision, 304
belief
    and action, 311n7
    formation, 322

body, 273, 321
    as factor in interpretation, 30, 31, 32, 59, 89, 261n15
    resurrection of, 105, 256, 290, 335
    and soul, 273–74, 321
    spiritual, 256

Canons of Dort, 145n106, 278n77, 285n91, 289n107
catechesis, 50
character formation, 50n156, 330
Christ. See also Jesus.
    ascension of, 33, 82, 103, 242–43, 245, 249–51, 291, 323, 324n26, 332
    as covenant head, 140, 141, 147, 153, 186, 323
    as covenant mediator, 102–3, 112, 153, 186, 323
    died for all, 288n104
    divinity not restricted by humanity, 282n84
    forsaken by Father, 287n99
    as head of creation and humanity, 291
    imitation of, 55n174
    inseparable from Spirit, 293
    as king, 82, 103, 239n187, 250, 286–87, 291, 299, 323
    mediator of creation, 207, 270, 270n44, 274n61
    mediator of new covenant, 102–3, 112, 121, 153, 186, 291
    mind of, 32–35, 36n90, 56, 59, 91, 96n169, 247, 297, 301, 320, 323, 326, 335

385

SUBJECT INDEX

Christ (*continued*)
  as model of image of God, 206, 207, 212, 274–75, 318
  participation in, 5n25, 35, 74, 147, 158, 159, 174, 187n270, 193–94, 243, 274, 283, 289, 293, 294, 296–97, 319, 324
    cosmological vs. redemptive, 270n45, 274n62
    kingly ministry, 250, 274, 299, 319
    prayers, 250
    priestly ministry, 249–50, 274, 299, 319, 323
    prophetic ministry, 250, 299
    sufferings, 249
    worship, 249–50, 323–24
  person of, 282–84, 316
  as priest, 82, 103, 239n187, 250, 286–87, 291, 299, 323
  as promised one, 283
  as prophet, 82, 102, 239n187, 250, 286–87, 291, 299, 323
  putting on, 23, 34–35, 55, 60, 98, 104, 247, 254, 293, 296, 297, 302, 303, 325, 329–30
  as representative,
    of Adam, 279, 284
    of the elect, 284n91
    of humanity, 33, 283n86, 284n91, 315, 320
    of Israel, 156, 157, 233, 234, 235, 236, 237, 239, 240, 246, 279, 283–86, 288, 290–91, 315, 320
  return as judge, 251–55, 303–6, 317–18
  rule in church, 83, 179
  rule in world, 83, 179
  as savior of world, 288
  as substitute, 33, 103, 109, 233, 234, 235, 236, 237, 240, 246, 251, 279, 283–86, 290n108, 315, 320
  union with, ix, 2–3, 12, 34, 48, 73, 75n71, 104, 106, 172, 186, 192, 193–94, 199, 204, 247, 250, 278n77, 293, 296–97, 300–302, 309, 319, 320, 321, 333, 336
    covenantal, 73, 106, 115
    energies, not essence, 104, 106, 115, 163–64
    external, 71, 106, 115, 184, 186
    and imputation, 149n160
    and justification, 75n71, 76, 171, 172, 186
    legal/ethical, 73, 109, 110, 115, 184
    as matrix of *ordo salutis*, 104, 115, 169
    mystical, 147
    ontological, 2, 158
    as source of authentic humanity, 320
    transformative aspects, 104, 105, 172–73, 186, 301–2
  work of, 284–91, 320
Christendom, 177n241, 183
"Christian" as adjective, 117, 175–77, 182–83
Christian faith, 310
Christianity,
  as culture, 117, 177, 182–83
  as system of truth claims, 117, 177, 182
Christology, 121, 196–97, 282n83, 288n104. *See also* Christ; Jesus.
  distinguished from pneumatology, 288n104
  inseparable from soteriology, 282n83
church, 4, 5, 52, 82–83 87, 97, 100, 105–7, 111–18, 124, 136, 152, 155, 175, 177, 179, 181, 183, 187, 198, 200–201, 233n176, 272n53, 291, 296–99, 304–5, 317, 319, 322, 325n28, 326n30, 329–30, 332, 333–34

SUBJECT INDEX

as community of cultural agents, 334
as community of love, 333–34
as context of covenant, 121
creation of, 105–6, 296–99
dependent on Christ, 297
and disruptive witness, 334n47
doctrine of, 55, 82, 121, 154
as eschatological community, 296
essence, 297, 319
grounded in heaven, 299
and hospitality, 334
and Israel, 70–71, 107, 154, 251, 279, 296
living for the other, 334
marks of, 107, 117, 177
mission, 98, 105, 107, 116, 117, 176–77, 183, 187n270, 198, 264n24, 298, 321
as mixed community, 296n128
as new covenant community, 39, 82, 111, 112, 113, 179, 246, 251, 293, 294, 295, 296, 297n132, 298, 305, 319, 321, 326, 328, 330, 333
as participant in theodrama, 23, 49–50, 60, 258
as pilgrim community, 82, 299, 333, 336, 337
and political engagement, 334n48
as preliminary, provisional form of new creation, 296, 299, 321, 333, 337
as reconstituted, expanded Israel, 244, 251, 279, 333
in secular culture, 6, 11–14, 307, 308–9, 312, 322n22
and social issues, 177, 182
as theater of theodrama, 97, 217n115, 244–51, 317
and theology, 5, 28, 42, 44, 56, 57–58
watchful and waiting, 252, 299, 304, 337–38
church discipline, 87, 107, 117, 136, 250

church government, 106–7
church order, 62, 87
common curse, 176
common grace, 83, 100, 101–2, 110, 117, 175, 176, 180, 181, 182, 187, 272n53, 292
communicatio idiomatum, 282n84
confessions, 48n147, 294n141
consumerism, 312
councils, ecumenical, 48n147, 294n141
counter-cultural life, 248
counterdrama, 85–86, 97, 115, 187
courtroom drama, 25, 102
covenant, covenants, 142, 213n98, 218n119, 330
 with Abraham, 4, 69, 70, 80, 102, 113–14, 119, 133, 134, 140, 148, 149, 152–53, 155, 160–61, 162, 217, 219–23, 229, 281
 blessings, 104–7, 112, 121
 as center of theological framework, 2, 4, 62, 99, 119, 121, 339
 conditional and unconditional aspects, 160–61, 220n130
 consummation, 107–8, 121
 of creation. *See* covenant, covenants: of works.
 establishing relationship, 24, 120, 122, 139, 150, 152, 214, 223
 with David, 4, 69–70, 80, 102, 119, 129, 132–33, 153, 155, 161, 217, 228–31, 281
 of grace, 4, 63, 64, 65, 68–72, 74, 80–81, 83, 88, 102–4, 106–7, 109, 110, 112, 113, 114, 115, 116–17, 119, 120, 128n41, 134, 138, 139, 140, 141, 142n97, 148, 150–62, 175, 179–80, 184–86, 302n152
 biblical and theological support for, 151–62
 bilateral in continuation, 152

covenant, covenants (*continued*)
  of grace (*continued*)
    conditional in
      administration, 114,
      160–61
    depends on meritorious
      covenant of works,
      68–69, 141, 153
    external vs. internal, 71,
      114, 184
    includes all post-fall
      covenants, 151
    includes non-elect
      members, 71
    as meta-covenant, 151
    Michael Horton's
      differences from
      classical view, 153–54
    one overarching covenant,
      68–70, 185
    as royal land grant
      covenant, 68–70, 153
    supra-historical, 151
    unconditional, 68, 70, 114,
      153, 160–61
    unilateral in origin, 152
  and headship, 140, 141, 147,
    153, 186
  and Hittite treaties, 66, 68, 153,
    161–62, 220n130
  with Israel, 4, 66, 67–70, 103,
    113–14, 140, 141, 148–49,
    152–53, 154, 155, 156, 162,
    185, 197, 217, 223–28, 229,
    230, 231, 232, 239, 279,
    287, 315. *See also* covenant,
    covenants: new.
    conditional, 67
    as covenant of grace,
      141n95
    as republication of
      covenant of works, 67,
      103, 113, 141, 148–49,
      153–54, 185
    as scaffolding, 70
    second covenant mediated
      by Moses, 227
    subordinate to Abrahamic
      covenant, 223
    as suzerainty covenant, 67
    two layers, 68
  maker, 99–100, 121
  meaning of *bĕrît*, 122–23, 143
  mediator, 102–3, 112, 121, 153,
    186
  missional intent of, 126, 143,
    182, 194, 195, 281, 315
  Mosaic. *See* covenant, covenants:
    with Israel.
  new, 4, 39, 70, 80–81, 82–83, 86,
    101, 106, 109, 111–14, 119,
    120n5, 129, 132, 134, 140,
    149, 151, 153–54, 155, 161,
    179, 184, 198, 217, 220, 228,
    231–33, 234, 236, 240, 241–
    42, 244–45, 246, 251, 279,
    287, 290, 291, 293, 294–98,
    305, 315, 317, 319, 321, 323,
    326, 328, 330, 333, 335
    Christ as mediator of, 291
    conditional in
      administration, 70,
      154, 161, 184
    eternal, 232
    governed by election, 114,
      184
    hidden character of,
      296n128
    irrefragable, 231n171
    not all members believers,
      233n176, 296n128
    and Spirit, 232
    unconditional in essence,
      70, 114, 154, 161, 184
    with Israel, 132, 155, 217,
      231–32, 241, 244, 279,
      315
  with Noah, 4, 24, 70, 101, 119,
    140, 150, 152, 160, 175, 182,
    201, 215–16, 219, 220, 223,
    281
  old, 106, 120n5, 149, 152,
    233n176, 241
  partner, 100–102, 121

SUBJECT INDEX

pre-fall. *See* covenant, covenants: of works.
of redemption, 4, 64, 71–72, 99–100, 102–3, 104, 114, 119, 121, 126–35, 150, 151–52, 153, 184, 190n3
   basis of other covenants, 72
   and election, 71
   exegetical support for, 128–35
redemptive and non-redemptive, 182
as redemptive instruments, 126, 143, 182, 194, 281, 315
reframed understanding of, 5, 6, 14, 62, 187–88, 189, 201, 257, 340
as relationship, 120–24, 142–43
Sinai. *See* covenant, covenants: with Israel.
as structure of God's counterdrama, 85
and uncertainty, 126, 143, 182, 194, 194n23, 215, 216, 219, 220, 221, 223, 226, 228, 231, 281, 315
as unifying theme, 24–25
of works, 4, 63–70, 72, 80, 81, 83, 101, 102, 103, 109, 110, 112, 113, 117, 119, 121, 125, 135–50, 153–54, 156, 179, 185–86, 285, 286
   beginning with creation, 64, 73, 123–24, 140
   biblical and theological support for, 139–50
   in effect today, 66, 110, 142, 145, 185
   Michael Horton's differences from classical view, 140–41
   and merit, 65, 68–69, 110, 125
   republication, 67, 113, 141, 148–49, 153–54, 185
covenant theology, 2, 4, 14, 119, 125, 138, 142n97, 147n113, 151n130, 155, 339. *See also* covenant.
classic (federal theology), 25, 60, 62, 119–20, 135–36, 139, 140, 147n113, 153–54
covenant as integrative center, 4
as framework, 2, 4, 14, 60, 62, 63–79, 99–108, 119, 121, 339
Michael Horton's, 5, 6, 14, 60, 62, 63–79, 110, 113, 118, 119–188, 189, 339–40
and nominalism, 124–26, 144
and social contract theory, 124, 125–26
creation, 266–71
of angels, 267
beauty of, 203–4
compatible with God, 204, 317
in, by, for Christ, 203
Christ-shaped, 203, 270n44
doctrine of, 54, 196–97
of earthly stage, 269–71, 313, 331
enchanted, 8, 269, 270, 272, 313, 324, 331
ex nihilo, 269n42
goal of, 81, 271, 303–4, 337
God's presence in, 274
as grace, 269n42
groaning, 212
of heavenly stage, 266–69, 313
invisible aspects, 270n47
kingly rule over, 335–36
as participant in theodrama, 270n47
porous, 269, 270, 273, 313, 318, 331, 335
priestly care for, 335–36
sacramental, 270n46
and scientific conclusions, 270n47
self-sufficient, 8, 313, 320
as stage of theodrama, 201–5, 266–71, 313, 331
as temple, 80, 101, 201, 202–5
cruciform life, 55, 247–248, 248n213, 249, 251, 303

SUBJECT INDEX

cultic mandate, 83, 102, 116, 175, 187. *See also* Great Commission.
cultural engagement, 116–18
cultural mandate, 83, 102, 175, 179–80
    as covenant of works, 179–80
"curse of the law," 156–57

dangers, mortal, 20–21
death, 21
deification. *See* glorification; *theosis*.
deism, 72. *See also* Moral Therapeutic Deism.
design study, 2
devil. *See* Satan.
disciplines, spiritual, 34–35, 35n88, 56, 115–16, 187, 332n43
doctrine, doctrines,
    and Christian identity, 53–55, 98, 257
    and Christian practice, 55–56, 98, 257
    appeal to imagination, 46, 60, 95, 257–58, 330
    dialogical, 46, 257–58
    and drama, 45–50, 95–96, 257–58, 260n8. *See also* drama; theodrama
    as dramatic direction, 50–52, 60, 96–98, 307
    as grammar, 42–44, 94–95, 108, 258, 259
    as interpretive lens, 96
    as mental habit, 50, 53, 55
    nature of, 15, 42–56, 94–98
        canonical-linguistic model, 45, 51
        cognitive-propositional model, 42, 44, 45, 95
        covenantal model, 95
        cultural-linguistic model, 42–44, 45, 51, 95
        emotional-expressive model, 44, 45
        experiential-expressive model, 42, 95
        narrative models, 95
    pastoral function, 50, 56
    performance of, 43–44, 45, 49–50
    as second-order propositions, 43
    as spiritual formation, 56, 57, 58, 98
    as training in wisdom, 50, 56, 58, 60, 96, 99, 108, 112, 259
drama, dramas, 3, 21–22
    and Christian faith, 85–86
    and doctrine, 45–50. *See also* theodrama.
    competing, 52
    essence of, 45
    etymology, 45n131
    as handmaid to theology, 22
    vs. narrative, 21–22
    as words and action, 22

ecclesiology. *See* church.
ecological repentance, 336n56
Eden, as temple, 202n50
effectual calling, 74, 75n70, 76, 104, 153, 169, 170, 172n221, 174, 300n141, 301, 302
    and regeneration, 75, 76, 169, 170, 301
election, 71–72, 80, 81, 100, 102, 103, 104, 105, 109, 111, 112, 114, 115, 127, 128, 129, 133, 140, 151, 153, 156, 157, 184, 186, 280n79, 284n91, 288n107, 292n115, 302, 303
    and covenant, 280n79
    of Israel, 201, 217–18, 231, 279–281, 314–15, 330
    placement in theology, 302n152
    and reprobation, 303n153
    two kinds, 280n79
embodiment. *See* body.
encyclopedia, theological, 1, 13, 56, 339
environmental moralism, 336n56
epistemology, 30, 35, 164
    analogical, 90, 164, 166
    and certainty, 32, 35n90, 60, 89, 91
    covenantal, 90

and dualism, 94
as hermeneutical starting point, 35n90
limitations, 30, 31, 32, 59, 89, 261n15
eschatology, 54, 56, 59, 91, 195–96, 303–5, 317–18. *See also* creation: goal of.
and ontology, 199n40
and orientation of theodrama, 195–96, 199n40
precedes soteriology, 65n20, 82
and Sabbath, 197, 271
Eucharist. *See* Lord's Supper.
evangelism, 14, 118, 322n22. *See also* gospel, communication of.
evil, problem of, 276n71
evolution, 270n47, 277n74
expiation, 286, 286n94
expressivism, 8–9, 307, 314, 316, 323, 329, 332, 333
and doctrine, 42, 44, 45, 95

faithful presence, 176
fall into sin, 54, 275–78
fear of the Lord, 330–31
federal theology. *See* covenant theology.
filioque, 260n13
finitude, as factor in interpretation, 30, 31, 32, 59, 89, 261n15
formation, spiritual, 187
foundationalism, 35n90, 63, 295n122
framework hypothesis, 271n48
framework, theological, 1, 13–14, 15, 56, 59, 60, 339
and Christian identity, 1, 6, 56, 60, 318, 339–40
and Christian practice, 339–40
and communication of gospel, 1, 6, 56, 60, 312n10, 339–40
covenantal. *See* covenant theology.
participation as center, 2–3, 5, 6, 59, 62, 189, 339–40

theodramatic, 3–4, 5, 6, 14, 15, 60
design features, 6, 15–60
free will, 275n67. *See also* humanity: freedom of.

glorification, 75, 104, 105, 112, 153, 169, 283n92, 302, 317–18. *See also* Trinity: mutual glorification.
and *theosis*, 164, 168, 168n207, 193n16, 199n39
Gnosticism, 72
God. *See also* Trinity.
analogical knowledge of, 90, 91, 93, 109, 166–68, 265n26
attributes,
communicable and incommunicable, 266n30
and God's glory, 264n26
and human attributes, 274n63
performative, 264
as perspective on God's being, 264n26
as "theatricals," 264n25
as "transparencies," 264n26
canceling promise, 161
communicative, 38–39, 80, 189–90, 215n107, 217, 260n8, 261, 263, 264, 265, 268, 272, 273, 282, 285, 292, 293–94, 295, 300, 312, 313, 321, 327, 328, 330
as covenant blessings, 104–7, 112, 121
as covenant consummation, 107–8, 121
as covenant maker, 99–100, 121
as covenant mediator, 102–103, 112, 121
as covenant partner, 100–102, 121
desiring communion with other, 28, 87, 265, 312–13, 331

God (*continued*)
- essence and energies, 77–79, 92, 100, 109, 115, 163–69, 186, 304
- ethically distant from creation, 72, 109
- fatherly discipline, 253n251
- glory of, 189–92, 255. *See also* God: mission for glory of.
- identity defined by Jesus, 284
- immanence, 266
- impassibility, 265n26
- incomprehensibility, 164–65
- judgment, 253, 255, 304
- known in work, not essence, 78, 90, 109, 164–65, 186
- love, 190, 265, 265n27, 284, 312–13, 317, 331
- mission for glory of, 24–25, 29, 45, 46, 48, 54, 155, 189–90, 192n11, 194, 195, 199, 201, 207, 208, 210, 213, 214, 217, 221, 223–26, 228, 229, 231, 232, 233, 240, 243, 244, 251, 254, 255, 256, 257, 267, 268, 269n43, 276, 279, 281, 282, 285, 291–94, 305, 306, 311, 312, 317, 321, 323, 326, 328, 330, 333, 336
- modes of activity, 263n20
- not hampered by creatureliness, 31
- not wearing mask, 167–68
- and meeting a stranger, 72–73, 108
- metaphysical distance from creation, 123, 184
- missional activity, 54–53
- oneness, 99, 259n7
- our image of. *See* God: view of.
- participation in life of. *See* participation in God's life.
- presence of, 8, 25, 28, 38, 89, 126, 181, 202, 204, 205, 213, 224, 239, 241, 251, 270, 271n50, 272, 274, 293, 313, 317, 324, 327, 331
  - practice of, 331
- punishment by, 253n231
- qualitatively distinct from creation, 73, 95, 109
- simplicity of, 264n26
- speaking in Scripture, 38–40
- and suffering, 276n71
- transcendence, 266
- unity with creation and humanity,
  - ethical, 5, 62
  - ontological, 62
- view of, 38, 109–10, 138, 185, 187n270, 266n30
- vision of, 304
- wrath of, 265, 283, 306n165

gospel,
- being gospel, 97
- communication of, 6, 15–16, 30, 59, 60, 79, 83, 94, 108–14, 118, 120, 184–87, 258, 261n15, 311–18, 322
- vs. effects of gospel, 76–77, 170, 172, 186–87
- equated with justification, 111–12, 170, 185
- doing gospel, 97
- law before gospel, 184
- living gospel, 97
- and social issues, 117–18

grace
- before fall, 140–41, 146–47
- covenant of. *See* covenant, covenants: of grace.
- creation, as act of, 269n42
- definition, 146

Great Commission, 83, 175, 179, 180, 187. *See also* cultic mandate.

habits, infusion of, 74, 76, 169, 170, 173, 174
headship, covenantal, 140, 141, 147, 186
Heidelberg Catechism, 187n270, 272n51
hermeneutical circle, 31, 90
hermeneutical groaning and redemption, 32–33

SUBJECT INDEX

hermeneutics,
  historical-critical method, 16
  and language, 35–41, 92–94
  and mind of Christ, 32–35, 91
  nature of, 15, 30–41, 56, 59, 79, 89–94
  starting point, 35
history, 30, 71, 80, 84, 86, 87, 89–90, 92, 95, 97, 98, 100, 101, 102, 104, 116, 124, 130, 166, 181, 198, 200, 213, 214, 241, 242, 244, 257, 261, 265n26, 280, 283n85, 291, 292, 294, 298, 302n152, 323, 327n31, 329
  Christocentric view, 132
  as factor in interpretation, 30, 31, 32, 59, 89–90, 261n15
  and faith, 17–18
  of redemption, 20, 22, 29, 39, 41, 49, 67, 70, 71, 83, 84, 88, 113, 132, 154, 155, 163, 185, 199, 258, 267
  as theater, 23, 25, 27
Holy Spirit. *See also* pneumatology.
  as creator of new covenant community, 296–99, 317, 329, 331, 333
  and new creation, 316
  as director of theodrama, 22, 263, 264n24, 292, 293–95, 317, 329, 331
  as downpayment, 198, 251
  as gift, 293, 316–17, 328
  gifts of, 298
    special, continuing, 250n223
  as giver of life, 33, 292–93
  as improvisation of God, 264
  inseparable from Christ, 293
  opening hearts, 300n142
  outpouring of, 29, 59, 83, 197–99, 201, 244–45, 251
  prayer to be filled by, 328–29
  as prompter of theodrama, 263n21, 264n24
  as prop master of theodrama, 263n21

  as renewer of humanity, 299–303, 329, 331, 335
  threefold relationship to Christ, 292–93
humanity. *See also* anthropology; image of God.
  as anthropological duality, 273, 321n19
  attributes of, 274n63
  capable of union with God, 204
  creation of, 273–75
  embodied and finite, 30, 31, 32, 59, 89, 261n15
  and eschatology, 196
  essence of, 318–20
  freedom of, 272, 275, 276
  as kings and priests of creation, 21, 208–9, 212, 274
  limited by time and history, 30, 31, 32, 59, 89, 261n15
  male and female, 273n57
  porous, 274, 314, 321, 324
  psychosomatic unity, 273
  relational capacity, 274n63
  renewal by Spirit, 299–303
  spiritually dead, 301n145
  as temple, 101
  union with Adam, 278n77
hypothetical universality, 288n107

identity, Christian, 1–2, 5, 6, 14, 15–16, 29, 53–56, 59–60, 79, 91, 96, 98, 108, 114–18, 120, 158, 182, 184, 186, 187, 257, 258, 307, 318–21, 322
  and justification, 115, 185–86
  narrative, 9, 53, 97, 323, 329
  and self-image, 114, 185–86
  and union with Christ, 115. *See also* Christ: union with.
image of God (*imago Dei*), 65, 73, 81, 100–101, 140, 144, 147, 196, 201, 205–210, 212, 212n95, 273n56, 274n63, 275, 275n64, 276, 329
imagination,
  appeal to, 46, 60, 95, 257–58, 309, 330, 340

imagination (*continued*)
  biblically formed, 46, 48
  cognitive faculty, 47, 47n141, 308
  and communication of gospel, 309–10
  and eschatology, 48
  integrative faculty, 47, 308
  and reason, 47n142
  theodramatic, 15, 46, 48, 50, 53, 60, 96, 258, 260, 264, 267, 269, 271, 273, 276, 279, 282, 284, 292, 293, 296, 300, 303, 309–10
immanent frame of life, 7, 10–11, 13n64, 307, 313, 317, 319–20, 321, 325, 329, 332, 333, 335, 336, 340
improvisation, 4, 48, 50n152, 53, 60, 95, 258, 264, 294n121
imputation, 65, 69, 70, 141, 147, 149n160, 153, 159, 171
incarnational life, 247, 248, 251
individualism, 7, 307, 312–13, 314, 332
injustice,
  perpetrators of, 316
  victims of, 290–91, 316
institutions, Christian, 117
Israel,
  covenant with. *See* covenant, covenants: with Israel.
  election of, 217–32, 279–81, 314–15, 330
  future ingrafting into church, 71, 107, 251, 279, 280n80, 296, 333
  history reveals human sinfulness, 67, 88, 113, 154, 155, 185, 279
  parenthesis in history of redemption, 70, 88, 113–14, 154, 155, 185, 279
  pedagogical function, 152, 153, 154, 155, 185, 279, 314
  priestly nation, 156
  reconstituted and expanded, 244, 251, 279, 332
  as theater of theodrama, 217–32, 234, 246, 330
  typological function, 67–68, 70, 88, 148–49, 152, 153, 154, 155, 185, 279, 314

Jesus. *See also* Christ.
  absent in present, 12, 320, 329
  active obedience of, 68–69, 70, 80, 103, 104, 109, 141, 147, 153, 156, 159, 171, 186
  as authentic human being, 315–16
  baptism, 235–36
  death, sacrifice of, 239–41, 286–87, 315
  exorcisms, 238–39
  healings, 238–39
  hiddenness, 243, 319
  in historical context, 19
  incarnation, 233, 234, 243n198, 282
  life, sacrifice of, 236–39, 284–86, 315
  and merit, 68–69, 69n41, 109, 110, 112, 138, 141, 156
  partial, 12, 308, 309, 320, 329, 330
  passive obedience of, 68–69, 70, 80–81, 104, 109, 141, 147, 153, 156, 159, 171, 186
  private prayers of, 332
  prophet, priest, and king, 82, 239n187, 286–87, 291, 299, 323
  reception of Spirit, 235–36, 236n181
  resurrection, 82, 241–42, 290–91
  solitude, 332
  as theater of theodrama, 233–43, 286
justification, 74–77, 104, 254n234
  equated with gospel, 111–12, 170, 185
  extra nos, 74, 169, 174
  as heart of covenant ontology, 74, 185

394

SUBJECT INDEX

and imputation, 65, 69, 70, 141, 147, 149n160, 153, 159, 171
and judgment according to works, 305n160
as legal fiction, 74, 76, 170, 171, 172, 173, 174
second, 305n160
source of *ordo salutis*, 74–75, 76, 112, 169–74
transformative, 76, 104, 171, 172, 174
and union with Christ, 75n71, 76, 171–72, 186

kingdom, kingdoms,
common, 102, 175–77, 181–82
of God/heaven, 19, 23, 24, 25, 41n109, 47n141, 48, 49, 81, 82–83, 84, 98, 102, 107, 111, 112, 113, 117, 130, 133, 155, 157, 175–79, 181–82, 187n270, 194, 236–239, 241, 249n217, 250, 252, 254, 260n11, 267, 285, 290n108, 291, 298–99, 303–4, 323, 327, 333, 335, 336–37
announced by Jesus, 236–37
nearness of, 236–37, 238, 337–38
as realm, 179, 237
as rule, 179
transfer to, 249n217
Israel, 82, 152, 224–25, 227n155, 230, 239
sacred. See kingdom: of God.
in Scripture, 179
two kingdoms, 175–79, 181–82, 183
and nature-grace dualism, 181n263
kingdom work, 176–77

language, 30–31, 36–41, 42. See also speech acts.
and Scripture, 37–38
as toolbox, 36, 42

law and gospel, 58, 63, 65, 65n19, 66, 83, 97, 102, 105, 106, 110–11, 113, 117, 136–38, 141, 145–46, 152, 175, 177, 182, 184, 185
lawsuit, 25, 102
lectio divina, 26, 328
literature, Christian, 176
liturgy. See worship.
Lord's Supper, 85, 86–87, 96, 106, 136, 163–64, 298, 326–27

man of lawlessness, 253n230
means of grace, 88, 298n134
meganarrative, 80n93
merit,
condign, 125, 139, 141
congruous, 125
and covenant of works, 65, 68–69, 110, 125
covenantal (*ex pacto*), 125, 139, 141, 144
and Jesus, 68–69, 109, 110, 112, 138, 141
quid pro quo, 110, 136n72, 139, 143, 185
strict justice, 125, 139, 141, 144
metanarrative, metanarratives, 80n93, 97
mindfulness, 332
mission, 24–25, 29. See also under church; covenant; God; Scripture.
"Moralistic Therapeutic Deism," 11–12, 308, 312–13
mutual indwelling, 5, 14, 73, 85
mysticism, 72, 77, 164

natural law, 83, 102, 117, 175, 180, 181, 187
New covenant theology, 135n70
new creation, 4, 21, 24, 25, 29, 33, 41n109, 48, 59, 67, 71, 79, 81, 82, 86, 103, 105, 111, 114, 131, 151, 182, 195, 197–99, 202, 204–5, 232, 234, 241–42, 246, 247, 248, 251–52, 255–56, 283, 290,

SUBJECT INDEX

new creation (*continued*)
    293, 296–99, 303, 316, 319,
    321, 323, 326, 333, 335, 336
    after destruction of old creation,
        255
    and Sabbath rest, 256
    as stage for theodrama, 255–56
    and termination of marital life,
        256
new heavens and new earth. *See*
    new creation.
neutrality, religious, 181n260
Newton, John, 176
nominalism 124–26, 144

ontology, 72
    Christian-platonic, 40n108,
        199n40, 270n46
    of correspondence, 115
    covenant, 4–5, 14, 62, 72–77, 90,
        91, 85, 108, 109, 115, 119,
        171, 173, 187n270, 339
    eschatological, 199n40
    forensic, 75, 169
    hyper-immanent, 72, 108
    participatory, 4–5, 14, 62,
        72–74, 77, 85, 119, 169, 171,
        173, 187n270, 199n40, 339
    Platonic, 41n108, 72, 108, 109,
        270n46
    sacramental, 40n108, 270n46
    hyper-transcendent, 72, 108
    univocal, 72–73
ordo salutis, 74, 75n70, 112, 115,
    153, 159, 302
    generated by justification, 74–
        75, 76, 112, 115, 169–74
    revised, 159, 302
    union with Christ as matrix of,
        104, 115

pactum salutis. *See* covenant,
    covenants: of redemption.
Palamas, Gregory, 77, 78, 163
panentheism, 77
pantheism, 72, 77, 164
parousia, 253n232

partaking of divine nature, 3, 104,
    163, 164, 192, 205, 293, 297,
    298n134, 302, 319, 325, 326,
    328
participation in God's life, 2–3, 5,
    6, 14, 25, 62, 72, 87, 98,
    104, 108–9, 184, 188, 189,
    191–94, 257, 266, 279, 282,
    292, 303, 319, 339–40
    as center of theological
        framework, 2–3, 5, 6, 59, 62,
        189, 339–40
    Christological, 193
    cosmological, 5n25
    mediated by Spirit, 193
    natural, 184, 204
    ontological, 109, 193, 318
    soteriological, 5n25
penance, 112n218, 136–37, 290n108
perichoresis, 262n18, 282, 292
Pentecost, day of, 244n204
Platonism, 41n108, 72, 108, 109,
    270n46
plausibility structures, 7, 10, 12–13,
    14, 308–10
plumbing, Christian, 176
pluralism, 10–11, 36n90, 308, 312
pneumatology, 82, 288n104,
    292n113. *See also* Holy
    Spirit.
    distinguished from Christology,
        288n104
political engagement, 334n48
politics, Christian and secular,
    176–77
postmodernism, 16, 19, 36n90, 63,
    309
practice, Christian, 2, 5, 6, 14, 15–
    16, 26, 45, 53–56, 59–60, 79,
    91, 96, 98, 108, 114–18, 120,
    182, 184, 186, 187, 257, 258,
    307, 322–37
prayer,
    contemplative, 332
    conversational, 332
    via Jesus, 332

396

SUBJECT INDEX

preaching, 82, 85, 86, 87, 94, 104, 106, 107, 115, 117, 145n106, 297–98, 323, 325n29
   biblical-theological, 325n29
   God's sacramental presence in, 105
   Jesus', 238, 250
   mystagogical, 322n20, 324–25
   one-sided emphasis on, 325n30
   sacramental, 325n29
   and Spirit, 297–98
   and spiritual formation, 325n29
   to the heart, 325n29
   transformational, 325n29
predestination, 100, 133, 184, 196, 280n79, 289n107, 302n152. *See also* election; reprobation.
process theology, 72
progressive covenantalism, 135n70
propitiation, 286n94
protevangelium, 69, 152, 179n253, 213n100
providence, 13, 38, 100, 271–72
   concursus, 271n50
   as drama, 271–72
   and sin, 271n50
   and Trinity, 272

ransom, 287n96
receptivity, spirituality of, 329
regula fidei, 27, 57
redemption, 20, 21, 54, 69, 72, 73, 80, 84, 89, 102, 103, 104, 114, 127, 128, 152, 153, 173, 179, 182, 213, 214n103, 217, 269, 282, 283n85, 285n92, 287–90, 315
   because of Christ, 283n85
   covenant of. *See* covenant, covenants: of redemption.
   drama of, 22, 23, 45, 50–51, 55, 85–87, 94–97, 115, 116, 187, 258, 295, 327
   future, of bodies, 251
   goal of, 65n20, 82
   hermeneutical, 34
   hidden quality of, 290

history of, 4, 20, 22, 41, 49, 67, 71, 80, 83, 88, 152, 154, 155–56, 163, 185, 258, 262, 267
   and Scripture, 39
   in spite of Christ, 283n85
regeneration, 74, 75, 76, 104, 153, 154, 169, 170, 233n176, 246, 300n144, 301, 302, 324
   and effectual calling, 75, 76, 169, 170, 301
   and moral suasion, 300n144
relationship to God,
   legal/ethical, 73, 85, 108–9, 110, 115, 119, 139, 184, 339
   of love, then law, 185
   natural, 8, 62, 123, 126, 144, 184, 204, 270, 274, 313, 324, 331
   ontological, 109, 119, 339
   porous, 313, 314, 318, 324, 331
reprobation, 303, 303n153
resurrection, 107, 111
   of Jesus, 290–91
   and spiritual bodies, 256n238
   as *telos* of Christian story, 81–82
resurrectional life, 248, 249, 251, 303
revelation,
   general, 83, 117, 175, 177, 180, 181, 182, 187, 293n118
   Scripture as, 40
   special, 117, 147, 177, 180, 181, 187, 293n118

Sabbath, 24, 25, 65, 67, 68, 70, 80, 81, 105, 107–8, 109, 124, 140, 151, 155, 179, 194, 197, 198, 204–5, 209, 218, 226n152, 255–56, 271, 283, 298–99, 327, 331, 333, 334, 335, 336
sacraments, 18, 35, 82, 83, 86–87, 96, 106–7, 112n218, 116, 117, 136–37, 145n106, 250, 264n24, 290n108, 297, 298, 322n20, 323, 325n28, 326–327. *See also* baptism; penance; Lord's Supper

SUBJECT INDEX

sacraments (*continued*)
  mystagogical approach to, 326–27
sanctification
  by Spirit, 285n93
Satan, 20–21, 29, 59, 83, 210, 212–14, 236, 239, 240, 241, 246, 252, 255, 253n230, 267–68, 276, 278, 283, 285, 286, 287, 289, 290, 314, 335
  as antagonist, 210, 268
  binding and release of, 289, 304n158
  as communicative being, 268, 272
  and depersonalization, 268n38
  fall, 267–68
Satan (*continued*)
  as father of lies, 268
  freedom, 268
  God's authority over, 268, 272, 276
  head crushed, 155, 213–14, 218, 225, 230, 238, 255, 278
  kingdom of, 178
  victory over, 80, 81, 101, 103, 305
scientific conclusions, 270n47, 277n74
Scripture,
  accompanied by Spirit, 39, 94, 295
  as canon, 88, 93, 295n124
  and Christ, 40
  Christ's reading of, 328
  as divine communication, 28, 38–40, 46, 92–93, 294, 295, 327–28
  as drama, 59
  in economy of redemption, 39
  fourfold sense, 26, 41n109, 294n120
  genres, 51
  as God's covenant document, 39–40, 88, 93
  God's presence in, 28, 87, 327
  historical-critical approach, 16, 17n4, 19, 27
  Jewish approach, 16, 19
  and language, 37–38
  as means of grace, 88
  mission of, 39, 40, 295
  modeled on suzerainty treaties, 88
  and moral formation, 87
  mystagogical reading, 294, 327–28
  narrative approach, 16–19, 20, 29, 79–83
  nature of, 15, 16–29, 79–89
  plotline, 17, 80–83
  postmodern approach, 16, 19
  reader as performer, 41, 59
  reader's typological inclusion in, 41n109
  redemptive-historical approach, 19–21, 29, 41, 49, 59, 83–85, 108, 258
  requires Spirit, 94, 295
  as revelation, 40
  as script, transcript, prescript, 23, 49, 59, 60, 86, 108, 258, 294, 299, 307, 328, 333
  self-authenticating, 93
  as Spirit's instrument, 28, 29, 59, 87–88
  spiritual reading, 328
  stability of meaning, 40, 295
  theodramatic approach, 21–25, 29, 46, 49, 85–87, 96
  theological approach, 26–28, 29, 87–89
  and tradition, 28, 94
  transformative, 295
  unity of, 20, 27, 59, 79, 83, 295
secular, secularity, 6–7
  crisis, 309
  opportunity, 309
  realm, 102, 175–76
  vs. sacred, 102, 116–18, 187, 334n53
  state, 181n260
secular culture, 5–14, 15, 31, 43–44, 60, 63, 182, 307–36, 339–40
  and church, 11–13
  consumeristic, 312

disenchanted, 7–8, 307, 311
distracted, 10, 308, 322
experiential, 9–10, 308, 323, 329
expressive, 8–9, 307, 314, 316, 323, 329, 332, 333
goal of, 333
imagination of, 330
immanent frame of, 313, 321, 332
individualistic, 7, 307, 312–13, 314, 332
lies of, 334n47
malaise, 8, 311, 321
open to transcendence, 321, 329, 331, 336
plausibility structure of, 7–14, 308–10
pluralistic, 10–11, 36n90, 308, 312
social imaginary of, 7–14, 306–8
technological, 10, 308, 322
theory-laden, 6
self, selves,
　"buffered," 7, 8n36, 307, 313, 314, 320, 328
　enclosed, 7, 10, 32, 33, 34, 59, 91, 182, 211, 212, 232, 246, 268, 276, 277, 301, 307, 313, 314, 318, 320, 328, 332
　individual, 7, 307, 312–13
　porous, 7–8
　rational, 7, 313
self-image, Christian. *See* identity, Christian.
sermon. *See* preaching.
sin, 19, 20–21, 29, 32, 53, 54, 58, 59, 80, 83, 86, 100, 109, 139, 145, 146, 147, 176, 194, 196, 210, 214, 215, 216, 218, 219, 235, 236, 240, 241, 242, 245, 246, 248n213, 249n215, 253n231, 255, 271n50, 272, 276, 277, 279, 283, 285, 286, 287, 288n103, 290, 292n115, 303, 306n165, 315, 335
　Adam's, 18, 101, 225, 230, 240, 277, 278n77, 279. *See also* fall into sin.
　confession of, 137
　and darkened understanding, 182
　and death, 19, 20–21, 201, 212, 239, 267
　and decay, 211
　and division, 21
　effects, 233n176, 296n128
　essence of, 276, 277n72
　and guilt, 20–21, 111–12
　incurvatus in se, 182, 210, 212, 220, 232, 246, 277, 314
　knowledge of, 110–11
　noetic effects, 254n233
　not ontological, 276
　original, 212, 277, 278n77
　as pollutant, 21
　as power, 21, 103, 211, 248, 249n216, 268, 287n96
　social imaginary, 7, 10, 12, 13, 14, 303n154, 307–309
　secular vs. biblical, 12
　in worship, 324n26
*sola*s, 184n268
solitude, 332
soteriology, 36n90, 121, 169, 172, 287, 315
　appropriationist, 157, 186, 315n13
　and Christology, 282n83
　and determinism, 128n41, 184
　as earning and applying benefits, 112, 157–58, 186, 246n209, 286n95, 315n13
　extrinsic, 157, 186, 315n13
　as hermeneutical starting point, 35, 35n90
　and participation in Christ, 5n25
　preceded by eschatology, 65n20, 82
　"schizophrenic tendency" in, 75
　twofold structure of, 112, 157–58, 186, 246n209, 286, 286n95, 315n13
soul,
　and body, 273–74
　porous, 273, 321

SUBJECT INDEX

soul (*continued*)
    receptive and responsive, 273–74, 309n3, 320–21
speech acts, 15, 23, 36–37, 39, 41n110, 46, 49, 50, 53, 56, 92, 94, 174n230, 258, 260, 264, 267, 269, 271, 273, 276, 279, 282, 284, 292, 293, 294, 295, 296, 303, 303, 324
"spiritual but not religious," 10, 322
spiritual warfare, 249, 267
spirituality, contemplative, 26, 116, 187, 332
structure. *See also* framework, theological.
    covenantal, 147. *See also* covenant theology.
    nature of, 16, 56–59, 99–108
structure (*continued*)
    pastoral, 56
    and pedagogy, 56–59, 99, 108, 112
    redemptive-historical, 112
suffering, and God's will, 276n71
supercessionism, 155–56

Tarot cards, 11
theater, 3, 199. *See also* drama; theodrama.
    Christians, 183, 236, 293, 306
    church, 55, 97, 217n115, 244, 247, 251, 317, 321, 328, 333
    creation, 65, 100, 205, 217n115, 270, 335, 336
    history, 23, 27
    Israel, 205, 217, 218, 223, 224, 226, 231, 246, 279–80, 314, 315, 330
    Jesus, 233–34, 284–85, 286
    new heavens and earth, 217n115
    in Scripture, 45
    and temple, 217n115
theodrama, 3–4. *See also under* doctrine: as drama; framework, theological; imagination; theodramatic; Scripture: theodramatic approach.
    acts, 3–4, 199–201
    beginning in Trinity, 23
    and biblical narrative, 6
    church as theater, 97, 217n115, 244–51, 317
    as comedy, 54
    creation as stage for, 201–5, 266–71, 313, 331
    and discipleship, 97
    eschatological orientation of, 195
    Father as author, 22, 203, 263, 267, 269–70, 272, 273, 275n67, 312, 314
    history as theater, 23, 27
    and imagination, 15, 46, 48, 50, 53, 60, 96, 258, 260, 264, 267, 269, 271, 273, 276, 279, 282, 284, 292, 293, 296, 300, 303, 309–10
    Israel as theater, 217–32, 234, 246, 330
    Jesus as theater, 233–43, 286
    ourselves as participants, 22–23, 41, 59, 60, 86–87, 97, 108, 115, 206–7, 258, 263n22, 295
    Scripture as script, transcript, prescript, 23, 49, 59, 60, 86, 108, 258, 294, 299, 307, 328, 333
    Son as protagonist, 22, 263, 267, 269, 273, 278, 282, 312
    Spirit
        as director, 22, 263, 264n24, 267, 269, 273, 292, 293–95, 312, 317, 329, 331
        as prompter, 263n21, 264n24
        as prop master, 263n21
    structured by covenant, 85
    and systematic theology, 6, 257–306
    and tension, 48, 49, 258
    unifying themes, 24–25
    and urgency, 48, 258
    world as audience, 217

SUBJECT INDEX

world as stage, 23
theology. *See also* doctrine.
   archetypal, 78, 90, 164, 166, 168
   covenant. *See* covenant theology.
   definition, 5, 311n9
   ectypal, 78, 90, 164, 166, 168
   framework. *See* framework, theological
   of cross, 78, 84, 164, 166, 168
   of glory, 78, 84, 164, 166, 168
   integrative center of, 2–3, 5, 6, 58, 59, 62, 99, 339
   methodology, 1, 28n6, 46, 84, 339
      Michael Horton's, 84
   "Platonizing," 84–85
   and theory-laden practice, 5–6
theosis, 81n99, 164, 168, 193n16, 199n39
time, 303n154
   and eternity, 302n152
   as factor in interpretation, 30, 31, 32, 59, 89, 261n15
   God's interaction in, 128n41, 133, 184, 202, 205, 251, 261, 262, 263, 282, 284, 292
tradition, 28, 30, 52n163, 94
transcendence, 8, 10–11, 72, 86, 265, 266, 308, 312, 316, 317, 319, 321, 325, 326, 327, 328, 329, 331, 332, 336
transsexuality, 53
treaties, Hittite, 66, 68, 153, 161–62
   not unconditional, 162
trinitarianism, social, 262n18
Trinity. *See also* covenant, covenants: of redemption; God.
   as archetype of covenant, 121
   as beginning of theodrama, 23
   and communication, 23, 38–39, 189–90, 217, 261, 263, 273, 285, 292, 293, 300, 321
   covenantal relations between members, 99
   doctrine, 1, 53, 55, 71, 128, 259, 260, 262n18
   as beginning of doctrine of God, 259n7
   generated by biblical narrative, 260
   and mystery of salvation, 259
   drama of, 259–64, 272
   economic, 38, 39, 300, 54, 100, 165, 166, 189, 262, 269n42, 293
   enacting perfect life, 313, 317
   and fullness, 23n31
   immanent, 23n31, 38, 39, 54, 100, 189, 260n10, 262, 293
   inner life of, 23n31, 100, 260n10
   and kenosis, 23n31
   mutual glorification, 189, 190, 202, 204, 205, 210, 217, 231, 236, 246, 251, 256, 267, 270, 273, 276, 285, 286, 293. 295, 303, 306, 312, 314, 317, 318, 328, 330, 335, 337
   mutual indwelling, 99
   ontological, 165, 166
   participation in life of, 62, 102, 119, 120, 163, 193, 301
   persons of,
      passable, 163
      as relations of origin, 260–61
   and speech acts, 39n102
   subordination in, 261n16
   and will, 261n16
typology, 26, 40, 41n109, 67, 69n41, 70, 88, 132, 148, 152, 153–55, 161, 185, 279, 295, 314

virtues, 330
vocations, Christian, 117, 175–77, 182–83
voluntarism, 124–26

Westminster Confession of Faith, 120, 123n21, 126, 136
Wilberforce, William, 176
wisdom, training in, 50, 56, 58, 60, 96, 99, 108, 112, 259

works, judgment according to,
     305n160, 317
worship, 86–87, 97, 115–16
   and Christ's pattern, 324n26
   and discipleship, 324n26
   as echo of heavenly worship, 250
   enacting God's drama, 86, 97,
     115, 250
   eschatological, 324n26
   and formation of imagination,
     324n26
   human and divine agency in,
     324n26
   liturgy as covenant renewal, 86
   supplemented, 87n125, 116
   theodramatic, 323

Author Index

Adams, Marilyn McCord, 54n172
Alexander, T. Desmond, 24n37, 25, 196n27, 198n36, 202n50, 209n78
Allen, David, 127n39, 289n107
Allen, Leslie C., 232n173
Allen, R. Michael, 33n77, 34n85, 120n5, 127n39, 135n72, 150n125, 151n130, 262n16, 299n138, 330n39
Allison, Gregg R., 203n56, 203n57, 204n58, 207, 237n183, 243n198, 261n14
Anderson, Bernhard W., 223n141
Anderson, Kenton C., 325n29
Andrews, Alan, 35n88
Ashford, Bruce Riley, 191n5, 278n77
Asselt, W. J. van, 120n5, 128n41, 184n269
Augustine, 17n4, 135n72, 177–78, 262n17
Aulén, Gustaf, 290n108
Austin, J. L., 36

Bailey, Justin Ariel, 47n141, 309–11
Balthasar, Hans Urs von, 3, 22–23, 25, 26n51, 27n58, 46n135, 48n146, 49n150, 52n163, 53n167, 54nn169–172, 55n173, 55n175, 201n46, 210n86, 260n7, 261n15, 263n21, 264n24, 266n31, 269n41, 273n56, 277n72, 282n82, 284n90, 293n117, 296n126, 299n140, 303n154
Barach, John, 280n79

Barr, James, 122n15, 122n18, 209n79
Barringer, Laura, 334n51
Barth, Karl, 27, 39n102, 142n97, 146n108, 257n1, 259n7, 261n15, 263n20, 266nn30–31, 269n41, 271nn49–50, 273n56, 276n69, 281n80, 282n82, 284n90, 292n114, 293n117, 296n126, 297n131, 299n140
Barth, Marcus, 25
Bartholomew, Craig G., 4, 17n4, 26n46, 27n53, 28n60, 121n8, 140n89, 150n127, 191n5, 194n23, 218nn119–20, 237n183, 278n77
Bass, Diana Butler, 11, 322n21, 322n23
Bass, Dorothy C., 331n42
Bauckham, Richard J., 192n13, 195n25
Baugh, S. M., 134
Bavinck, Herman, 120, 123, 127n39, 135n72, 147n111, 150n125, 151n130, 152, 165, 166nn197–99, 180n258, 190–91, 257n1, 259n7, 261n15, 262n17, 266nn30–31, 267n34, 268n37, 269n41, 271n49, 273n56, 276n69, 278n77, 280n80, 282n82, 284n90, 292n114, 293n117, 296n126, 299n140, 303n154, 304n155
Beach, J. Mark, 127n39

AUTHOR INDEX

Beale, G. K., 3n11, 18n12, 24, 25, 132n58, 135n72, 150n126, 192n14, 196n27, 198, 202n50, 204n62, 206n70, 208, 209n79, 209n82, 210n85, 237n183, 274n63, 305n160
Beek, A. van de, 334n47
Beeke, Joel R., 127n39, 135n72, 145n106, 151n130, 165n190, 257n1, 259n7, 261n15, 266nn30–31, 273nn56–57, 276n69, 282n82, 284n90, 292n114, 292n117
Behr, John, 196n29
Bekkum, Koert van, ix, 66n28, 123n20, 162n175, 202n50, 205n65, 208, 210nn84–85, 211n89, 269n42, 271nn47–48
Belcher, Richard P., Jr., 120n5, 135n72, 151n130, 216n113, 220n131
Bergquist, Randall A., 149n118
Berkhof, Hendrikus, 281n81
Berkhof, Louis, 120, 123n22, 127n39, 135n72, 151n130, 205n66, 259n7, 261n15, 266n31, 269n41, 271n49, 273n56, 276n69, 282n82, 284n90, 292n114, 293n117, 296n126, 299n140, 303n154
Berkouwer, G. C., 142n97
Berlin, Tom, 334n52
Bianchi, Enzo, 328n34
Billings, J. Todd, 2n2, 3, 27, 28nn60–61, 28n63, 168n207, 193, 199n40, 247n211, 270n46, 294n120, 300n140, 304n155, 327n31
Bintsarovskyi, Dmytro, ix, 77, 79n92, 90n142, 92n148, 92n150, 163n176, 165–66, 166nn195–96, 166n199, 167, 168–69, 304n157
Bird, Michael F., 160n161
Block, Daniel I., 202n50,
Boa, Kenneth D., 35n88, 311n8

Boer, Harry R., 196n29
Boersma, Hans, 26n51, 270n46, 290n108, 304n155, 324n26, 325n29, 328nn34–35
Bolt, John, 135n72, 147n112
Bonhoeffer, Dietrich, 98, 334n49
Booram, Beth A., 331n41
Booram, David, 331n41
Booth, Susan Maxwell, 195n25
Borg, Marcus J., 17n8, 18n10
Boulton, Matthew Myer, 334n45
Bourke, Vernon J., 178n246
Bowald, Mark Alan, 35n90, 39n102
Bowman, Robert M., Jr., 311n8
Bowsher, Clive, 3n11
Boyer, Steven D., 33n77, 261n16
Bradshaw, David, 77n84, 77n86
Braun, Gabriele G., 203n50
Brink, Gijsbert van den, 158, 197n35, 240nn189–90, 257n1, 259, 260n13, 261n15, 262nn17–19, 264n26, 265nn27–28, 266nn29–31, 267n32, 268n38, 269n41–42, 271nn49–50, 272n51, 272n55, 273nn56–57, 274n60, 274n63, 275n67, 276nn69–71, 277n74, 280n80, 281n81, 282nn82–83, 283n85, 284nn89–90, 285n92, 287n99, 290n108, 292nn113–14, 293nn116–18, 294n122, 295n123–24, 296nn126–27, 297, 298nn134–35, 299n140, 302n152, 303n154, 321n18
Brown, Michael G., 121n8
Browning, Don S., 6n28
Bruce, F. F., 280n80
Brueggemann, Walter, 99n181, 203–4, 334n54
Bruggen, Jakob van, 134n67, 134n69, 145n104, 149n120, 149n123, 157, 179, 211n92, 236nn182–83, 238nn184–86, 248n212, 249nn216–17, 252nn227–28, 253nn229–30, 253n232, 254n233,

AUTHOR INDEX

256n239, 270n47, 275n68,
280n79, 281n80, 287n98,
302n151, 305n160, 337n57
Bruijne, A. de, 30n65, 32n74,
179n254, 183n266,
251nn223–24, 297n133,
326n30, 330n38, 331n40,
334n48, 336n56
Burger, Hans, ix, 3, 5, 6n28,
7n31, 12, 21n22, 30n65,
33nn79–80, 34nn82–84,
34n86, 35nn89–90, 37n93,
38n98, 39n102, 41nn109–
10, 58–59, 110nn214–16,
112n219, 113, 122n14, 123,
125, 126nn36–37, 136n74,
137n78, 137n80, 138n86,
139n88, 143n97, 143n100,
144n102, 145, 146n108, 147,
150nn128–29, 152nn133–
35, 153n136, 154n139,
154n141, 156n144, 157,
158–59, 160nn161–62,
162n175, 171n219, 173n223,
187n270, 192–93, 193n16,
194n23, 195n25, 198n38,
199n40, 209nn81–83,
210n86, 211nn87–88,
211n91, 212, 215n109,
215n111, 216n113,
218nn119–120, 220n129–
31, 221n132, 221n134,
222n138, 223n139–40,
226n152, 227nn153–55,
228nn156–60, 230n165,
231n169, 233n176,
235n179, 236n180, 239n185,
240nn192–93, 241nn195–
95, 242nn196–98,
243nn199–201, 244nn202–
3, 247n210, 248n213,
249nn215–16, 250nn220–
23, 251, 253n231, 254n234,
255n235, 259nn4–5,
262nn17–18, 270n46,
275n68, 277n72, 279n78,
283n86, 284n87, 284n91,
285n93, 286nn94–95,

287nn96–98, 287n100–102,
288n104, 288n107, 290n108,
291nn111–12, 295n125,
296n128, 302n150, 311n9,
324, 327, 336n55
Butterfield, Rosaria, 334n46

Calhoun, Adele Ahlberg, 35n88
Calvin, John, 2, 58, 78, 90, 92,
104n199, 106n207, 177–78,
193, 217n115, 246n209,
254n233, 259n7, 261n15,
266n29, 266n31, 269n41,
270n44, 270n47, 271n49,
273n56, 274n61, 276n69,
277n72, 278n77, 280n79,
281n80, 282n82, 284n90,
292n114, 293nn117–18,
296n126, 299n140, 300n144,
302n152, 303n154, 304n155,
305n160, 327n31
Campbell, Constantine R., 3n11,
296n128
Canlis, Julie, 3, 158n153, 159n160,
168n207, 193, 199n40,
204n61, 210n84, 270n44,
274n61, 277n72
Carson, D. A., 156, 183n266
Caughey, Christopher Earle, 141n95
Chandler, Diane J., 35n88
Chapell, Bryan, 325n29
Charry, Ellen T., 50n155
Childers, Jana, 325n29
Childs, Brevard S., 16n4
Clapp, Rodney, 299n136
Clark, John C., 262n18, 284n88–89
Clark, R. Scott, 127n39, 128n44,
129n46, 129n48, 130nn50–
51, 130n53, 131n57, 134n65,
164n67
Clines, D. J. A., 206n70
Cocceius, Johannes, 129n46,
129n48, 130nn50–51,
130n53, 131n57, 151n130
Colorado, Carlos D., 7n31
Courtenay, W. J., 124nn26–27,
125n30
Cranfield, C. E. B., 280n80

Crisp, Oliver D., 288n107
Crouch, C. L., 207n71
Crouse, Robert C., 178
Cullmann, Oscar, 305n159
Cumin, Paul, 270n44
Currid, John D., 151n130
Curtis, Byron G., 150n125

Dalferth, Ingolf U., 34nn83–84, 263n20
Davidson, Ivor J., 282n84
Davies, Glenn, 149
Dawkins, Richard, 11n55
Dawn, Marva J., 334n49, 334n54
Dean, Kenda Creasy, 11n58, 12n59
De Boer, Erik, 280n79
Demarest, Bruce A., 134n65
Dempster, Stephen G., 24n38, 207n71, 213n100,
Dennison, James T., Jr., 149n118
Denton, Melinda Lundquist, 11n58, 12n59, 312n11
DeYoung, Kevin, 121n8
Dijstra-Algra, N., ix, 143n97
Dodd, C. H., 191n7
Dolezal, James E., 262n18
Dooley, Kate, 137n79
Douma, J., 280n79, 292n115, 303n153
Douma, Jos., ix, 35n88, 314n12, 325n29, 328n34
Dumbrell, William J., 24, 25, 149n125, 196n27, 197n32, 197n34, 204nn62–63, 210n85, 214n106, 216n113, 218n119, 222n137, 224, 225n150, 226n152, 227n154, 228n158, 231n171, 233n176
Duncan, Mike, 227n155
Dunn, James D. G., 211n92, 277n73, 280n80
Durham, J. I., 224n143, 224n146, 225n150
Dusseldorp, K. van, 17n4
Duvall, J. Scott, 237n183

Eck, J. van, 203, 244n204, 245nn206–7, 249n215

Edmonson, Stephen, 270n44
Edwards, Jonathan, 127n39, 190n3, 263n20
Egan, Kieran, 47n141
Elam, Andrew M., 149n118
Enns, Peter, 226n152
Estelle, Bryan D., 135n72, 149n119
Evans, C. Stephen, 18n11
Evans, William B., 2n2, 3, 34n86, 157n152, 171n219, 193n16, 193n18

Faber, Jelle, 144
Fairbairn, Donald, 3, 168n207, 191n8, 193nn17–18, 196n29, 199n40, 205n66, 207n73, 284n88
Fanning, Buist M., 302n151
Farlow, Matthew S., 4, 41n112, 46n139
Fee, Gordon D., 251n223
Ferguson, Sinclair B., 265n28
Ferry, Brenton C., 142n95
Fesko, J. V., 17n4, 123n22, 127n39, 128, 129, 130nn50–51, 130n53, 131nn55–57, 133, 135n72
Finlan, Stephen, 168n207
Foster, David, 328n34
Foster, Richard J., 35n88, 328n35
Fowl, Stephen E., 28n60, 28n62
Frame, John M., 35n90, 97n172, 121n8, 127n39, 143n97, 151n130, 165n190, 167, 180n259, 181, 182n264, 192n14, 257n1, 259n7, 261n15, 266nn30–31, 268n37, 269n41, 271nn49–50, 272n53, 273nn56–57, 275n67, 276n69, 278n77, 282n82, 284n90, 292n114, 293n117, 296n126, 299n140, 303n154
Francis, 336n55
Franke, John R., 35n90
Frei, Hans, 16n2, 17n4

AUTHOR INDEX

Gadamer, Hans-Georg, 6n29, 27n56, 30nn66-68, 31nn69-70, 32nn73-74, 38n97, 52, 57n179, 89
Gaffin, Richard B., Jr., 149n118, 159n158, 160n161, 171n219, 191n8, 256n238
Garcia, Mark A., 138n85, 160n162
Garvey, Jon, 202n50
Gattis, Lee, 289n107
Genderen, J. van, 121n8, 127n39, 128n41, 151n130, 184n269, 207n71, 257n1, 259n7, 261n15, 266nn30-31, 269n41, 271n49, 273n56, 276n69, 277n75, 278nn76-77, 282n82, 284n90, 292n114, 293n117, 296n126, 300n140, 303n154
Gentry, Peter J., 24n41, 135n70, 135n72, 150n128, 151n130, 160n162, 195n25, 202n50, 215n111, 216n113, 218n120, 220nn130-31, 226n152, 233n176, 237n183
Gerrish, B. A., 210n84, 277n72
Gladd, Benjamin L., 202n50
Godfrey, W. Robert, 289n107
Goheen, Michael, 4, 17n4, 26n52, 121n8, 195n25, 218n120, 237n183
Golding, Peter, 120n5, 142n95
Goldingay, J., 122n14, 194n23
Goldsworthy, Graeme, 24n38, 237n183
Gorman, Michael J., 248n214
Gould, Paul M., 47n141
Graaf, S. G. de, 121n8, 127n39, 142n97, 146n108, 151n130
Green, Joel B., 27n56, 28nn62-64, 57n179
Greenman, Jeffrey P., 35n88
Greidanus, Sidney, 213n98, 214n103
Greijdanus, S., 280n80
Grenz, Stanley J., 16n3, 35n90, 36n90, 196-97, 257n1, 259n7, 261n15, 266nn30-31, 269n41, 271n49,
273nn56-57, 276n69, 282n82, 284n90, 292n114, 293n117, 295n123, 296n126, 299n140, 303n154
Grudem, Wayne A., 127n39, 135n72, 151n130
Gumbel, Nicky, 21n20
Gundry, Robert H., 160n161
Gunton, Colin E., 262n19, 265n27, 266n30, 269n42
Guthrie, Steven R., 41n112

Habets, Myk, 55n174, 168n207, 199n40, 260n13
Hahn, Scott W., 24n41, 222n138
Hamilton, James M., Jr., 24n40, 191n6, 191n9, 202n50, 203n56, 209n82, 210n85, 213n100
Hansen, Collin, 7n31
Harris, Max, 4
Hart, Trevor A., 41n112
Hastings, W. Ross, 290n108
Hays, J. Daniel, 237n183
Hays, Richard B., 17, 18n11, 21n21, 201n45
Heide, Gale, 57
Heidegger, Martin, 17n4, 30nn66-67, 31n69
Helmers, Kathryn A., 328n35
Hendriksen, William, 280n80
Heppe, Heinrich, 127n39, 135n72, 254n233
Hiestand, Gerald, 12n61
Hitchens, Christopher, 11n55
Hodge, Charles, 127n39, 135n72, 151n130
Hoekema, Anthony A., 143n97, 280n80
Hoeksema, Herman, 142n97
Hoglund, Jonathan, 172nn220-21, 174n230, 300n142, 300n144, 301n145, 301n148
Holland, Tom (*Dominion*), 183n266
Holland, Tom (*Tom Wright...*), 19n18
Holmes, Christopher R. J., 303n154

Holmes, Stephen R., 196n29, 266n30
Holt, Robby, 28n60
Horrell, J. Scott, 262n18
Horton, Michael S., 2, 4nn21–23, 5, 14, 61–119, 121, 123–24, 125n31, 127, 131, 136n75, 138, 140n90, 141, 142n96, 145n105, 146, 147n112, 148n115, 151, 153–54, 160–62, 163–65, 167–87, 196, 197n32, 198n36, 199n40, 202n50, 205, 210n85, 243n199, 257n1, 259n7, 260n8, 261n15, 266n30, 273n53, 273n56, 274n63, 276n69, 282n82, 284n90, 292n114, 293n117, 296n126, 299n136, 299n140, 301n148, 302n152, 303n154, 304n156, 308n2, 325n29, 339
Houwelingen, P. H. R. van, 192n13, 243n198, 255nn236–37, 267, 281n80
Howard, Thomas, 319n16
Hugenberger, Gordon P., 122
Hughes, Philip Edgcumbe, 196n29
Huigen, Arnold, 199n40, 259n7, 270n46, 274n59, 293n118, 294n119, 304n157, 306n165, 328n35
Hyde, Daniel R., 121n8

Immink, F. Gerrit, 323n25
Irenaeus, 17n4, 57, 135n72
Irons, Lee, 125, 139n88

Jenson, Matt, 210n86, 277n72
Jenson, Robert W., 198
Jeon, Jeong Koo, 143n97
Johnson, Jan, 332n42
Johnson, Marcus Peter, 262n18, 278n77, 284n88–89
Jones, Joe R., 257n1, 258n3, 259n7, 261n15, 266n30, 267n32, 269n41, 271n49, 273n56, 274n63, 276n69, 277n72, 282nn82–83, 284n90, 292n114, 293n117, 296n126, 299n140, 303n154,
Jones, L. Gregory, 334n50
Jones, Mark, ix, 121n8, 127n39, 135n72, 141n95, 143n99, 145n106, 146–47, 151n130
Jong, H. de, 121n8, 229n161, 230nn163–65, 230n167, 231, 280n79
Jong, J. M. de, 334n48

Kalantzis, George, 35n88
Kalluveettijl, Paul, 122n16
Kamp, H. van de, 304n158
Kamphuis, B., 243nn199–200
Kamphuis, J., 127n39, 151n130
Kärkkäinen, Veli-Matti, 259n7, 261n15, 266n30, 269n41, 271n49, 273nn56–57, 276n69, 277n74, 282n82, 284n90, 292n114, 293n117, 296n126, 299n140, 303n154
Karlberg, Mark W., 142n95
Kasper, Walter, 259–60
Keele, Zach, 121n8
Keller, Timothy, 146n107, 176, 181n260, 182n264, 183n266, 325n29
Kelly, J. N. D., 193n13
Kersten, G. H., 128n41
Kevan, Ernest F., 146n110
Kidner, Derek, 210n85
Kilner, John F., 192n12, 196n29, 205n66, 206n67, 206n70, 207n71, 208n75, 209n79, 212n95, 274n63, 275nn64–65
Kim, Mark, 64n12, 69n41, 137n84, 161n167
Kim, Mitchell, 24n37, 196n27, 198n36
Kistemaker, Simon J., 243n198, 256n238
Kittel, G., 190n4
Klassen, Justin D., 7n31
Kline, Meredith G., 61, 65n17, 66, 68–69, 73n61, 88, 102n19, 127n39, 129n45, 129n48,

130n50, 135n72, 148n115, 151n130, 196n29, 197n32, 202n50, 207n71, 209n82, 271n48
Klink, Edward W., III, 16n1, 17nn4-5
Kloosterman, Nelson D., 180, 182n264
Knoppers, Gary N., 162, 220n130
Kooi, Cornelis van der, 158, 197n35, 240nn189-90, 257n1, 259, 260n13, 261n15, 262n17, 262n19, 264n26, 265nn27-28, 266nn29-31, 267n32, 268n38, 269n41-42, 271nn49-50, 272n51, 272n55, 273nn56-57, 274n60, 274n63, 275n67, 276nn69-71, 277n74, 280n80, 281n81, 282nn82-83, 283n85, 284nn89-90, 285n92, 287n99, 290n108, 292nn113-14, 293nn116-18, 294n122, 295n123-24, 296nn126-27, 297, 298nn134-35, 299n140, 302n152, 303n154, 321n18
Köstenberger, Andreas J., 134n65, 203n56, 203n57, 204n58, 207, 207n72, 213n100, 243n198, 261n14, 288n103
Kuhrt, Stephen, 19n18
Kutsch, E., 122n18
Kwakkel, G., 32n75, 122n14, 122n18, 160n162, 161, 214n106, 215nn108-10, 216n113, 220nn127-28, 220n130-31, 224n145, 225nn149-50, 226n152, 227n153, 227n155, 230n166, 271nn47-48, 272n54

Ladd, George Eldon, 237n183
Lane, Tony, 265n28
Lash, Nicholas, 50n152, 259n5
Latzel, T., 187n270
Lawrence, Brother, 331n41

Leder, Arie C., 24n37, 25, 126n37, 143n98, 147n112-13, 194, 195n24, 209n78, 213, 214n105, 216n112, 218n120, 220n129, 221nn132-34, 223n139, 281n81
Lee, Amhi, 325n29
Lehrer, Steve, 135nn70-71
Leithart, Peter J., 147n111, 181n260, 183nn266-67
Letham, Robert, 3, 120n7, 135nn71-72, 142n95, 148, 149n118, 149n120, 151n130, 162n175, 165n190, 168n207, 192, 193n18, 194, 196n29, 199n40, 203, 204, 205n65, 206, 234n178, 257n1, 259n7, 261n15, 266n30, 269n41, 270n46, 271n49, 273n56, 276n69, 282n82, 284n90, 292n114, 293n117, 296n126, 299n140, 303n154
Levering, Matthew, 26n51
Lewis, C. S., 47n142, 48, 311n8
Lewis, Gordon R., 134n65,
Lillback, Peter A., 120n5, 125n31, 125n34, 126n36, 135n72
Lindbeck, George A., 42-44, 173, 174
Lister, J. Ryan, 196n27, 202n49
Littlejohn, W. Bradford, 178n248
Lockett, Darian R., 16n1, 17nn4-5
Longman, Tremper W., III, 192n12,
Loonstra, B., 120n7, 127n39, 128n41, 134n70
Lubac, Henri de, 40n108
Luther, Martin, 136, 137, 167, 177-78, 210n86, 277n72

Macaskill, Grant, 3n11, 158n153, 158n156, 193n16, 296n128, 301n149, 330n39
Macchia, Frank D., 199, 207n72, 234n177, 236nn180-81, 256n238, 287nn96-97, 290n109
MacIntyre, Alasdair, 56n177

Macleod, Donald, 4nn21–22, 62n3, 119nn3–4, 120n5, 127n39, 135n72, 151n130, 203, 259n7, 269n41, 270n44, 273nn56–57, 276n69, 282n82, 284n90, 286n94, 292n114, 293n117, 296n126, 299n140, 303n154
Magee, Bryan, 17n4
Martin, Ralph P., 288n104
Matthews, Kenneth A., 199n39, 207n71, 210n85, 211nn89–90, 219n125
McCarthy, Dennis J., 122n16, 123n18
McComiskey, Thomas E., 143n101, 149n125, 209n83
McConville, J. Gordon, 122n15, 123n20
McCormack, Bruce L., 73n62
McGowan, A. T. B., 120n5, 138n86, 142n97, 147nn111–12, 149n122, 159n158, 162n173, 275n66, 277n75, 278n77
McGrath, Alister, 11n55, 44n128, 61, 124nn27–28, 271n47, 323n24
McGrath, Joanna Collicut, 11n55
McGraw, Ryan M., 138n85, 145n106, 171n218
McKenzie, Steven L., 122
McKnight, Scot, 334nn50–51
Melanchthon, Philip, 57–58
Michelson, Jared, 77n81, 171n218, 172, 173, 174,
Middleton, J. Richard, 202n50, 206n70, 208n75, 209n80
Millar, J. Gary, 35n88
Millard, Kent, 334n52
Miller, Timothy, 171n219
Moes, Dick, 12n59
Moltmann, Jürgen, 197
Moo, Douglas J., 277n75
Moo, Jonathan A., 208n74, 209n82, 211n88, 212nn93–94
Moore, Jonathan D., 288n107, 296n126
Moore-Keish, Martha, 327n31

Morris, Leon, 301n146, 304n158
Mosser, Carl, 168n207, 199n40
Muether, John R., 120n5
Muller, Richard A., 127n39, 128, 135n72, 136n73, 151n130, 262n16, 289n107
Mullins, Jim, 195n25
Murphy, Nancey, 35n90
Murray, John, 135n71, 143n97, 147n112, 151n130, 277n75, 280n80

Nichols, Aiden, 22n24
Nicholson, Ernest W., 122n15, 123n18, 225n150
Noble, Alan, 10nn46–47, 334n47
Noort, E., 194n23
Noppen, Koos van, 299n137
Nouwen, Henri J. M., 35n88

O'Donnell, Laurence, 127n39,
O'Donovan, Oliver, 33nn78–79, 33n81, 34nn82–84, 157n148, 158n156, 182n264, 183nn266–67 210n86, 246n208, 277n72, 287n98, 288n104, 288n107, 291n112, 334n48
Oldhoff, M., 274n60
Oliphint, K. Scott, 123n22
Ordway, Holly, 47n141
Origen, 57
Orthodox Presbyterian Church, 148n114
Osborne, Grant R., 31n71
Ouweneel, William, 181n263
Overstreet, Jeffrey, 328n33

Paas, S., 121nn8–9, 181, 282n82, 336n56
Packer, J. I., 121n8, 135n72, 151n130, 286n94, 306n165, 319n16
Paddison, Angus, 27n53, 27n58, 28nn60–61
Pannenberg, Wolfhart, 259n7, 260n11
Pattison, John, 334n49

AUTHOR INDEX

Pauw, Amy Plantinga, 296nn126–27
Peels, H. G. L., 214n104, 265n28
Pelikan, Jaroslav, 136nn76–77, 137n79
Perkins, Larry, ix, 262n18
Perrin, Nicholas, 237n183
Peterson, Eugene H., 328n33, 328n35, 330n37, 331n40, 331n42
Peterson, Jonathan, 87n125
Plantinga, Alvin, 35n90, 254n233
Pleizier, T., 325n29
Plummer, Robert, 27n58
Pohl, Christine D., 334n46, 334n49
Poythress, Vern S., 180n259, 182n264
Pratt, Richard, Jr., 160n163, 160n165, 221n135
Provan, Iain, 41n108, 270n46

Rad, Gerhard von, 192n12
Rae, Murray, 27nn54–55
Rahner, Karl, 262n19
Redd, John Scott, 220n131
Reeling Brouwer, Rinse H., 57n182, 58n183, 58n185, 58nn187–88, 125n34
Reeves, Michael, 331n40
Reid, J. Nicholas, 120n5, 142n95
Renihan, Samuel D., 65n19, 138n86
Rhodes, Jonty, 120n5
Richard, Guy M., 127n39
Ricoeur, Paul, 17n4, 32n73, 37, 38nn96–97
Ridderbos, Herman, 196n29, 237n183
Rietkerk, W., 282n82
Rishmawy, Derek, 10,
Robertson, O. Palmer, 121n8, 134n70, 150nn25–26, 151n130, 220n130, 230n167, 232n175, 233n176
Root, Andrew, 7n31, 9, 12n60, 309n3, 332n44
Rosa, Hartmut, 309n3
Rose, Wolter, 191
Ross, Allen P., 213n101, 220n130
Ruijter, C. J. de, 324n26, 325n29

Sailhamer, John H., 210n85, 212n97
Saliers, Don E., 324n26
Sanborn, Scott F., 149n118
Sanders, Fred, 203n51, 260n10, 263n19
Sandlin, P. Andrew, 138n86
Sarot, Marcel, 35n90
Satterlee, Craig A., 325n28
Sayers, Dorothy L., 49n147
Scheuers, Timothy R., 178n244, 180n258
Schilder, K., 121n8, 127n39, 135n72, 143n97, 183n266
Schmemann, Alexander, 324n26
Schreiner, Thomas R., 121n8, 135n72, 147n112, 150n126, 237n183
Schweitzer, William M., 263n20
Searle, Alison, 48n143
Searle, John, 36n92
Seifrid, Mark A., 159n158, 160n161, 171n219
Seitz, Christopher R., 17n7
Shepherd, Norman, 149n120, 151n130
Smail, Thomas A., 205n66, 206
Smalley, Paul M., 127n39, 165n190, 257n1, 259n7, 261n15, 266nn30–31, 273nn56–57, 276n69, 282n82, 284n90, 292n114, 293n117
Smalley, Stephen S., 288nn105–6
Smith, C. Christopher, 334n49
Smith, Christian, 11n58, 12n59, 312n11
Smith, Gordon T., 327n31
Smith, James K. A., 7n31, 10n52, 11n55, 17n4, 35n88, 47n141, 178n246, 183n266, 324n26
Smith, Mark S., 202n50, 209n79
Smith, Ralph A., 121n8, 121n10
Smits, Cees-Jan, 288n104
Soulen, R. Kendall, 156n144
Spanje, T. E. van, 288n104
Spears, Aubrey, 28n60
Spencer, Archie J., 265n26
Spijker, G. J., 7n31

Spykman, Gordon J, 135n72, 151n130, 257n1
Stam, Clarence, 121n8, 151n130
Stanislavski, Constantin, 24n36, 50n156
Starr, James, 192
Stek, John H., 122n14, 123n22, 194n23, 218n119, 220n130
Stinissen, Wilfrid, 328n34
Stob, Henry, 180, 182n264
Stolk, Maarten, 306n165
Storer, Kevin, 40n108
Stott, John R. W., 244n204, 245n205
Strachan, Owen, 207n71
Strange, Alan D., 146n109
Strange, Dan, 181n260, 182n264
Strauss, S. A., 143n97
Strehle, Stephen, 120n5, 125n31
Stroup, George W., 17n4
Swain, Scott R., 27n56, 28n60, 28n63, 33n77, 57n179, 127n39, 134n65, 134n70, 262n16
Swinburnson, Benjamin W., 149n118
Swoboda, A. J., 334n54

Tanner, Kathryn, 196n29
Tate, Marvin E., 230n163
Taylor, Charles, 6–11, 12n60, 13, 269n40, 309
Terlouw, I., 12n61
Thate, Michael J., 3n11, 296n128
Thiessen, Gerd, 309n3
Thistleton, Anthony C., 6n27, 30n65, 31n71, 32n74, 311n7
Thomas, Derek, 232nn172–73
Thomas, Heath A., 26n46, 27n53, 28n60, 28n63
Thomas, Michael G., 289n107
Tipton, Lane G., 171n219
Torrance, James B., 142n97, 146n108, 234n177, 239n187, 250nn218–19, 250n222
Torrance, Thomas F., 33n77, 142n97, 165n193, 166n196, 193n17

Treier, Daniel J., 22n23, 26nn46–50, 26n52, 27n53, 28nn62–63, 293n117
Troost, P., 35n88, 329n36, 330n37, 331n41
Turner, Laurence A., 216n114
Turretin, Francis, 127n39, 129n46, 129n48, 130n50, 135n72, 149n118, 151n130
Tylenda, Joseph N., 270n44
Tyson, Paul, 47n141

Van Dam, Cornelis, 273n57
Vander Lugt, Wesley, 4, 22n23, 24n36, 50n153, 50n156, 52nn162–63, 55n174, 201n47, 217nn117–18, 263nn22–23, 264n24
Vander Zee, Leonard J., 327n31
VanDrunen, David, 24n40, 121n8, 127n39, 128n44, 129n46, 129n48, 130nn50–51, 130n53, 131n57, 134n65, 135n72, 178, 191n5
Vanhoozer, Kevin, 3, 5n25, 12–13, 14, 22n23, 23, 24n36, 25, 27n57, 28n60, 28n63, 33nn76–77, 33nn79–80, 35n89, 36nn90–91, 37n92, 37n94, 38–39, 40nn104–8, 41, 42n116, 44–56, 76, 96n169, 121n8, 127n39, 134, 170, 189n1, 190nn2–3, 191n7, 192n11, 199–200, 202n48, 217n118, 258n2, 260nn8–9, 260n11, 261nn14–15, 262nn16, 262nn18–19, 262nn20–21, 264nn24–25, 267n35, 268nn38–39, 269n42, 270n45, 272nn51–52, 272n54, 275n67, 284n90, 294n119, 294n121, 295nn123–25, 296n128, 300n141, 300n143, 301n148, 324n26, 334n53
Van Kooten, Robert C., 149n118
Van Pelt, Miles V., 182n265

AUTHOR INDEX

Van Raalte, Theodore G., 275n67
Van Til, Cornelius, 121n8, 121n10
Veldhuizen, P., 143n97
Velema, W. H., 121n8, 127n39,
   128n41, 151n130, 184n269,
   207n71, 257n1, 259n7,
   261n15, 266nn30-31,
   269n41, 271n49, 273n56,
   276n69, 277n75, 278nn76-
   77, 282n82, 284n90,
   292n114, 293n117, 296n126,
   300n140, 303n154
Venema, Cornelis P., 142n95,
   178n250, 182nn264-65,
   183n266, 281n80
Versluis, A., 259n7
Vlach, Michael J., 135n70
Volf, Miroslav, 334n50
Vorster, Nicholaas, 196n29, 197
Vos, Geerhardus, 86, 120n5,
   127n39, 135n72, 151n130,
   171n219, 180n259, 197,
   237n183, 281n80
Vos, P., 330n38
Vriezen, Th. C., 191n8, 214n104,
   265n28

Waaijman, Kees, 274n60
Waddington, Jeffrey C., 180nn258-
   59
Waltke, Bruce K., 151n130, 210n85,
   212n97, 218n123, 220n130,
   233n176, 237n183, 331n40
Walton, John H., 202n50, 204n62
Ward, Roland S., 121n8, 143n97
Warner, Michael, 7n31
Warren, Tish Harrison, 35n88,
   331n41
Waters, Guy Prentiss, 120n5,
   135n72
Watkin, Christopher, 260n7,
   269n41, 273n56, 276n69,
   281n81, 282n82, 284n90,
   296n126, 303n154
Webber, Robert E., 319n16, 322n22,
   324n26, 325n29
Webster, John, 33n77, 190n2
Weeks, Noel, 162n175

Weinandy, Thomas, 260n12
Weir, David A., 120n5, 135n72,
   136n74
Wells, Samuel, 4, 50n152, 52n162,
   200-201
Wellum, Stephen J., 24n41, 135n70,
   135n72, 150n128, 151n130,
   160n162, 195n25, 202n50,
   215n111, 216n113, 218n120,
   220nn130-31, 226n152,
   233n176, 237n183
Wendt, H. T., ix, 143n97
Wenham, Gordon J., 202n50,
   208n78, 210n85, 216n112
Westerman, Edian, 156n144
Westermann, Claus, 197, 204n62
Wielenga, B., 195n25
Wigley, Stephen, 22n24
Willard, Dallas, 35n88, 332n43
Williams, Brian M., 48n144, 311n8
Williams, Michael, 121n8, 135n72,
   143n97, 149n120, 150n125
Williamson, Paul, ix, 25, 122nn13-
   16, 127n39, 128n42,
   129n47, 129n49, 130, 132,
   133, 134n70, 135n71,
   143n100, 150nn125-26,
   151n132, 194n22, 195n26,
   210n85, 213n100, 214n103,
   216nn112-14, 218n121,
   219nn124-26, 220nn130-
   31, 221n133, 222nn136-37,
   223n141, 224nn144-45,
   225nn147-48, 225n150,
   226nn151-52, 227n155,
   228n160, 231n168, 231n170,
   233n176
Wilson, Andrew, 331n41
Wilson, Jonathan, 336n56
Wirzba, Norman, 334n54, 336n55
Witsius, Herman, 127n39, 130n51,
   131n53, 131n57, 135n72,
   151n130
Wittgenstein, Ludwig, 17n4, 37n92,
   42, 311n7
Wolters, Al, 183n266, 255n236

Wolterstorff, Nicholas, 35n90, 38n98, 40n105, 44n127, 50n152, 92, 324n26
Woo, B. Hoon, 127n39, 128nn41–42, 130n51, 134n67
Wood, W. Jay, 35n90
Woolsey, Andrew A., 120n5, 125nn29–31, 126n36, 135n72
Woude, A. S. van der, 191n9
Wright, Christopher J. H., 4, 24, 25, 26n52, 45n133, 157n148, 160n163, 192n11, 195, 202n50, 216n113, 218n120, 219n125, 224, 229, 232n174, 237n183, 255n236, 281n81
Wright, N. T., 3–4, 17–19, 24, 25, 36n90, 156n147, 157n148, 194n23, 200, 201, 202n48, 218n120, 236n181, 237n183, 241n194, 241n196, 244nn202–4, 281n80, 287n98, 287n101, 330n38
Wright, Shawn D., 120n5

Yarbrough, Robert W., 237n183
Yinger, Kurt L., 305n160,
Young, Frances, 50n152

Zimmerman, Jens, 30nn65–68, 31nn69–71, 32nn72–74, 319n16
Zizioulas, John, 209n81, 336n55
Zorgdrager, H. E., 166n196

Scripture Index

Genesis	197, 214n103, 216n114	3:16a	211
1–3	139, 202n50	3:16b	211, 211n89
1–2	197	3:17–19	211
1	143, 175, 195, 196, 202n50, 203n56, 206n70, 216n114	3:19	211
		3:22	211
		3:23–24	211
1:1	269n43	3:23	208n78
1:2	203, 267, 269	3:24	267
1:6–8	216n114	4	211n89
1:26–28	207n71, 208	4:2	208n78
1:26	205–6, 208	4:7b	211n89
1:27	273n57	4:9	208n78
1:28	180, 208, 275	4:12	208n78
1:31	203	5	207n71
2	143, 195, 203n56	5:1–3	207n71
2:5	208n78, 209n79	5:3–31	207n71
2:7	207, 207n72	5:3	207n71
2:9	209	6	150
2:15	208, 209n79	6:5–8	214
2:16–17	64, 139, 180, 209, 275	6:5–7	214
		6:5	216n112
2:17–18	143	6:8	24
2:17	287, 292n115	6:18	150, 214, 215, 215n108
3	113, 152, 155		
3:1–5	210	8:20	215
3:7	211	8:21	215, 216n112
3:8	211	9	150
3:10	211	9:1–7	216n113
3:12	211	9:4	225n149
3:14	212	9:8–17	161, 215, 216n113
3:15	69, 152, 155, 179n253, 213, 213n100, 215, 218, 241, 255, 290	9:9	150
		9:11	150
		9:17	150
		11:1–9	218
		11:4	219n124

415

SCRIPTURE INDEX

Genesis (continued)

12:1–3	152, 218n119, 218n121
12:1	218
12:2	218–19, 219n124
12:3	179n253, 219, 225, 241, 245
12:7	220
12:28	218n123
12:31	218n123
13:14–17	220
15	152, 159, 160, 195, 222n138
15:2–3	219
15:4–5	219
15:6	159, 161, 219–20, 221
15:7	220
15:8	218n123, 220
15:9–21	220
15:13–14	223
15:18–21	161, 220n128
17	152, 160, 195, 220, 222n138
17:2	221n134
17:4–5	222
17:4	221n134
17:6–8	222
17:6	229
17:7	221n134
17:9–14	221
17:9	208n78; 221, 221n134
17:10	221n134
17:13	221n134
17:14	221n134
17:16	229
18–19	267
22	152, 222n138
22:1	222
22:13	222
22:15–18	222
28:12	267
30:31	208n78
32:1	267
45:8	222

Exodus

3:14	223
4:22–23	223, 224, 235
5:1	34
5:2	225n148
6:4	214n106
16	197
16:7	191
18:11	191
19–24	195, 223
19	227n154
19:3b–8	226n150
19:5–6	152, 224, 241, 281
19:6	250
19:8	225
19:16–25	225
19:22	227n155
19:24	227n155
20	225n147
20–23	225
20:11	271n48
21–23	225n147
24	152, 227
24:1–8	225
24:3–8	226n150
24:3–4	225
24:5	225
24:6–8	225
24:7	225
24:8	223, 241
28–29	227n155
30:30	227n155, 235
31:13	226n152
31:16–17	226n152
31:16	197
31:17	271n48
32	152, 227n154
32:1–6	226
32:7	226, 226n151
32:9	226n151
32:10	226
32:14	226
32:34	226
33	78
33:2	226
33:12–22	191
33:12–16	226

SCRIPTURE INDEX

33:12–13	227	6:4	191, 259
33:16–17	227	7:6–8	281
33:17	226	7:6	227n155
33:18–19	191	8:5	228
33:19	226, 227	8:18	214n106
34	227	9:4–6	281
34:6–7	191, 226, 227	10:12–22	228
34:9	226, 227	10:17	191
34:10–28	227n153	14:1	228
34:10	226, 227n153	18:15	20, 235
34:11	227n153	18:17–19	235
34:13	227n153	27:26	240
34:22	244n204	28	141, 228
34:27	227	28:36	231
40:34–38	243	28:54–68	231
40:35	243	29:1	228
		29:16	227n155

Leviticus

		30:1–10	228, 231
9:23–24	191	30:1	231
17:11	225n149	30:6	232
17:14	225n149	30:16	149
18:5	67, 141, 149, 208n78	31:16	228
		31:20	228
19:2	22	32:46–47	149
23:15–17	244n204		
26:9	214n106	**Joshua**	233
		3:16	149
		13:13	229

Numbers

		15:63	229
3:3	235	16:10	229
3:7–8	208n78, 209n78	17:11–13	229
3:11–31	227n155		
4:23–24	208n78	**Judges**	229
4:26	208n78	1:21	229
5:7	34	1:27–36	229
8:16–19	227n155	2:1–5	229
13:29	245n206	2:11–13	229
25:1–13	228	2:19–20	229
25:12–13	227n155	3:7	229
25:12	220	3:12	229
28:26	244n204	4:1	229
		6:1	229

Deuteronomy

		6:25	229
4:1	67	8:33	229
4:19	208n78	10:6	229
5:24	191		
5:33	149		

417

SCRIPTURE INDEX

1 Samuel

2:30	161, 230
4:21–22	191
8:7	229
10:1	235
10:19	229
13:14	229
15:17	235
15:23	229
15:26	229
16:1	229
16:7	229
16:13	235

2 Samuel

2:4	235
5:1–12	229
6	229
7	153, 161, 229, 230n163
7:1–2	229
7:12–16	241
7:14	230
7:14b	161
7:16	229
7:24	229
8:5	229
8:20	229

1 Kings

1:39	235
2:4	153, 161, 230
8:10	243
8:11–12	243
8:46	278n76
9:4–5	161, 230
19:16	235

2 Kings

6:15–17	267
17:7–23	231
19:15–19	35
24:10–25:11	231

1 Chronicles

17	153
17:22	229

Nehemiah

9:14	197
9:29	149

Job

14:4	278n76
33:4	207
38–41	269n43
38:7	267

Psalms

	16, 20, 128, 132
1:2	35
2	131, 132
2:7–9	20
8	270
19	201
19:1–6	270
19:1	191
24	269n43
29	270
32:5	34
33:6	269
36:6–7	191
44:25	212
51:5	278n76
62:1	35
62:5	35
63:6	35
65:9–13	270
69:10	34
69:34	270
72	132
72:9	212
72:19	191
78:56–64	229
78:69	202
88:8	191
89	132, 153
89:3–4	229
89:7–9	191
89:19–20	230
89:24	231

89:28	229	21:21	149
89:34	229		
89:39	229	**Isaiah**	
90	269n43	2:2-4	322n23
96:3-4	191	6	267
96:11-12	270	6:3	191
98	201	7:14	20
99:5	35	8:18	71, 131
103:20	267	9:6	20
103:21	267	11:2	332
104	269n43, 270	11:9	25
104:1-2	202	13-23	181
104:30	25, 203, 204, 267, 269, 270, 274	14:3-21	268n37
		14:32	231
106:33	228	24:4	212
106:34-39	229	25:12	212
110	131, 132, 133	32:15	232, 245
110:1-2	235	40-44	269n43
110:4	235	42:1	146, 225
113:4	191	42:6	225, 232
113:5-6	191	43:5-6	287
113:5	191	44:3	232, 245
119:93	149	44:6	191
130:3	278n76	44:8	191
132	132, 153, 230n167	44:23	270
132:5	229	45:14	191
132:8	229	48:13	269
132:11-12	229, 230, 230n167	49:6	225, 232
132:12-13	231	49:13	270
132:13-18	230n167	51:3	232
132:13	230	52:8	19
132:17-18	230	53	21, 132
132:17	231	53:10	130, 287
133:1-3	34	54:1-10	231
145:7	34	55:3-5	232
145:11-12	191	55:3	232
148	201, 269n43	55:3b-4	230
148:1-4	270	55:12	270
148:2	267	56:4-8	232
148:5	269	56:9-12	234
		57:1-13	234
Proverbs		58:1-14	234
4:4	149	58:8	191
4:22	149	59:1-13	234
8:30-31	204	59:21	232, 245
8:35	149	60:1-3	191
19:16	149	61:1-2	235, 237

Isaiah (continued)

61:8	232
63:10	228
63:11–14	228
63:16	223, 235
64:8	223, 235
65:17	213, 255
65:25	212
66:1	202
66:18–24	232

Jeremiah

1:4–19	218n123
4:28	212
10:6	191
11:3	240
11:10	231
12:4	212
12:11	212
15:19–21	218n123
30:21–22	230
30:22	232
30:24	232
31–33	153
31:9	223, 235
31:31–34	231
31:33	198, 232, 244n204, 245, 301
31:34	232
32:38	232
32:40	232
33:9	232
33:20–21	140, 149–50
33:25–26	149–50
34:18–20	220
50:4	232
50:5	232

Ezekiel

16:59	231
16:60–62	150
18:4	240
18:21	149
20:11	149
20:13	149
20:18–26	228
20:21	149
20:25	228
26:25	232
28:2–19	268n37
28:25	232
34:23–24	230
34:23	232
36–37	153
36:20–23	232
36:22–28	231
36:26–27	198, 232
36:27	232, 245
36:28	232
36:33–38	232, 241, 242, 290
36:33	232
36:34–35	232
36:36	232
37:1–14	232, 241, 242, 290
37:14	232, 245
37:15–28	232
37:26	232
37:28	232
39:28	232
39:29	245
40–48	232

Daniel

2:44	179n253, 237
7:11–14	179n253, 237
10:13	267
10:20	267

Hosea

4:3	212
6:7	67, 140, 149
11:1	223, 224n142, 235

Joel

2:28–29	232, 245

Amos

5:14	149

Micah

7:17	212

7:18–19	238

Habakkuk

2:14	25

Haggai

1	37

Zechariah

4:1–6	235
6	131, 132
6:13	130, 130n51
8:19	34
12:10	232

Malachi

1:3	280n79
1:4	280n79

Matthew

1:18	234
1:20	234
1:23	282
3:1–12	237
3:2–3	235
3:7–12	235
3:9–10	250
3:11	252
3:13–17	235
3:15	239
3:16	235
4:8	213
4:9	213
4:17	237
4:23–24	238
4:24	238
5–7	239, 248
5:3	237
5:8	304
5:10–12	249
5:16	238
5:17	239
5:20	179, 237
5:22	252
5:29–30	254
5:44	35
5:45	238
5:48	238
6:1	238
6:8	238
6:9	238
6:10	267
6:14	238
6:16–18	34
6:26	238
6:28–30	208
6:32	238
7:11	238
7:13–17	237
7:13–14	237
7:19	252
7:21	237
8:12	305n163, 306n164
8:16–17	238
9:2	238
9:6	238
9:27–31	247
9:35–38	247
9:35	238
9:36	207
10:1	238
10:18–22	249
10:25	249
10:28	254, 273
10:29	208
10:38	248
10:39	248
10:40	133n64
11:10–24	250
11:24–30	237
12:24	208
12:28	238n186, 239n186
12:36–37	253
13:34	256
13:40	252
13:42	252, 254, 306n164
13:50	252, 254, 306n164
14:13–21	247
14:14	207
14:23	35
15:24	133n64
15:32	207
16:19	250

Matthew (continued)

16:21	240, 242
16:22	242
16:24–27	306
16:24	248
16:25	248
16:27	253
17:1–8	199n39
17:22–23	240, 242
18:3	179, 237
18:8–9	252
18:9	254
18:14	238
18:15–20	250
18:20	291
18:23–25	237
19:24	237
20:1–16	237
20:18–19	240, 242
20:28	240, 287
20:34	207
21:1–17	240
21:18–27	237
21:33–44	237
22:1–14	237
22:13	305n163
22:30	256
22:37–40	191, 225, 265
22:42	235
24:1–25:46	237
24:1–31	252
24:9	249
24:12	253
24:13	302n151
24:27	253
24:29–30	253
24:42	252, 299
24:44	252
24:51	306n164
25:1–13	305
25:10	252
25:13	252, 299
25:14–30	305
25:21	255
25:30	305n163
25:31–46	305
25:34	237, 254
25:41	252
25:46	254
26:26–29	250
26:26–28	241
26:29	241
26:36–46	241
26:36	235
26:39	235
26:42	235
26:44	235
26:47–56	241
26:57–68	241
27:11–26	241
27:43	330
27:51–53	238
27:51	214n103
28:1–10	242
28:9	242
28:18–19	250
28:20	291

Mark

1:3–8	237
1:14–15	237
1:35	235
1:39	238
5:35–42	238
6:5–6	238n185
6:34	207
6:46	235
8:31	240, 242
8:34	248
8:35	248
9:31	240
9:43	252, 254, 305n162
9:45	252
9:47	237, 252
9:48	305n161, 305n162
10:33	240
10:45	157, 240, 287, 287n96
11:1–11	240
11:15–18	240
12:35–37	243
13:3–27	252
13:29	252
13:32	252

13:35–37	252	10:14	253
14:22–24	241	10:16	133n64
14:25	241	10:18	286, 290
14:32–42	241	10:28	149
14:43–50	241	11:1	235
14:53–65	241	11:13	238, 250
15:2–15	241	11:20	239n186
		12:32	254

Luke

		12:37–40	299
		12:40	252
1:17	235, 237, 250	12:47–48	250, 253
1:31–33	235	12:49	252
1:32–33	291	13:1–8	237
1:35	234, 234n177	13:22–30	237
1:68–75	230	14:14	255
1:69	231	14:27	248
2:40	146, 235	16:1–31	237
2:42	235	16:24	305n162
2:46–47	235	17:5–28	252
2:49	235	17:21	239n186
2:52	146	17:26–30	253
3:2–27	237	17:33	248
3:16	252	18:1–8	237
3:38	207n71	18:32–33	240, 242
4:1–13	236	18:34	242
4:14	238	19:29–40	240
4:18	235, 237	19:45–46	240
4:43	133n64	20:9–18	240
5:16	235	20:36	256
5:17	238	21:24–27	253
6:12	235	21:27	243
6:18	238	21:31	237n183
7:11–17	238	22:19–20	241
7:13	247	22:22	287
7:47–48	238	22:29	130, 133, 254
7:47	290	22:29–30	255
7:50	238	22:31–32	250
9:18	235	22:40–46	241
9:22	240, 242	22:47–53	241
9:23	248	23:2–3	241
9:24	248	23:18–25	241
9:28	235	23:34	239
9:29	235	24:1–49	242
9:34–35	243	24:13–30	242
9:44	240	24:19	19
9:45	242	24:26	287
9:48	133n64	24:27	16
10:12	253	24:30–31	35

Luke (continued)

24:31–32	300n142
24:31	242n197
24:34	242
24:36–49	242
24:36	242n197
24:45	301
24:46–47	16
24:50–53	242
24:51	291

John

1:1–5	207
1:3–5	203
1:3	262n17
1:4	261, 297n131, 304
1:9	33, 261
1:12–13	247
1:14	199n39, 262n17
1:18	199n39, 304
1:29	156, 284n91, 288
1:33	236
3:3–5	278n76
3:3	237
3:4–5	247
3:5	237
3:16–17	156, 284n91
3:16	207, 254, 288n105
3:17	133n64, 288n103
3:18–19	306
3:34	133n64, 236, 250
3:35	265
4:10	250
4:13–14	247
4:34	133n64
4:42	288n103, 288n105
5:19	190, 261
5:20	265
5:23–24	133n64
5:26	203, 261
5:30	190, 330
5:36–38	133n64
6:12	208
6:29	133n64
6:35	247
6:38–39	133n64
6:38	190
6:39	71, 130, 131, 133, 190
6:44–45	301
6:44	133n64, 156, 284n91
6:53–58	247
6:57	34, 133n64, 248
6:63	33, 261
7:16	133n64, 190, 235
7:18	133n64
7:28–29	133n64
7:37–39	247, 250
7:38–39	236
8:12–20	252
8:12	33
8:16	133n64
8:18	133n64
8:25–30	252
8:26	133n64, 190
8:28	235
8:29	133n64
8:31–32	247
8:42	133n64
8:44–47	252
8:44	213, 268
8:54–58	252
8:54	189
9:4	133n64
9:5	33
10:3	247, 301
10:11	291
10:17–18	54
10:18	133n64
10:27	247, 301
10:29	71, 130, 131, 133
10:36	133n64
10:38	304
11:25–26	242, 290
11:37–44	238
11:41–42	235
11:42	133n64
12:12–19	240
12:25–26	248
12:28	189, 206
12:31	213, 286, 290
12:44–45	133n64
12:47	156, 284n91
12:49–50	235

Reference	Pages
12:49	133n64, 190
13:5	179
13:15	290
13:20	133n64
13:31–32	206
14:2–3	254
14:6	261
14:7	165, 304
14:9–10	206, 304
14:9	165
14:10	190, 262
14:13	189
14:16–17	250
14:19	247
14:21	247
14:23	256
14:24	133n64, 235
15:1–8	297
15:1–7	248
15:4–5	247
15:5	158, 301
15:6	252
15:7–8	247
15:9	265
15:10–12	247
15:13	265
15:15	190
15:16	247
15:18–25	249
15:21	133n64
16:5	133n64
16:8–9	245
16:11	287
16:13	291
16:14	189
17	235
17:1	189, 206
17:2	71, 130, 131, 133, 156, 284n91
17:3–4	133n64
17:4–10	71, 131
17:4	190, 199n39, 206
17:5	189, 196, 242, 262
17:6	130, 131, 133, 156, 190, 284n91
17:8	133n64, 190
17:9–21	250
17:9	156, 284n91
17:11	247, 299
17:19	285, 290, 299
17:20–23	247
17:21–24	256
17:21–23	299
17:21	133n64, 193, 262, 297
17:22–24	304
17:23–24	265
17:23	133n64, 297
17:24	130, 131, 133, 156, 190, 242, 262, 284n91
17:25	133n64
17:26	247, 265
18:12–13	241
18:19–24	241
18:36	179
19:30	214n103
20:11–18	242
20:16	242
20:19–29	242
20:19	242n197
20:21	133n64, 247
20:22	236
20:24–29	242
21:1–14	242
21:21	254n233
21:22	254n233

Acts

Reference	Pages
1:1–11	242
1:5	236
1:9–11	242
1:9	243
1:11	243
2:1	244
2:2	245
2:4–11	245
2:13	245
2:17	236, 291
2:22–36	245
2:23	200, 240, 287
2:24	242, 290
2:33	234, 236, 244, 291
2:34–35	291
2:37	290

Acts (continued)

2:39	245
2:42	35
2:46	35
3:15	261
3:22–23	235
4:24	249n215
4:31	250
5:41	249
7:4	218n123
7:51	228, 234
8:12	291
8:15	250
10:38	247
10:44–47	236
13:1–3	35
13:22	229
14:22	291
16:14	300n142, 301
17:28	25, 204, 270, 271n50, 274, 331
19:8	291
19:29	45
19:31	45
20:25	291
28:23	291
28:30–31	291

Romans

	27, 61, 61n1
1	61n1, 145
1:3–4	171
1:4	290
1:17	34
1:18–32	280n79
1:18–23	32
1:18–20	182, 254n233, 306n165
1:21	182
1:24–32	249n216
1:28–32	268n38
1:28	182
1:32	254n233, 306n165
2	145
2–3	157
2:1–13	280n79
2:4–5	250
2:6–16	253
2:9	250
2:11	253
2:14–16	254n233, 306n165
2:15	180
3:5–7	287
3:21–26	153, 287
3:23	277
3:24–26	286
3:24	286
3:25	286
4	152, 153, 159
4:3	161
4:13	213
4:16–18	213
4:16–17	222
4:17	172n221, 269n42
4:23–25	171
4:25	160, 160n161, 171, 290, 291, 301
5:6–8	239
5:8	265
5:9	254n234
5:12–21	140, 209, 249n216
5:12–19	277
5:12	249n216, 277n75
5:12a–c	277n75
5:15–19	277n75, 287
5:18–19	278n77
5:19	239
6:1–11	35, 171
6:2	248
6:3–11	33, 245, 247
6:7	248
6:9	242, 290
6:11	289
6:12–14	248
6:15–23	248
6:16–18	248
6:22	248
6:23	240, 287
8:1–11	248
8:1	254
8:3	133n64
8:5–9	277
8:9–10	247
8:12–13	248
8:14–17	238
8:17–25	242n197

8:17–23	249
8:17	254, 255
8:18–25	277
8:18	249
8:20–23	21
8:20–21	211
8:21	256
8:22–25	201
8:22–23	32, 212
8:22	252
8:23–25	251
8:23	244n204, 251
8:26–27	250
8:26	33
8:29–30	71, 131, 256, 302
8:29	196, 249
8:30	153, 199n39
8:34	250, 291
8:37	249
9–11	280n80
9:4	223, 235
9:7–8	280n79
9:11–21	248
9:11–12	280n79
9:13	280n79
9:17–18	280n79
9:22	280n79
10:16	146
10:17	47n141
11	71, 154, 296
11:11–24	279
11:17–24	251, 280n80
11:20	302n151
11:25–16a	280n80
11:28	279
11:30–32	251
12:1–2	251
12:1	250
12:2	34, 248, 298, 301
12:3–8	298
12:4–17	35
12:4–5	247
12:5	247
12:6–8	250
12:17	248
12:19	248
12:21	248
13:1–10	248
13:8	191, 265
13:10	191, 265
13:12	237n183, 299
13:13–14	248
13:14	247, 248
14:1–23	248
14:17	237, 291
15:1–7	248
15:3	247
15:5	247
16:20	214n103, 255

1 Corinthians

1:2	290
1:10	33
1:26–28	248
1:30	153, 160, 239, 285, 286, 286n95, 299
1:39	290
2:9	254
2:16	32, 247
3:9–10	297
3:10–15	254n234
3:11	247
3:14	255
3:16	247, 297
3:16–17	248
4:5	254n234, 255
4:20	291
5:1–5	250
6:1–20	248
6:9–10	179, 237, 248
6:9	254
6:12–19	248
6:17	247
6:19	247
7:1–40	248
7:7	250
7:31	299
8:1–13	248
8:6	259n7, 262n17, 270
9:4–6	248
9:12	248
9:15	248
9:18	248
10:11–12	302n151

1 Corinthians (*continued*)

10:16	247
10:23–33	248
11:1–34	248
11:1	247
11:7	199n39
11:17–31	250
11:22	253
11:32	250
12–14	298
12:1–31	250
12:12	247
12:14–20	247
12:27	247, 297
13:1–13	248
13:8–10	250n223
13:12	304
14:1–40	250
15:3	146
15:5–7	242
15:15	289
15:20–23	242, 290
15:20	33
15:21–22	140, 209, 277
15:23	33
15:26	255, 256
15:28	25
15:35–44	242n197
15:42–44	256
15:44b–49	140
15:45–49	209
15:45	196, 283n86, 286, 291
15:49–50	238
15:50	179, 237, 256
15:53–54	256
15:55	54, 286
16:1–2	248
16:13	299

2 Corinthians

1:5–11	248
1:5	249
1:22	251
2:16	249
3:14–16	301
3:18	41, 199n39, 256, 304
4:4	196, 199n39, 205, 206, 213, 256
4:6	190, 196, 199n39, 301, 304
4:9–12	249
4:16–18	249
4:16	34, 273
4:17	256
5:4	256n238
5:5	251
5:8	273
5:10	253
5:14–17	249
5:14	171, 288n104
5:17	5n25, 12, 48, 246, 286, 296
5:18–21	288n104
5:19–21	290
5:19	288
5:20	288n104
6:14–18	248
6:18	238
7:9–10	250
7:10	248
8:1–14	248
9:6–15	248
10:3–5	249
12:9–10	249
12:20–21	248

Galatians

1:4	133n64
2:19–20	249
2:20	12, 25, 33, 34, 158, 172, 193, 247, 248, 249, 296, 301
2:21	34
3	152, 153, 157, 159, 195, 228n159
3:1–5	247
3:6–14	235
3:6	161
3:8	213, 218n121
3:10–14	153, 156, 284n91
3:10–13	157

3:10	240	2:6	249n217, 319
3:13	287	2:7	249
3:14	245, 287	2:10	160, 248, 250n222, 299
3:19–20	134		
3:19	134, 267	2:15	246, 286, 296
3:20	134	2:19–22	297
3:24	152	2:21–22	247
3:27	35, 160, 247	3:14–19	250
4:3	248	3:16–17	248
4:4–5	156, 239, 284n91	4:4–6	299
4:4	133n64	4:8	291
4:6	247	4:9–16	250
4:9	248	4:10	243, 247
4:19	25, 248, 249, 296	4:11–16	298
4:21–31	66, 149	4:12	247
4:25	149	4:13	247, 256
5:4	302n151	4:15–16	35
5:19–21	238, 248	4:15	291
5:21	179, 237, 254, 291	4:20–24	33
5:22–23	248	4:22	247, 248
5:24	248	4:23	34
6:1–10	248	4:24	247, 248, 275n65, 286
6:14	248		
6:15	246, 296	4:25–31	248
		4:25	248
		4:28–29	248

Ephesians

1:3–14	130, 131, 133, 190	4:32	248
1:3–11	287	5:1	248
1:3–6	302	5:2	247, 290
1:3	291	5:3–7	248
1:4–12	71, 131	5:5	179, 237, 238, 254, 291
1:7	286		
1:10	21, 190	5:11–12	248
1:11–13	71, 131	5:15–33	248
1:11	254, 280	5:18	248, 250
1:14	251	5:23–32	297
1:17–18	301	5:23	247, 291
1:18	48n143	5:26	299
1:19–20	248	5:30	247
1:20–22	291	6:1–20	248
1:20	249	6:10–20	249
1:22–23	247	6:10–12	305
1:23	247	6:12	213
2:2	213, 248	6:18	35
2:3	248, 278n77		
2:5–6	243	## Philippians	
2:5	248	1:9–11	248

Philippians (continued)

1:21	248
1:27	248
1:29	249
2	156
2:1–5	248
2:5–8	54
2:5–6	203n51
2:5	290
2:6–7	234
2:8	239
2:9–10	243
2:10–11	54, 253
2:12–13	271n50
2:12	253n232
2:13	248
2:14–18	248
2:15	248
3:9	239
3:10	249
3:17	248
4:1–9	248
4:4	34
4:8	35
4:13	248

Colossians

1:13	48, 249n, 249n217, 287
1:14	286
1:15–20	207
1:15–16	196, 205
1:15–20	207
1:16–17	203
1:16	5n25, 203n52, 267, 269, 270
1:17	25
1:18	242, 247, 290, 291
1:19	236
1:24	249
2:3	33
2:6–7	248
2:8	248
2:9–10	247
2:10	248, 291
2:11–13	247
2:11–12	245
2:14	286
2:15	286, 287, 290
2:19	247
2:20	248
3:1–4	171
3:3	243, 297, 319
3:4	256
3:5–11	33
3:5–9	248
3:8–17	35
3:9	247, 248
3:10–25	248
3:10	34, 275n65, 286
3:12	247
3:14	191, 265
3:18–24	35
3:24	254
4:1–6	248

1 Thessalonians

2:12	291
4:3–6	248
4:9–12	248
4:13–18	253
5:6	252, 299
5:12–18	248
5:22	248

2 Thessalonians

1:8	146
1:9	254
2	253n230
2:1–12	253
2:8	253
2:15	248
3:3	249
3:5	249
3:13–15	249

1 Timothy

1:9–10	130, 131
1:17	304
2:1–4	250
2:5	235, 291
3:16	171, 290
4:16	324n26

5:1–6:2	249	2:12	250
5:22	248	2:13	71, 131, 330
6:11–21	249	2:14–15	256, 286, 287
6:16	304	2:14	214n103, 236n181, 290
		2:15	289
2 Timothy		2:16–18	291
1:3–14	249	2:17	286
1:9–10	133	3:7–19	302n151
1:10	286, 290	4:1–11	249
2:1–26	249	4:9	197
2:3	249	4:11	302n151
2:9	249	4:12	51
2:10	256	4:13–16	250
2:11–13	248	4:14–16	235, 291
2:12	254	5:1–10	235
3:1–4	253	5:7	235
3:1	245n206, 291	6:4–8	302n151
4:1–5	249	6:20	250
4:1	291	7:11–28	235
4:6–8	248	7:20–22	130, 131, 133
4:8	255	7:25–8:6	250
4:9	248	7:25	291
		7:28	133
Titus		8	153
2:11–3:11	249	8:1–13	287
2:12	248	8:2	250
2:14	286	8:6	291
3:3	248	9:11–15	134
3:5	71, 131	9:11–14	235
3:7	254	9:12	286
		9:14	287
Philemon		9:15	291
17–18	249	9:24	250
		10	153
Hebrews	302	10:1–18	287
1:1–3	207	10:8–12	235
1:1	245n206, 291	10:19–22	235
1:2–3	304	10:22–25	249
1:2	270	10:25	237n183, 299
1:3	25, 32, 190, 196, 204, 205, 270, 274	10:26–31	302n151
		10:32	249
1:13	291	11:3	269
1:14	267	11:16	254, 299
2:5–10	21, 199n39	11:17–19	222
2:9	207	12:1–17	249
2:10	256	12:1–2	290
		12:4	291

Hebrews (continued)

12:5–11	253
12:22–24	250
12:24–25	250
12:28	35, 254, 291
13:1–19	249
13:17	35
13:20	134

James

1–5	249
1:27	248
2:5	238, 254, 291
2:22–23	161
3:14–16	248
4:1	248
4:4	248
4:7	35, 249
5:8	237n183
5:9	252
5:10	249
5:13	249
5:16	34

1 Peter

1:1	299
1:4–5	254
1:4	256
1:5	71, 131
1:13–25	249
1:16	22
1:17	253
1:18–19	286
1:20	245n206, 291
1:23	247
2:5	250, 297
2:8	303
2:9	250
2:11	248
2:13–3:7	249
2:19–20	249
2:21	247, 290
2:22–23	239
2:24	248
3:14	249
3:17	249
3:18–19	242n198
3:20	182
3:22	242n198
4:1–4	248
4:1	247
4:7–11	249
4:7	237n183, 299
4:10–11	250, 298
4:13–16	249
4:17	146, 250, 253
5:1	256
5:8–9	249
5:8	252
5:19	256

2 Peter

1:3	192
1:4	256, 289, 319
1:5–7	192
1:11	254, 291
1:14	192, 248
1:17	199n39
2:4	254
2:5–10	253
2:10–11	281
2:18–22	302n151
2:20	248
3:3	245n206, 291
3:9	304
3:10	253, 255, 255n236
3:12	252, 255
3:13	255

1 John

1:5	253n230, 261
2:1–2	250, 291
2:2	284n91, 286, 288, 288n103
2:4	156
2:6	247, 290
2:15–17	248
2:18	245n206, 252, 291, 252
2:22–23	252
2:29	232
3:1	238

3:2	242n197, 248, 256, 297, 304	2:17	302n151
		2:21–22	250
3:4	248	2:25–26	302n151
3:8–9	248	3:3	250
3:8	213, 286, 290	3:19	250, 253
3:9	232	3:21	255
3:12	213	4:11	269n42
3:13	248	5:9	157, 286
3:16	248, 265, 290	5:11	267
3:24	193	6:1–8	253
4:3	252	6:11	249n215
4:4–6	248	7	156, 284n91
4:7	232	7:14–17	248
4:8	265, 265n27	8:6–12	253
4:9–10	133n64	9:1–21	253
4:10	286	11:15	237, 291
4:12	249	11:18	255
4:14	133n64, 156, 284n91, 288, 288n103	12:9	210, 212
		12:11	248
		12:13–17	249
4:15–16	193, 232, 247, 249	12:17	213
4:16	265, 265n27	13	253n230
5:1	232	13:8	71
5:4–5	248	14:4	157, 286
5:4	232	14:12	213
5:18	232	16:1–16	253
5:19	213, 248, 288n106	16:15	299
5:20	193, 247	19:7	252
		19:11–21	253
2 John		19:16	235
7	252	20:2–3	290, 304
		20:3	304n158
		20:8	304n158
Jude		20:10	253n230, 255
6	268n37	20:12–13	253
7	253, 254	20:14	255, 256
18	245n206, 291	21–22	195, 202, 213, 255
25	196	21:3–5	255
		21:3–4	194
Revelation	66, 86, 181, 303n154, 304n158	21:4	238, 255, 256, 286, 289
1:5	235, 242, 290	21:5	246, 296
1:8	291	21:6	291
1:18	242, 286, 289, 290	21:7	255
2–3	249, 291	21:8	254
2:5	250'	21:10–27	202
2:10–11	248	21:16	202
2:10	302n151	21:22	202

Revelation (*continued*)

21:23	205
22:3	256
22:4	304
22:5	205
22:12	253
22:13	291
22:14	252
22:17	305

www.ingramcontent.com/pod-product-compliance
Lightning Source LLC
Chambersburg PA
CBHW071235300426
44116CB00008B/1041